Enclosed CD-RO[

LearnKey™ Self-Paced Video Training Demo

- Features full CD-ROM #1 from LearnKey's Designing Directory Services (Exam 70-219) Self-Paced Multimedia Training Series

- Includes more than 60 minutes of full-motion video with glossary, quizzes, and more as taught by expert MCSEs Aaron Spurlock and Michael Storm

- **LearnKey's** effective presentation format lets you test your knowledge before and after each topic and move between topics to skip or review specific subjects. You can pause the video to complete an exercise or check the Glossary.

All-in-One Practice Test Software

Realistic and challenging questions to help you learn

Graded by topic for easy review

- 300+ questions covering three MCSE Designing Exams:

    Exam 70-219: Designing a Microsoft Windows 2000 Directory Services Infrastructure

    Exam 70-220: Designing Security for a Microsoft Windows 2000 Network

    Exam 70-221: Designing a Microsoft Windows 2000 Network Infrastructure

- Practice mode with access to answers to help you learn as you test

- Powered by Total Seminars' NEW Java-based test engine

ALL · IN · ONE

MCSE
Windows 2000
Designing

EXAM GUIDE

ALL ▪ IN ▪ ONE

MCSE
Windows 2000
Designing

E X A M   G U I D E

Harry Brelsford &
Michael Hinrichsen

Osborne / McGraw-Hill
New York • Chicago • San Francisco • Lisbon • London
Madrid • Mexico City • Seoul • Singapore • Sydney • Toronto

Osborne/**McGraw-Hill**
2600 Tenth Street
Berkeley, California 94710
U.S.A.

To arrange bulk purchase discounts for sales promotions, premiums, or fund-raisers, please contact Osborne/**McGraw-Hill** at the above address. For information on translations or book distributors outside the U.S.A., please see the International Contact Information page immediately following the index of this book.

MCSE Windows 2000 Designing All-in-One Exam Guide

1234567890 DOC DOC 01987654321

Book P/N 0-07-212935-2 and CD P/N 0-07- 212934-4
parts of

ISBN 0-07-212936-0

Publisher
Brandon A. Nordin

Vice President & Associate Publisher
Scott Rogers

Acquisitions Editor
Michael Sprague

Senior Project Editor
Betsy Manini

Acquisitions Coordinator
Jessica Wilson

Technical Editor
Evan Morris

Copy Editor
Andy Carroll

Proofreader
Stefany Otis

Illustrator, Compositor, and Indexer
MacAllister Publishing Services, LLC

Cover Design
Greg Scott

This book was composed with QuarkXpress.

DEDICATION

Again and again, my family provides the strong support needed to
complete one of these books and, while I can never fully repay them,
I do offer my heartfelt thanks and love (if not olive branch).
Thanks to my wife, Kristen, and sons, Geoffrey and Harry. Even our beloved
Springer Spaniels, Brisker and Jaeger, deserve part of this dedication.

Harry Brelsford

I want to thank my darling Kim, who is the love of my life and my
biggest supporter and advisor along with my two kids, Ryan and Sierra,
who are the best children a father could have.

Michael Hinrichsen

ABOUT THE CONTRIBUTORS

Author **Harry Brelsford** is the founder and CEO of NetHealthMon.com, a Seattle-based firm providing fee-based consulting and remote network monitoring for BackOffice 2000 and Small Business Server 2000. Harry holds the following technology vendor certifications: MCSE, MCT, CNE (retired), CLSE, and CNP, as well as an MBA from the University of Denver. He writes monthly columns for *Microsoft Certified Professional Magazine* (where he is a contributing editor), *IT Contractor Magazine, IT Insider,* and *Computer Source*. He is a long-time instructor in Seattle Pacific University's MCSE certification program (a Microsoft AATP).

When free time allows, you'll find Harry and his family sampling cross-country ski resorts from Vermont to Alaska! The author of eight technology books, Harry can be reached at harryb@nethealthmon.com or www.nethealthmon.com. Harry is a resident of Bainbridge Island, Washington

Author **Michael Hinrichsen** is a Senior Trainer and Consultant who lives and works in Skagit Valley, Washington. He holds the two Microsoft systems and network certifications (MCP, MCSE) in addition to an MBA from Pacific Lutheran University in Tacoma, Washington. Michael is an adjunct faculty member of the Seattle Pacific University's MCSE AATP training program and teaches graduate-level networking courses.

Additionally, Michael is the Director of Information Systems for Small Planet Foods, a division of General Mills, Inc., and has over 20 years of IT systems and business-related experience. In July of 1997, Michael participated in an intensive professional seminar at the Harvard Graduate School of Business focused on melding an organization's business and technology strategies. He lives in Washington State with his wife, Kim, and his two children, Ryan and Sierra. When not trying to make the world a better place for people and computers, Michael can be found spending time with his family, golfing, walking the beach, or gardening. He can be reached via email at michaelhinrichsen@hotmail.com.

Technical editor, **Evan Morris**, MCSE, MCT, and Master ASE, is a System Engineer at Compaq's Redmond Office. His focus is on technical research and consulting in the areas of Active Directory design, storage area networks, and hosted Exchange deployments. He also delivers training on Windows 2000 and Exchange 2000.

BRIEF CONTENTS

Foreword . . . . *xxvii*

Acknowledgments . . . . *xxxi*

Introduction . . . . *xxxiii*

Part I Exam 70-219: Designing a Microsoft Windows 2000
Directory Services Infrastructure 1

Chapter 1 Defining Directory Services 3

Chapter 2 Analyzing Business Requirements 33

Chapter 3 Analyzing Technical Requirements 57

Chapter 4 Designing a Directory Service Architecture 77

Chapter 5 Designing Your Service Locations 113

Part II Exam 70-220: Designing Security for a Microsoft
Windows 2000 Network 139

Chapter 6 Introduction to Security 141

Chapter 7 Analyzing Business and Technical Requirements 157

Chapter 8 Analyzing Security Requirements 197

Chapter 9 Designing a Windows 2000 Security Solution 231

Chapter 10   Designing a Security Solution for Access
Between Networks 309

Chapter 11   Designing Security for Communication Channels 363

Part III   Overview of Designing a Network Infrastructure 395

Chapter 12   Overview of Designing a Network Infrastructure 397

Chapter 13   Analyzing Business and Technical Requirements 431

Chapter 14   Designing a Network Infrastructure Using TCP/IP 485

Chapter 15   Designing an Automated IP Configuration Solution
Using DHCP 529

Chapter 16   Creating a DNS Name-Resolution Design 569

Chapter 17   Designing with WINS Services and DFS 627

Chapter 18   Designing Internet and Extranet Connectivity
Solutions 671

Chapter 19   Designing a Wide Area Network Infrastructure 703

Chapter 20   Designing a Management and Implementation
Strategy for Windows 2000 Networking 753

Part IV   Bringing It All Together 771

Chapter 21   The Holistic Windows 2000 Design Process 773

Part V   Appendixes 779

Appendix A   More Case Study Analyses and Questions 781

Appendix B   MCSE Certification Specifics 843

Appendix C   Case Study Analysis Approach 877

Index 897

CONTENTS

Foreword . . . . *xxvii*

Acknowledgments . . . . *xxxi*

Introduction . . . . *xxxiii*

Part I Exam 70-219: Designing a Microsoft Windows 2000
Directory Services Infrastructure I

Chapter I Defining Directory Services 3

Common Understanding of Directory Services 4

    Directory Services and Meta-Information 6

    History and Types of Directory Services 7

    Predicting the Future: Meta-Directories 9

Active Directory from the Top Down 10

    Forests 11

    Trees 11

    Domains 11

    Organizational Units 13

    Lower-Level Objects 13

    Data and Attributes 15

    Sites 16

    Directory Services in Different Versions of Windows 16

Top Reasons to Implement Windows 2000 and Active Directory 17

    Top Reasons to Implement Windows 2000 18

    Top Reasons to Implement Active Directory 25

Chapter Review 31

    Questions 31

    Answers 31

Key Skill Sets 32

Key Terms 32

Chapter 2   Analyzing Business Requirements 33

Analyzing the Existing and Planned Business Models 34

   Analyzing the Company Model and the Geographical Scope 35

   Analyzing Company Processes...44

   Management 47

   Company Organization...48

   Vendor, Partner, and Customer Relationships......................................51

   Acquisition Plans 52

Analyzing Factors That Influence Company Strategies 53

   Identifying Company Priorities 53

   Identifying the Projected Growth and Growth Strategy 53

   Identifying Relevant Laws and Regulations 54

   Identifying the Company's Tolerance for Risk 54

   Identifying the Total Cost of Operations...54

Chapter Review 55

   Questions 55

   Answers...55

   Key Skill Sets 56

   Key Terms 56

Chapter 3   Analyzing Technical Requirements 57

Evaluating Existing and Planned Technical Environment 58

   Analyzing Company Size and User and Resource Distribution...........59

   Assessing Available Connectivity 62

   Assessing Net Available Bandwidth 64

   Analyzing Performance Requirements...65

   Analyzing Data- and System-Access Patterns 66

   Analyzing Network Roles and Responsibilities....................................67

   Analyzing Security Considerations 69

Analyzing the Impact of Active Directory...70

   Assessing Existing Systems and Applications 70

   Identifying Existing and Planned Upgrades and Rollouts...................70

   Analyzing the Technical Support Structure...71

   Analyzing Existing and Planned Network and Systems Management.................72

Analyzing the Business Requirements for Client-Desktop Management.....................72

Chapter Review 74

   Questions 75

Answers...75
Key Skill Sets 75
Key Terms 76

Chapter 4   Designing a Directory Service Architecture 77

Designing an Active Directory Forest and Domain 78
Designing a Forest and Schema Structure 79
Designing a Domain Structure...83
Analyzing and Optimizing Trust Relationships 85
Designing an Active Directory Naming Strategy....................................87
Establishing the Scope of the Active Directory................................88
Designing the Namespace 89
Planning DNS Strategy 90
Designing and Planning Organization Units 93
Developing an OU Delegation Plan..94
Planning Group Policy Object Management 97
Planning Policy Management for Client Computers........................99
Planning for Coexistence 100
Designing an Active Directory Site Topology 100
Designing a Replication Strategy 101
Defining Site Boundaries 102
Designing a Schema Modification Policy...103
Designing an Active Directory Implementation Plan..........................105
Single-Domain Windows NT System 106
Single-Master-Domain Windows NT System 106
Multiple-Master-Domain Windows NT System 107
Complete-Trust-Domain Windows NT System..............................108
A New Windows 2000 Domain 108
Chapter Review 109
Questions 110
Answers 110
Key Skill Sets 110
Key Terms 111

Chapter 5   Designing Your Service Locations. 113

Designing the Placement of Operations Masters.................................115
Understanding the Roles of Operations Masters 115
Schema Master...115
Domain Naming Master 117

Primary Domain Controller Emulator...118
Infrastructure Master...118
Relative Identifier Master 119
Role Placement 119
Permissions 120
Role Changing...120
Disaster Recovery...121
Designing the Placement of Global Catalog Servers 122
Global Catalog Servers 122
Global Catalog Server Placement Considerations 123
Designing the Placement of Domain Controller Servers 125
DNS Zone Planning..129
DNS Lookup Zones 130
DNS Zone Types 130
Where, Oh Where Should My DNS Go?..131
Designing the Placement of DNS Servers 132
Design 1 133
Design 2 133
Design 3 134
Design 4 134
Next Steps 135
Chapter Review..135
Questions 135
Answers 136
Key Skill Sets 136
Key Terms 137

Part II Exam 70-220: Designing Security for a Microsoft
Windows 2000 Network 139

Chapter 6 Introduction to Security........................... 141
Intruder Perspectives...141
The Business Case...142
Technical Tangents of Networking and Security..144
User and Group Account Management..144
Machine Security..145
Network and Communication Security 146
Public Key Infrastructure (PKI)..149

The Security Life Cycle...151
    Discovery..151
    Design...151
    Testing..151
    Deployment..152
    Evaluation...152
    Final Steps–Feedback...152
Chapter Review...153
    Questions...154
    Answers..154
    Key Skill Sets...154
    Key Terms..155

Chapter 7 Analyzing Business and Technical Requirements 157
Defining Security in the Enterprise 158
Evaluating Business Factors That Affect Security Planning.........................160
    Analyzing the Existing and Planned Business Models...........................161
    Analyzing Business Factors That Influence Company Strategies 163
Evaluating Your Technology Options in Security Planning..........................168
    Analyzing the Physical and Information-Security Models 171
    Understanding the Logical Layout of Services and Applications...........174
Understanding the People Factor in Security Planning 179
    Analyzing Business and Security Requirements for the End User 180
    Analyzing Network Roles and Responsibilities.....................................180
Evaluating Specific Security Vulnerabilities 182
    Lack of IT Staff Education 183
    Ineffective, Incomplete, or Missing Corporate Security Policies...........184
    User Education...185
    Proactive Anti-Hacking Measures 186
    Disaster-Recovery Plan 188
    Security Hotspots...189
Chapter Review...192
    Questions...193
    Answers 193
    Key Skill Sets 194
    Key Terms..194
    Additional Resources and Information 195

Chapter 8 Analyzing Security Requirements...................... 197

Assessing Your Current Environment...198
   Vulnerabilities 198
   Creating a Baseline 202
Developing a Security Policy 206
   Authenticating All User Access to System Resources.............................206
   Applying Appropriate Access Control to All Resources 209
   Establishing Appropriate Trust Relationships Between Multiple Domains.......212
   Enabling Data Protection for Sensitive Data 213
   Setting Uniform Security Policies..214
   Deploying Secure Applications 221
   Managing Security Administration 222
Implementing Your Security Policy...223
Chapter Review..229
   Questions 229
   Answers..230
   Key Skill Sets 230
   Key Terms 230

Chapter 9 Designing a Windows 2000 Security Solution 231

Windows 2000 Security Policies...232
   Audit Policies 233
   Delegation of Authority..243
   Policy Inheritance 249
   Encrypting File System (EFS) 253
Design an Authentication Strategy 260
   Authentication Methods...260
   Security Group Strategy 270
Design a Public Key Infrastructure..271
   Certificate Authority Hierarchies..271
   Certificate Server Roles 273
   Managing Certificates 277
   Third-Party Certificate Authorities 281
Design Windows 2000 Network Services Security 284
   DNS Security 285
   Remote Installation Services (RIS) Security 286
   SNMP Security 294
   Terminal Services Security 296

Chapter Review 306

    Questions 306

    Answers 307

    Key Skill Sets 307

    Key Terms 308

Chapter 10 Designing a Security Solution for Access
Between Networks **309**

Accessing the Internet 310

    Proxy Server 310

    Firewall 311

    Gateway 311

    Internet Connection Server 311

Common Internet File System (CIFS) 315

IP Security (IPSec) 317

    Windows 2000's Default IPSec Policies 318

    Policy Configuration 321

    Testing Your IPSec Configuration 333

Virtual Private Networks (VPNs) 333

    The VPN Server 336

    Installing a VPN Client 343

Remote Access Service 346

    Remote Access Authorization 353

Chapter Review 359

    Questions 359

    Answers 360

    Key Skill Sets 361

    Key Terms 361

Chapter 11 Designing Security for Communication Channels **363**

Common Communication Channel Attacks 364

Designing a Signing Solution with the Server Message Block Protocol 366

    SMB Signing Implementation 368

Designing IP Layer Security 369

    Selecting IPSec Mode 369

    Planning IPSec Protocol Usage 371

    Using Predefined IPSec Policies 372

    IPSec Implementation Components 374

    Designing an IPSec Management Strategy 377

Defining Security Levels 378
Designing Negotiation Policies...379
Designing Security Policies and Policy Management 382
Designing IPSec Encryption 384
Designing IPSec Filters 384
IPSec Best Practices 387
Verifying IPSec Communications 387
Chapter Review 391
Questions...391
Answers 392
Key Skill Sets 393
Key Terms 393

Part III Overview of Designing a Network Infrastructure 395

Chapter 12 Overview of Designing a Network Infrastructure 397
Windows 2000 Networking Services Design Overview................................397
The Networking Services Deployment Cycle................................401
Designing the Networking Services 402
Testing the Design...404
Implementing the Design 404
Managing the Network Services...405
Microsoft Windows 2000 Networking Services 405
Lab Exercise 12.1: Developing a Design Approach.......................406
The Network Foundation..408
Base Protocol Support—TCP/IP 409
Automated Client Configuration—DHCP.....................................410
Resolving Host Names—DNS..411
Lab Exercise 12.2: Solving a Name Resolution Design Problem 412
Resolving NetBIOS Names—WINS...412
Designing Internet Connectivity...413
Network Address Translation—NAT 414
Microsoft Internet Security and Acceleration Server 415
Designing Routing and Remote-Access Connectivity 416
Remote Access 416
RADIUS and IAS...417
IP Routing..417

Putting It All Together: Integrating the Network Services Infrastructure 418
    Creating Performance Monitor Log Files 419
    Defining the Network Design Attributes 426
Chapter Review 428
    Questions 429
    Answers 429
    Key Skill Sets 430
    Key Terms 430

Chapter 13   Analyzing Business and Technical Requirements 431
Analyzing the Business 433
    Analyzing the Geographical Scope and Existing and Planned
        Business Models 434
    Analyzing Company Processes 439
    Analyzing the Existing and Planned Organizational Structures 442
    Analyzing Factors That Influence Company Strategies 446
    Analyzing the IT Management Structure 450
    Business Requirements Analysis Checklist 457
Evaluating the Company's Technical Requirements 458
    Documenting the Existing Infrastructure Design 458
    Analyzing Client Computer Access Requirements 468
    Analyzing the Existing Disaster-Recovery Strategy 470
    Directions 475
    Business Background 475
    Current System 476
    IT Management Sample Interviews 477
    Envisioned System 477
    Case Study Questions: BTI Analysis 480
Chapter Review 481
    Questions 481
    Answers 482
    Key Skill Sets 483
    Key Terms 483

Chapter 14   Designing a Network Infrastructure Using TCP/IP 485
TCP/IP Background 487
    TCP/IP Protocol Suite 488
    TCP/IP Standards 488
    TCP/IP Protocol Architecture 490

Key TCP/IP Design Considerations 493
    Windows 2000 TCP/IP Features...493
    Windows 2000 TCP/IP Services 495
Designing a Functional TCP/IP Solution 495
    IP Addressing Review...496
    Private Network IP Addressing...499
    Subnet Requirements..503
    IP Configuration Approaches 504
TCP/IP Design for Improving Availability 505
TCP/IP Design for Improving Performance 507
    Optimizing IP Subnetting 507
    Optimizing Traffic on an IP Network...509
    Using QoS Mechanisms 510
TCP/IP Security Solutions 514
    Packet Filtering Techniques 514
    Data Encryption Design..515
    IPSec Encryption Algorithms..516
    IPSec Authentication Protocols 517
    IPSec Internet Key Exchange 517
Chapter Review..525
    Questions 526
    Answers 526
    Key Skill Sets 527
    Key Terms 527

Chapter 15   Designing an Automated IP Configuration Solution
              Using DHCP. **529**
Key DHCP Features...531
    Management Features...532
    Enhanced Monitoring and Statistical Reporting..............................532
    DNS and WINS Integration...533
    Rogue DHCP Server Detection...533
    User-Specific and Vendor-Specific Option Support...........................534
    DHCP Server Clustering..534
    Multicast IP Address Allocation 534
    DHCP Client Support..535
    Automatic Client Configuration 535
    Local Storage 535
    BOOTP Client Support..536

Combining DHCP with Other Services 536

    Active Directory Integration 536

    Dynamic Updates in the DNS Namespace 537

    Routing and Remote Access Integration 537

DHCP Design Choices 539

Functional Aspects of Designing a DHCP Solution 539

    Using DHCP Servers on the Network..540

    Configuring and Selecting TCP/IP Options on the Network 541

    Providing IP Configuration Management to BOOTP and
       Non-Microsoft Clients 542

    DHCP Sample Design for a Single Subnet LAN 543

    DHCP Example Design for a Large Enterprise Network..................................544

    DHCP Example Design for a Routed Network 545

    Relay Agent Deployment..545

    DHCP and Routing and Remote Access 547

    DHCP Server Placement 547

Creating a DHCP Solution to Ensure Service Availability 548

    Distributed Scope Solution 549

    Clustering Solution 550

Creating a DHCP Solution to Enhance Performance..550

    Increasing Performance of Individual DHCP Servers.....................................550

    Increasing Performance by Adding DHCP Servers 554

Designing a Secure DHCP Solution 554

    Preventing Unauthorized Windows 2000 Servers 555

    Security Risks Using DHCP in DMZ Networks..556

    Directions..557

    Scenario 557

    Design Requirements and Constraints..558

    Envisioned System 558

    Availability 559

    Performance...559

    Security..559

    Proposed System..559

    Chief Technology Officer's Comments..560

    Case Study Questions 560

Chapter Review..563

    Questions 564

    Answers 565

    Key Skill Sets 566

    Key Terms 567

Chapter 16 Creating a DNS Name-Resolution Design 569

The Domain Name System Solution 570

New Features in the Windows 2000 Implementation of DNS 571

Key Components of DNS 574

DNS Resolution Process 575

Resource Load-Sharing Control 576

Collecting Information for the DNS Design Decisions 579

Creating a Functional Windows 2000 DNS Strategy 579

DNS Zones and Zone Types 580

DNS Server Placement and Zone Type Considerations 585

Integrating DNS and WINS 588

Integrating with BIND and Windows NT 4.0 DNS Servers 590

Internet Access Considerations 598

Existing Namespace Integration Issues 599

Hands-On Section Exercises 599

Availability Considerations in Windows 2000 DNS Designs 601

Optimization Strategies in Windows 2000 DNS Designs 602

Server Capacity Optimization 602

Monitoring Server Performance 603

Query Resolution Optimization 609

Reducing the Impact of Server-to-Server Traffic on the Network 611

Security Strategies in DNS Designs 611

Secured Dynamic Update 611

Controlling Update Access to Zones 612

DNS Dynamic Updates from DHCP and Windows 2000 612

DNS Zone Replication 613

DNS in Screened Subnets 613

Hands-On Section Exercises 613

Chapter Review 623

Questions 624

Answers 624

Key Skill Sets 625

Key Terms 625

Chapter 17 Designing with WINS Services and DFS 627

The Microsoft WINS Solution 627

WINS Background 628

NetBIOS Name Resolution 629

Creating a WINS Design 635
   Initial WINS Design Steps 636
   Designing a Functional WINS Solution 637
   Enhancing WINS Availability 646
   Optimizing WINS Performance 648
   Securing a WINS Solution 651
Designing a Distributed File System (DFS) Strategy 652
   DFS Architecture 653
   DFS Platform Compatibility 653
   DFS Features 654
   Key DFS Terms 656
   Placing a DFS Root 657
   DFS Root Replica Strategy for High Availability 658
Chapter Review 667
   Questions 668
   Answers 669
   Key Skill Sets 670
   Key Terms 670

Chapter 18   Designing Internet and Extranet Connectivity
           Solutions 671

Firewalls 673
   Common Firewall Technologies 675
   Firewall Placement 679
   Demilitarized Zones or Screened Subnets 679
Routing and Remote Access 680
Windows 2000 Network Address Translation 681
   Designing a Functional NAT Solution 682
   Designing for NAT Availability and Performance 685
   NAT Security Considerations 686
   Outbound Internet Traffic 686
   Inbound Internet Traffic 687
   VPNs and Network Address Translators 687
Internet Connection Sharing 687
Web Caching with a Proxy Server 688
   What Does a Proxy Server Do? 688
   Protecting the Network 689
   Microsoft Proxy Server 689

Designing a Functional Proxy Server Solution 691
Designing for Proxy Server Availability and Performance................................693
Proxy Server Security Considerations 694
Comparing Internet-Connection Sharing Solutions 695
Scenario...696
Case Study Question 697
Chapter Review...698
Questions 699
Answers..700
Key Skill Sets 701
Key Terms..701

Chapter 19   Designing a Wide Area Network Infrastructure 703
Connecting Private Networks Using RRAS...705
Installing and Configuring RRAS 707
Routing for Connectivity Between Private Networks 713
Designing a Functional Routing Solution 716
Securing Private Network Connections 728
Optimizing a Router Design for Availability and Performance 729
RRAS Solutions Using Demand-Dial Routing 730
Designing Remote-User Connectivity 730
Designing a VPN Strategy...732
Designing Remote-Access Dial-Up Solutions...733
Designing a Dial-Up or VPN Solution in a Routed Network..............................734
Performance and Availability Design Considerations....................................734
Security Considerations...735
VPN Best Practices 737
Dial-Up Best Practices 738
Designing a Remote-Access Solution Using RADIUS...739
Integrating Authentication with RADIUS...740
Why Use IAS? 743
Designing a Functional RADIUS Solution 743
RADIUS Fault-Tolerance and Performance Solutions 744
Security Considerations for RADIUS...745
Chapter Review...747
Questions 748
Answers..750
Key Skill Sets..751
Key Terms 752

Chapter 20   Designing a Management and Implementation
Strategy for Windows 2000 Networking. **753**

Network Services Management Strategies 754
   Identifying Management Processes 755
   Monitoring the Network Services Status 755
   Analyzing the Information 762
   Reactive and Proactive Response Strategies 763
Combining Networking Services 763
   Benefits of Combining Networking Services 763
   Constraints on Combining Networking Services 764
   Security Issues Related to Combining Services 765
   Combining Networking Services That Are Cluster-Aware 765
   Optimizing Performance by Combining Services 766
Chapter Review 767
   Questions 768
   Answers 769
   Key Skill Sets 770
   Key Terms 770

Part IV   Bringing It All Together. **771**

Chapter 21   The Holistic Windows 2000 Design Process. **773**

Building Blocks 773
   Active Directory 774
   Security 775
   Network Infrastructure 775
   Common Elements 775
Next Steps—Life as an MCSE 776
Chapter Review 778

Part V   Appendixes. **779**

Appendix A   More Case Study Analyses and Questions **781**

Four Case Studies for Analysis 781
Exam Questions on the Topics Presented in this Book 813
   Encrypting File System (Six Questions) 813
   Auditing (Three Questions) 816
   Public Key Infrastructure (11 Questions) 818
   Internet Protocol Security (Six Questions) 825
   Active Directory Services (27 Questions) 830

Appendix B MCSE Certification Specifics. 843

Microsoft's New Certification Track 843

Your Commitment to Getting Certified 844

Role of Real-World Experience. 844

Opportunities for MCSEs. 846

Compensation 847

Ongoing Certification Requirements 850

Life as an MCSE Professional 851

    Work. 851

    Continuing Education 851

    Conferences. 852

    User Groups 852

Certification Exam Objectives 852

    Exam 70-210: Installing, Configuring, and Administering
        Microsoft Windows 2000 Professional 853

    Exam 70-215: Installing, Configuring, and Administering
        Microsoft Windows 2000 Server. 857

    Exam 70-216: Implementing and Administering a Microsoft
        Windows 2000 Network Infrastructure. 860

    Exam 70-217: Implementing and Administering a Microsoft
        Windows 2000 Directory Services Infrastructure. 863

    Exam 70-219: Designing a Microsoft Windows 2000 Directory
        Services Infrastructure 866

    Exam 70-220: Designing Security for a Microsoft Windows
        2000 Network 869

    Exam 70-221: Designing a Microsoft Windows 2000
        Network Infrastructure. 872

Appendix C Case Study Analysis Approach 877

Case Study Method 878

Management Value. 878

How to Approach a Case 880

Index 897

FOREWORD

If you think you have picked up just another book about becoming a Microsoft Certified Systems Engineer in Windows 2000, think again! This particular book happens to be written by Harry Brelsford and Michael Henrichsen who are definitely not just average MCSEs. What you will find, as in Harry's previous books, is a writing style that is understandable by not only the technical professional working in the field today, but also by the person considering a career transition to the technical profession—and that includes people with no technical background at all. Harry and Michael present the material in a scenario-based format, presenting problems and describing solutions with detailed explanations. This is very similar to the way the Windows 2000 exams are presented, although Harry and Michael admit early on in the book that the text alone will probably not prepare a person to take the certification exams. Hands-on experience with the product is extremely important and is strongly emphasized in the new curriculum.

I've managed a Certified Technical Education Center (CTEC) for more than two years with Paladin Data Systems in Poulsbo, Washington. It was a challenge to absorb the MCSE NT 4.0 requirements and then articulate these requirements to potential students in an understandable way. In comparing the MCSE NT 4.0 with the Windows 2000 certification, I discovered quickly that there is really very little to compare. The exams now measure the ability of a person to think on their feet and solve real-world problems. On the positive side, with the certification becoming more of a challenge to complete, we probably won't see MCSEs saddled with the denigrating sobriquet of "paper MCSE," a term made common in many magazine and newspaper articles about the MCSE field. In the good old days, it was possible for students to pass the exams through memorization and self-study of exam materials. The new program has shifted the focus to real-world problems and situations, and the new exams reflect this change. Be prepared to think and solve problems when taking the Windows 2000 exams.

Today, Paladin is moving into the network support business and we are employing our own staff of MCSEs, MCSDs, and MCDBAs. We talk to customers every day who ask our advice on the different types of hardware and software they should buy to meet their business requirements. That's when the help of a qualified networking professional is indispensable. Like many employers, we know that the MCSE designation implies a certain level of expertise in the field. The good news is that we have not been disappointed! The readers of this book should know that the technical qualifications are not the whole story and Harry and Michael do a great job of investigating the other qualities a good MCSE should have to be successful. For instance, they both talk about the value of integrating MCSE technical know-how with the business savvy of the MBA. Instead of the technical person and the financial person or decision-maker sitting at opposite ends of the building, they are sitting at the same table, developing a business strategy that meets the customer's needs.

MCSEs today are in a position to make technical recommendations that impact the bottom line and they must be prepared to provide concrete justification for their recommendations. In other words, the MCSE must be an interpreter, someone who can translate a company's functional requirements and specifications and communicate them to the decision-maker. This means presenting data and information in a logical format and being prepared to discuss alternatives or options. The MCSE is also a negotiator and should be prepared to explain benefits and trade-offs for each alternative course of action.

Harry and Michael cover all the bases of network design, infrastructure, and security. They know the mind-set of the techno-professional, so they are able to address the issues that matter most to their readers. How many MCSEs are waiting for the right company to come along and ask them to design a brand-new network from the ground up? A lot! But, realistically, how often is that going to happen? As Harry and Michael point out, an MCSE typically will inherit a network and then have to make it work—a challenging job when working with limited resources.

In presenting the topic, "Designing a Security Solution for Access Between Networks," Harry and Michael reiterate the importance of security on a network and identify the different types of security available with Windows 2000. Security and privacy are major initiatives and concerns throughout the industry. MCSEs need to be prepared to explain to a customer the different types of network security that can be activated and the possible impacts to performance or vice versa.

The essence of networks is communication and Harry and Michael's book takes this once step further. Their emphasis on the MCSE needing to be a skilled communicator is right on. One of the most frustrating moments for a customer is the not knowing what's wrong with a network and when it will be fixed. The MCSE must not only be a skilled technician to analyze the problem and ultimately solve it. He or she must also be able to communicate the extent of the problem to a non-technical user, explain the possible solutions in layman's terms, as diplomatically as possible explain how long each solution will take, and how much it could cost. In many instances, an MCSE may not have the answers either, but the MCSE needs to be able to analyze a problem and communicate with the customer. The lack of communication can leave doubt in the customers' mind.

I congratulate Harry and Michael on this book, their writing style, and approach in explaining Windows 2000. This is not only a knowledge-based book, but also an excellent reference book to use while pursuing your MCSE Windows 2000 certification. Good luck and have fun!

Peggy J. Roy
Vice President
Paladin Data Systems
Poulsbo, Washington

ACKNOWLEDGMENTS

Where do we begin with the thanks on such a mammoth undertaking?

The authors would certainly like to start with the team at Osborne/**McGraw-Hill** who helped us slay every dragon we found around every corner on this road trip. And believe us, there were more dragons than we anticipated. These helpers include Jessica Wilson, Michael Sprague, Gareth Hancock, Betsy Manini, Andy Carroll, Stefany Otis and good old John Read.

Next up are all of the worker bees who worked hard in the background and under deep cover to pull together a million bits and bytes in completing this work. A tip of the hat to Anita Varghese, who started assisting us with case study development while being a full-time graduate student in the Information Technology program in the Graduate School of Business and Economics at Seattle Pacific University. Anita has since finished her Masters and is gainfully employed in the technology industry in the Pacific Northwest (you go girl!). We called on Mike Toot and Dave Mackey to assist us with some prickly security chapters and we're forever grateful. We owe special thanks to George Oakes, and Kim Hinrichsen for their help with Test Question development, and to Bruce Rudd for helping us with the CD-ROM. A few ardent BackOffice Professional Association (BOPA) members—Russell Rosco (a college professor at Shoreline Community College in Seattle), Timothy R. Smith (Major, Network Control Center Manager, U.S. Army in Tacoma, Washington), and Alice Goodman (Network Analyst at Airborne Express in Seattle, Washington)—pitched in with pages of valued content, advice, and review.

Others who deserve mention include the staff and faculty at Seattle Pacific University, where both of us teach MCSE courses to people just like you who are reading this book! These special people include George Myers, Gerhard Steinke, Alec Hill, Kristen Gauche, Travis Voltz, and David Wicks. And our employers and clients have provided countless war stories (as well as bona fide technical experiences) that have ended up on these pages. All told, the above parties have greatly contributed to the positive outcome of this book.

A Special Note from Harry Brelsford

Speaking in the first person, I'd like to thank Michael's ongoing commitment to this book. I think Michael would now agree that the experience was as valuable (if not more) as the time he spent studying at Harvard University. Michael, shall we dance again (after a long vacation, of course)?! I also thank the staff at *Microsoft Certified Professional Magazine* for winks, nods, backslaps, and other forms of encouragement (these made no small difference in completing this work!).

A Special Note from Michael Hinrichsen

I think Harry will agree that whenever we take on a project as enormous as this one, it sounds very good. It usually takes some time before we realize the enormity of the task before us and we start looking at things like page count. Then, before you know it, someone is asking for dedications and acknowledgments. The time does fly . . .

I would like to thank my partner, Harry Brelsford, for offering me this opportunity and Osborne/**McGraw-Hill**. Harry originally recommended me to Osborne and is a true friend, a true professional, and someone whom I respect deeply. He also has a great "Texas accent," which was used throughout this book to its benefit. The folks at Osborne/**McGraw-Hill** have also been a pleasure to work with and I would work with them again in a heartbeat.

INTRODUCTION

Perhaps you shared in the surprise expressed by many certification candidates seeking to earn the Microsoft Certified Systems Engineer (MCSE) designation under Windows 2000: things have changed since the old days (the days of Windows NT Server 4.0, that is). To say that the MCSE program has been revamped is an understatement. One of the most notable changes is the emphasis on information system design, the focus of this book.

Why the emphasis on design topics? Microsoft is attempting to turn the technical nature of the MCSE designation into a professional designation with a technical emphasis. Instead of being a photocopier repair person, which is analogous to how some business people have viewed the MCSE historically in its technical realm, the new MCSE should be viewed very differently. Microsoft is elevating the MCSE designation into the ranks of physical engineers who earn the PE designation after passing exams administered by a board of peers. I'm not sure the MCSE designation is ascending to the level of the certified public accountant (CPA), medical doctor (MD), or state bar-approved attorney, but Microsoft is clearly raising the bar of professionalism for the MCSE under Windows 2000.

Defining the Windows 2000 MCSE

Microsoft has changed the Windows 2000 MCSE program in the following ways:

- **Design and planning emphasis** As we mentioned, the design and planning dimension is a new addition to the MCSE program. We'll discuss this more in a moment.

- **Four core exams with no consumer desktop operating system** The MCSE title has sharpened its focus on Microsoft networking and server-based solutions. The consumer desktop operating systems, such as Windows 9x and Windows ME, are being de-emphasized in the land of MCSEs. It is possible that these desktop operating systems will be supported by Microsoft's Office Users Specialist (MOUS) program, which is a Microsoft certification program for desktop applications, such as Microsoft Word, Excel, and PowerPoint.

- **Limited electives** Another shift in the MCSE program is the focus on networking infrastructure at the expense of supporting other BackOffice and Microsoft server applications, such as SQL Server. Microsoft is saying that an MCSE will have more than a half-dozen networking and infrastructure exams under his or her belt. Certifications in individual server-based applications will either occur because the title was earned in the legacy Windows NT Server 4.0 MCSE days, or additional exams will be passed above and beyond the stringent Windows 2000 MCSE requirements.

- **No paper MCSEs here** Clearly stung by public criticism, Microsoft has vowed to make the MCSE designation a respectable title that is difficult to earn. My assessment, and that of other test takers, is that Microsoft has clearly succeeded. Even long-time MCSEs are fearful about meeting the MCSE renewal requirements, sensing that the days of the paper MCSEs have come to an end. In the sense that no MCSE candidate could reasonably read and memorize the exam topics, the exams are more experienced-based. My take on it is that the exams now draw from multiple areas, requiring you to integrate unrelated subjects. For example, the Windows 2000 Professional exam (70-210) has questions that address Group Policy, a server-side issue. If you've had experience working with Windows 2000 Professional and Group Policy, the exam questions on this topic might not be so daunting. However, if you're a loyal reader and have read about Windows 2000 Server, Professional, and Active Directory, it's unlikely you'd be as proficient at integrating these disparate topics as someone who's actually been there and done that! The point that we're making here, later in this Introduction, and many other times in this book is that your success as an MCSE will be directly correlated to the amount and quality of technical experiences you have (and enjoy!).

- **Thinning the ranks** As suggested in the previous point, some qualified and experienced MCSEs will be left behind in the Windows 2000 era. Why? In part, it's the time commitment required to master the world of Windows 2000 and pass the seven MCSE exams. Legacy MCSEs, already earning significant salaries, are going to ask hard questions about investing up to several hundred hours to retain a designation once they've "made it" in the eyes of their mothers, themselves, and their bank accounts (flush with earnings, which many consider a sign of success). One interesting consideration when discussing the thinning of the MCSE ranks is the economic effect. When times are good and people are making money, working overtime, and so on, it's hard to justify the hours pulled away from money-making endeavors to go pursue education. This is known as the counter-cyclical effect of education: class enrollments boom in bad times and lag in good times. Depending on whether you believe the economy will thrive or falter, the economy may clearly affect the number of MCSEs in the Windows 2000 era. Finally, we've already witnessed some legacy MCSEs move into management due, in part, to hands-on technology burnout and to career maturation (higher salaries in management). One night, at a BackOffice Professionals Association (BOPA) monthly meeting, we saw a long-time member look agitated and head for the exit halfway through a Windows 2000 MCSE exam preparation speech. Curious as to whether the member didn't enjoy the speaker, we intercepted this disgruntled dude in the parking lot. "We've had it! I'm not renewing our MCSE in Windows 2000. I'm not that big of a gear head," he offered, arms waving. Turns out this individual had gone as far with the MCSE designation (circa Windows NT 4 MCSE) as he wanted to. He was going to accept the management position at the dot-com company. We suspect other MCSEs will arrive at the same conclusion.

TIP Ironically, the last class of MCSEs, the ones moving into management, can benefit most from this book and the designing exams in the Windows 2000 MCSE certification track. Why? Because the new MCSE program, with its design exams, embraces many tried-and-true management approaches. Read on for more of our insights on the role of "management" in the Windows 2000 MCSE program.

The New Design Paradigm

So where can Microsoft's changes, making life tougher for Windows 2000 MCSEs, be best displayed? We'd say the introduction to the designing exams is one of the best examples of raising the bar. The designing paradigm is truly a shift in thinking, as we'll explain next, and it is a theme we will repeat often in this book. Already, test takers (including the authors of this book) are reporting that these designing exams are more difficult than other MCSE certification exams. And that's all the evidence the authors' need that the design exams have raised the testing standards that must be met to earn the coveted Windows 2000 MCSE designation.

Backroom to Boardroom

You're no longer just the computer repair guy—you're now the technology advisor as well. You have to be both hands-on and a thinker. Not only must you have the skills to perform step-by-step configurations in Windows 2000 and replace RAM memory sticks, but you need the wisdom of Solomon to map out the information system infrastructure on the white boards of the corporate boardroom. We can just imagine the prototypical image of the Windows 2000 MCSE: Superman. Not only are the performance expectations higher, but you'll need to quickly stop in and change from coveralls to suit and tie as you are pulled out of the back room and rushed to the boardroom. Clearly, life as an MCSE under Windows 2000 is only going to be more interesting and challenging, not less. Perhaps this is best shown in Figure I-1.

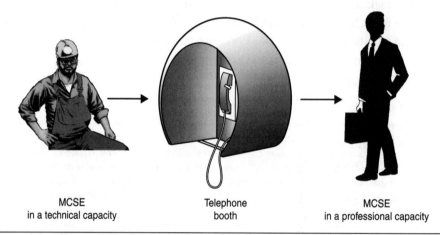

MCSE
in a technical capacity

Telephone
booth

MCSE
in a professional capacity

Figure I-I The modern-day Superman!—The Windows 2000 MCSE

Cultural Revolution: Blue Collar Meets White Collar

Clearly, a large number of old-school MCSEs rose through the ranks of the break-fix computer community. Many started out repairing printers and the like. Some even punched time cards in a time clock (and some still do). Fast-forward to the new Windows 2000 MCSE and you'll find, with the introduction of the design paradigm, a white-collar MCSE. This will be a challenge for some from the blue-collar community, long taught to view professionals with skepticism. We'll pay good money for front row seats to witness this convergence of cultures!

Analytical Advancement: MCSEs and MBAs

The MCSE meets the MBA! The Windows 2000 design process is an analytical process, not a step-by-step cookbook approach to computers. This design process is much more ambiguous, much like strategic planning in business. Design alternatives will emerge from your MCSE design process, each with its own merits. In fact, there may be no one correct answer as to how the Windows 2000 network should look. Rather, each design alternative may stand on its own, technically, resulting in you and the other design team members making a judgment call on how to proceed.

The muddled picture we've just presented is the world that management team members in a company live in. Welcome to MBA country. If anything, the MCSEs will develop keener business-process skills as a result of the design exams in the Windows 2000 MCSE track. And who knows, with MCSEs working side by side with MBAs, maybe a little BackOffice technical know-how will rub off on the business people, making the world a better place, eh?

Communication Skills

In the past, being a great communicator wasn't necessarily a success factor in the technical community. That is, a grumpy guru holding the MCSE designation could make a very good living on technical know-how alone. That's changing with the design paradigm in the Windows 2000 MCSE. No longer can you fuss with a server, do a reboot, and walk away as an honored god. The design process demands much greater communication, both oral and written. Why? Because you'll be working with a wide range of stakeholders as you endeavor to create and implement your vision of what the Windows 2000 network should look like. On any given day, when you have your MCSE designer hat on (perhaps even designer clothing, but that comes with the money, which we'll discuss shortly), you'll talk with fellow MCSE tech-heads, unsophisticated end users, and sophisticated executives who can single-handedly eliminate your budget.

The point is this. The business community that you'll interact with, as part of the Windows 2000 network design process, expects and requires sufficient, if not superior, written and spoken communications. Here communication skills are truly a success factor. The good news is that if you're an MCSE who, shall we say, had technical limits in the legacy Windows NT era but you are smooth as silk when it comes to speaking, then this MCSE is for you! Granted, you'll need the requisite Windows 2000 technical knowledge, but your communication skills will really kick in with the design process. Trust us!

Professional Politics

We feel compelled to tell you straight up, that the design process is a political process. We can just hear you saying "ouch!" And we don't blame you. On some days, when we're in an introverted mood, we still prefer to just close the barn door and play with the server farm, not allowing pesky people to ruin a good time. But the design process isn't nearly that insular. Rather, you'll conduct needs analysis, attend meetings, tolerate kind and unkind comments behind your back, and be befriended by people who really aren't your friends. Welcome to the big leagues!

The Abstract—Poets, Artists, and MCSEs

The freeform design process, as exemplified in the arts community, likely has a role in your Windows 2000 MCSE thinking. In the Apple Macintosh community, long a haven for turtleneck-wearing artistic types, the emphasis has always been less on the bits and bytes of the technology and more on the design process. The Mac people have traditionally been less interested in the computers themselves and more interested in what the computers allowed them to do. You and I, as Windows 2000 MCSEs, can learn something here. Isn't the abstract element really one of questioning "why are we here?" Indeed. By viewing the desired outputs, such as "what if we could do this?" you'll have more creative designs that address the end result and place less emphasis on the bits and bytes.

Oh—Higher Pay!

So far we've cast a long but realistic shadow on the path to becoming a Windows 2000 MCSE. But there is, of course, a pot of gold awaiting those who make it. The revamped MCSE program really reflects a value-added process. Not only does earning the MCSE title add value to your professional career, but the Windows 2000 MCSE offers added value over the legacy MCSE title from the Windows NT 4.0 days.

Here's what we mean. The old MCSE focused on technical solutions, agreed? And the new Windows 2000 MCSE adds the design elements, right? It has been our experience that the marketplace financially rewards those with more abstract skills, such as design and planning, over those who efficiently perform routine tasks time and time again. That's something to consider as you attempt to maximize the return on your MCSE investment.

Bringing It All Together—The Exams

Obviously, the designing exams are nearly half of the Windows 2000 MCSE certification experience. That much is apparent by looking at the qualifying MCSE exams, from which you pick seven to complete. However, the exams bring together many of the points we raised earlier. Although the exams are presented under the guise of being more experienced-based, in reality the exams are more analytical, which means you not only need more hands-on experience, but you also need greater thinking skills. One example of this is the reading comprehension skills. Those with strong reading skills will do well when it comes to the long case studies that are standard on the Windows 2000 MCSE design exams.

The designing exams also integrate all of your core Windows 2000 knowledge. The good news is that the hard work you did to pass the core exams is reused here, with a few twists. These twists are in the design paradigm that builds on the core exams. Think of it this way. An architect in the building trades fancies herself as more of a designer than a hands-on builder. Fair enough. But for an architect to create buildings that don't fall down, she must, of course, have a core knowledge of building techniques, materials, specifications, and building codes. It's the same for a Widows 2000 MCSE who is taking the designing exams. You can't really design a Windows 2000 network until you know the finer points of Windows 2000 networking. This was the mindset in placing the designing exams after the core exams in the Windows 2000 MCSE track.

Sample Company—Catywhompus

As a long-time Microsoft Certified Trainer (MCT), we've learned that students learn best when the information being presented is put in some type of context. There are a number of ways to do this in both writing and in the classroom: war stories, fables, analogies, and sample companies. For this work, we've collaborated with Marcus Barton, the author of *MCSE Windows 2000 Core All-in-One Exam Guide* (Osborne/McGraw-Hill, 2001), ISBN: 0-07-212747-3. We have created a sample company that crosses over both books and is presented in each chapter. This allows you to put the technical and design information in a familiar context while enjoying the ins and outs of Catywhompus Construction, Inc., a California construction company.

Details

So here are the facts on Catywhompus. The real details follow over the next several hundred pages as you observe how Catywhompus develops as an integral part of this book's storyline and facilitates your understanding of the Windows 2000 MCSE design process.

Company Name	Catywhompus
Industry	Construction (commercial general contractor)
Headquarters	Oakland, California
Other Locations	New York City, Los Angles, Chicago, London, Tokyo
President	Bob Smith
Major Departments	Constructions, Operations, Project Management, Marketing, Finance and Accounting, Human Resources
Business Basics	The company is doing well and is profitable. May consider merging with another firm within the next year. May acquire other firms within the next year.
Networking Basics	Windows 2000–based network. Wide area network (WAN) linking all sites. Remote construction sites not listed under "Other Locations" are linked via virtual private network (VPN) connection over the Internet. Professional staff often will connect to the network via VPN from home and while traveling. Major use of fax over IP to transmit construction specifications, documents, and drawings. Online storage of specifications, documents, and drawings has been implemented in the last 12 months.
Internet Domain Name	Catywhompus.com

A graphical representation of Catywhompus is displayed in Figure I-2.

Storyline Continuity

The continuity provided by having a sample company in this and also in Burton's *MCSE Windows 2000 Core All-in-One Exam Guide* is considered to be an especially effective instructional design mechanism. Not only do you have a familiar storyline, but if you are ever lost in the discussion, you can simply fall back to an earlier point of reference in the Catywhompus tale to regain your footing.

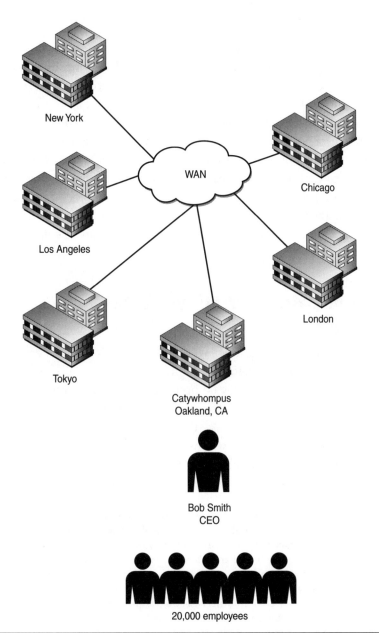

Figure I-2 Welcome to Catywhompus, the sample company used for case studies and examples in this book.

Truly All in One

The use of Catywhompus is consistent with the all-in-one nature of this MCSE study guide. Please pardon the pun, but this book is designed to bring all of the Windows 2000 MCSE design exams under one cover. That's easily accomplished by creating an outline that lists the 70-219, 70-220, and 70-221 exams. So far, no problem. What is much more difficult to accomplish is tying the design exams together into some coherent framework so you emerge not only certified, but are more than satisfied with the MCSE certification experience. The use of Catywhompus is our approach to meeting and exceeding your expectations in this area. More importantly, as a practicing MCSE, we suspect you'll long appreciate how the divergent design topics of directory services, networking infrastructure, and security were blended into a coherent and holistic model of understanding by having a recurring sample company to guide the way.

Learning Microsoft Windows 2000 Technologies

No matter who you are, this book alone will not likely result in your becoming a Windows 2000 MCSE. You need experience to supplement your education. For many of you working long MCSE hours already, say 60-hour weeks, getting experience is clearly not the problem. Finding time to study is. For others using the MCSE avenue as a chance to better themselves and change careers, getting experience can be more difficult. At a minimum, every reader of this book will need a Windows 2000 network with at least one server machine and one client machine. This will allow you to better follow the discussion in the book by using your own network for test-preparation purposes.

TIP It has been our experience that all MCSE candidates have a test network somewhere to gain experience, and this test network often consists of more than one server, so you can truly have a tree of domain controllers, and so on. Even if you work with Windows 2000 in a production environment by day, it's in your best interest to have a test network available to practice what we're preaching in this book. We would be remiss if we advised otherwise. Do not practice for your MCSE designing certification exams on a production network! Enough said.

Here are a few tips we've shared with readers over the years for getting more hands-on experience with Microsoft networking solutions such as Windows 2000:

- *Read the "Professionally Speaking" column in Microsoft Certified Professional Magazine.* You'll find it at www.mcpmag.com. It's great for the latest tips and tricks for gaining more bona fide work experience. The entire magazine is a good read for certification matters in general, and we will often refer to it in this book.

- *Volunteer.* Select a non-profit and help the political candidate of your choice to implement a Windows 2000 network. These tend to be wonderful, and forgiving, learning environments for gaining experience.

- *Go to school with your kid!* Assuming you have children (or even if you don't), join other parents who are working for free (there's that "volunteering" term again) to help network the school, serve as lab aides, and so on.

- *Hang out with the networking gurus.* At work, maybe you are in a department such as Finance, but you really yearn to be an MCSE. Our advice? Go hang out with them. You'd be surprised that, in most cases, existing MCSEs are willing to mentor MCSE candidates.

- *Seek out and attend user groups.* Seek out and attend the monthly user-group meeting of your choice in your community. In many cities and towns, there are Windows 2000 and MCSE user groups. Often these groups have donated equipment that has been used to create a test lab. "Seek, and ye shall find" (and get a leg up in passing the Windows 2000 MCSE exams!).

Next Step—Start the MCSE Journey!

So your next step, assuming you either have Windows 2000 experience or have put a plan in place to gain such experience, is to reflect for a moment on the design paradigm discussion presented here. In short, do you "feel" the MCSE Zen underlying Windows 2000? Do you "get it?" If so, great! Let's move on to Chapter 1 and jump into the heart of the MCSE journey! (And if not, hang in there. After a few chapters, we assure you that it'll all come naturally.)

PART I

Exam 70-219: Designing a Microsoft Windows 2000 Directory Services Infrastructure

- **Chapter 1**   Defining Directory Services
- **Chapter 2**   Analyzing Business Requirements
- **Chapter 3**   Analyzing Technical Requirements
- **Chapter 4**   Designing a Directory Service Architecture
- **Chapter 5**   Designing Your Service Locations

Defining Directory Services

This chapter covers the following key mastery goals:

- Understand directory services, including knowing what directory services are and are not
- Understand Active Directory from the top down

Without question, as an aspiring MCSE candidate and practitioner, you've heard much ado about directory services. Perhaps you heard the term discussed some years back in the context of competing operating systems, such as Novell NetWare. Or perhaps you heard of directory services more recently with the release of Windows 2000 and the much-touted Active Directory. Active Directory is, of course, the subject of this and the next several chapters as part of Exam 70-219, "Designing a Microsoft Windows 2000 Directory Services Infrastructure."

The Windows 2000 hype is more subdued now than when it was launched in February 2000 and Active Directory was cited as one of the top reasons to purchase Windows 2000. However, several reasons for implementing Active Directory are explained in this chapter. We'll also look at some of the top reasons for implementing Windows 2000, to provide both foundation information and context. That comes later in the chapter after we've taken several pages to define Active Directory.

Introducing Catywhompus Construction

No chapter in this book is complete without some discussion of our sample company, Catywhompus Construction, Inc. As mentioned in the Introduction of this book,

continued

Catywhompus is a hypothetical international construction company based in Oakland, California. Catywhompus is really a composite of companies that have gained experience in planning for and deploying Active Directory. When that experience wasn't enough, we had coffee with fellow Windows 2000 MCSEs to pick their brains for more Active Directory war stories. In this chapter, we often visit Catywhompus and relate it to the discussion.

Common Understanding of Directory Services

Let's take a look at some of the common elements of a directory-services solution. You'll note that we frame this directory-services discussion in the context of Active Directory (which shouldn't surprise the Windows 2000 MCSE). Directory services are often thought of in the following ways:

- **Ultimate computer-network telephone book**   This is a popular view of directory services that speaks to the management of computers, groups, users, and numerous other types of objects (including custom objects that you can create).

- **Ultimate unification provider**   A goal of all directory services, and one that is achieved by none, is setting a single sign-on standard for everything on the network (literally having one logon, no others). That means the accounting software you work with would use the network username and password for logon purposes, and information changes made to a user inside the accounting system would be duly noted by the directory services. The current generation of directory services is making strides toward this ultimate unification goal. For example, Exchange 2000 is very Active Directory-aware. Unification also means that different networks and operating systems should share critical authentication and configuration information, but the ultimate unification strategy is a meta-directory, which is still the stuff of Ph.D. theses—we'll discuss this later in the "Predicting the Future: Meta-Directories" section.

- **Ultimate computer network index**   This refers to the ability to query the information system infrastructure for information, locations of data, settings, and so on.

- **Ultimate war room and mission-control center**   One goal behind directory services is the ability to organize your network. For example, with Active Directory, you can organize your network as you see fit and create domains and organizational units (OUs) that reflect the geopolitical structure of your firm. You can also manage the namespace, such as the Internet domain names, used in your organization. And don't forget security, which is another important role for directory services. Finally, the directory services schema contains definitions of objects and the attributes (the data) for those objects.

- **Ultimate reliability** A directory-services mechanism must be accessible and available, backed up (or at least recoverable), accurate, and otherwise reliable. It contains core information about your information-system infrastructure, and it must necessarily maintain the confidence of you and your users. At all locations, this is typically accomplished by replication between domain controllers (those god-like Windows 2000 Server machines). That is, all or a part of the directory-services database is maintained on different servers. Two terribly complex little devils called *bridgehead servers* and *global catalog servers* (these names are designations of honor for these servers) play a huge role in facilitating the replication process. (For more information on replication, see the "Replication and PDAs" sidebar.)

- **Ultimate growth path** As a system-wide database, a directory service must be able to accommodate growth in the organization, including mergers and divestitures.

- **Customizable database** Believe it or not, you can use Active Directory to perform some minor database functions (but we'd certainly recommend using SQL Server instead). For example, you can store user contact information along with photos and other graphic images, if you desire.

Replication and PDAs

Not sure you completely understand replication? Don't worry. There is a very easy way to understand the replication being performed by Active Directory. Simply look at a personal digital assistant (PDA), such as the generic Pocket PC, or a brand such as Phillips Nino or one of the Palm handhelds. These business-class PDAs have the capability to connect your PDA directly to your computer to synchronize your appointments, contacts, tasks, and e-mail with your network-based e-mail system. This is

continued

commonly done using the Windows Pocket PC (formerly Windows CE) operating system which synchronizes with Microsoft Outlook. If the PDA doesn't use Windows Pocket PC, it likely uses the Palm OS to accomplish the same type of synchronization.

At startup, when your PDA is connected to your computer, the two devices synchronize information in both directions. That is, if you've made an appointment while outside of the office and "tapped" it into your PDA, this appointment time-slot is outdated on the scheduler on your computer. When the information is synchronized, only the delta (the changed) data is synchronized. It's not as if your entire appointment, contacts, and tasks databases are downloaded to the PDA each time you synchronize them.

The same thing occurs periodically with Active Directory. Active Directory replication involves transferring changes and modifications to other servers that hold copies of the Active Directory database. In Texas and the testing lab, we might call these changes the *delta data*; the point being that the entire database isn't replicated.

Directory Services and Meta-Information

As an MCSE, you will probably interact with some of the underlying building blocks of directory services each day (such as the management and recycling of information), without even thinking much about it. Take, for example, the idea of meta-information. Meta-information is high-level information that is used for multiple purposes. Database administrators (DBAs) would think of this as a one-to-many relationship. But for those of us who aren't DBAs, think of meta-information as "information about information" (as odd as that admittedly sounds).

Directory services, and thus Active Directory, contain meta-information. This is object information that is searchable and that is used across the Active Directory, such as a username. Now extend this thinking on meta-information to include custom objects and data in the Active Directory database and you can begin to see how powerful Active Directory can be in managing enterprise meta-information. Truly, the old phrase of "the possibilities are endless" applies here. Stick with us as we continue to define meta-information (we understand it can be a difficult topic to grasp).

So how will this apply in a practical sense? Perhaps someday in the future you'll check into a hotel, and not only will the staff know your entire customer history with that hotel chain, but they'll quickly identify and start the in-room movie that best fits your personality. What's important to understand here is that this movie would likely come from some distant database elsewhere on the Internet that contains a listing of every movie ever made.

History and Types of Directory Services

To understand directory services like Active Directory, it is critical to understand their history. What is the evolution of directory services that resulted in Active Directory?

All software development is subject to learning-curve analysis, and the development of Active Directory is no exception. For those of you who skipped the college lecture on learning curve analysis, the idea here is that basically there is a steep learning curve when introduced to a change in technology (it takes a long time to initially learn about Active Directory). Later on, after you've worked with Active Directory, you will still learn more about the product, but the learning curve will have a less steep slope. So while you clearly have a lot to learn in this text and the real world about using Active Directory, the following sections are a historical primer on other directory services. We strongly believe by learning about our past (in this case, directory services), we're not doomed to repeat failures.

Much as Catywhompus Construction would start one of its commercial building projects by pouring the foundation, we will lay the intellectual foundation of directory services by outlining their history. We'll start with X.500.

X.500

First things first. X.500 is a standard that basically defines the placement of address elements in an order so that every object has a unique address. The best example of this is how telephone numbers are organized. Reach under your desk or across the room, and grab your telephone directory (white or yellow pages). Congratulations! At a simplified level, you are holding X.500 and each telephone number in that book is unique.

The white pages allow you to browse for information in a somewhat inefficient manner (limited to A to Z sorting). By sorting through directory entries, you find what you are looking for. The yellow pages are somewhat different. Their filter (categories and subcategories) result in a more refined search.

But perhaps the best relationship between your telephone book and X.500 is this. X.500 might be used as the basic model from which systems like our telephone system can be constructed. If you've made a telephone call overseas, it's possible you employed terms that map very closely to X.500: country code, area code, prefix, number, extension. Telephone numbers are a hierarchical form of information that is based on X.500.

The X.500 directory service is a mechanism for managing details related to network users, systems, services, applications, and the business entity itself. Highlights of X.500 include:

- **Simplified management**   Maintenance is performed locally, with each portion of the tree being responsible only for its own maintenance.

- **Extendable framework** A key point of X.500 is that it defines a directory services framework that can be extended. Active Directory is based in part on X.500.

- **Single namespace** A highlight of X.500 is its support for a single homogeneous namespace. In that sense, X.500 sounds something like DNS, but X.500 is a directory service, not a name server. X.500 supports *distinguished names* and *relative distinguished names.* A distinguished name is a unique name. A relative distinguished name is a name that is unique within its container or immediate location.

- **Powerful querying** X.500 supports both simple and complex queries, as suggested earlier with the white and yellow pages example.

- **Approved standard** The X.500 standard is really a set of protocols that have been approved by International Telecommunications Union (ITU) as a formal standard. The X.500 standard is also recognized by the International Organization of Standardization (ISO), which is another organization that oversees standards.

- **Clearly defined goals** The implicit goal of X.500 is to rule the world as an open, worldwide, distributed directory service. Resistance is futile.

- **Object definition** X.500 is the foundation for defining country, organization (O), organizational unit (OU), and common name (CN) objects. These should look familiar in your study of Active Directory. Why? Because Active Directory uses Os, OUs, and CNs.

NDS

Many networking professionals credit Novell's Network Directory Services (NDS) with saving the company during some dark days in the 1990s. Novell, best known for its NetWare network operating system, was an early player in the directory services market with NDS. NDS is a highly regarded and well-respected directory-services solution in the networking community, so it should be on your MCSE radar screen as you master and promote Active Directory. To learn more about NDS, see www.novell.com.

The current NDS version from Novell, known as NDS Corporate Edition is a directory-enabled solution for creating a seamless, unified network from heterogeneous systems. Corporate Edition integrates Windows NT, Sun Solaris, and Linux user management functions into NDS eDirectory so that you can allegedly, easily, and inexpensively manage a network comprised of multiple platforms and operating systems.

X.400, Banyan

When the votes are counted (and recounted), X.400 will be a first-round choice for the directory services hall of fame, believe me. X.400 is the basis for message-handling services (message handling services, by definition, manage the flow of messages on a computer network) and is the standard upon which modern e-mail is based. Some e-mail systems, such as Novell's GroupWise, are X.400-adherent. Other e-mail systems, such as Microsoft Exchange Server 2000, provide support for X.400.

One last directory service we should mention is Banyan StreetTalk, which you can learn more about at www.banyan.com.

LDAP

Granted, the Lightweight Directory Access Protocol (LDAP) isn't a directory service, but rather is a protocol for directory services (which is why we are mentioning it to you). Defined by RFCs 1777, 1778, and 2251, LDAP performs something of a support role in the world of network infrastructure, allowing network hosts to query the directory-services database. Simply stated, the LDAP standard facilitates client access to the directory-services database and its information. LDAP also defines how a directory service stores the directory information and how it names the directory objects. LDAP relates most closely to Active Directory's schema, which defines object classes and information attributes in the database. The base information in the Active Directory schema is provided by LDAP.

ADSI

Active Directory Services Interface (ADSI) isn't a directory service, but it's a tool for interacting with Active Directory and thus demands an introduction. To exploit and extend many of the great features in Active Directory, programmers and developers alike need a way to get inside. Typically, operating systems provide application program interfaces (APIs) that allow such access. With Active Directory, the access occurs via ADSI. We'll mention ADSI later in this chapter as a compelling reason to implement Active Directory.

Predicting the Future: Meta-Directories

Meta-directories are historically the realm of Ph.D.s and other deep thinkers (which might well include MCSEs). The marketing professionals in the technology community have embraced the term meta-directory to describe NDS and even Active Directory, but true meta-directories don't exist yet (at least not in a reliable form you would trust your enterprise to!). A meta-directory is an umbrella directory service that wraps around other directory services (akin to a trade association for trade associations—one of which really exists).

Here are several key aspects of the meta-directory concept:

- **Centralized management** A meta-directory should make your job easier to perform, not more difficult. A meta-directory should have the ability to manage the underlying directory services it is wrapped around.

- **Centralized security authority** Another key paradigm is security. By having a meta-directory manage the directory-services process in your information system, you can have one central security authority.

- **X.500 roots** X.500, with its goal of "taking over the world," is really positioning itself as the standard for a meta-directory. It has several architectural features, such as being a globally distributed database using Os, OUs, and CNs (this is a short list of four features, but there are others that we won't mention for the sake of brevity). You should note that a deeper discussion of the finer points of X.500 is beyond the scope of the Windows 2000 MCSE exams.

- **LDAP connectivity** LDAP is the communication medium for connecting different directory services. Today's conventional wisdom is that LDAP will continue to be the communication standard implemented by meta-directories.

- **Synchronization vs. brokering** There are two major approaches that a meta-directory may take to organizing and maintaining information: synchronization and brokering. *Synchronization* is accomplished by replicating information from one data store to another. *Brokering* is more akin to a view in Microsoft SQL Server —it retrieves and displays information from a distant data store (say another directory service) without actually performing any update against that data store.

Active Directory from the Top Down

Time to present Active Directory in top-down fashion. In the remaining chapters of this part of the book, you'll study many of the points we're about to raise in much greater detail.

Active Directory is typically viewed from a logical perspective without regard for the physical location of your offices, servers, or people (the one exception being the use of sites to map out physical locations). The primary logical objects related to Active Directory are forests, trees, domains (note that these first three—forests, trees, and domains —can be thought of in the context of namespace; that is, these objects are part of the DNS namespace), and lower-level objects (including organizational units).

TIP   If you read the following explanations and find yourself confused, don't despair. Several of the concepts are interrelated, and because of the top-down approach, some definitions are used that, quite frankly, won't be fully explained until a paragraph or two later. You will better understand forests after you know something about trees, and vice versa. Read these sections all of the way through, focusing only on the basic meanings. Then, after pausing, reread the section again.

Forests

A *forest* is a collection of trees, much like in the real world. It is the highest-level or broadest object we'll discuss in the context of Active Directory. You can have multiple forests in your Active Directory, and you might well want to do so to accommodate sub-sidiaries, outside business entities, or merger partners. This ability to have multiple forests in your Active Directory is a real-world lifesaver, as it allows for unforeseen events, such as hostile corporate takeovers. Your namespace might change and Active Directory can accommodate such namespace changes.

Graphically, a forest is sometimes represented by a large box that contains everything else. In Figure 1-1, you will see a forest. Speaking from an Active Directory management perspective, you're most likely to discuss forests in only the largest enterprises. Small organizations and medium-size organizations (SOMOs) won't typically use the word *forests* much in their directory-services implementation since they only have the one.

Trees

Simply stated, *trees* are a collection of DNS domains, typically arranged in a hierarchic view. One defining characteristic of trees is that they share a common root domain name, such as expectationmanagement.com.

It is larger organizations, such as enterprises, that would actually speak of trees. SOMOs are unlikely to have much to do with trees, working with one tree at best. A tree appears as lines connecting multiple domains, but it doesn't have a shape itself. You can see two trees in Figure 1-1.

Domains

Windows 2000 domains are domains as you've known them under Windows NT, with a few new twists. Officially, Microsoft defines a *domain* as a container of objects that share:

- Security requirements
- Replication processes
- Administration

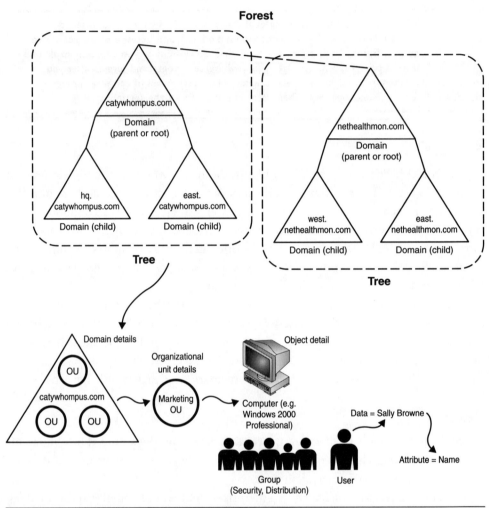

Figure 1-1 Viewing the forest and other Active Directory details

Domains are considered to be the core unit in Active Directory, and they are assumed to take on the name of your registered Internet domain name. In fact, your internal network domains (similar to your old Windows NT domain) and your registered Internet domain can have the same exact name. Also note that the top-level domain is called the *parent domain* and the lower-level domains (typically placed beneath the parent domain in a diagram) are *child domains*. For Internet geeks, this would translate into second- and third-level domain names. Organizations of all sizes would both use and speak about domains. The relationship between domains and organization size is direct—larger organizations would have multiple domains, while many SOMOs would have just one domain. It is the practice of Active Directory architects in this day and age to have a domain that is represented by a triangle in a drawing of a Windows 2000 Server-based network.

TIP From a directory-services perspective, all domain controllers are "equal" in functional status under Windows 2000 (although the first domain controller is slightly more equal than the others, a topic discussed in the final section of this book on Exam 70-221). Domain controllers are Windows 2000 Server machines charged with performing security, administrative, and replication duties. Note that there are no primary and secondary domain controllers in Windows 2000.

Organizational Units

Organizational units (known as OUs) are one of the coolest things in Active Directory —they represent logical administrative units. An OU is a container that holds other objects, such as nested OUs, users, computers, and so on. We especially like OUs for the pragmatic role they assume and for the assistance they bring to the design effort. For example, the fact that the Marketing department has an OU titled Marketing is very practical. Also, we recommend that Active Directory design inherently starts with a simple OU. Successive OUs should be added only when all parties to the directory-services planning process reach consensus and such a move is justified.

An OU is typically represented in a diagram by a circle, and it is in effect a container. All organizations implementing Windows 2000 and Active Directory would use OUs, some more than others, depending on their needs and size. The relationship should be linear: larger and more complex organizations would use more OUs in the directory-services implementation. However, a Windows 2000 MCSE should also be aware that OUs are used to apply group policies or to delegate administrative tasks, so a large centralized organization could have just one OU, or a small company with many branch offices needing delegated control could have several OUs.

Lower-Level Objects

A picture is worth a thousand words. In Figure 1-2 you will notice that several objects, ranging from computers to shared folders, can be added to an OU.

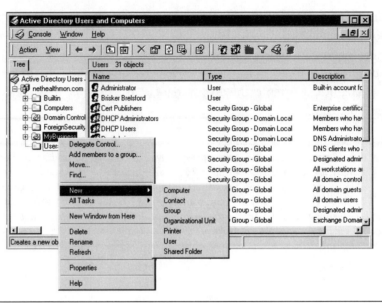

Figure 1-2   Several types of objects can be added to an OU.

Here is a brief description of each object type:

- **Computer**   This is the computer account for all Windows 2000 and pre-Windows 2000 machines. This allows the computer to participate in the Windows 2000 security model.

- **Contact**   This is an Active Directory contact record, not a Microsoft Outlook or Microsoft Exchange contact record. It isn't very useful (yet). It is here so a Windows 2000 MCSE can add an SMTP address for external recipients.

- **Group**   This is where a Windows 2000 MCSE creates a security or distribution group. Security groups are assigned rights and permissions. Distribution groups send messages to a group of accounts. Groups are discussed in several places in this book, including Chapter 3.

- **Printer**   The administrator can create a printer object, which allows the Windows 2000 MCSE to manage printer access and at least six other printer rights (such as the ability to delete a print job and other printer controls). You will recall a printer is a device that uses paper to create output of the information displayed on a computer screen.

- **User**   The Windows 2000 MCSE often creates the user account object as part of his or her day-to-day network administration duties. This is considered an ordinary task. The creation of the user object includes the user logon name for Windows 2000 environments (this name looks very much like an Internet address and the user logon name for pre-Windows 2000 environments).

- **Shared folder**   You can create a shared folder object that can be recognized and managed by Active Directory. This is useful for searching for shares (folders designated for access by other network users).

- **Custom**   A Windows 2000 MCSE can add your own objects to Active Directory (and to any directory-services solution worth its salt). You would likely do this in conjunction with a third-party software developer who is seeking to install a business application that will interact with Active Directory and needs some form of custom object.

These types of objects are the lowest level of interaction you will have with Active Directory. All organizations of any size using Windows 2000 and Active Directory will use objects.

Data and Attributes

The next step down the directory-services food chain is data. Every object will have data associated with it. For example, if the object is a printer, the *data* might be "HP5 Color." Furthermore, the *attribute* for the data might indicate that it is the "Printer name." The relationship between data and attributes is shown in Figure 1-3.

Figure 1-3
Relating object, data, and attributes with a printer example

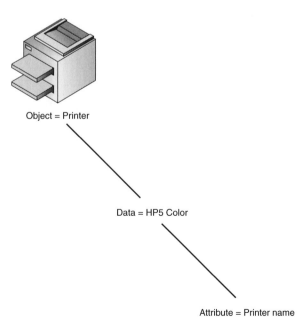

Object = Printer

Data = HP5 Color

Attribute = Printer name

Sites

On a distant but related note, sites are used to describe the physical network (typically the TCP/IP subnet). As such, physical sites don't match up very well with the logical object-based views of the forest we have been considering in the preceding sections. Organizations of all sizes would discuss sites in the context of the physical network. Figure 1-4 displays the relationship between sites and the traditional Active Directory view.

Directory Services in Different Versions of Windows

Table 1-1 compares and contrasts Windows 2000's Active Directory with the directory services in Windows NT and the way that such system information was managed in Windows 3.*x* or Windows for Workgroups 3.*x* (WFW). This should help you understand how directory services available through Active Directory in Windows 2000 relate to previous Microsoft operating-system releases.

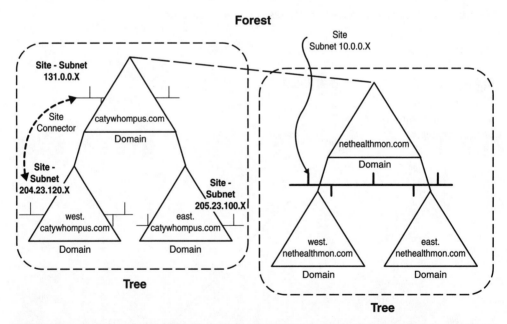

Figure 1-4   The physical concept of sites overlaid on the logical Active Directory view

Table 1-1 Comparing and Contrasting Directory Services

Item	Windows 2000	Windows NT	Windows 3.x WFW
"Directory" or "Directory Services"	Active Directory	Domains	Workgroup, folders, and subdirectories
Single sign-on available	Yes	Yes	No
Interoperability between OS and applications	Yes for Active Directory–aware applications	Interoperability between OS, Microsoft Exchange, and SQL Server for user authentication	Account management: managed at each workstation, no central domain administration
Interoperability between different OSs	Stronger than ever with LDAP standard	Limited; had to use NFS clients and NetWare Gateway (GSNW) to achieve limited interoperability	Used multiple network clients (NetWare and a Microsoft client) to achieve interoperability
Information Systems Configuration Settings	Active Directory, Registry	Security Accounts Manager (SAM), Registry	*.ini files
Standards-based	Draws on X.500 and uses LDAP	Domain model not based on published standard	N/A
Domain Icon	Triangle	Circle	N/A

Top Reasons to Implement Windows 2000 and Active Directory

So why implement Windows 2000 and Active Directory in your organization? Some of our thinking in this section might surprise you. For example, while Active Directory is certainly an important component of Windows 2000, as you'll see in our top-ten list for Windows 2000, it's not the first reason to implement Windows 2000 in your organization. Active Directory comes in just above the middle of the pack, at number four.

NOTE On an annual basis, we update our top reasons to implement Windows 2000 and Active Directory for one of the monthly publications that we write for. Not surprisingly, the list can change somewhat from year to year reflecting purchasing behaviors, trends, and technology. What follows is our current thinking as of the early 21st century.

Top Reasons to Implement Windows 2000

Windows 2000 is now a rambunctious toddler quickly heading to maturity, having been on the market long enough to have service packs available. The aging of Windows 2000 has allowed us practicing MCSEs to reflect on why customers are purchasing and implementing it. Here's our top-ten list of reasons to implement Windows 2000.

- Business applications
- More stability
- Fewer reboots
- Active Directory
- Group Policy
- Terminal Services
- Hardware support
- VPN support
- Wizards
- Improved relations

Business Applications

Topping our list this round is a rather old fashioned and somewhat staid topic from any "Introduction to Computers" course: determining your business needs first. Business needs typically manifest themselves in terms of business applications that need to be deployed.

A practicing MCSE consultants, we're constantly reminded that the "theory" we learned in MIS courses in college has become reality. In the old days, IS purchase decisions were made based on the needs of the business. These needs were often identified after extensive needs analysis was performed by a consultant. Little regard was initially given to the operating system or vendor (although there was an important need to go through vendor qualification steps as well).

Then, somewhere along the way, many of us became more interested in the operating system's features and functions than the end results desired from line-of-business applications. In the late 1980s through late 1990s, it was easy to get caught up in the war of the day, including Microsoft versus Apple, or Windows NT versus NetWare. Our customers suffered, to say the least.

Along came Windows 2000 with some mysterious powers and a revamped MCSE program that focused on needs analysis. All of a sudden, business needs were back in fashion. More importantly, there have been positive developments in the Windows 2000 business-application area.

First, more and more line-of-business applications are being launched with the Windows 2000 seal of approval, meaning that the software has been enhanced to leverage Windows 2000 features and functions. More importantly, business applications are starting to integrate with Active Directory by modifying the schema (database structure). This is done in several ways, including exploiting ADSI, the Active Directory API that we'll discuss in the "Top Reasons to Implement Active Directory" section.

The bottom line here is that you should implement Windows 2000 immediately because your application vendor will drive you toward it. As more and more line-of-business applications become Windows 2000–compliant, support and desire will dry up for older editions of your business software. Business applications that are Windows 2000 compliant will do more cool stuff, making this the most compelling reason to embrace Windows 2000.

More Stability

We're having lots of success introducing Windows 2000 Server to our customers based on its increased stability. We're very much enjoying the fact that blue screens of death (BSODs) are much fewer and farther between. In fact, we're truly scratching our heads to recall a BSOD since the commercial release of Windows 2000 (we did see a couple back in the beta test period in 1999, but all's fair in pre-release versions).

Fewer Reboots

Closely related to the previous point, but coming third in our Windows 2000 top-ten list, is fewer reboots. We don't have to come into the office late at night as much either to perform a reboot or to disrupt people at mid-day because we've absolutely got to reboot. While reboots still exist, and they still can't be done at mid-day, we find ourselves catching our favorite shows on TV at night more than we used to.

Active Directory

We're a big fan of Active Directory. We like many of its features, such as the replication capabilities that ensure our critical "database" of user settings and system configuration information is stored in more than one place in a multiple domain-controller (DC) scenario. And we like the removal of physical limitations on domains (allowing our clients to typically operate with a single domain). Join us in saying goodbye to complex trust relationships and hello to organizational units (OUs), which have largely replaced the need for many domains (especially resource domains). A popular view of Active Directory, the Active Directory Users and Computers snap-in, is displayed in Figure 1-5.

But accolades aside, the momentum for Active Directory is building from a slow start. Part of the reason is that Active Directory is complex, and people are still learning it and thinking of ways to use it. Also, Windows 2000 MCSEs are still trying to pass their certification exams, such as Exam 70-219, "Designing a Microsoft Windows 2000 Directory Services Infrastructure."

Our prediction? Look for Active Directory to make it to the top of our list in the future, as more Windows 2000 MCSE candidates (that's you) pass all of their exams to

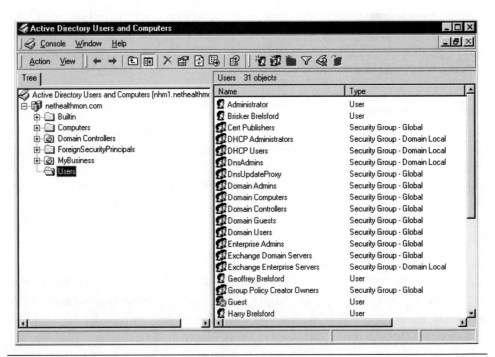

Figure 1-5 One of Active Directory's most-used tools, the Active Directory Users and Computers snap-in

earn the MCSE title. It's a chicken-and-egg scenario—you've got to learn about Active Directory and pass the MCSE certification exams before you start working on Active Directory, and you've got to get bona fide work experience with Active Directory before you can be assured of passing the demanding MCSE exams. It'll all work itself out in the long run, providing ample opportunities for all MCSEs.

Group Policy

Group Policy is moving up and gaining serious momentum. Group Policy is the ability to automate the administration and configuration of your Windows 2000 network by performing several functions. Examples of this would be the ability to lock down a workstation, install software, and manage user settings. It is surprisingly powerful and a very welcome friend.

Since Group Policy only works in the homogeneous Windows 2000 networks (the client workstation must be running Windows 2000 Professional), we believe that Group Policy is the "killer application" that is driving much of the success of Windows 2000 Professional, thus earning a place in the top half of our list. A common view of Group Policy is displayed in Figure 1-6.

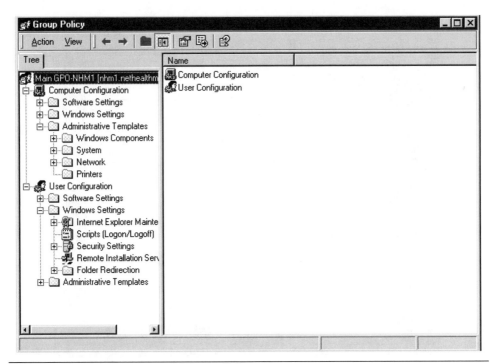

Figure 1-6   A common view of Group Policy

Terminal Services

Coming on strong in the Windows 2000 MCSE community is Terminal Services. In Figure 1-7 you can see that the inside window is a Terminal Services session, where the user runs a full Windows 2000 session remotely.

The use of a Terminal Services solution is a remote-host approach, where only the delta screen images are passed on, rather than *all* of the network traffic. (Remember that *delta* is the Latin word for "change.") There are several popular uses for Terminal Services, including working from remote locations over the Internet and enjoying full network capabilities at seemingly high speeds, and using thin clients, such as the WinTerm clients (basic monitor, keyboard, and mouse without a CPU box). Our favorite use of Terminal Services is performing remote administration, such as running the Active Directory snap-ins on our client's servers from many miles away!

 TIP No one argues that Terminal Services is cool. What people have a problem with is the expense associated with licensing Terminal Services clients (and the confusion about what those licenses really are all about). We have to admit that we learned about Terminal Services licensing the hard way—when the 90-day licensing grace period expired. See the Terminal Services licensing white paper at www.microsoft.com/windows2000/library/technologies/terminal.

Figure 1-7 Observe a Terminal Services session in the inner window

Hardware Support

A favorite worthy of the top-ten list is the increased hardware support found in Windows 2000. We're seeing this on several fronts. Starting with the initial installation of Windows 2000 Server, we're no longer hitting the F6 key nearly as much (right after the first setup disk runs in character-based mode) to add unsupported or OEM drivers for RAID and SCSI controller drivers. That is a joy, as Windows 2000 Server supports many more controller cards than was our experience in Windows NT.

Equally important, the automatic and accurate device detection has become a fast friend of ours. This means we don't need to run some convoluted setup program on a manufacturer's drivers diskette, followed by a reboot or three.

In Figure 1-8 you will see the Device Manager in Windows 2000. This is very much like the Device Manager found in Windows ME/9x, and it's a very welcome addition from the Windows NT days.

VPN Support

Not that you couldn't do this before, but the ability to create a virtual private network (VPN) connection is not only easier between locations with Windows 2000, but we're

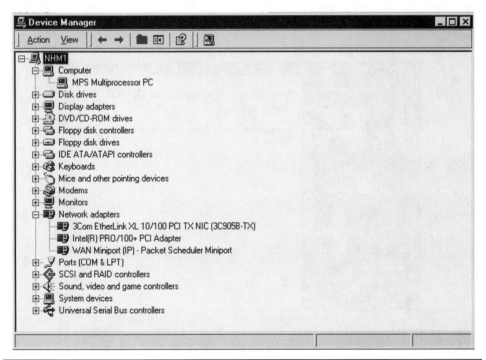

Figure 1-8 The Device Manager in Windows 2000—another cool tool

finding it's much more stable. We now have clients running mission-critical network connections between offices via a VPN connection in Windows 2000. Cool!

CAUTION When you configure the server-side VPN capabilities using the configuration wizard in Routing and Remote Access Service (RRAS), note that this wizard believes the server will only be used for VPN activity when it comes to remote communication. It has a nasty way of shutting down other port openings you might need for Microsoft Internet Security and Acceleration (ISA) Server. Ouch! Note the VPN capabilities of Windows 2000 are discussed much more in Part III of this book, on Exam 70-221, "Designing a Microsoft Windows 2000 Network Infrastructure."

Wizards

We've always been a fool for a pretty face, so we can express our enduring love for the wizards in Windows 2000. Each time we turn the corner in Windows 2000, we're seduced by some sexy wizard or another. If the question is "Can we configure Windows 2000 without wizards?" the answer is yes. But we prefer the ease of administration afforded by the extensive collection of wizards in Windows 2000, and for that reason, wizards make our top-ten list this year. Whenever possible, use the wizards! A Windows 2000 wizard is shown in Figure 1-9.

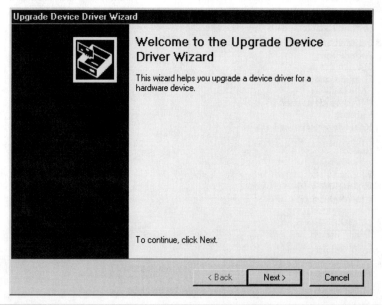

Figure 1-9 There are wizards for nearly every configuration task in Windows 2000.

Improved Relations

"The doggone thang just works better" is our final pitch to you on implementing Windows 2000 today. As MCSE consultants, we're finding that our client relations improve when we implement Windows 2000. And by virtue of fewer late-night site visits to reboot servers, our family relationships are stronger to boot!

Top Reasons to Implement Active Directory

Our top reasons to implement Active Directory, and thus implement directory services in your organization, are divided into technical and business sections. Not surprisingly, there is some thought behind the division—it mirrors the technical and business roles of Active Directory.

Technical Side of Active Directory

Here are five technical reasons to implement Active Directory (and we're sure there are many more):

- Active Directory's scope
- Relationship to X.500 directory services
- AD loves LDAP
- Open environment
- Active Directory Services Interface (ADSI)

Active Directory's Scope   Clearly, the scope of services provided by Active Directory is one of its greatest strengths. In Figure 1-10, we've tried to capture the essence of Active Directory's scope.

At a glance, it should be apparent that the breadth of capabilities provided by Active Directory is impressive. These include:

- **Query**   This is the ability to find an object in the directory, including printers, computers, and users.
- **Replication and storage**   This is the ability to distribute the database to multiple locations to ensure high availability and protection.
- **Address book**   This is standard white-pages capabilities for managing user objects and attributes, including user-profile information.
- **Recipient lookup**   This includes the ability to resolve recipient naming in an e-mail application, and it also provides secure e-mail services.
- **Credential management**   Basic and advanced security features include the capability to handle logins for registered applications and services.

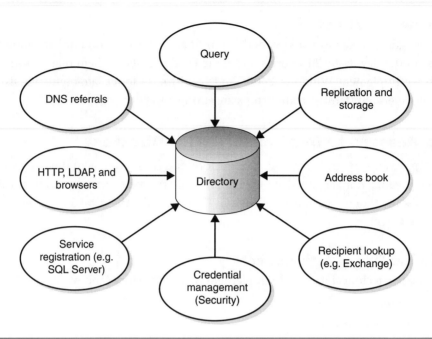

Figure 1-10   The services provided by Active Directory are varied and robust.

- **Service registration**   Applications and services are registered in Active Directory. These components provide identifying information, such as class store. (Class stores are a computer programming concept and don't require further discussion for your success as a Windows 2000 MCSE, but it is a term necessary to make the point in this paragraph about the registration of services.) The concept of classes isn't related to the bricks-and-mortar educational experiences you have had, but rather to object classes typically defined by developers. These are similar to classes in programming environments such as C++.

- **HTTP, LDAP, and browsers**   HTTP and LDAP queries are passed and returned via browsers. Also, there is support for secure Web access via HTTPs queries. You may know secure Web access from a more practical point of view: safely accessing your online stock-trading account via a Web browser over the Internet.

- **DNS referrals**   If host names are not resolved within the Active Directory database, host-name resolution activity is passed to DNS. The results are returned to Active Directory.

Relationship to X.500 Directory Services   The dark and detailed world of X.500 is, in general, beyond the scope of Windows 2000 MCSE experience (earlier in this chapter we spent a few pages on X.500 and we assure you, that was sufficient). If, for some reason, you'd like to master the finer points of X.500, you might read a book on X.500, and the best ones out there are the X.500 Requests For Comments (RFCs) and X.500 standards, managed by both the International Telecommunications Union (ITU) and the International Organization of Standardization (ISO). But for starters, go to the Internet Activities Board Web site at www.iab.org and search on X.500.

Briefly, the X.500 directory-services model defines the *directory schema*, which defines how information is stored in a table. A business-software correlation to this might well be a business accounting package, such as Great Plains Dynamics. The accounting data is stored in a data file as you would expect, but the index files (*.idx) are critical files that describe where and how the data is stored. If you make one of those *.idx files unhappy, your data is really unhappy!

Active Directory implements the parts of the X.500 standard that work for it. This is a common practice with other directory services, including Novell's NDS. Microsoft would prefer to have you believe that Active Directory uses a scaled-down X.500 schema.

As we mentioned before, the X.500 design can be likened to the design of the world-wide telephone system. The X.500 standard accounts for such objects as root, country, organization, organizational unit, much as the telephone system uses country code, area code, prefix, suffix, and extension.

Here are a few of X.500's features:

- It is decentralized, allowing for local administration.
- It has powerful querying capabilities to allow for searching.
- It allows for a single, unified namespace.
- It provides for a structured method of storing information.
- It is a published standard, which means that applications using X.500-based directory services can expect certain things to behave in certain ways, avoiding guesswork and errors on behalf of the application developers.

AD Loves LDAP   The Lightweight Directory Access Protocol (LDAP) can be thought of as the child of the Directory Access Protocol (DAP), which is the mechanism that allows access to X.500-based directories. DAP is also especially burdensome and not easily adaptable to new implementations. LDAP is a simplified implementation of DAP, and it supports the TCP/IP protocol (DAP supported the Open Standard Interconnection (OSI) protocol). LDAP processes requests, such as queries, much faster than DAP could.

LDAP consists of the following components:

- **Querying and modification rules**   LDAP defines how query and modification operations against the directory will be performed. Note that read and write is new to LDAP version 3.

- **Integration** LDAP's topological model defines how different directory services can and will be integrated.

- **Data dictionary** LDAP provides the data model that defines the syntax of the data in a directory.

- **Tree** LDAP's organization model defines how a directory organizes its data.

- **SSL** Secure Sockets Layer-based security provides a high level of security for directory access. The Simple Authentication and Security Layer (SASL) implementation is also used.

Open Environment Because Active Directory has incorporated several de facto standards in its design, it sports a certain sense of openness. These standards are X.500, LDAP, and TCP/IP. Other access protocols are supported, such as ADSI (discussed next). This openness is very encouraging to other vendors who want to support Active Directory. Such support might take the form of an application developer writing applications that interact with Active Directory.

Active Directory Services Interface (ADSI) Too much openness often means too much compromise. It's a case of too much of a good thing. For those developers who ascribe to this viewpoint, Microsoft has introduced a proprietary directory-services API known as Active Directory Services Interface (ADSI), mentioned earlier in this chapter. ADSI's mission is simple: provide developers with a single API to deal with Active Directory (and other directories). That not only hides a lot of Active Directory's complexity from the developers, but it facilitates integration with competing directory services such as Novell's NDS (which ADSI supports). Developers will use ADSI to build administrative tools as well as applications.

ADSI not only replaces multiple software development kits (SDKs) that developers would otherwise have to deal with when interacting with Active Directory, but ADSI allows for the simplified and uniform manipulation of directory-service objects in a heterogeneous environment of competing directory services. Developers can easily create reusable, namespace-portable applications for common administrative and end-user tasks, such as "pause my jobs in the map room printer."

Business Side of Active Directory

So now you're clearly sold on Windows 2000 Server and Active Directory, right? Good, but that's only half the battle. It's likely you will have to gain the support of management on both the Windows 2000 Server and Active Directory fronts so that you will have the political and financial support you need.

Many of the features discussed in the course of this chapter can be translated into MBA-speak that management can understand. With respect to Windows 2000 Server, the MBA-speak might include the following points:

- Ease of administration will save time and prevent configuration mistakes. That adds up to increased efficiency and to accomplishing more with the same or fewer staff resources.

- Centralized enterprise management will save time.

- The data management and protection in Windows 2000 Server will make better use of storage and result in greater uptime.

- Windows 2000 Server not only interoperates with other computer environments, but Active Directory provides a directory-services tool that can manage the heterogeneous world typically seen in companies.

So all things being equal, we assume at this point that you're a Windows 2000 MCSE candidate who, given the choice of networking solutions available worldwide, would select Windows 2000 and implement Active Directory. That said, selecting Windows 2000 and implementing Active Directory places the chosen networking solution in alignment with Microsoft's historic Digital Nervous System and Microsoft's forthcoming "dot-NET" (.net) initiative. In order to lay the historic foundation so you have depth of knowledge in Microsoft networking solutions, consider the following. The Digital Nervous System (or its successor, the .net initiative) is meant to metaphorically emulate the human nervous system, which is the system inside us that makes everything happen. In the context of business computing, the Digital Nervous System is meant to be a Microsoft technology implementation based on Microsoft solutions, such as Windows 2000, Active Directory, and BackOffice, that will motivate workers. These allow you to manage your business processes (such as Enterprise Resource Programming, or ERP), and allow you to remain competitive and stay ahead. You could say that this is the old "no one ever got fired for buying Microsoft" argument (which, of course, is based on the old "no one ever got fired for buying IBM" argument). Microsoft is positioning the Digital Nervous System paradigm, shown in Figure 1-11, as the best way to position your business for the new e-commerce world. And as you know, e-commerce is a very powerful word in the MBA community!

The following Active Directory pitch for management is slightly more complex and will require a certain deftness on the part of the Active Directory architect. These are again presented in MBA-speak.

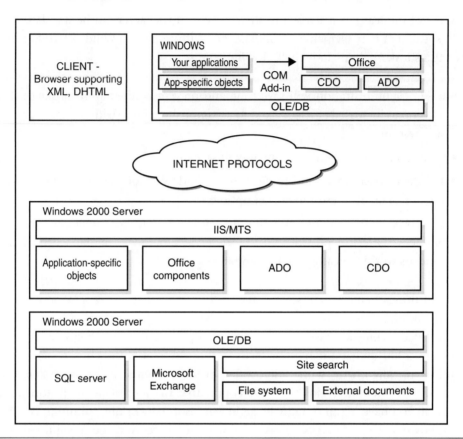

Figure 1-11 Microsoft's Digital Nervous System (DNS) paradigm created the momentum for the .NET successor paradigm.

- Directory services provide fault tolerance and access to the directory services database (which contains object information) via distribution and replication.

- Logons are simplified with a single sign-on (or at least fewer sign-ons) to all systems and applications.

- Administration is simplified by having a central and single point of administration for all systems and applications.

- Directory services provide robust security for authentication purposes and resource authorization purposes.

- Active Directory will grow with changing needs. It has good scalability to handle any size and type of network infrastructure.

- Active Directory can be easily and extensively customized to meet needs and accommodate specific situations.

Chapter Review

This chapter introduced you to the concept of directory services. Now that you've learned the fundamentals of directory services and received a gentle introduction to Active Directory, you're ready for the specifics that follow in the next few chapters, and which will prepare you for Exam 70-219, "Designing a Microsoft Windows 2000 Directory Services Infrastructure."

You should now have a basic understanding of directory services and understand the top-down view of Active Directory. You should also know several reasons to implement Windows 2000 and Active Directory.

Questions

1. True or False. Directory services are always X.500-based.

2. Which of the following are directory-services solutions?
   a. Novell's NDS
   b. LDAP
   c. Microsoft's Active Directory
   d. Banyan's StreetTalk
   e. Answers A, C, and D

3. True or False. A Windows 2000 network can function without Active Directory.

Answers

1. **False.** Many, but not all directory services are based on the X.500 standard.

2. **E.** It's likely you knew about NDS and Active Directory. Banyan's StreetTalk is a popular directory-services solution in some technology communities. LDAP is a protocol.

3. **True.** You can implement the workgroup model instead of the Active Directory-based forest/tree/domain model for your network. You will (of course) limit the effectiveness and capabilities of the network by using the workgroup model.

Key Skill Sets

- You should understand what directory services are.

- You should understand how directory services are used.

- You should understand that the directory-services solution in Windows 2000 is called Active Directory.

- You should understand that Active Directory is not the only directory-services solution available.

Key Terms

Active Directory
Active Directory Services Interface (ADSI)
Attributes
Classes
Data
Directory services
Domains
Forests
Lightweight Directory Access Protocol (LDAP)
Meta-directory
Network Directory Services (NDS)
Objects
Sites
Trees
X.400
X.500

Analyzing Business Requirements

This chapter covers the following key mastery goals:

- Introduce the planning and design MCSE mindset
- Understand that Active Directory represents, in many ways, the merger between the technical and business communities
- Develop an appreciation for a wide range of business matters, including business models
- Have the ability to understand different types of organizational structures and business relationships
- Develop a rich understanding of company strategies so you can really understand where the business is headed and appreciate whether your Active Directory design fits or not

For the MCSE working with Microsoft technologies, such as Active Directory, at some level it all starts and ends with business. It's the business that needs your services, the business that will benefit from directory services, and most importantly, the business that will pay for your services as an MCSE.

With the core MCSE exams behind you, this book (covering the three planning exams) represents a paradigm shift away from nuts-and-bolts practice to planning. No longer is the emphasis placed on hands-on keystrokes. Rather, the emphasis is placed on design. From this point forward, instead of thinking of yourself as a technician, it is more appropriate to think of yourself as an esteemed architect, and in this section of the book, an Active Directory architect.

TIP And we won't let you go one step further without understanding that Microsoft's 70-219 exam area of "Analyzing Business Requirements" (the title of this chapter and a bona fide exam area) is synonymous with the phrase "business-needs analysis." Understanding this tidbit will aid in your understanding of the discussion presented in this chapter.

This point is a milestone in your journey as an MCSE candidate. It is nothing short of a merger between the business and technology communities, with a focus on Active Directory. This is where the Masters of Business Administration (MBA) meets the MCSE, the white-board flowchart meets the keystroke, and the BackOffice meets the boardroom.

The early Windows 2000 MCSE courses and exams were oriented toward providing you with the technical base you need on a day-to-day level. The technical base you've acquired from passing the core exams (and hopefully from working with Windows 2000 Server) is critical for making network design decisions. Imagine trying to design a network without sufficient knowledge of the underlying technologies! Assuming you completed the lower-level course work, you've matured as an MCSE candidate and can now move on to the more advanced topics and the ambiguity that accompanies the design process. You're entering an area of study where there isn't necessarily one right answer, and there are different ways of reaching goals.

Analyzing the Existing and Planned Business Models

Business people use a different terminology than MCSE technical professionals. If you've worked in business or with business people, this shouldn't surprise you. Business people speak about *business models*, the framework in which a business organization attempts to operate and function in a profitable way.

Business models are dynamic entities, and business people are fond of tweaking these models in order to squeeze out more profit and search for long-term opportunities for accumulating wealth. This is akin to MCSEs tweaking Windows 2000 Server network and machine configurations to boost performance. This section of the chapter will analyze business models from several different perspectives. First, we'll look at company models built on geographic scope, including regional, national, international, subsidiary, and branch-office scenarios. We'll also look at company processes, including information flow, communications flow, services, and product life cycles. This is followed by a look at the management model used by the organization, including discussion on decentralized, centralized, project, and matrix organizations. The discussion continues with vendors, partners, and customers in the context of stakeholders that impact the organization. The section concludes with how acquisition plans can impact a company's future.

Analyzing the Company Model and the Geographical Scope

A critical design consideration in both Windows 2000 and Active Directory is geographically-dispersed operations. With affordable telecommunications solutions and access to the Internet, as well as the changing nature of businesses in general, even small firms are working with customers at the regional, national, and international levels.

When analyzing the company models, consider the regional, national, international, subsidiary, and branch office geographic considerations.

Regional

So exactly what is the process for analyzing a business in the regional geographic context? To be honest with you, you've entered an ambiguous area of business where even court rulings resulting from litigation contradict each other when it comes to defining the term *regional*.

For some of you reading this book, when you hear the term *regional* in the context of business-needs analysis, you might be thinking of an area defined by political boundaries (such as the four-county region). Others who are reading this book may view *regional* as an appreciation for the customs, culture, or manner of conducting business. When we say "conducting business," we are attempting to impart the understanding that different regions have different ways of doing business, such as by handshakes, lots of preliminary social discussion (weather and sports) before discussing business, or the distinctly regional diversity concerning the acceptance of personal checks.

Merchants in a geographic area may accept checks that are local to the area, but not checks from out-of-state. And why do we say this is a regional characteristic? Because it has been the authors' experience that some regions actually *do* accept checks as a medium of exchange from *both* local residents and those who call from other parts of the world. (Thank goodness! Could you imagine having to barter for things otherwise?) But other regions are more strict and will only accept checks from local residents who present two or more pieces of identification. (This identification might include a drivers license and some other form of photo-based identification card such as an employee ID card from a job.) So why these differences between regions with respect to the businesses attitude toward check acceptance? As near as the authors can tell, it might be that the more liberal region (that is, the region where businesses accept checks from all) has not had negative experiences like the more conservative region may have (the conservative region being the region in this example that only accepts checks from local residents with two or more pieces of identification).

The term *regional* may also apply to a situation in which a very large company has offices in different regions. These offices away from headquarters would be called regional offices.

Finally, some view *regions* from a geographical perspective: the wine region or the ski-resort region.

EXAM TIP Granted, we've probably stirred the pot here with more confusion than clarity. Who would have guessed the term "regional" could be so many different things to so many people? So what's our answer to that? A short and sweet "welcome to the real world" where things are much more ambiguous than the hallowed halls of higher education (and we include your core Windows 2000 MCSE exams in this sweeping statement!). We realize it's highly unlikely that you fell off the pumpkin wagon yesterday; you've likely heard the term regional before in your lifetime. The main point is that the whole act of "design" and the Windows 2000 MCSE designing exams are much more ambiguous than other certification exams you've likely encountered. So when you bump into the word "regional" in a case study on the Windows 2000 MCSE designing exams, stop and reflect so you can determine how the term "regional" is being used. It could be any of the numerous definitions of regional given in the previous section. Whew!

The authors have observed yet another context that fits the term *regional*. The merchants also tend to know both their regional customers and vendors better than those at the national and international levels. In short, a business tends to know its smaller, regional markets best. Not true, you say? We encourage you to think again as you work with businesses in designing Active Directory solutions and see if you don't agree at a future point in time that you're likely to know your regional markets (perhaps defined by geography or political boundaries) better than far away global markets.

Often, the regional analysis as part of your business-needs analysis for the purpose of designing an Active Directory solution (the purpose of this chapter) has the greatest level of detail and includes customer types, vendors, labor supply, demand for the firm's products and services, and so on. In Figure 2-1, a regional firm is displayed (this is a grocery store with several locations in the Pacific Northwest). That is, you're likely to exert more effort to gather more information about regional matters than you would to write up your business-needs analysis report on distant international markets.

On a technical note, consider the following. Will the network infrastructure need to support a connection between offices? Will there be Windows 2000 domain controllers (DCs) at each location to support replication of the Active Directory database? Will you

Figure 2-1   A regional grocery store chain

treat each location as an Active Directory site, or will the entire collection of store networks be treated as a single site? Would it make the most sense to have a single Active Directory domain, with each store location being an organizational unit? All of these, and more technical matters, need to be considered in the design process for a regional business.

National

The definition for a firm that operates nationally is a company that has a nationwide presence.

Safeco, which is Seattle-based with nationwide operations, has very limited international activities and is widely considered a national company. As if to make a statement about its national presence, Safeco purchased the naming rights to the professional baseball stadium in the Seattle area (baseball being America's national pastime). Consequently, Safeco Field, as the baseball stadium is called and is shown in Figure 2-2, represents a subtle form of corporate communication about how Safeco perceives itself (something the information-systems architect should honor during the directory-services design phase).

National issues (such as military spending appropriation increases being debated in Congress) have less impact on the day-to-day operations of most firms than closer-to-home regional matters (such as a change in local zoning laws), but still have important long-range, strategic implications (perhaps your firm is interested in opening a new office somewhere that has a large military population that will benefit from a larger defense budget at some point in the future).

Figure 2-2   Safeco Field

Another discussion that we can have in the context of "national" issues faced by businesses is transportation. For a business that produces goods for shipment to market, distribution issues have a particularly interesting national perspective. In many areas of commercial transportation, regulations occur primarily at the national level such as speed limits, permits, hours the loads can be moved, and so on. It has been the observation of the authors that firms rely on trucking and rail, both shown in Figure 2-3, as domestic shipping methods. Contrast our observation that trucks and trains tend to shoulder the distribution burden domestically with how products are distributed internationally (which we've noted tends to be more by airplane and ship).

Even national-level topics such as fiscal and monetary policies, and interest rate and inflation indicators, are of concern to businesses. One excellent site for this type of quantitative economic information is The Federal Reserve at www.federalreserve.gov. The top executives of nationwide enterprise track movements in interest rates, and other financial and political information, which can significantly impact the earnings of the firm (and the ability to fund your Active Directory implementation).

TIP   It has been the author's experience that executives that manage firms that are national in scope may well monitor political and news Web sites such as MSNBC (www.msnbc.com, which is a joint-venture of Microsoft and the National Broadcasting Corporation). What that means to you is that, as the technology architect in the Active Directory design process, you might score quick "hero points" with the executives by facilitating a high-speed Internet connection that will allow the executives to monitor news Web sites during the business day.

Figure 2-3   Rail and trucking are attractive transportation options for shipping goods across the country.

International

Not all firms sell goods and services to the international community, but those that do, such as Boeing and Microsoft, will tell you that international considerations are of paramount importance in business-model discussions. Distant economies, world-geopolitical events, and monetary-exchange rates are just a few international factors that affect firms with international operations. Believe it or not, one of the top exporters in the United States, based on dollar amount, is The Boeing Company, an aerospace company shown in Figure 2-4.

Boeing is one of the largest employers of MCSEs in the world, in part due to its location in Seattle, Washington, and its generous tuition reimbursement for MCSE candidates taking certification courses. Boeing also recognizes the MCSE designation with higher pay. In fact, Boeing has over 5,000 IT employees, many of whom hold the MCSE designation.

International business issues are tracked by looking at organizations that are global in scope, including The World Bank, which maintains a Web page at www.worldbank.org. Day-to-day issues, such as shipping, shown in Figure 2-5, require the attention of managers in international companies to get goods from supplies to purchasers.

Subsidiary

The term *subsidiary* is as much an accounting and taxation definition as a generic business definition (used loosely in conversation between business people). Technically

Figure 2-4   Production facilities at The Boeing Company

Figure 2-5   Ports as the epicenter of international shipping activity and thus international trade

speaking, a subsidiary is an entity that is more than 50 percent owned by a parent entity. That is, a company with its majority owned by another company is called a subsidiary to the company that owns it. In a general business sense, subsidiaries are typically wholly owned by a parent company (allowing you to avoid highly technical accounting debates about percentage of majority ownership). A practical issue for the MCSE to be keenly aware of is the role of subsidiaries in the firm's business operations.

At a minimum, the existence and role of subsidiaries should not be overlooked. Making that mistake would possibly result in a poorly-designed Windows 2000 network, especially when it comes to Active Directory.

In the case of directory services, should the subsidiary have a third-level domain name that is a child domain to the parent company? Or should the subsidiary have its own internal-domain namespace, effectively forming another tree in the Active Directory forest? Or should the subsidiary share the same internal domain as the parent company, perhaps "main.local," in Active Directory, and maintain a separate Internet identity via a DNS A record maintained at the ISP (these are resource records and are discussed in great detail in Chapter 16). What about the use of virtual directories in Internet Information Server (IIS)—assuming the firm hosts its own Web pages—and the use of recipient policies in Microsoft Exchange 2000 for SMTP e-mail addresses?

These are all technical decisions that must be made based on how the subsidiary relates to its parent company. An example of a firm with several subsidiaries is Pepsico with its Pepsi bottling, Tropicana, and Frito-Lay subsidiaries (see www.pepsico.com).

Branch Offices

Another structural consideration is branch offices. For example, would the network be best designed if a power user were selected to serve as a part-time network administrator at each branch office? This could be accomplished by emphasizing the use of organizational units (OUs) in Active Directory. Figure 2-6 shows the Active Directory Users and Computers tool (a snap-in tool found in the Administrator Tools program group) which can be used to create OUs.

How should the infrastructure be implemented? This directly pertains to Active Directory. For example, should BackOffice 2000, which installs Windows 2000 Server and BackOffice applications, such as Microsoft Exchange, in a manner designed for branch offices, be selected over stand-alone Windows 2000 servers? Should each branch office have its own domain controller or not? These are all valid questions, often with different correct answers (in design issues there isn't necessarily one right answer).

A well-known business that emphasizes the branch-office concept is banking. It should be noted that banks, built on the backs of branches, are large and enthusiastic implementers of technology such as Windows 2000 and Active Directory. That's something to think about as an MCSE candidate studying for the last exams in the design series, and possibly soon to be seeking gainful employment.

Wells Fargo, a large bank in the United States, is representative of a bank with a large network of branch offices. A photo of an actual branch is displayed in Figure 2-7. The authors have it on first-hand knowledge that Wells Fargo has deployed Microsoft-based networking solutions.

Figure 2-6
OUs matching company branch names

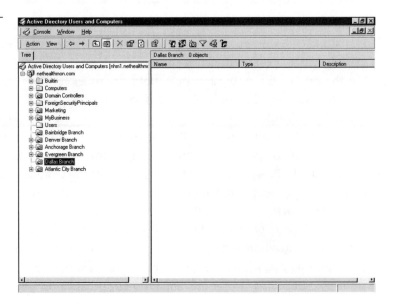

Figure 2-7   The Bainbridge Island Washington Branch of Wells Fargo

Bringing It All Together

Perhaps you live in a diversified community that has some or all of the geographic business models present. Seattle, Washington (seen in Figure 2-8), for example, is home to firms with significant international sales activity, such as Boeing and Microsoft. It is also home to companies with nationwide operations, such as Safeco. And, of course,

Figure 2-8   Seattle has companies that use many of the geographic business models.

there are regional firms, such as grocery stores, accounting firms, and law firms. Many subsidiaries of national and international companies have Seattle offices. And like nearly every community, Seattle has many firms with branch offices. The community you will operate in as a practicing MCSE may well have some or all of these geographic business-model elements.

Windows 2000 and Active Directory reflect these business realities of geographically dispersed operations and increased scalability and connectivity. Windows 2000 and Active Directory address geographic business issues in the following ways:

- Windows 2000 international support includes fonts, characters, and language options.

- Windows 2000 communications permit low costs and secure virtual private networks (VPNs).

- Active Directory, being a distributed database, allows domain controllers at distant locations to maintain an Active Directory database.

- Active Directory supports the use of organizational units to map the directory to geographic locations or subsidiaries.

- Active Directory allows the use of multiple domain structures to support multi-tiered business models, such as third-level DNS domains, multiple Internet identities, and so on.

Analyzing Company Processes

Welcome to the proverbial world of the Masters of Business Administration (MBA) and process analysis. *Process analysis* inside an organization is an opportunity to create flow charts that map out how information, communications, and the delivery of services flow through an organization. Process analysis provides information needed by business decision-makers in order to make critical business decisions. We liken this area to what used to be called Manufacturing Resource Planning (MRP), and is now called Enterprise Resource Planning (ERP). The idea with ERP is to detail the flow of sub-components down to the lowest level and order any and all components for a product when it is sold to a customer. For example, the ERP system might order six, size "A" flathead screws, when a reseller orders the company's product. And now, like any good journalist, the preceding MBA speaks about communication avenues, information management, and ERP with the MCSE viewpoint. The MCSE viewpoint might be to embrace Microsoft's dot-NET (.NET) strategy, which is the application of e-business solutions to company processes. For more information on the dot-NET solutions from Microsoft, visit www.microsoft.com/net. Several types of company processes should be analyzed, which include

- **Information flow** (With a look at formal communication overlaid by information communications)

- **Communication flow** (With the sender-receiver model and via the Myers-Briggs Type Indicator). You will recall from Communications 101 in college that communication occurs between a sender and receiver and this is typically presented as the Sender/Receiver (S/R) model.

- **Service and product life cycles** (With the MCSE life cycle as an example)

- **Decision-making** (With decision tree analysis)

Note that each of these points is further discussed next.

Information Flow

It is necessary to appreciate the foundation of information flow. Formal communications are vertical between organizational layers and can also be horizontal between peers. Informal flows of information can be, in a sense, whatever isn't formal, such as a subordinate speaking with a superior in another area of the organization.

One of the first roadblocks in many Windows 2000 and Active Directory implementations is the discovery that formal information and communication flows aren't in alignment with informal information and communication flows. That is, the way in which memos and official e-mails are routed doesn't match up well with the communication grapevine. On one hand, this is an issue between centralized and decentralized communication inside of the firm. Does the communication occur through official channels (centralized) or casually (decentralized)? The trend as of late in the business community has been towards decentralization with the advent of e-mail technologies, such as Microsoft Exchange, that have fostered and promoted informal communication channels.

TIP And why do we discuss Microsoft Exchange–based communications in the 70-219 section on Active Directory? Simple. Microsoft Exchange 2000 is heavily integrated with Active Directory, in terms of managing user accounts. And how does this integration occur you ask? Simply right-click a user account in Active Directory Users and Computers, and view the E-mail Addresses, Exchange Features, and Exchange General tabs. So in that sense, these apparently separate concepts are tied together!

Communication Flow

Closely related to and intertwined with information flow is communication flow. Admittedly, this is a tough area to tie into the very technical professional area that historically has been the type-cast world of the MCSE. But it's on the 70-219 exam, so we're honor-bound to present this information to you. To present the information to you, we've decided to use a popular communications model called the Myers-Briggs Type Indicator (MBTI).

The idea is that by engaging a consultant to work through the MBTI assessment tool, you can understand how people communicate and understand communication. Once you understand how people communicate and how they understand communication, you can assess if the communications, occurring in the organization, is empowering to the individual, promote leadership, or not (that is, whether the communications are meant to make people feel insignificant and unimportant). Communicating better because you understand how different people communicate and how people perceive the communication that is occurring certainly won't hurt you along the way as you work with other MCSEs and business types in the design of your directory services. In the old days, it was called getting along with people in business, before all these fancy models with ten-dollar words started appearing.

There are eight personal preferences identified by MBTI, which I've grouped by general category.

- *Extrovert* and *Introvert* focus on personal energy level.
- *Sensate* and *Intuitive* are perceptions of information.

- *Thinking* and *Feeling/Valuing* differentiate decision-making styles.

- *Judging/Organizing* and *Perceiving* are ways of managing daily lifestyle.

While there is more to know about MBTI, this text is dedicated to the MCSE certification journey. To find out more, visit the Web page for the Association for Psychological Type (APT) at www.aptcentral.org.

Service and Product Life Cycles

Business people like to speak about service and product life cycles. Technology people, such as MCSEs, are familiar with this concept, having watched the latest high-technology gadgets rendered obsolete in relatively short periods of time. To drive home the point about life cycles, I present the poignant and oh-so-true MCSE life cycle, as seen in Figure 2-9.

As you can see, the MCSE life cycle displays the MCSE candidate from birth, through MCSE candidacy, through the MCSE working life (including recertification requirements) to MCSE retirement and ultimately MCSE expiration. Be sure to get yourself certified before *your* cycle comes to its end stage—but hey, no pressure, guys!

Decision-Making

The term *decision-making* means many different things to different people. For example, it might mean that you have a strong leader in your organization who can make decisions, not look back, and march forward. Or it might be a visit to the MBA classroom to learn about decision-tree theory. With decision-tree theory, you start at the left side

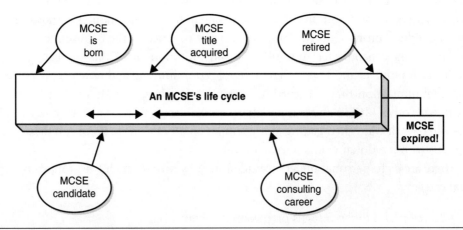

Figure 2-9   The MCSE life cycle

of the decision tree and work your way to the right, taking forks in the road along the way to arrive at the best decision possible. There are many good software products available for decision-tree analysis, including DecisionPro from Vanguard Software Corporation (visit www.vanguardsw.com).

Analyzing the Existing and Planned Organizational Structures   MCSEs are now expected to know about organizational structures and take them into consideration when designing the Active Directory. Why? Because the essence of much Active Directory design work is undertaken with the organizational structure in mind. Much of the time, there is creative friction between trying to recast the organization to fit Active Directory and vice versa—making Active Directory fit the organizational structure.

Management

The term *management model* is one of those broad terms that can be interpreted many different ways. In this case, we're interested in driving home two practical points that we think will contribute to your success as a practicing MCSE in the Active Directory design area.

First, there is the notion of the Chief Executive Officer (CEO), one of whom is shown in Figure 2-10. The CEO is ideally the firm's chief salesperson and perhaps the visionary leader behind the organization. CEO styles vary widely, ranging from distant and detached to micro-managers. Under any circumstances, though, the CEO is one of the most powerful people in the entire organization, a fact of life in business you must honor.

Figure 2-10   The CEO

Second, there are key people on the staff who, in many cases, perform the "real" work. This real work may range from making many day-to-day decisions that the CEO doesn't have time to make to acting as a gatekeeper, limiting access to the CEO. It is critical that you learn how to work with these key people, one of which is shown in Figure 2-11.

Company Organization

Basically, you should be concerned with four organizational structures: centralized, decentralized, project, and matrix.

- **Centralized** This is the traditional business structure with a vertical chain of command, as shown in Figure 2-12.

- **Decentralized** This business structure is informal, with a lot of peer-to-peer level communications. The structure is shown in Figure 2-13.

Figure 2-11 Every organization has a key manager you must successfully work with.

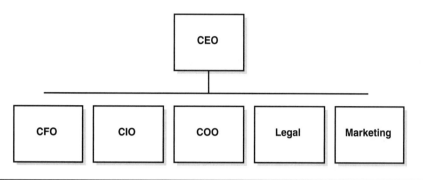

Figure 2-12   Centralized company structure

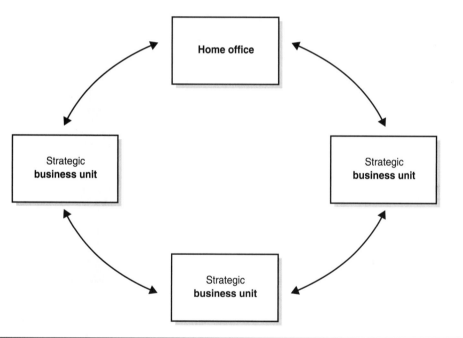

Figure 2-13   Decentralized company structure

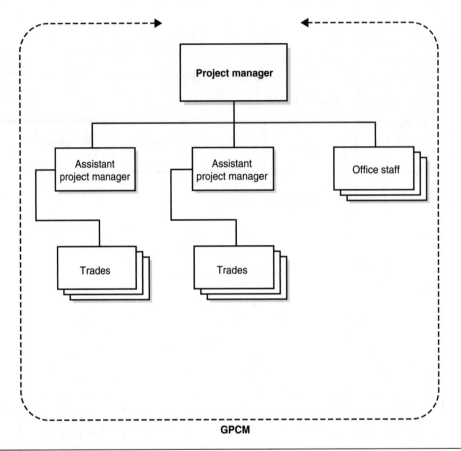

Figure 2-14 Project organization structure

- **Project** Project organizations are characterized by their limited durations. Teams are brought together for a specific project with start and end dates. At the end, the project team is disbanded, with many participants going on to the next project. A project organization is shown in Figure 2-14.

- **Matrix** Matrix organizations are a cross between traditional business organizations and project teams. Here functional employees are placed on project teams, often having dual reporting relationships. This is shown in Figure 2-15.

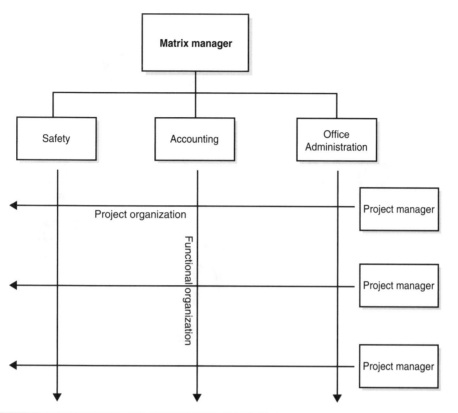

Figure 2-15   Matrix reporting relationship

Vendor, Partner, and Customer Relationships

When discussing the vendor, partner, and customer relationships, we're really talking about stakeholder analysis. That is, external stakeholders directly affect the success of the organization. Vendors typically supply goods, while partners provide and use goods and services, often interacting with the organization on a peer level. Customers are critical to the success of the organization, regardless of what type of organization you are speaking about (yes, even not-for-profit organizations). In Figure 2-16, you will see a stakeholder wheel that outlines how the various stakeholders interact with the organization.

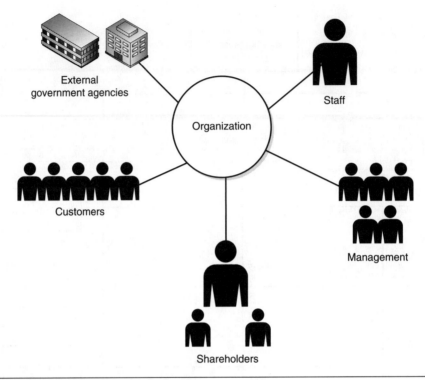

Figure 2-16   Stakeholder wheel of analysis

One area where the Windows 2000 MCSE has to be concerned with vendor, partner, and customer relationships is the use of extranets and secure Web sites. For example, Microsoft has a password-protected Web site, accessible from the Internet, where vendors may submit invoices for payment. At a minimum, exposing such an important business process entry point raises network security concerns. It also raises legitimate questions about the checks and balances of the accounts payable process in the accounting departments. Are there enough process gateways in place to prevent fraud?

Acquisition Plans

Another Active Directory architectural and design issue is the possibility of an acquisition. This includes being acquired or acquiring other firms. The Windows 2000 MCSE needs to be concerned about this area because it could affect the Internet and network namespace. Would the firm being acquired be rolled into an organizational unit in an existing domain? Would the acquired company require a new forest in Active Directory, in order to retain a separate identity? These are examples of the many questions related to Active Directory that need to be answered when a company is acquired.

Analyzing Factors That Influence Company Strategies

Several business-analysis factors influence how the company operates. These include company priorities, anticipated growth, growth strategies, the regulatory environment, the tolerance for risk, and the total cost of operations.

Identifying Company Priorities

Part of Microsoft's motives in presenting business topics to Windows 2000 MCSEs is to make you savvier at the enterprise level. Microsoft is using Windows 2000 Server to push into the enterprise marketplace, and it depends on support from business-minded Windows 2000 MCSEs.

One of the first tests of working successfully in an organization is to have a sense of what the company's priorities are. This can be accomplished by asking the firm's employees, reading the company's newsletter or Web site, or just watching how the company operates. The point is, you need to be smart and determine what areas are emphasized and what areas are de-emphasized. Knowing a company's priorities is an important part of making the best technology decisions possible.

As an example, Amazon.com, like many dot-com firms, has had to recently shift its priorities from growing madly with little regard to profit to controlling costs and achieving the profitability its investors demand. Such a shift has resulted in layoffs and, more importantly, could impact an MCSE working on infrastructure projects, such as Active Directory design and implementation.

Identifying the Projected Growth and Growth Strategy

Some firms are trying to grow rapidly while others prefer controlled growth in an orderly manner. Knowing what the growth strategy is can significantly affect what you want to accomplish with the Windows 2000 network.

Perhaps the firm's forecast is to stay the same size for the foreseeable future. This would suggest that the network design will be somewhat static. On the other hand, perhaps you are working with a start-up firm. Today this firm might have 20 employees using Small Business Server 2000 with a single Active Directory domain. Tomorrow the company could have 300 employees running BackOffice 2000 with two domains.

Anticipating this type of growth is important to making the best technology decisions (including Active Directory design solutions) you can, given the information you have available to you.

Identifying Relevant Laws and Regulations

With the introduction of the Windows 2000 MCSE program, Microsoft effectively has its Windows 2000 MCSEs (including you) on the path to being management consultants with suggestions about identifying relevant laws and regulations. The idea is well taken, but areas such as this are not emphasized on the MCSE exams. To be honest, we feel this specific exam objective is Microsoft's attempt to enhance your understanding of business issues, as esoteric as such business issues may appear.

We can suggest two resources you can use to educate yourself on laws and regulations. This first is a site used by our attorney clients, a legal service called Westlaw, which can be accessed at www.westlaw.com. Another source for learning about relevant laws and regulations would be the Web sites for your state, county, and local governments. For example, the Web site for King County, Washington, is at www.metrokc.gov.

Identifying the Company's Tolerance for Risk

Some firms have a high preference for risk taking, while others do not. Risk tolerance is based as much on the founder's or top-management's philosophy as anything. As a practicing Windows 2000 MCSE, you should assess how much risk the company tolerates. This information will help you determine whether, for example, a network that has a lower cost with certain safeguards, such as redundancy, would be the best design for the company. In contrast, if you work for a risk-adverse firm that is willing to pay heavily for their risk aversion, they might be a good candidate for a high-availability (and expensive) system, such as Windows 2000 Advanced Server with its clustering capabilities.

Identifying the Total Cost of Operations

A goal in the business community in recent years has been to lower the technology-related total cost of operations (TCO). A big design goal behind Windows 2000 and

Active Directory has been the push to lower TCO. For example, Active Directory attempts this by allowing you to delegate administration at the OU level. The idea here is that by selecting a power user at the OU level, and by not having to make this person an administrator at the domain level, you can delegate tasks down the organizational structure, freeing your administrator's schedule for more pressing (and costly) matters.

Chapter Review

Hopefully, you've finished this chapter with a heightened awareness of business issues in the context of technology. Too often, MCSEs are focused on the bits and bytes of a technology solution while not seeing the greater business purpose. More importantly, you, the Windows 2000 MCSE candidate, should be starting to formulate a Windows 2000 and Active Directory deployment road map. You have now been exposed to business-needs analysis, a function performed by many Windows 2000 MCSEs in a consulting capacity.

Questions

1. The CEO of a company mentions that they are an acquisition target. What do you believe might be going on?

2. True or False? Business models have little to do with Active Directory.

3. True or False? A centralized organization could also be a project-management organization.

Answers

1. The company might be purchased by another company. This could impact your Active Directory planning and design by having to account for how a new entity would be merged into your Active Directory forest.

2. **False.** Business models speak volumes about how a firm operates. This will affect the type of Active Directory solution you create as an MCSE.

3. **True.** Nothing inherently prevents a centralized organization from using project-management techniques. Perhaps a project manager leads the organization.

Key Skill Sets

The following skills sets meet the Microsoft Objectives for the 70-219 exam:

- Undertake the analysis of business requirements as part of the Active Directory planning and design process.

- Be able to assess business models from a geographic and company-process perspective.

- Have an appreciation for how an organization's structure will likely relate directly to the Active Directory solution you design as an MCSE.

- Know what company strategies are important and being implementing by looking at priorities, growth strategy, the laws and regulations that affect the company, and the company's risk preference.

Key Terms

Business models
Company processes
Priorities
Risk

Analyzing Technical Requirements

This chapter covers the following key mastery goals:

- Perform an evaluation of the company's existing and planned technical environments
- Consider how Active Directory will impact the existing and planned technical environments
- Focus on end-user desktop-management issues

After the MCSE completes the business-needs analysis described in Chapter 2, the focus shifts to an analysis of technical needs. Interestingly, it is here that the focus shifts from a high-level business discussion (which included economic, organizational, and management considerations) to the bona fide technical requirements. This chapter follows the traditional needs-analysis methodology of gathering information first, and then analyzing that information.

You may be wondering why Microsoft is placing greater emphasis on planning topics now with the Windows 2000 MCSE program than the old days of MCSE life under Windows NT Server 4.0? For example, why topics such as analyzing technical requirements? The answer is simple, and it amounts to a paradigm shift in Microsoft's thinking. The new Microsoft mindset represents a significant departure from the old view of the MCSE as only a technician. There are at least two reasons for this new thinking.

First, Microsoft is turning the MCSE designation into an analytical, not just a technical, designation. That is, once you earn the Windows 2000 MCSE, you should have both technical and architectural/design skills. This shift in the MCSE program will undoubtedly present some of the biggest certification challenges for some MCSE candidates. Other MCSE candidates will thrive on this planning and design paradigm.

Second, on a broader level, Microsoft and the technology-solutions industry as a whole realizes that improvements are necessary in the way the technology projects are planned, designed, and implemented. In the Microsoft white paper, "MS Solutions Framework: Enterprise Architecture Essentials—Achieving Business Value with IT" (available on Microsoft TechNet by either the CD-ROM subscription service or at www.microsoft.com/technet), it is claimed that only 16 percent of technology-implementation projects have been successfully completed over the last 20 years (Standish Group Report, 1995). Approximately 31 percent of the projects were cancelled outright (as was the case with the $38-million mainframe payroll software project with the King County, Washington, government in mid-2000), and over half (53 percent) of the technology projects resulted in disappointment. Needless to say, few other industries have such a poor track record of accomplishment. This low-success rate has contributed to the restructuring of the MCSE program under Windows 2000 to both acknowledge and emphasize planning, design, and architectural issues.

It is incumbent upon you, the Windows 2000 MCSE candidate, to understand the role of technical-needs analysis, the underlying theme of this chapter. While it's simple enough to present the old adage that "proper planning prevents poor performance," such phraseology understates the true importance of technical-needs analysis. The main justification for technical-needs analysis is to gather critical technology information about an organization so that the solution you plan, design, and implement will result in a technology solution aligned with the business processes. The point is that you are trying to align information technology (IT) goals with corporate or business goals. This type of alignment, while not guaranteeing the success of any given technology solution, will prevent the outright failure of such a solution.

Evaluating Existing and Planned Technical Environment

Microsoft is turning its MCSEs into technology consultants. As you likely know, the traditional role of consulting is to gather information about an existing situation and then synthesize and process that information to create a technology plan. As a Windows 2000 MCSE, you will view the company from a technology perspective (Chapter 2, of course, viewed the company from a business perspective).

Let's jump right in, starting with a view of a smaller company's existing technical environment (see Figure 3-1) followed by the meat of the matter (analyzing company size and user and resource distribution).

Figure 3-1 A small firm's existing technical environment

Analyzing Company Size and User and Resource Distribution

As a practicing MCSE who will at times act like an MBA (that is, wearing both the technology and business hats), you'll find that you work from a checklist when performing technology-needs analysis for a client. How can we make such an observation? Simple. By watching experienced MCSEs work (including observing our own work habits), it becomes apparent that work is accomplished much like completing a to-do list (or checklist). In fact, some people use the Tasks capability in Outlook 2000 to do exactly this (others keep a mental checklist in their head to complete tasks). In this chapter, we present much of the information we want to convey to you in the context of creating a needs-analysis checklist. You will see this in the form of questions. To be honest, you could take our questions in this chapter and recast it into a checklist to help you perform your design-related tasks.

When analyzing company size and user and resource distribution, your needs-analysis checklist should address the following questions:

- How many full-time equivalent (FTE) employees does the company have? This can be an interesting number to derive. First, some employees may only work part-time (that is, half-time, 3/4-time, and so on), so it would take two half-time employees to equal one FTE. Second, there may be more FTEs than meets the eye. Take a large law firm, for example. During the daytime hours, it is easy to observe how many employees are present. But many of the largest law firms also have night shifts of typists, and so on. Thus, the FTE count under this scenario might be significantly larger than you imagined. Another consideration is that many companies are motivated to minimize the number of FTEs for reporting purposes. This often results in firms where the political advantage accrues to a manager who maintains a minimal FTE head count. So what tricks do savvy managers play to lower FTEs? Quite simply, they use temporary employees, contractors, and consultants!

- How many users does the company have? On the surface this might sound simple: just count the number of users that the company has. However, it's not always that straightforward. Not only might you have two users on different shifts sharing one desktop computer (as the law firm does in the preceding point), but counting the number of users may not be that meaningful in your needs analysis. Some software-licensing mechanisms relate more to how many computers are connected to the network infrastructure than to the number of users utilizing the software. For example, consider Microsoft Small Business Server 2000 (SBS), a BackOffice solution for smaller firms. The licensing relates to client computers connected to the network (which is limited to 50 in SBS). You can have 100 users on the SBS network (added to Active Directory Users and Computers) and still be in conformance with the 50-license limit. This just points out that you need to count what's truly meaningful.

- If the employee and user counts are different, why? Many companies are not white-collar firms where each employee has a computer. Rather, a company may work in the trades or natural resources, such as fishing. One client we served was an Alaskan fishing company of significant size (often over 1,000 employees during the peak season). However, the home office has just 30 PCs. Not every fisher or ship captain needed (or wanted) a PC. The result was a significant difference between the employee and user counts.

- Does the company make use of part-time workers, contractors, and temps? And if so, how many? We've already mentioned the use of part-time workers, contractors, and temps, and the point here is that many firms have business models based on the use of this type of labor. Microsoft is a prime example. Whereas Microsoft now reports having over 39,000 full-time employees worldwide, it has been our experience that it has at least that number of contractors and temps (making the 39,000 seem like a case of underreporting).

- Does the company have different shifts where one computer is used by multiple users over a 24-hour period? Although we've made this a separate point, we've already mentioned the idea of shift work. However, we do want to add that this sharing of computers can present unique challenges. For example, we once served as MCSE consultants to a theater that had a bank of computers used by different shifts of volunteers and employees. It was our experience that these computers suffered excessive wear and tear not just from hours of use, but also from the indifference of volunteers towards the computer. One solution that was pursued was the use of dumb terminals in a Windows NT Server 4.0 Terminal Server Edition–based network. Having a terminal instead of a workstation seemed to limit the volunteers' ability to trash the machines.

- Do the contractors and vendors that serve the company that is implementing Active Directory provide their own PCs for your use? As an MCSE consultant, when we've been vendors serving a client, we've been in engagements where the price of our services included providing our own computer resources. This observation can affect you in two opposing ways. First, if you're an MCSE consultant who is acting as a vendor or a contractor and providing services to a company, you obviously need to adjust your price to account for the deployment of your own technology assets on the engagement. Second, if you're an MCSE on the inside of the organization (working for the company as an employee), and you interact with contractors and vendors who are providing services to your organization, how will you account for and secure the company-owned technology assets that are not owned by the contractors and vendors? Quite frankly, managing others' computers (which in this day and age also includes personal digital assistants—PDAs) and other equipment can be a bigger job than you might anticipate.

- Can employees purchase PCs to use while performing company-related work at home? Does the IT staff support these PCs for employees performing company work at home? It is common these days for companies to offer financial assistance for employees who want to purchase and deploy technology solutions at home. And it is also increasingly common for employees to perform company work at home (this can be work performed after hours during the evening, weekends, or even working one or more days per week at home). Certainly, one of the most popular selections is to help employees purchase a personal computer for both personal and business use. We've participated in agreements where a loan for the purchase of a PC is made by the firm to the employee. The loan is then forgiven on a sliding scale, depending on the tenure of the employee (for example, at the end of each year, 20 percent of the loan is forgiven, resulting in a free-and-clear computer for the employee to use at home by the end of year five). But financial arrangements aside, the crux of the matter is whether you, the MCSE, will be dragged (kicking and screaming) into supporting an employee's home (company-subsidized) PC? Our advice to you would be to assess how prevalent the situation is at your firm and to insist on boundary definitions that work for you. Perhaps you don't mind supporting home users, but we tend to offer this support only to senior management and other critical business stakeholders.

Assessing Available Connectivity

All of us occasionally fall victim to provincial thinking and view the world through our own eyes and experiences. In the context of network connectivity, we've found ourselves assuming that other locations are like the locations we work in, and that they have readily-available broadband connectivity solutions. We were surprised when we consulted for a large federal agency in Washington, D.C., with outposts in over 76 countries. The available connectivity between the work sites was often analog telephone (at best, and when it worked). Analog telephone lines accounted for over 70 percent of the computer-related connectivity for this agency. Modern solutions, such as broadband connectivity, were not part of the picture. Suppose this agency was looking at a Windows 2000–based solution as part of its network architecture, and you'll quickly see that available connectivity was a major consideration. Figure 3-2 shows a view of geographic connectivity.

By compiling information about the firm's existing WAN connections and what connectivity options are available, you will be able to address the following Active Directory planning issues:

- **Site placement and structure**   The general assumption is that Windows 2000 will be set up on a WAN to connect the remote locations. But don't discount other alternatives. The government agency mentioned earlier ultimately selected Microsoft Small Business Server as its solution for remote worksites, which allowed each site to be self-contained. E-mail became the primary communication link.

- **Domain controller (DC) placement**   The DC placement issue is a big one for WAN-based Windows 2000 Server solutions. For example, sites with expensive connections can benefit from having a DC placed at each remote location to han-

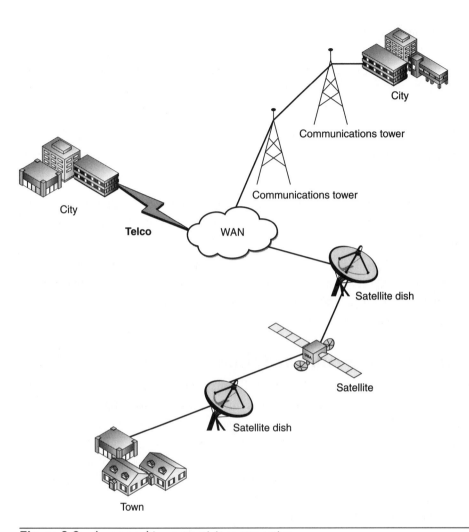

Figure 3-2   A geographic connectivity perspective

dle many administrative duties, including logon authentication. In the aforementioned government agency example, it was noted that many sites had telco-related connectivity charges in excess of $1/minute (thus, the attractiveness of Microsoft Small Business Server in this particular situation, where the single server is a DC).

- **Global catalog (GC) server placement**   In order to speed network response, the placement of Windows 2000 servers holding the GC role may be to your advantage. A GC facilitates rapid searches of Active Directory.

- **Replication requirements** A significant planning consideration is how replication will be handled. This topic is covered in much greater detail in Chapter 4, but the point is that while a DC placed at a remote site will minimize certain forms of traffic (such as logon authentication), it will increase other forms of traffic (such as the replication of Active Directory delta information) between domain controllers.

Here are a couple of connectivity questions to include on your technical-needs analysis:

- How are company work sites and remote locations connected today? For example, are some employees still using analog modems for computer-related communications?

- Do different communication alternatives exist? For example, has a digital subscriber line (DSL) service been introduced? Will satellite connections be necessary or even possible (such as VSAT)? It has been our experience that broadband communication services are not available in all areas.

Assessing Net Available Bandwidth

Needs-analysis, the focus of this chapter and analogous to planning, can be divided into two categories: link speed and bandwidth utilization. *Link speed* relates to the connection itself—the bits-per-second rating. *Bandwidth utilization* is the percentage of the communication channel that is being utilized. For example, perhaps the Windows 2000 network design calls for using the Quality of Service (QoS) capability to restrict traffic to a percentage of bandwidth. Or perhaps you should consider implementing the bandwidth throttling settings in both Microsoft Proxy Server 2.0 and Internet Security and Acceleration (ISA) Server 2000. In other words, you have a set amount of bandwidth, and you can restrict how much of that bandwidth can be used by an individual or application so some of the bandwidth is available to others. Figure 3-3 is a representation of the bandwidth pipe, both in thickness and utilization.

When assessing net available bandwidth, the Windows 2000 MCSE should obtain answers to these questions:

- What is the link speed between geographic locations?
- What is the link speed between buildings?
- What is the link speed between network segments?
- What is the network utilization on a daily and monthly basis during normal business conditions?

Figure 3-3
Bandwidth link speed (size of pipe) and percentage consumed (bandwidth utilization)

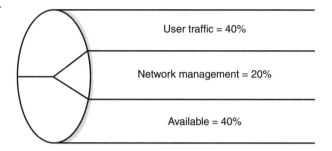

User traffic = 40%

Network management = 20%

Available = 40%

- What is the network utilization on a daily and monthly basis during busy business conditions?

- What is the network utilization on a daily and monthly basis after business hours?

- What other peak utilization periods exist (such as bi-weekly payroll, end-of-month accounting, and night batch-processing runs)?

- Are all of the networking protocols that are currently implemented actually required?

- Can any of these networking protocols be eliminated to increase network efficiency? (Fewer networking protocols reduce broadcast-related traffic.)

Analyzing Performance Requirements

Who can realistically argue against performance requirements? Everyone wants the best performance, right? Unfortunately, performance often comes at a price, both financial and sometimes at the cost of the stability of a system. For example, you might be inclined to use the very latest Intel microprocessor to gain the greatest speed advantages you can. However, suppose the chip is brand new (and so is very expensive). And because the chip is new, it is a risky proposition because it has not been in production very long (what if a flaw is discovered in the chip?).

The motivation for better performance is typically based on application issues, not the MCSE's need for speed. We've sat in more meetings than we care to count, with application software vendors listing system requirements for their applications to run properly on the computer network. Sometimes these stated requirements are right on target and reflect realistic load conditions. Often, though, these system requirements are understated to make the product seem lean and mean (that is, to suggest it will run on smaller or older machines with less processing power and RAM). Even now, Microsoft will understate the system requirements for many of its solutions. (To Microsoft's credit, there is some truth starting to appear in advertising—Microsoft now typically lists the minimum and the recommended system requirements, and other vendors are starting to follow.)

Our point is that it's the performance of the software applications that will typically drive the firm to make financial outlays to improve the computer network. If the accounting system or corporate database are performing at substandard levels, the case for obtaining better equipment or a software upgrade will be far better.

For performance issues, the Windows 2000 MCSE should obtain answers to the following questions:

- Does the firm place an emphasis on high availability, high performance, or both?

- Is the firm willing to make the necessary capital investment to achieve performance targets?

- Are users generally satisfied with the performance of the system?

- Have benchmarking tests been performed, measuring network and application performance (such as Microsoft SQL Server benchmark measurements)?

- Are these benchmark reports available?

- What, if any, quantifiable performance improvements is the firm seeking to achieve with the implementation of Windows 2000 Server and Active Directory?

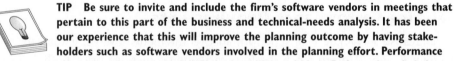

TIP Be sure to invite and include the firm's software vendors in meetings that pertain to this part of the business and technical-needs analysis. It has been our experience that this will improve the planning outcome by having stakeholders such as software vendors involved in the planning effort. Performance issues are not just operating-system-specific, and you'll greatly benefit from the mind share offered by all of the participants. Mind share is a technical term currently in favor with "tech heads"; it refers to multiple parties (managers, MCSEs, stakeholders, and so on) making analytical contributions to a task, project, or meeting. Try using this term with your MCSE buddies to show off sometime!

Analyzing Data- and System-Access Patterns

The basic role of any computer system (regardless of the operating system) is to access and manage data. This area of planning and analysis (data system and access patterns) isn't so much about having a histogram that shows peak system-usage periods (for example, a histogram that shows the data is accessed mostly between 8:00 A.M. and 11:00 A.M.) but rather to step back and observe how the data is used.

TIP   Our advice here is to include a "data mining" specialist in this phase of the planning. Data mining is still a relatively new concept and includes looking at access patterns. Not many people have specialized in this field yet, so we recommend you contact the Computer Science department at a local college or university for resources in this area. It is possible that one of the faculty members both specializes in this field of study and will provide consulting services after hours or between terms (perhaps even forgoing a spring break in Florida to assist your planning efforts!). And if you find you really enjoy working with data, consider that Microsoft has a premium technical certification called the Microsoft Certified Database Administrator (MCDBA) that focuses on database administration. It is something for you to consider after earning your MCSE if you have the desire to earn more technical certifications from Microsoft. See www.microsoft.com/trainingandservervices for more information on the DBA.

Regarding data- and system-access issues, the Windows 2000 MCSE should obtain answers to the following questions:

- How is data stored on the network? Microsoft SQL Server? Microsoft Exchange public folders? Oracle? ISV business applications, such as Great Plains accounting systems? And what about the distributed file system in Windows 2000 Server (DFS)? DFS is discussed in Chapter 17.

- How is data merged and compiled in the organization? ODBC? DDE? Copy and paste? Import/export routines?

- What changes in data management might occur in the foreseeable future? Consider XML, SQL-based data management, and especially the Web components!

- What types of data- and system-access relationships exist between locations, business units, divisions, outside vendors, customers, and joint-venture partners? Had there been sufficient discussion about Internet access for these parties (listed in the preceding sentence) and data sharing via XML.

- Are any version-control tools, such as Microsoft Visual SourceSafe, being used to control software code, documents, and applications? Visual SourceSafe is a powerful way to check-in and check-out code and documents, storing them in a secure library.

Analyzing Network Roles and Responsibilities

Analyzing network roles and responsibilities is truly nothing more than human resources management. It generally involves starting with the traditional look at the existing situation (such as reviewing the organizational chart) and thinking outward from there.

TIP A quick-and-dirty way to learn who's who in enterprises is to observe the tabs and fields for entries in the Microsoft Exchange Global Address List (GAL) recipients. If you compose an e-mail in Outlook, click the To button, and display the firm's GAL, you'll see all of the usernames. For a particular user, highlight the username and then click the Properties button. In the dialog box that appears, the information in the fields (if they are filled in) will reveal the reporting relationships that person participates in.

Regarding network roles and responsibilities, the Windows 2000 MCSE should obtain answers to the following questions:

- How is the IT function managed today by the organization? Is there strong centralization or strong decentralization? Are there both centralization and decentralization approaches present in the organization? Centralized would speak towards centralized decision-making housed in the IT department. Decentralized would speak towards dispersed technology decision-making with functional departments and branch offices making technology purchasing decisions.

- Are all network administrators from the IT department?

- Who currently performs administrative tasks, such as creating groups, creating and maintaining share points on the network (such as shared folders), changing passwords, and configuring object attributes?

- Are any users allowed to perform administrator functions?

- Are users allowed to manage their own accounts? Change passwords?

- If appropriate, list resources (machines or printers) that might be appropriate administrative task delegation candidates using organizational units (OUs) in Active Directory. Remember with Active Directory, you can delegate administrative tasks to users (typically power users).

 TIP We've used the Web to search for job descriptions to use as templates in creating human resources manuals for a technology department. For example, look up an enterprise on the Web, click the Jobs link, and copy and paste a network engineering job description into your Word document as the starting point for creating a job description in your technology department. That approach can save you hours!

Analyzing Security Considerations

Part II of this book is dedicated to the security topic (and more importantly, to Exam 70-220, "Designing Security for a Microsoft Windows 2000 Network"). You'll need to review that material carefully in preparation for the Active Directory planning work you may perform, and to bone up for the Active Directory–planning certification exam (70-219) that this section of the book is dedicated to. But since the devil is in the details, the following list of questions can be used to analyze the organization's computer security. Figure 3-4 shows one security consideration that is often overlooked: the physical.

Regarding security considerations, the Windows 2000 MCSE should obtain answers to the following questions:

- What are the policies concerning the rights to gain access to, view, and change data and resources?

Figure 3-4   The proverbial locked door representing sound physical security

- Are users grouped together for security management purposes?

- How is access to applications restricted? (For example, is there overall network security or is security native to the application?)

- What types of information are available to all users in the organization?

- What user and enterprise security policies currently exist?

- What types of guidelines exist regarding appropriate network use?

- What security and encryption standards are currently in use or are planned for the future?

Analyzing the Impact of Active Directory

The technical-needs analysis should also take Active Directory into account. Technical issues can affect Active Directory, so your technical-needs analysis should involve the following:

- Assessing existing systems and applications

- Identifying existing and planned upgrades and rollouts

- Analyzing the technical support structure

- Analyzing existing and planned network and systems management

Assessing Existing Systems and Applications

The Windows 2000 MCSE should inventory existing hardware, software, and applications. This information is very useful for forward-planning purposes. This is a huge task in the real world, requiring you to work across departments and with many different vendors. The outcome of this part of the job is typically a large notebook that identifies where the organization is at from a technology viewpoint.

Identifying Existing and Planned Upgrades and Rollouts

A list of current and future upgrade projects should be created. Do any of these upgrade projects negatively affect Active Directory (such as introducing Novell Network Directory Services)? Are any of these upgrade projects negatively affected by Active Directory (will Active Directory break any upgrade)?

Analyzing the Technical Support Structure

The analysis of the technical support structure is both technical- and human resources-related. We're basically talking about the help desk here. A view of a help desk operation is shown in Figure 3-5. To be honest, we find this is an opportunity crying out for the use of two popular MBA management paradigms: talk to your customers, and management by "walking around." First, if you really want to know how your technical support is structured and functioning in an organization, conduct a survey of end-users asking them to answer numerous questions about the process for getting computer help and how effective that help has been. Second, instead of looking at organization charts that tell you what the technical support structure should be, walk around the technical support department during different times of the week and observe how people work, interact and so on.

Figure 3-5 The help desk operations (affectionately called "the pit" by old-time MCSE professionals)

TIP Keep an eye on turnover in this area. Many new MCSEs use the technical support path as a foot in the door to launch their MCSE careers. These people are typically gone in six months. You need to factor this observation into your planning when determining what the technical support structure will look like for the enterprise.

The Windows 2000 MCSE should consider the following question: How is technical support provided today? Via a help desk in the IT department, a Web-based subscription, or an outsourced support partner?

Analyzing Existing and Planned Network and Systems Management

The Windows 2000 MCSE needs to look at how network and systems management is currently set up. This is also a chance to consider how things could be done better. For our purposes, network management would clearly relate to the ordinary and necessary tasks performed by a network professional to keep the network up and running (and the end-users happy). Systems management should be considered a broad term and might include the application development, database administration, and even telecommunications areas in an organization.

The Windows 2000 MCSE should consider the following questions:

- What network management tools are currently being used? An example of this is Simple Network Management Protocol (SNMP)-enabled devices. You may know that many devices such as printers, routers, and switches are SNMP-compliant.

- What systems management tools are currently being used (such as Microsoft Systems Management Server 2000 [SMS])? If you've worked with SMS, you would know this tool provides network monitoring, inventory management, and remote control capabilities. Other tools in this software category include Computer Associates UniCenter and IBM's Tivoli.

Analyzing the Business Requirements for Client-Desktop Management

Talk about another thick study to perform. Analyzing the business requirements at the workstation-level, at first blush, appears to be huge. But in reality, it's more a matter of bringing together much of the information you've already gathered in this chapter and

Chapter 2 and putting a client-desktop spin on it. The traditional client desktop, for both laptop and desktop machines, is shown in Figure 3-6.

Here are some general questions to consider concerning the client desktop:

- What are the requirements of business applications running on the desktop? For example, does the new accounting system require more RAM memory on the workstation?

- When analyzing end-user work needs, consider whether the PCs are appropriately allocated to users? Do mobile users have laptops? Are workstations shared? Are the workstations secure?

- When identifying technical-support needs for end-users, consider whether the end-users have been surveyed regarding their current technical-support needs. (If they haven't, do so now.)

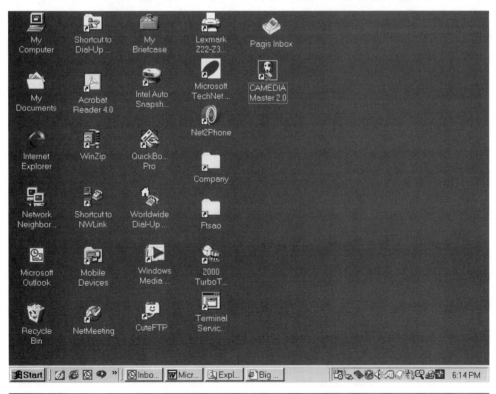

Figure 3-6   The client desktop as seen from an end-user's workstation

- When establishing the required client-computer environment, consider whether the firm is planning to use Group Policy once Active Directory is implemented. Are all client machines going to be upgraded to Windows 2000 Professional to accommodate Group Policy–based management?

Update: Catywhompus Construction, Inc.

It is safe to say that the technical-needs analysis presented in this chapter applies to our beloved Catywhompus Construction. The management at Catywhompus is not only interested in the "20 questions" nature of the technical analysis process, but has decided it needs to use the process to learn as much about its current and future technical infrastructure as it can from its MCSE consultants. (Rememeber that *you* are acting as an MCSE consultant who serves Catywhompus Construction.) By observing how you and your associate MCSE consultants undertake the planning process in the context of technical analysis, the Catywhompus management team will be able to make its own determination as to whether it's being well served or not.

Chapter Review

This chapter focused on technical-needs analysis. This is a big area of study and is certainly multifaceted, but technical-needs analysis is more often than not about the identification and assessment of the company's existing technology environment. However, we didn't stop there as technical-needs analysis is also about looking to the future. We also discussed the impact of Active Directory on the technical environment. Active Directory is unique in that it impacts the organization in many ways such as the organizational structure and the technology infrastructure.

The underlying purpose of this chapter was to provide a framework for Windows 2000 MCSEs to understand and conduct technical-needs analyses. Although not the primary learning outcome of this chapter, along the way you've increasingly learned how to integrate technology and business goals as part of your Active Directory design and planning process. To see this, revisit many of the questions presented in this chapter and observe how they relate to business as well as technology. This stage in the process allows you to be both an MCSE and a business consultant, by virtue of conducting business-needs analysis with a focus on technical requirements.

Questions

1. True or False. Planning is an unnecessary expenditure as part of the Active Directory-implementation process.

2. What does the first "D" in DDNS stand for?
   a. Design
   b. Domain
   c. Dynamic
   d. Data

3. An organization called Independence Incorporated is known for its strong branch office system. The company has a total of 300 employees and 10 branch offices. It's not worried about bandwidth considerations on its wide area network (WAN). Should a single domain with OUs for each branch office be the fundamental design?

Answers

1. **False.** Planning is a very good use of money and time. However, as a Windows 2000 MCSE, be advised that you might meet resistance from the business types in the real world of business and commerce, who might see planning as money down the drain. You'll have an educational challenge in front of you in that case.

2. **C.** The full term is Dynamic DNS.

3. The authors support having fewer domains that emphasize OUs with smaller firms. However, as with any design matter, answers may vary. It is possible that you would prefer to have each branch office act as its own domain.

Key Skill Sets

You should be able to perform the following tasks to meet the Microsoft Objectives for the 70-219 exam:

- Extend your needs analysis to technical issues.
- View technical issues from a business perspective.

- Understand the impact of Active Directory today (in the existing technical environment) and tomorrow (in the planned technical environment).

Key Terms

Applications

Minimum requirements

Organization

Recommended requirements

Systems

Technical support structure

CHAPTER 4

Designing a Directory Service Architecture

This chapter covers the following key mastery goals:

- Design an effective Active Directory forest and domain structure
- Create a design that optimizes trust relationships if such trust relationships exist
- Design an Active Directory namespace that is consistent with the organization's DNS strategy and scope of its Active Directory implementation
- Design a practical organizational unit scheme that is both effective and efficient
- Plan for implementing Group Policy in the organization to improve network management
- Decide how and where to implement Active Directory sites that are functional and accommodate replication needs
- Design an Active Directory implementation plan

Directory services provide a method of organizing information about objects (files, users, printers, and the like) with the capability to manage and apply security configurations to those objects. A good directory-services design should make the actual physical directory structure invisible to the user. The user should be allowed to focus on using information rather than on searching the directory. A directory can be a part of the operating system, such as Novell Directory Services (NDS), or part of the application, such as Microsoft Exchange.

Microsoft's latest version of directory services is called Active Directory. This directory service becomes an integral part of the operating system when a Windows 2000 Server is promoted to a domain controller. Active Directory utilizes the International Organization for Standardization's X.500 directory service protocol. In this chapter, we will concentrate on the design elements of a Windows 2000 Active Directory, and we will also consider other directory services in relationship to Active Directory.

In the past, the administrator was able to be somewhat removed (perhaps even isolated) from the business goals of the company. With the advent of Active Directory, the goals of the business will, more than ever, dictate the structure of directory services, especially decisions concerning forests, domains, and organizational units. System analysts have been proclaiming for some time that in order for the Information Technology (IT) department to add value to the company and to help create best practices, the IT goals needed to be aligned with those of the business. To avoid a bad deployment of Active Directory and to minimize maintenance of Active Directory in the future, the IT department needs to know and address the strategic goals of the company. This may very well be unfamiliar territory for your company, but it is necessary for you to create and/or foster a cooperative exchange of information between the IT department and business management. This will necessitate the IT department taking a crash course in business administration and for the business-management team to be exposed to IT.

As an IT administrator, you will no longer function as the person who has all the answers; you will now have to be the one asking all the questions. It will be management that has the answers required to properly set up a network that will support the current and future needs of the company. While this paradigm shift may be a difficult one, it is not impossible.

Designing an Active Directory Forest and Domain

Before jumping into forest and domain design specifics, let's look at Active Directory. Active Directory provides the administrator with several benefits:

- **Scalability** Active Directory scales to the largest organizations and enables domains to interoperate easily. This is perhaps one of its strongest points. Active Directory allows for several organizational units (OUs), and these OUs can be combined into a domain (although, practically speaking, the OUs are really containers in a domain). Domains, via the namespace, are combined into a domain tree, and the trees are combined to create a forest.

- **Domain Name System (DNS)**   Active Directory is integrated with DNS, and Active Directory and DNS namespaces are the same. Windows 2000 DNS uses Active Directory for the replication of primary DNS zones, and Active Directory helps to provide security for the DNS service.

- **Global catalog**   Active Directory enables the querying of the global catalog rather than querying each and every domain. The global catalog is created initially on the first domain controller and is essentially an efficient index that points to objects in Active Directory, and it can then be moved to another domain controller—it is possible to have a global catalog on more than one domain controller. The global catalog is used when logging on in native mode or, in other words, in a Windows 2000 environment with no Windows NT Backup Domain Controllers (BDCs). Not all class attributes are in the global catalog because the global catalog is operating as more of an index than a full database. Only attributes that assist with querying for an object and that remain constant should be in the global catalog. (Global catalog servers are discussed in greater detail in Chapter 5.)

- **Multi-master replication**   Active Directory uses a multi-master replication model, allowing you to update the directory from any domain controller. In Windows NT, the person who was logged on to the network as an administrator could only make changes to the Primary Domain Controller (PDC), which in turn replicated a read-only copy to the BDC. With a Windows 2000 domain controller, the administrator can make changes to any domain controller, and those changes are replicated to the other domain controllers.

- **Two-way trusts**   Active Directory has implicit two-way trusts, which means that the administrator is freed from the tedious task of creating trusts as in Windows NT 4.0.

- **Lightweight Directory Access Protocol (LDAP)**   Active Directory uses LDAP, which means Active Directory is interoperable with other applications and directories. Every object in the Active Directory has a globally unique LDAP name, which enables you to find things more easily.

- **NTFS 5**   Active Directory requires the use of NTFS 5. NTFS security is, of course, a large topic and is woven into many passages in Part II of this book. For more on the security protection provided by NTFS, see Chapter 9.

Designing a Forest and Schema Structure

A forest is a grouping of domain trees, and all trees in the forest use the same schema and global catalog. A *tree* is a set of domains within a contiguous namespace, while a

forest is a set of trees that do not share a contiguous namespace. A new or separate forest is created when it is impossible or impractical to merge or consolidate domains,
such as when you already have multiple root domains, or when you need to create
more than one view of the company (this slightly understates the process with a dose
of business-speak). In reality, forests are distinguished by their schema, and while we're
talking reality here, the fact of the matter is that, on a day-to-day basis, you won't really
deal with or pay attention to forests. But as you see in the example in this section,
forests become much more front and center on your radar screen when a firm merges
with another firm where both are using Active Directory.

In the spirit of learning to crawl before walking, let's look at the evolution of the
Microsoft forest. Figure 4-1, reading from the top, displays the evolution of the

Figure 4-1
Evolution of the
Microsoft forest
as three separate
epochs

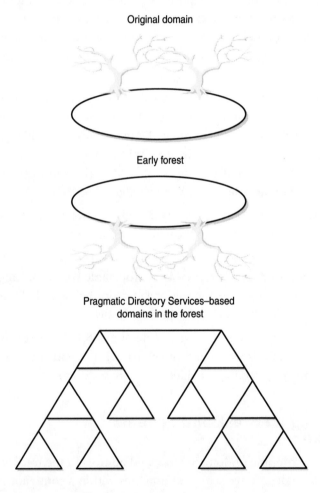

Original domain

Early forest

Pragmatic Directory Services–based
domains in the forest

Microsoft forest from our viewpoint. The top of the figure represents the first epoch when the idea of basing directory services was implemented. The middle of the figure represents when a directory services design architect was able to merge the world of technology with the forest concept (even though the trees point downward). The bottom of the figure represents the final epoch where an Active Directory tree is represented by interconnected domains (domains are the triangle shape).

Now suppose Catywhompus were to merge with Doggywhompus, a company that already has its own Windows 2000 structure, which is not compatible with Catywhompus's Windows 2000 structure. As we all know, cats and dogs cannot get along, but here we're really talking about the merger of forests. Neither Doggywhompus nor Catywhompus want to give up their current Web presence or Active Directory schema. Doggywhompus's Active Directory forest structure is broken down by geographical boundaries, whereas Catywhompus's Active Directory forest structure is broken down by function. After the merger, we would end up with a forest that looked like Figure 4-2.

If Catywhompus wanted to have an external namespace for their Web presence and a different internal namespace for their employees, you would have a forest that looks like Figure 4-3. Here you see the traditional Internet-registered domain name being used as the external domain name and a simple abbreviation, CW (short for Catywhompus), being used for the internal domain name.

The best time to consolidate and attempt to create a single contiguous namespace is before you promote any Windows 2000 server to be a domain controller. This early planning stage is the time to deal with the political issues of reorganizing domains that

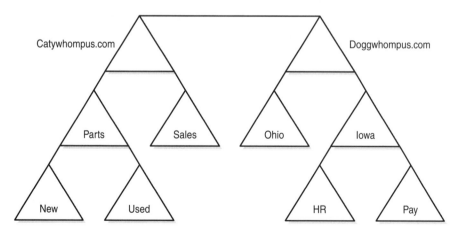

Figure 4-2   The Catywhompus-Doggywhompus merger

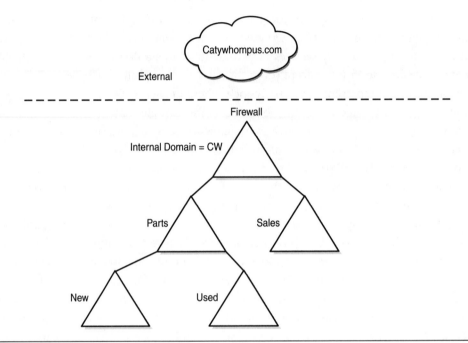

Figure 4-3 Catywhompus internal-external forest

are presently being used. It should be easier to make these organizational changes at this stage because people are more likely to give up control when this is accompanied by other changes, such as getting new equipment and network operating systems.

Windows 2000 domains within a tree have implicit two-way trusts, meaning that users who are logged on as administrators don't have to create these trusts manually; these trusts are created automatically. These trusts that exist between domains are also transitive, meaning that if domain A trusts domain B, domain C trusts domain D, and if domain A trusts domain C, then domain B trusts domain D (as shown in Figure 4-4).

Trusts between trees in a forest still require the administrators of each domain to add the other domain as a trusted domain. This is different from Windows NT 4.0 where the administrator was required to set up each and every one-way (and two-way) trust relationship.

You will need to carefully plan your forest before you start using Active Directory, since Windows 2000 does not provide a method to merge multiple trees or domains (as of this writing, but solutions are under development). Windows 2000 also does not presently have any tools to manage multiple forests, thus giving you more incentive to

Figure 4-4
Domain trust
relationships

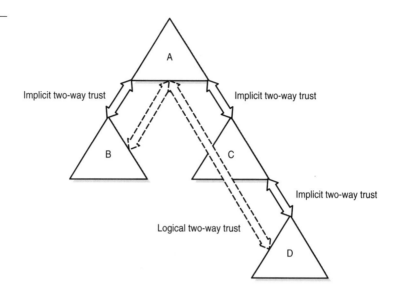

have a single-forest design. If you need to manage multiple forests, you will need to set up explicit nontransitive trust relationships.

A *schema* is a description of the objects and attributes that are in the directory. Since an attribute is only defined in the schema once and can be used by any class, you should take great care when naming and defining attributes, which may well be used by very different classes. The schema also makes a reference to its parent object. You can think of this as the glue that binds the family of Active Directory objects.

Applications can use the schema to determine what attributes the object has. One object is the user object, shown in Figure 4-5. It has several attributes, such as the name-related fields. The administrator can add attributes to an object. However, the administrator is not allowed to delete an attribute, only to mark the attribute as deactivated.

You will need to load the Active Directory schema snap-in using the Windows 2000 Administration Tools to manipulate the schema. See Chapter 5 for more information on using the Active Directory snap-in tools (and, to be honest, if you are taking these design-level exams, you should already have mastered these tools).

Designing a Domain Structure

Your first domain is created when you run dcpromo.exe and create that first domain controller. A domain in Windows 2000 is capable of holding a million or more objects

Figure 4-5
Screenshot of
user object

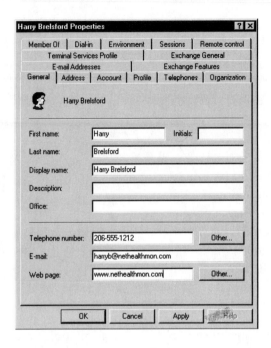

(Microsoft reports that it is capable of holding 10 million objects). With Windows 2000, you can now keep all of your objects in one domain, something that was not a possibility in Windows NT.

In the real world, the authors have found the following to be universally true. If you have more than one domain, it is because you have a reason to do so, such as having different Internet names, organizational differences, geographical divisions, or for network administration reasons. The domain serves several functions, including security, replication, and centralized administration.

A domain is primarily a security boundary. Windows 2000 introduces a third security group, called a *universal group*, in addition to NT's *local* and *global groups*. Universal groups enable you to put global and universal groups from one domain in your forest into another domain. Universal groups are only available in native mode.

Administrative authority is also bound by domain boundaries. This allows the granting of administrative authority to a user in one domain, while not allowing that user to have administrative rights in another domain. Note that the administrator of one domain can be explicitly granted administrator rights in another domain (via the two-way transitive trust mechanism discussed in the "Designing a Forest and Schema Structure" section earlier in the chapter). This helps to prevent the compromising of the overall security of the organization.

Analyzing and Optimizing Trust Relationships

A *trust* is a means for the users in one domain to be authenticated in another domain. Windows 2000 has two types of trust relationships: explicit and transitive. The one-way *explicit trusts* are the trusts that were used in Windows NT, which required action by the administrator to be set up. Two-way *transitive trusts* are created automatically when Windows 2000 is in native mode.

If you want to set up a trust between Windows 2000 and Windows NT, the administrator will be required to set up explicit trusts. These trusts will only function in one direction—just because domain A users are trusted by domain B does not mean that domain B users are trusted by domain A (the one-way trusts shown in Figure 4-6). The administrator will need to set up each one-way trust relationship.

When Windows 2000 is placed in native mode, two-way transitive trust relationships are formed. Thus, if domain A and domain B trust each other, and domain B and domain C trust each other, then domain A and domain C trust each other (the two-way implicit trusts in Figure 4-6). When a domain is created in a tree, Windows 2000 forms the new domain using a two-way, transitive-trust relationship with the rest of domains in the tree without any administrator intervention.

When your Windows 2000 forest begins to grow, you will want to consider using shortcut trusts and external trusts. A *shortcut trust* is a means of connecting two non-adjacent domains within the same forest, whereas an external trust is a means to connect two domains in separate forests (see Figure 4-7). Both of these trusts are one-way trusts that the administrator will need to set up.

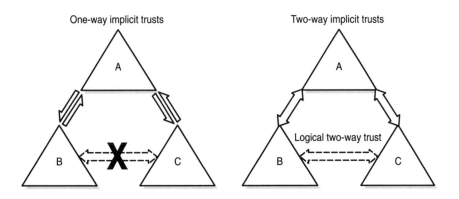

Figure 4-6   One one-way trusts versus two-way trusts

Figure 4-7
A shortcut trust

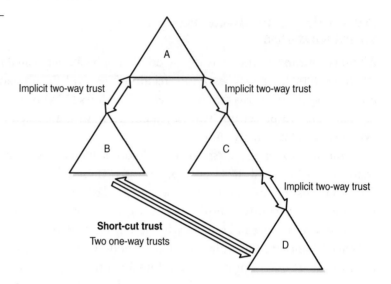

You are probably asking yourself why you would want to set up a one-way trust within a forest that already has a two-way transitive trust. Well, the answer is that the trust path (or the link between domains that is a trust) needs to be created by Windows 2000 before an account is given access to a resource in another domain in the forest, and it takes more time to create the trust paths as the forest becomes larger and more complex. A shortcut trust allows the administrator to shorten the time for an account to gain access to a resource. You may want to create two one-way shortcut trusts between the two domains, much as you did in Windows NT. The use of the shortcut trusts allows you to optimize your use of trusts.

External trusts are a way for the administrator to allow accounts to use resources in another Windows 2000 forest or a non-Windows 2000 domain. The external trust allows the administrator to establish a trust between a new Windows 2000 domain and an existing Windows NT domain. Remember, an external trust is a one-way trust relationship (see Figure 4-8).

During the upgrade process, the existing trust relationships will be preserved. If you are a believer in Murphy's Law (if it can go wrong, it will), as we are, you will want to document and test each trust relationship prior to upgrading your current Windows NT system.

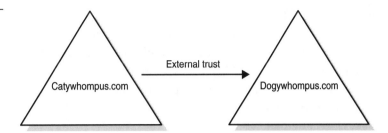

Figure 4-8
A one-way
external trust

External trust

Catywhompus.com

Dogywhompus.com

Designing an Active Directory Naming Strategy

Once you are ready to name your domains, you should start with a root name that will not change. It is almost impossible to change the root name later, so choose this name very carefully.

NOTE For Active Directory–integrated zones, the default value for the Dynamic Update setting is Allow Only Secure Updates. This is set on the property sheet for a DNS zone. The exception to this is the default value for Active Directory–integrated root (or ".") zones. For these zones, the default value is None. This behavior is by design because the root zone should not undergo dynamic changes. See the Microsoft TechNet article Q232187 at www.microsoft.com/technet.

You will want your domains to have short, descriptive logical names that are easy to remember. You have chosen a good name if a non-IT user can easily determine the physical, geographical, operational, functional, or divisional nature of the domain. Each domain name needs to be unique within the DNS namespace, and an individual domain name can be up to 63 characters. You are allowed to use uppercase and lowercase letters, numbers 0 through 9, and the hyphen, as defined in RFC 1035. Unicode (RFC 2044) characters are additional characters used by other languages.

With a 255-character limit for a fully qualified DNS name, you will need to limit the number of domain levels. A fourth or fifth domain level with a host name truly starts to become a run-on sentence. Also, as you create more domain levels, keeping track of names becomes more cumbersome. Keeping the "seven plus-or-minus two" rule in mind should help you to limit the number of domain levels. This rule is an old trick for helping you remember to limit the depth of your domain naming, but we won't leave you hanging there. What we're really saying is you should try to keep your domain structure as flat as possible and not go deeper than nine layers and preferably not deeper than five layers (thus the "seven plus-or-minus two rule").

When considering whether you will only need one domain or several, examine the business's strategic planning goals (for example, look three to five years into the future) and ask the following questions:

- Are you growing?
- Are you going to be acquiring another company?
- Are you going to be spinning off a company?
- Are you going to be expanding into new geographical locations, which may require different object attributes?

Establishing the Scope of the Active Directory

The scope of Active Directory includes every object within the forest, and it has the capability of holding millions of objects.

Part of defining the scope (or breadth and depth) of Active Directory is to look at the components that affect Active Directory. When setting the scope, you'd look at the two types of groups in Windows 2000: security and distribution. *Security groups* have a scope or range in which they can operate. These scopes can be local, global, or universal. The first two group scopes, local and global, are carried forward from Windows NT, and thus should be familiar.

In networking, you will recall that one of the main reasons to have groups on a computer network is to manage permissions. The permissions for a *local group* pertain only to local domain resources. The members of this group have a need to use local resources, and the members can include users, other local groups, global groups, and universal groups.

The members of the *global group* come from the domain in which they are created and can be given permission for any resource in any domain. Members of this group can include individual user accounts and other global groups that come from the same domain.

When running a mixed-mode domain, you will be limited to the global and local groups, just as you are in Windows NT. With some creativity and planning, you should be able to use these two security groups to do most of what you want to accomplish. With global groups, you can combine users who have common job responsibilities or needs, especially those located in other domains. Local groups can be created for local resources that users will need to use.

Windows 2000 introduces a new group, the *universal group*, whose members come from any domain and who can be given permissions to any resource in any domain. Members of this group can be individual user accounts, global groups, and other universal groups. Universal groups are only available when Windows 2000 is running in native mode. You may not want to put every user in a universal group because of the additional time needed to create the security token when the user logs on (though this is computer time in the nanosecond realm). Such a security token is used for resource authentication purposes. Finally, universal groups cannot be placed in global groups.

Group names should be easily recognizable. If you or other administrators have to guess who might belong to a group, or what the name means, then you should select another name. It is also good to name a group and then add a geographic prefix. For example, you could initially create a group called Production Managers and then create the following groups: Brazil Production Manager, African Production Manager, Canadian Production Manager, and U.S. Production Manager. However, at the end of the day, the naming issue will most likely be dictated by the naming standards already in place for your company (or your client if you're an MCSE consultant).

To get maximum benefit from the use of universal groups, and to minimize network traffic and administrative maintenance, you should consider putting only global group accounts in universal groups. If you place individual accounts in universal groups, every change to the individual account will have to be replicated to every domain, not just the domain in which the individual account resides. Just as in Windows NT, it is always a good policy to put individuals into global groups and place these global groups into local groups when crossing domain boundaries (this is the traditional "users go into global, which go into local" groups approach, well known in MCSE-land).

Windows 2000 provides us with several built-in groups:

- **Local groups**   Administrators, backup operators, guests, power users, replicators, and users

- **Domain local groups**   Account operators, administrators, backup operators, guests, print operators, server operators, and users

- **Global groups**   Domain admins, domain computers, domain controllers, domain guests, domain users, enterprise admins, and group policy admins

Designing the Namespace

A *namespace* is any bounded area in which a given name can be resolved. In planning your namespace, you will need to start with the root domain, and keep in mind that once you name a domain, you cannot rename it without reinstalling Active Directory. Each internal domain name has to be unique, so it cannot be a name that is already in use by your company (for example, you could not have two internal domains named MAIN).

If you already have a DNS namespace, you may want to use the existing Internet (or external) domain name as your unique internal domain name. Or you may want to create a new root domain and a new DNS namespace (for example, if the company name changes). Keeping in mind that the company as a whole will have to live with the name, you will need to seek suggestions and approval from the business types in the corner-window offices.

There are two types of namespaces: contiguous and disjointed. A Microsoft tree is an example of a *contiguous namespace*, where the child domain contains the name of the parent domain. A forest is an example of a *disjointed namespace*, where the parent objects (the trees, which are a collection of related domains) are not directly related to each other with respect to namespace (the trees could have different namespace considerations). Granted, there will be some relationship between objects in a forest or else they wouldn't be there. Perhaps the objects are under the larger umbrella of a corporate conglomerate.

In Windows NT, you put all user and machine accounts in an accounts domain, but with Windows 2000, you will only want to create administrative accounts in the root domain. Other user and machine accounts should be created in the domains where they will do most of their work. The point is that in Windows 2000, the distinction between an accounts and a resources domain has been removed.

Once you have decided upon your domain name, you can set up the root domain. You will want to create other domain controllers soon thereafter for redundancy. Microsoft recommends that you install DNS on each domain controller, unless, of course, you have DNS elsewhere (such as on a Unix system). Over time, you will then add child domains based on the directory structure you developed.

Planning DNS Strategy

Domains have a contiguous DNS namespace and are given DNS names. Domains use the same naming conventions as DNS, so you would use your second-level name (Catywhompus.com) with subdivisions to create domains. These subdivisions or child domains can be based upon such things as physical, functional, organizational, geographical, or work groups. Thus, we could divide Catywhompus into four major divisions of Administration, Construction, Sales, and Purchases. We could also further break Construction into Single Home, Multiple Unit Housing, and Commercial. The Single Home domain could be further broken down into New Construction and Remodeling. Thus, Remodeling would have a fully qualified DNS name of remodeling.singlehome.construction.catywhompus.com. Hopefully, the pattern of putting the child domain name in front of the parent domain name will feel comfortable from the time you have spent surfing the Web. As shown in Figure 4-9, the format is *host.domain* (IIS_Server.Consumer.Catywhompus.com).

You will want to keep the domain name down to the NetBIOS naming limit of 15 characters or less in order for the host name to be completely visible in legacy Microsoft networking environments that are NetBIOS-based. Be careful of name choices—the name you choose may be very descriptive and useful in your native language, but it may be offensive or meaningless in another language.

Figure 4-9
The "domains use DNS namespace" convention

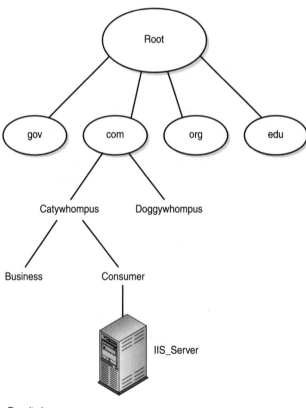

Results in:
IIS_Server.Consumer.Catywhompus.com

EXAM TIP We've just mentioned the NetBIOS naming considerations, but don't forget that DNS permits 63 octets per label when it comes to naming.

You should register your name with the governing bodies of the Internet, even if you only intend to use the name internally. Failure to register your DNS name as an Internet domain name can cause DNS resolution errors if somebody should use the same name. If you choose to use separate external and internal DNS namespaces, we would recommend that you use two different names, and you will need to register both of them. By having two different names, you can easily configure your proxy clients by having an exclusion list that contains the external namespace when identifying external resources. One of the drawbacks to having two different names is that your logon and e-mail names will be different, although Microsoft Exchange 2000 and other e-mail solutions provide ways to deal with this by managing different mail exchange (MX) records. This should be a design consideration as a Windows 2000 MCSE! Here are some issues about having different external and internal domain names:

- Your users may become confused as to which DNS namespace they are in if the names are the same, but the resources are different.

- It will be difficult to maintain or update both DNSs, especially if you want them to basically have the same resources.

- It is possible that an error may occur, and internal information may accidentally get published on the external DNS.

- Your proxy configuration will be more complex.

Microsoft recommends that you use Microsoft DNS Server supplied with Windows 2000 Server as your DNS server. However, Microsoft DNS is not required. The DNS server that you use

- Must support the SRV RR (RFC 2052)

- Should support the dynamic update protocol (RFC 2136)

Version 8.1.2 and later of BIND, a popular DNS server implementation, supports both the SRV RR and dynamic update (this is explained in the TechNet Knowledge Base article Q237675 found at www.microsoft.com/technet).

You must have the DNS settings configured correctly on the Windows 2000 Server machine before promoting it to a domain controller in an existing domain. During the

promotion process, the Windows 2000 Server machine needs to resolve the fully qualified domain name of the domain (this is explained in the TechNet Knowledge Base
article Q238369 found at www.microsoft.com/technet).

There are two types of DNS servers that are installed on domain controllers in the
Active Directory. A *root server* is installed to be the source for resolving names for a hierarchical namespace. The root is the top of the hierarchy, containing all organizational
domain zone names. Names that cannot be resolved in the DNS zone are passed to the
root DNS server.

Granted, we're assuming you've configured your network to use additional DNS
servers as forwarders. The *DNS forwarder* is a DNS server that contains one or more
domain zones in an enterprise, and this DNS server can be configured to forward
names it cannot resolve to the root server for the domain. See the Microsoft TechNet
article Q231794 at www.microsoft.com/technet for more information.

If you aren't using DNS forwarders, you'll likely receive a message stating that
the query was unresolved (like a 404 error message when your browser can't find a
Web page).

Designing and Planning Organization Units

A new concept for Windows 2000 is the OU. The OU is like a resource domain, but it
does not have the resource overhead of a domain controller, nor is it involved in handling replication traffic.

OUs are containers that can contain other containers or objects. If you have
done object-oriented programming, the term *object* will be familiar. An object has
attributes or properties. Attributes help to define or further describe the object. If your
object is a user, the attributes could be first name, last name, username, and social
security number. If the object is a server's network adapter card, the attributes could be
MAC address, IP address, physical location, and operating system. You can use OUs to
organize objects.

OUs are the base units upon which you can assign administrative authority. They
enable you to break a domain into smaller subunits, which enable you to organize
users and resources. You can then delegate administrative-level authority (that is, the
ability to act as an administrator account) to a user within that OU without having to
give the user administrative authority over the whole domain. This delegation of
administrative authority does not need to be based on object locations. Thus, if you create an OU based on a departmental unit, such as the Sales department, and create
objects (users, printers, and computers) for the Sales OU, you can allow a user in the

Sales OU to have the administrative authority to manage that OU. Figure 4-10 shows three OUs within a domain.

An OU serves as a means to divide a domain into partitions for administrative control and for policy application. OUs can be based on such things as business functions (such as management, sales, production, or research), geography (such as continents, countries, states, or cities), departments, or projects. It is usually better to base the OUs on geography rather than on the other business-driven components, because a business may be reorganized frequently, but it is less often physically moved. OUs can also be based upon a combination of the factors, such as business functionality and geography. To aid in the design process, you may want to consider what properties or characteristics OUs would have in common with each other, as shown in Figure 4-11.

A nice feature of OUs is that they can be moved between domains, which effectively allows you to promote an OU to a domain by simply creating a new domain and moving the OU to the new domain. At that point, the contents of the moved OU are placed in the new domain.

Developing an OU Delegation Plan

OUs can be used during the migration of existing Windows NT resource domains. It is very easy to replace each resource domain with an OU. After you have migrated to Windows 2000, you can easily combine OUs with other OUs.

However, the primary use of an OU is to provide a boundary for delegating administrative authority. As an administrator, you can now give a user complete administrative

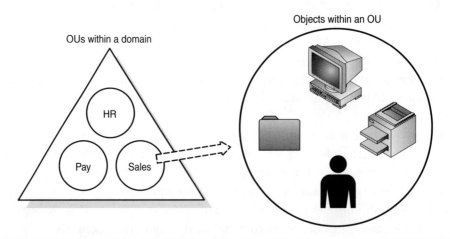

Figure 4-10   Organizational units within a domain

Figure 4-11
The beginnings of
an OU design

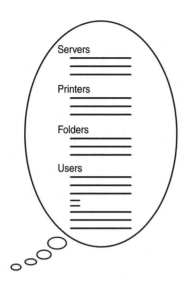
Servers

Printers

Folders

Users

control over an OU without having to give that user complete administrative control over the entire domain. The ability to delegate routine or daily maintenance of the system will be a welcome relief, and you can pay more attention to the larger picture as the network grows.

With the Delegation of Control wizard, the administrator can control the amount of administrative control a user will have. You are able to delegate tasks from property permissions (which control access to the object's attributes) to general permissions (which control the entire object).

The key point is that you can make some users part-time administrators on the network with "limited" administration capabilities (perhaps completing administrative tasks within a single OU). This is called partial delegation. We could list all the items the administrator could delegate, but that would involve a list of 6 predefined tasks, 16 types of general permissions, 54 individual property permissions, and 88 individual permissions. You will have to settle for the knowledge that there are over 150 different items you can control.

OUs inherit security policies from the parent domain by default, but it is possible to disable the inherited security policies so that an administrative user or group cannot control all OUs in a nested structure.

NOTE Perhaps you assumed that you could assign administrative authority to users by using the Managed By tab. Sorry. This is just an informative contact name.

The Managed By tab is displayed in Figure 4-12.

Just as too many cooks can spoil the broth, we find that too many Active Directory architects can spoil the management of OUs at a company. As in Windows NT, you should be conservative in delegating administrative rights to individuals, especially to a user in an OU. You should only give users the permissions that are necessary to perform their tasks. If a permission can affect more than one OU, give administrative control to a user in the nested OU (a nested OU is a child OU inside of a parent OU). Even if you trust an OU user, you may want to reserve permissions such as Modify Permissions and Access Control. Why? Because these two permissions, while not granting the keys to the kingdom, are certainly a start in lowering the drawbridge across the moat. How? The Modify Permissions command allows the holder of this permission to modify permissions for other users and so on. The Access Control permission allows the holder of this permission to control access to the OU for other users. Powerful stuff.

If you attempt to create an OU in the parent domain with the same name as an OU in a child domain, the following error message is displayed:

```
Active Directory
    Windows cannot create the object because: An attempt was made
to add an object to the directory with a name that was already in
use.
  Name-related properties on this object might now be out of sync.
  Contact your network administrator.
```

Figure 4-12
The Managed By
tab of an OU

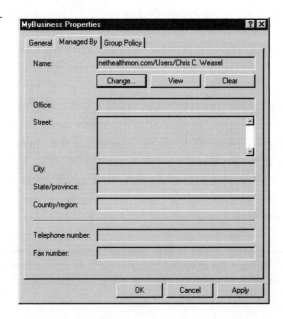

If you attempt to create a child domain with the same name as an OU in the parent domain, the following error message is displayed:

```
Active Directory Installation Failed
    The operation failed because: The Directory Service failed to
create the object CN=Name of the Child Domain, CN=Partitions,
CN=Configuration, DC=DomainName, DC=Com. Please check for possible
system errors. "The directory service is busy"
```

To understand more about this, see the Microsoft TechNet article Q240147 at www.microsoft.com/technet.

Planning Group Policy Object Management

Group Policy is one of the coolest areas in Windows 2000 and Active Directory. Group Policy can be applied to OUs, domains, and sites by linking the Group Policy Objects (GPOs) to the Active Directory container holding the users or computers. Group Policy has several components, and some of the components of Group Policy that can be fine-tuned via the Group Policy Editor are folder redirection, scripts, security settings, and software.

Group Policy is applied in the following object order:

1. Local group policy

2. Site

3. Domain

4. OU

5. Child OU

By default, group policies are applied to all users and computers in the container. The administrator can explicitly change this by not having the Apply Group Policy and Read permissions both set to Allow as members of a security group (members of a security group are users that have security group membership). Figure 4-13 shows the Security tab for applying permissions to a GPO.

Group Policy applies system settings to users when they log on. (It applies settings to workstations at boot time, and that will be discussed in the following "Planning Policy Management for Client Computers" section.) GPOs determine what resources are available to a user. For example, GPO software-management options can determine what application users will have access to when they log on.

Scripts can be used for both logon and logoff. Although the Windows 2000 MCSE exams do not delve deeply into scripting, we can recommend that you read some articles that focus on scripting by Chris Brooke, a monthly columnist for *Microsoft Certified*

Figure 4-13
Apply Group
Policy and Read
permissions are
set to Allow

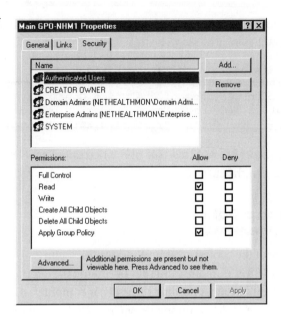

Professional Magazine (www.mcpmag.com). Additional user settings can also specify desktop appearance, logon and logoff scripts, file deployment options, and security issues.

GPOs enable the user with administrator-level permissions to manage individuals in a group instead of the overwhelming task of managing a large number of individual users (say, thousands of users). By manage, we mean perform the ordinary and necessary tasks performed by someone logged on as a user with administrative rights (change permissions, change username, and so on). Applying GPO settings to a group is very similar to using groups in Windows NT—it is much easier to keep track and modify a few groups than it is to handle hundreds if not thousands of users.

Special folders located under the Profiles folder (Documents and Settings) for users contain Application Data, Desktop, Favorites, Local Settings, My Documents (with a My Pictures subfolder), NetHood, PrintHood, SendTo, Start Menu, and Programs (with a Startup subfolder). We won't get into Group Policy at the implementation level, but you should recall from the Windows 2000 MCSE core exams that Group Policy is capable of redirection by policy. This is, of course, very valuable in managing roaming laptop users.

EXAM TIP   You can control the priorities with which policies are applied, but remember that the last policy applied wins!

Planning Policy Management for Client Computers

GPOs for controlling workstations determine how the resource is configured for use, and they are enacted when the computer boots up. This is easily seen in the Windows 2000 start-up screens that show policies being applied. The rules and implementation of GPO for workstations is very similar to that for users.

You can use GPOs to control the appearance of the desktop. The special folders for computers are Application Data, Desktop, Start Menu, and Programs (with a Start-up subfolder). You will probably have noticed that the special folders for the computer are also special folders for users. Whether the setting applies to the computer or user depends on whether the setting is applied when the computer boots or when the user logs on. User settings will only be available to the specific user regardless of which Windows 2000 Professional computer they use (which makes sense when you consider that it's a user policy). If there is a conflict between a computer or user policy, the computer policy is the one that gets applied.

You can use software policies to mandate Registry settings on the workstation or scripts to control workstation start-up, shutdown, and security setting. Windows 2000 has several security areas, including Account Policies, Event Log, File System, IP Security, Local Policies, Public Keys, Registry, Restricted Groups, and System Services. It has been our experience with Windows 2000 Professional that these areas of settings are especially valid when you are implementing third-party software applications (such as business accounting applications) that depend on and expect certain Registry settings and configurations.

Windows 2000 allows you to have policy settings in the following functional areas:

Control panel	Offline files
Dial-up connections	Printers
Desktop	Software installation
Disk quotas	Start menu
Folder redirection	Task scheduler
Logon scripts	Taskbar
Logoff scripts	Windows components
Network connections	

Planning for Coexistence

Active Directory not only coexists with other directory systems, but it can get along with them. Active Directory uses the following two application programming interfaces (APIs): Active Directory Service Interface (ADSI) and Lightweight Directory Access Protocol (LDAP). ADSI permits processes to access Active Directory by allowing access to the objects in the directory as Component Object Model (COM) objects. Currently, ADSI providers exist for Novell's Network Directory Services (NDS) and NetWare 3 (bindery), Windows NT, LDAP, and IIS. Microsoft supports the LDAP API as defined in RFC 1823.

ADSI is a set of COM programming interfaces that programmers can use to build applications that let Active Directory interact with and manage other directory services. This helps to provide both the administrators and users with a single point of access to various directory services that are listed here:

- Novell's Network Directory Services (NDS)

- Microsoft Exchange 5.5

- GroupWise

- Lotus Notes

- Netscape Directory Services

- Banyan StreetWise

- Sun Microsystems' Sun Directory Service 3.1

Novell NDS uses the LDAP protocol via LDAP Services for NDS, which is a server-based interface between NDS and the operating system, clients, and even other directory services. LDAP is not native to NDS, and LDAP Services for NDS acts as a translator.

Sun Microsystems' Sun Directory Service 3.1 uses the LDAP 3 protocol. Sun requires no translation and is integrated with the DNS, like Windows 2000.

Designing an Active Directory Site Topology

A domain controller has three types of replication data that can be replicated: domain data, schema data, and configuration data. *Domain data* contains the objects within the domain, and it is only replicated within that domain between domain controllers. *Schema data* and *configuration data* are replicated to all domain controllers in the forest. Schema data is just what you think it would be—data containing all object types and their related attributes. Configuration data is primarily information concerning replication topology and contains some information used by applications.

If the domain controller is also a global catalog server, it will also require a partial replica of domain data. The global catalog server is a list of all objects in the forest and a selected subset of the object's attributes that help to resolve client queries locally. A partial replica is a read-only replication that occurs only between global servers.

Designing a Replication Strategy

An Active Directory site represents the boundaries for replication between domain controllers. Regardless of boundaries set by geographical, functional, or political entities, a change can be made to one domain controller, and that change is replicated to all other domain controllers in that domain.

There are two types of replication: *intra-site replication*, which is replication within a site, and *inter-site replication*, replication between sites.

For intra-site replication, Active Directory provides for redundancy by attempting to establish at least two connections to every domain controller. The Knowledge Consistency Checker (KCC) service of Active Directory will automatically evaluate and adjust the replication topology when a domain controller is added, unavailable, or removed. The KCC also has the responsibility of triggering replication events. Within a site, the data is replicated frequently, and it is done automatically. Since the priority for replication within a site is to keep the data as up-to-date as possible, there is no compression of the data—it is assumed the network (internally speaking) has the available bandwidth to support this traffic.

Inter-site replication requires more effort on the part of the administrator. You will be required to manually create a site link using the Active Directory Sites and Services snap-in (found in the Administrative Tools program group). A site link is a transitive link between two or more sites via a slow non-LAN link or a fast link. You will also be required by Windows 2000 in a dialog box when building a site link to provide information concerning replication availability, relative cost, and replication frequency. Active Directory uses the information you provide to create connection objects.

These connection objects use the links to replicate data with the preferred connection at each site being called the bridgehead server. Each site may also have optional connection points. Inter-site replication occurs between the bridgehead servers and then is replicated to other servers and domains within the site. The data transferred between bridgehead servers is compressed to minimize the usage of the slower and more expensive bandwidth in the WAN environment.

Windows 2000 has a peer-to-peer relationship between domain controllers; in other words, all domain controllers have a read/write copy of the directory at basically an equal level. This peer-to-peer relationship provides redundancy by allowing any domain controller to act as the bridgehead server (the bridgehead designation is specified by the administrator) or as an optional connection. Once the site-link's schedule, which says when the link is available and other configuration information is completed, replication of schema data and configuration data to all the domain controllers in the forest becomes automatic.

Directory information is replicated using IP or SMTP protocols. IP uses remote procedure calls (RPCs) for both intra-site and inter-site replication, provided you have a physical connection. If you have no permanent connection but are able to make a connection via SMTP, you can replicate data between sites via what is called a mail-based connection—a mail-based connection cannot be used to replicate data between domain controllers within the same domain. SMTP also limits the data that can be replicated. You are only allowed to replicate schema, configuration, and global-catalog partial-replica data. Figure 4-14 displays SMTP-based replication between sites.

SMTP-based Active Directory replication uses public key encryption and certificates to authenticate and provide for digital signatures during the replication process. See the Microsoft TechNet article Q222962 at www.microsoft.com/technet.

Defining Site Boundaries

Sites use the low-cost, high-speed communication connections of LAN technology to provide replication services, workstation logon, and authentication. Sites can span

Figure 4-14
SMTP connection between domains

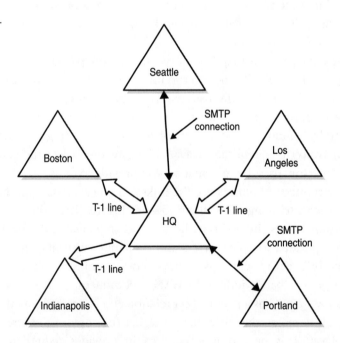

domains and are not dependent on the boundaries of the domains. Sites are more concerned with connection speeds and geographical boundaries than the logical construction of the domains. Windows 2000 uses existing IP subnets to define the boundaries of the site.

Within a site, a client can request services from a domain controller within the same site and can minimize replication latency for intra-site replication. Sites provide the ability to minimize bandwidth consumption across links. For example, you can define bandwidth requirements when performing replication and the ability to schedule when that replication will occur.

Designing a Schema Modification Policy

Modifying an Active Directory schema is an advanced operation that should only be performed by experienced programmers and system administrators. Changes to the schema should not be made on a regular basis, because every change you make will affect the whole forest. If and when you decide to make changes (which often include the addition or modification of database fields), you will need to make sure your naming conventions comply with LDAP naming rules. And note that if you add a field to the Active Directory schema, it cannot be deleted (a fact that should give you reason to pause).

Since only experienced individuals should make changes to the schema, Microsoft has placed several limitations on how schema modifications are made:

- By default, domain controllers permit only read access, and modifying that requires a change to the Registry (how to make this change is addressed in the list on the following page).

- Only members of the Schema Administrators group are allowed to make changes to the schema (the administrator is a member of the Schema Administrators group by default).

- The schema Flexible Single Master Operations (FSMO) is the only domain controller that is allowed to write to the schema. Therefore, you must log on locally at the FSMO as administrator to write to the schema.

Since changing the schema is supposed to be an infrequent activity, you will need to add the Microsoft Management Console (MMC) Schema Manager snap-in manually. This is demonstrated in the next chapter, Chapter 5.

> **CAUTION** Do not make up your own object IDs (OIDs). OIDs use the IDs supplied by the standards people at such places as the International Telecommunications Union, and making up your own can cause problems when you decide to use an Active Directory object that has been assigned the same OID. Microsoft warns that improperly changing the schema can impair or disable Windows 2000 Server and possibly your entire network.

A good schema modification policy would have to address the following questions:

- What is the need for changing the schema?
- Do you fully understand what the change to the schema will affect?
- What will the name of the new attribute or object be?
- Is the name already in use?
- Is there a name that looks similar?
- Is the person making the change a member of Schema Administrator or Administrator group?
- Have the changes been tested on non-production servers and workstations?

So assuming you have bona fide reasons to modify the Active Directory schema, understand that Active Directory enables you to modify the schema at any domain controller in the enterprise using the Active Directory Schema snap-in.

The FSMO Schema-Master (a server role) can be chosen in the Active Directory Schema snap-in by selecting Operations Master from the secondary menu that is displayed when you right-click on the Active Directory Schema object in the left pane of the Active Directory Schema snap-in. The present domain controller can be made a schema writable domain controller (this is a domain controller that has an editable Active Directory schema). The Schema Master computer should also have the following Registry key (you can verify or add as necessary via Registry Editor):

KEY_LOCAL_MACHINE\SYSTEM\CurrentControlSet\Services\NTDS\Parameters\
Schema Update Allowed REG_DWORD 0x00000001

If changes to the schema are made at a domain controller that is not a schema writable domain controller, the settings will not be applied (not surprisingly) and a message is generated in the Active Directory Schema snap-in:

```
The displayable status could not be changed. (Q229691)
```

By default, Windows 2000 domain controllers permit only read access to the schema. If you have only a single Windows 2000 domain controller in your network, it is always the schema FSMO. Management of the Active Directory schema is not a frequently performed task (thank goodness!), and care must be exercised when modifying the schema.

To modify the registry to allow write operations to the schema, create a new REG_DWORD value named "Schema Update Allowed" with a data value of "1" in the following registry key:

HKEY LOCAL MACHINE\System\Current Control Set\Services\NTDS\Parameters

It is not necessary to reboot the computer. The Active Directory service automatically detects the change. To disable schema updates on this domain controller, change the data value to 0. Note that an Active Directory–aware application may do this programmatically (for example, Exchange 2000). See the Microsoft TechNet article Q216060 at www.microsoft.com/technet for more information.

Let's take a brief moment to consider Active Directory modifications. For example, if you create an attribute "abc" and add it to a class, you are unable to add another attribute called "abc<x>" to the class, where <x> is any valid character or combination of characters.

To resolve this issue, use Ldp.exe to add the optional attribute or auxiliary class, or reverse the order in which you add the attributes to the class. For example, add "abc<x>" before you add "abc." See the Microsoft TechNet article Q243978 at www.microsoft.com/technet for more information.

Designing an Active Directory Implementation Plan

You are probably faced with one of the following five options, each of which is discussed shortly:

- Upgrading a single-domain Windows NT system
- Upgrading a single-master-domain Windows NT system
- Upgrading a multiple-master-domain Windows NT system
- Upgrading a complete-trust-domain Windows NT system
- Creating a new Windows 2000 domain

NOTE To make life easier, you will want to make most changes to domains after switching to native mode. Once the two-way transitive trust relationships are created, it will be easy to move objects with their permissions. If you make these changes prior to going to native mode, you will need to recreate object permissions. The only major decision that needs to be acted upon when setting up that first domain controller is the naming of the root domain.

Single-Domain Windows NT System

Upgrading a single domain is one of the easiest forms of upgrades between Windows NT and Windows 2000. The existing domain, provided everyone is content with its name representing the company, becomes your root domain. Remember that the domain name you use will be the name that will be used in the DNS as the human-understandable component. You can use OUs to subdivide the domain and to delegate your administrative authority.

Single-Master-Domain Windows NT System

Again, if everyone is happy with the name of the domain, you can use the former master domain as the root domain, and make the resource domains into child domains. Alternatively, you could use OUs in place of the resource domains. This may be a good time to use OUs to reorganize by geographical, functional, administrative, or project needs.

This is the perfect time to consider consolidating multiple Windows NT domains into one Windows 2000 domain. You will need to determine the historical rationale for having more than one domain. If the reasons have vanished with technology and time, you can decrease the number of domain controllers. This should help to reduce your up-front costs for the upgrade. Other benefits of a reduced number of domain controllers is the reduction in the amount of time it takes to log on or to resolve queries (note this might not be the case if the servers are already over-utilized).

You can use OUs to organize your domain and reduce your administrative burden by delegating administrative duties to an OU super-user. The process of converting a Windows NT master (or accounts) domain into a Windows 2000 domain is shown in Figure 4-15.

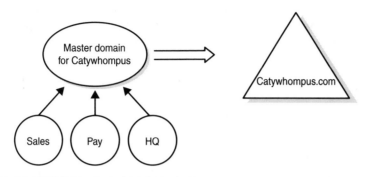

Figure 4-15   Converting a single-master Windows NT domain to a single Windows 2000 domain.

Another option with the single-master domain is to convert the resource domains into one Windows 2000 domain because your company may not want to maintain several domains. This will allow you to place the user accounts and the resources in the same domain, thus helping to reduce network traffic. If you are not comfortable with this or do not want to waste a lot of time creating all the one-way trusts you will need to move all the users into the old resource domains, you might want to wait to move users until the transitive trusts are created when the network is placed in native mode.

You may also pursue a combination solution. It is possible to combine some of the resource domains into one Windows 2000 domain. You can then make the balance of the resource domains into OUs in other domains. The number of combinations is limitless. The primary limits placed upon you are the strategic goals of the organization.

Multiple-Master-Domain Windows NT System

Since Windows 2000 makes it practical to have a single-domain system and offers many advantages to the administrator, you will want to consider combining all the domains into one domain. During the creation of the first domain controller, you can use one of the current master domains or a new domain as the root domain. The decision as to which domain you should use, or whether to create a new name, is based upon the strategic goals of the company. Thus, this is not a decision made in the IT department but should be a joint effort of the IT department and the management team. Once the root domain name has been chosen, you can add the other domains as the children that help to create your Windows 2000 tree.

TIP To make your life easier, you should opt to make most of your changes to the actual domains after going to native mode.

Another option is to keep each master domain and create a Windows 2000 forest. Each master domain will become a tree with the former master domain becoming a root domain. You will need to use the same inquiry and decision-making process concerning root domain names as you have in the other upgrade scenarios.

After you have created your root domain for your Windows 2000–based network, or root domains for your tree, you have the same options concerning turning resource domains into Windows 2000 domains and/or OUs as you had with the single-master Windows NT system described in the previous section.

When creating a new domain, you will want to start with a clean install of Windows 2000. After creating the new root domain and a couple of domain controllers, you can then upgrade the PDC into the tree as a child domain.

Complete-Trust-Domain Windows NT System

The complete-trust-domain system in Windows NT is much like the multiple-master-domain system. The biggest distinctions between the two trust models (complete trust versus multiple-master) are the independence and flexibility of each master domain with an increase in administrative complexity.

You will use the same design process you would use for the multiple master-domain system; that is, consider the following issue. To keep the independence and flexibility of the current system, you will probably favor a forest over a single domain or tree.

One thing you will want to remember about Active Directory is that all the trusts are two-way transitive when Windows 2000 is in native mode. If you do not want a totally transitive model, Windows 2000 does allow you to replace any transitive trust with a one-way Windows NT trust. If you use these one-way trusts, the trusted domain will not have any access to any other domain, even if the other trusts are transitive. This can be a plus or a minus and it must be examined carefully before making any changes.

A New Windows 2000 Domain

This appears to be one of the easiest options to implement, but it may surprise you in some cases and actually be more difficult (although nothing compares to the utter hell you may go through in a rough Windows NT upgrade to Windows 2000).

The organization will need to decide if they will need a forest or a tree. Then the organization will decide how to break the tree(s) into domains and then into OUs. Once the domains have been decided, a choice concerning your DNS structure will need to be made. A decision will also have to be made concerning internal and external naming.

What can make this one of the most difficult installations is that this situation often occurs in young organizations with little organizational culture in which to make these decisions. New organizations are also more likely to want to change their organizational structure within the next three to five years, and this is probably not accounted for during the initial planning and installation of a Windows 2000 system.

Catywhompus Construction Update

In this chapter, we've tried to skillfully weave Catywhompus into the storyline. You would have noticed this in the DNS domain-naming discussion, where we hopefully proved cats and dogs can live in harmony. Aside from that, we would emphasize that Catywhompus is indeed interested in a planning paradigm that places an emphasis on fewer domains and more OUs. This is sound advice for a Windows 2000 MCSE to ascribe to.

Chapter Review

If you read this chapter in hopes that we would be able to give an exact blueprint of your upgrade, you are probably very disappointed. If you read this chapter to gain insight as to the questions you will need to ask before upgrading your current system or when trying to pass the exam, you have the right mindset.

As we have hopefully made perfectly clear, there are no black-and-white questions and answers. It is time to become more of a system analyst—an individual with a multiple personality who works in both IT and management circles equally well. You will need to be both an introvert and an extrovert and have the ability to switch between the two several times a day. You will also need to be able to switch rapidly between the logical and physical makeup of your system.

Questions

1. Another vendor with its own directory services contacts Microsoft and proposes a plan to integrate its offering with Active Directory. Microsoft agrees and recommends using the following tool to make this happen smoothly.
   a. DNS
   b. DHCP
   c. WINS
   d. ADSI
   e. All of the above

2. True or false? OUs can be named after department titles, geographic locations, or both.

3. Switching from mixed mode to native mode is
   a. A one-way trip that can't be reversed
   b. A two-way trip that can be reversed
   c. You can run in both mixed mode and native mode, so no switching is required
   d. None of the above

Answers

1. **D.** The vendor will use the Active Directory Services Interface (ADSI) as the application program interface to hook into Active Directory.

2. **True.** There is really no implicit problem with naming OUs after departments or locations. The key point is to try and adhere to a naming standard.

3. **A.** This is an irrevocable decision.

Key Skill Sets

The following skill sets meet the Microsoft Objectives for the 70-219 exam:

- Understanding the broad issues involved in directory services design
- Understanding and engaging in planning for DNS in the organization
- Appreciating and incorporating issues related to Active Directory trees, forests, and domains into the planning process
- Understanding the role of trust relationships

- Developing a consistent and meaningful naming strategy for the organizational units

- Understanding and planning for Group Policy

- Understanding how Active Directory can coexist with other directory services

Key Terms

Active Directory

Active Directory Services Interface (ADSI)

Delegation

Domain

Forest

Organizational units

Tree

Trust relationship

5

Designing Your Service Locations

This chapter covers the following key mastery goals:

- Understand the roles of your domain's operations masters and where to place them to maximize performance
- Know what factors to consider in designing the placement of your global catalog server
- Identify the best places for your domain controllers to maximize performance, enhance fault tolerance, increase functionality, and improve manageability

The last area of knowledge responsibility on the 70-219 "Designing a Microsoft Windows 2000 Directory Services Infrastructure" exam is *service locations*. Granted, this area is very specific. First off, you must understand exactly what Microsoft is talking about when they introduce terms such as "operations masters." It sometimes seems that all of this new vocabulary is designed solely as a means of confusing people, but it actually helps you to define what you want a particular server to do, what role you want it to play in the Active Directory design.

Operations masters were originally called Flexible Single Master Operations (FSMO) servers. Fortunately, Microsoft decided to shorten the name to operations masters, but you may see both terms used interchangeably. The focus of this chapter is on understanding the various roles of operations masters, and determining where you should put them in your domain for maximum performance. Factors that will weigh in your design placement decisions will be a combination of trade-offs between budgetary concerns, performance issues, fault tolerance, availability, functionality, and manageability.

Under Windows 2000, each operations master controls its own piece of the Active Directory turf, depending on its operations masters role (five roles wil be discussed in a moment). Some of the operations masters are found with only one per forest, and others must be within each domain of the forest.

The first Windows 2000 domain has five operations master roles, and these roles could all be on one machine, or on any combination of machines, depending on your design strategy. The five operations master roles are: Schema Master, Domain Naming Master, Primary Domain Controller (PDC) Emulator (providing support for legacy NT systems), Infrastructure Master, and the Relative Identifier (RID) Master. The Schema Master or Domain Naming Master exist only once per forest, so additional Windows 2000 domains that follow would not have those roles.

Introduction to Case Study 5:
Advanced Active Directory Design Issues
for Catywhompus Construction

Many of the topics discussed in this chapter relate to optimization. You have learned about the mechanics of Active Directory in order to complete the core Windows 2000 MCSE exams. The first couple of chapters in this section further prepared you to tackle the directory-services needs at Catywhompus from a business- and technical-needs perspective. At this point, you should be able to create a functional Active Directory design for your client, Catywhompus.

But now, let's take it one step further. How can we make the directory-services solution operate more effectively and efficiently? That is the question you should keep in mind as you read this chapter and study the placement of service locations. The management team of Catywhompus will be oblivious to the details of this discussion, but they will certainly benefit from a more efficient network. At the end of this chapter, when we revisit the Catywhompus case study, you'll have a chance to evaluate some additional design considerations.

Designing the Placement of Operations Masters

By default, Windows 2000 puts all five operations master roles on the first domain controller you install in the forest. Naturally, if this were the optimum solution for all companies, large and small, then this would be the end of the chapter. However, as you shall see, life is not always so simple. MCSEs would not be able to properly justify their huge salaries if everything worked perfectly with the default settings. Where you decide to put your operations masters is a critical decision that can make your life as an administrator easy or a living nightmare. Why? Because performance is the key.

Let's take a look at the different roles of operations masters, and why it can be important to design where they are in the domain structure.

Understanding the Roles of Operations Masters

In this section, we discuss the Schema Master, Domain Naming Master, Primary Domain Controller Emulator, Infrastructure Master, and Relative Identifier Master.

Schema Master

Imagine for a moment that Catywhompus (the sample company that is referenced throughout this book) stores all information about the company in a database and circulates the file to multiple computers in the company so that people can make changes. Someone decides to reorganize our divisions, while someone else reorganizes in another copy of the document. How are the differences reconciled? The solution would be to designate only one copy of the document as the source for such important changes to our company's structure.

Similarly, the Schema Master, as its name implies, has the only writable copy of the schema for the entire forest. The schema is simply the formalized framework used by Active Directory to catalog all the objects and their attributes within a Windows 2000 forest. There can only be one schema per forest. In order to make any changes or updates to the schema, you must have access to the Schema Master. This access can either be local, at the server itself, or through the Active Directory Schema MMC snap-in.

> **TIP** The Active Directory Schema snap-in is not available by default. To use the snap-in, you must first register the DLL with the operating system by typing regsvr32 schmmgmt.dll at the command prompt. You will then see a dialog box telling you that the DLL has been successfully loaded. As shown in Figure 5-1, the Active Directory Schema snap-in then becomes a choice that you can add to your Microsoft Management Console.

Editing the schema is not recommended unless you are very sure of what *all* the ramifications are! The schema is like an elephant—once an object is added to it, it is never forgotten and cannot be deleted. All you can do is deactivate objects, which prevents any new instances of the object from being stored in the Active Directory and prevents all current instances of the object from being replicated throughout the entire forest.

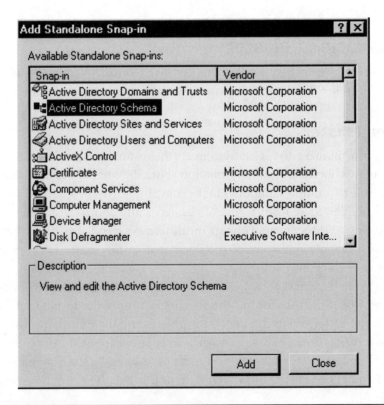

Figure 5-1   The Active Directory Schema snap-in is now an available choice.

Changes to the schema propagate to all domains and domain trees contained in the forest. Because of this effect on the entire forest, only members of the Schema Admins group have the ability to change the schema, by default, and it is a good idea to limit who becomes a member of the Schema Admins group. Also, it is a good idea not to log on as a member of the Schema Admins group *unless* you specifically want to change the schema. In fact, you can use the Run As command to log on as a lower-level user account to run the process.

In the days of Windows NT 4.0, you could load an application on one machine on the network and not have to worry about crashing the entire network if the application behaved badly. Your worst-case scenario was having to rebuild the one machine. However, with Windows 2000, your worst-case scenario is now an entire enterprise network meltdown. It is possible to load a badly behaved application that takes full advantage of the power of Active Directory and can make undesired and irreversible changes to the schema. Bottom line? Be vigilant—understand how your application is modifying the Active Directory schema and affecting your entire forest of domains.

Here's a way to recover from Active Directory Schema disaster. Besides seizing the role as just discussed above, to recover from such a disaster is to restore the Schema Master from tape backup (you *do* have a current tape backup, don't you?) before it has a chance to replicate all the evil changes of the badly written application. Tape backups are nearly always an appropriate way to recover from disasters! But back to the Active Directory issue at hand. If it replicates before you discover what happened, it's time to polish up that resume!

Domain Naming Master

The Domain Naming Master controls "who's who in the zoo." If you need to add another domain, or domain tree, to your forest, you must do it from this operations master server. The operations master server is also one to a forest, which may lead you to think Microsoft should have named it the "Forest Naming Master." At any rate, it contains the only writeable copy of the forest's naming configuration. If the Domain Naming Master is offline, you will have to wait until it comes back online or is replaced (has the role seized) before you can add, change, or delete any domain groupings. Since this server is also the one used to configure interdomain trusts, should a domain trust "break" while the Domain Naming Master is unavailable, you will not be able to fix the trust until this operations master becomes available again. However, it must be noted that the loss of the Domain Naming Master is completely transparent to users and even administrators, except when you are trying to change which domains are members of the forest.

Primary Domain Controller Emulator

As you can probably guess from the name, this operations master emulates the role of a Primary Domain Controller (PDC) for legacy NT 4.0 workstations and servers. Each Windows 2000 domain has one PDC Emulator, which contains the only writable version of the user account database and the workstation/server membership database, replicating all changes to the NT 4.0 Backup Domain Controllers. It also serves as the Domain Master Browser. Note that you can only have one domain controller being the PDC Emulator (which stands to reason, since you can only have one PDC in an NT 4.0 domain) in each domain within the forest.

The PDC Emulator receives preferential treatment, even after your domain has switched from running in mixed mode to Windows 2000 native mode. This is because there has to be at least one domain controller that has the most current user-account database. For example, suppose you decide to change your password on your Catywhompus Windows 2000 native mode domain. The domain controller that registers your successful password change immediately replicates that change to the PDC Emulator. The change to your user account takes time to propagate from the domain controller you changed it on to all the other domain controllers in the network. Say you now try to log on to another machine that is on a different subnet and that talks to a different domain controller for user authentication. You type in your new password, but the domain controller trying to authenticate you does not yet have your new password. The authentication fails because it still has your old password paired up with your username. However, instead of immediately issuing a failed-logon type of message, the domain controller forwards your authentication request to the PDC Emulator for authentication. Since the PDC Emulator has your new password, it authenticates your username and generates your access token, allowing you to log on.

Infrastructure Master

The Infrastructure Master updates group-to-user and group-to-group information when you change group membership in other domains or change the group name. It should be called the "Cross-Domain Group Membership Consistency Checking Master," since that more accurately tells us what it does (but granted, that title is more than a mouthful!). For example, say you need to change a user's account name (perhaps because of a marriage or divorce) in the Catywhompus HRO domain. But suppose that user is also a member of groups in both the Project Management domain and the Marketing domain. Without an Infrastructure Master, that user's name would only appear correctly in the HRO domain (where the change was made). It is the job of the Infrastructure Master to update any cross-domain references and to replicate those changes to the other domain controllers so that everyone is on the same sheet of music.

Relative Identifier Master

Each object in a forest has a unique identifier. When a new object is created, a domain controller needs to be able to issue the object an ID that is guaranteed to be unique. The Relative Identifier (RID) Master allocates blocks of RIDs to each Windows 2000 domain controller within the domain.

A RID is the number at the end of the SID, and the SID is, of course, the same as it was in NT 4.0—a unique "serial number" for all objects in the domain. The RID Master issues blocks of 500 RIDs to each domain controller (DC) to use each time the DC creates a user account, a group, or a computer object. When the DC has used 80 percent of its assigned RIDs, it requests another block of 500 from the RID Master. It is the RID Master's job to keep track of the RIDs it has assigned. If the RID Master is down, and a domain controller runs out of RIDs to assign, it cannot create any objects. It cannot borrow any RIDs from other domain controllers and must wait for the RID Master to come back online.

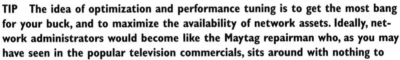

TIP The idea of optimization and performance tuning is to get the most bang for your buck, and to maximize the availability of network assets. Ideally, network administrators would become like the Maytag repairman who, as you may have seen in the popular television commercials, sits around with nothing to do—unfortunately, network administrators generally have users out there whose job seems to be inventing new ways to cause mischief. Also, you have bosses who like to make sure that you are gainfully employed in worthy endeavors.

Role Placement

So to avoid all the unpleasantness of a mismanaged network, the first step is to plan how you are going to transfer the different operations masters' roles to other domain controllers in order to maximize their availability to the network. First of all, you should document which computers are running which operations master roles. Annotate changes as you make them. This will both save you time and make it look like you know what you are doing. One of your main design goals is to figure out the most efficient design for maximum network performance. This is simply stated but not always so easy to achieve. In your domain, if you have enough domain controllers, then each role should be on a separate domain controller. However, there are some caveats.

By default, when you install the first Windows 2000 domain controller in the forest, it will house all the operations master roles discussed earlier in the chapter. The Schema Master and Domain Naming Master roles should both remain on the same domain controller. These are very powerful and important roles, but they are not going to see the type of traffic that the PDC Emulator does.

If you have an extremely dynamic organization, the PDC Emulator will have all sorts of traffic coming to it: users changing their passwords or administrators adding, changing, or deleting accounts, groups, group memberships, and so on. For performance reasons, you should put the PDC Emulator role by itself on a domain controller. After that, it's likely the remaining roles would reside on individual server machines.

Another caveat is that the Infrastructure Master needs to have a good connection to a global catalog server. However, if both roles are on the same box, the Infrastructure Master will not send out an update of any changes to the domain controllers because the Infrastructure Master checks for differences between what it knows about objects in other domains and what a domain controller in its own domain knows. It then replicates the updates to all the domain controllers in its own domain. However, since the global catalog already has the most current information, the Infrastructure Master sees no differences in the two versions, and so it issues no updates to any of the domain controllers in its domain. As you can tell, this is only an issue in multidomain configurations. If your forest is a single domain, then this will not affect you.

Permissions

In order to move the roles to different domain controllers, you need to have the correct permissions to make the changes. Note that the groups listed next might contain a common account, such as Administrator (so logging on as the Administrator would accomplish this for you). Note that you don't inherently have to log on as a different user to assume the powers needed to interact with the roles listed here.

- The Schema Master role can only be changed by Schema Admins.
- The Domain Naming Master role can only be changed by Enterprise (forest) Administrators.
- The PDC Emulator role is changed by Domain Administrators.
- The Infrastructure Master role is changed by Domain Administrators.
- The RID Master role is changed by Domain Administrators.

Role Changing

Now that you have figured out where you want to move the roles of your Windows 2000 operations masters and you have the correct permissions, it is time to put your plan into motion. You can use either the Command Line Interface (CLI) or the GUI, whichever you are most comfortable with, to transfer operations master roles from one domain controller to another. To use the CLI, open up a command prompt and then type **ntdsutil.exe**. For the GUI approach, use the appropriate snap-in listed in the following table.

Role	Snap-In
Schema Master	Active Directory Schema
Domain Naming Master	Active Directory Domains and Trusts
Relative Identifier Master	Active Directory Users and Computers
PDC Emulator	Active Directory Users and Computers
Infrastructure Master	Active Directory Users and Computers

Disaster Recovery

When one of your operations master domain controllers fails, you need to have a good disaster-recovery plan ready to execute. The actions you take will depend largely on the nature of the failure and what sort of failover redundancy you have in the way of node clustering. As you know, disaster recovery approaches such as clustering are highly recommended to ensure the health and wealth of your Windows 2000 network. The roles can either be transferred or seized, depending on whether the shutdown is scheduled or unscheduled.

If you are scheduling an operations master for maintenance, or are upgrading its hardware, and it will not be available for a while, you can transfer the role to another domain controller before taking down the current operations master. This gives the two domain controllers the opportunity to synchronize their databases so that the new operations master will have the most current information.

However, if your operations master takes a hard crash, you will have to seize the role. The former operations master did not have a chance to synchronize its database with anybody, so some recent changes may be lost.

Any domain controller can seize any of the five operations master roles. There is one caveat, though: if you have seized the Schema Master, Domain Naming Master, or RID Master roles, it is imperative that you do *not* bring them back online. Format the drives and reload Windows 2000. If you do not, the machines will continue to believe that they hold their former operations master role and will attempt to resume their duties, the results of which are not always predictable.

Now granted, we've done nothing more here than recite the litany and verse of the published Microsoft "best practices." Without question, you can find secrets, tips, and tricks in other published references and in dubious Internet chat rooms and e-mail lists that suggest handling this process in other ways. But remember the old adage, "you get what you pay for." More importantly, as a Windows 2000 MCSE candidate, particular attention should be devoted to the Microsoft way of doing things. Let's face it. The Microsoft way is the MCSE certification examination way, correct?

If the Schema Master comes back, any recent schema changes can be lost. If the Domain Naming Master comes back, your domain controllers will be caught in a tug-of-war, not knowing which is the real naming master. If the RID Master comes back, it may attempt to issue blocks of RIDs that have already been given out. This sort of problem is analogous to a DHCP server having its scope deleted and re-created—the server has no idea what is already out there, and so it starts giving out numbers it thinks are legitimate. The results would not be pretty: objects with different attributes could have the same RID, confusing the Active Directory and causing unpredictable behavior.

However, if you have to seize the roles of the PDC Emulator or Infrastructure Master, they can be brought back online safely. They will resume their former roles and behave themselves quite nicely, synchronizing their databases and carrying on like they were never gone.

Designing the Placement of Global Catalog Servers

In the preceding discussion, we talked a little bit about global catalog servers and their relation to the roles of operations master servers. We alluded to a few design considerations, such as what happens if you put the role of Infrastructure Master on one of your global catalog servers in a multidomain forest. Now, however, we need to define the design elements that determine where to put your global catalog servers for maximum performance.

Global Catalog Servers

A global catalog server is simply the server that houses the Active Directory global catalog. The global catalog is analogous to a library's card catalog, something that those under 30 have probably never used since libraries are now mostly computerized. If you want to find a book, you could just start looking through all the shelves until you found what you were seeking, but this would be a very time-consuming way to spend your time. This method works for a very small library, but it does *not* scale well if you are looking in the Library of Congress, or even a moderately sized university library.

To maximize your performance in searching for your book, you would go straight to the catalog and search the index. This allows you to sort through a record set containing thousands and thousands of entries easily and rapidly. You could find out where any book in the library's system was located, even if it were at another branch. This is the function of the global catalog. It helps users and applications efficiently find objects housed in the Active Directory. You can find things within your domain, and you can find things in other domains in the forest.

The global catalog also provides information to the Netlogon services. When a user logs on, the domain controller checks the global catalog to determine the user's universal group membership information so that it can generate an access token with the proper permissions.

To find an object in the global catalog, simply click Start, click Search, and then select where you want to go today.

Global Catalog Server Placement Considerations

By default, Windows 2000 only creates one global catalog server. It is created on the first domain controller in the first domain in the forest. As your forest grows more and more trees, it is easy to see just how big the global catalog will become—it is an index to every single object in every single domain in the forest. Because of this, you will want to have one global catalog server located at each *site* of your forest (remarkably, this is Microsoft's recommendation too, and if Microsoft recommends it, you should pay heed to this advice in the context of the Windows 2000 MCSE exams).

> **NOTE**   A site is a term that is applied to a TCP/IP subnet. In other words, each TCP/IP subnet is a site in Windows 2000 Server.

For Catywhompus Inc., you would have a global catalog server in Oakland, New York, Los Angeles, Chicago, London, and Tokyo. This serves two purposes: first, it cuts down on traffic between the WAN links connecting your sites, since searches will not have to travel across the link to be answered; second, it provides fault tolerance should the WAN link go down. Granted, the network would be running at a low level of functionality with an out-of-date global catalog.

Now that you have determined that you will have a global catalog server at each site within the forest, you need to find the best place to put them within the site. If you only have one domain in your forest, your job is done. You can safely leave the global catalog server in its default location and be happy. However, since that does not make for interesting exam scenarios, you should know where to put your global catalog servers in a forest with multiple sites and multiple domains. Those of you who are familiar with Microsoft Exchange Server will notice many similarities between the considerations used to determine the placement of an Exchange server and a global catalog server.

A bridgehead server is the domain controller in your site that talks to a domain controller at other sites, and your bridgehead server should always be a global catalog server configured to replicate between sites. You can either let Windows 2000 select the server for you through the Knowledge Consistency Checker (and hope it made the "right" choice) or select it manually through the Active Directory Sites and Services snap-in via the following step list.

Lab Exercise 5.1:
Manual Selection of a Server

1. Click Start | Administrative Tools | Active Directory Sites and Services.

2. Expand the Sites node in the console pane to display the sites in the forest.

3. Select the site where the domain controller resides (for example, Default-First-Name) and expand the Servers folder. Note that the default is, ironically, called Default First Name in the user interface.

4. Right-click the domain controller object and select Properties.

5. On the Server tab, in the left column, select the intersite transport or transports for which this computer is the preferred bridgehead server, and then click Add. The transport is moved to the This Server Is a Preferred Bridgehead Server for the Following Transports box.

6. Click OK.

For more information on creating a bridgehead server, see the Microsoft TechNet article at http://support.microsoft.com/support/kb/articles/Q271/9/97.ASP.

Once you have created a bridgehead server, the Intersite Topology Generator will always choose your preferred server as the one to host the inbound replication traffic.

This use of bridgehead servers serves two purposes: first, it reduces intersite traffic required by replication in a multiple domain environment, and second, it reduces latency in synchronizing the information stored in the databases. This will result in faster and more up-to-date query responses for users at both ends of the connection.

Designing the Placement of Domain Controller Servers

The first domain controller created in a forest is also the first domain controller in the root domain and the first domain controller in the site. As a result, it is the single most important computer in your entire enterprise. Initially, it houses all of the operations master roles (Schema Master, Domain Naming Master, PDC Emulator, Infrastructure Master, and the RID Master). Of course, based on your knowledge of operations masters from the earlier part of this chapter, you can move the roles to different domain controllers to maximize performance and implement fault tolerance.

Windows 2000 servers are different from other types of Microsoft servers we have worked on over the years as technology professionals. You can promote a member server to become a domain controller at any time after you have installed Windows 2000 by using the dcpromo command line utility. The server must have at least one partition formatted as NTFS version 5.0 because this is—if you believe Madison Avenue phraseology—a "new and improved" version of NTFS (it really is, but it's not necessary to understand the finer points of NTFS for the purposes of the Windows 2000 MCSE Designing exams). If you try promoting a server that does not have an NTFS version 5.0 partition, you will get an error message to this effect, letting you know that you need to change the FAT partition to an NTFS partition. This would be accomplished from the Computer Management snap-in found in the Administrative Tools program group (this is a tool you should be familiar with from your journey through the Windows 2000 MCSE core exams).

Similarly, you can demote a domain controller to become just a member server, and it will no longer house the Active Directory database. The side benefit of being able to demote a domain controller is that you can move that server, or any domain controller, from one domain to another without having to reinstall the operating system. You can even promote the moved server to make it a domain controller in the new domain.

You can also promote a server to domain controller status via the Windows 2000 Configure Your Server tool (launched from Configure Your Server in the Administrative Tools program group) as shown in Figure 5-2.

As you will recall from your studies and practice for the core Windows 2000 MCSE, Active Directory is installed from the Active Directory Installation wizard, shown in Figure 5-3.

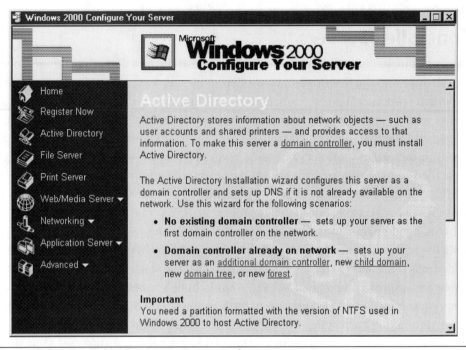

Figure 5-2   The Active Directory server configuration menu

Figure 5-3   Implementing Active Directory

The end of the Active Directory process, which is several wizard pages later in the process, summarizes the changes made and is displayed in Figure 5-4.

Each domain controller contains a shared system volume, conveniently named sysvol, and it is this volume that requires an NTFS version 5.0 partition. At first it might seem that this is because it will be housing the Active Directory. However, this is not the case. The sysvol, by default, contains a scripts folder for logon scripts and system policy files, and a policies folder for the group policy template files. In other words, sysvol contains many files that are used by the Active Directory but does not contain the Active Directory information itself. The sysvol information is replicated to all the domain controllers within the domain.

When considering where to place the domain controllers within your domain, you must take into account the speed of the links between the various sites. To be considered "fast," your network connection should be at least 512Kbps. However, you must still have sufficient bandwidth for the directory replication. For example, if your users have Web applications that suck up 450Kbps on a routine basis, then your connection will not support the replication of Active Directory—it is not a "fast" network connection.

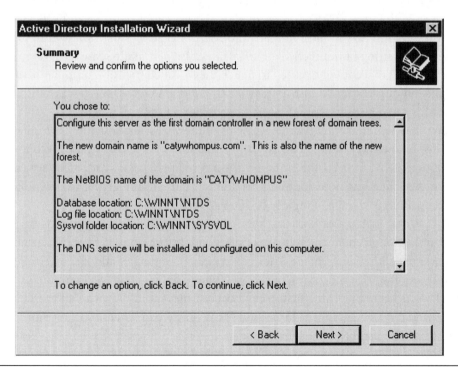

Figure 5-4   Completing the Active Directory installation

This bandwidth connection issue is even more interesting in domains with multiple sites. In your design planning, you must first determine whether a location even needs a domain controller. This is a decision that would be made, in part, based on your perception of network traffic at the site. If the site is a victim of debilitating network traffic to the main network (say across a WAN link), then the site could benefit greatly from having a domain controller with its own replica of critical system state data, such as the Active Directory.

But hang on for just a minute. As we discussed in the "Global Catalog Server Placement Considerations" section earlier in the chapter, you want to put the global catalog on the bridgehead server to maximize its performance and minimize unnecessary local traffic. In fact, in a bona fide, large-scale Windows 2000 network, it's a fact of life that there is an abundance of global catalog servers.

A Brief History of DNS

The Domain Name Service (DNS) originated from the ARPANET (which became the Internet) in the early 1970s. At that time, there were very few hosts connected to each other on the ARPANET. Since humans can remember names like "Catywhompus" far better than a string of numbers like "192.168.32.157," it made sense to develop a text file (hosts.txt) that could be parsed to match the so-called friendly computer name to a globally unique IP address. However, while the solution was simple, it was far from elegant. This name resolution method had two major flaws.

One flaw was that the hosts.txt name-resolution was not scalable. Each new host required a new entry in the hosts.txt file. As the number of hosts swelled into the tens of thousands, so too did the number of lines required. Also, each new host added meant that there was now another host adding to the traffic, trying to download the newest edition of the file. It rapidly became an unworkable solution.

The second major flaw was that the hosts.txt name-resolution method was easily broken. The Stanford Research Institute's Network Information Center (NIC) had control over the addressing scheme. They could make sure that all addresses were globally unique, but they had no control over host names. So if you had two computers named "Fred," whichever one came first in the hosts.txt file would be where all traffic would go. It would really get ugly if the second "Fred" entry happened to be a major hub of the ARPANET, disrupting most traffic.

continued

In 1984, Paul Mockapetris released RFCs (Requests For Comments) 882 and 883, which described the Domain Name System. These RFCs were refined and superseded by RFCs 1034 and 1035, which define the current specifications of DNS. For Windows 2000, DNS has been further enhanced by compliance with RFC 1995 (incremental zone transfers), RFC 2052 (outlining the DNS service that supports SRV records— required by Active Directory), and RFC 2136 (supporting dynamic updates).

In order to ensure globally unique host names, name resolution went from the flat namespace of the hosts.txt file to the hierarchical namespace of DNS. The root domain is the period (.). The top-level domains are .com, .edu, .gov, .mil, .net, .org, and the in-addr.arpa domains (you will recall from the core Windows 2000 MCSE exams that in-addr.arpa is a default DNS configuration related to reverse name resolution). As of this writing, several new domain name suffixes have been proposed for specific user communities and market segments, but it is highly unlikely that you'll be held responsible for these on the designing exams on the Windows 2000 MCSE track. For more information on domain names, see http://www.networksolutions.com.

DNS Zone Planning

The DNS service allows you the flexibility of dividing up your DNS namespace into one or more zones, depending on the structure of your forest. You can design your forest all under one namespace, or split it into multiple namespaces based on domains, sites, or political divisions. How you configure your namespace is going to involve a balance between what makes sense for your enterprise forest, how you can optimize performance, and where you need fault tolerance.

For example, Catywhompus is merging its organization with Vanillafudge, so you now need to extend your namespace to include all the subdomains of Vanillafudge. It probably makes more sense to add DNS zones to accommodate the new organizational structure.

What if Catywhompus wants to delegate control of the Marketing and HRO subdomains to those domain administrators? The answer is simple: divide up your namespace and delegate the DNS management to those domains.

Of course, you must always consider performance issues. Perhaps the network traffic has increased significantly, and dividing your DNS zone would help to eliminate some of the traffic. Also, you may have to create more fault tolerance by placing additional DNS zones within your namespace.

continued

DNS Lookup Zones

There are two types of lookup zones you can implement in your DNS structure: forward and reverse. You must configure at least one forward lookup zone in order for the DNS service to work. Reverse lookup zones are not required, but some command line utilities will not return any information unless you have a reverse lookup zone configured. For more information on DNS lookup zones, refer to Chapter 16.

DNS Zone Types

The Standard Primary zone server contains the writable DNS database for the portion of the namespace for which it is authoritative. The Standard Primary server is the one that accepts changes to the zone data. For fault tolerance and load balancing reasons, it is always a good idea to house the data on an additional server on your network (for example, another Windows 2000 Server). However, you must be concerned about keeping the data current. This concern is addressed by having the additional server maintain a read-only copy of the data. That way, updates are maintained on one server and propagated out to the other servers.

This is where a Standard Secondary zone server comes in. The Standard Secondary server contains a read-only copy of the DNS zone information, receiving all updates from the Standard Primary server. You can have multiple secondary servers, but there can only be one primary for the zone.

Caching-Only DNS servers do not maintain any copy of the zone database. As the name implies, their sole function is to hold information in cache and to resolve DNS queries. The information only stays in the cache until its time to live (TTL) expires, or until it is renewed by another forward lookup (the TTL gets reset). For a really busy forest, with many DNS queries going on, this is a good server to have around, as it reduces the load on the primary and all secondary servers.

The Active Directory–integrated zone server contains the writable zone database, but in Active Directory form. Instead of storing zone information in the text format of a Standard Primary server, the Active Directory–integrated zone server uses the power of Active Directory to store the zone information as Active Directory objects. This accomplishes two things for the administrator: First, since the zone information is now an Active Directory object, the information is replicated to all the domain controllers along with all the other Active Directory data. Second, you can now run the DNS service on any of your domain controllers. Since they are all replicating Active Directory information anyway, DNS zone information now comes along for the ride. So if you find that you need to add another zone to your Active Directory domain, the new information is automatically replicated to any new domain controllers.

continued

Not surprisingly, Microsoft strongly recommends the use of Active Directory–integrated zone servers. Along with the simplified administration and faster replication benefits, these DNS servers can also help to enhance security through the security protections afforded by Active Directory. Also, because the writable copy of the DNS zone database is kept in the Active Directory, the DNS service has the ability to update zone information on any domain controller in the domain. In plain east Texas talk, would you rather have your DNS zone information stored as a text file that is unprotected or as part of the Active Directory database structure that is protected (and that has many other wonderful features)?

For more information on Active Directory–integrated zone discussion, see Chapter 16.

Where, Oh Where Should My DNS Go?

Basically, you have two choices to consider when implementing your DNS structure: external and internal. In other words, your namespace design can be either the same as your registered domain name (external), or you can have a separate, private one that "only locals seem to know about" (internal). You can achieve this by placing a firewall between your internal, private network and the public Internet. The use of a separate and distinct DNS zone is usually driven by security concerns about your network assets, but it may also be from a merger or reorganization.

Names Are the Same, Public and Private   The goal of this type of arrangement is that all hosts in the company's internal network be able to access resources located both on the outside of the firewall (on the Internet) and on the inside of the firewall (on the intranet), while denying access from the outside to internal resources.

This scenario requires two separate DNS zones to work. The zone outside the firewall provides name resolution for resources on the Internet. This zone must not be configured to resolve internal names. If it is, then you have defeated its purpose, for you are trying to prevent outside sources from contacting your internal resources.

The main advantage of this arrangement is that the external and internal domain names are identical. The downside is that the hosts must be configured to be able to distinguish internal resources from external resources. Because the names are the same, this will be confusing. The confusion could result in someone posting confidential information on an external server, wide open to the world, thinking that they were posting to an internal server with the same name. Users will also see a different topology when connecting from the outside versus connecting from the inside. In addition, you will have to duplicate your efforts to maintain a separate set of DNS servers.

continued

Names Are Different, Public and Private   In this case, you are using a separate DNS namespace on the outside of the firewall (on the Internet) from that used on the inside of the firewall (on the intranet). Of course, this requires having two separate domain names registered with InterNIC to prevent possible future confusion, should another organization register your private domain name on the Internet.

This plan has the advantage that the users will always know which resources are internal and which resources are external, simply by the name. Also, there is no need for duplication of effort in maintaining DNS zone servers. The downside is that your logon domain name would have to be different from your e-mail domain name.

Designing the Placement of DNS Servers

Still hanging on to that hat from the last section? Good, because this next section is a critical part of your real-world life as a Windows 2000 MCSE acting in the capacity of a network or enterprise architect. It's also known as, shall we say, a *popular* area in the designing certification exams on the Windows 2000 MCSE track. So take a moment and catch your breath. *This is one of the most critical steps in your Active Directory planning!*

The Domain Name System (DNS) and how it operates is a huge topic that could easily fill its own book, and in many cases already has! What is DNS? It is a hierarchical namespace, it is a service that resolves host names, it is a query-result caching service, it provides reverse lookup queries, and it is the means Windows 2000 uses to locate domain controllers. DNS is all these things and more. However, our focus here is on where to place the DNS servers in your domain design so that you maximize performance, establish fault tolerance, increase functionality, and improve manageability.

The most significant change in DNS with Windows 2000 is that it now has dynamic update ability, Dynamic DNS (DDNS). You also have the ability to control which servers and clients in the domain can initiate these updates. Your Dynamic Host Configuration Protocol (DHCP) server and your Windows Internet Naming Service (WINS) server can now dynamically add all the required DNS records to the DNS zone database automatically. You will recall from your core Windows 2000 MCSE days that DNS databases are based on zones.

> **CAUTION**   The Windows 2000 Active Directory cannot function and will not install without access to (or the ability to create) a DNS server. As with any new, powerful tool, you must give some serious thought to where these servers will live in the domain. Since the Windows 2000 Netlogon service uses the DNS server to locate your domain controllers, a good design will streamline your network traffic; a bad design will give you problems you don't need.

Case Study 5:
Advanced Active Directory Design
Issues for Catywhompus Construction

We will now revisit Catywhompus in the context of domain controller placement and global catalog servers, two critical topics in this chapter. This fulfills the promise we made at the start of the chapter wherein we asked you to think about how to make the Catywhompus network more efficient and effective in the context of the service locations for Active Directory.

As you know, the Catywhompus head office is in Oakland. The Chicago branch office is connected by a T-1, but the link to the Los Angeles branch office is only a 56Kbps frame-relay circuit. Having a domain controller in Chicago makes sense, but having one in LA will not work. Even if you increased the bandwidth to 256Kbps, some of the users in LA would get frustrated with the inevitably slow logon process. If you have more than two to five workstations logging on across a slow WAN link, you will need to have a domain controller at that branch office.

Let's take a look at another example at Catywhompus, Inc. The headquarters is in Oakland, there is a big branch office in London, and a small branch office in Tokyo. The connection from Oakland to London is a T-1. The connection from London to Tokyo is a 56Kbps frame-relay. We'll consider four design alternatives in the following sections.

Design I

You construct the network as one domain, and all three locations have domain controllers to guarantee fast logons. You add a new user in Oakland, and the user's information is replicated to all domain controllers. The Active Directory updates are pushed out from Oakland to London, and then from London to Tokyo. Since it is the first time this information has existed, all of the attributes are sent out, as well. You realize that you need to make a correction to the user's group membership, and so you make the change—only the changed property gets replicated to the other sites.

Design 2

Each site has its own domain, and hence, its own domain controller. Administrators at each site create users at each site, and since each domain is its own Active Directory, there is no data to replicate between sites (however, depending on the placement of the

continued

domain controllers, you would clearly have intrasite replication between global catalog servers and operations masters). The only traffic that needs to go over the WAN links would be schema changes and RID requests. Since you have no updates to the forest, there is none of that traffic either. If heavy replication traffic is what you are trying to avoid, then this would be an excellent solution. However, if users from the Tokyo domain start querying the directory for information about network resources in Oakland, the queries and the answer traffic would get sent all over the network. The advantages of not having all the replication traffic fade rapidly. In reality, there would probably be at least a few applications that would send out these types of queries (especially for sales people checking their quota figures, and other similar functions).

Design 3

Each site has a domain controller for each domain (Oakland has a Tokyo domain controller and a London domain controller in addition to its own domain controller, and so on). This solution solves the problem discussed in the second design. Queries are now local operations, and new or changed objects are replicated only once over the network. However, the trade-off is that now all Active Directory objects have to be copied to all sites. Another factor to consider is hardware cost. The Tokyo office may only have five people, and one domain controller would have been sufficient for their branch. This design requires them to have two more server boxes.

Design 4

Each site is its own domain, but now each site also has a global catalog server. Since the global catalog servers contain a complete replica of their own domain's Active Directory, and the global catalog (index) of all objects in the forest, each site now has a server that knows where to find the resources located in all the different domains. If the administrator in Oakland creates a new user account, it is only the catalog entry for that object that gets replicated to the other global catalog servers. Users looking for specific resources can sift through the entries of the local global catalog server without adding to the WAN link traffic. Even if the global catalog does not contain all of the object attributes that the user or application needs, it will give the fully qualified domain name so that the resource can be located and used. This is an excellent solution for any design scenario in which network traffic is a major concern but all objects need to be accessible to all clients in all domains.

Next Steps

Your mission, should you choose to accept it, is to take all of the valuable knowledge and insights that you have gained from this portion of the book, and add to that all of your Windows 2000 experience (or develop a plan to acquire such experience). The resulting synthesis of material will not only make you a valued and highly respected Windows 2000 Administrator, but will also enable you to pass Microsoft's Designing Windows 2000 Directory Services Infrastructure exam. Do you feel ready? If so, great! Time to schedule Exam 70-219!

Chapter Review

This chapter explained the role of operations masters in your forest, and where they are located in the forest. The five operations master roles are: Schema Master, Domain Naming Master, PDC Emulator, Infrastructure Master, and RID Master. You learned the importance of properly placing your global catalog servers in terms of maximizing performance, providing fault tolerance, improving network functionality, and improving manageability. You then looked at the ramifications of where you place the domain controllers in your design. There are many solutions, but only one will best fit the bill for the goals and constraints imposed on the network infrastructure. The DNS servers under Windows 2000 support dynamic updates. This is a powerful feature, but one that must be implemented with some thought.

Questions

1. In designing the placement of your domain controllers, what is the most important factor to consider in your decision (choose all that apply)?
   a. Budgetary concerns
   b. Performance issues such as link bandwidth and media saturation
   c. Fault tolerance
   d. Required availability
   e. Robust functionality
   f. Easy manageability

2. List the various roles of operations masters.

3. True or False: Only Schema Administrators can change the domain schema.

4. What are some reasons for creating more than one domain in your design? Note that you may need to consult other chapters in the book to answer this question (consider it a research project and start with chapters in Part III, "Designing a Microsoft Windows 2000 Network Infrastructure").

5. What are some advantages of using Active Directory–integrated zone types?

6. What is the function of a bridgehead server?

Answers

1. **A through F.** Not surprisingly, each of the answers is applicable to the domain controller placement issue.

2. The answer is Schema Master, Domain Naming Master, Primary Domain Controller Emulator, Infrastructure Master, and Relative Identifier Master.

3. **True.** Only members of the Schema Admins group have the ability to change the schema, by default.

4. **Answers will vary,** but certainly two reasons come to mind. The first is performance. You might find that dividing resources into separate domains results in improved network performance. The second is politics. Try as you might otherwise, the political forces inside the organization may require you create multiple domains for resource control and naming reasons.

5. **Answers will vary,** but certainly one benefit is the fact the Active Directory security is applied to the zone file (otherwise the zone file is a text file). Another benefit is replication via the Active Directory replication mechanism.

6. A bridgehead server is the domain controller in your site that talks to a domain controller at other sites, and your bridgehead server should always be a global catalog server configured to replicate between sites.

Key Skill Sets

- Understanding the roles of your domain's operations masters and where to place them to maximize performance.

- Knowing what factors to consider in designing the placement of your global catalog server.

- Identifying the best places for your domain controllers to maximize performance, enhance fault tolerance, increase functionality, and improve manageability.

- Recognizing the importance of properly placing your Domain Name Service (DNS) servers and how they best integrate with your security strategy.

Key Terms

Bridgehead servers
Domain Naming Master
Global catalog server
Infrastructure Master
Operations master
PDC Emulator
RID Master
Schema Master
WAN links

PART II

Exam 70-220: Designing Security for a Microsoft Windows 2000 Network

- **Chapter 6** Introduction to Security
- **Chapter 7** Analyzing Business and Technical Requirements
- **Chapter 8** Analyzing Security Requirements
- **Chapter 9** Designing a Windows 2000 Security Solution
- **Chapter 10** Designing a Security Solution for Access Between Networks
- **Chapter 11** Designing Security for Communication Channels

Introduction to Security

This chapter covers the following key mastery goals:

- Understand the skill set required to design security for a Windows 2000 network
- Understand the business aspects of designing Windows 2000 security
- Understand the technical aspects of designing Windows 2000 security
- Understand the life cycle of a security design

Your network is installed and running. Active Directory is working wonderfully. Your new SQL Server is running like a well-oiled machine. IIS is serving up Web pages like there's no tomorrow. And then it happens—from absolutely nowhere, an external foe gets into the network from the Internet. Before you know it, the HR database has been raided, the corporate Web site has been defaced, and the Active Directory schema has been trashed.

Sound familiar? We certainly hope not! And, of course, this is an extraordinary circumstance, but it illustrates what can happen if a security plan is not designed along with the network and directory infrastructure.

Intruder Perspectives

You must take the perspective of an intruder to determine what needs to be locked down, as suggested in Figure 6-1. What perspective does the intruder hold? Is the intruder motivated by a need for attention, achievement, or simple financial gain? What kinds of targets does the intruder seek? Sites that have high public visibility? Is the intruder's preference to seek out small sites instead of large sites?

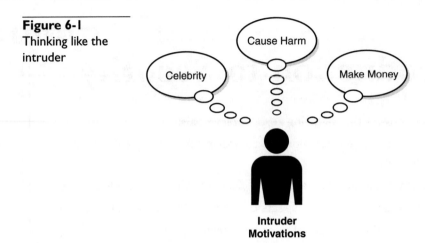

Figure 6-1
Thinking like the
intruder

Once you've taken the viewpoint of an intruder, I'm sure your next question is "How can I make my network bulletproof?" The simple answer is that you can't. Not unless you have a network that is not connected to the Internet and only allows internal logons under the strictest monitored conditions to dumb terminals without floppy or hard disks.

What you can do, however, is decrease the likelihood that a hacker can go on a veritable shopping spree at your company's expense. This will require a great deal of planning, and you will need to stay current with security trends and apply large doses of MCSE common sense. You will need a great deal of knowledge about the Windows 2000 operating system before you can embark on this arduous journey. Your technical skills have to be top notch.

If you don't have an outstanding network and directory design in place, your security design will most certainly fall apart, simply because there are holes in your infrastructure's core. Like a car, you can have the best engine in the world, but if the car has a bad frame, your car is still in bad shape.

The Business Case

Having technical knowledge is imperative in your journey to devising a security design, but if you don't have the business sense, you're not going to make it very far. If you're just a technical person, you will not have the political finesse to navigate the minefield of upper management. You're always going to want the most expensive toys (who wouldn't?), and the CIO and executive staff will probably cut you down. You need to finely tune your business mind to figure out which battles to fight and which ones to let go. Focus your efforts where they are likely to produce results and don't let the lost causes consume your time. With your available time, focus on security success factors.

As consultants, we had to learn very quickly to recommend the lowest common denominator in a given situation. Sure, we absolutely love the perks that come with installing and configuring new high-tech toys, but we learned to ask ourselves, "Do they really need this?" If we can find another solution that doesn't put a damper on network management or costs and that still uses their existing systems, we usually choose it. If you can come in under budget, by all means, do so!

A lot of technical consultants don't do business cases. This is where the problems start. The business case is there to assist both you and your client. It defines the company's current infrastructure, their goals, and why you've been hired as a consultant. They have a problem, and you're supposed to fix that problem in the best way possible.

The business case will also serve as a guideline for you as you work on the project. It will provide you with milestones, due dates that ensure everything is going smoothly, and often a budget for the entire project if you're the project manager. It can also let you know what you're getting into. After you've compiled all the data about your client's organization, you can see whether this is a major or minor project, and whether or not you can completely fulfill each of their needs.

If you decide against doing a business case, we can guarantee that you'll be sorry. No job is too small for a business case. It provides both you and your client with a set of expectations that are agreed upon after the analysis portion of the project. You know exactly what your client expects of you, and the client knows exactly what you'll do. There's no room for argument if everything is letter perfect. You'll want to make sure everything is covered—if you don't outline everything, you will find a significant amount of additional adrenaline coursing through your bloodstream. You think skydiving and bungee-jumping are scary?

 TIP Make sure you thoroughly review the business case with your client and sign off on it. That way you'll have a paper trail to follow throughout the process. Make sure that you document and sign off on any changes your client wants made when you're in the middle of the project. Leave nothing undocumented!

Technical Tangents of Networking and Security

Once you have the business case figured out, you need to get the logistics finished for the technical aspect relating to networking and security. You need to have a good draft of how the Windows 2000 Active Directory infrastructure is going to be laid out, as well as a good diagram of the network and the services you'd like to implement. Designing security is something you're going to do while designing your directory and network, since both the directory and the network have security-related issues.

Now, let's take a look at the technical issues that you're going to have to account for in our security design:

- **User and group account management**   Adding, modifying, and deleting user and group accounts

- **Machine security**   This includes physical and computer-based security (logons and so on)

- **Network and communication security**   Firewall, protocol, and Internet

- **Public Key Infrastructure (PKI)**   Authentication-related security

User and Group Account Management

You need to make sure that you've adequately planned your users and groups. Remember the "A-G-DL-P" rule: "*accounts* go into global groups, *global groups* go into domain local groups, and *domain local groups* get assigned *permissions.*"

Make sure you create and organize groups to match the security policy of your organization. You need to ensure that small details don't go unnoticed. For instance, did you make sure the Administrator account is renamed? Is the Guest account disabled? Does the IUSR_<computername> account have too many permissions? These are the obvious tasks. Less obvious ones would include

- Disabling recently terminated employee accounts

- Deleting terminated employee accounts a reasonable amount of time after termination

- Creating low-level accounts for temporary employees

- Logging on as a low-level user instead of a power user (or higher)

If you haven't locked these accounts down, any user who knows even a little bit about Windows 2000 can seriously injure or cripple your network with very little effort.

Delegation of authority is also a critical topic associated with accounts. Make sure that you only give users the access they absolutely need. For example, don't make somebody a domain administrator if they only need to administer a single OU! The fewer permissions a user has, the less likely they are to cause trouble. And if they do cause trouble, it's at least on a limited scale, not on an enterprise basis. For example:

- Can you give a user account the change permission instead of the full-control permission?

- Can you give a user account the read-only permission where appropriate?

Another tip for the real world would be to have administrative accounts separate from everyday-user accounts. By this, we mean that your administrator should only log on to the administrative account when performing administrative functions (or use Run As to elevate privilege). We know, you've probably heard this one a million times, and you're rolling your eyes thinking "Oh boy, there they go talking about this academic nonsense again." However, we have often seen an administrator walk away from his or her desk only to have a sly user walk by and begin using the administrator machine. Most of the time, the user doesn't have any malevolent intentions, but there are nearly always disastrous results. The user ends up deleting something or causing damage that requires the administrator (after a good deal of vile language) to restore a backup or spend time fixing the problem.

Why doesn't the administrator just lock the workstation? Well, all users should lock their workstations, regardless of who they are. Doing so involves a little inconvenience, but it can certainly save a lot of headaches in the long run. One such headache would be a co-worker walking up to a machine and reading the private e-mail of another co-worker. We've seen this done, and this is how sensitive information, such as salary levels, gets into the wrong hands quickly!

Let us reiterate our cardinal rule: users on a network should have the lowest amount of access they need to perform their jobs. No more, no less. This is critically important for a production environment.

Machine Security

Machine security encompasses two areas: physical security and operating system security.

For physical security, you need to consider the physical locations of the machines. For example, are they located in areas that could be accessed by anyone? Could a hacker get into the building and find them easily? If the answer is yes, you may want to find a better solution. If the hacker can't get to the machine, they can't physically destroy anything or play with the hardware. Here is a quick checklist to think about when it comes to machine security:

- Is the machine locked in a secure room?

- Is the machine serial number (and other unique identification numbers) recorded somewhere (to trace a theft, for example)?

- Is the machine physically restrained with a chain or cable that is attached to something permanent?

Operating system security is more complicated. At the basic level, this involves ensuring that only authorized users can log on to specific machines (especially domain controllers), and that appropriate policies are present and enforced on the network. One aspect of this security is in training users to respect the machines used by co-workers by only logging on to their assigned machines (user education plays a huge part of your success in security matters).

 TIP Ensure that Active Directory Group Policy is appropriately restrictive for your environment. If it's not, you'll find your chances of keeping a secure network are about as high as winning the Publishers Clearing House sweepstakes. Don't forget that Group Policy only applies to homogeneous Windows 2000 environments.

Network and Communication Security

Secure communications in today's world are a must. You never know who might be lurking around with a copy of Network Monitor or NetXRay, waiting to strike and steal your passwords. If you transmit data in clear text, you're a very likely candidate to be attacked this way.

What to do? Take this scenario where we've configured IPSec appropriately for network communication. IPSec, as you likely know, encrypts transmissions between the clients and servers (IPSec is discussed more in Chapter 11). Of course, only Windows 2000 clients support IPSec, so this limits you if you use older legacy operating systems. In fact, if you are using Windows ME, Windows 9x, or Macintosh clients, you'll possibly be able to justify the move to Windows 2000 Professional–based clients (upgrades and new machine purchases) for security reasons alone.

You need to think about your company's Internet access as part of your technology planning effort. Remember, the Internet is the most dangerous environment for employees to use, so you need to ensure that they can access what they need to and not expose the corporate network to an external risk. Microsoft Proxy Server is an excellent solution, because it provides the services of an application-level firewall, it can keep the bad guys out, and the good guys in! See Chapters 12 and 20 for more discussion of Microsoft Proxy Server.

EXAM TIP Many Ph.D.s can speak at length about the merits of hardware-based firewall solutions over software-based firewall solutions, and vice-versa. That's not what this book is about. Rather, in preparing for the MCSE exams, you want to know that Microsoft, having its own software-based firewall solution in Microsoft Proxy Server (recently upgraded and renamed as Internet Security and Acceleration Server 2000), will have a testing bias on the MCSE certification exams toward software-based firewall solutions. Make sure you honor that perspective.

Physical security of computer networks (such as a secure area with locked doors and alarm systems) is also important, and although Microsoft Proxy Server is a good tool for this, nothing beats having the appropriate network hardware, such as firewalls and routers, to keep things safe. Setting up screened subnets or demilitarized zones (DMZs) is also an excellent way to provide an extra layer of security. The DMZ concept is explained in Chapter 10.

Integration with third-party devices must be considered in the overall communication security plan (an overall communication security plan involves safety on networks and in telecommunications). For example, how many enterprise networks do you truly see out there that have only one operating system installed in their entire organization? Between us, we've been consulting for years now, and have never seen that yet. There's always that "one lone NetWare server" out there on the horizon. Well, believe it or not, that counts for something. How does this NetWare server fit into the networking infrastructure mix?

Third-party integration can actually be a blessing in disguise. For example, we can sleep a little easier knowing that our internal network runs IPX/SPX instead of TCP/IP. With the evolution of the Internet, and TCP/IP becoming the standard networking protocol (even Novell uses it natively in NetWare 5), it's easier to break into corporate networks knowing that they all talk in the same protocol. One way to help matters is to have a router run multiple protocols, so that the Internet connection can run on TCP/IP (of course) and the internal network can run another protocol, like IPX/SPX or NWLink. Granted, you'll need some type of gateway to translate between these two protocols, such as Microsoft Internet Security and Acceleration Server 2000. NetBEUI is not practical, in this case, because it's nonroutable. Figure 6-2 shows how such translation activity occurs. Using different protocols doesn't guarantee that nobody will break in, but the differences can certainly put a crimp in a hacker's day, nonetheless.

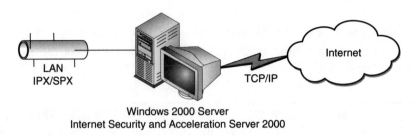

Figure 6-2 Translating between protocols

No network is completely safe. It just depends on how determined the hacker is. If you can find ways to keep the hacker busy on the front lines, he or she may give up in hopes of finding an easier target.

The bottom line is simply that you have to know how to integrate the major network operating systems into your security design. For example, how do you interoperate UNIX DNS (BIND, which stands for Berkeley Internet Name Daemon) and Windows 2000 DNS. Are there special security implications here? Are there special DNS replication implications? Of course, the answers to these questions are yes, but you'll have to read on to find out more!

Don't be surprised if you run into a few shops out there that integrate older products that use mainframe technology, such as Systems Network Architecture (SNA). Microsoft had a product called Host Integration Server (HIS) 2000 for integrating Windows 2000 into the mainframe environment. It is to your benefit to approach network security from all angles and realize that legacy systems may very well be present on the network. Know how to integrate them if need be.

EXAM TIP This book has a limited discussion of host-integration issues for one simple reason: the Windows 2000 MCSE has a very limited focus in this area.

What about remote users, you ask? Well, you always have Remote Access Service (RAS) for dial-in users, but Microsoft has added a host of new security protocols, such as the Microsoft Challenge Handshake Authentication Protocol, version 2 (MS-CHAPv2), and Transport Layer Security (TLS). Windows 2000 uses these protocols to provide better security.

In Windows 2000, Microsoft extends the ability to host a virtual private network (VPN) server (we feel the VPN capabilities in Windows 2000 are more stable than the predecessor Windows NT versions). A VPN allows clients to dial-in to the Internet from virtually anywhere, and then connect to a Windows 2000 server that has an Internet presence, establish a tunnel, and enjoy the benefits of encrypted communication with the internal network. As of this writing, VPN solutions based on encryption are considered to be acceptable in both the business and technology communities. This, of course, could change with future events, such as the discovery of successful hacks into this type of solution set.

During our present day, when much of the focus of the technology community (including Microsoft) is on corporate enterprise networks, the administrators and managers alike need to have ways to determine the costs of designing, implementing, and maintaining the network. Many upper-level executives see IT as a money pit, and strictly from the black-and-white income reports, that's true. IT does not generate a profit for the company, but the service it provides is invaluable.

Many companies nowadays charge the functional departments that use IT services based on what IT services are actually used (you can almost think of this as cost metering). How does Windows 2000 help with this, you ask? Well, with the Remote Authentication Dial-In User Service (RADIUS), any of the Windows 2000 Server family can account for who is connected to the corporate network via a RAS line and for how long. One possible use of this is to allow the company to determine how much of the company's money is being used to keep that user dialed in. Then the IT department can bill the user's department on a per-month rate or for an incidental charge, whatever the company has decided to do.

Another practical use for RADIUS and Windows 2000 is the role of an ISP. The ISP can use RADIUS to account for how long a user stays logged in to the system and then bill the client according to company policy. The Windows 2000 implementation of RADIUS has many implications and will be discussed at greater length in Chapter 9.

Public Key Infrastructure (PKI)

In the Windows NT 4.0 Option Pack, Microsoft introduced a new product called Certificate Server. Certificate Server was used to issue SSL certificates and other security certificate types to provide Web site security (if your company was already a certificate authority or self-signed), allow secure e-mail, and issue certificates for client authentication. Little did we know that Certificate Server would become an integral part of the operating system. In fact, Certificate Server is the basis for establishing a Public Key Infrastructure (PKI) in a Windows 2000 environment.

With PKI, you are now able to attach a smart-card reader to any Windows 2000 Professional client and allow your users to log on to the network. On the smart card is the user's certificate, known as the smart-card application certificate. The client is then authenticated without any more fuss. This allows corporations to require a physical security component to workstation logon. No longer can someone just steal a password —they'd have to have the user's smart card, as well. This increases security dramatically, because of the physical burden placed on the would-be hacker.

Also new to Windows 2000 is the Encrypting File System (EFS). EFS allows the network administrator to use the existing PKI to implement encryption on files and folders. Of course, this can only be done on machines that are running Windows 2000, so integration can become a little bit more nightmarish in this situation, but who ever said being on the cutting edge of technology was easy?

With Windows NT 4.0, anyone who was a member of the Administrators local group on the domain basically had the ability to reassign themselves permissions to anything in the domain. All they had to do was take ownership of an object and viola! Full access is granted with no questions asked. Auditing was also a problem because when a user was a member of Administrators, the owner of an object was simply displayed as "DOMAINNAME\Administrators" rather than as the individual user that took ownership of the object. Now in Windows 2000, EFS allows a user to have true privacy over files. Not even an administrative user can open the file without the appropriate key to do so. More on this in Chapter 9.

So, what if an administrator actually needs to get into encrypted files? That's simple. The administrator can perform a series of recovery steps and then assume the role of the Recovery Agent. The Recovery Agent's certificate can gain access to any encrypted file so that it's not lost forever if a certificate server fails or an administrator needs access. The process to gain Recovery Agent status is complicated enough that it can't be done by accident, either.

Of course, with the increased security functionality of PKI, there are also administrative drawbacks. A PKI infrastructure of certificate servers must be installed and maintained in conjunction with Active Directory. Also, policies must be in place for the issuance and revocation of certificates and smart cards. This means a cost/benefit analysis must be done to determine whether or not this is a good move for your corporation.

 NOTE PKI is discussed in much greater detail in Chapter 9.

The Security Life Cycle

A security infrastructure, unlike diamonds, doesn't last forever. You have to be able to adapt as needs change. After all, one of your greatest weapons against hackers is to constantly change small things about your network. A stagnant network attracts trouble.

You should be diligent in applying appropriate service packs and hot fixes for your network (a point made repeatedly in the core Windows 2000 MCSE exams on Windows 2000 Professional and Server). Remember that no network is completely secure, so loopholes can be found. If you change things on a regular basis, however, this can greatly lower the risk of intrusion.

Security design falls into five phases: Discovery, Design, Testing, Deployment, and Evaluation.

Discovery

The first phase of security design is *discovery*. In the discovery process, you should interview the client and come up with an appropriate business plan and documentation for implementing the plan. This is actually the most important part of the entire process. If you don't meet the clients' needs and expectations, you can do the best implementation job in the world and still fall short of the goal.

The discovery phase is where you and the client get to know each other, set dates, and agree to general terms of the project. It is important that explicit communication takes place here. This sets the stage for all future dealings, so make sure it's a good start!

Design

The second phase of the life cycle is the *design* phase, which is a large part of the security section of the book. This is where you take the business plan and figure out exactly what the client needs for a successful organization. You must assess current security policies, interview the users, and plan for the future. When you design a security infrastructure, you should have the design plans of the network and directory readily available for informational purposes. And, as the Windows 2000 MCSE, don't assume the client (or your employer) is aware of the security risks (either external or internal threats). You need to act as the client's advocate and think for them when it comes to security risk assessment in the design phase.

Testing

We'll assume you will join us in recognizing the importance of *testing* (and testing again). The fact of the matter is that you cannot release a security plan on the firm's network infrastructure without first engaging in appropriate testing. You'll need to create a test lab, run the tests, and perhaps retain an outside security consultant to verify the fitness of your security architecture. Enough said.

Deployment

Once the design plan is in place, you need to set up a *deployment* schedule. Make sure all roles are carefully planned when deploying. Everybody should know exactly what their role is, whether it's a primary or backup role, and when they're supposed to do their job. If there is mass confusion on day one of a deployment project, there are bound to be many mistakes that neither you nor the corporation can afford. Planning well ensures success!

Deployment begins once roles are assigned to the assorted people involved in the project, and when they are very clear about what they are doing. Deployment should be done reasonably quickly, but not so quickly that all changes irreversibly change a user's life. If you lock everything down too quickly, you could cause the users some extreme "network whiplash" and prevent them from doing their jobs. On the other hand, if you deploy the plan too slowly, you could leave the network too insecure during the transition period and allow a hacker to get into the network. Balancing all activities, and knowing the consequences of every action, is critical during this phase of the life cycle.

Evaluation

The final phase, *evaluation*, involves giving the network a "once over" to ensure that nothing was missed. It's also important to set measurable guidelines to see whether or not the design and deployment is a success. Be sure to check everything out, and see if there are any obvious (or not so obvious) holes in your design. If there are, fix them. If not, don't pat yourself on the back yet! Check again. Chances are you did miss something the first time. And once you've done that, check again. Don't hesitate to use the SECEdit tool to test your security design.

Final Steps—Feedback

Whew! Well, we bet you're thinking that everything is all done now, right? Wrong! You need to ensure that the network stays secure by changing things around every once in a while. If you're a consultant, check back with the client from time to time and make sure that your design still meets their business needs. If you're a staff network administrator or engineer, it never hurts to give things a quick look every now and then. Check the auditing logs. Change the administrator passwords. Make sure nobody unauthorized has gotten into the network.

Catywhompus Construction Update

The discussion we've used was to "set the table" for the security chapters that follow, and how security applies to our sample company, Catywhompus. As an enterprise in a competitive industry, Catywhompus places a premium on having a secure network. As we dig into the security specifics over the next few chapters, you will learn, in great detail, how the security design applies to Catywhompus. But in the interim, this chapter, which serves as the introductory chapter for the designing security section of this book, highlights a few general security planning issues that Catywhompus has addressed:

- **User and account management** It is the intent of Catywhompus to, whenever possible, limit permissions assigned to individual user accounts.

- **Machine security** Catywhompus would like to physically secure each machine with the security cables that can be attached to machines.

- **Network and communications security** In addition to computer network security considerations, Catywhompus understands that there are telecommunications security considerations, such as changing the passwords frequently on voicemail system accounts.

- **PKI** By using Windows 2000 Professional workstations on a Windows 2000 network, Catywhompus can take advantage of advanced Windows 2000 security architectures such as PKI.

Chapter Review

There you have it, a warm welcome to the world of Windows 2000 security. This chapter sets the framework for you to proceed with security matters as both an MCSE candidate and a practicing MCSE professional.

A final thought on security. If you do need to make changes in your security plan as you go, that's okay. In fact, we'd expect to have to make regular tune-ups to the big picture. If you don't, you're probably not looking closely enough for problems. No security design is perfect. Just make sure you do everything in your power to keep the bad guys out. How, you ask? Keep reading.

Questions

Consider the following computer security problems with each of the following scenarios:

1. You forget to change the door locks of your businesss after an unfriendly employee termination.

2. You give a key to the doors of your business to a janitorial services firm that provides cleaning services at your site.

3. The computer consultant that you use has a key to your building and office for after-hours access.

Answers

Answers will vary, but should include the following:

1. Remember that an "inside" party, including current and past employees, with after-hours access (such as keys to a door) can represent a major security breach.

2. It's not uncommon to trace security breaches back to the cleaning staff from a janitorial company (some out-sourced personnel may surf the Internet on client computers during breaks, and so on).

3. It is important that you have a relationship based on considerable trust if you plan to issue an after-hours key to your computer consultant. Not only does the key give access, but the computer consultant likely has the knowledge to cause great damage.

Key Skill Sets

The following skill sets meet the Microsoft Objectives for the 70-220 exam:

- Understand the skill set required to design security for a Windows 2000 network.
- Understand the business aspects of designing Windows 2000 security.
- Understand the technical aspects of designing Windows 2000 security.
- Understand the life cycle of a security design.

Key Terms

Group accounts

Internet Protocol Security (IPSec)

Intruder

Machine accounts

Public Key Infrastructure (PKI)

SECEdit

Security life cycle

User accounts

PART II

Analyzing Business and Technical Requirements

This chapter covers the following key mastery goals:

- Understand the business-specific factors that affect your security plan's strategic objectives
- Understand the technology-specific factors that influence your tactical choices in meeting those security objectives
- Understand the people-specific factors that may limit your security strategy and tactics

"Web Site Hacked!" screams one headline. "Thousands of Credit Card Numbers Stolen!"

Everyday, stories like these appear in a newspaper or on a Web site. The affected company races to engage damage control in the media, while belatedly trying to find out what happened, how to minimize the damage, and how to fix the problem so it will never happen again.

Meanwhile, behind the scenes, the Windows 2000 MCSE in the IT organization gets a personal visit from a corporate vice president who wants to know why this happened, why protective measures weren't in place, and why the Windows 2000 MCSE is just standing there talking when this person should be off fixing something. Hopefully, any Windows 2000 MCSE is smart enough to realize this isn't the time to point out that he or she has been advocating stronger security measures for the last year, but haven't been able to get past the infernal internal politics. Instead, it's likely this person (not willing to argue with a business executive) takes a deep breath, sighs, and says, "I'll get on it right away."

Sound familiar?

It should. More than ever, IT professionals are being required to know all about security and how to implement it. Yet most professionals have never participated in an arms-length, unbiased, thoroughly researched security analysis for any given company, much less the one they work for. Instead, security is typically a reactive process; new services are added to the company's Web site, corporate mergers and acquisitions happen with lightning speed, and whole divisions are right-sized out of existence. Through it all, the IT staff is scrambling to keep up with continuous corporate demands for new hardware and software that incidentally has to be easy to use and has to be online tomorrow. Somewhere in this organized chaos, you are supposed to implement "security," whatever that is. Want to bet that nobody has a common understanding of what security is, what it should be, and what the options are for your organization?

Not a pretty picture, is it? Let's take a breather from this nightmare, take a step back, and consider some of the factors that make up security. This chapter will use broad brushstrokes to cover a large amount of area—enough to make you aware of what should be considered when designing a corporate security plan. Later chapters will delve into specifics and show you how to put the plan into action using Windows 2000 tools and technologies. To use a wartime analogy, we are engaging in the battle for security. Your corporate security plan will identify the strategic objectives in this battle, and Windows 2000 will provide the tactical means you'll use to achieve those objectives.

Defining Security in the Enterprise

Stripped of the confusion, mysticism, and paranoia that normally accompany the word, security is really just about protecting yourself or your business against loss. That's it.

When most people think about security, they think of passwords and identification badges, burglar alarms, night security guards, and large steel doors on bank vaults. They don't think about crashed hard drives, flooded server rooms, stolen laptops, unpatched software, or yellow sticky notes with passwords written on them. Security isn't a discrete planning element that can be labeled and managed under a single umbrella, like accounting. It is more of a pervasive way of thinking and a set of technologies that impacts all areas of business (a starting point is the basic business network displayed in Figure 7-1). It is also a system with a single point of failure: If one security element is compromised, then loss occurs or is highly likely to occur. You, as an IT professional, must be aware of all the points of failure in the enterprise and understand the strong and weak points before you can create your strategic plan.

Here are some questions you should ask to help define security requirements for any given business:

Figure 7-1
Viewing a business
network

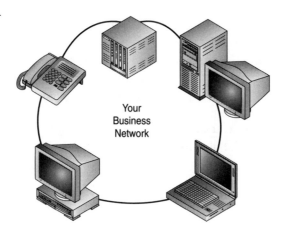

Your
Business
Network

- *What can the business afford to lose?* The nature and volume of the business will help identify key data sources and services, as will thinking about the business factors discussed later in this chapter. For instance, accounting information is almost always critical to the success and operation of any business, and even one day's loss of data means a severe negative impact to the company's ability to do business. In contrast, not having access to forms for ordering office supplies probably won't send a company spiraling into bankruptcy.

- *How long can the business go without a service?* One day's data from a Web-based commerce site could make or break the business, while Internet access for internal employees is probably not as crucial. You need to ask questions and find out how critical various information and services are to the business. Some companies may need internal Web access all the time (a brokerage house or a news bureau). Most companies may not think that e-mail is a critical business system, but ask around. These days, most businesses rely heavily on e-mail to keep in touch with suppliers, trading partners, business ventures, and financial institutions. Don't overlook services like instant messaging just because "everybody knows" that IM is only used for chat rooms. What about the tech support teams, online catalog shopping assistants, and the help desk and security personnel? Don't assume anything. Ask!

- *What contingency plans or systems are in place?* It's a sad truth that there are very few crisis planning or contingency procedures in place at most businesses. You will need to ask your co-workers to find out what they know and establish a procedural baseline. If Sarah is the only person in your department who knows how to restore the Web server in case of failure, what are you going to do on that tragic day when the server crashes, a flood washes out the bridge and power lines between Sarah's home and work, and the new kid Phil is the only one who can make it in to the office? Don't laugh—this scenario happened to someone, somewhere, every day last year. Ask anyone in IT about his or her favorite "war story," and you will be bombarded with examples. The odds of having one happen to you are quite good.

These generalities give you a starting point for discussing and analyzing a business's security needs. You should also use a systematic approach that goes into the security factors in more detail. The rest of this chapter is devoted to discussing these several security factors and helping give you ideas of questions to ask.

Evaluating Business Factors That Affect Security Planning

Every business's key asset is information. Information about customers, information about products, information about financial plans—all these are unique to each business and have value to the business and its competitors. This information could involve trade secrets, customer lists, pending litigation, source code, patented business methods, or supplier contracts with pricing information. At the end of the day, how well a business uses and guards this information determines whether it will open for business the following day.

When you are performing a security evaluation or audit for a company, you should know as much about the company as possible. You can't make recommendations in a vacuum, and if you propose a security plan without knowing how the business works, you will be shot down by a VP who smoothly states, "We can't do that because our partnership with VeryBigCo means we have to keep those ports open on our router in order to exchange information." You don't want to be on the feeble end of that conversation, do you?

This section of the book focuses on two areas: (1) analyzing business models and (2) analyzing business factors. You can get the information you need for both types of analysis from the following sources:

- **The corporate business plan**   This is one document all businesses should have. It basically sets forth these simple ideas: "Here's how we're going to make money. Here's what we need to do. Here's what we have to work with. Here's what we need." The business plan is used to obtain financing, plan the company's next fiscal year, and drive the business processes that will help everyone make money and go home at night better off than they were before.

- **Corporate annual and quarterly reports**   If your company is publicly traded on a stock exchange, you can learn a lot about what it does for a living by reading its financial statements for the preceding period. This will give you an idea about what types of business it's in, what markets are pursued, who its strategic partners are, and perhaps who the competition is.

- **Department and division executives**   These are the people who make the wheels go round and who handle the big-picture vision for their area of the company. You can talk with them to gain insight on what is currently going on, what is planned for the future, and whom they work with internally and externally.

- **Corporate literature, Web site, and marketing brochures**   These will have a lot of information in them about the company and what its business is. (Yes, you can find helpful information in marketing literature. Sometimes you just have to dig very, very deep.) White papers and corporate success stories can tell you about specific incidents that illustrate what the products are and how they help customers work better.

- **Previous consultant reports or security analyses**   The odds are good that you're not the first person asked to evaluate the business. Previous reports can be helpful to either confirm your findings or point out new areas of investigation. They can also help you determine how willing the company is to undergo corrective action if it's needed.

Analyzing the Existing and Planned Business Models

The corporation's current business model will tell you a lot about what's important to the company and how it plans to make money. This will identify the key technologies or information that make the company valuable to its investors and employees. Is the business focused around manufacturing? Or is it software? Do internal service departments contribute to the bottom line (or are they cost centers such as general management), or is the corporation set up solely as a service provider? You will need to ask these questions and get answers to them before you can identify what the corporation considers its information gold mine.

Analyzing the Company Model and the Geographical Scope

You need to take a look at the applicable business model, as this will identify new areas of investigation. There are numerous forms a business can take, such as a corporation, partnership, wholly owned subsidiary, joint venture, and sole proprietorship. These have very different means of conducting business and are subject to different operational rules. The interrelationship of different business entities means that each will likely have its own set of security concerns and different priorities, many of which will conflict.

Business-Model Impact on Day-to-Day Operations

We once worked for a company that was a venture capital–funded start-up. It was a corporation that held intellectual property assets it purchased from a bankruptcy proceeding, and it was engaged in a joint venture with a second company that produced electronic components built using the intellectual property of our company. Our company also handled all the product-marketing and business-development functions.

This particular business model and business relationship meant that neither company held the upper hand, and neither company trusted the other. This effectively kept both companies from exchanging information, from exchanging documents such as requirements specifications or product plans, or even from allowing e-mail between people in the two companies without "upper management review." This was a dysfunctional business model, yet it drove the security plan and mandated what would be made available and what would be kept private.

Geographic models will also have an impact on your security analysis. Geographic spread can include regional, national, international, subsidiary, and branch or field office operations, each of which needs to be considered both independently and as part of a larger whole. Any geographic model (see Figure 7-2) that spans multiple time zones—and sometimes even just area codes—will have security implications, such as time synchronization between servers, task schedules, such as server backups, and desktop application licensing. For example, some truly large multinational corporations have enough clout to negotiate "follow-the-sun" client licenses, rather than much more costly per-desktop or per-user license models. Managing the licenses as they "flow" from site to site will be a major IT concern.

Also, internationalization and localization considerations must be made if your business spans multiple countries. In some cases, you may not find applications that support particular code pages (use of keyboard characters and symbols) that are needed by users in one country, and so data passed between these countries may not be

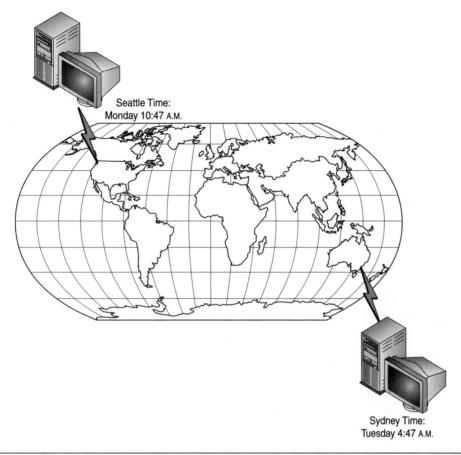

Seattle Time:
Monday 10:47 A.M.

Sydney Time:
Tuesday 4:47 A.M.

Figure 7-2   Thinking globally from an IT viewpoint

readable or usable. There are also issues with products using encryption—what levels of encryption are permissible are determined by the local government (and even the U.S. government that limits what encryption standards can be exported). See the "Identifying Relevant Laws and Regulations" section a bit later in this chapter for more on this.

Analyzing Business Factors That Influence Company Strategies

Although business models and geographical scope tend to be strategic and will be unchanged for a long time, other factors are more tactical and will likely change over the course of a year. These factors will have an impact on how a company does business; few businesses can design and develop new products overnight, can retool a factory to meet market whims, or can expand into new markets or geographic regions without affecting the corporate strategies. Thus, it will be your job to stay in tune with the near-term goals for your company and to change your security planning and security models accordingly.

Identifying Company Priorities

What are your company's priorities? You may see several broad concepts listed on the company's intranet Web site or printed communications, but they generally boil down to just a few major ideas: maintain or increase market share, increase revenue, or increase profitability. (If you are an MBA, you can stop snickering at our simplified description; this is for folks who have never read a business plan before.) You may see all of these listed in one business plan, but be aware that they frequently conflict with each other—it's very, very difficult to both increase your market share while increasing profitability. It costs far more money to get new customers than it does to retain existing customers, so expenses rise proportionately.

You can identify business priorities using a very simple guideline: How much money will the business spend on each item in the business plan? Most businesses won't toss a lot of money at an idea without some type of risk analysis or calculations of return on investment. If a company says a product is strategically important, but they spend less than one percent of the budget on it, then you have a rough idea as to how important it is to the company (and, by extension, to its investors). If your company is nervous about making this information available, then obtaining specific financial information may not be possible. However, you can still get a rough idea by talking to other people in the company and using the corporate grapevine to find out what's hot and what's not.

Identifying the Projected Growth and Growth Strategy

A company's growth strategy will tell you a lot about how the executives see the future. A growth strategy can be as simple as "increase revenue by 10 percent per year," or as complex as "divest unprofitable divisions while reducing risk from hostile takeovers or leveraged buyouts." The company could be striving towards an IPO, which means installing executives with solid management histories and revamping internal procedures to have them conform to industry best practices. Or it could be pursuing an exit strategy that is simply to cash out when a good bidder comes along. This information will help you determine the company's overall health and how management intends to keep doing business.

Identifying Competitors and Competitive Situations

"You can tell a lot about a man by the enemies he keeps." This is especially true in business, where new companies and products spring up overnight with an eye toward getting some of that market share you are so jealously protecting.

Who are the competitors in your market space? Are you the big kahuna or the underdog? Do you rely on marketing to provide competitive differentiation in a field filled with look-alikes and imitators? Do you offer products that are viewed as commodities, or are your products or services unique or difficult to develop and produce? All these questions are helpful in identifying the view your customers have of the marketplace in general, and your company specifically.

This view helps provide some objectivity to balance out internal corporate optimism, and it gives some insight into the soundness of the overall business plan. For example, if no one else is doing what your company is proposing, it's usually not because no one else thought of doing it. In most cases, there are reasons why no one else is getting into that business—there is poor return on investment, the products are difficult or expensive to develop, or the business model has failed before. Take a good, hard look at the competitive landscape to discover if there really is opportunity there or just a heap of fool's gold.

Identifying Relevant Laws and Regulations

What a surprise: Businesses have to operate by all kinds of laws and regulations. These can come from many sources and will usually be determined by the local and national government. These laws govern the forms a business can take, how a business can operate, the protections and penalties that apply, employer-employee relationships, and what taxes are collected.

All these regulations can be tricky, which is why interpretation and compliance with these regulations nearly always require an expert in that area. Manufacturing and heavy industry have environmental regulations to comply with, Internet-based sales may need to collect local taxes, and even service businesses need to worry about which cities, counties, and townships they are licensed to practice in.

If you are involved in a multinational corporation or are purchasing or selling software, you need to worry about import/export regulations and encryption levels. The United States used to have a very restrictive policy on what cipher or key strength could be exported to other countries. The maximum used to be 40-bit encryption, which is not strong in terms of computing cycles needed to crack it when compared to 128-bit encryption. Exporting 40-bit encryption required quite a bit of paperwork with the U.S. government, including submission of the software for review. 128-bit encryption was strictly controlled and special exemptions were required to ship this encryption level overseas. Recently, the policy has been relaxed somewhat, so that 128-bit encryption products may be exported to other countries. However, there is still paperwork that must be filed with the government prior to shipment, and approval must be received before making the product available for export.

Encryption levels also become important in larger corporations or when you are doing business with international partners (see Figure 7-3). They may not be able to use strong encryption software for trading-partner links and may not be able to use a business channel that requires strong encryption for data exchange.

For all of these legal and regulatory factors, you need to talk to an expert, either within the company or hired from outside the company, to conduct a review and discuss the implications of local and national regulations. Ignorance of the law is no excuse. Exercise your due diligence in this area.

Identifying the Company's Tolerance for Risk

Some companies are risky by nature; they are new to the market, with untried products or services, and they hope to turn a profit before any financing or funding runs out. Others are risk-tolerant and are capable of funding new or ongoing operations without being crippled by downturns in revenue. Still others are risk-adverse, seeking to have stable revenues or profits year after year. Banks and insurance companies are risk-adverse; your typical dot-com start-up lives with lots of risk. By looking at a company's risk tolerance, you can get a good feel for where they place the most value. Naturally, you want to ensure that your paycheck keeps coming in, so it is never out of place to inquire about a business's stability and risk tolerance.

Figure 7-3 You will need to understand what encryption levels are permissible overseas.

Identifying the Total Cost of Operations

Although the total cost of operations (TCO) is sometimes overlooked, it helps you understand what funding has been allocated for IT matters. Budget wars are never pretty, especially when you are faced with implementing two different mission-critical projects with only finite people and funding available. If your department is expected to "just do it," but you are not given the ability to make it happen, then your chances of success are very slim indeed.

Analyzing the Organizational Structures, Including Staffing

It often helps to look at how the company is formed into groups: the corporate management and administration organization; the production and services divisions; the third-party vendor, partner, and customer relationship management, including technical support; sales and marketing organizations; and, of course, the IT infrastructure group. Traditional management models group common functions together into a department or division. Newer styles, such as matrix management or virtual teams, will group along product or task lines, with members from other organizations taking part in the management and development efforts. Each group will commonly require access to the same sets of business information, will require similar resource management and service management, and will be able to restrict access from other groups. This concept is displayed in Figure 7-4.

Additionally, in all these groups, there are hirings and layoffs, rapid growth or absorption into other existing groups during reorganization, vacations and sick leave, and other people-oriented changes. These changes will require you to respond quickly to ordinary changes, such as adding a new user account or helping integrate two businesses during a merger-and-acquisition phase.

Analyzing Company Processes

Analyzing company processes is a fancy way of looking at how stuff moves between organizational groups. These processes include information flow, communication flow, service and product life cycles, and decision-making trees that span multiple groups. From a high-level perspective, just knowing that Marketing wants to roll out a customer-relationship management (CRM) application will give you a heads-up that major changes are afoot in how data is made available to customers.

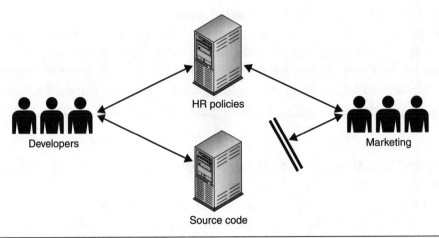

Figure 7-4   You will need to appreciate all of the users of business information and how that business information is used.

Evaluating Your Technology Options in Security Planning

It doesn't do any good to identify factors that impact security if you can't do anything about them. Technology is an equal-opportunity enabler. It enables businesses to create new and useful ways of sharing information, while at the same time allowing unauthorized access and use of that information. In a Zen-like manner, technology provides the same tools for the good guys to make security and for the bad guys to break it.

At a very high level, security planning involves six attributes. By an amazing stroke of luck, these attributes all begin with the letter "A" and provide an easy mnemonic for security planners everywhere:

- **Access**   Access formerly referred to physical access to a server or to network equipment where someone had control over the machine itself, including power switches, floppy drives, and hard disks. In today's networked environment, access also refers to availability over the Internet, because someone could gain remote control to the piece of network equipment.

- **Authentication**   This usually requires you to have two out of three pieces of information: who you say you are (identification), something you know (shared secret or password), and something you are (biometrics, such as fingerprints or voice scans). The bottom line is that you're either authenticated or you're not, as shown in Figure 7-5. Companies today are increasingly relying upon smart cards and biometric technology to help provide secure authentication.

- **Authorization**   Authorization is the means of restricting access to only those users who have permission. Everyone may be authorized to see the online HR manual, but not everyone is authorized to see HR's list of people's salaries.

- **Accuracy**   Accuracy of data is simply another way of saying that you need to keep data free from tampering. This means that a person or process should not be able to change data without permission, and the data should remain intact when moving between applications. In some cases, data accuracy may also involve encryption; if encrypted data comes through garbled, the chances are good that the data has been compromised or changed somehow.

- **Accountability** (also called Auditing)   Accountability involves keeping a log or record of certain actions and events in your network. For instance, an unusually high number of failed login attempts on a user account usually means that the account is being hacked. Accountability also provides for non-repudiation—you can prove someone received the money if the check cleared his or her bank.

- **Administration**   The difficult part for security measures is, of course, administration. Being able to implement, manage, monitor, and modify security attributes across an enterprise requires both technical sophistication for the administrator and sufficiently robust and powerful tools. You could include Analysis as another factor to consider in this list, though we consider it to be a part of Administration.

Figure 7-5
Depicting an
authenticated and
unauthenticated
user

User ID: SLaPlume
Password: ++++++++

User ID: VLaPlume
Password: ++++++++

These six attributes help provide a framework for analyzing the technical security capabilities of a given enterprise or company. Try using these attributes as a starting point the next time you're asked to provide a security analysis for a company.

Where Security Is a Slogan!

One of our consulting opportunities was for a small law firm that shared office space with other tenants. In surveying the office, we found that the network server was sitting physically unsecured in the same room as the photocopier and office supplies. We went up to the mouse, bumped it, and—surprise!—the screen saver disappeared and we were logged in as Administrator. A quick look showed that this server held confidential client information as well as the Exchange mail server and backup financial data from an accounting program.

We told the managing partner (who also wore a hat as the office network administrator) that she needed to lock up the server or, at the very least, secure the screen saver with a password. Her reply: "I'm not worried about that; no one here is that smart about computers." After we picked our jaws up off the floor, we put our recommendations in writing, bold face and italics, in our network survey.

About a year later, she caught one of the "not very smart" co-tenants surfing some very questionable Web sites on the company server. Based on the cookie files, it looked like he'd been doing it for three months before getting caught. She's still not sure whether the tenant viewed or changed any confidential data; no word on whether she finally enabled that screen-saver password or not.

As an IT professional, it is your job to understand technology and its impact on business information. The specific information presented in the following two sections, "Analyzing the Physical and Information-Security Models," and "Understanding the Logical Layout of Services and Applications," are not exhaustive or exclusive, but illustrative of some ways you need to analyze business information and its coexisting infrastructure.

Analyzing the Physical and Information-Security Models

At its core, your network is a collection of interconnected devices, servers, and applications that provide services, data, or both. When you connect your network to other networks, you make those services and data instantly available to those other networks, unless you implement some form of security.

What is challenging about the Internet is that it was designed to be as open and flexible as possible. Because it is so open, many access points into a company exist that aren't monitored or shut down to prevent unauthorized access. These access points can include modem banks for remote access, unsecured Web servers, FTP servers, router ports left open for tech-support troubleshooting, and remote-control software loaded on a user's desktop.

Before you can create an effective security plan, you must analyze the ways that information can enter your company and ways that information can leave your company. The connections between the network and the outside world, and the connections to other sites, are a starting point in analyzing your company's security plans.

Analyzing the Network Architecture and Its Connection Points

Companies have many different ways to connect their information infrastructure to the outside world. They may use dedicated leased lines, DSL lines, wireless connections, high-speed satellite links, or BISYNC connections between trading partners. These are just a few of the ways that information flows between people outside your company and people within your company. Data and services may also be accessed through dial-up lines into your network that enable users to gain access to their e-mail or to work with files on a server share.

The first place to start is to draw a network schematic or architecture diagram. In a small company, this will be a fairly simple task; in a larger company, this task may be best handled by automated software that diagrams the network structure for you. Many companies have added hardware and software without much thought to the infrastructure, usually as a reaction to changing business conditions. Perhaps marketing needed a new server for its projects, or accounting was running out of room for its financial application. In some cases, especially in medium-sized companies, it may be impossible to draw a diagram that accurately represents how all the pieces interrelate. In that case, you should start at the known entry points into your network, such as a router connecting you to an ISP. From there, you can make a diagram of computers and servers that are directly connected to the outside world and determine which applications and services may be at risk. An example of this is displayed in Figure 7-6.

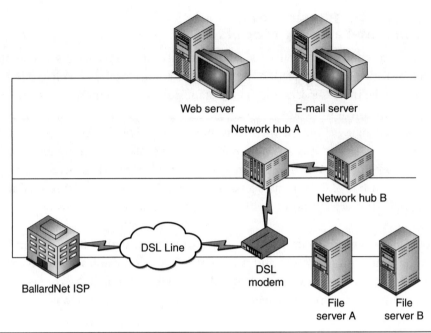

Web server   E-mail server

Network hub A

Network hub B

DSL Line

BallardNet ISP

DSL modem

File server A   File server B

Figure 7-6   A network schematic

This diagram becomes especially important when you make services and data available to people outside your company. Common sense dictates that you only make available the specific data and services that are needed by your suppliers, trading partners, or customers. At the very least, you should have a firewall between the applications and servers that are exposed to the outside world and your internal business systems and confidential or proprietary data. Many companies create a demilitarized zone (DMZ) that has a firewall between the outside world and your server, and another between the server and your company. This gives you a greater degree of control over who has access to your data, and it isolates your internal network from your exposed servers.

However, none of this will be possible if you don't know which servers are vulnerable. Find out how your company connects to the outside world, and then find out how information might move between the two. If you're lucky, someone will have made a network diagram already, and you can compare the diagram to your existing network architecture. Then you can begin analyzing the network for any obvious vulnerable places.

The second area to look at is the type of network protocols you are carrying. Most networks today use TCP/IP as the protocol of choice; however, many networks still use IPX for their internal networks, with NetWare file and printer sharing systems, and companies with mainframes will use DLC to communicate between the workstation and the mainframe.

Each protocol has benefits and disadvantages. DLC and IPX are sometimes used in internal networks as one means of isolating the internal network from the Internet. Because a TCP/IP hack will not work on IPX, this adds an additional layer of security for businesses concerned about hackers gaining access to network resources. It also adds another layer of management and complexity, and introduces a different set of management systems and network requirements that may not be acceptable to a business wishing to consolidate on one system (that is, the multiple protocols are supported and managed for reasons such as interacting with multiple systems). Heterogeneous environments are on the way out in a general sense. It takes a lot of time (and thus, costs a lot of money) to maintain multiprotocol environments, and most companies are removing non-TCP/IP protocols from their networks.

In smaller companies, or in remote branch offices, NetBIOS or NetBEUI may be in heavy use. Those protocols are very fast and efficient where there are 25 or fewer workstations, but larger numbers of workstations increase the amount of local broadcast traffic and reduce overall performance. In addition, NetBIOS and NetBEUI have well-known and well-publicized vulnerabilities that make any network susceptible to attack from hackers. Most "serious" companies use TCP/IP rather than NetBIOS or NetBEUI for precisely that reason. If your network is running these protocols, you should seriously consider replacing them with TCP/IP.

Assessing the Available Connectivity Between Sites

Once you have completed a survey of your own network, you must do the same for any WANs your company uses, and any connections between your company and any trading partners or suppliers. If your company has offices in far-flung locations, you should make a diagram of how the sites interconnect, including any primary and backup connections between them. Do these connections pass information in clear text, or are the connections encrypted? Do you require any authentication, such as a user ID and password, or do you use certificates for authentication? This information will help determine whether any of your data is at risk when it moves between locations.

You should also determine how much information is flowing across your network. Your WAN may be supporting high amounts of data moving between sites, such as frequent database backups or file replication and synchronization. Heavy volumes can slow down other traffic, such as authentication for users and applications, or network management information, such as DNS zone replication. If your network is handling too much traffic, that can lead to problems, such as corrupted data, services timing out, and applications becoming unavailable. A complex WAN that might be subject to these management maladies is displayed in Figure 7-7.

You can also use a network sniffer to determine what type of traffic is moving across your LAN and WAN. You may be surprised to find out what traffic your network is carrying; you may find that Napster is in heavy use or that someone is running a Web server without your knowledge.

Some companies may not have a dedicated hardware sniffer in order to analyze network protocol traffic. Fortunately, both Windows NT and Windows 2000 have simple network-monitor utilities that can be used to detect what type of traffic is moving over the network.

Understanding the Logical Layout of Services and Applications

Any good survey of network services and applications includes both a physical schematic of interconnected networks and a logical diagram that overlays the physical one. This is an important step in your security assessment and is expanded upon in the

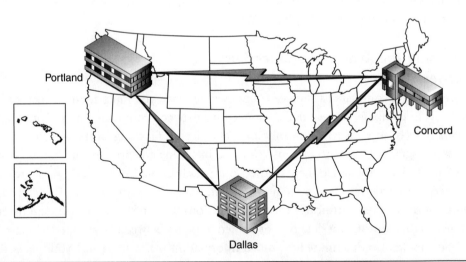

Figure 7-7 A complex WAN requires more management to resolve performance problems than smaller and simpler networks.

following sections: "Assessing Systems and Applications," "Analyzing the Method of Accessing Data and Systems," "Identifying Upgrades and Rollouts," "Analyzing Network and Systems Management," "Reviewing Security Threats and Hacking Methods," "Analyzing Your Security Design," and "Analyzing the Technical and IT Support Structure."

Assessing Systems and Applications

For all its apparent complexity, hardware inventory and analysis can be fairly easy. You can walk into a wiring closet or go into the server room and get a rough idea of which systems are in your environment. On the other hand, services and applications are much more difficult to identify. You must look at each machine and its operating system, determine which services and applications are running, and then determine an interrelationship between that machine and other machines in your environment. The problem is magnified because the machine may be providing a passive service, such as file or data storage. In those cases, it is not readily apparent how the passively stored data may be used in the enterprise.

In these cases, a mere service and application inventory may not be enough. You'll need to talk to people in your company, find out which applications and services they use on a daily basis, and then begin sketching in the interrelationships. It is likely you'll overlook something, and you'll need to adjust your plan later to accommodate a suddenly remembered application or set of data that is needed for an urgent report. This is why you will include full backups of all systems as part of your security plan.

When you are conducting your survey, don't overlook applications, such as mail server quotas and user data storage quotas, which address the way that applications are configured. Most administrators set limits on how much mail may be kept on a mail server, and most companies place quotas on how much storage is available to a user. These limits balance competing interests: the desirability of backing up frequently accessed and frequently changed data, and the desirability of keeping storage-space costs to a minimum.

Analyzing the Method of Accessing Data and Systems

How do your users get access to data and applications on your network? Are they limited to local logon access only, do they have browser-based access across the Internet, do they use dial-up access via RAS or a RADIUS server, or do they use VPN to tunnel into your network? Do they (God forbid) use some form of remote-control software running unencrypted over the Internet? Although there are probably good reasons for using any of these methods to access data on your network, some present greater security risks than others, and you'll need to identify these problem areas in your security plan.

Windows 2000 improves on security by providing better authentication and encryption mechanisms. However, if your users are using offline file synchronization on a laptop, you may have confidential documents and data walking out of your corporation every day that are subject to theft, inadvertent loss, or even malicious editing and changing of the data. In order to help your security planning, you can talk to end users or a few key individuals in your corporation about their daily habits and ways of using data or applications.

Lastly, there may be security and authentication systems in the enterprise that you may need to interoperate with. For example, some mainframe systems use a system called RACF that enables you to provide single sign-on capabilities for your users.

Identifying Upgrades and Rollouts

Few, if any, corporations have a static environment. Even though you may be designing a security plan from scratch, there are probably other plans for hardware and software upgrades in the works. Corporations may already have a desktop replacement system in place or may be planning a major rollout of new hardware along with Windows 2000 to hundreds or thousands of users in the enterprise. Smaller companies may be inadvertently using "stealth upgrades" to upgrade an operating system or an application, where an end user gets a copy of the new application and decides to install it on a work PC "just to see what it does." It doesn't take a genius to figure out that upgrading an operating system may be the single largest environmental change with the greatest potential for mischief-making. It is up to you and your security plan to account for present or future upgrades to operating systems and applications—it's not a question of whether it will happen, but when.

Changes, whether planned or unplanned, can have security implications, depending on the type of application. Users who subscribe to streaming media through the firewall require open ports to your network that may present a hazard to other data. In other words, all technical talk aside, an open port at a very basic level is a breach in the old barbed wire fence out on the ranch.

Consider this technical matter: Suppose other departments may be planning on rolling out a new collaborative application that uses peer-to-peer networking. You need to talk with end users and key individuals within different departments to find out what they are planning with regards to new applications and services.

Analyzing Network and Systems Management

Once you know what systems you have in your environment, you can plan how to manage the servers, applications, and data sources. Most networks already have tools and utilities to manage and monitor hardware and software; these tend to be underutilized, especially when there isn't a cohesive management strategy or security plan in place.

Although Windows 2000 contains a comprehensive set of programs and utilities for managing Windows 2000 and Windows NT servers and desktops, they are not a panacea for managing all the hardware and software in your environment. For instance, though Windows 2000 provides SNMP management and support, it still lacks the strength and robustness of an enterprise-wide SNMP management program. Your company may be using specialized tools to handle some of these network management tasks, such as router alerts, or you may find that you need a particular tool in order to provide some aspect of security for your network. As with any analysis area, you should engage in a cost/benefit analysis to determine whether the tool should be purchased immediately or put off until funding is available.

Networking system management is also important where there are quality-of-service arrangements between you and the service provider. If a service falls below bargained-for levels, you'll need documentation showing how long the service was below those levels. A combination of alerts and logging files will help you provide this information; of course, it's only useful if you know what the information means and how to take advantage of it.

One area that is sometimes overlooked involves data backups and disaster recovery. If a server goes down or a hard drive fries, how will you replace it? What about when the CEO deletes the only copy of a file and wants to recover a saved one from the previous night's backup? Do you have offsite storage for your backup tapes, or are the backups all sitting in the cabinet under the water pipe to the second floor? In effect, your servers are always the "bull's eye" for pending disasters and trouble (see Figure 7-8).

More than one IT executive has been fired for not having contingency or disaster plans in place, and not a few of those were fired because they had plans, but had never

Figure 7-8
Don't become complacent and ignore the fact that your servers are just one bad backup away from disaster.

tested them. You should include information on data recovery, uninterrupted power supplies (UPSs), disaster planning (or lack thereof), and hardware replacement in your analysis.

Reviewing Security Threats and Hacking Methods

It is possible to identify security holes merely by knowing which services and applications are open and available to others. However, it is not always possible to identify what types of attacks are possible, based on this information. For instance, a bug or flaw in a router's operating system can make your whole network susceptible to spoofed IP address attacks. Short of being the subject of an attack, the best way to learn about these security flaws and vulnerabilities is to maintain an accurate inventory of the hardware, software, and applications in your network, and then conduct some research on the Internet about your findings.

You will be surprised to find out how much information about your enterprise is readily available to hackers. Port scanners can find out which ports and services are available to people inside your enterprise and outside of it, "war dialers" can find out which telephone numbers have modem banks attached to them, and even some simple DNS queries to a name registrar can reveal IP address information about your routers, Web servers, and mail servers. Some of this information can be protected from discovery; other information must always be available in order for services to work across the Internet. It will be up to you and your security plan to define how much of this can be protected and what is an acceptable risk.

Uncovering this information is really the first phase of a concerted attack against an enterprise. Once a hacker discovers information about your network, such as which IP addresses and port numbers have significant network services running on them, an attack can be mounted against that machine or operating system based on known security holes or exploits (these would be widely published security holes or exploits). The ones most commonly reported in the news include denial-of-service attacks, buffer overflows, Trojan horse or remote-control exploits, and, of course, e-mail viruses of all shapes and flavors.

Knowing what your weaknesses are and where they are located is half the battle; finding out how to reduce or eliminate those weaknesses is the next major step in validating your security plan.

Analyzing Your Security Design

By now, you should have a good idea of what your environment looks like and how it works. Based on the factors we have discussed, you should also be able to formulate a security plan. As the saying goes, however, "no battle plan ever survives contact with the enemy." During the design and review process, you'll need to identify which solutions are feasible, which ones would be difficult or costly to implement, and which ones cannot be done due to technical or budget constraints. With that information in hand, you can prioritize the solutions that should be implemented based on a balance between the cost to implement and the security risk or severity of loss, should that weakness be exploited.

Analyzing the Technical and IT Support Structure

No security plan would be complete without an introspective look at your own capabilities. What tools do you have available, and which do you use on a day-to-day basis? How is your staffing—do you have the right skills and abilities in the right amounts to get the job done? Does your help desk keep answering the same questions over and over again, such as, "What is my password?" or "The server isn't responding—why not?" Answers to these questions will help you pinpoint where the trouble spots are with respect to managing the information infrastructure and will perhaps suggest a course of action toward improvement.

Understanding the People Factor in Security Planning

One of the least measurable, yet most significant, factors in any security plan is the effect it has on end users. If the restrictions are too complex or difficult, the average end user will try to circumvent them or just plain not use them. For instance, it may seem like a good idea to require complex passwords of 12 characters or longer, and require them to be changed every 30 days, but most users find this unworkable; they will write down the password on a yellow sticky note and keep it underneath a keyboard, stuck to the side of the drawer, or "hidden" on the next page of a Joke-a-Day desk calendar. This type of circumvention is common where a security plan is put into place without consulting with the people who are affected by it.

Security plans will always walk a fine line between implementing safety and security measures, and restricting the ability of people to do their business. If you want your security plans to succeed, you are strongly advised to consult with those who will be affected by your plan, and to discuss the risks and the options available. That way, you stand a better chance of getting a buy-in from the affected groups, and a better likelihood of having your plan implemented and your security procedures followed.

Analyzing Business and Security Requirements for the End User

There seem to be as many business and security requirements as there are users in the enterprise. Your typical CEO wants access to everything, all the time, with as little interference as possible. Your typical frontline end user wants the same thing. Your typical "power user" also wants the same thing, along with the ability to run new operating systems, play with Web servers, install and uninstall software with abandon, and have an instant reset button to automatically restore things when something goes wrong.

This is where your knowledge of the organizational structure with respect to network service and data availability becomes important. If you work in conjunction with groups of users who have similar needs, you can design a security plan that meets most of those needs for most of the users, and then deal with exceptions on a case-by-case basis. You may even be able to suggest new or easier ways for people to do their jobs without a lot of expense or retraining.

You will also face challenges when dealing with remote sites or users who use a laptop and are on the go all the time. Supporting these users' technical needs and keeping the connection and the data sufficiently secure will provide a significant challenge to your IT organization.

As with any organization, spend time with the end users who will be affected by your plan, and collaboratively design a solution that meets everyone's needs. Be aware that not everyone will be completely happy with any compromise that is reached, and that some inconvenience may be a part of the solution. The objective is to get a buy-in from all affected groups, including upper management. Without that buy-in, you stand a good chance of having your plan circumvented, ignored, or shelved.

Analyzing Network Roles and Responsibilities

If you have done your homework, you will have defined the various business organizations and user groups, and their need for network resources and applications. The intersections and relationships between network roles and responsibilities help define what types of network accesses are required and what roles each group in the organization will play in your network structure.

For instance, your company may observe a rigid hierarchy based on department membership. That means you can assign roles and responsibilities based on membership in a particular department. Other companies may have membership based on site location or geography. Still others may use a combination of the two, where membership is determined both by site location and by membership in a particular group within the organization (see Figure 7-9). There are also companies whose organizations are determined

Figure 7-9
Considering what
business factors
impact directory
services

Organization by
Geography

Irvine, CA   New York City

Organization by
Department

Marketing   Development

not by geography or by hierarchy, but by matrix-management or dotted-line reporting into a project-specific tiger team. It will be part of your responsibility to determine the center relationships and resolve conflicts that may arise.

The single best thing anyone can do is spend a lot of time up front understanding the business and planning what the directory structure will look like. Active Directory is powerful and flexible, and will hurt you if you don't do your homework. Active Directory design and implementation goals were presented in the first section of this book that focused on the 70-219 exam.

To make your life even more interesting, you shouldn't look just at relationships between people and groups; you must also look at the interrelationships between applications and services on the network. Applications and services will need to authenticate to a security provider, such as a Web-based application requiring authentication against an SQL Server account. Don't forget the legendary anonymous user account that many applications install by default, and which should be included on your "hotspots to watch" list.

Typical roles you may encounter include administrator, user, service, resource owner, and application. Most operating systems install default groups with default sets of rights, and you may find that some companies seldom change these groups or authorizations. Other companies may have wildly differing groups and user rights with conflicting and overriding sets of permissions and authorizations. If you can, figure out how they interrelate; if you can't, consider working with the affected groups to help define a clean and more streamlined set of roles and authorizations.

"Who Do You Want to Be Like?"

One of the companies we've had the pleasure of working for had one of the most confusing ways of determining permissions and authorizations. They had experienced fairly rapid growth and had added both remote offices and internal servers and resources at an almost explosive rate. It was a mixed environment, with Windows NT file servers, Novell NetWare file and print servers, and a host of other stand-alone machines with frequently accessed resources. When we joined the company, we found we needed access to several servers within the development organization. We sent an e-mail to the IT help desk asking if we could be added to the developer group so we could gain access to servers. They sent us back an e-mail asking, "Who do you want to be like?"

We resisted the urge to fire off a witty response and went to the help desk in person. After a few moments of surreal conversation, we found out that they didn't assign permissions based on group membership; instead, they copied a user account with permissions similar to those you wanted, renamed it, and modified it further if you had additional specialized needs. They had no easy way of telling who had access to what, or whether any of the users could be placed into a group with similar access needs.

Sadly, we don't think this method is that uncommon. If your organization is like this, we wish you luck should you ever want to rename a server that is accessed by many people.

Evaluating Specific Security Vulnerabilities

Although you should consider a lot of factors when evaluating a company's security, there are specific ones you will see repeatedly that should be a part of your security plan. These specific vulnerabilities can have a very narrow scope; others will span multiple factors or have very broad-reaching implications.

One of the main reasons you will see these come up repeatedly is because anyone looking to exploit security weaknesses will probably go after these areas. They are ones that are either widespread, easy to exploit, or have a high rate of success. You can use a similar method to evaluate these factors and provide some form of measurement when consulting with a client. The formula is

$$\text{Degree of risk} = [(\text{severity of loss}) + (\text{likelihood of attack})]/2$$

where both severity of loss and likelihood of attack are measured on a scale of 1 to 10 (1 being low, 10 being high). For example, the likelihood that someone would try a social engineering attack against your company may be low (give it a 6) and the severity of loss, should it succeed, is high (give it a 10). This gives you a risk factor of 8, which puts the risk at the high end of the scale. If you evaluate specific vulnerabilities using this method, it gives you and your client a prioritized list of vulnerabilities. Then work your way down the list, proposing ways to plug holes, fix walls, and educate customers on technical and non-technical solutions.

A word of advice: If you are a consultant on technical security matters, you are almost always assured of repeat business. *Every* system has vulnerabilities, and new exploits are created every day. You will never have a dull day as a security consultant!

The following sections identify several standard security risks.

Lack of IT Staff Education

Likelihood of attack	10
Severity of loss	10
Risk factor	10

The number one challenge is to get the IT staff up to speed on security matters. Every day that goes by without any training or education is a day fraught with risk. Your company will incur loss, whether through misplaced passwords, deleted files with no backups, or insecure systems. If your IT staff is inexperienced or new to the IT role, your first priority is getting the staff trained to prevent the obvious problems, and then later work on fixing the long-term problems.

For administrative staff that are not new to IT, but may be unfamiliar with new attacks and vulnerabilities, numerous Web resources and books cover security. See the end of this chapter for a resource starter kit. Subscriptions to security newsletters or e-mail listservers providing immediate information and updates should be mandatory, while a one-day training class on security issues should be required of everyone who is responsible for the day-to-day maintenance of the IT infrastructure. Hands-on training should be provided to anyone who works with network-specific equipment, such as routers, CSU/DSU equipment, and telephony or modem banks. Here is a list of ways and means to stay current with security topics:

- Subscribe to security bulletins, listservers, and newsletters.
- Provide classroom training on security issues.
- Provide hands-on training for network and telephony technicians.
- Read books on security practices, hacks, and countermeasures.

Ineffective, Incomplete, or Missing Corporate Security Policies

Likelihood of attack	9
Severity of loss	9
Risk factor	9

Many companies do not have official security policies. Instead, they have relied upon measures put into place as a reaction to events as they occur. For example, a company may have a policy to protect classified documents, but may lack a policy for destroying documents once they become obsolete. This can result in employees just throwing documents out in the garbage, where someone may "dumpster dive" and obtain valuable company information.

A company may also lack policies regarding personal versus company usage and be unclear about whether employees can use company assets for personal use. It is important to set out the rights that employees can expect with respect to Internet surfing, e-mail usage, Internet messaging, and shareware. If only authorized applications are to be used on company systems, then it would be a violation of company policy to install a screen saver or shareware application from the Internet that has not been approved by management. Your company may require that this be enforced in a systematic way using group policies, or your company could rely on the honor system as a means of enforcement. Which is it, and do your users know about it?

Company security policies also extend to passwords, access to server rooms and network cabling rooms, discussing company business in public places, laptop usage at home and on the road, palmtop or PDA device usage, and other technologies. A good company security policy will address these areas:

- Physical security
- Information protection and disposal
- Clean desk policy
- Internet access
- Public area behavior
- Laptop security
- Telecommuting policy
- Cell phones
- PDA usage

Thus, you should review existing security policies and procedures to see how they address these areas. Ideally, you should be able to test the policies to see how well they work, and then determine the degree of risk presented by the existing policy. You can then make recommendations based on your findings. This list summarizes these immediate sentiments:

- Review policies
- Evaluate findings
- Determine risk

User Education

Likelihood of attack	8
Severity of loss	10
Risk factor	9

Once you have a set of security policies in place, you need to communicate that information to the end user. You need to discuss the importance of these policies with the employees and help them understand their role in keeping company information safe. Although you can just mail out a link to the company policy posted somewhere on the intranet Web site, a better education program involves multiple means of education. A written policy is good, but a show-and-tell meeting is better. You can demonstrate how to use security programs and features, with specific examples of compliance and noncompliance behavior. For instance, one security training session we conducted had a mock-up desk, complete with computer, monitor, and personal memorabilia. The computer was hooked up to an overhead projector so that everyone could follow along with any programs we used during the demonstration.

Our first demonstration had four different ways to guess the password to gain entry into the system. We asked volunteers in the audience to come up and try simple techniques to gain access. Of the three volunteers, only one of them was able to find one of the four ways. The method she found? Using the default password "12345" that everyone was issued when they first joined the company. So the first problem was not having changed our password. Here were the other three ways:

- The password was taped to the underside of the keyboard.
- Our wives first names were the passwords.
- Our favorite sport (sailing) was the password.

We were then able to point out how easy it was to guess the password using a few simple tricks, and that probably half the audience was at risk for having their account hacked. It was then a simple matter of suggesting that they should change their passwords or remove the little reminders they had scattered around their offices and cubes.

You should also provide education on how to recognize "social engineering." Social engineering is one of the most effective methods of gaining access to information and to breach the security perimeter of your enterprise. Social engineering usually involves subterfuge or impersonation of someone in your enterprise, usually of a help desk technician. This person will contact an unsuspecting employee in your company and persuade the victim to hand over user identification and password information, often on the pretext of conducting troubleshooting or virus-prevention measures. The poor victim, having no reason to distrust the person on the other end of the phone, hands over the information, convinced they are doing a good thing. This is the same as handing over the keys to the kingdom, especially if the user has elevated rights to systems or information within the company. Natural targets for social engineering include executive assistants or administrators to company officers, accounting department personnel, research assistants, and other people who may have access to sensitive information.

Finally, make sure you provide education on the mechanism used to report non-compliant behavior from colleagues, anything suspicious or unusual. There should be a way for employees to report security lapses or system behavior that just doesn't feel quite right. That way, you are encouraging them to report irregularities that may affect everyone, such as a sudden virus attack or a hacker bringing down a Web site. These points are summarized as

- Communicate company security policies.
- Stress the importance of security for everyone.
- Provide instruction on using security tools and programs.
- Provide examples of good and poor security.
- Provide education on social engineering.
- Provide a reporting mechanism.

Proactive Anti-Hacking Measures

Likelihood of attack	10
Severity of loss	10
Risk factor	10

It is not a question of if you will be hacked, but when. Today's hacking tools can run against large numbers of IP hosts, logging security vulnerability findings for later exploitation. Large sites make especially good targets; for some, the lure of hacking a Web page or crashing a Web site via denial-of-service attacks is too good to resist. If your business connects to the Internet in any way, you are guaranteed to encounter some type of hacking attempt within minutes of making a connection.

Most initial hacking attempts are launched with the idea of exploiting well-known vulnerabilities. Several software packages are out there that, when installed in a default configuration, provide an open door for hackers to walk right in. Fortunately, these attacks can be prevented by installing the necessary security patches. When you conduct a hardware and software inventory, make sure you note all applicable version numbers. Then go to the Internet sites listed at the end of this chapter, and do a search for those products; if there are any security breaches and patches available, they will be noted there. Obtain the patches and install and test them on a system before you roll them out to the entire company. That way, you can be confident that the patches solve the problem, and that they do not destabilize any of your existing systems.

You should also disable any unnecessary services on your servers and close down any ports on your routers and firewalls that are not explicitly needed. A popular way to get hacking tools into your enterprise is by using an unsecured FTP server. By closing down FTP and not allowing it in your enterprise, you take away one of the key tools in a hacker's arsenal. For example, Microsoft provides white papers on how to harden IIS 5.0 and improve your Web server's security. You can find the link at www.microsoft.com/technet/security/iis5chk.asp. Additional security links can be found at the end of this chapter.

However, just putting locks on the door does not mean your house is safe. You also want to know if a burglar's rattling the knob or is attempting to open a window. In the IT world, you put in the equivalent of a burglar alarm: You set up audit logs that monitor specific events, such as failed logon attempts and port-scanning activities, and send alerts to a pager or send an e-mail notification to a security mail queue. These will provide you with the notification that somebody is knocking at the door, so to speak, and give you the opportunity to respond.

Finally, you should develop investigation and incident-response protocols. When an alert happens, who gets notified? How serious is the threat? Is it merely somebody forgetting a new password, or is it the leading edge of a denial-of-service attack? Depending on the nature and severity of the attack, you may need to notify several different groups in your company and work with security and law enforcement officials from other organizations. Make sure you brainstorm the different types of attacks and provide written guidelines for how you will respond to them. IT folks have a big advantage over hackers. They know, or should know, their own internal systems with great specificity and can determine weak points or failure scenarios. Yes, hackers will hack and will probably surprise someone. But if you use research, planning, and preventative measures, you can minimize or even defeat a hack before damage occurs. You read it here first. But seriously, these points are summarized as

- Install and test all security patches.
- Disable unnecessary services and close unneeded ports.
- Enable logging for key events.
- Monitor logs and alerts for suspicious log events.
- Develop investigation and incident-response protocols.

Disaster-Recovery Plan

Likelihood of attack	4
Severity of loss	10
Risk factor	7

Consider the following matters, as each question is related to disaster recovery planning (as we know from first-hand experience and observation). How well equipped is your company to withstand a disaster? What do you do if a Web server's hard drive crashes, or your e-mail server gets infected with a virus and fires off infected e-mails to everyone in the global address book? If the power goes out, do you have a UPS in the server room? What about your routers—are they on a UPS? When was the last time you made a complete backup of the company's data, and where is the backup stored? All of these areas qualify as disasters because they do not happen in the normal course of business, and they have the potential to do a great deal of damage or wreak a great deal of financial loss to your company.

In order to develop a disaster-recovery plan, you need to sit down with your IT team and brainstorm the types and scope of disaster incidents that could happen to your organization. Although this is a serious topic, have fun with it. Maybe a bus full of enraged protesting nuns won't shut off power to the campus, but a march or a protest could disrupt business or make access to certain buildings impossible. If you were cut off from the server room, would you still be able to manage the servers? Your disaster-recovery plan should outline the types of incidents you can expect, though not necessarily the causes.

Next, you should define disaster response teams and notification measures. Define the teams so that someone always has a backup in case you cannot reach the designated team leader. If the team is large, you should have a phone-tree contact system so that one person is responsible for making all the phone calls.

The next task is to document your recovery plans. The plans should be a step-by-step list that takes the team through recovery measures. Don't assume anything; include item names and descriptions, locations, configuration details, and diagrams where appropriate. A sentence like, "Get the backup server from the closet and plug it in," won't be much help to the new guy who has only been working in the group for a day when disaster strikes and who doesn't know where the closet is, much less which server is the backup server. Where possible, assign team members to particular tasks.

Part of your disaster planning should also include time to test the recovery plans and modify them as needed. See if you can restore your e-mail server from a backup tape, or bring a backup Web server out of cold storage and put it online in the shortest amount of time possible. Chances are you'll discover glitches along the way, and you'll need to modify your plans accordingly.

Lastly, you will need to keep logs of your recovery activities in the case of a real emergency. This may seem difficult to do, especially when a crisis is crashing down around your ears, but you should have at least one team member or crisis coordinator whose job is to track your disaster-recovery activities. These logs will become much-needed evidence in case you need to make an insurance claim or need to present evidence about criminal activity to law enforcement officials. These points are summarized as

- Brainstorm the types and scope of disaster incidents.
- Define disaster response teams and notification measures.
- Document your recovery plans.
- Assign team members to particular tasks.
- Test the recovery plans and modify as needed.
- Keep logs of recovery activities.

Security Hotspots

Likelihood of attack	8
Severity of loss	10
Risk factor	9

You should be on the lookout for several other security hotspots in your network. Some of these have been touched upon in earlier parts of this chapter, but because they are so important and there is a high degree of risk associated with them, they are worth calling out for individual attention.

- **Improperly configured routers** Many companies have improperly configured routers that lack appropriate rules, that have conflicting rules, or that provide wide-open ports into your network. Older routers or routers running older versions of software may not have been patched to prevent security holes. A properly configured router is one of the best first steps you can take to secure your network.

- **Unsecured remote-access mechanisms** It doesn't help to have locks and bars on your front door when you leave a window wide open. Companies often have employees who run remote-access software on their workstation so they can dial in and control their work desktop from home. Or a company may be running a modem bank for customer-support testing purposes, but the modem bank connects directly into an unsecured server on the network. These unsecured remote-access mechanisms are an open invitation to hackers using war dialers. Modems in employees' desktop computers and remote-access servers must be strictly controlled and monitored to prevent security breaches.

- **Running NetBIOS on your network** NetBIOS or NetBEUI are great protocols for very small networks with very few computers or services connected to them. Unfortunately, they are wide-open protocols that provide far too much helpful information to the would-be hacker. NetBIOS can be used to identify your domain controllers, your administrator account name, users and groups on your network, and routing information about the network. It is like handing a roadmap to a hacker with all the points of interest clearly circled in red pen. One of the first things you should do is eliminate NetBIOS from your network, and secure ports 135 through 139, which provide replies to NetBIOS queries on your network.

- **Running unneeded or unsecured services** You should make every effort to discover and disable any unneeded services in your network, especially if they are running it in your DMZ or outside your firewall. These include FTP, finger, telnet, SNMP, or SMTP, and they should not be accessible to anyone outside your business.

- **Weak or nonexistent password policies** Having a weak password policy is almost worse than having no policy at all; it can create a false sense of security and give the impression that the service is secure when, in reality, it can be easily guessed or hacked. You need to strike a fine balance between complex, difficult-to-hack passwords, and passwords that are easy to remember and use. If the password is too difficult, a user will write it down and stick it in a drawer, thus bypassing any security you were trying to build into the system. Good passwords are at least six to eight characters long, use at least one number or punctuation character, and do not consist of words found in the dictionary.

 TIP In the real world, when two MCSEs get together for a cup of coffee and discuss password policies, the discussion inevitably turns to passwords versus secure phrases (a secure phrase might read "keepsecure!101"). Here's our take on this debate. "Secure phrase" is not technically accurate (there is nothing inherently secure about "keepsecure!101"), and this terminology is not used anywhere in Windows 2000 that we're aware of in place of "password." We're all welcome to have our opinions, but on the MCSE exams, the proper term is "password."

- **Misconfigured Web servers** Some servers, especially earlier versions of Windows NT Web servers, were susceptible to misconfiguration. Too many services were left wide open, and a determined hacker could discover too much information. Things to watch for include read/write access to root directories, execute permissions on non-script directories, and CGI scripts that permitted buffer overflow conditions.

- **Administrator and guest account maintenance** It's crazy, but it's true. One of the most frequently overlooked security precautions is administrator and guest account management. The administrator account should be renamed and a difficult password assigned; the guest account should be disabled. Most system administrators know they're supposed to do this, but they forget in the rush to get the system up and running, and leave the system vulnerable as a result.

- **Secure or limit telnet access** This has been mentioned before and is more applicable to Unix systems and routers. These type of systems are accessed across a network by a terminal program (also called "headless mode"), and these systems, especially routers, should only be accessible via a direct connection. If you must manage them across a network, use ssh (secure shell) or another encrypting mode.

- **Limit access to scheduling services** Hackers will frequently upload programs that run as part of a scheduled task. Services like AT or cron should be secured so that only administrators or system-level services can use them.

Catywhompus Construction Updates

No discussion on analyzing business and technical requirements is complete without a look at the impact on our sample company, Catywhompus Construction, Inc. Assuming you are wearing your MCSE consulting hat, many good billable hours await you in completing the type of analysis discussed here.

You've read about defining security in the enterprise, early in this chapter, followed by evaluating business factors that affect security planning (including taking a look at existing and planned business models). You've looked at how to evaluate your technology options in security planning and even how to understand the people factor in security planning. Finally, though, it really comes back to this: Does it make sense? Is this discussion of business and technical issues relevant to security matters at hand? And does it all make sense from a cost/benefit perspective—are you starting toward security solutions that aren't cost-effective, given the amount of financial damage that can be inflicted by the bad guys?

Do as the Catywhompus management team does, and constantly ask whether the cures make sense. That is, the cost of the cure for a security matter doesn't outweigh the money saved if the security matter went unaddressed (this is basic cost/benefit analysis).

Chapter Review

Security is not a single topic, but permeates all levels of an enterprise. It will be affected by numerous business, technical, and social factors, all of which can and should be considered when designing a security plan or conducting a security assessment. This chapter is not meant to be an exhaustive discussion, but is a starting point for your investigations and discussions. Trust us, the security discussion is a never-ending topic, because security needs constantly change.

Questions

1. Which of these are among the "A"s of security? Choose all that apply:
   a. Administration
   b. Access
   c. Angst
   d. Authentication
   e. Auditing

2. What is a network demilitarized zone (DMZ)?
   a. An area you set up to ambush hackers
   b. A physical security perimeter around the server room
   c. An area along the 48th parallel in Korea
   d. An isolated network zone set between firewalls that contains Web servers or other network service providers

3. NetBIOS is (choose all that apply)
   a. An early network protocol and API that is still in use
   b. The default networking protocol for earlier versions of Windows
   c. Used to share resources on a network
   d. A significant security vulnerability that should be corrected
   e. All of the above

4. Good resources for up-to-date information on security topics are (choose all that apply)
   a. Security-centric Web sites, such as CERT and SANS
   b. Vendor Web sites, such as Microsoft
   c. Books and magazine articles from security professionals
   d. Movies with computer geeks in them like *Hackers*, *Sneakers*, and *The Matrix*

Answers

1. **A, B, D,** and **E.** Among the "A"s of security are securing physical *access* to systems and equipment, *authorization* of users and services, *auditing* events that occur on the system, and *administering* the system to keep security functioning properly. Angst is likely to occur if you mishandle one of the other "A"s.

2. **D.** A DMZ is a network zone set between firewalls that contains only the applications and services you want exposed to the outside world and that provides protection from internal and external attacks. A, B, and C are not correct for various reasons, though they could be entertaining alternatives if you propose them to a client.

3. **E.** NetBIOS was invented as a networking and application protocol and was designed to make it easy for data and services to be shared. It was also installed by default on earlier versions of Windows, including Windows for Workgroups and Windows 95. However, NetBIOS is highly susceptible to attack from outside your network and should be removed at the earliest opportunity.

4. **A, B, and C.** There is a lot going on in the security world, and new threats and countermeasures are announced every day. You should collect security information from a variety of reputable sources. Unfortunately, most Hollywood movies are not considered reputable sources of information about computer security.

Key Skill Sets

The following skill sets meet the Microsoft Objectives for the 70-220 exam:

- Analyze business factors that affect security planning.
- Understand the "people factor" in security planning.
- Prioritize security risks.
- Develop good, proactive security practices and procedures.
- Communicate your proposed security plans to all affected parties.
- Develop disaster-recovery plans and test them.
- Educate yourself and others about security risks and resources.

Key Terms

Access
Accountability
Accuracy
Administration
Authentication
Authorization
Corporate security policies
Disaster recovery

Network architecture

User education

Additional Resources and Information

As fast as vulnerabilities are found, people develop exploits to take advantage of them. Sometimes this is first found by the bad guys, and systems are compromised before patches or isolation measures can be developed. In those cases, rapid response is required. Here are some additional resources for staying current and well educated in the security field.

Web Sites

Numerous Web sites and Internet resources are dedicated to security issues, and some provide daily newsletters or security alerts when new hacks or viruses are discovered. The ones listed here should be considered "must-subscribe" sites, and depending on what software and hardware your client or employer uses, other vendors should be added to the list to keep your routers, e-mail software, and virus scanning software safe.

- **SANS Institute (http://www.sans.org)** The SANS Institute is a worldwide watchdog organization dedicated to providing up-to-the-minute information on security breaches and countermeasures. They maintain daily and weekly e-mail newsletters and alert notifications, and a list of the top 10 security vulnerabilities found on the Internet. They cover Windows NT, Solaris, Novell, Unix, and other operating systems.

- **CERT (http://www.cert.org)** CERT provides an incident reporting service and incident response team. They track security vulnerabilities and virus activities and help coordinate countermeasures among the Internet's service providers and backbones, as well as for corporate clients. They have newsletters, alerts, and advisory services available via their subscription link.

- **Microsoft (http://www.microsoft.com/security)** This should be on your list because you're working with Microsoft's flagship operating system. If any bugs or patches are discovered, Microsoft will announce them here. Subscribe to the bulletins for late-breaking information about security holes. You can also read Microsoft's list of security best-practices white papers, though they tend to be specific to Microsoft products.

- **SecurityFocus (http://www.securityfocus.com)** This site, formerly known as BugTraq, provides news and information on security hacks and vulnerabilities. It is not tied to a particular product vendor and is considered more of a "gray hat" site; it often has news from the hacker community long before anything official is posted at Microsoft, Sun, or Unix-related sites. It is a must-subscribe site precisely because it provides a view from the other side of the security fence.

Books

The following books are excellent sources of in-depth information about security measures, hacks, and countermeasures. They range from global musings on the nature of security to minutely detailed instructions on how to launch a security attack using freely available tools. They are required reading for anyone in the security business and are worth reading just for the links and cross-references to other books and sites.

- Donald L. Pipkin, *Information Security: Protecting the Global Enterprise* (Upper Saddle River, N.J.: Prentice Hall PTR, 2000), ISBN 0-13-017323-1. This is an entire book dedicated to the big picture of security, which we have discussed only briefly in this chapter. It is required reading if you are creating a written security proposal for your corporation and need a solid framework on which to hang your proposal.

- Stuart McClure, Joel Scambray, and George Kurtz, *Hacking Exposed: Network Security Secrets and Solutions,* second ed. (Berkeley, Calif.: Osborne/McGraw-Hill, 2000), ISBN 0-07-212748-1. This book goes into depth about ways people can gain access to information in your enterprise. It discusses specific tools and programs that can be used to prevent, detect, or stop hacking attempts. Although it is not for the beginner, it is perhaps the single best resource if you are serious about stopping intruders from accessing your network, with very detailed instructions on the available tools and countermeasures you can take.

- Bruce Schneier, *Secrets and Lies: Digital Security in a Networked World* (New York: John Wiley & Sons, 2000), ISBN 0-47-125311-1. Schneier's book is a wry yet sobering look at the history of information security and its implications in today's interconnected world. It falls midway between the previous two books, covering both the big picture and some technical implementation issues. Highly recommended.

Periodicals

When reading magazines related to your chosen career, be sure to check out Roberta Bragg's monthly "Security Adviser" column in *Microsoft Certified Professional Magazine,* www.mcpmag.com. She is a well-respected security expert and resource.

Analyzing Security Requirements

This chapter covers the following key mastery goals:

- Design a security baseline for a Windows 2000 network that includes domain controllers, operations masters, application servers, file and print servers, RAS servers, desktop computers, portable computers, and kiosks

- Identify the required level of security for each resource, including printers, files, shares, Internet access, and dial-in access

All too often, IT personnel don't see the creation, implementation, and enforcement of a security policy as a priority. With stability and reliability being the prime motivators, security is all too often overlooked. A security policy, however, should provide a foundation for *all* IT operations. From desktops to servers and network devices to user account creation, a security policy should outline the various policies and procedures that will help you keep your computing environment hardened against attack. Without a security policy (and its implementation and enforcement), you'll have even more help to ensure the stability and reliability of your systems—just ask the various "helpers" that have administrative access to your computer systems.

This chapter will focus on the Windows 2000 Security Configuration and Analysis tool to first help you assess your current computing environment. Then, after you sit down and plan your security policy, you can use the Security Configuration and Analysis tool to implement your chosen security settings.

Assessing Your Current Environment

Perhaps the most important standards that you can employ in your computing environment are your security standards. These standards should be housed in a clear, concise, and overarching security policy that covers all aspects of your computing environment. Sound a little daunting? You bet. You must weigh the needs of the computer users against potential threats to your computer systems—a task that would surely strain King Solomon.

You have two tasks to complete before you can begin developing a security policy and implementing its standards. First, you must assess the current vulnerabilities within your computing environment, and the possible vulnerabilities your systems may have in the future. After you've chewed on that problem for a while, you must take a security inventory (a baseline) of your environment and assess your network's current security posture.

Vulnerabilities

Before you develop a sound security policy, you need to spend some time assessing the vulnerabilities of your network. To do so, you must inventory your computers, servers, and network devices. After you've collected a long list of the physical assets of your network, you must also determine the software and services that run on your network. Then, after you're done there, you must investigate the various methods of data entry into your network—everything from Internet connections and remote access to VPN and tunneling solutions.

Once you have your hardware inventory, your list of current software, and a network diagram ready, it's time to match your environment against common types of security attacks and assess your vulnerabilities. A variety of possible dangers exist, including social engineering attacks, viruses, Trojan horses, worms, intercepted authentications, denial-of-service attacks, attackers masquerading as valid users, and even inside jobs.

Social Engineering Attack

Social engineering attacks are listed first for good reason—they are perhaps the most commonly perpetrated attacks against organizations. A *social engineering attack* is when an attacker gains information from an organization's human assets. A common ploy utilized by attackers is masquerading as the IT department and asking for a user's remote-access or network username and password. Another common ploy is gathering information under the guise of a survey or telephone questionnaire.

Socially engineered attacks are common, easy to use, and extremely difficult to prevent. Since you can't apply a Windows Group Policy to a computer's human counterpart, you must develop sound security education that alerts employees to the possible dangers. Any sound security policy should include the following to help deter a socially engineered attack:

- Guidelines to help employees guard confidential company information
- Steps that an employee should follow if confronted with a possible information thief
- Security-incident reporting procedures
- Provisions for a security controller officer who can investigate and escalate possible security breaches

Viruses, Trojan Horses, Worms, and Other Malicious Computer Code

Most system administrators are familiar with viruses, Trojan horses, worms, macro viruses, malicious Web pages, and other deviant computer code. Unfortunately, these items are part of the reality of doing computing business. Although definitions may vary as to the function of each type of malicious computer code, Table 8-1 provides a quick overview.

Interception

One type of interception attack involves "recording" the authentication process between a client and server. The malicious user can then replay this conversation to gain access to the server. Oddly enough, this special interception attack is commonly referred to as a *replay attack*. Other types of interception attacks can be done, including the old over-the-shoulder method. An example of this might be a villain standing behind you while you type your password on the screen. And even though your password appears as asterisks on the screen, the villain is watching your keystrokes on the keyboard. Implausible, you say? Not really. The approach of looking over your back has been used for a long time at public telephone booths where villains watch the calling card code you enter to make long-distance calls. Once such a villain has your long-distance calling card code, they can make free long-distance calls to other villains in far away lands.

Denial of Service

Denial of service (DoS) attacks received much attention when such attacks blocked access to some of the Web's most popular sites. During this type of attack, the malicious computer user floods a network with an overwhelming number of network packets.

Table 8-1   Types of Malicious Computer Code

Type of Malicious Computer Code	Action	Prevention
Virus	The term *virus* is starting to become a common term referring to all malicious computer code. However, a virus is generally defined as a program that can attach itself to another program, thereby infecting it. Using the host program, it propagates itself through various files on one system or many systems connected on a network. A virus can also damage existing data while it travels.	Generally, anti-virus programs do a good job of detecting and eliminating viruses. However, anti-virus programs must be maintained and kept up to date to combat the latest viruses.
Worm	A *worm* is similar to a virus in that it can propagate itself. However, it does not normally attach itself to another program. A worm can also damage existing data.	Anti-virus programs can detect and eliminate worms.
Trojan horse	A *Trojan horse* is a malicious program that masquerades as a benign or friendly program. For example, an attacker might replace the Notepad application with one that looks like Notepad, but upon execution, deletes files from your system.	Anti-virus programs can detect and eliminate Trojan horses.
Macro virus	A macro virus is a small deviation from normal viruses. Instead of creating an entire application or program, an attacker uses the macro commands available in applications, such as the Microsoft Office suite. Using these simple commands, attacks can be launched when the user opens a particular document or the macro virus can propagate itself by e-mailing itself via Outlook.	Anti-virus programs can detect and eliminate macro viruses.
Malicious code or scripts	Using ActiveX, VBScript, JavaScript, Java, or other Web programming languages, many attackers have been able to destroy data on Web surfers' local machines. This type of attack utilizes vulnerabilities in a Web browser to affect data on a Web surfer's local system.	Patch your Web browsers often, and stay on top of security vulnerabilities. Microsoft offers a security newsletter to alert users of these types of exploits. In addition, you can set the policy of a Web browser to disallow code of any kind to prevent this type of attack.

Once the network devices and systems are saturated with data, normal users are unable to gain access to the network.

 NOTE   The infamous Web attacks on Amazon.com, CNN, and Microsoft were distributed denial of service (DDoS) attacks, which means that many computer systems flooded the Web sites with network data. This coordinated attack crippled the Web sites and denied access to millions. In order to accomplish this type of attack, the attacker(s) broke into other systems scattered over the Internet, and remotely installed the application that perpetrated the attack. Improper security on these systems ultimately affected the target of the DDoS attacks.

Masquerade

Like the party of the same name, a *masquerade* attack is one where the malicious computer user pretends to be someone else—and in the case of network security, the attacker pretends to be a valid computer user. The attacker can then gain the same access to your network's resources as the valid user.

IP spoofing is just the opposite. Instead of impersonating a host or server on the network, a malicious computer user tries to impersonate a client using a valid IP address. Using an assumed IP address, the attacker can gain access to your network and possibly the systems on your network. For Unix, VMS, and other host-based systems that use IP addresses as a method of authentication, IP spoofing is a dangerous exploit.

For Windows systems, IP spoofing is not a common threat. And because Windows requires user authentication for access to server resources, it's difficult to pull off man-in-the-middle attacks. All political correctness aside, the well-known industry term *man-in-the-middle* refers to an intermediary that "reads" packet traffic between sender and receiver. The exception to both of these general statements is the use of FTP and Telnet. Since any Windows 2000 machine can act as a Telnet server, and the personal Web servers grant the ability to serve files via FTP, a solid security policy should severely limit the use of either. If Telnet and FTP must be used, try to implement encrypted clients and follow the best practices on securing each.

Inside Jobs

A common mistake made by most companies is to focus on the security threats that may originate outside a company. More commonly, however, security incidents and destruction occur at the hands of company employees or individuals who have access to your systems. Never underestimate the possibility of employee data theft, sabotage, or destruction! When you build your security policy, be sure to include security policies that also help to protect company assets from employees. That means restricting employees' access to only job-specific data. In addition, compartmentalize data to prevent the unnecessary sharing of sensitive information.

Creating a Baseline

Bear with us as we use a convenient example from the medical community to introduce the baselining concept. When you start a medical relationship with a physician and have your first checkup, often extensive testing occurs, X-rays are taken, and so on. These records are then saved in a medical file. This becomes your personal baseline against which future medical reports are compared. Now back to the world of Windows 2000 networks. You would perform tasks in these areas to create your baseline that future network performance can be compared to inventory and security configuration and analysis.

Inventory

These areas should be inventoried as part of your baseline analysis:

- Number of systems
- Type of system (for example, router, switch, server, workstation, and so on)
- Type of operating system (for example, Windows 2000, Windows 98, Cisco IOS, and so on)
- Network protocols used (for example, TCP/IP, IPX/SPX, and so on)
- User access (for example, who has access to this device, and what type of access is allowed)
- Resource access (for example, what device resources are available to network users, and what type of access is allowed)
- Who has administrator access to the device?

Security Configuration and Analysis

With the introduction of Windows 2000, Microsoft has been kind enough to include a utility to assess your current security settings—the *Security Configuration and Analysis* tool. This MMC snap-in will assess the major security areas of your Windows 2000 system and report on its current settings. In addition, you can compare these settings against a *security template* and report on the differences. A security template is a built-in form (or template) in Windows 2000 that saves time and efforts in the security area.

Once you have developed a security policy, you can return to the Security Configuration and Analysis tool to actually implement these security settings.

NOTE Microsoft also includes the command-line tool SECEdit, which performs the same actions as the Security Configuration and Analysis MMC snap-in. With SECEdit, you can run the security analysis from a batch file, schedule the task using the Task Scheduler, or even deploy security configurations using SECEdit and a remote management tool, such as Microsoft System Management Server (SMS).

Lab Exercise 8.1:
How to Discover Your Current
Security Configuration

1. Ensure that you are logged on to the Windows 2000 system as an administrator.

2. Select Start | Run.

3. In the Run dialog box, type **MMC /A** to start an MMC console in Author Mode and then press ENTER.

4. In the Microsoft Management Console, select Console Menu | Add/Remove Snap-In Menu.

5. In the Add/Remove Snap-In dialog box's Standalone sheet, click the Add button.

6. From the list of available snap-ins, choose the Security Configuration and Analysis snap-in, and click the Add button. Click Close to close the Add Standalone Snap-In dialog box.

7. In the Add/Remove Snap-In dialog box, click OK to close the dialog box.

8. Right-click the new Security Configuration and Analysis entry under the Console Root, and select Open Database from the shortcut menu.

9. In the Open Database dialog box, choose the path and filename of the security database. This database will hold the results of the security analysis. Click OK.

 NOTE When using Security Configuration and Analysis for the first time, you will be prompted to compare your environment against a security template. Which template you choose will not matter since you're simply trying to understand the settings that are currently in place.

10. The Security Configuration and Analysis tool will now display the Import Template dialog box. In this dialog box shown in Figure 8-1, you will be presented

Figure 8-1
Selecting from the existing security templates to import

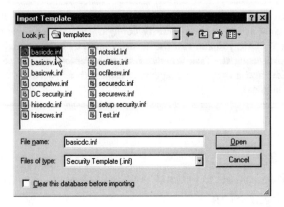

with a list of security templates. For purposes of the initial analysis, choose the BASICDC.INF template for a Windows 2000 domain controller, BASICSV.INF for a Windows 2000 server, and BASICWK.INF for a Windows 2000 workstation. It doesn't matter which template you use—this basic security template simply gives you a beginning baseline to use for comparison. Click the Open button.

NOTE The security templates, by default, are stored in the %SYSTEMROOT%\SECURITY\TEMPLATES directory.

11. Once you've created your database and associated the security template, right-click the Security Configuration and Analysis item, and choose Analyze Computer Now from the shortcut menu (shown in Figure 8-2).

12. The Security Configuration and Analysis tool will now prompt you to enter a path and filename for the log file that records the various security checks that are performed and their results (shown in the following illustration). Click OK to continue.

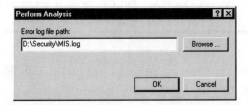

PART II

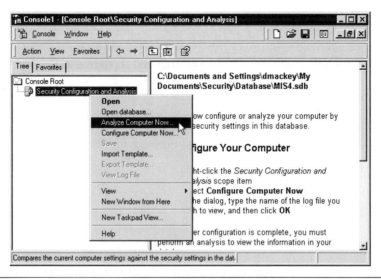

Figure 8-2   Selecting the Analyze Computer Now menu item

13. The Security Configuration and Analysis tool will now perform the security analysis (see the next illustration).

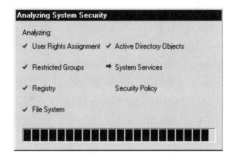

14. Once the security analysis is complete, the system's security settings will be displayed. Search through the various results to understand how the system is currently configured.

Developing a Security Policy

When you create your security policy, you'll want to include a variety of business-specific security issues. In addition, Microsoft advises that you include seven critical points:

- Authenticate all user access to system resources.

- Apply appropriate access control to all resources.

- Establish appropriate trust relationships between multiple domains.

- Enable data protection for sensitive data.

- Set uniform security policies.

- Deploy secure applications.

- Manage security administration.

For a thorough security policy document, you'll want to analyze these areas for each of your technologies. Regardless of whether you have Sun systems, telephony devices, or old Windows 3.11 workstations, no technologies should be exempt. However, since this book's main focus is Windows 2000 and the associated MCSE exams, let's explore these security areas and how they apply to the technologies of Windows 2000.

Authenticating All User Access to System Resources

One of the most important security tasks a system administrator can perform is to ensure that network users can access the proper resources. In the older network days, this meant that every user had to have a user ID on every server in the environment. If you were lucky, all of the user accounts were identical. In other words, John Sweeney used the JSweeney user ID on all servers to which he needed access. If you were unlucky, you had a JSweeney on this server, a JSween on that server, and a SweeneyJ on yet another server.

With Windows NT, Microsoft introduced the idea of the domain to try to avoid the problem of multiple user accounts for one computer user. By using domain user accounts, a user can log on and authenticate once to the domain and obtain access to all the appropriate servers. In addition, a computer user can walk to any number of computers within the organization, log on, and receive his or her user account information and settings. The problem, however, is that Windows NT domains are not extensible. Once you implement a Windows NT domain, it's hard to add more organizations or to authenticate users from one domain to another domain's resources.

Borrowing a page from Novell's Network Directory Services (NDS), Microsoft has introduced Active Directory to provide the truly single-sign-on authentication method.

Authenticating from organizational unit to organizational unit, or from domain to domain, is easier and hopefully more convenient for users. Using Active Directory, you can control access for valid users to all resources within your organization—servers, printers, shared folders, and other computer resources. Additionally, Active Directory provides authentication mechanisms not only for user accounts, but also for computers and services. This allows system administrators more granular control over which security measures are applied to a machine or application and which are applied only to user accounts.

More importantly, Active Directory offers a large improvement over the old Windows NT domain in terms of security. Each object housed within the domain can be secured with object rights, much like the NTFS permissions afforded to files. User accounts, printers, organizational units, and any number of other Active Directory objects can have access restricted by the click of a mouse.

The following sections, "Kerberos," "Password Policies," "Smart Cards," and "Remote Access," are all germane authentication methods in Windows 2000 Server.

Kerberos

Active Directory, by default, implements *Kerberos* for authentication purposes. The Kerberos authentication protocol is used to ensure that users are whom they claim. Much like a unique fingerprint, Kerberos uses a digital key to uniquely identify users. This key is then embedded in network communications to verify the sender.

When planning your security policy, think seriously about implementing Kerberos as the sole authentication protocol (unless you have older versions of Windows, in which case, you will have to use NT LAN Manager [NTLM] authentication also). For more information regarding Kerberos and NTLM, refer to Chapter 9.

Password Policies

Active Directory and the variety of other authentication mechanisms are only as strong as their weakest link. In terms of security, the weakest link is almost always the people using the computers. Obtaining usernames and passwords is still an easy and powerful way to gain access to the network. Education remains the key in avoiding the disclosure of this type of sensitive information—don't write usernames and passwords on a sticky note under your keyboard, don't give out password information to anyone, don't make the password the same as your username, and so on.

To help administrators, Windows 2000 also enables you to invoke password policies to enforce stricter password schemes and more frequent password changes. For example, you can force users to change their passwords every 60 days, require a minimum password length, and ensure users don't repeat the same password by keeping a history of used passwords.

Additionally, Windows 2000 includes an option within the Group Policy object to enforce *complexity requirements*. These requirements specify that the password:

- Does not contain all or part of the user's account name

- Is at least six characters in length

- Contains characters from three of the following categories:

  - English uppercase characters (A to Z)

  - English lowercase characters (a to z)

  - Base 10 digits (0 to 9)

  - Nonalphanumeric characters including, but not necessarily limited to: !, @, #, $, ~.

NOTE These complexity requirements are enforced by enabling an option within the Group Policy MMC snap-in. However, the real tool is the passfilt.dll file that is included with Windows 2000. This file will filter passwords for the preceding rules. With a little programming work, you can create a custom password filter. Refer to the Microsoft Developer Network for more information.

Smart Cards

Windows 2000 includes support for smart cards, which eliminate the need for users to remember multiple usernames and passwords. Instead, the user inserts a card into an attached card reader and supplies one password or code to authenticate to all resources on the network. The smart card provides a double layer of security by storing security information on the smart card and also requiring the proper code from the user. In this case, if the smart card is lost or the PIN is stolen, an attacker would still not have all of the necessary tools to access your network. For more information regarding smart cards, refer to Chapter 9.

Remote Access

Your authentication security policy should also encompass remote access to your network. With Windows 2000, remote-access security has been tightened to eliminate the possibility of unauthorized remote access. For example, for a client to gain access to your remote access server, the user must

- Meet the criteria outlined in the remote-access policies.

PART II

- Have a user account that is enabled for remote access.

- Authenticate successfully using proper protocols, network information, a username, and a password.

For more information on remote-access policies, refer to Chapter 10.

Applying Appropriate Access Control to All Resources

Once you have covered the various ways users can authenticate onto your network—through Active Directory, using remote access, or even through the use of older Windows clients—you must ensure that each user has the appropriate level of access to network resources. This serves two functions. First, you limit the damage that can be done if an attacker assumes the identity of a legitimate network user, and second, you limit the damage that can be done by your company's own employees. Never underestimate the importance of either of these objectives. Attackers and disgruntled, mischievous, and vengeful employees all exist, and they rarely show themselves until after damage is already done to your network.

Security Groups

In order to manage the daunting task of security control over all of your network objects, you should use *security groups*. This is new; in Windows NT 4.0, security groups were simply referred to as "groups." Within Windows 2000, security groups are collections of user accounts that can have security rights associated with them and can also be used as distribution lists by certain applications. The other major type of group is a *distribution group*, and they are solely used as distribution lists.

Under the umbrella of security groups are four classifications:

- **Local Group**   A *local group* is specific to a computer. This group cannot be granted access to any resources other than those found on the associated computer. In a business organization, you'll probably want to steer clear of using local groups because of the overhead associated with changing group membership on each computer. Instead, you may just want to ensure domain administrators are also included in the local group Administrators, so that system administrators can log on to every machine within your organization.

- **Domain Local Group**   If your domain is running in *mixed mode* (Windows NT 4.0 and Windows 2000), a *domain local group* is a local group that exists on the domain controller only. Within a *native mode* domain (Windows 2000 only), a domain local group can contain users from within the same domain, and users from without. Also known as a *resource group*, this type of group is generally used to grant access to system resources, such as printers, shared folders, and files. The drawback to a domain local group is that it cannot be nested within a local, global, or universal group. For example, you cannot use a domain local group to house all of the administrators within your domain, and then include this group on every system's local Administrators group.

- **Global Group**   Within a Windows 2000 environment, you will probably use global groups most often for holding user accounts. *Global groups* allow you to group user accounts logically, by department, business function, or mission. For example, you can create an Accounting global group that has access to shared accounting information, two shared accounting printers, and a dedicated financial server. The benefit to using a global group is that it can be included in all other groups. For example, if Accounting and Marketing share one printer, you can create a domain local group with access to the shared printer, and then include both the Accounting and Marketing global groups. The drawback to using a global group is that included user accounts must reside within the same domain.

- **Universal Group**   *Universal groups* are only used in organizations with multiple domains. A universal group can bridge several domains and offer a user in domain A access to resources in domain B, as can domain local groups. Since universal groups and their memberships are included in the Active Directory global catalog, you will want to minimize the number of additions, modifications, and deletions you perform on a universal group's membership. All of these operations require replications among the various global catalog servers located in your organization. Instead, include local domain or global groups as members of the universal group, and make modifications to the included groups only.

Now that you're familiar with the various security groups available within Windows 2000, you should keep some things in mind when setting up your security groups:

- *The built-in Everyone group includes every user within your system or domain—properly authenticated or not!* Generally, Windows tries to restrict access to read-only for the Everyone group. You may need to go further and remove access altogether for sensitive information or in situations where the Everyone group has access to sensitive operating system resources.

- *Users have a limit to the number of combined local, domain local, global, and universal groups to which they can be members.* In a single domain, a user cannot be a member of more than 1,000 groups. Hopefully, you won't need to exceed that limit. However, in a multiple domain model, the limit will be 1,000 per domain.

PART II

- *When creating security groups, use group nesting to reduce administration.* For example, if you have a security group that should contain all members of your company, create department groups and include those in the more general All-Company group. In this way, you only have to add or remove users from the individual department groups to affect the more general group.

- *If you're using Windows 2000 in a mixed-mode environment, you may find that you cannot nest groups or that domain local groups behave differently.* Upgrading all servers to Windows 2000 and switching to native mode will correct these problems.

- *When a Windows 2000 system joins the domain, the Domain Administrators global group is automatically added to that system's local Administrators group.*

- *Try to refrain from granting users administrative access to their own systems.* Use the Users group for typical users to prevent program installation and configuration changes. Use the Power Users group to grant more privileges, but prevent the installation of hardware and other administrative functions. Restrict Administrative access to IT personnel.

With all of the information on security groups, you'll probably have to draw a picture for yourself so you will know which groups to create. You'll need to assess which resources should have their own domain local group and which users should be grouped together. In general, you'll want to build a logical model to house your network's users. Then use the groups to manage access to individual resources.

Restricting User Access

Now that you have a handle on security groups, you'll need to use them to restrict access to your network resources. In particular, you will want to focus on the following areas when restricting access:

- **Shares**   In general, drives, folders, and printers will be the resources most often shared within a Windows environment. Ensure that each is properly controlled. Since shared resources are accessible over the network, this is your first line of defense.

- **Files and folders**   You can restrict access to drives, folders, or even individual files using NTFS permissions. Due to the overwhelming number of drives, folders, and files you'll have among all of your servers, this is hard to manage. But NTFS permissions are very effective for sensitive information. This provides a second line of defense for attackers coming over the network, and a first line of defense for attackers that have physical access to your computer.

- **Applications security**   Although most current applications will not be directly controlled by Windows 2000 Active Directory security, future applications may be Active Directory–aware, which enables you to control access to the application from the Active Directory side.

Establishing Appropriate Trust Relationships Between Multiple Domains

When planning your overall security policy, you must take into account your organization and its structure. Are there multiple domains? If so, are they contained within one forest? If not, will they have trusts established between them?

Sit down and sketch out your various domains and decide whether the users within one domain should have access to resources within another domain. (Actually, you probably won't decide whether users should have access between domains—it'll probably be dictated by business needs or by business whiners, but it's nice to pretend.) If you only have one domain within your organization, you can bypass this section—you won't have a need for trust relationships.

Trust Relationships

Within Windows 2000, the idea of *trust relationships* has evolved tremendously. In Windows NT 4.0, separate domains had to trust each other in order for users contained within one domain to access resources in another domain. There was a *trusted* domain and a *trusting* domain. If domain A is a trusted domain to domain B, then B allows A's domain users access to its resources. In this scenario, B is the trusting domain. Both were hard to keep track of, but vital for the MCSE exam.

In addition, there were several other terms to learn when describing a trust relationship:

- **Transitive trust**   This means that if domain A has a trust relationship with domain B, and domain B has a trust relationship with domain C, domain A also has a trust relationship with domain C.

- **Nontransitive trust**   This is the opposite of a transitive trust relationship—if domain A has a trust relationship with domain B, and domain B has a trust relationship with domain C, domain A does not have a trust relationship with domain C.

- **One-way trust**   In this situation, domain A trusts domain B, but B does not trust A. Authentication requests are only sent from the trusting domain to the trusted domain. One-way trusts are also non-transitive.

- **Two-way trust** Here, domain A trusts domain B, and domain B trusts domain A. Authentication requests are passed back and forth between domains.

In Windows 2000, all domain trusts within the same forest are automatically linked by two-way transitive trusts between the parent and child domains. This simplifies your life as an administrator by not requiring manual trust establishment.

Don't get us wrong; you can still establish manual trusts, but most of the trusting is now automatic. For example, you can also create manual trusts among various branches of the domain tree structure to allow faster authentication to take place. Additionally, you can create explicit nontransitive trust relationships to block the authentication between domains.

 NOTE Windows 2000 can only establish a one-way trust between a Windows 2000 domain and any of the following: a Windows 2000 domain in a different forest, a Windows NT 4.0 domain, or an MIT Kerberos V4 realm.

For purposes of your security policy, you should keep track of any trust relationships. Related to the trust issue is access across trust relationships. Ensure that you know who has access to your domain or forest at all times.

Enabling Data Protection for Sensitive Data

Encryption has become a powerful tool for thwarting would-be attackers. One user scrambles data on one end, and an authorized user on the other end unscrambles the data. In between, the data looks like gibberish. Of course, no security precaution is foolproof, but encryption offers an easy method of protecting data. Windows 2000 includes two new important tools in this area that should be able to better protect sensitive data: EFS and IPSec.

Windows 2000's Encrypting File System (EFS) enables you to encrypt files and folders. As long as the authorized user is logged into the operating system, Windows 2000 automatically encrypts and decrypts the files behind the scenes. It does take some overhead, but the operation is seamless to the end users. In cases where an attacker has physical access to the computer, EFS is invaluable. For instance, if an attacker uses another operating system to boot the computer, Windows 2000 using the EFS process has effectively encrypted data to further protect the data from prying eyes. For more information on EFS, refer to Chapter 9.

IP Security (IPSec) is another important feature that helps protect sensitive data. Like EFS, it encrypts data to protect it from attackers. However, the data is encrypted while in transit over a network. In this case, if an attacker steals the data while "listening" on the network, the data is still encrypted and hard to view. For more information on IPSec, refer to Chapter 10.

When building your security policies, seriously consider implementing EFS on laptops, and using IPSec in situations where network traffic may be monitored (for example, when it is passed over the Internet).

Setting Uniform Security Policies

Outside the context of the broader corporate security policy that you are trying to develop for your company, you should also be aware of policies that are built into Windows 2000. These security policies are called *group policies*—a term that is a holdover from older Windows NT days. These group policies hold security settings that can be applied to local computers and users, organizational units, domains, or sites. Be wary, however. You should implement group policies at only one level, if possible. The inheritance of group policies may lead to an administrative nightmare. To learn more about policy inheritance, refer to Chapter 9.

Group policies cover nine major areas and involve the most sensitive parts of your operating system. It is definitely worth your while to plan which settings you want to implement and at which level. These are the nine areas:

- **Account Policies** This group policy object includes Password Policy, Account Lockout Policy, and Kerberos Policy. The Password Policy object includes password restrictions, such as minimum password length and password history (see Figure 8-3). The Account Lockout Policy object specifies when the user account is automatically locked out after invalid logon attempts (see Figure 8-4). The Kerberos Authentication Policy object allows you to modify properties of the Kerberos authentication process, such as ticket lifetime, user logon restrictions, and tolerance for clock synchronization (see Figure 8-5).

- **Local Policies** This group policy object includes Audit Policy, User Rights Assignment, and Security Options. The Audit Policy object specifies which events Windows 2000 will record within the event logs (see Figure 8-6). For example, you can log user login and logoff attempts, file access attempts, or policy changes. The User Rights Assignment object allows you granular control over security tasks, such as shutting down the system, backing up files, taking ownership of files, or changing

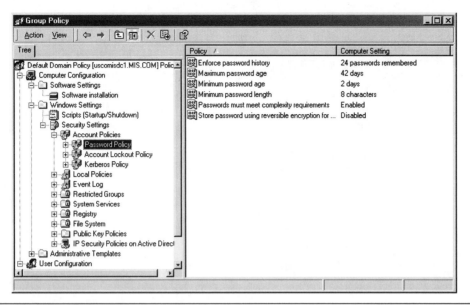

Figure 8-3   Observing Password Policy details

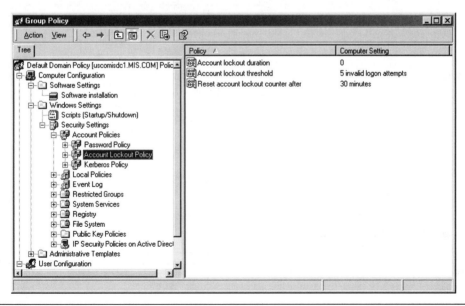

Figure 8-4   Account Lockout Policy information

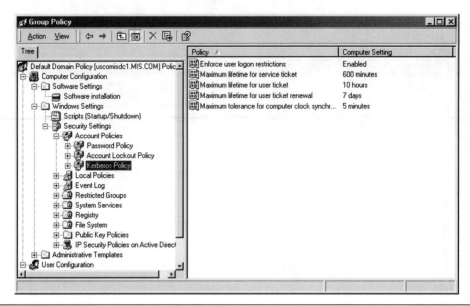

Figure 8-5   Details on Kerberos Policy

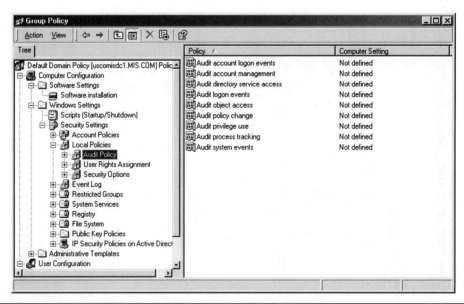

Figure 8-6   Details on Audit Policy

the system time (see Figure 8-7). The Security Options object enables you to control a variety of valuable security options, such as requiring the key combination of CTRL-ALT-DEL to log on, clearing the pagefile on shutdown, and forcing users to log off during off-hours (see Figure 8-8).

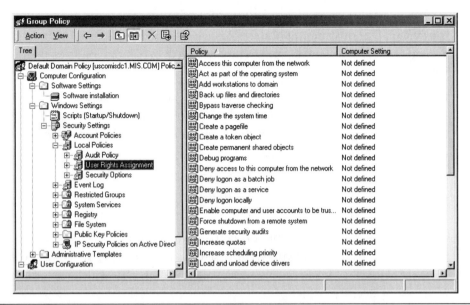

Figure 8-7   Specific information is displayed for User Rights Assignments.

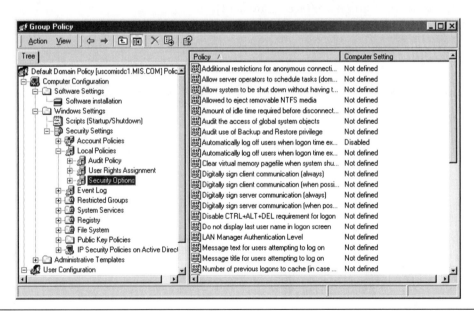

Figure 8-8   Observe the security options that are available to you.

- **Event Log** This group policy object enables you to control the various features of the System, Security, and Application logs within Windows 2000 (see Figure 8-9). You can modify how long logged events are stored, maximum log sizes, or actions when a security event is detected.

- **Restricted Groups** This group policy object can be used to manage membership of Windows 2000 built-in groups, such as Administrators, Power Users, or Print Operators (see Figure 8-10). For example, you can ensure that no members are ever added to the Administrators group.

- **System Services** This group policy object enables you to modify the startup mode for services, to disable services, to designate access rights for services, and even refine the auditing levels for various services (see Figure 8-11).

- **Registry** This group policy object is perhaps an overlooked component of security. You can use it to modify the security settings of various Registry keys and sub-keys (see Figure 8-12). You can also designate which user has which types of rights to access the Registry.

- **File System** Use this group policy object to restrict which users have access to various files on your system (see Figure 8-13).

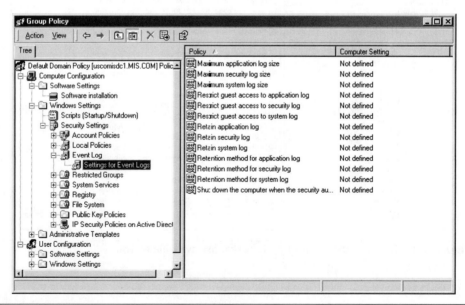

Figure 8-9 Details on policy settings for Event Logs

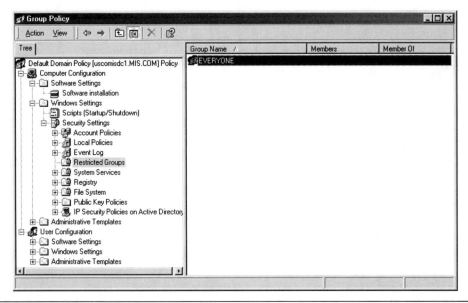

Figure 8-10   Restricted Group settings

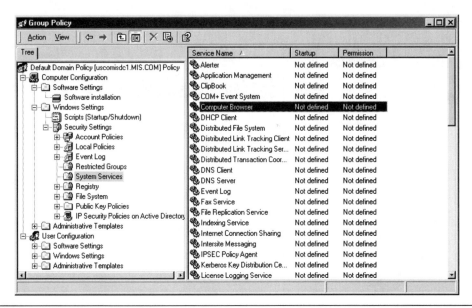

Figure 8-11   Setting a policy for services

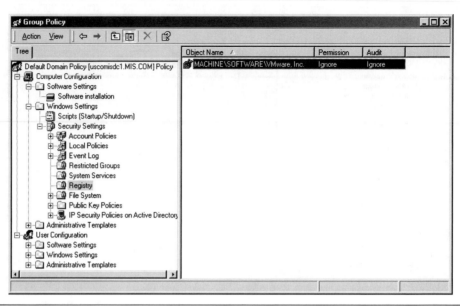

Figure 8-12   Using a policy to protect Registry editing and settings

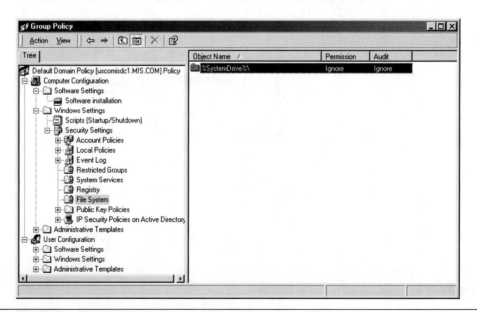

Figure 8-13   Protect the file system with a group policy.

- **Public Key Policies**   The various settings under the Public Key Policy object help you manage your Public Key Infrastructure (PKI) by adding encrypted data-recovery agents and automatic certificate requests (see Figure 8-14).

- **IP Security Policies on Active Directory**   Use this group policy object to specify how your system uses or does not use IP Security when transmitting data over TCP/IP (see Figure 8-15). In addition, you can modify how your system reacts to IPSec data requests received.

Look over the various settings included in the group policies and decide which settings apply to your environment. Then decide where to implement those settings and how strictly you'd like to enforce them. You'll use your settings decisions later in this chapter when we return to the Security Configuration and Analysis tool.

Deploying Secure Applications

Developing your security policy should not stop with your servers' operating system; you must also secure the applications that run on the operating system. You must ensure that communications are secure, passwords are encrypted and safely stored from prying eyes, and that all data remains confidential. The problem, however, is that with

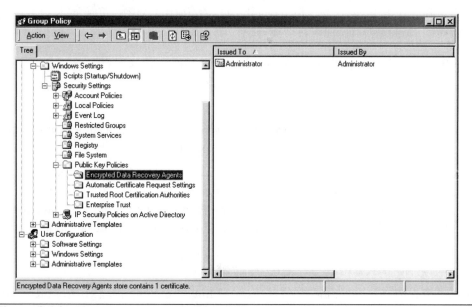

Figure 8-14   Managing settings related to PKI

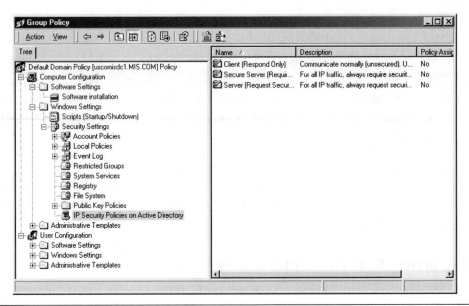

Figure 8-15   Configuring IP Security

the myriad of applications out there, a separate security book could be written about each application. Instead, let's focus on the guidelines that Microsoft suggests to secure your applications:

- Run them on properly secured Windows 2000 servers.

- Use single-sign-on authentication with Kerberos and Active Directory authentication.

- Develop user accounts for application services. Avoid using the Local System account, since that account has full system privileges.

- Only apply digitally signed applications and drivers (this may not be realistic in the near future, but it sure is a great goal). This ensures the application comes from the stated source. Authenticode is one such mechanism that was implemented within Internet Explorer; it uses standard x.509 certificates to prove software is authentic.

Managing Security Administration

In addition to managing the normal users within your computing environment, you must also pay close attention to the users with special access. For example, if you have an IT department that splits the administration of your Windows 2000 servers, you must ensure that these users, in particular, have closely controlled accounts and conform to security standards. Often, administrative user accounts are the least secure and the least auditable, simply because these users can turn the group policy off for their particular account.

Administrative Access

For these special administrative users, you must do some extra planning within your security policies. You must ensure that administrative accounts are included within the normal user-account processes for creation, modification, and removal. If you verify user accounts every month, administrators should be included. If you verify access needs for your users every quarter, then—you guessed it—administrators should also be included.

In addition, you can compartmentalize administrative functions. Ensure that a handful of administrators control only a handful of servers, another group controls another handful of servers, and so on. By dividing the administrative access, you ensure that not one administrator has destructive capacity across your entire environment. You can easily compartmentalize administrative functions using Windows 2000's Delegation of Authority wizard. For more information on delegating authority, refer to Chapter 9.

Auditing

You should consider enabling auditing on your Windows 2000 server. Although it has some processing overhead, Windows 2000 can log and record events for future reference and possible security investigations. Try keeping a month or two worth of system logs. For more information on auditing, refer to Chapter 9.

Implementing Your Security Policy

Once you've got a clear picture of your current security situation as it relates to your computing environment (existing security settings and so on), and you've developed a security policy, it's time to go to work to ensure that both match. Luckily, the Security Configuration and Analysis tool can also be used to *implement* your security policies.

The first step, before you return to the Security Configuration and Analysis tool, is to create a security template that matches your new security policy. This template, in turn, can be used by the Security Configuration and Analysis tool to implement the settings you designate.

Lab Exercise 8.2:
How to Create a New Security Template

1. Select Start | Run.

2. In the Run dialog box, type **MMC /A**, and then press ENTER.

3. In the Microsoft Management Console, select Console | Add/Remove Snap-In.

4. In the Add/Remove Snap-In dialog box's Standalone sheet, click the Add button.

5. From the list of available snap-ins, choose the Security Templates snap-in, and click the Add button. Click the Close button to close the Add Standalone Snap-In dialog box.

6. In the Add/Remove Snap-In dialog box, click OK to close the dialog box.

7. In the Security Templates tool, click the \WINNT\Security\Templates folder. You can see in Figure 8-16 that Windows 2000 already comes with a variety of security templates.

8. The easiest way to create a new template is to start with a built-in template and save it as your own. Use the basic*x* templates for a basic level of security, secure*x* templates for a medium level of security, and hisec*x* templates for a highly restrictive security environment.

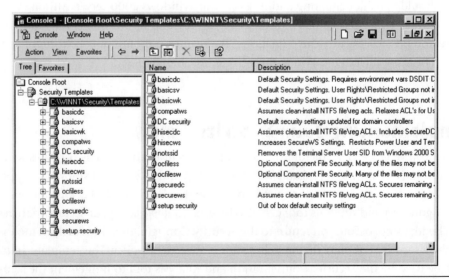

Figure 8-16   Select an existing template.

9. Once you've chosen your template, right-click it and choose Save As from the shortcut menu. Save the template under an appropriate name and within an appropriate folder.

 NOTE You can also right-click the WINNT\Security\Templates folder and choose New Template from the shortcut menu. You can then create a template from scratch. This is a little more work, but you will only get settings that you expressly set.

10. Once you've created your template, click it in the left pane. In the right pane, you'll see the variety of settings that you can manipulate. Drill down through the template and change the settings to match your security policy (see Figures 8-17 and 8-18).

Now that you've created your template, you can use the Security Configuration and Analysis tool to implement your security settings.

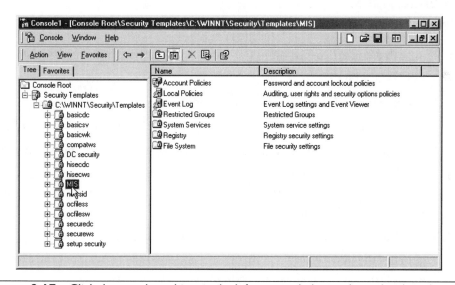

Figure 8-17 Click the template object in the left pane and observe basic details in the right pane.

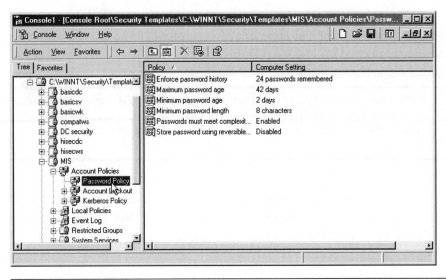

Figure 8-18 Drilling down into template details

Lab Exercise 8.3:
How to Implement Your New Security Policy

1. Ensure that you are logged on to the Windows 2000 system as an administrator.

2. Select Start | Run.

3. In the Run dialog box, type **MMC /A** and press ENTER.

4. In the Microsoft Management Console, select Console | Add/Remove Snap-In.

5. In the Add/Remove Snap-In dialog box's Standalone sheet, click the Add button.

6. From the list of available snap-ins, choose the Security Configuration and Analysis snap-in and click the Add button. Click the Close button to close the Add Standalone Snap-In dialog box.

7. In the Add/Remove Snap-In dialog box, click OK to close the dialog box.

8. Right-click the new Security Configuration and Analysis entry under the Console Root and choose Open Database from the shortcut menu.

9. In the Open Database dialog box, choose the path and filename of the security database. This database will hold the results of the security configuration. Click OK.

10. The Security Configuration and Analysis tool will then display the Import Template dialog box. In this dialog box, you will be presented with a list of security templates. Choose the template you created earlier. Click the Open button.

11. Once you've created your database and associated the security template, right-click the Security Configuration and Analysis item and choose Configure Computer Now from the shortcut menu (see Figure 8-19).

12. The Security Configuration and Analysis tool will then prompt you to enter a path and filename for the log file that records the various security checks that are performed and their results, shown in the next illustration. Click OK to continue.

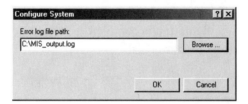

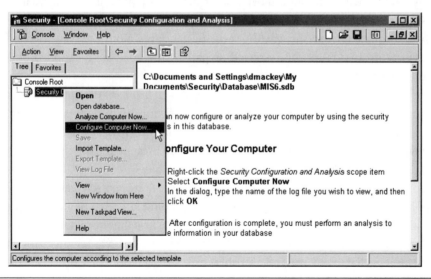

Figure 8-19 Selecting the Configure Computer Now command

13. The Security Configuration and Analysis tool will then perform the security analysis (shown in the following illustration).

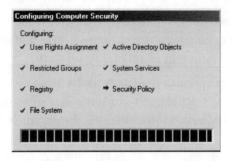

14. Once the security configuration is complete, you may need to reboot your computer for some settings to take effect.

Catywhompus Construction Update

Like other companies, Catywhompus can benefit greatly from the process of analyzing security requirements. You should begin with an assessment of its current environment. Not only will this serve as a snapshot looking at current security conditions, but it will also be a chance to revisit the existing security standards. Both the security conditions and security standards can be reviewed as part of the baseline creation process presented earlier in this chapter.

As in most companies, the social engineering attack is one of the greatest concerns at Catywhompus, which has developed a trusting and non-blaming business culture. As the ardent MCSE consultant retained by Catywhompus, it is also assumed that you have reviewed the types of malicious computer code presented earlier in Table 8-1.

Next in your security analysis process, you take the baseline information and the feedback you've received from the Catywhompus management team to create a revised security policy. This process was presented in the middle of this chapter and includes authenticating all user access to system resources (including the use of password policies), applying appropriate access control to all resources (such as via security groups), and understanding what, if any, trust relationships exist between domains. And don't overlook how to use group policy, and how to deploy secure server-side applications.

Last, and certainly not least for Catywhompus, is the process of implementing a security policy, which was covered extensively in the last part of this chapter.

Chapter Review

Windows 2000 provides valuable security analysis tools: Security Configuration and Analysis and Security Templates. With a thorough knowledge of your environment and a solid security policy, you can significantly reduce the chances of security breaches within your Windows 2000 environment.

Questions

1. Which type of attack includes the man-in-the-middle and IP-spoofing techniques?
   a. Masquerade
   b. Virus
   c. Social engineering
   d. Sniffer

2. What is Security Configuration and Analysis's command-line equivalent?
   a. SecPolicy
   b. SECEdit
   c. SecureAudit
   d. AuditSec

3. Which group is designed to control access to resources?
   a. Local group
   b. Domain local group
   c. Global group
   d. Universal group

4. Which type of trust relationship is created automatically between domains located in the same forest? (Choose all that apply.)
   a. One-way trust
   b. Two-way trust
   c. Transitive trust
   d. Nontransitive trust

5. Where are security templates stored by default?
   a. C:\
   b. \WINNT\SYSTEM32\CONFIG
   c. \WINNT\SYSTEM32\DRIVERS
   d. \WINNT\SECURITY\TEMPLATES

Answers

1. **A.** A masquerade type of attack involves an attacker that pretends to be another user or system.

2. **B.** SECEdit is a command-line equivalent to the Security Configuration and Analysis tool. You can use this to create a batch file or schedule to run on a regular basis.

3. **B.** A domain local group is designed to control access to individual domain resources, such as printers, folders, and files.

4. **B** and **C.** By default, domains located within the same forest have two-way transitive trust relationships established.

5. **D.** Security templates used by the Security Configuration and Analysis tool are stored, by default, within the \WINNT\SECURITY\TEMPLATES folder.

Key Skill Sets

The following skill sets meet the Microsoft Objectives for the 70-220 exam:

- Be aware of possible attacks.
- Assess your current computing environment.
- Develop a security policy.
- Implement security settings.

Key Terms

Audit
Encrypting File System (EFS)
Group policy
Kerberos
NT LAN Manager (NTLM)
Smart card
Trust relationship

Designing a Windows 2000 Security Solution

This chapter covers the following key mastery goals:

- Know what constitutes sound Windows 2000 security policies
- Understand how to design an authentication strategy
- Appreciate the key considerations in designing a Public Key Infrastructure solution
- Master the steps for creating a Windows 2000 network services security design

You've seen the news: viruses tie up corporate e-mail systems, distributed denial of service attacks shut down Web sites, and hackers steal financial and confidential data. For a system administrator, the news is frightening. You may, however, want to sit down for *this* news—your company's biggest security threat is *its employees*. Estimates place the likelihood of a computer security breach by a company's own employees in the 80 percent range, according to several studies and security Web sites (we concur with that whole heartedly!). So, in addition to the many security threats that come from outside your company, you also have to maintain a watchful eye on the practices and actions of your own colleagues. Paranoid yet? If not, you will be.

As you probably already know, implementing a proper security policy protects your company's operations, reputation, and critical data. It's an unfortunate reality for today's MCSEs, and IT staff in general, that so much is riding on security. Luckily, Windows 2000 has built upon the security model of Windows NT 4.0 and has added a rich array of features and tools to help you further secure your environment. This chapter will help you understand Windows 2000's security tools and features, and will help you implement them to create an effective security policy.

Update: Catywhompus Construction Must Implement Windows 2000 Security Solutions

You are an IT consultant that has been hired by Catywhompus Construction to help the in-house IT staff protect client data. Security is a crucial component of today's computing environment and, fortunately, your customer has crossed the first major hurdle in realizing that security needs to be implemented in its computing environment. You have already developed the skills from Chapter 8 to be able to analyze the company's needs and security requirements. Now you must use these skills to determine which Windows 2000 security features need to be implemented.

In this chapter, you will learn the vital Windows 2000 security components that relate to securing your Windows 2000 desktops and servers, authenticating users, ensuring users' identities, and implementing security within key Windows 2000 services. By the end of the chapter, in the Catywhompus Case Study, you will address key security questions that will help you in implementing security features based on your new skills.

Windows 2000 Security Policies

Windows system administrators, and thus MCSE candidates, must be vigilant in defending the networks, servers, and desktops within their charge. That means that security concerns should be part of your everyday operations. In particular, you must ensure that

- Computer users are who they say they are. You can accomplish this type of identity checking through authorization and authentication practices.

- Authorized users are only allowed access to the data and resources that are absolutely necessary.

- Unauthorized users are denied all access to your systems' data and resources.

- Malicious users cannot compromise the security measures that you employ.

With these charges in mind, you must also circumvent the obstacles that each computing environment imposes.

First, the spectrum of security stretches from a completely secure environment with little flexibility or usability from the user's point of view to an environment with tons of flexibility and usability, but little real security. In reality, most environments lie somewhere in the middle. As an administrator, it is your job to understand where this middle lies.

Second, you must not be fooled into thinking that security threats will only come from strangers or company outsiders. Unfortunately, as mentioned earlier, your colleagues offer the highest security threat to your computing environment. They have access, they know the systems, and they may imagine a very real motive in causing damage. Never underestimate security threats from within your company.

Finally, each company has different security needs. Your company may be spread over a large geographical area with many business units or may be a small operation with one physical location. The company characteristics will play a vital role in determining which security policies you employ.

Now that you understand the importance of knowing your company and its security needs, it is important to understand the various security tools and features that Windows 2000 offers. The following sections will walk you through the various tools, show you the best practices, and guide you to making the best decisions when it comes to security.

Audit Policies

Auditing can be an important way to ensure that your Windows 2000 systems and security measures are not compromised. *Auditing* is the overall process of tracking the actions of users, programs, and other systems upon your Windows 2000 system. Consequently, an *audit policy* determines which events are tracked and how these events are reported to you, the administrator. There are many decisions to make when implementing an audit policy and, as is the case with most administrative decisions, planning goes a long way.

Planning

Mapping out your audit policies *before* you implement them will allow you to plan an effective auditing strategy and save you the headache of nested iterations of audit settings. In this context, "nested" means that one set of audit policies may be at odds with another set of audit policies, so the question clearly becomes which audit policy applies. The following sections outline the six main planning areas that you should focus on when building your audit policy.

To Audit or Not to Audit   In Windows 2000, auditing is disabled by default. So, the first question you must answer is whether auditing is necessary for your computing environment. Auditing does allow you to track various security events, such as login failures, changes in user rights, successful file accesses, and many others. From a security standpoint, auditing is a must have. However, auditing also has some technical baggage that you must weigh (forgive the pun):

- *Manually churning through the Security log can be a tedious process depending on which events you are auditing.* The auditing process records events in the Security log, and normally, to view the various events, you must use Windows 2000's Event Viewer. If you are recording a large number of events, you should think about investing in a third-party tool that will help you filter the Security log and only report those events you wish. TNT Software's Event Log Monitor, NetIQ's AppManager, and Aelita Software's EventAdmin are just three of many such products on the market.

- *The auditing process requires additional process and memory usage on each Windows 2000 system for which auditing is configured.* For older machines or heavily used machines, auditing may not be logistically feasible.

- *Audit logs can consume a large amount of disk space.* You can, however, adjust the Security log to overwrite itself, thereby avoiding this problem.

  1. Right-click on the Security log object in the Computer Management snap-in and select Properties.

  2. On the General tab, select one of the overwrite options under the Log size area.

  3. Then click OK to accept the new settings for overwriting.

Audit Where?   Once you've decided that you should turn on auditing, you must decide which systems will be audited. Since auditing is a function of the local system, each system records the audited events to the local Security log. If you only want to audit the events of a Windows 2000 workstation, your task is easy. You can simply enable auditing on each individual computer by using the Windows 2000 Local Security Settings tool, as shown in Figure 9-1.

If, however, you would like to enable auditing for a wider group of computers, you should use Group Policy to implement the auditing policy (for example, in the default domain Group Policy Object, select Computer Configuration | Windows Settings | Local Policy | Audit Policy). This will save you a tremendous amount of time in configuring auditing on each workstation and server. Instructions for implementing audit policies will be covered in the following sections. For more information on group policies, refer back to Chapter 4.

Audit How?   After you've determined the scope of your auditing, you must design a plan to check your Security logs. Auditing is a passive process that simply records events. As such, it requires constant vigilance from an experienced system administrator. You're welcome to turn on every auditing event that Windows 2000 offers, but a warm human body must still interpret the logs and determine where security

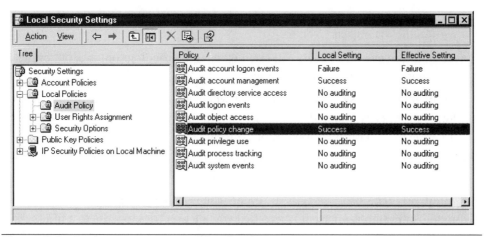

Figure 9-1   Implementing security-related auditing

breaches have occurred. More importantly, this is really a call to fix the underlying audit policy so that you are advised of critical events and not about unimportant events.

As mentioned earlier, you'll have to decide who will check the Security logs and how often. If you decide that manual intervention is too time-consuming, one of the third-party tools mentioned earlier may be more suitable.

Which Events?   Again, auditing should be meaningful and easily deciphered by the system administrator. If you're auditing all events that Windows 2000 offers, the Security logs will probably be too cluttered to be useful and will eventually be neglected. Therefore, it's important to select only the events that are important and meaningful in your overall security strategy.

In addition, there are two levels of auditing in Windows 2000: *action* and *object*. The following action-auditing events are available:

- **Audit account logon events**   Records an event whenever a user account is validated. For local accounts, this event occurs on the local system. For domain accounts, this event occurs on the domain controller.

- **Audit account management**   Records an event whenever

    - A user or group account is created, modified, or deleted

    - A user account is renamed, enabled, or disabled

    - A user account's password is modified

- **Audit directory service access**   Records an event whenever an Active Directory (AD) object is accessed. This audit event is only available on Windows 2000 domain controllers. You must enable this audit event in order to specify auditing on specific AD objects.

- **Audit logon events**   Records an event whenever a user logs on, logs off, or makes a network connection to this computer.

- **Audit object access**   Records an event whenever a specified file, folder, registry key, or printer is accessed. You must enable this audit event in order to specify auditing on specific files, folders, or printers.

- **Audit policy change**   Records an event whenever user-rights assignment policies, audit policies, or trust policies are modified.

- **Audit privilege use**   Records an event whenever a user tries to exercise a user right. For example, an event is recorded when a user tries to write to a file.

- **Audit process tracking**   Records an event whenever the system detects an application that is tracking program activation, process exit, and other low-level events.

- **Audit system events**   Records an event whenever the system is restarted, the system is shut down, system security is affected, or the Security log is modified.

Once you have addressed the higher-level action-auditing events, you can take the next step and audit object events. For example, when you enable the Audit Directory Service Access event, you can then audit specific events within Active Directory, as shown next. In the default domain Group Policy Object, select Computer Configuration | Windows Settings | Local Policy | Audit Policy.

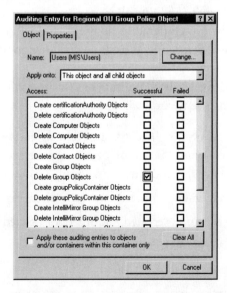

In addition, when you enable the Audit Object Access event, you can audit file, folder, and drive access, Registry access, and printer access, as shown in the following three illustrations.

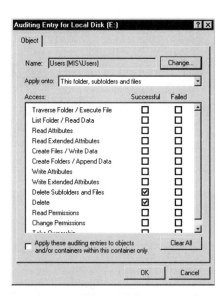

We find the next illustration to be especially interesting: the ability to audit local hard disk access. So many times, access concerns are thought of in the context of network access. It's easy to overlook concerns about local disk access.

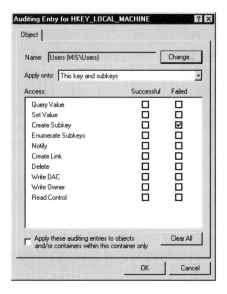

Another auditing area that hasn't received near the attention it should is Registry access. It's not lost on us and other long-time MCSEs that access to the Registry was one of the big security headaches in the Windows NT era.

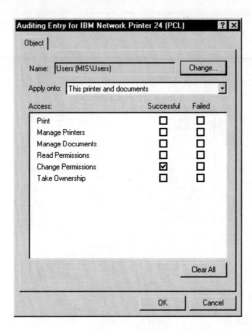

Success vs. Failure   Whenever you enable an audit event, you can choose whether you would like to audit instances where the event was successful, failed, or both. As you can see in Figure 9-2, each event allows you to check Success, check Failure, or check both options.

These options give you the flexibility to audit only the events you want. For example, if you would like to catch the times when a user successfully deletes a file from a particular folder, you can audit the success of the Delete event. Alternatively, if you want to catch someone trying to hack into your Windows 2000 server, you could monitor the failure of the Audit Logon Events event.

Security Log Behavior   The last item you must plan is how to control the Security log. Since auditing will write your chosen events to the Security log, it can fill up quickly. You must contain the size of the log to fit within the available disk space but also maintain enough audit events to ensure your newly developed audit policies and procedures are effective.

Figure 9-2
Types of audit
events

To modify the behavior of the Security log, follow these steps:

1. Click Start | Programs | Administrative Tools | Event Viewer.

2. Right-click the Security Log and choose Properties.

3. On the General tab, modify the log behavior as needed, using the options shown here.

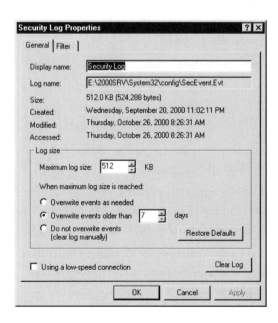

Implementation of Audit Policy

Now that you've thought through and extensively planned your audit policy, it's time to implement it. Before you do, though, you must ensure that you are logged on as Administrator to the local machine or domain controller, are a member of the local or domain Administrators group, or have the following special permissions added to your account:

- Generate Security Audits
- Managing Auditing and Security Log

Lab Exercise 9.1: Implementing Audit Policy

Audit Action Events   There are various ways to audit the higher-level action events.

- **Propagating a Domain-Wide Audit Policy**   As a domain administrator, you can propagate a specific auditing policy to various systems within the domain. To implement an audit policy on domain systems, follow these steps:

    1. Click Start | Programs | Administrative Tools | Active Directory Sites and Services to implement an audit policy at the site level; or alternatively, click Start | Programs | Administrative Tools | Active Directory Users and Computers to implement an audit policy at the domain or organizational unit level.

    2. Right-click the directory object where you would like to implement the audit policy, and choose Properties.

    3. In the Properties dialog box, click the Group Policy tab.

    4. In the Group Policy page, select a group policy in the Group Policy Object Links area, click the New button to create a new group policy for the object, or click the Add button to associate an already-created group policy.

    5. Once you have chosen a group policy, click the Edit button. Windows 2000 will launch the Group Policy tool.

    6. In the Group Policy tool, navigate to Computer Configuration | Windows Settings | Security Settings | Local Policies | Audit Policy, as shown in Figure 9-3. Double-click an event from the right pane to modify its properties.

- **Implementing an Audit Policy on a Domain Controller**   Your next task as a domain administrator might be to implement an audit policy on a domain controller by following these steps:

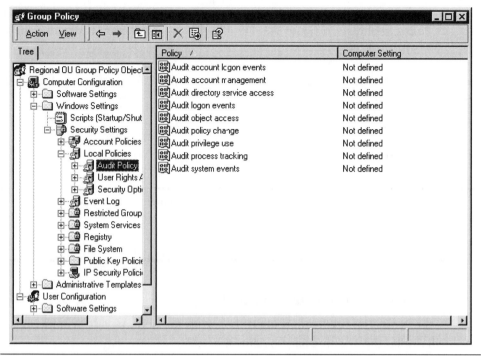

Figure 9-3 Selecting an audit policy

1. Click Start | Programs | Administrative Tools | Active Directory Sites and Services to implement an audit policy at the site level; or alternatively, click Start | Programs | Administrative Tools | Active Directory Users and Computers to implement an audit policy at the domain or organizational unit level.

2. Right-click the directory object where you would like to implement the audit policy, and choose Properties.

3. In the Group Policy tool, navigate to Windows Settings | Security Settings | Local Policies | Audit Policy, as shown in the previous illustration. Double-click an event from the right pane to modify its properties.

- **Implementing an Audit Policy on a Stand-Alone Server, Member Server, or Workstation**   To implement an audit policy on a stand-alone server, member server, or workstation, follow these steps:

    1. Click Start | Programs | Administrative Tools | Local Security Policy.

2. In the Group Policy tool, navigate to Security Settings | Local Policies | Audit Policy, as shown in figure 9-3. Double-click an event from the right pane to modify its properties.

Audit Object Events   To audit object events on a drive, folder, file, printer, or AD object, follow these steps:

1. Right-click the object that you would like to audit, and select Properties.

2. In the Properties dialog box, click the Security tab.

TIP   If you don't see the Security tab for your chosen AD object, select Advanced Features from the AD tool's View menu.

3. In the Security page, click the Advanced button.

4. In the Access Control Settings dialog box, click the Auditing tab. Windows 2000 will display the Auditing page, as shown here.

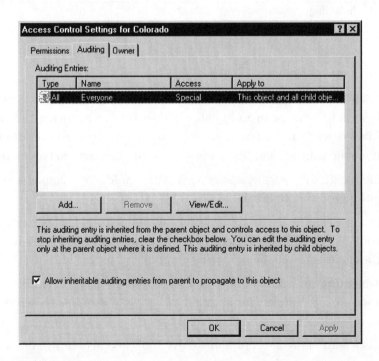

PART II

5. On the Auditing tab, click the Add button to add a new auditing event or select a listed audit event, and click the View/Edit button to modify audit properties. In addition, you can uncheck the Allow Inheritable Auditing check box to ensure that audit settings on any parent objects are not propagated to this object.

Delegation of Authority

One major problem with Windows NT 4.0 was that there was no good way to compartmentalize and delegate various administrative rights—at least, no good way built into the operating system. And why is this important? Speaking only for ourselves, we can well remember the August afternoon when we were running for a flight at Seattle-Tacoma International Airport and performing an administrative function or two on the Windows NT Server on the way out the door. In this case, it was the last day of employment for a low-level staff member, and the account was to be disabled (not deleted). Clearly, we could have delegated this relatively safe task to a power user, but we didn't want to provide the "keys to the kingdom" to this same power user by allowing him to log on as an administrator. We got the account disabled, but nearly missed our flight. This is an example of where we had to do something ourselves instead of being able to delegate it out to someone else at work. And just how did we disable this account under Windows NT Server 4.0? By using the User Manager for Domains tool found in the Administrative Tools program group.

With the introduction of Active Directory and Windows 2000, administrators can now divvy out their tasks and responsibilities. After all, it's important to share the wealth, or at least the administrative duties that can be *safely* assigned to power users. ("Safely," as in not inflicting massive damage to the network inadvertently or intentionally!)

For all intents and purposes, a domain forms the most fundamental security container available within Windows 2000 (which, believe it or not, is the same foundation as Windows NT Server). Group policies, security groups, and organizational units all give you vital tools for administering rights and privileges for your domain users. Our rule of Windows 2000 security is that if your domains are in order, the rest will follow.

Other chapters and sections within the book will deal in more detail with group policies and security books, so this section will focus on organizational units (OU) and how to use them for security purposes.

Planning

When designing your Active Directory structure, one major concept to keep in mind is the idea of delegation. By structuring your domain with logical grouping of objects

Figure 9-4
Company domain
structure

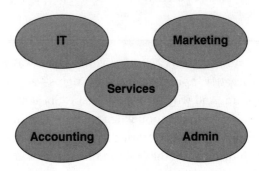

MIS' Only Domain
MIS.COM

under OUs, you can guarantee easier delegation of administrative tasks. For example, suppose MIS has one location in Denver that is comprised of five departments: IT, Admin, Marketing, Accounting, and Services. Figure 9-4 displays a possible domain structure for a company (a sample company name of MIS) that allows an organized delegation structure.

By organizing the domain into these various OUs, you can delegate administrative privileges to another responsible computer user or administrator for a specific OU. In addition, Windows 2000 gives you the flexibility of delegating explicit administrative tasks. For example, suppose the company has a power user in the Marketing department. Instead of constantly having the IT department administer objects within the Marketing OU, you could delegate that authority to your Marketing hotshot. What? Don't trust your power user that much? Then grant the hotshot only limited rights— limit her to only being able to reset passwords for the Marketing OU.

When you have an idea of how you want to delegate administrative privileges, it's time to use the Delegation of Control wizard. This wizard walks you through the steps to delegate rights to other users.

Lab Exercise 9.2:
Delegation of Control Wizard

- To use the Delegation of Control wizard to delegate common administrative tasks, follow these steps:

    1. Click Start | Programs | Administrative Tools | Active Directory Users and Computers.

2. Right-click the domain or organizational unit where you would like to delegate control, and select Delegate Control. Windows 2000 will launch the Delegation of Control wizard.

3. In the wizard's Welcome screen, click the Next button to continue.

4. In the Users or Groups screen, click the Add button, which will allow you to include the users or groups to which you would like to delegate authority (see the following illustration). Click the Next button to continue.

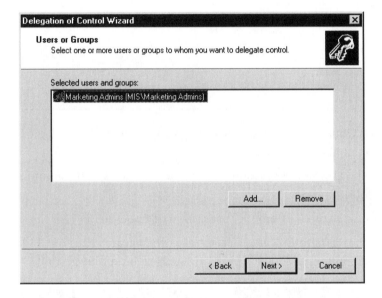

 TIP When delegating authority, it is much easier and safer to delegate authority only to security groups. Whenever you need to delegate authority to more individuals, simply add the user to the designated security group. If an individual leaves the company, you can swap the authority delegation with another user account quickly and easily.

5. In the Tasks to Delegate screen, select the Delegate the Following Common Tasks radio button, and check one or more of the listed administrative tasks to delegate. For example, if you want to grant your Marketing user the right to reset passwords, check the Reset Passwords on User Accounts option, as shown here. Click the Next button to continue.

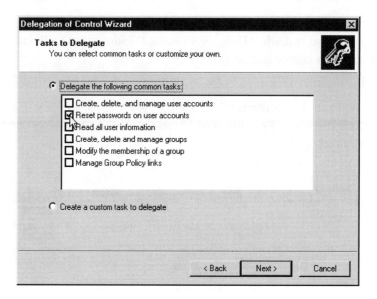

6. In the final screen, review the changes you've made and click the Finish button to complete the wizard.

- To use the Delegation of Control wizard to delegate specific administrative privileges, follow these steps:

   1. Follow steps 1–4 from the first section of this exercise.

   2. In the Tasks to Delegate screen, select the Create a Custom Task to Delegate radio button, as shown here. Click the Next button to continue.

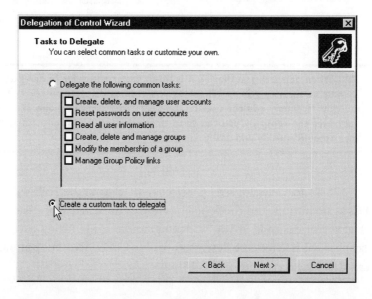

3. In the Active Directory Object Type screen, select the This Folder . . . radio button if you would like to delegate control to all objects within this particular domain or OU, or select the Only the Following Objects in the Folder option to specify which objects the delegate should control (as shown next). Click the Next button to continue.

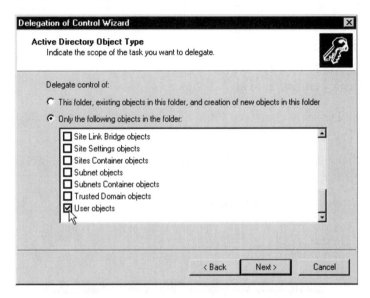

4. In the Permissions screen, select the various permissions that you would like to assign to your delegate, as shown next. These permissions will govern what access rights your appointee will have over your previously selected objects. Click the Next button to continue.

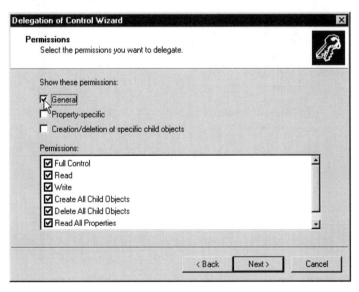

5. In the final screen, review the changes you've made and click the Finish button to complete the wizard.

Would you like even more granular control over how you delegate control? Well, Active Directory offers it. Like most other Windows objects, you can simply modify the security properties of an AD object and grant (or deny) specific permissions to groups or users.

Lab Exercise 9.3:
Delegating—More Options

To assign specific permission to an AD object:

1. In Active Directory Users and Computers, select Advanced Features from the AD tool's View menu.

2. Right-click the object to which you would like to grant or deny access, and then select Properties.

3. In the Properties dialog box, click the Security tab.

4. In the Security page, you can grant or deny general rights to specific users or groups, as shown here.

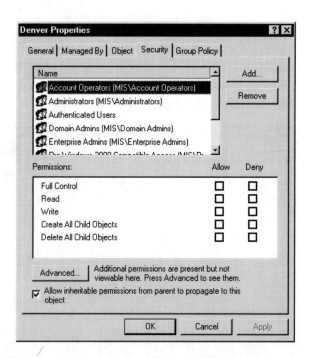

5. For more granular control, however, click the Advanced button. In the Advanced dialog box, click the Permissions tab. Select a specific permission that you would like to modify, and click the View/Edit button. You can see here that Windows 2000 offers greater control over very specific administrative tasks using this method.

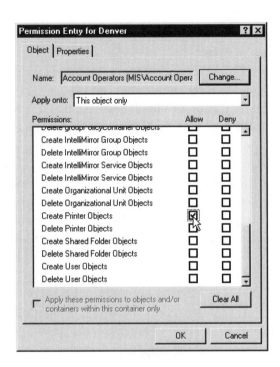

Policy Inheritance

The MCSE exam objective, "Design the Placement and Inheritance of Security Policies for Sites, Domains, and Organizational Units," is less about learning a new skill and more about applying already-learned skills. To fully understand this objective, you must go back to Chapter 1 and review the concepts of a site, domain, and organizational unit. These concepts are important because administrators can configure group policies only for these AD objects.

In Microsoft-speak, group policies are synonymous with security policies, setting aside the power-configuration capabilities of Group Policy for just a moment (as you know, Group Policy is used for security, software distribution, and configuration purposes). Group policies form the security core by offering features to control user-account properties, local-computer properties, event logs, groups, services, the Registry, the file system, public key policies, and IP Security for any and all computers within your domain. And since you learned back in Chapter 4 that there is a many-to-many relationship between group policies, sites, domains, and OUs, you should understand how these policies are inherited.

Group Policy Inheritance

Group policies can be a tricky business. As mentioned previously, you have the ability to implement group policies at the site, domain, and OU level. However, you can also implement policies at a local-computer level. And what happens when you have nested OUs—which group policy wins out? The Zen answer is they all do and only one does. Group policies are cumulative, meaning that the settings from all group policies are applied. For example, a computer may have a local group policy, and the user using that computer has group policies implemented at her site, domain, and OU. When she logs into her computer, all settings from the group policies will be implemented. However, and here's the catch, if any settings are in conflict, the settings from the last group policy to be processed are implemented, and group policies are processed in the following order:

1. **Local user and computer policies**.

2. **Site group policies** (in the order listed within the object's Properties dialog box, Group Policy page).

3. **Domain group policies** (in the order listed within the object's Properties dialog box, Group Policy page).

4. **Organizational unit group policies** (in the order listed within the object's Properties dialog box, Group Policy page).

5. **Nested OU policies** (OU within an OU; in the order listed within the object's Properties dialog box, Group Policy page). Policies are applied at the parent before the child OU for nested organizational units.

For example, if the site group policy mandates that the minimum password length is three characters, the domain group policy mandates six characters, and the user account's OU mandates five characters; then the user's minimum password length must be five characters.

Blocking Inheritance

We now know that group policies are inherited and their properties are cumulative once they reach the intended user or computer. Windows 2000, however, comes with several ways to block group policies from taking effect. The most effective way is to remove or disable a group policy. This keeps the policy landscape simple and easy to maintain; however, it is not always possible. Instead, you may simply want to block the inheritance of a group policy from a parent container.

For example, suppose an IT department doesn't want the default domain group policy applied to its employees (despite the fact that IT employees are more likely to cause damage!). Instead, the IT department has a more "flexible" group policy that its employees would like to apply to users only within the IT OU. By blocking the inheritance of a stricter domain group policy, the IT department is free to set its own group policy. (There are also ways to get around a block of a stubborn department. Read on.)

Lab Exercise 9.4:
Removing a Group Policy from
a Site, Domain, or OU

To remove a group policy from a site, domain, or OU, follow these steps:

1. Click Start | Programs | Administrative Tools and select Active Directory Users and Computers to modify a domain or OU or select Active Directory Sites and Services to modify a site's group policy.

2. Right-click the site, domain, or organizational unit that you would like to modify, and select Properties.

3. In the Properties dialog box, click the Group Policy tab.

4. Select the group policy object that you would like to remove. Click the Delete button to completely remove the link to the group policy object, or click the Options button and select Disabled (as shown here) to disable the group policy.

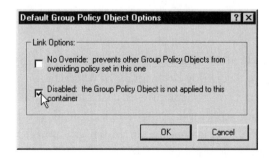

Lab Exercise 9.5:
Blocking a Group Policy Inheritance
from a Parent Container

To block group policy inheritance from a parent container, follow these steps:

1. Click Start | Programs | Administrative Tools | Active Directory Users and Computers.

2. Right-click the domain or OU where you would like to block inheritance, and select Properties.

3. In the Properties dialog box, click the Group Policy tab.

4. Click the Block Policy Inheritance check box (as shown here) to ensure that group policies are not propagated to this container's objects.

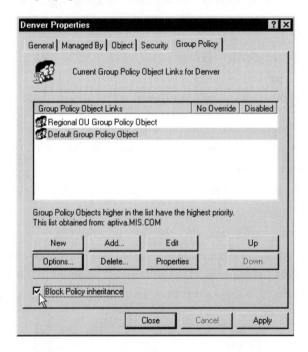

Overriding Blocked Inheritance

You just learned that a discerning department or organization can politely refuse the group policies of a parent container. However, as the administrator of a site, domain, or parent OU, you may not accept this polite refusal. Instead, you may decide to override this block and force the acceptance of your chosen group policy. Is it a drastic move? Yes. Is it an administrator's prerogative? Absolutely.

Lab Exercise 9.6:
Forcing the Inheritance of Group Policy

To force the inheritance of group policy, follow these steps:

1. Click Start | Programs | Administrative Tools and select Active Directory Users and Computers to modify a domain or OU or select Active Directory Sites and Services to modify a site's group policy.

2. Right-click the site, domain, or organizational unit that you would like to modify, and select Properties.

3. In the Properties dialog box, click the Group Policy tab.

4. Select the group policy object that you would like to enforce. Click the Options button and select the No Override check box (as shown here) to enforce the group policy.

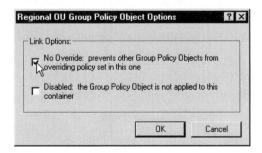

Encrypting File System (EFS)

One of the major security holes in any operating system is the vulnerability of data once an attacker has physical access to your computer. For example, if your laptop were ever stolen, Windows 2000 could do a pretty good job of stopping an attacker by requiring a valid user account and password when Windows booted. In addition, file and folder permissions could add another layer of protection against data loss. If, however, the malicious computer attacker had physical access to the machine and did a parallel operating installation on the NTFS partition, the folders and files (along with sensitive data) would be subject to compromise.

In order to shore up the defenses against this type of security weakness, you can encrypt your files and folders to protect them from theft. The encryption ensures that only authorized users can view the contents of your files. And fortunately, Windows 2000 employs the Encrypting File System (EFS) to allow you and your company's users to encrypt files.

As with everything else that relates to security, encryption does require a bit of planning before you turn it loose on your company.

Planning

There are several important points to keep in mind when deciding if and when you will use EFS.

- As with most advanced features, EFS can only be used on NTFS volumes.

- If you've encrypted a file under NTFS and move it to a non-NTFS volume, the file is decrypted automatically.

   Moving encrypted files over the network will decrypt them. In addition, encrypted files do not remain encrypted during network transmission. To protect files during a data transfer, you have to use another method, such as a virtual private network connection using Point-to-Point Tunneling Protocol (PPTP) or Internet Protocol Security (IPSec). You will recall that these terms have previously been defined on the core Windows 2000 MCSE exams (we'll continue to assume you have passed those exams prior to starting the design series exams that this book is dedicated to).

   You cannot encrypt files or folders that are compressed. If a volume, folder, or file is compressed, you must first uncompress it in order to use encryption.

- Only the user that encrypted the file, or a data-encryption recovery agent (see the "Disaster Recovery" section later in this chapter), can decrypt an encrypted file.

- System files cannot be encrypted—luckily for you and your users. That is because access can't be denied to system files.

- Encrypted files can still be deleted. You must still employ the other security measures to protect your data (such as locking up your machines when it is not in use). And don't forget data backup methods such as tape backups to recover deleted files.

- Macintosh and NFS (Unix-based) clients will not be able to use EFS.

- The CHKDSK command is run if upgraded from NT4. You will recall from your experience as a networking professional that the "check disk" or CHKDSK command is run at the command prompt. The CHKDSK command can negatively impact settings such as EFS when it's trying to perform its function of checking disks.

- Files that are moved by dragging and dropping will decrypt, even if they are moved to an encrypted folder (instead, you must perform a true copy and paste function first and then remove the old files from the old location).

Best Practices As you can see from the preceding list, there are more than a few points to consider; however, it's important to keep these items in mind when planning how and where data encryption is employed. In addition, to help you plan a data-encryption policy, here is a list of recommended best practices when using EFS:

- **Encrypt the folder or folders where a user stores most of his or her documents** This ensures that all user documents are encrypted by default.

- **Encrypt any folders that hold applications' temporary files** Since temp files often contain the same sensitive data as your original documents and are not always promptly removed from the system, encrypting them should be a priority. As a general rule, temp files have a .tmp file extension and are stored in one of four places: a temporary folder at the root of the volume's file system (`c:\temp`), in a folder used by the application (for example, `c:\accounting`), in each user's Documents and Settings folder (`c:\documents and settings\{user name}\local settings\temp`), and in the Windows folder (for example, `c:\winnt` or `c:\windows`). You should check with your application vendor to determine how it uses temp files. Encrypt folders instead of files to ensure the greatest number of files is protected and to reduce administrative overhead.

EFS Disaster Recovery Since only the user who encrypted a file, by default, can open it, it is important to have a backup strategy in case an employee is unavailable to decrypt a necessary file—this is a form of disaster recovery. Another disaster recovery scenario is when a file-encryption certificate and associated private key are damaged or lost.

By default, the domain administrator is the only recovery agent for your domain; however, Windows 2000 allows you to elect other disaster recovery agents via *recovery policies*. At the domain, organizational unit, or computer level, administrators can set three different types of policies:

- **Recovery Agent Policy** Designated users can recover encrypted data within their area of responsibility (their domain, OU, and so on). The default recovery agent for the domain is the domain administrator.

- **No Recovery Policy** When the Encrypted Data Recovery Agents policy is removed, a no-recovery policy is in place. No recovery agents have been designated to recover encrypted data; however, each computer's local policy is in effect. The default recovery agent in this case is the local administrator.

- **Empty Recovery Policy** When all recovery agents and associated certificates are removed, EFS is effectively turned off. No one can encrypt or decrypt data within the scope of the policy.

Lab Exercise 9.7:
Enacting a Recovery Policy
at the Site, Domain, or OU Level

To enact a recovery policy at the site, domain, or OU level, follow these steps:

1. Click Start | Programs | Administrative Tools, and then select Active Directory Users and Computers to modify a domain or OU, or select Active Directory Sites and Services to modify a site's group policy.

2. Right-click the site, domain, or organizational unit that you would like to modify, and select Properties.

3. In the Properties dialog box, click the Group Policy tab.

4. Select the specific group policy object where you would like to enable the recovery policy and click the Edit button. We are, of course, assuming you know the group policy you want to work with, or that you will be creating a new group policy object.

5. In the Group Policy snap-in, navigate to Computer Configuration | Windows Settings | Security Settings | Public Key Policies | Encrypted Data Recovery Agents, as shown in Figure 9-5.

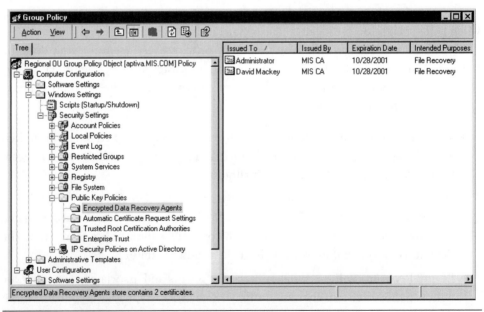

Figure 9-5 Configuring the Encrypted Data Recovery Agents

6. In the right pane, right-click an empty space and select Add to add recovery agents or select Delete Policy to enforce a No Recovery Policy. To enforce an Empty Recovery Policy, select all listed users, right-click the selection, and then choose Delete.

NOTE   To add a recovery agent, that user or group must have an associated file-recovery certificate. To learn more about certificates, see the "Design a Public Key Infrastructure" section later in this chapter.

For individual Windows 2000 systems (say a Windows 2000 Professional workstation), the process of designating recovery agents is just as straightforward. Simply open the Local Security Policy tool and select Security Settings | Public Key Policies | Encrypted Data Recovery Agents.

Recovery Tool Security   Having a recovery agent is a great and necessary backdoor for accessing encrypted files on your company's computers, under legitimate pretext, of course. And since the recovery agent must have a verified certificate to perform this type of work, you can be assured that a safeguard is in place to ensure that not all users can access sensitive encrypted data. But what would happen if a malicious computer user gained access to your agent's file-recovery certificate? Would that not defeat the purpose of encryption?

Absolutely! So if you are acting as the company's file-recovery agent, you can avoid having the precious file-recovery certificate stolen by exporting the certificate to a secure location, deleting the certificate from your personal store, and then importing the certificate only when file-encryption recovery is needed.

Lab Exercise 9.8:
Securing Your File-Recovery Certificate

To secure your file-recovery certificate, follow these steps at the Windows 2000 machine:

1. Assuming you are logged on as an Administrator, start MMC and add the Certificates snap-in to reference your user account.

2. Navigate to Certificates | Personal | Certificates.

3. In the right pane, right-click the file-recovery certificate, select All Tasks, and then select Export. Windows 2000 will launch the Certificate Export wizard.

4. Using the Certificate Export wizard, export the certificate and private key to a secure location. (By default, the wizard saves the export certificate to a file at the root of your system drive.) You should also assign a password to the file.

NOTE You can also use the previous step to simply make a backup copy of your file-recovery certificate to prevent against loss or damage.

5. Once you have exported the certificate, store the resultant file in a secure location.

6. Return to the Certificates tool, navigate to Certificates | Personal | Certificates. Right-click the file-recovery certificate once again and select Delete. Once you confirm the deletion, the certificate will be removed from your personal store.

7. Whenever decryption is necessary, return to the Certificates tool and navigate to Certificates | Personal | Certificates. Right-click an empty area within the right pane, select All Tasks, and click Import. Windows 2000 will launch the Import Certificate wizard to allow you to restore your file-recovery certificate.

Lab Exercise 9.9:
Encrypting a File or Folder

With EFS, each designated file or folder is encrypted using a combination of an operating system-generated encryption key and the user's public key. The user must then use his or her own private key to decrypt the file and access the data.

To encrypt a file or folder, follow these steps:

1. In Windows Explorer or a similar file-management tool, right-click the desired file or folder, and select Properties.

2. In the Properties dialog box, click the General tab.

3. In the General page, click the Advanced button. Note that you won't see this on a non-NTFS volume.

4. In the Advanced Attributes page, select the Encrypt Contents to Secure Data check box, as shown here.

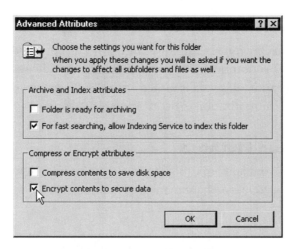

If you have chosen to encrypt a file that does not reside within an encrypted folder, Windows 2000 will display the following warning message. This dialog box gives you the opportunity to encrypt the parent folder or simply encrypt the file.

To decrypt a file, follow the same procedure and simply uncheck the Encrypt Contents to Secure Data check box.

TIP You can also encrypt and decrypt files from the command prompt using the CIPHER command. Type CIPHER /? for more details.

Design an Authentication Strategy

Authentication forms the foundation for security within your Windows 2000 network. In simple terms, authentication makes computer users prove they are who they say they are. Once a user is authenticated, you then have the power, as the administrator, to determine the user's authorization to access various network resources and services.

Authentication Methods

In Windows NT 4.0, your authentication options were limited. However, with the introduction of Windows 2000, you have many more options.

Certificates

During the discussion of EFS and its recovery agents earlier in this chapter, you learned a little about certificate-based security. In order to designate an EFS recovery agent for your domain, that user had to have a file-recovery certificate. This prevents unauthorized users from decrypting sensitive files and data.

The basic premise behind the certificate, then, is to associate one of these critical digital keys with each of your Windows 2000 users. This key is then used to ensure that the user is authorized to access specific network resources or administrative functions. Certificates are also versatile in that you can use certificates to identify yourself to Web-based entities or other network entities that exist outside of your organization.

The Windows 2000 certificate holds several important pieces of information, including the following:

- The owner's public key, which is one-half of Windows' Public Key Infrastructure (PKI); the second half—the private key—is retained solely by the owning user

- The identification information about the certificate

- The dates that the certificate is valid

The following illustration shows how the information discussed previously is presented.

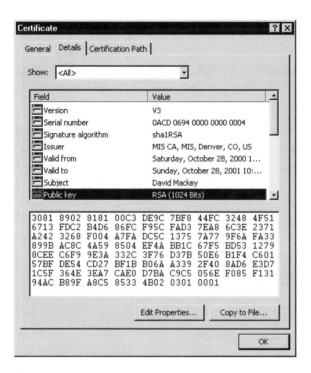

Once a user has been issued a private key and a certificate, he or she can then gain access to various Windows applications and services that use certificates for authentication. Specifically, Windows 2000 can use certificates in support of smart-card authentication, EFS, and secure e-mail.

For more information on certificates, see the "Design a Public Key Infrastructure" section later in this chapter.

Kerberos

Kerberos was developed by MIT to help securely authenticate users. Like certificates, Kerberos uses the idea of a digital key to verify that users are who they say they are. This key is then imbedded in network communication to verify the sender.

The first publicly released version was Kerberos v4. Windows 2000, however, has implemented Kerberos v5, and although it isn't yet a public standard, Microsoft's implementation closely followed RFC 1510. There are a few major benefits to the Windows 2000 implementation of Kerberos:

- **No additional software**   A Key Distribution Center (KDC) performs the critical function of authenticating networked systems. Luckily, Windows 2000 implements a KDC automatically on every domain controller, so there are no additional components to install.

- **Kerberos is paranoid** Kerberos does not assume that every server on the network is a valid system. Through its paranoia, it requires that every client and server validate their identity.

- **Fewer authentication requests** Clients obtain authentication credentials once per network session. Instead of having to authenticate with the domain controller each time a user accesses a network resource, Kerberos allows all servers to accept the authentication credentials presented by the client.

One of the major drawbacks, however, is that you cannot use Kerberos to communicate with older Windows NT systems. All systems involved in the Kerberos request and authentication process must use Windows 2000.

Authentication Process The Windows 2000 Kerberos service has several major components:

- **Key Distribution Center (KDC)** A Kerberos security system has three parts: a client, a server, and a trusted third-party authenticator. The KDC is the trusted third-party authenticator. As such, the KDC contains information about every security "principal" within its realm, which, in the case of Windows 2000, is your domain. A *principal* can be a user, machine, service, or application, and along with the principal's account information, the KDC stores a key, known as a *long-term key*, within its database. A long-term key is usually derived from the principal's account password and is used to encrypt and decrypt information transferred between the KDC and the principal. The KDC itself uses the domain account `krbtgt` to derive its own key. The `krbtgt` account cannot be renamed or deleted, and its password is modified automatically by Windows 2000 to avoid compromise. The primary purpose of the KDC's key is to encrypt and decrypt issued ticket-granting tickets (ticket-granting tickets are discussed next, with the Authentication Service).

- **Authentication Service (AS)** Part of the KDC, the Authentication Service issues ticket-granting tickets (TGTs). The TGT, in turn, allows a system to access the Windows ticket-granting service (TGS). A ticket is exactly what it sounds like. It is a virtual ticket that grants the holder certain rights, in this case related to authentication.

- **Ticket-Granting Service (TGS)** Another component of the KDC, the ticket-granting service issues sessions tickets that allow a system to access network resources, or the TGS issues a TGT for another TGS in another trusted domain.

If a Windows 2000 Professional workstation, w2kpro1, would like to connect to a service running on the Windows 2000 Server, w2ksrv1, the Kerberos authentication would work like this:

1. w2kpro1 requests a TGT from the KDC's AS. Since a KDC and its associated authentication service exist on every domain controller, the TGT request can be fielded by any domain controller within your domain.

2. The AS checks to see if the client is included in the KDC's database of security principals. If the client exists, the AS issues a TGT to the client.

3. The client then sends the TGT to the TGS to request access to the service located on w2ksrv1.

4. The TGS then issues a session ticket, or *session key*, back to w2kpro1 to use when communicating with w2ksrv1 that confirms w2kpro1's identity. This session key can then be used by w2kpro1 for any subsequent requests to w2ksrv1, thereby eliminating the need to reauthenticate through the KDC.

5. w2kpro1 then presents the session ticket to w2ksrv1 to access the necessary service. w2ksrv1 decrypts the session ticket to ascertain whether the client has properly authenticated through the KDC. If the client's session key is confirmed, w2kpro1 is granted access to the requested service.

6. Depending on how Kerberos is configured, w2ksrv1 may also send confirmation back to w2kpro1 once the session key has been accepted.

Configuring Kerberos Policy   Windows 2000 gives you some granularity for modifying the properties and operation of the Kerberos protocol, such as controlling the lifetime of the TGT, controlling the lifetime of the session ticket, or specifying the maximum length of time for which a TGT can be renewed. These settings are only available at the domain level, and you must be a domain administrator to modify them.

To access the Kerberos policy settings, follow these steps:

1. Click Start | Programs | Administrative Tools | Active Directory Users and Computers.

2. Right-click the domain that you would like to modify, and select Properties.

3. In the Properties dialog box, click the Group Policy tab.

4. Select the group policy where you would like to modify the Kerberos settings, and click the Edit button.

5. In the Group Policy tool, navigate to Computer Configuration | Windows Settings | Security Settings | Account Policies | Kerberos Policy, as shown in Figure 9-6.

NTLM

Kerberos is the authentication protocol of choice within Windows 2000. However, since a wholesale upgrade of network systems to Windows 2000 is a bit impractical for most organizations, the need for backward compatibility to the Windows NT 4.0 authentication protocol is still necessary. NT LAN Manager (NTLM) is the default authentication mechanism for Windows NT 4.0, and to provide backward compatibility, Windows 2000 is also packaged with the ability to use NTLM. You must use NTLM whenever the client, server, or both are running Windows 3.11, Windows 95, Windows 98, Windows ME, or any flavor of Windows NT 4.0.

Authentication Process   The NTLM authentication process is fundamentally different from that of Kerberos. If a Windows 2000 Professional Workstation, w2kpro1,

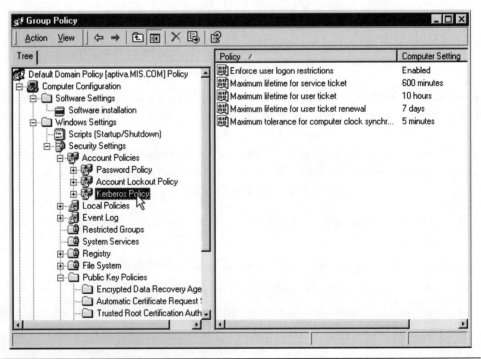

Figure 9-6   Configuring the Kerberos policy

would like to use a printer resource attached to a Windows NT 4.0 Server server, `nt4srv1`, the NTLM authentication process would work like this:

1. `w2kpro1` logs into a Primary Domain Controller (PDC) or Backup Domain Controller (BDC).

2. With the proper credentials, the PDC or BDC authenticates `w2kpro1` into the domain.

3. `w2kpro1` then requests permission from `nt4srv1` to use its printer.

4. `nt4srv1` checks with the PDC or BDC to ensure `w2kpro1` has the proper permissions.

5. The PDC or BDC authorizes `w2kpro1` to access the requested printer.

6. `nt4srv1` then allows `w2kpro1` to access its printer.

One of the major weaknesses of NTLM is that every time a client would like to access a network resource, the server must check with a PDC or BDC to verify the client's credentials. In other words, steps 3 through 6 are repeated for every request.

Smart Cards

A *smart card* is simply a credit-card-sized device that holds its own memory or processing chip. This additional chip allows it to store a variety of information, such as personal data, user account name, passwords, PINs, security codes, and other critical information, or it can provide low-level computations or interactions with smart-card readers. Unlike the normal username/password combination, smart cards offer one huge advantage—if the card is stolen or lost, the user knows this immediately (or relatively soon). Why? Because the belief is that you would notice the loss of a physical card sooner than the loss of a username or password (granted, this belief is optimistic, but when a smart card is missing, much like your car keys in real life, you would notice it). The card then can be replaced and the access granted to the missing card can be removed.

Generically, the process of using a smart card works like this:

1. The user inserts the smart card into a hardware device called a *smart-card reader*.

2. The smart-card reader and its associated software read the appropriate personal information from the smart card and pass that to the application requesting the information.

3. The user must then normally input a PIN or password to activate and authenticate the information stored on the card.

4. The requesting application then authenticates the user.

Windows 2000 also includes support for smart cards with a simple extension to the Kerberos protocol. As a result, the Windows 2000 smart-card process can work like this:

1. The user inserts the smart card into the smart-card reader.

2. The smart-card reader, its associated software, and a properly configured Windows 2000, signal an event to the operating system.

3. The Winlogon process displays a PIN prompt.

4. The user enters the appropriate PIN or password for the account.

5. Windows 2000 uses the PIN to access the information stored on the smart card.

6. The client computer sends a public key certificate to the domain KDC.

7. The KDC validates the certificate and uses its public key to encrypt a logon session key. The KDC then sends the encrypted logon session key and TGT to the client computer.

8. The client decrypts the logon session key using its private key and then uses it in all future communication with the KDC.

RADIUS

With the proliferation of remote employees, satellite offices, and connected travelers, most companies have implemented some sort of remote-access solution to allow access to network resources. In the case of Windows, most companies rely on the Remote Access Service (RAS) to handle this task. A RAS server is simply a Windows service that runs on an existing Windows server. RAS acts as a gateway that allows up to 256 simultaneous remote connections via dial-up, ISDN, or other types of connections.

The Remote Authentication Dial-In User Service (RADIUS) protocol, on the other hand, is an industry standard that provides the authentication and authorization necessary for remote employees using an ISP to dial in to their corporate networks. RADIUS can eliminate the need for RAS servers and the ever-expanding banks of remote connections. RADIUS, which is relatively new to the Windows world, works in this way:

1. A remote employee uses DUN or another type of remote connection client to access his or her ISP.

2. Once connected to the ISP, the client tries to authenticate into the corporate network a dial-up connection configured for a VPN network connection (it dials the IP address of the distant host that accepts VPN calls).

3. The ISP's remote access server, in turn, takes the request, acting as a RADIUS client and tries to authenticate the user using a known RADIUS server located within the corporate network.

4. If the user credentials are confirmed, the RADIUS server will then authenticate and authorize the user, based on Active Directory or local Windows accounts, to use the corporate network's resources.

Using this method, the system administrators have eliminated a need for separate user account and password databases, RAS servers, modems, telephone lines, and their associated cost, and they have even installed a level of auditing to show when users log in to the network. And perhaps the biggest benefit to RADIUS is that it allows you to interact with other types of heterogeneous RAS servers, thus providing a seamless connection for your remote users to access your Windows 2000 network resources.

 NOTE   If you would like to keep your own Windows 2000 RAS servers, you can still use RADIUS to add another layer of security and centralized user administration.

Installation   It is simple to convert your Windows 2000 server into a RADIUS server —just install the Internet Authentication Service (IAS). IAS is normally installed by default; however, if you must install it manually, it's located under the Networking Services Windows component. Once IAS is installed, you have only to list the various RADIUS servers that will be using your server for authentication purposes.

Lab Exercise 9.10:
Setting Up a Trust Between Your RADIUS Server and a RADIUS Client

To set up a trust between your RADIUS server and a RADIUS client, follow these steps:

1. Click Start | Programs | Administrative Tools | Internet Authentication Service.

2. In the IAS management tool, right-click the Clients folder and select New Client.

3. In the Add Client wizard, type in a name to identify this new client, and select the RADIUS protocol, as shown here. Click the Next button to continue.

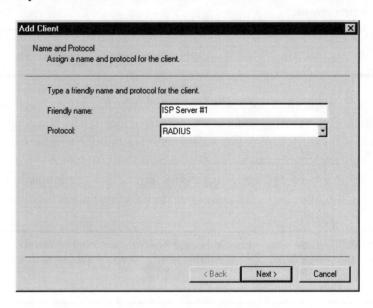

4. In the Add RADIUS Client screen, type in the IP address or DNS name of the RADIUS client. Also, type in a shared secret (a form of password) that the RADIUS client must use to authenticate with the RADIUS server, as shown here. Click the Finish button to complete the process.

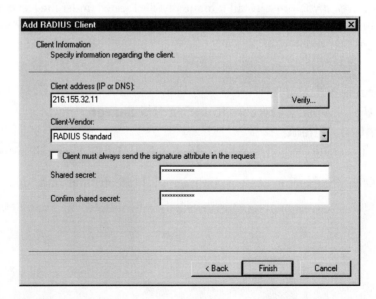

TIP   Just like any password, you should arrange to change the shared secret between RADIUS clients and servers on a regular basis.

Clear-Text Passwords

Clear-text passwords only deserve brief mention in this chapter because using them will be considered an insecure authentication. Clear-text passwords, however, do offer one benefit, which is that they can be employed with any system across any networks, and they can be used to authenticate between heterogeneous systems. Popular uses include HTTP 1.0 browsers and forms, Telnet, FTP, SMTP, POP3, and other network protocols that weren't designed with secure authentication in mind. Clear-text passwords, however, provide no real security because they can easily be intercepted by sniffers or crafty network users. If it's at all possible, eliminate the use of clear-text passwords on any and all of your computer systems.

Digest Authentication

Because of the obvious and glaring weaknesses of clear-text passwords, the World Wide Web Consortium (W3C) responded with RFC 2069 to create Digest Authentication (DA). Since clear-text passwords were the default with the HTTP 1.0, DA is included with HTTP 1.1 to provide stronger security in the transmission of sensitive information.

The basic operation works like this:

1. The Internet Information Services (IIS) server prompts the user to enter a username and password within Internet Explorer.

2. The user enters the proper username and password via the browser. Using a *hash*, or *message digest*, the username and password are encrypted for secure transmit to the IIS server.

3. Once received, the IIS server then decrypts the contents and tries to authenticate the user based on the passed username and password.

With regards to Windows 2000, HTTP 1.1 is only supported by IIS 5.0 and a browser that supports HTTP 1.1, such as Internet Explorer 4 and above.

SSL

Secure Sockets Layer (SSL) is in wide use on the Internet today. You probably have encountered sites that use SSL to securely transmit personal or credit card information.

The tip-off to an SSL-secured page is its beginning with the HTTPS:// protocol tag. SSL also uses private/public key algorithms to encrypt data for travel across data lines. The net effect is that your sensitive information is protected en route and is only decrypted by the intended recipient. Most modern Web browsers support SSL technology on the client end, and IIS 5.0 supports its use on the server end.

Security Group Strategy

Earlier in this chapter, you learned about group policies, OUs, and some of the considerations you must elucidate when planning your network. It's now time to bring all of these concepts together in providing comprehensive security settings and policies. Here's a planning checklist to help you develop an overall security plan that doesn't consume all of your administration time and energy.

- Organize users into security groups that reflect the functional nature of the group and also its security needs. For example, you may have an Accounting group that includes all users from the Accounting department to specify access to shared folders. However, from a group policy standpoint, you may want to divide those Accounting users further to apply strict security settings for contractors and more leeway for regular employees.

- Decide where you want to implement group policies. Do you want to implement group policies at the site, domain, OU, or local level? Of course, there are planning and design considerations ranging from the reasonable to the repugnant (such as politics and egos) that will weigh heavily in where Group Policy is implemented (and you thought the design track would be an easy high-paying career track!). For administrative ease, you should probably try to stick with a generic domain-level group policy and further specify security settings at the OU level. Avoid local policies if at all possible.

- Modify the group policies to match your organization's security needs. In addition, you may want to modify desktop settings and other minor features to display corporate logos or defaults. Make sure you refer back to the "Policy Inheritance" section earlier in this chapter to understand the inheritance of security policies.

- Try to delegate administrative control wherever possible, but limit the administrative access for your delegates. You want them to take the superfluous administrative tasks, such as password resets and folder access, but limit their ability to do damage or unleash major network resources. We consider the ability to delegate (with limitation) to be a good thing in our day-to-day world of MCSE consulting in Windows 2000 environments!

Design a Public Key Infrastructure

As mentioned previously in this chapter, digital certificates form an important part of the overall Windows 2000 security structure. By carrying the public key of the private-key/public-key combination, certificates can be freely distributed without causing a break in the security structure. And better yet, certificates work behind the scenes, so users are not forced to remember additional usernames and passwords.

Certificates, however, are but one piece of the overall Public Key Infrastructure (PKI). Unlike many other security measures, PKIs are not an established standard with the Internet or other network committees. Instead, PKI is a loose system of certificates, Certificate Authorities (CAs), and other security measures. In particular, Windows 2000's PKI consists of the following features, services, and applications:

- Internet Information Services (IIS) and Internet Explorer (IE) support PKI for Web-based applications.

- Microsoft Outlook and Outlook Express support PKI for certificate-based e-mail.

- Encrypting File System (EFS) uses PKI to verify that users can encrypt files or specify recovery agents.

- IPSec uses certificates to authenticate the identities during data communication.

- Smart cards can support the use of certificates as mentioned previously in this chapter.

- Active Directory can publish certificates.

- Microsoft Certificate Services enable organizations to issue their own certificates and PKI.

- Microsoft PKI provides support for third-party certificate authorities, such as VeriSign, Netscape, and others.

Certificate Authority Hierarchies

Viewing the previous list of PKI applications and services, you can see that digital certificates are becoming a larger part of Windows' security infrastructure. The certificate is the digital equivalent of a user's signature, and the security involved is hard to break. However, the big problem with certificates is that they have to be created and issued by a trusted source. After all, if anyone could issue certificates, the whole process breaks down.

Certificate Authorities (CAs) are the entities that perform the crucial task of creating and issuing certificates to the necessary users. In theory, a CA is a simple concept;

however, the implementation of a CA system is more difficult. In most organizations, multiple CAs are needed to issue and verify certificates in a *certification path*. This path is the progression of CAs that a PKI application or service must check to determine the authenticity of a certificate.

For large organizations, the recommended certification path should follow a progression such as the one shown in Figure 9-7. It has the following CAs:

- **Root CA** The root CA is the topmost, end-all, be-all certification authority. It has the final say by signing subordinate CAs' certificates. For smaller organizations, there may only be a root CA without the other intermediate or issuing CAs. Since the root CA is, by far, the most critical piece of the PKI puzzle, it's recommended that once you've issued the necessary certificates, the root CA is taken offline and stored in a secure location.

- **Intermediate CA** Depending on your organization's needs, you may need to install intermediate CAs to sign certificates for issuing CAs. These act like the root CA, but help to disseminate certificates to specific organizations. The next level down from the root CA should also be taken offline and stored in a secure location.

- **Issuing CA** This CA actually issues the certificates to users, computers, or applications. As such, it must be connected to the network. As mentioned previously, the

Figure 9-7
Recommended
certification path for
larger organizations

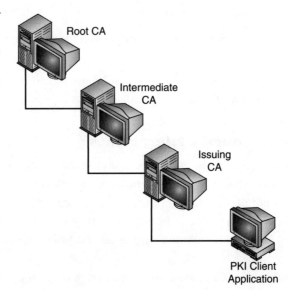

issuing, intermediate, and root CAs may all be one and the same for smaller organizations. This is not the most secure hierarchy, but it is probably the most feasible.

Certificate Server Roles

When implementing the PKI, you must determine which type of certification authority to install. You have two choices: an *Enterprise CA* or a *stand-alone CA*.

The Enterprise CA is for explicit use with Windows 2000 Active Directory. For example, if you have a domain and Active Directory installed, you can use an Enterprise CA to handle the issuance, revocation, and validation of certificates within your organization. This offers automated certificate approval and issuance. In addition, the Enterprise CA must be used when deploying smart-card technology. The biggest benefit is that certificates are tied into AD, so they can be issued based on group policies.

If, however, you must integrate with a third-party CA or don't have Active Directory installed within your organization, you can still use a stand-alone CA for certificate management. Unfortunately, stand-alone CAs, in the most secure situation, require more administration—a CA administrator must manually approve certificates. This process can be automated, but at the expense of a secure certificate-management process.

Lab Exercise 9.11:
Installing a Certification Authority

To install a CA on your Windows 2000 Server:

1. From the Control Panel, launch the Add/Remove Programs tool and select Windows Components.

2. From the Windows Components list, select Certificate Services. Windows 2000 will begin the installation process for your CA.

3. In the Certification Authority Type screen, select the type of CA that you would like to install, as shown here.

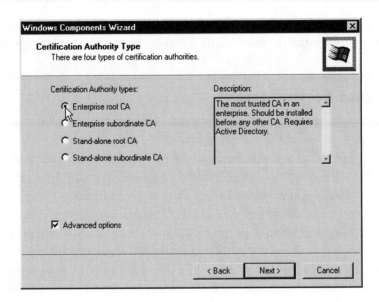

In addition, you can select the Advanced Options check box to access advanced settings on public and private key generation, as shown here. Click the Next button to continue.

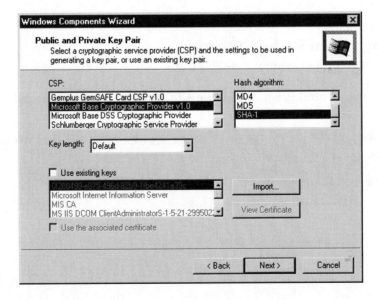

4. In the CA Identifying Information screen, enter the appropriate description and identification for your new CA, as shown here. Click the Next button to continue.

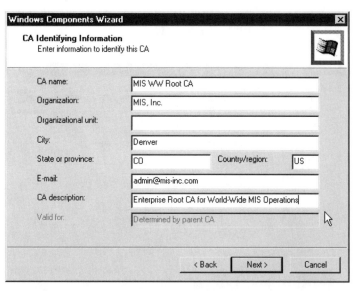

5. In the Data Storage Location screen, select folders where you would like to store the Certificate database and log, as shown here. As you can see, you can also choose to store the information on a shared network folder. Storing the Certificate database and log on a shared network folder is a bit riskier, because it can be accessed by other network users. If you decide to use this option, make sure your share and file permissions are tightly regulated. Click the Next button to continue.

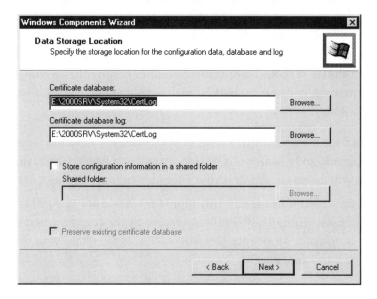

6. If you chose to install a subordinate CA, the wizard's next screen will allow you to request a CA certificate from the root CA or next highest CA in the hierarchy, as shown here. Click the Next button to continue. Windows 2000 will then install the necessary files and utilities for your CA.

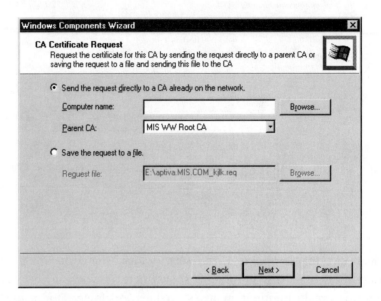

CA Disaster Recovery

There are two situations to fear when using CAs. First, the server running the CA service could have a hardware failure or crash. To prevent this damaging situation, you must have a backup procedure and restore policy in place for your CAs. If these servers fail and you have no way to restore the CA, you're looking at building new CAs and reissuing all certificates within your enterprise—obviously, a nightmare at best.

The second situation should, hopefully, be a rarer occurrence—a compromised CA. If, however, your CA is compromised by malicious computer users, there are several steps that you'll need to take:

1. First, and most importantly, shore up your defenses. Find out how the CA was compromised and restore your shields. Installing a new CA and issuing new certificates will do no good unless your environment is secure once again.

2. Revoke the CA's certificate. This will annul the CA and any subordinate CAs. Additionally, this will annul any certificates issued by the compromised CA and by all of its subordinates. Hopefully, this will convince you to take your root CA offline and store it in a secure area.

3. Remove the compromised certificates from all Trusted Root Certification Authorities stores. These stores indicate to users, computers, applications, and services, which CAs are to be trusted. You can access these stores using the MMC Certificates snap-in or Group Policy tool.

4. Install a new CA and reissue certificates to the appropriate users, computers, and applications. You should notify all appropriate users that the original certificates are being revoked and new ones will be issued.

Managing Certificates

Certificates go through a life cycle of usefulness to your PKI system. The life cycle includes the following events:

- Installation of the root CA and any subordinate CAs
- Issuance of CA certificates
- Issuance of certificates to users, computers, services, or applications
- Revocation of certificates
- Renewal of certificates
- Expiration of certificates
- Removal of CA

 NOTE Some of these events are optional to the certificate life cycle and may not occur in your specific environment.

Each part of this life cycle is critical to the overall security represented by the certificate. The previous section on server roles discussed the installation of the CA, issuance of CA certificates, and removal of CAs; this section will cover the certificate life cycle: issuance of certificates, revocation, renewal, and expiration.

Certificate Life Cycle

The life cycle of a certificate begins when it's issued and ends when it expires. Fortunately, you, as the administrator, have some administrative choices between these points.

Issuance   The first step in the certificate's life cycle is for a computer, user, or application to request a certificate from a CA. There are several common methods for doing so:

- Users can use the Certificates snap-in to explicitly request a certificate. A user can right-click the Certificates | Personal | Certificates section and select the All Tasks | Request New Certificate. Windows 2000 will then begin the Certificate Request wizard to start the process, as shown here.

- As an administrator, you can specify a group policy that will force client computers to automatically request a certificate. To do so, edit your desired group policy and navigate to Computer Configuration | Windows Settings | Security Settings | Public Key Policies | Automatic Certificate Request Settings. In the right pane, right-click an empty area and select New | Automatic Certificate Request. Windows 2000 will launch the Automatic Certificate Request Setup wizard, as shown here.

- For Web clients looking to gain certificates for their browser, e-mail client, or other applications, Certificate Services is automatically installed with its own Web-based certificate-request system. By default, the Windows 2000 Certificate Services Web pages can be found at `http://CA's servername/certsrv`. Once the user is granted access to the Web pages, he or she can request a certificate, as shown in Figure 9-8.

- You can also use the CertReq, a utility that requests certificates. The CertReq utility is a command-line tool that is fully documented in the Windows 2000 Server online help system under Certification Services.

Revocation   There also may be instances when you'll need to revoke certificates that have been issued by a CA. Specifically, you may want to cancel a certificate in cases where

- A user's private key has been compromised.
- A CA has been compromised.
- A user leaves your organization. This is probably one of the most important steps that often is overlooked.
- A computer that owns a certificate is retired or replaced.
- A user changes a name.

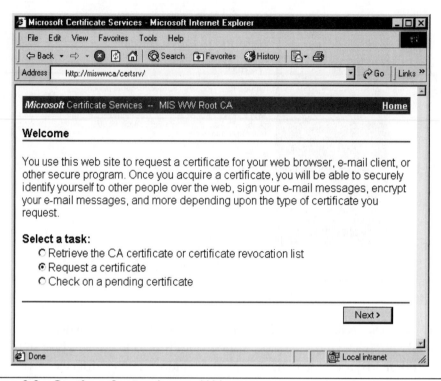

Figure 9-8   Certificate Services Intranet Web page

To revoke a certificate, you actually publish the certificate to a CA's Certificate Revocation List (CRL). The CRL is, by default, published weekly to all subordinate CAs and certificate clients. Once the certificate appears on the CRL, it is no longer valid.

NOTE   You can modify the CRL publishing interval on the CA by using the Certification Authority tool, right-clicking Revoked Certificates and choosing Properties. Additionally, you can manually publish the CRL immediately by right-clicking the Revoked Certificates folder and selecting All Tasks | Publish.

To revoke a certificate:

1. On the CA, click Start | Programs | Administrative Tools | Certification Authority.

2. In the Certification Authority tool, select the Issued Certificates folder.

3. In the right pane, right-click the certificate you would like to revoke and select All Tasks | Revoke Certificate.

4. The CA tool will then ask you to select a reason for the revocation. Select the appropriate reason and click OK. The certificate will then be moved to the Revoked Certificates folder and published at the set CRL interval.

Renewal   Every certificate has an expiration date. Only between the time the certificate is issued and the time it expires is a certificate valid. Like a password, a certificate is subject to attack and should be strengthened on a regular basis. The certificate's renewal process provides this added strength. When a certificate is renewed, the user can request a new certificate for the same purpose, under the same name, with a new serial number and even a new key pair.

The renewal process does come at a price—administrative hassles. The shorter the lifespan of the certificate, the more secure, but the more administrative work must go into the process. The converse is also true. The longer the lifespan of a certificate, the fewer administrative tasks needed, and the weaker the security it provides.

The renewal process is also important for certificates held by CAs. In the case of renewing a CA's certificate, you should try to request a new key pair as often as possible. This will optimize the security for your CA, and thus for all issued certificates.

To renew a certificate for a user, computer, or application using Windows 2000, open the Certificates MMC snap-in, right-click the certificate you'd like to renew, point to All Tasks, and select either Renew Certificate with New Key or Renew Certificate with Same Key.

To renew a certificate for a CA, follow these steps:

1. On the CA, select Start | Programs | Administrative Tools | Certification Authority.

2. In the Certification Authority tool, right-click the CA name and select All Tasks | Renew CA Certificate.

Expiration   As mentioned in the previous section, a certificate is only valid from the time it was issued to the time it expires. Unfortunately, Windows 2000 cannot currently modify the expiration-date policies of issued certificates, so expiration is controlled through the renewal process. For example, if a certificate's expiration date is two years in the future, you may still want to renew the certificate every three or six months. This ensures tight security, but also ensures administrative overhead.

Third-Party Certificate Authorities

PKI solutions are relatively new. Not all solutions are interoperable, and PKI, some would say, is still immature in today's security world. Within the murky waters of today's PKI solutions, some organizations have already pioneered a certification-management system using third-party CAs, and as these organizations migrate to Windows 2000, it may become necessary to integrate these existing CAs into the total Windows 2000 certificate solution.

There are several different PKI situations that you might encounter:

- Enterprise CAs only
- Third-party root CAs
- Third-party root CAs only
- Certificate mapping

These situations are described in the following sections.

Enterprise CAs Only

As stated earlier, Enterprise CAs are integrated with Active Directory and are only available for organizations that use Windows 2000. In an environment where you only have Windows 2000–based CAs, you can use Active Directory to distribute certificates. No CA trusts must be established with external CAs.

Third-Party Root CAs

If your organization is a pioneer with a previously installed third-party root CA, and you want to integrate your Windows 2000 CAs to use this root CA, you can accomplish this by specifying the third-party root CA as a *Trusted Root Certification Authority*. Essentially, you're telling your Windows 2000 CAs that the third-party CA is the root for the organization and thus the master of all certificates.

To designate a trusted root CA, follow these steps:

1. Go to your third-party CA and export the CA certification to a file.
2. Edit the Group Policy at the site, domain, or OU level.
3. Navigate to Computer Configuration | Windows Settings | Security Settings | Public Key Policies | Trusted Root Certification Authorities.
4. In the right pane, right-click an empty space and select All Tasks | Import. Windows 2000 will launch the Certificate Import wizard to import your third-party CA's certificate.

Third-Party Root CAs Only

In the case where you already have third-party CAs installed and have no desire to install Windows 2000–based CAs, you can designate a trust between your AD organization and the third-party CA. You specify this relationship using an *enterprise trust policy*. Additionally, you can use an enterprise trust to establish a relationship between your AD organization and other Windows 2000–based CAs located in another organization.

The most powerful feature of the enterprise trust is that you can limit the duration of the trust and can even limit the scope of activities that your Windows 2000 organization will trust the external CA. Using a *Certificate Trust List* (CTL), you can specify a list of trusted external CAs, the duration of the trust, and the specific actions you want your Windows 2000 certificate to authenticate from them. For example, you can limit the trust to one month and only allow the external CA to authenticate e-mail certificates.

To establish an enterprise trust with a third-party CA, follow these steps:

1. Go to your third-party CA and export the CA certification to a file.

2. Edit the Group Policy at the site, domain, or OU level.

3. Navigate to Computer Configuration | Windows Settings | Security Settings | Public Key Policies | Enterprise Trust.

4. In the right pane, right-click an empty space and select All Tasks | Import. Windows 2000 will launch the Certificate Import wizard to import your third-party CA's certificate.

Alternatively, if you would like to create a CTL, follow the first three steps in the preceding list, right-click an empty space in the right pane, and select New | Certificate Trust List. Windows 2000 will launch the Certificate Trust List wizard, which you can use to add a trust to external CAs and provide any desired limitation, as shown here.

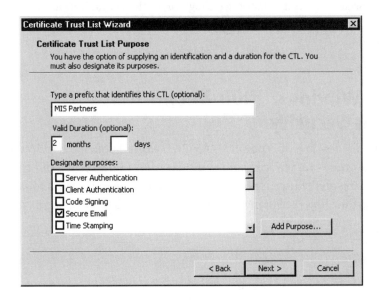

Certificate Mapping

In cases where you have to integrate your Windows 2000 organization with a third-party CA, you also have another powerful option in handing out certificates to your AD users—you can map certificates to user accounts. This allows you to associate a third-party certificate, or even a Windows 2000 CA-issued certificate, to a specific user account. In this way, specific rights and accesses to network resources are still managed via Active Directory; however, whenever the user needs to access Web-based resources or other certificate-based systems, the certificate is readily available.

There are several restrictions to certificate mapping, specifically:

- If your organization doesn't use roaming profiles, the user can be limited to only using the certificate when the user is logged into his or her own computer. This is mainly because the user's private key is located locally on that user's computer.

- Certificates can only be mapped to user accounts, not security groups. In fact, you can map one or multiple certificates to one user account.

To map a certificate to a user account:

1. Click Start | Programs | Administrative Tools | Active Directory Users and Computers.

2. In Active Directory Users and Computers, select Advanced Options from the View menu and navigate to the user account to which you'd like to map a certificate.

3. Right-click on the user account and select Name Mappings.

4. In the Security Identity Mapping dialog box, click the Add button to add a certificate.

5. Select the certificate and click OK.

Design Windows 2000 Network Services Security

Most of our discussion to this point has revolved around policies, certificates, and other security measures to authenticate and authorize users into your Windows 2000 organization. Focusing on the user aspect is crucial to laying the foundation for a sound security infrastructure; however, there are also several network services on which you should focus to round out the entire security framework.

DNS Security

When securing your DNS infrastructure, there are three main areas on which you should concentrate. First, you should secure the DNS list. You don't want malicious computer users modifying the properties or configuration of your DNS server. Second, you want to ensure that zones cannot be modified without your knowledge, so only proper personnel should be allowed to manage DNS zones. And finally, you should ensure that unauthorized users cannot create or modify DNS entries. The ability to create or modify DNS entries may give a malicious computer user the ability to redirect network traffic to an unwanted destination, such as a cracker's computer. (For a detailed discussion of Windows 2000's implementation of DNS, its features, and its functions, refer to Chapter 16.)

Securing the DNS Server

If you have chosen to integrate your DNS server into Active Directory, managing access is no problem. All authenticated Windows 2000 users automatically have Read access to use DNS, most Admin groups have Full Control, and non-Windows 2000 machines have no access. To modify these default accesses, simply right-click the DNS server within the Active Directory Users and Computers tool and select Properties. Then from the Properties dialog box, click the Security tab and modify access as needed.

If you choose, however, not to integrate your DNS server with Active Directory, all bets are off. For example, if you choose to use your current Unix DNS system, Active Directory obviously cannot help. You'll have to implement a security policy that protects the text file that houses your DNS records and the replication procedures using the security practices and procedures specific to your platform.

Managing DNS

By default, the DNS Admins group has Full Control access to the DNS server and all of its zones. However, if you need to segment and grant administrative access to specific users or groups to certain zones, it's a little trickier. The recommended process works like this:

1. Create a zone-admin group for each zone you would like to distribute administration to.

2. Give that zone-admin group Full Control access to the administered zone.

3. Add the zone-admin group to the Domain Admins group.

4. Restrict the rights of the Domain Admins group to Read access only on every zone within the domain. The problem is that to administer a zone within DNS, the users or groups must be members of the Domain Admins group. Limiting access for the entire Domain Admins group allows you more granularity in choosing zone administrators.

Protecting DNS

You should also ensure that unauthorized users cannot create or modify DNS records. By default, any AD-integrated DNS zone will have the Only Secure Updates option set. This option requires that clients authenticate through AD and have proper security rights to the zone before making updates. Also, by default, only authenticated Windows 2000 users have the Create All Child Objects right enabled to allow this type of dynamic update to occur. For a Windows 2000 only environment, therefore, DNS is fairly secure with its default settings.

If, on the other hand, you have a mixed environment with older Windows clients that use the Windows 2000 DNS server, you will not be able to make dynamic updates to DNS. There are, however, two ways around this:

- You can manually add DNS records for other systems. For example, the company's Unix server, older Windows clients, and other IP systems can be added by using the Add Host option with the DNS tool. This is a convenient option, but extremely painful if you have hundreds of systems that you'd like to add to the DNS records.

- If you use Windows DHCP to hand out IP addresses, you can have the DHCP server register clients by proxy. Simply add the computer running the DHCP server to the DNSUpdateProxy group. Then, when computers grab IP addresses from the DHCP server, those records can be inserted into DNS. The records created by the DHCP server are not secure, however. These unsecure records pose a large security weakness to your DNS structure, so it's important not to install the DHCP server on a domain controller or on the same computer as the DNS server.

Remote Installation Services (RIS) Security

For those of you who have had a job where you had to support dozens, hundreds, or thousands of computers, you undoubtedly used software products that let you take an image of a machine, store it to a shared network location, and use it to populate new computers that came into the organization. And if you never used Ghost, Drive Image, or other similar products, you sure wasted your time setting up new computers. With all the Nexts, Continues, and Press x to begins, you probably dreamt the setup procedures every night. Luckily, with Windows 2000, you don't have to dream installations anymore.

Remote Installation Services (RIS) works like Ghost or those other imaging products. You can create an *image*—a copy of all of a computer's installed software and settings, store that image on the network, boot a brand new computer using a pre-boot execution environment (PXE)-enabled (v.99c or later) BIOS or by using a RIS remote boot disk, and load the image on your new machine. The whole process saves you tons of valuable time. However, unlike Ghost or those other imaging products, RIS has the following requirements and limitations:

- You must have a Windows 2000 domain controller and Active Directory installed on the network.

- You must have an AD-integrated DNS server installed on the network.

- You must have a DHCP server installed on the network so the RIS process can grab an IP address when installing a new image.

- RIS cannot be installed on the boot or system partition.

- RIS can only deliver Windows 2000 Professional client images.

- RIS only supports a small number of PCI network cards. Any other type of network card and even less-popular PCI network cards cannot benefit from RIS.

- RIS only images the C drive.

Installation

Installing RIS is a bit trickier than most other Windows 2000 components. There are several steps to follow. Before you can actually install an RIS server, you must authenticate the soon-to-be RIS server with Active Directory. This way, not any server can serve out images to the AD environment. To do this, you must be an administrator and have access to the DHCP administrative tool.

To add the RIS server into Active Directory, follow these steps:

1. In the DHCP administrative tool, select Action | Manage Authorized Servers, as shown here.

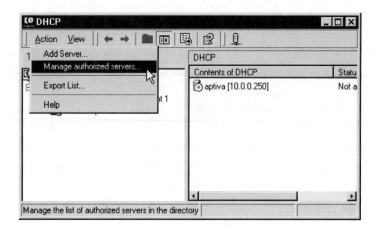

2. In the Manage Authorized Servers dialog box, click the Authorize button.

3. In the Authorize DHCP Server dialog box, type in the host name or IP address of the new RIS server, and then click the OK button.

4. Windows 2000 will ask you to confirm your choice. Click Yes.

To install a RIS server, follow these steps:

1. From the Control Panel, launch the Add/Remove Programs tool and select Windows Components.

2. From the Windows Components list, select Remote Installation Services. Windows 2000 will begin the installation process for RIS.

3. After all files are copied, you will be prompted to reboot your computer.

4. After you've rebooted your computer, go back into the Add/Remove Programs applet and select Windows Components. This time, Configure Remote Installation Services will be listed, as shown here.

5. Click the Configure button. Windows 2000 will launch the Remote Installation Services Setup wizard.

6. In the wizard's Welcome screen, click the Next button to continue.

7. In the Remote Installation Folder Location screen, select the drive and folder name where you'd like to store the images. As you can see in the following illustration, the drive must be formatted with NTFS, have enough space, and it cannot exist on the system volume. Click the Next button to continue.

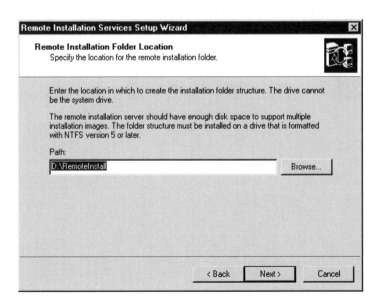

8. In the Initial Settings screen, unless you already have images stored on this server, leave all of the check boxes unchecked, as shown here. Click the Next button to continue.

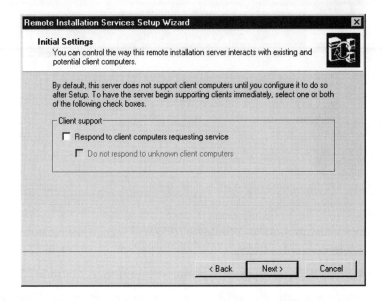

9. In the Installation Source Files Location screen, type in the path where RIS can find the Windows 2000 Professional setup files. You'll have to point to a location that contains the installation files from the full setup of Windows 2000 Professional—the upgrade version won't do. Click the Next button to continue.

10. In the Windows Installation Image Folder Name screen, select a name for the folder where the installation files will be stored. Click the Next button to continue.

11. In the Friendly Description and Help Text screen, enter a name and description for this image, as shown here. Click the Next button to continue.

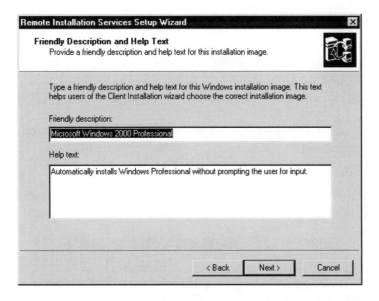

12. In the Summary screen, click the Finish button to begin the installation and configuration of the RIS server. Windows 2000 will display a progress screen showing you the current installation operation, as shown here.

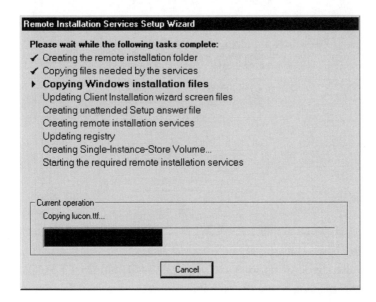

Configuration

After the RIS server installation is complete, the default Windows 2000 Professional image is in place, and you have added any additional images using the RIPRep tool (this tool is located at \\RIP server\REMINST\I386\RIPREP.EXE), you have to go back and enable the RIS server to accept client requests. To do so, follow these steps:

1. Use the Active Directory Users and Computers tool and navigate to the RIS server's AD object.

2. Right-click the server object and select Properties.

3. In the Properties dialog box, click the Remote Install tab and check the Respond to Client Computers Requesting Service check box, as shown here.

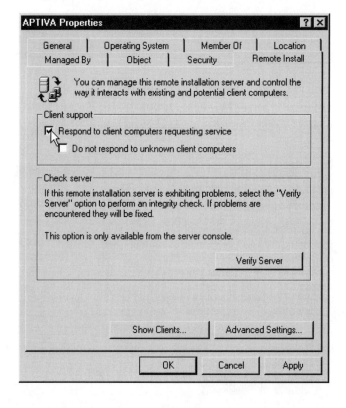

4. You can also check the option Do Not Respond to Unknown Client Computers. This option allows clients to use RIS even if they don't have a valid computer account. That may not be a big deal for plain vanilla images, but if you have images that contain default applications or settings, you may need to secure them a bit. To do so, leave the Do Not Respond to Unknown Client Computers option unchecked, and ensure that a valid computer account exists for the new computer before it's installed.

RIS Security

RIS doesn't have a large number of security options in place. You have to authenticate the RIS server into AD, you can force the computer account creation before the client computer is installed, and finally you can modify group policies to force the operation of the RIS installation process.

To access the RIS security settings, follow these steps:

1. Click Start | Programs | Administrative Tools | Active Directory Users and Computers.

2. Right-click the domain that you would like to modify and select Properties.

3. In the Properties dialog box, click the Group Policy tab.

4. Select the group policy for which you would like to modify the Remote Installation Services settings, and click the Edit button.

5. In the Group Policy tool, navigate to User Configuration | Windows Settings | Remote Installation Services.

6. In the right pane, double-click the Choice Options icon. Windows 2000 will display the Choice Screen Options dialog box, as shown here.

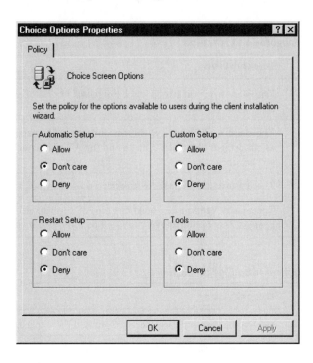

7. Select the various options and click OK to put your changes into effect. See Table 9-1 for a brief description of what the various options mean, and Table 9-2 explains the possible settings for each option.

SNMP Security

The *Simple Network Management Protocol* (SNMP) allows you to monitor various network devices from a central *SNMP manager* or several managers. With an *SNMP agent* installed, a network device (a workstation, server, router, smart hub, switch, and so on) can report back valuable information to a central computer running SNMP management software. This information can include computer name, IP address, MAC address, and a variety of error and informational conditions specific to the network device. The agent then sends this information in the form of a *trap* to the SNMP manager, which, in turn, collects all of this information and either stockpiles it for reports or alerts a member of the IT staff for immediate action. Yes, SNMP is a valuable protocol to implement from a network-management perspective.

Windows 2000, however, does not have SNMP management software installed with the operating system. In other words, your Windows 2000 system cannot act as an SNMP manager—it can only act as an SNMP agent.

Table 9-1 RIS Configuration Options

Option	Description
Automatic Setup	The client machine installing the image will not be offered any choices during the installation process.
Custom Setup	The client is offered a few choices during the RIS installation process, such as choosing the computer name and the AD container where the computer will be stored.
Restart Setup	The RIS installation process is restarted if a previous attempt failed.
Tools	Third-party vendors can build custom RIS tools to aid in the RIS installation process. This option allows the client to use those tools.

Table 9-2 RIS Configuration Option Settings

Setting	Description
Allow	Within this group policy, users are granted the explicit right to the option.
Don't Care	This group policy will defer to the group policy from the parent container.
Deny	Within this group policy, users are explicitly denied access to this option.

Lab Exercise 9.12:
SNMP Agent Installation
and Configuration

To install the SNMP agent software on a Windows 2000 system, follow these steps:

1. Launch the Add/Remove Programs applet from the Control Panel.

2. Select Add/Remove Windows Components and select the Management and Monitoring Tools option.

3. Click the Details button and select the Simple Network Management Protocol.

To change any configuration options with SNMP, follow these steps:

1. Launch the Control Panel and double-click the Administrative Tools icon.

2. In the Administrative Tools window, double-click the Services icon.

3. In the Services tool, right-click SNMP Service and select Properties. As you can see here, the Properties dialog box offers you two import security-related pages on which you can change options: the Traps and Security pages.

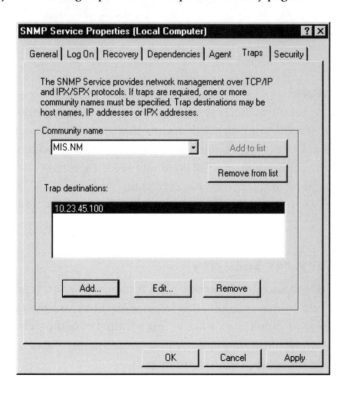

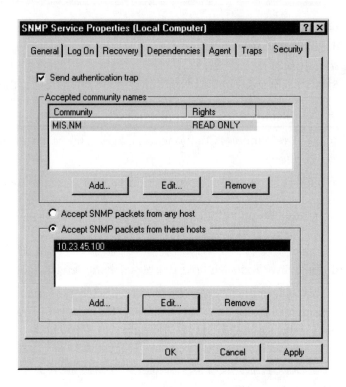

Security Measures

SNMP can be a security risk, because when an agent sends information to the SNMP manager, it is usually in plain text. This means that anyone monitoring the network between the agent and manager could see computer names, IP addresses, passwords, and other sensitive information. SNMP does have several security features that should help slow an attacker's advance when hacking SNMP packets.

Table 9-3 outlines some of the security measures, their benefits, and where you can find them.

Terminal Services Security

Unlike its stand-alone ancestor, Windows NT 4.0 Terminal Server, Terminal Services is now integrated into Windows 2000. This integration offers you the flexibility to run Terminal Services to run applications like a Unix terminal or in the style of mainframes. Users run all the applications on the server in separate session spaces without affecting other users (unless the server resources are maxed).

Table 9-3   SNMP Security Measures

Security Measure	Benefit	Location
Community Name	An SNMP agent will only accept requests from systems that belong to the same community name. Creating a hard-to-guess community name will help secure SNMP.	SNMP Service Properties—Traps page.
Trap Destinations	Specifies the destination computer or IP address where the SNMP agent will send its traps. Setting this value will help to ensure that critical information is not sent to an unauthorized computer.	SNMP Service Properties—Traps page.
Send Authentication Trap	Whenever an SNMP agent receives a request from an unauthorized source, or an authorized source tries to perform an unauthorized action, the SNMP agent can send a security notice in the form of an authentication trap.	SNMP Service Properties—Security page. Check the Send Authentication Trap check box.
Accepted Community Names	Listing accepted community names forces the SNMP agent to only accept traps from systems with the listed community names. Any SNMP traps received from communities not on the Accepted Community Names list will generate an authentication trap.	SNMP Service Properties—Security page.
Rights	Allows you to specify how the SNMP agent will react to a request from the listed community name. Here are the available rights: **None** The agent will not process any requests, but will generate an authentication trap. **Notify** Same as None. **Read Only** The agent will allow SNMP requests that ask for information only. Any requests to modify information will generate an authentication trap. **Read Create** The agent will process all SNMP requests from the listed community name. **Read Write** Same as Read Create.	SNMP Service Properties—Security page. Listed within the Accepted Community Names field.
Accept SNMP Packets from Any Host	All SNMP packets are accepted from any network name or address.	SNMP Service Properties—Security page.

continued

Table 9-3 SNMP Security Measures (*continued*)

Security Measure	Benefit	Location
Only Accept SNMP Packets from These Hosts	This provides a higher level of security, since the SNMP agent will only accept SNMP packets from those listed hosts. SNMP packets from all other hosts are rejected and cause an authentication trap to be sent.	SNMP Service Properties—Security page.
	By changing the network port numbers that SNMP uses to communicate, you can foil malicious users seeking to find SNMP packets on ports 161 and 162. Unfortunately, you must make the port changes on all SNMP agents and managers.	Port numbers can be changed in the file `\WINNT\SYSTEM32\ DRIVERS\ETC\ SERVICES.`

This is nothing new; Windows NT 4.0 Terminal Server offered the same centralized application server functionality. Now, however, Terminal Services can be used to remotely administer servers or other workstations. For example, if you have critical Windows 2000 servers running Terminal Services, you can connect to these servers and remotely administer them as if you were standing at the console.

NOTE Like pcAnywhere, LANDesk, or other remote administration tools, Terminal Services establishes a session with the target Terminal Services server by actually logging in as if you were at the console. However, Terminal Services is multisession.

Also, with its implementation of the Remote Desktop Protocol (RDP) over TCP/IP, Terminal Services uses less bandwidth than most remote-control clients. These benefits may prove to give Terminal Services the most power yet.

This section will not go into the details of installing and configuring Terminal Services; an entire book would be needed to cover all of Terminal Services' features and configuration options. Instead, this chapter focuses on securing Terminal Services from those lurking malicious users.

Encryption

Like IPSec or other security measures, Terminal Services allows you to encrypt data while it is in transit between the Terminal Services server and Terminal Services client. There are three different encryption levels:

- **Low**   Encrypts data sent from the client to the server. A Windows 2000 Terminal Services server will use a 56-bit key when communicating with Windows 2000 clients and a 40-bit key when communicating with older Windows clients.

- **Medium**   Encrypts data sent in both directions between the server and the client. A Windows 2000 Terminal Services server will use a 56-bit key when communicating with Windows 2000 clients and a 40-bit key when communicating with older Windows clients.

- **High**   Same as medium encryption, however, it uses a 128-bit key. This is only for Terminal Servers deployed within the U.S. and Canada.

Lab Exercise 9.13:
Configuring the Terminal Services
Connection Encryption

To configure the Terminal Services connection encryption, follow these steps:

1. Click Start | Programs | Administrative Tools | Terminal Services Configuration.

2. In the Terminal Services Configuration tool, select the Connections folder.

3. In the right pane, right-click the RDP-TCP connection, and select Properties.

4. In the Properties dialog box, click the General tab.

5. On the General tab, select the type of encryption you'd like to use from the Encryption Level drop-down box, as shown here.

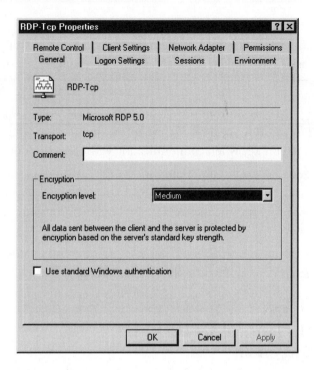

Session Limits

One often-overlooked security feature of Terminal Services is its ability to configure session limits. These limits ensure that users cannot leave a connection open forever. An open connection is an open invitation and open door into your Terminal Services server.

You can set session limits on a per-user basis, which may require a good deal of administrative effort in larger organizations, or on a per-connection basis, as with the encryption level.

Lab Exercise 9.14:
Configuring Session Limits

To configure session limits on a per-user basis, follow these steps:

1. Click Start | Programs | Administrative Tools | Active Directory Users and Computers.

2. Right-click the user whose Terminal Services session settings you'd like to modify, and select Properties.

3. In the Properties dialog box, click the Sessions tab.

4. In the Sessions page, modify the session limits as desired (shown here).

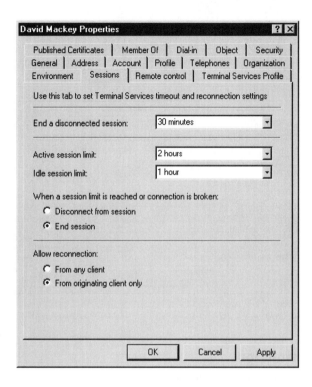

To configure session limits on a per-connection basis, follow these steps:

1. Click Start | Programs | Administrative Tools | Terminal Services Configuration.

2. In the Terminal Services Configuration tool, select the Connections folder.

3. In the right pane, right-click the RDP-TCP connection, and select Properties.

4. In the Properties dialog box, click the Sessions tab.

5. In the Sessions page, modify the session limits as desired (shown here).

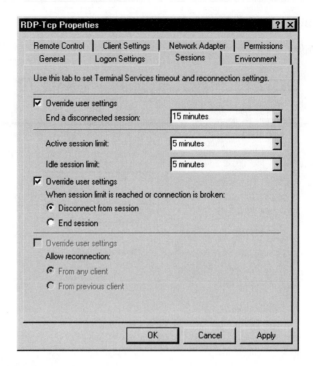

Connection Permissions

Like most Windows objects, the Terminal Services connections have their own set of permissions: Full Control, User Access, and Guest Access.

Full Control permission allows users to perform the following actions:

- Start a session.
- Get information about a session.
- Send a message to other user sessions.
- Connect to another session.
- Modify connection parameters.
- Reset a session.
- Remotely control another session.
- End a user's session.
- Disconnect a user's session.
- Use RDP's virtual channels to connect between Terminal Services and client devices.

User Access permission allows users to perform the following actions:

- Start a session.
- Get information about a session.
- Send a message to other user sessions.
- Connect to another session.

Guest Access permission allows users to perform the following action:

- Start a session.

To modify these permissions, follow these steps:

1. Click Start | Programs | Administrative Tools | Terminal Services Configuration.
2. In the Terminal Services Configuration tool, select the Connections folder.
3. In the right pane, right-click the RDP-TCP connection, and select Properties.
4. In the Properties dialog box, click the Permissions tab.
5. In the Permissions page, add or remove the desired users or groups and modify permissions as needed (shown here).

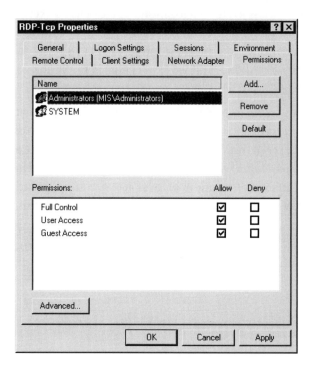

Case Study 9: Catywhompus Construction Must Implement Windows 2000 Security Solutions

Now you will apply your newly gained knowledge of the various security solutions covered in this chapter to Catywhompus Construction. Review the following case information and pay particular attention to the security issues that are presented. We start with the questions and follow with the suggested answers. (You should understand that your answers might vary slightly from ours.)

Case Study Questions

1. You have taken seriously the integration requirement for the Active Directory integrated zones, and you believe it is the best solution for a variety of reasons. You will recall from Part I and from the knowledge you gained while preparing for the Windows 2000 Core MCSE exams that an Active Directory integrated zone incorporates the DNS zone information directly into Active Directory (making it secure and replicated instead of the traditional text file–based DNS zone). Name at least four reasons why Catywhompus Construction should use integrated zones. Should the firm use them exclusively in all situations?

2. Catywhompus needs to create a location plan for DNS servers. Based on the existing network structure and management's expectation for system-wide stability, identify the quantity, type, and location of each DNS server for the headquarters and outlaying offices. Also, address how clients in the various subnets will contact DNS servers.

3. Catywhompus wants to be sure that all nodes including clients and servers have "A" resource records in DNS and are available from any DNS server on the network. You will recall from studying for the Windows 2000 MCSE core exams (and perhaps your past work with DNS) that resource records are entered into the DNS tables to facilitate the location of host using a fully qualified domain name (FQDN). How would you create the design to accomplish this objective?

4. What design enhancements can you add to ensure DNS server availability in the case of a single DNS failure, and how does this change your DNS location design?

continued

5. If the outlying, small Catywhompus offices (including temporary construction sites) have limited bandwidth over the WAN connection to the Internet, how can you configure the DNS servers at those offices to minimize traffic related to zone transfers?

6. What type of zones would you put in the construction company's screened subnets to provide Internet accessibility? Why?

7. Recommend a zone replication strategy for the Catywhompus network.

Suggested Solutions

(Your solutions vary.)

1. Four answers that come to mind are

   a. having the DNS zone part of the Active Directory security model

   b. having the DNS zone stored as part of a real database instead of a simple text file

   c. zones are replicated and synchronized to new DCs automatically whenever a new one is added to an Active Directory domain

   d. directory replication is faster and more efficient than standard DNS replication

2. At each location, a robust server acting as a DNS server should be present. One DNS server per location will be sufficient. Clients will receive DNS server information from the DHCP scope used to lease the IP address.

3. Use the Dynamic DNS capabilities of Windows 2000 Server to accomplish the creation of resource records for each host. In the DHCP service, select Automatically update DHCP client information in DNS on the server property sheet.

4. As planned, use multiple DNS servers on the network to ensure high availability.

5. Use Active Directory sites to manage the transfer of Active Directory database to outlying, low bandwidth sites.

6. Both forward and reverse lookup zones are needed.

7. Use Active Directory-integrated DNS zones to manage zone replication.

Chapter Review

Windows 2000 provides a variety of security features to help you secure your environment and ensure that only authorized users can access network resources and services. The features reviewed in this chapter cover a broad range of topics and technologies, so you may need to review this chapter a few times to understand all of the security concepts.

Questions

1. In what order are group policies implemented?
   a. OU, domain, local, site
   b. Domain, local, site, OU
   c. Local, site, domain, OU
   d. OU, site, local, domain

2. Which authentication method requires a Key Distribution Center (KDC)?
   a. Kerberos
   b. NTLM
   c. Clear-text passwords
   d. Digest

3. What is the purpose of a TGT?
   a. A TGT authenticates a user to the KDC.
   b. A TGT allows a user to request a session ticket.
   c. A TGT allows a user to access a Kerberos-protected network resource.
   d. A TGT issues a TGS to the user after authentication is complete.

4. Which type of certification authority must be integrated with Active Directory? (Choose all that apply.)
   a. Enterprise root CA
   b. Stand-alone root CA
   c. Enterprise subordinate CA
   d. Stand-alone subordinate CA
   e. Third-party CA

5. True or False? Remote Installation Services (RIS) can be used to image Windows 98 clients and later deploy the image to a new computer.

PART II

Answers

1. **C.** Group policies are processed and implemented in the following order: local policy, site policy, domain policy, OU policy, and then nested OUs' policies.

2. **A.** Kerberos requires the use of a Key Distribution Center (KDC) to handle the issuance of TGT and session tickets.

3. **B.** A ticket-granting ticket (TGT) allows the user to request a session ticket from the ticket-granting service (TGS) to ultimately access specific network resources.

4. **A and C.** The Enterprise types of CAs require integration with Active Directory.

5. **False.** Currently, RIS can only be used to image Windows 2000 Professional workstations.

Key Skill Sets

- Have the ability to design an audit policy.

- Use your skills to design the group policy strategy between sites, domains, and OUs.

- Competently design an EFS strategy.

- Have the ability to select the proper authentication method for specific environments.

- Undertake the tasks necessary to design a certificate-management system.

- Implement a secure DNS solution.

- Plan and design for secure RIS.

- Understand how you would secure the use of SNMP.

- Plan for and design a secure Terminal Services solution.

Key Terms

Audit
Certificate Authority (CA)
Certificate Revocation List (CRL)
Certificate Trust List (CTL)
Digest Authentication (DA)
Encrypting Files System (EFS)
Hash
Kerberos
Key Distribution Center (KDC)
NTLM
PKI
RADIUS
Remote Installation Services (RIS)
Smart card
SSL
Ticket-granting ticket (TGT)
Ticket-granting service (TGS)

CHAPTER 10

Designing a Security Solution for Access Between Networks

This chapter covers the following key mastery goals:

- Accessing the Internet
- Common Internet File System (CIFS)
- IP Security (IPSec)
- Virtual private networks (VPNs)
- Remote Access Service

In the ever-changing corporate landscape, providing constant, reliable communication is a necessity. Not only must you, the administrator, worry about seamless data flow among your local network users, but you have to manage data traffic between corporate sites, integrate newly acquired businesses, and, of course, allow remote users to access network resources from home or on the road. Seem like a lot to chew on? It is. Luckily, Windows 2000 offers many new tools to help you perform these tasks and gives you the security features necessary to allow secure data communication on your networks.

This chapter's focus will be to help you understand Windows 2000's security features and help you provide secure data communication among all of your company's constituents. Additionally, this chapter will cover the following key mastery goals for Exam 70-220, "Designing Security for a Microsoft Windows 2000 Network:"

- Provide secure access to public networks from a private network
- Provide external users with secure access to private network resources

- Provide secure access between private networks
- Provide secure access within a LAN
- Provide secure access within a WAN
- Provide secure access across a public network
- Design Windows 2000 security for remote access users

Accessing the Internet

It's hard to find businesses today that don't require some sort of connection to the Internet. Whether it's for Web browsing, e-mail, or newsgroups, businesses in general must find a way to allow your users *out* to the Internet without letting malicious users *in* to your network resources. And with today's emphasis on security, there is a variety of hardware and software products that help you do just that.

Proxy Server

A *proxy server* serves as a middle man when your corporate users are accessing the Internet. To your end users, accessing the Internet is seamless; there is no additional work or actions required. However, in the background, the proxy server first intercepts the

Catywhompus Construction Updates: Secure Remote Communications

As we near the end of the security section of the book, the management team at Catywhompus has reminded you to design their secure remote communications solution. There are several important reasons for doing this, the least of which is the nature of the commercial construction business. It is common for Catywhompus to set up work sites for a limited duration of a few months. However, management's expectation is that these remote work sites will have the same access to the corporate network as an established office. Also, you're smart enough to know by reading between the lines that many of the executives are secretly craving robust and secure access to the corporate network from their home offices or while on the road. Keep these considerations in mind as you read this chapter.

request for Internet resources from the client so that the client never has to communicate beyond the company network. The proxy server then, with a proper connection to the Internet, accesses the requested Internet site and grabs the necessary content. This content is then passed back to the company network and ultimately to the client.

The biggest benefits to a proxy server are these:

- *A proxy server can cache site content.* This allows it to serve out the cached content to users who make the same requests for Internet resources, thereby speeding content delivery to the client.

- *A proxy server can also filter Internet content.* This allows administrators to configure the proxy server to decline the return of content that has been deemed inappropriate by corporate policies.

Firewall

A *firewall* can also act like a proxy server, but it's usually a more secure defense mechanism against unwanted network traffic trying to enter your network. Firewalls can lock down TCP and UDP ports, secure application traffic, or encrypt data leaving the network. And most importantly, firewalls can be implemented on a router, which can more effectively protect data communications by touching each network packet.

Gateway

A *gateway* is a server or device that connects two heterogeneous networks. In regards to network security, gateways can be effective in that you can employ *Network Address Translation* (NAT). NAT allows you to have a private network with its own network addresses that are separate and distinct from the Internet. Because of the two sets of networks, NAT requires two network interfaces—one connected to your local network and the other connected to the Internet. Whenever a system tries to access the Internet, it can use a separate, external IP address that is valid for use on the Internet and keep its real network address hidden from prying Internet eyes. Using NAT, the gateway hides your local network addresses from the Internet for greater security and protection.

Internet Connection Server

Bear with us as we walk you through this area of certification study. The Windows 2000 MCSE exams focus on Microsoft Proxy Server 2.0, a solution that provides proxy-server functionality and was in use at the time the exams were written. However, Internet Security and Acceleration (ISA) Server is now here and provides proxy server caching, firewall, and gateway functionality. Needless to say, Microsoft will continue to develop a host of security products to protect your environment from unwanted—and as yet unnamed—intrusions. But separate solutions such as ISA Server aside, there are internal Windows 2000 capabilities for facilitating shared connections to the Internet.

Using Windows 2000 Server, you can set up a gateway to the Internet using Routing and Remote Access Service (RRAS), or more specifically, NAT. Using one server system, two network interfaces, and Windows 2000, you can use NAT to securely connect your internal network to the Internet.

To do this, Windows 2000 establishes a connection to the internal network just as any other system would. The Windows 2000 server also connects to the Internet and provides an IP address, DNS configuration, and any other Internet-connection properties. Whenever network clients request Internet resources, the Windows 2000 server routes the request out and then routes the returned data back to the client. Windows 2000 can accomplish these routing tasks using the Internet Connection Server application.

Lab Exercise 10.1: Configure an Internet Connection Server

Follow these steps for practice configuring an Internet connection server:

1. You must first ensure that your Windows 2000 server is configured with two network interfaces. One network card must be connected to your local network and your other network card or modem must be configured to access the Internet.

2. Choose Start | Programs | Administrative Tools | Routing and Remote Access.

3. From the Action menu, choose the Configure and Enable Routing and Remote Access option. Windows 2000 will start the Routing and Remote Access Server Setup wizard.

4. In the wizard's Welcome screen, click the Next button to continue.

5. In the Common Configurations screen, select the Internet Connection Server option (as shown here), and then click the Next button to continue.

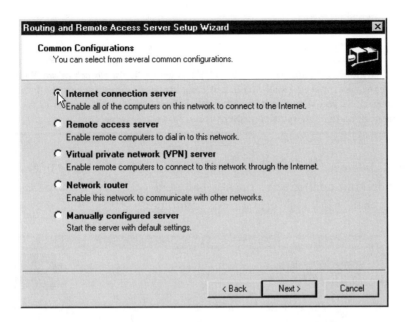

6. In the Internet Connection Server Setup screen, select the Set Up a Router with the Network Address Translation (NAT) Routing Protocol option, as shown here. Click the Next button to continue.

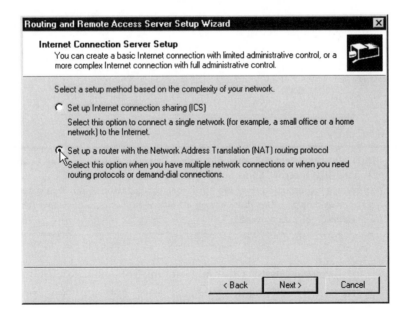

NOTE You'll also notice on the Internet Connection Server Setup screen that you have the option to set up Internet Connection Sharing (ICS). In addition to Windows 2000's server family, ICS is available to Windows 2000 Professional, Windows ME, and Windows 98 SE. ICS is generally for homes or small offices where you want to connect a small number of computers on one subnet to the Internet. For larger organizations, you should install RRAS with NAT to enable greater security for your internal network and enable multiple subnets to access the Internet.

7. In the Internet Connection screen, choose the Use the Selected Internet Connection option, and then select the network interface that connects to the Internet, as shown here. Click the Next button to continue.

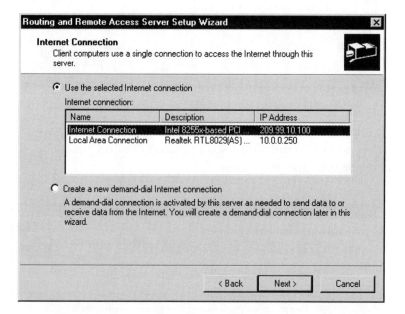

 NOTE In the Internet Connection screen, you can also choose the Create a New Demand-Dial Internet Connection option to use a modem that dials an ISP for an Internet connection. However, in larger organizations, you'll want to steer clear of this option. Imagine sharing a 56Kbps modem connection with dozens or hundreds of other users!

8. The wizard will finish with a summary telling you that the NAT protocol was installed on your chosen adapter. Click the Finish button to close the dialog box and wizard.

9. Now that you've finished with the Internet Connection Server Setup wizard, you must now confirm that the network connection that connects your server to the Internet has the proper IP address or DHCP settings and DNS configuration information. This information will be passed out to the other systems on the network, so it's important to get this right. To confirm this information, type the following at the command prompt: **ipconfig | all | more**. If you look closely at the information returned on your computer screen, you will be able to verify the configuration you created.

Common Internet File System (CIFS)

Server Message Block (SMB) is the protocol that allows Windows servers and clients to share files, printers, named pipes, and other Windows resources. With the introduction of Windows 2000, Microsoft has enhanced SMB with additional functionality in the form of the Common Internet File System (CIFS). This additional capability allows users to access shared resources over the Internet. There has also been improvements in performance with CIFS in the form of optimizing performance over a slow dial-up connection. With this Internet integration, security is even more important.

One of the weaknesses of Windows is the high number of vulnerabilities that Microsoft's implementation of SMB allows, and once an SMB weakness is exploited, a malicious computer user can gain access to a variety of shared resources on the system.

Despite the vulnerabilities, Microsoft's implementation of SMB does contain two main security methods. First, you can secure shared resources using a single password, which must then be supplied for users to gain access. This is called *share-level security*, and the problem with it is that everyone shares the knowledge of this one password. This makes it next to impossible to determine who knows this password and also to change the password and inform all of the appropriate users. Share-level security is available in the Windows *ME/98/95* clients.

The second level of security is called *user-level security*, and it requires that every user enter a unique username and password to gain access to the resource. Windows NT and Windows 2000 offer this type of security to further protect your shared resources. User-level security is much easier to administer (since you can assign access to resources via security groups) and provides a tougher layer of security.

To add yet another layer of security, Microsoft implemented an SMB signing solution. This requires that every SMB packet be signed and verified. This type of signing is only available with Windows 98, Windows ME, Windows NT 4.0 running Service Pack 3, and Windows 2000 clients. While this increases the security of SMB communication, signing does increase the CPU usage on the client machines. Fortunately, no additional network traffic is generated, but the CPU performance degradation is around 10 to 15 percent—enough to scare away many administrators.

SMB signing is helpful in securing SMB communication on your Windows LAN. By default, Windows 2000 systems are enabled with SMB signing, but when communicating with a system lacking signing ability, the system will revert back to a less secure method. You can, however, force signing-only communication on both the server and client.

Lab Exercise 10.2: Implement SMB Signing on a Windows 2000 System

For practice implementing SMB signing on a Windows 2000 system, follow these steps:

1. Choose Start | Programs | Administrative Tools | Local Security Policy.

2. Navigate to Security Settings | Local Policies | Security Options.

3. In the right pane, double-click the Digitally Sign Client Communication (Always) option when enabling signing on clients, or Digitally Sign Server Communication (Always) option for servers.

4. In the Local Security Policy Setting dialog box, select the Enabled option, as shown here. Click the OK button to put your changes into effect.

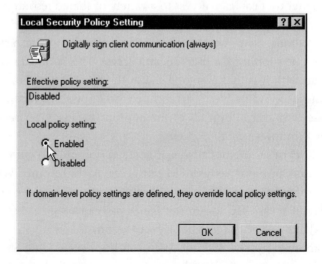

IP Security (IPSec)

SMB signing is great for securing SMB communications between Windows clients. However, in heterogeneous environments and when using other network protocols, Windows 2000 includes a much more powerful tool in the fight against malicious computer attacks—IP Security (IPSec). IPSec encrypts IP traffic, repels a variety of TCP/IP attacks, and ensures communication privacy.

Encryption and encryption algorithms have long been used (since long before the advent of the computer) to hide the contents of confidential messages. When the computer rolled onto the scene, some of the same encryption methods were adapted to hide confidential electronic data. However, many of the early encryption methods and tools operated at higher levels of the Open Standards Interconnection (OSI) model, and therefore did not have a chance to affect both the data and headers of a network packet. Let us assume that at this point in your journey, as an MCSE candidate and technology professional, you've been introduced to the seven layers of the OSI model. You will recall that the first layer is physical, dealing with the network adapter card. The middle layers relate to networking protocols and the upper layers relate to session and application matters. If for some reason you've not been exposed to the OSI model, refer to an elementary text on networking.

For example, Secure Sockets Layer version 3 and Transport Layer Security (SSL3/TLS) are still used by browsers to protect confidential data; however, this solution is usually implemented within specific applications, such as Internet Explorer, to protect documents transmitted over the Internet. The packet headers of this data are left unprotected and are thus vulnerable to attack.

It is only recently that IPSec has become widely available and can be used to hide both the contents of network data and the packet itself. The greatest benefit of IPSec is that it offers end-to-end security, meaning that both the sender and receiver must have IPSec-aware systems. Any intermediate routing device just forwards the packet on. These intermediate devices are oblivious to the fact that the packet is encrypted.

 NOTE   When routing IPSec traffic, a network device does not need to have the same IPSec settings as your hosts, since these devices will simply pass the encrypted packets on to their final destination. If, however, you must send IPSec traffic through a firewall, secure gateway, or proxy server, IPSec traffic may be blocked by default. You should refer to Microsoft's Knowledge Base article at http://support.microsoft.com/support/kb/articles/Q233/2/56.ASP for information on how to configure your network systems to allow IPSec traffic.

There are currently two basic IPSec modes: *tunnel mode* and *transport mode*. When using transport mode, only the data carried by each packet is encrypted. Tunnel mode, on the other hand, encrypts both the header information and the data. Obviously, tunnel mode is more effective in thwarting attacks involving IP spoofing and sniffers, because your IP address and various other pieces of IP addressing information are encrypted during transmission. This way, even if your packet is intercepted, the malicious computer user must break the IPSec encryption to discover any information.

Like TCP/IP, IPSec is really a collection of protocols. IP Security includes Authentication Header (AH), Encapsulating Security Payload (ESP), Internet Key Exchange (IKE), Internet Security Association and Key Management Protocol (ISAKMP), Oakley Key Generation Protocol, and a variety of other algorithms that help IPSec determine how your packets will be encrypted. For more information about IPSec, refer to RFC 2411.

ISAKMP and Oakley are two of the most important IPSec components. ISAKMP is the management system used to manage security associations, and the Oakley protocol generates and manages the various keys involved in the secure communication process. IPSec works by first establishing a security association (SA) between the data sender and data receiver. The SA is the common set of protocols, keys, and systems that the two systems will use to exchange the encrypted data. One of Oakley's main benefits is that it provides "cover" during the establishment of the SA, so that an attacker cannot eavesdrop on the data conversation during the vulnerable stage of SA establishment. Once the SA is established, the two communication parties then exchange encryption keys. During this process, the encrypting algorithm, integrity algorithm, and authentication method (Kerberos v5, public key certificate, or preshared key) are established. Once the keys have been exchanged, data is encrypted, exchanged, and decrypted.

Windows 2000's Default IPSec Policies

Windows 2000 offers many choices in implementing IPSec. Before you wade through the configuration choices of IPSec on your Windows 2000 system, you should think through your data-communication security needs and make your decisions. Here are some of the things you will want to consider:

- What types of information are being transmitted over your network?
- How sensitive is the transmitted information?
- Which network segments need improved security?

- What are your network's vulnerabilities and entry points for network attacks?

- Does your Windows 2000 server pass information to other network devices, such as routers, gateways, or proxy servers?

- Do you have any network devices or systems that might not forward IPSec traffic (such as a firewall)?

Understanding the overall scope of your security picture will help you decide whether to implement IPSec, where to implement it, and what type of settings you will use.

By default, Windows 2000's IPSec ships with the following three policies for your immediate use (this is very helpful and saves time in implementing IPSec):

- **Client (Respond Only)** The Client security level instructs Windows 2000 not to use IPSec by default. Instead, IPSec is only used when another host or device requests the use of IPSec.

- **Server (Request Security)** When using the Server security level, your Windows 2000 system requests IPSec secured traffic initially; however, it will accept unsecured communications if the other host or device is incapable of using IPSec.

- **Secure Server (Require Security)** The Secure Server security level offers the highest protection by requiring that all network traffic to and from the Windows 2000 system be secured. Any unsecured TCP/IP traffic is automatically rejected.

Lab Exercise 10.3:
Implement a Default IPSec Policy

For practice implementing one of the aforementioned default IPSec policies, follow these steps:

1. Launch the Microsoft Management Console, by typing **mmc** at the Run line.

2. In MMC, choose Console | Add/Remove Snap-In.

3. In the Standalone page, click the Add button.

4. From the list of snap-ins, select IP Security Policy Management (as shown here) and click Add.

5. In the Select Computer dialog box, select which computer or domain this console will manage. As you can see here, you have the option to manage the Local Computer, the domain to which the local computer belongs, another domain entirely, or another computer. Click Finish.

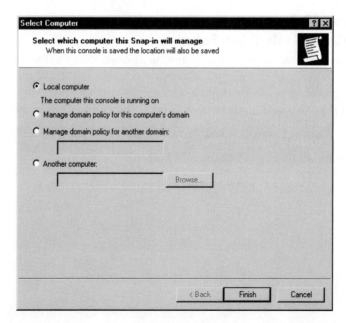

6. Click Close and then click OK to exit the various dialog boxes. You should then save this console by choosing Console | Save so that you can access the IPSec settings quickly at a later time.

Policy Configuration

If you feel that the default policies do not meet your needs, Windows 2000 gives you a great deal of granularity for choosing your own settings and configuration options. The following sections outline the various IPSec policy options and how to access each.

Security Rules

A *security rule* tells Windows 2000 how and under what conditions data communication is to be secured. Rules are applied to network or host IP addresses that are listed within the *filter list*. The filter list can contain specific network or host addresses or can apply to all detected traffic. Windows 2000 allows you to create your own filter rules.

Lab Exercise 10.4:
Create a Security Rule

For practice creating a security rule, follow these steps:

1. Using the IPSec snap-in that you created earlier, right-click the desired security policy and select Properties.

2. In the Properties dialog box, click the Rules tab.

3. In the Rules page, click the Add button. Windows 2000 will launch the Security Rule wizard.

4. In the Security Rule wizard's Welcome screen, click the Next button to continue.

5. In the Tunnel Endpoint screen, select The Tunnel Endpoint is Specified by This IP Address option if you need to specify a system on the other end of a VPN to handle secure traffic (shown here). If you're not creating a rule for a VPN connection, select the This Rule Does Not Specify a Tunnel option. Click the Next button to continue.

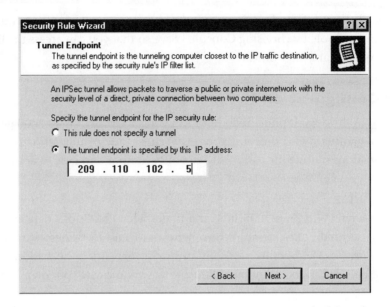

6. In the Network Type screen, select the type of network connection to which you would like to apply this filter rule, as shown here. Click the Next button to continue.

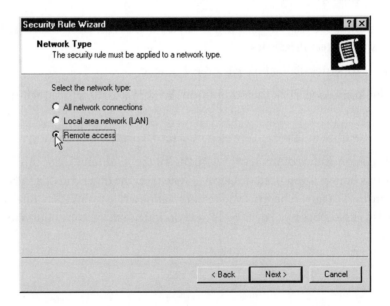

7. In the Authentication Method screen, choose the type of authentication you would like to use, as shown here. Click the Next button to continue.

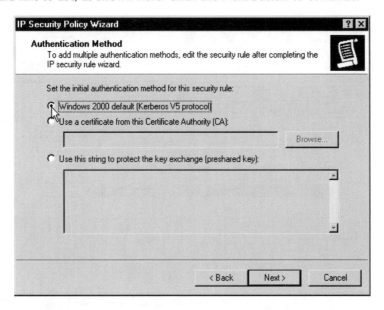

8. In the IP Filter List screen, choose a filter to apply to the IP traffic. For example, you can apply your new filter rule to all IP traffic (as shown here) or you can limit it to ICMP traffic only. Click the Next button to continue.

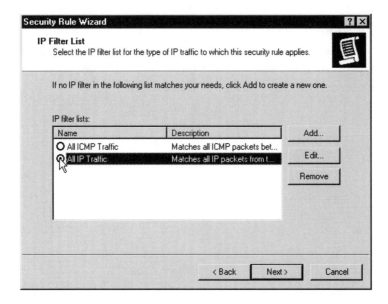

9. In the Filter Action screen, select the type of action you want Windows 2000 to perform on your chosen IP traffic, as shown here. Click the Next button to continue.

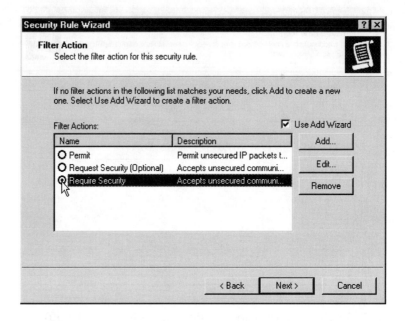

10. In the Finish screen, click the Finish button to complete the creation of your new security rule.

Security Method

IPSec allows you to specify the encryption schemes that your filter rule employs. You can choose between the authentication-encryption methods SHA1 or MD5, and between the data-encryption methods 3DES and DES.

Lab Exercise 10.5: Choose the Encryption Method Employed by Your Security Policy

To choose the encryption method employed by your security policy, follow these steps:

1. Using the IPSec snap-in that you created earlier, right-click the desired security policy and select Properties.

2. In the Properties dialog box, click the Rules tab.

3. In the Rules page, select your desired security rule and click the Edit button.

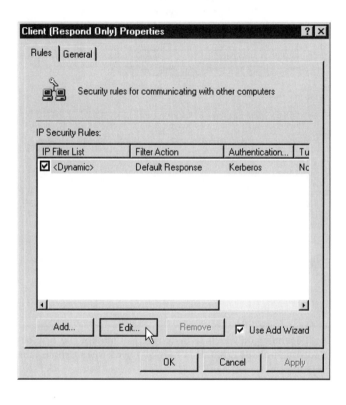

4. In the Edit Rule Properties dialog box, click the Security Methods tab.

5. The Security Methods page allows you to modify which methods are used (as shown next). You can also modify a specific encryption method by selecting it and clicking the Edit button.

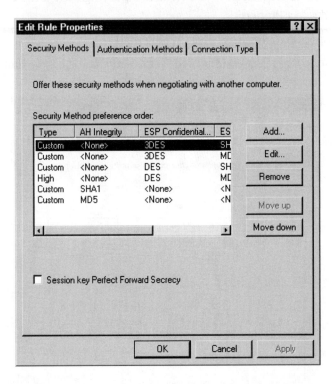

NOTE Depending on which security rule you modify, you may or may not see the Security Methods tab. This is normally used when defining the Default Action rule.

IP Filter List

As mentioned previously, you can specify which IP traffic is affected by your IPSec filter rule. This is accomplished by modifying the IP filter list.

Lab Exercise 10.6: Control IP Traffic by Modifying the IP Filter List

For practice modifying the IP filter list to specify which IP traffic is affected by your IPSec filter rule, follow these steps:

1. Using the IPSec snap-in that you created earlier, right-click the desired security policy and select Properties.

2. In the Properties dialog box, click the Rules tab.

3. In the Rules page, select your desired security rule and click the Edit button.

4. In the Edit Rule Properties dialog box, click the IP Filter List tab.

5. The IP Filter List page allows you to modify which IP addresses, network addresses, or types of traffic are affected, as shown here. You can also modify the properties of a specific filter list by selecting it and clicking the Edit button.

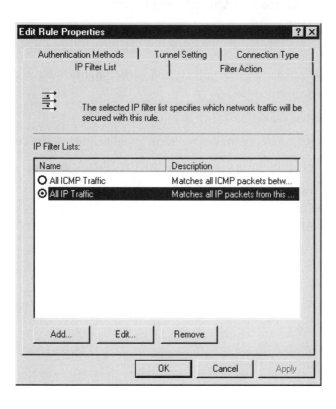

NOTE Depending on which security rule you modify, you may or may not see the IP Filter List tab. This is normally used when defining a rule other than the Default Action rule.

Filter Action

Filter actions allow you to instruct Windows 2000 how to handle security for the IP addresses specified within the filter list. The Permit option allows all traffic from IP addresses within the filter list. The Block option blocks all traffic from IP addresses within the filter list. The Negotiate option processes a list of security actions to try when negotiating security between your host and IP addresses within the filter list.

Lab Exercise 10.7: Modify the IP Filter List Using Filter Actions

For practice modifying the IP filter list using filter actions, follow these steps:

1. Using the IPSec snap-in that you created earlier, right-click the desired security policy and select Properties.

2. In the Properties dialog box, click the Rules tab.

3. In the Rules page, select your desired security rule and click the Edit button.

4. In the Edit Rule Properties dialog box, click the Filter Action tab.

5. The Filter Action page allows you to modify the security actions, as shown next. You can also modify the properties of a specific filter action by selecting it and clicking the Edit button.

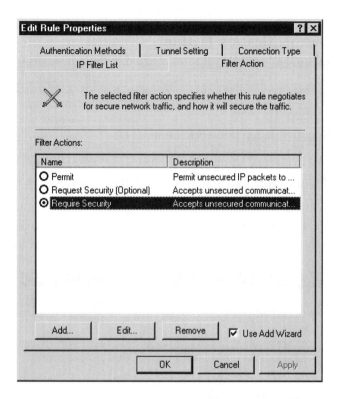

NOTE   Depending on which security rule you use, you may or may not see the Filter Action tab. This is normally used when defining a rule other than the Default Action rule.

Authentication Method

With Windows 2000's implementation of IPSec, you have three major options for verifying the identity of another network system. You can obtain the public key from the remote machine using Kerberos, use a public-key certificate from a trusted authority, or specify a preshared key. A preshared key is simply a string of characters, like a password. You must manually type in this string on all computers attempting to use IPSec with the preshared-key authentication method.

Lab Exercise 10.8:
Modify the Authentication Method

For practice modifying the authentication method, follow these steps:

1. Using the IPSec snap-in that you created earlier, right-click the desired security policy and select Properties.

2. In the Properties dialog box, click the Rules tab.

3. In the Rules page, select your desired security rule and click the Edit button.

4. In the Edit Rule Properties dialog box, click the Authentication Methods tab.

5. The Authentication Methods page allows you to add, remove or otherwise modify which authentication method(s) are used, as shown here. You can also modify the properties of a specific method by selecting it and clicking the Edit button.

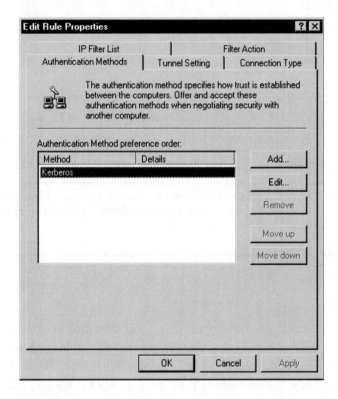

Security Mode

As we mentioned earlier, Windows 2000's implementation of IPSec offers two operating modes: transport and tunnel.

Lab Exercise 10.9: Specify the Security Mode
Used in the Implementation of IPSec

For practice choosing the mode used in the implementation of IPSec, follow these steps:

1. Using the IPSec snap-in that you created earlier, right-click the desired security policy and select Properties.

2. In the Properties dialog box, click the Rules tab.

3. In the Rules page, select your desired security rule and click the Edit button.

4. In the Edit Rule Properties dialog box, click the Tunnel Setting tab.

5. The Tunnel Setting page allows you to modify which IPSec mode is used, as shown here.

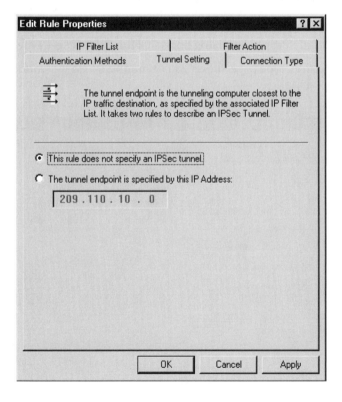

 NOTE   Depending on which security rule you modify, you may or may not see the Tunnel Setting tab. This is normally used when defining a rule other than the Default Action rule.

Connection Type

You can specify which network connection Windows 2000 will use IPSec with. For example, you could set up your Windows 2000 system to only use IPSec on the remote dial-up connection.

Lab Exercise 10.10: Specify the Network Connection for IPSec

For practice specifying the network connection for IPSec, follow these steps:

1. Using the IPSec snap-in that you created earlier, right-click the desired security policy and select Properties.

2. In the Properties dialog box, click the Rules tab.

3. In the Rules page, select your desired security rule and click the Edit button.

4. In the Edit Rule Properties dialog box, click the Connection Type tab.

5. The Connection Type page allows you to modify which network connection uses IPSec, as shown here.

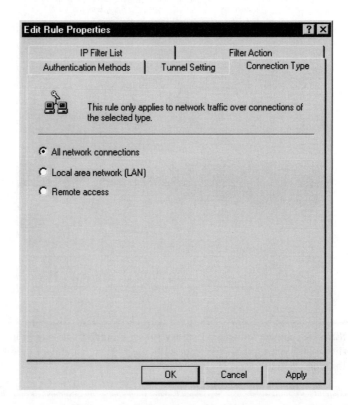

Testing Your IPSec Configuration

Once you have configured your computers, domain, or other systems to use IPSec, you should test the IPSec-protected communications to ensure that all systems are communicating using the same protocols.

Lab Exercise 10.11:
Test Your IPSec Configuration

For practice testing your IPSec configuration, follow these steps:

1. Choose Start | Programs | Administrative Tools | Computer Management.

2. Navigate to Services and Applications | Services.

3. In the right pane, right-click the IPSec Policy Agent service and select Start. Ensure the service is started on both the source and destination computer for which you are testing the IPSec communication.

4. Once the IPSec Policy Agent is running on all Windows 2000 systems to be tested, simply ping one computer from the other. You will recall from the earliest days of your career as a technology professional that the ping command is used to test connectivity (by pinging the IP address or host name of another computer). If for some reason you're not familiar with the ping command, type **ping /?** at the command prompt in Windows 2000.

Virtual Private Networks (VPNs)

Virtual private networks (VPNs) are a relatively new phenomenon in the business world. The corporate world, looking to harness the power of the Internet, needed to connect remote users and remote offices and provide links to external customers, vendors, and suppliers. VPNs provide this type of functionality and allow a cheaper solution than leased telephone lines by using the Internet. That is, the cost of a private WAN connection via frame relay or some other telecommunications solution typically exceeds the costs of a VPN-based solution over the Internet. Armed with those two benefits, VPNs have become standard in the corporate world.

VPNs link two (or more) private networks over a public network connection, such as the Internet. The key to this type of communication is implementing stringent security over the public network. With a VPN, this is accomplished by establishing a "tunnel" that protects data during the entire trip. The VPN tunnel simulates a point-to-point connection between private networks, and then uses encryption to protect the data in transit.

Here are some VPN terms you will need to know:

- **VPN server**   Accepts the VPN connection from a VPN client or from multiple clients.

- **VPN client**   Initiates a VPN connection to a VPN server. When using Windows 2000 as a VPN server, you can use any computer or router that supports the Point-to-Point Tunneling Protocol (PPTP) or the Layer Two Tunneling Protocol (L2TP) and IPSec as a VPN client.

- **Tunnel**   Refers to the two points where data is encrypted when sent and decrypted when received.

- **Transit network**   The shared or public medium that transmits the VPN-encapsulated data. For Windows 2000, the transit network must use TCP/IP.

- **Tunneling protocols**   Protocols that create and manage tunnels and encapsulate data.

As mentioned earlier, VPNs have two major purposes: remote access and connecting networks. The power of remote access is obvious—it can allow remote employees or external partners to connect to your private network using a standard Internet connection. On the other hand, you can also use VPNs to connect two private networks. That in effect creates a router-based solution as both the VPN server and VPN client can send protected data over a public network, like the Internet, to avoid the costs of leased lines. All of this and at a layer of acceptable security (via the VPN encapsulation approach).

NOTE   Throughout this section, the idea of cost reduction has been stated as one of the main benefits to choosing a VPN solution. The associated costs, as with anything in the IT world, can vary greatly by your environment. You may find, after crunching the numbers, that today's leased lines cost less than a VPN solution.

To set up a VPN, you'll need to implement various communication elements:

- **Encapsulation**   Using a special protocol, data is packaged with a special header that allows it to be routed properly over the public network. Windows 2000 can use PPTP (Point-to-Point Tunneling Protocol) or L2TP (Layer Two Tunneling Protocol) to perform this critical task.

  - **PPTP**   Based on the older Point-to-Point Protocol (PPP), PPTP uses Generic Routing Encapsulation (GRE) to encapsulate PPP frames. PPTP can encapsulate IP, IPX, or NetBEUI traffic with an IP header and send it over an IP network. In addition, PPTP provides one large benefit over L2TP in that it can be routed through NAT-defended systems.

- **L2TP** L2TP is a combination of PPTP and Layer 2 Forwarding (L2F) protocols. Like PPTP, L2TP can encapsulate IP, IPX, or NetBEUI traffic into PPP frames and send them over IP, X.25, Frame Relay, or ATM networks. Because of IPSec's use of Internet Key Exchange (IKE), the combination of L2TP and IPSec may prevent the ability to route packets through NAT.

NOTE Unfortunately, within Windows 2000, you can create VPN connections without using IPSec. This is obviously not the most desirable configuration, since data is transmitted across a public network without encryption, but it may be a workaround to route encapsulated packets through NAT.

- **Encryption** Since data transmitted within a VPN tunnel travels across a shared network, it's important that the data be encrypted. This prevents unauthorized people from intercepting the traffic and viewing its contents. The Windows 2000 implementation of VPNs offers two important types of encryption:

  - **IP Security (IPSec)** New to Windows 2000 and based on industry standards, IPSec provides a much-improved data-encryption method. Instead of relying on the operating systems or applications, IPSec encrypts data at the transport level. This lower-level security method is transparent to applications or services that must send and receive data. In relation to VPNs, IPSec can be combined with L2TP to form a strong encapsulation and encryption bond.

  - **Microsoft Point-to-Point Encryption (MPPE)** Obviously, this encryption method was developed by Microsoft. MPPE is used with PPTP to encrypt traffic and is generally used when IPSec is not an option. In addition, MPPE is supported by Windows 9x Dial-up Networking and Windows NT 4.0 Remote Access Services.

- **Authentication** The biggest challenge to VPNs is validating the identities of VPN clients and servers. As with any type of authentication, Windows 2000 must ensure that the systems are, in fact, the systems they identify themselves as. Windows 2000 supports the following authentication methods:

  - **Extensible Authentication Protocol (EAP)** EAP is an extension to PPP that allows a variety of arbitrary authentication methods. For example, EAP supports certificates, smart cards, password tokens, and Windows 2000's Internet Authentication Service (IAS).

- **Challenge Handshake Authentication Protocol (CHAP)**   CHAP uses an extra handshake between client and server to ensure that no password is sent unencrypted over the network during the authentication process. The CHAP server sends the client a key during the first step of authentication. The client, in turn, uses this key to encrypt its username and password and sends that information to the server. The server checks the authentication of the client and grants or denies access.

- **Microsoft Challenge Handshake Authentication Protocol (MS-CHAP)**   Like CHAP, MS-CHAP uses a three-step authentication process. However, in the case of MS-CHAP, the CHAP client uses the server's delivered key to encrypt the password. Then the client again uses the encryption key to encrypt the username and password one more time. MS-CHAP supports encrypted authentication for Windows 9x or Windows NT 4.0 clients.

- **MS-CHAPv2**   This is an updated version of MS-CHAP, and Microsoft implements it within Windows 2000. One of the biggest improvements within MS-CHAPv2 is mutual authentication between servers and clients. Use this updated version of MS-CHAP when authenticating Windows 2000 clients.

- **Dynamic Address and Name Server Allocation**   When establishing a VPN connection, both the VPN client and server must be assigned IP addresses. These addresses represent the *virtual interface* that must be used for communication. This provides another layer of security. However, to obtain these addresses, the VPN server hands out the IP addresses dynamically. In addition, the VPN server will also hand out the address of any DNS or WINS server for name resolution.

The VPN Server

You may want to install a VPN server on a Windows 2000 server system. Read on for a handy step list.

Lab Exercise 10.12: Install a VPN Server

For practice installing a VPN server, follow these steps:

1. Choose Start | Programs | Administrative Tools | Routing and Remote Access. If you have already configured your Windows 2000 server for Routing and Remote Access, skip to step 4.

2. In the Routing and Remote Access tool, click the Action menu and select Add Server, as shown in Figure 10-1.

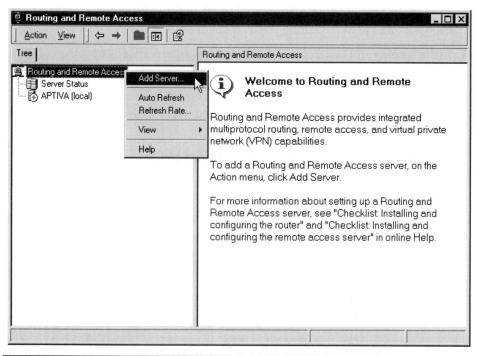

Figure 10-1   Using the secondary menu to add a server

3. In the Add Server dialog box, click the This Computer option and click the OK button (as shown here).

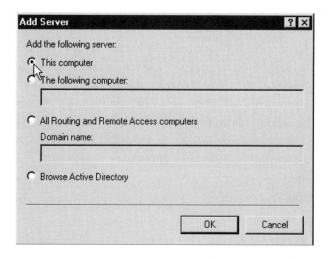

4. In the Routing and Remote Access tool, right-click the RRAS server and select the Configure and Enable Routing and Remote Access option.

5. In the Routing and Remote Access Server Setup wizard's Welcome screen, click the Next button to continue.

6. In the Common Configurations screen, select the Virtual Private Network (VPN) Server option (shown here), and then click the Next button to continue.

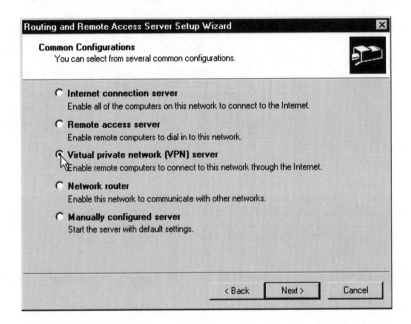

7. In the Remote Client Protocols screen, select the Yes, All of the Available Protocols Are on This List option if Windows 2000 has listed all of the protocols that VPN clients will use to connect to your VPN server (as shown in the following illustration). If you need to add any networking protocols (IPX/SPX, TCP/IP), you must install these protocols via your network connection's Properties dialog box (which can be accessed from the Control Panel). Assuming the proper protocols are installed (which is a safe assumption given TCP/IP is the default networking protocol when setting up Windows 2000 Server), select the No, I Need to Add Protocols option and select any additional protocols that you'd like to add. Click the Next button to continue.

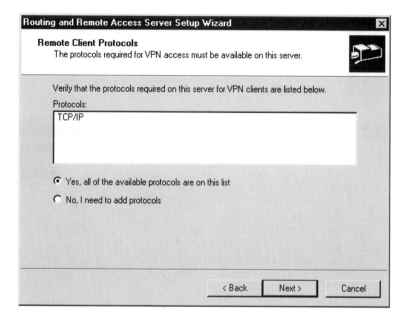

8. In the Internet Connection screen, select the network interface that you would like VPN clients to use for a connection, as shown here. Click the Next button to continue.

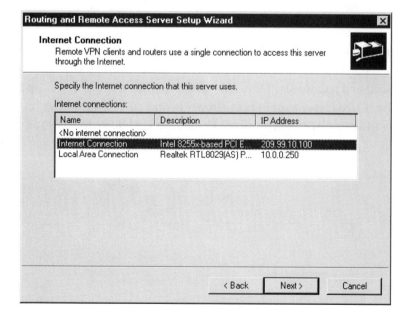

9. In the IP Address Assignment screen, choose the Automatically option, as shown here, if you already have a DHCP server on the network that can hand out dynamic IP addresses. Otherwise, choose the From a Specified Range of Addresses to have your VPN server hand out IP addresses from a range that you specify. Click the Next button to continue.

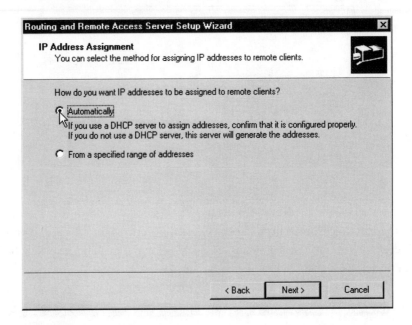

10. In the Managing Multiple Remote Access Servers screen, select the Yes, I Want to Use a RADIUS Server if you already have a RADIUS server set up to centralize user accounts and passwords. If not, choose the No, I Don't Want to Set Up This Server to Use RADIUS Now option, as shown here. You can always set up your VPN server to use a RADIUS server later. Click the Next button to continue.

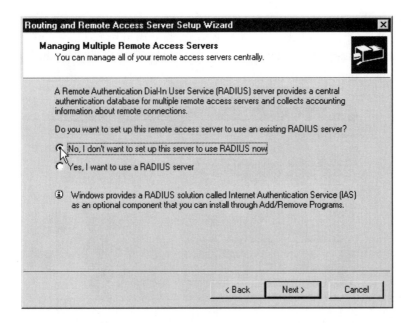

Routing and Remote Access Server Setup Wizard

Managing Multiple Remote Access Servers
You can manage all of your remote access servers centrally.

A Remote Authentication Dial-In User Service (RADIUS) server provides a central authentication database for multiple remote access servers and collects accounting information about remote connections.

Do you want to set up this remote access server to use an existing RADIUS server?

○ No, I don't want to set up this server to use RADIUS now

○ Yes, I want to use a RADIUS server

① Windows provides a RADIUS solution called Internet Authentication Service (IAS) as an optional component that you can install through Add/Remove Programs.

< Back   Next >   Cancel

11. In the Finish screen, click the Finish button to complete the setup of your VPN
    server.

After you have installed the VPN server, you may have to configure your DHCP Relay
Agent with the address of your DHCP server.

Lab Exercise 10.13: Configure Your DHCP Relay Agent with the Address of Your DHCP Server

For practice configuring your DHCP Relay Agent with the address of your DHCP server,
follow these steps:

1. Within the Routing and Remote Access tool, navigate to RRAS server | IP Routing
   | DHCP Relay Agent.

2. Right-click the DHCP Relay Agent and select Properties.

3. Within the DHCP Relay Agent Properties dialog box, type in the address of your DHCP server(s) and click the Add button, as shown here. Once you've added all of the necessary DHCP servers, click the OK button to complete the DHCP Relay Agent configuration.

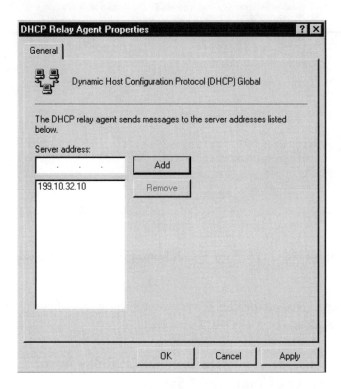

Lab Exercise 10.14: Configure Your VPN Server
After the Routing and Remote Access Wizard Setup

If you need to configure your VPN server after the Routing and Remote Access wizard setup, follow these steps:

1. Start the Routing and Remote Access tool again.

2. In the Routing and Remote Access tool, right-click the VPN server name and select the Properties option. The Properties dialog box will be displayed.

3. In the Properties dialog box, choose from a variety of configuration options, such as security authentication methods, as shown here.

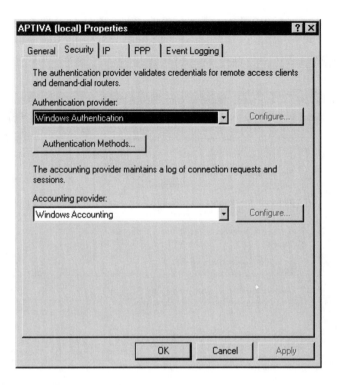

Installing a VPN Client

The following instructions will allow you to connect Windows 2000 workstations to a VPN server for remote access or to connect a Windows 2000 server to a VPN server to connect two separate networks.

Lab Exercise 10.15: Install a VPN Client

For practice installing a VPN client on a Windows 2000 system, follow these steps:

1. Choose Start | Settings | Network and Dial-Up Connections.

2. In the Network and Dial-Up Connections window, double-click the Make New Connection icon. Windows 2000 will launch the Network Connection wizard.

3. In the Network Connection wizard's Welcome screen, click the Next button to continue. (You may be prompted to configure the location information for your modem. Choose the appropriate settings, and then click the OK button to return to the Network Connection wizard.)

4. In the Network Connection Type screen, select the Connect to a Private Network Through the Internet option, as shown here, assuming that your Windows 2000 already has a connection to the Internet. Click the Next button to continue.

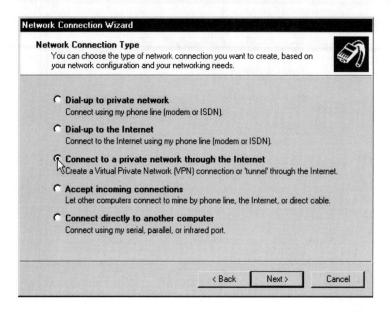

5. In the Destination Address screen, type in the host name or IP address of the VPN server, as shown here. Click the Next button to continue.

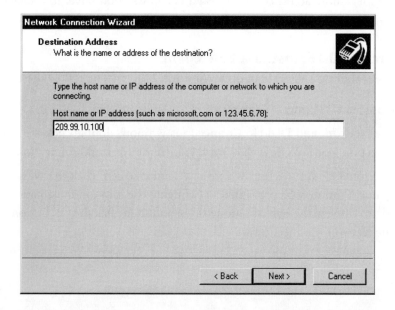

6. In the Connection Availability screen, select the For All Users option to make this VPN connection available for all users that log on to this Windows 2000 system, as shown here. On the other hand, if you'd like to keep the network connection private to your user profile, select the Only For Myself option. Click the Next button to continue.

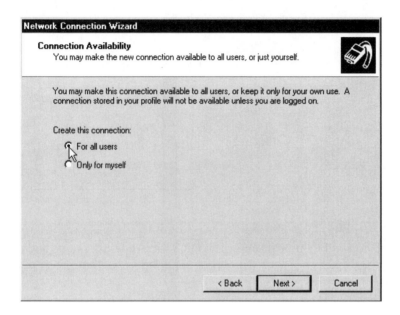

7. In the Internet Connection Sharing screen, select the Enable Internet Connection Sharing for This Connection option (as shown here) to allow other systems on the network to access this VPN connection. Once you've chosen this option, you can also choose the Enable On-Demand Dialing option to have this system dial the VPN server whenever a networked system requests resources accessible via the VPN connection. Click the Next button to continue.

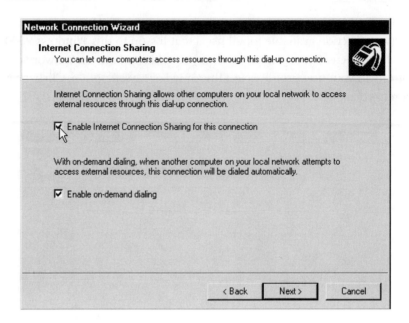

8. In the Finish screen, click the Finish button to complete the setup of the VPN client. You will then be prompted to enter the proper username and password to access the VPN server. Click the Connect button to establish the connection.

Remote Access Service

So far in this chapter, the topics of securing communications on a LAN, between LANs, and on WANs have been covered. In addition to these types of communication scenarios, most environments also have a need for employees to have remote access to network resources via a dial-up connection. So not surprisingly, you'd better do some planning to accommodate the organization's remote access needs (and such planning would, of course, include security considerations related to remote access).

The benefit of implementing a Remote Access Server within your Windows network is that you can use Windows 2000 security such as user authentication. You have to create a user account, manage password policies, and assign rights to users. In addition to this type of security (such as user authentication), Windows 2000 offers the ability to further secure the connection itself using the following features. For example, you can limit the time of day a user dials in, enable the Callback feature, or enable connection access based on group membership.

For older Windows clients and dial-up connections, RAS offers easy connectivity to remote network resources. Recall from the previous section that VPNs offer the same type of remote access as a simple telephone line-based dial-up connection. However, the key difference is that VPNs require an already-configured Internet connection (an ISP account) for connecting to the VPN. RAS allows you to hang a modem (or several modems) off the back of your Windows 2000 server and allow clients to dial-in.

Lab Exercise 10.16:
Set up a Remote Access Server

For practice setting up a Remote Access Server, follow these steps:

1. Choose Start | Programs | Administrative Tools | Routing and Remote Access. If you have already configured your Windows 2000 server for Routing and Remote Access, skip to step 4.

2. In the Routing and Remote Access tool, click the Action menu, and then select Add Server.

3. In the Add Server dialog box, click the This Computer option and click the OK button.

4. In the Routing and Remote Access tool, right-click the RRAS server and select the Configure and Enable Routing and Remote Access option.

5. In the Routing and Remote Access Server Setup wizard's Welcome screen, click the Next button to continue.

6. In the Common Configurations screen, choose the Remote Access Server option (shown here), and click the Next button to continue.

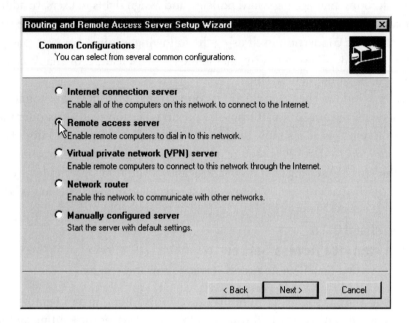

7. In the Remote Client Protocols screen, select the Yes, All of the Required Protocols Are on This List option if Windows 2000 has listed all of the protocols that RAS clients will use to connect to your RAS server, as shown in the following illustration. Select the No, I Need to Add Protocols option, and select any additional protocols that you'd like to add. Click the Next button to continue. For example, you might select the IPX/SPX protocol (which we assume you've previously added via the Networking applet in Control Panel, given your intention to use this networking protocol).

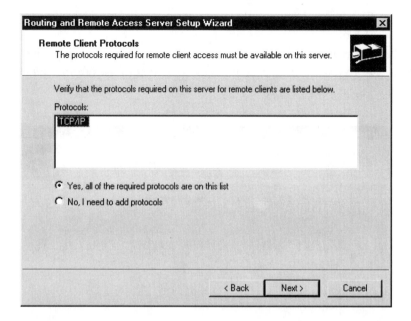

8. In the Network Selection screen, select the network interface that you would like RAS clients to use for a connection, as shown here. Click the Next button to continue.

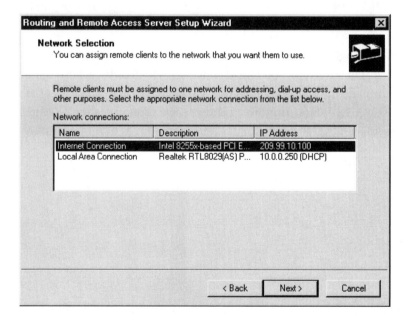

9. In the IP Address Assignment screen, choose the Automatically option if you already have a DHCP server on the network that can hand out dynamic IP addresses, as shown here. Otherwise, choose the From a Specified Range of Addresses to have your RAS server hand out IP addresses from a range that you specify. Click the Next button to continue.

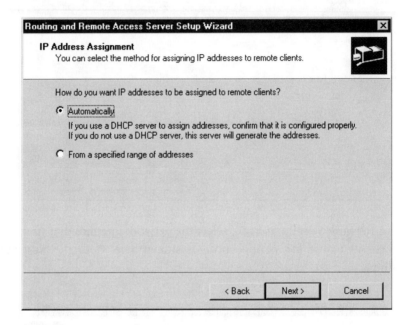

10. In the Managing Multiple Remote Access Servers screen, select the Yes, I Want to Use a RADIUS Server if you already have a RADIUS server set up to centralize user accounts and passwords. If not, choose the No, I Don't Want to Set Up This Server to Use RADIUS Now option, as shown here. You can always set up your VPN server to use a RADIUS server later. Click the Next button to continue.

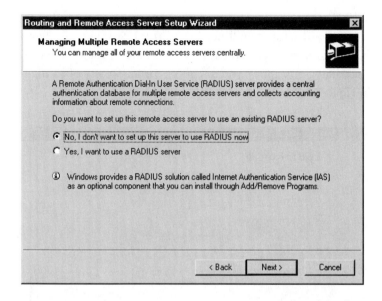

11. In the Finish screen, click the Finish button to complete the setup of the RAS server.

12. In the RRAS tool, expand the items under your RAS server and select the Ports option. You will then see all of the possible connections for your RAS clients, as shown here.

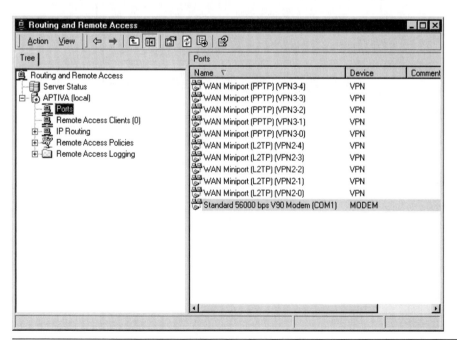

Figure 10-2 Configuring PPP for use

As with a VPN server, if you need to configure your RAS server after the Routing and Remote Access wizard setup, you'll need to start the Routing and Remote Access tool again. Within the tool, right-click the RAS server name and select the Properties option. The Properties dialog box allows you to choose from a variety of configuration options as shown in Figure 10-2.

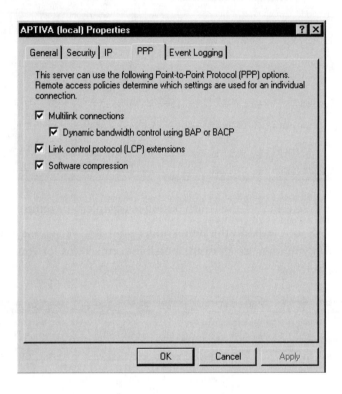

Remote Access Authorization

Windows 2000 allows you to control authorization on two levels: per user account and, as with most Windows 2000 security features, policies. As with Windows NT 4.0, you can enable and configure the properties for remote access by modifying individual user accounts, as shown here.

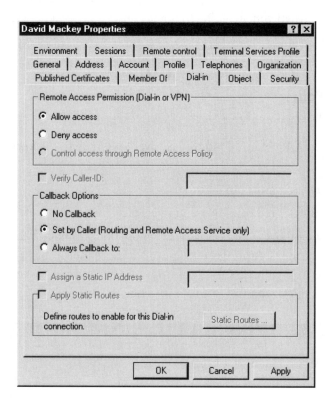

Even if you decide on using policies, which are easier to administer, you'll still have to modify each user account for remote access.

Lab Exercise 10.17: Enable Remote Access for Each User

For practice enabling remote access for each user, follow these steps:

1. Choose Start | Programs | Administrative Tools | Active Directory Users and Computers.

2. In the Active Directory Users and Computers tool, navigate to the user that you would like to grant remote access to.

3. Right-click on the desired user and select the Properties option.

4. In the Properties dialog box, click the Dial-In tab.

5. In the Dial-In page, click the Allow Access radio button.

6. If you plan on managing all RAS users' authentication and administrative policies by individual accounts, you may want to modify the Callback options and other security features. If you are going to manage RAS access via policies, click the OK button to put your changes into effect.

Lab Exercise 10.18: Manage Remote Access via a Group Policy

For practice managing remote access via a group policy, follow these steps:

1. Choose Start | Programs | Administrative Tools | Active Directory Users and Computers.

2. Navigate to the proper domain or OU.

3. Right-click the desired container and select New | Group.

4. In the New Object Group dialog box, type in a group name (for example, RAS Users), select the Security group type, and select the proper Group Scope, as shown here. You will use this group to house all of the users that need remote access. Click the OK button to create your new group.

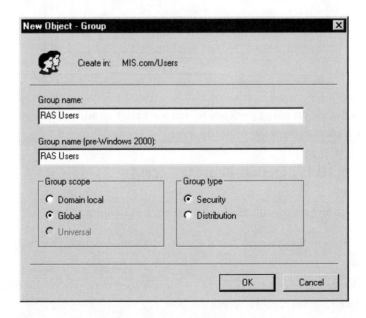

5. In the Active Directory Users and Computers tool, select all of the users you would like to add to the new group. Once you've selected all of the user accounts, choose Action | Add Members to a Group.

6. In the Select Group dialog box, select your newly created group. This will add all of the desired users to the new RAS group.

7. Choose Start | Programs | Administrative Tools | Routing and Remote Access.

8. Navigate to {RAS server name} | IP Routing | Remote Access Policies.

9. In the right pane, right-click somewhere within the empty space and select the New Remote Access Policy option.

10. In the Policy Name screen, type in a name to represent this new RAS policy, as shown here. For example, use the name RAS Policy. Click the Next button to continue.

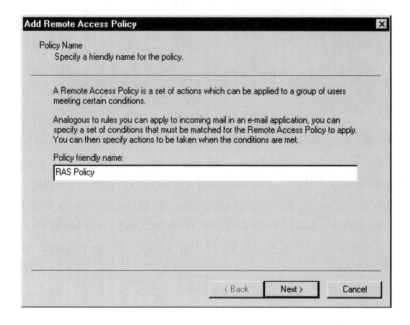

11. In the Conditions screen, click the Add button.

12. In the Select Attribute screen, select the NAS-Port-Type option (shown here) and click the Add button.

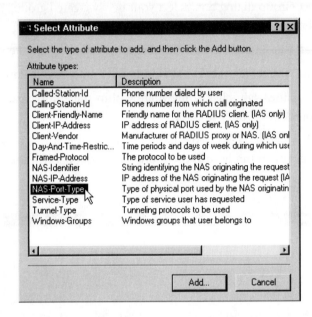

13. In the NAS-Port-Type screen, select the Async (Modem) option, and then click the OK button.

14. Repeat steps 11 and 12. This time select Windows-Groups option and click OK.

15. In the Groups dialog box, click the Add button. Select your new RAS group from the list, click the Add button, and then click the OK button to finish.

16. In the Groups dialog box, click the OK button to put your changes into effect.

17. In the Conditions screen (shown here), click the Next button to continue.

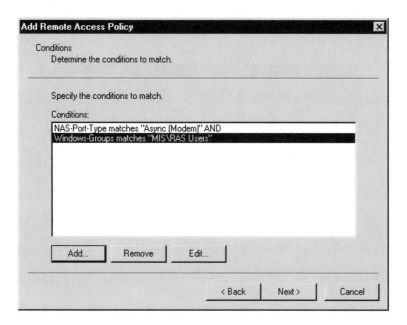

18. In the Permissions screen, select the Grant Remote Access Permission option, as shown here, and click the Next button to continue.

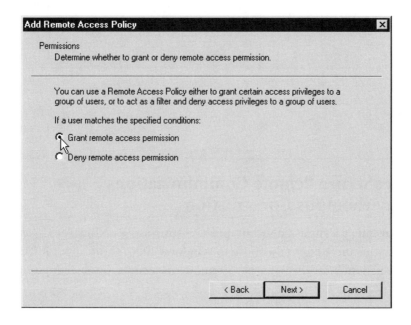

19. In the User Profile screen, click the Edit Profile button.

20. In the Edit Dial-In Profile dialog box, choose the variety of security options that you would like to implement with this policy, as shown here.

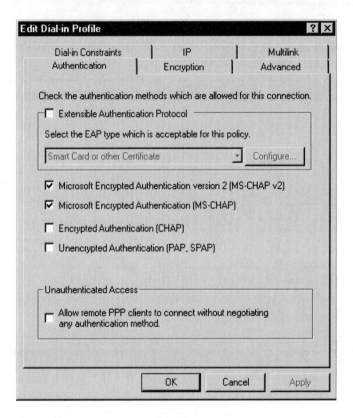

21. In the Permissions screen, click the Finish button.

Update: Secure Remote Communications for Catywhompus Construction

The management team at Catywhompus Construction has considered secure remote access a key justification for the move to Windows 2000. Think about it. The nature of the construction industry is to have remote sites for a limited duration (such as

continued

construction projects). And these remote sites have a need to communicate with the Catywhompus computer network. Thus, the need for secure remote access is a given.

The need for access between networks is just as clear for Catywhompus. Although it's a given the whole network will be a wide area network linking all Catywhompus offices, this can largely be viewed as one network. The connectivity between networks, say Catywhompus and a major client, isn't as big of a priority, given that much of the information that needs to be communicated between such separate entities can occur via e-mail and the use of the File Transfer Protocol (FTP).

Chapter Review

Windows 2000 provides a variety of security features to help you secure your network communications and ensure that only authorized users can access network resources and services. In particular, this chapter has covered intra-LAN communications, intra-WAN communications, and remote-access communications. Use all of these security features to ensure that your confidential data remains just that—confidential.

Questions

1. What are two of the biggest benefits to a proxy server? Choose all that apply.
   a. Content caching
   b. VPN tunneling
   c. Content filtering
   d. Network Address Translation (NAT)

2. What is the ultimate purpose of a virtual private network (VPN)?
   a. Filter Web content
   b. Transfer e-mail securely
   c. Create secure communication over a public network
   d. Connect to heterogeneous networks

3. What VPN term defines the bundling of data with a header that allows its transmission over a public network?
   a. Encapsulation
   b. Encryption
   c. Authentication
   d. Address allocation

4. Which of the following are tunneling protocols used by Windows 2000? Choose all that apply.
   a. PPTP
   b. TCP/IP
   c. IPX/SPX
   d. L2TP
   e. NetBEUI

5. True or False? Using a VPN, you are not able to connect two networks.

Answers

1. **A** and **C.** A proxy server can cache Web content for a number of network users and filter Web site content to remove unwanted subject matter.

2. **C.** A VPN allows you to securely transfer data over a public network, such as the Internet.

3. **A.** Encapsulation is the process of bundling the data to be sent over the VPN in a header that allows its routing over a public network.

4. **A** and **D.** PPTP and L2TP are the tunneling protocols that Windows 2000 supports.

5. **False.** There are two types of VPNs: remote access and router-to-router. The router-to-router VPN allows you to securely connect two networks and their systems and users.

Key Skill Sets

- Use Windows 2000 server as a NAT server
- Provide secure communication within a LAN using SMB
- Provide secure communication within a LAN or WAN using IPSec
- Design a VPN solution
- Design a RAS solution

Key Terms

Challenge Handshake Authentication Protocol (CHAP)
Common Internet File System (CIFS)
Extensible Authentication Protocol (EAP)
Firewall
Gateway
IP Security (IPSec)
Layer Two Tunneling Protocol (L2TP)
Microsoft Challenge Handshake Authentication Protocol (MS-CHAP)
Microsoft Point-to-Point Encryption (MPPE)
Network Address Translation (NAT)
Point-to-Point Tunneling Protocol (PPTP)
Proxy server
Routing and Remote Access Service (RRAS)
Server Message Block (SMB)
Virtual private network (VPN)

Designing Security for Communication Channels

This chapter covers the following key mastery goals:

- Design an SMB-signing solution
- Design an IPSec solution
- Design an IPSec encryption scheme
- Design an IPSec management strategy
- Design negotiation policies
- Design security policies
- Design IP filters
- Define security levels

Although it is important to secure both server and client data resources at a local level using NTFS and EFS, communication between computers must also be secured. In other words, just because data is encrypted or secured locally does not mean that when the data is transmitted it is still encrypted or secured. The local encryption and security is only on the volume where the data is stored, and it does not carry through the transmission.

Thus, there is a need to secure data transmissions, but each situation's requirements are potentially unique, and the solution must be based on the security policy of the organization. Some communications require more attention than others. The risks of each situation must be evaluated, and you will need to focus especially on sensitive servers that communicate over a public network segment. Secret data communications may also need to be protected on a private network, but transmission protection is not used as often as protection over public segments.

When communication takes place over public segments, two methods for securing communications are available: SMB signing and IP Security (IPSec). *SMB signing* provides for each individual packet in a server message block (SMB) being protected with SMB digital signing. SMB signing is used for backward compatibility with pre-Windows 2000 computers. *IPSec* is an IP-layer protocol that provides integrity, confidentiality, and authentication of communications over a network. IPSec can be used to protect the communications between Windows 2000 computers.

This chapter discusses the available design choices for both SMB signing and IPSec. However, IPSec is the preferred choice for most situations. Group policies can be used to enable and provide enforcement for either of these methods on a Windows 2000 network, and this chapter discusses how to enable group policies for each of these two strategies.

Common Communication Channel Attacks

Security measures and controls must be put into place to protect transmitted data from attack. Attacks come in the form of unauthorized monitoring where the attacker passively gathers data and then actively uses the data to harm the organization or its customers. Other attacks attempt to modify data in transit with the intention of destroying the data or critical network services.

The following are common communication channel attacks that require you to develop and deploy protective measures:

- **Eavesdropping** Most traditional and current network communication takes place in clear-text format. This enables attackers to "listen" to these transmissions if they have access to the data transmission path. This ability to read the traffic opens up what is often the biggest security problem that a security designer faces in an enterprise. Strong encryption capabilities are required to ensure that data will not be read as it moves over channels of communication.

- **Data modification** Once data is read, the attacker has the option to alter it or use it to gain access to once-secure resources. This ability to modify data can create invalid or corrupt data. For instance, if students were able to modify data, they could change their grades. Also, credit card transaction amounts could be modified.

- **IP address spoofing** Typically, network devices and network operating systems use the IP address of a computer to identify the sender and receiver for valid data transmissions. Hackers can assume an IP address and spoof an identity. In other words, the attacker can assume the network identity of an IP node and use programs to build IP packets that appear to come from a valid IP address. Once this is accomplished, the attacker can change or reroute the data.

- **Username and password combination-based attacks** Intruders may use tools to decrypt passwords that are encrypted. Password-cracking programs capture encrypted passwords and match the passwords to encrypted passwords that are known by using pattern-matching methods. For example, intruders can use a program named L0phtCrack to decrypt passwords from SMBs that are captured as they are transmitted across a public network. If an attacker finds a valid user account, the attacker has the same rights as the real user, and it is especially a problem if that user is an administrator. After gaining access to the network with a valid administrative account, an attacker can obtain lists of valid user and computer names and other network information.

- **Denial-of-service (DoS) attacks** The denial-of-service attack prevents normal use of your computer or network by flooding servers with traffic or sending invalid data to applications or network services. This flooding of services at best reduces the performance of network services and often overloads a server or network device until a shutdown occurs or invalid utilization exceeds the service capacity. DoS attacks therefore block traffic, and they result in network resource access.

- **Man-in-the-middle attacks** A man-in-the-middle attack occurs when someone has placed him- or herself between two devices communicating in a network to actively monitor, capture, and control your communication without detection. A man-in-the-middle attack is similar to someone assuming your identity in order to read a sent or received message. This attack can damage communications and provide bad information to the sender and receiver—it is capable of the same damage as an application-layer attack, described shortly.

- **Compromised access key attacks** An attacker can use the access key to gain access to a secured communication transparently. The attacker can decrypt or modify data and potentially use the key to compute additional keys, thereby compromising other secured communications.

- **Sniffer attacks** If transmitted packets are not encrypted, a network sniffer provides a view of the data inside the packet. Using a sniffer, an attacker can analyze your network's unencrypted data transmissions and eventually gain the information necessary to crash or corrupt the network.

- **Application-layer attacks** Application-layer attacks target servers by intentionally introducing errors in a computer's operating system or applications. The successful attacker gains control of an application, system, or network and can delete or modify your data or operating system. They can also modify other security settings to make openings for other attacks.

Figure 11-1 shows the common transmissions attack that you will have to develop design strategies to prevent.

Designing a Signing Solution with the Server Message Block Protocol

Several security methods on Windows 2000 networks provide authentication and data integrity. The SMB protocol is a file sharing protocol used by Windows computers. SMB has been enhanced by Microsoft. The new enhanced version is called the *Common Internet File System* (CIFS), and it is a protocol that computers use to share files across corporate intranets. CIFS provides for platform-independent file sharing and network file access.

CIFS defines commands used to move data between computers on a network. The presentation layer (OSI, layer 6) handles requests intended for remote computers in CIFS protocol structures. CIFS packages are sent over a network to remote nodes or devices. The redirector in the presentation layer can also use CIFS to make requests to the protocol stack of the local computer, but this does not create network communication security risks. Windows 2000 provides an enhanced version of the SMB protocol, and CIFS is a native file-sharing protocol in Windows 2000.

SMB moves file data between clients and servers and between servers. *SMB signing* mutually authenticates a client and server in a communication session by placing a digital signature in each message block—this does not encrypt the data but ensures that the proper client is communicating with the proper server, and it protects against various attacks, including IP spoofing and man-in-the-middle attacks. By using digital signatures, SMB signing prevents data in packets from being changed during transmission. When mutual authentication is required through SMB signing, attackers have difficulty proving that they are the impersonated client or server.

SMB signing can be used with Windows 2000–based computers and Windows NT 4.0–based computers with Service Pack 3 or later installed. SMB signing can also be implemented on Windows 98 and ME clients. The Windows 2000 version of SMB signing now includes support for mutual authentication and message authentication.

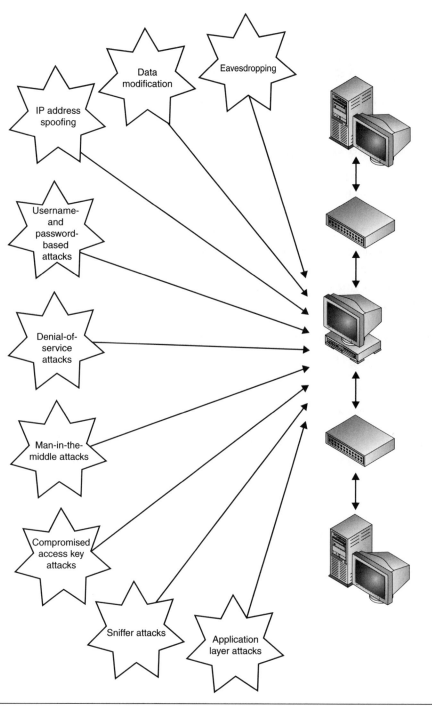

Figure 11-1   Common transmission attacks

> **NOTE** Mutual authentication is already provided by Kerberos on Windows 2000 clients. SMB signing is primarily needed for downstream (older) client versions, such as Windows NT 4.0 and Windows 9x. If there is no need to support downstream client communications, focus on using IPSec, as described in the "Designing IP Layer Security" section of this chapter.

SMB Signing Implementation

SMB signing is implemented by enabling the security signatures on clients and servers. SMB signing can be enforced by configuring group policies and local security policies for servers, and then configuring clients to use SMB signing when requested by a server.

Domain controllers by default have *EnableSecuritySignature* from Group Policy set to 1 (which signifies enabled) in the Local Security Snap-in. The Domain Controller's group policy object has this option enabled, and it takes precedence over any local settings on the specific domain controller. The following policy options are available for digital signing:

- Digitally sign client communications (when possible)
- Digitally sign client communications (always)
- Digitally sign server communications (when possible)
- Digitally sign server communications (always)

If you modify the EnableSecuritySignature and set it to require SMB signing, make sure that you also enable it. Figure 11-2 shows client digital signing enabled, but not required.

Figure 11-2
Digital signing
enabled

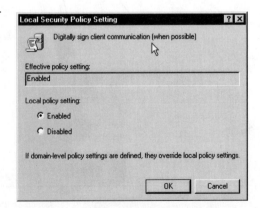

Consider the following when implementing SMB signing:

- SMB signing must be configured at both the client and the server. If the server is set to require SMB signing, communications cannot occur with clients that are not SMB signing–enabled.

- If you have Windows NT 4.0 clients with Service Pack 3 or later installed, SMB signing can be implemented to protect data transmitted between NT 4.0 clients and Windows 2000 clients.

- Use Group Policy to control SMB signing using domain, site, or OU levels to set SMB signing configurations.

Designing IP Layer Security

IP layer security works at lower layers than application layer security protocols, such as Secure Sockets Layer (SSL), and can protect network traffic at the IP layer. To put it simply, IP layer security can encrypt data for any application. The beauty of this is that applications or application protocols do not need to be aware that data encryption is occurring between client and server.

IP layer security is an emerging protocol and is still under development by the Internet Engineering Task Force (IETF), but it should be considered a long-term direction for secure networking. IPSec in Windows 2000 is the Microsoft implementation that, when properly designed by you, will provide a strong line of defense on your network against both private and public network attacks. IPSec focuses on achieving the following goals:

- Making sure IP packets are protected
- Providing a strong line of defense against transmission-based attacks

These two goals are met through encryption services, security protocols, and key management. These services and capabilities provide a strong and flexible way to protect communications between private network computers and public networks. It can also be used to filter or block certain traffic types between endpoints.

Selecting IPSec Mode

IPSec is used in one of two ways in Windows 2000 to send encrypted data between two endpoints. In an *end-to-end security model*, only the sending and receiving computers need to be aware of the data transmission. Each end handles security with the assumption that the communication media is not secure. Any computers that only route data (without modifying the IPSec-protected fields) from source to destination are not required to support IPSec. This end-to-end security model makes the transmission, in many cases, independent of the lower network layers, and it can be used for the following scenarios:

- **Local area network (LAN)**   Client/server or peer to peer
- **Wide area network (WAN)**   Router to router or gateway to gateway
- **Remote access**   Dial-up clients or VPN client Internet access to private networks

Figure 11-3 shows that IPSec can be deployed in transport mode or tunnel mode to provide endpoint-to-endpoint authentication encryption or authentication encryption when traversing a specific portion of a network.

NOTE IPSec cannot pass through a network address translator (NAT) because the NAT translates or modifies the IPSec-protected fields.

Transport Mode

In transport mode, IPSec will encrypt all traffic between a client and a server that passes through the IPSec filter. This mode is implemented on a network using IPSec policies between client and server. It is best to use the transport mode when two hosts are on the same private network and the communication does not need to traverse a NAT server.

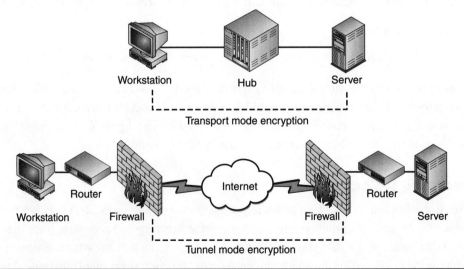

Figure 11-3   IPSec transport and tunnel modes

Tunnel Mode

In tunnel mode, all transmissions are encrypted and decrypted at the tunnel endpoints. This can be used between two routing devices where the data transmission crosses a public portion of the network. For example, you could use this mode between two locations that transfer data over the Internet. Each location could set up a tunnel between their firewalls or their NATs.

Lab Exercise 11:
How to Specify an IPSec Tunnel

1. In the Details pane of IP Security Policy Management MMC, right-click the policy you want to modify, and select Properties from the shortcut menu.

2. Select the rule you want to modify, and then click the Edit button.

3. On the Tunnel Setting tab, specify the computer that will be the tunnel endpoint.

4. Use "Tunneled communications to a specific computer" and click "The tunnel endpoint is specified by this IP address."

 NOTE To define IPSec policy for a computer, you must have appropriate administrator rights to Group Policy or be a member of the local system's Administrators group.

The tunnel endpoint is a static IP address at the computer to which you want to tunnel the packets, such as a firewall protecting a corporate network. Microsoft suggests that IPSec tunnels only be used for interoperability with other routers, gateways, or end-systems that do not support L2TP/IPSec or PPTP virtual private network tunneling technology. IPSec tunnel mode is supported as an advanced feature of Windows 2000, only to be used in gateway-to-gateway tunneling scenarios and server-to-server or server-to-gateway configurations. IPSec tunnels are not supported for client remote access VPN scenarios. L2TP/IPSec or PPTP should be used for client remote access VPN.

Planning IPSec Protocol Usage

IPSec is implemented in Windows as defined by the IETF, as a protocol and a driver, not as a service. IPSec uses an Authentication Header (AH) and an Encapsulating Security Payload (ESP). The AH provides data communication with source authentication and integrity without providing data encryption. The ESP provides confidentiality along with the aforementioned authentication and integrity. With IPSec, only the sender and recipient know the security key. AH is used when only data integrity is needed, and ESP is used when encryption is needed in addition to authentication and integrity.

Since Windows 2000 IPSec operates at and below the network layer, it is transparent to end users. Both AH and ESP support transport mode where endpoints are not identified, because multiple computers are involved in communication at the same time. They also support tunnel mode, where the endpoints are specified. It is possible to use IPSec alone as a form of tunneling when end systems do not support the use of other VPN tunneling technologies.

IPSec provides a number of security properties using the AH and ESP protocols. Table 11-1 shows the security properties IPSec provides for secured communications and which protocols support them.

 NOTE In Windows 2000, IPSec provides computer authentication but does not verify the user performing the data transmission. User authentication by way of Active Directory or the local security database must be used to control user access to an IPSec-enabled client computer. In other words, use strong password policies.

Using Predefined IPSec Policies

IPSec can be implemented either through Active Directory or by using local security settings. Whether you implement IPSec using Active Directory or local security settings, Windows 2000 comes with preset policies that define the IPSec role of a particular computer. These policies apply to a computer when they are assigned. The following are the default IP security policies available on Windows 2000:

- **Client (Respond Only)**   Used to communicate normally. This policy will use the default response rule to negotiate with servers that request security. Only the requested protocol and port traffic with that server is secured.

- **Secure Server (Require Security)**   Used for all IP traffic. This policy rejects unsecured incoming communications, and outgoing traffic is always secured. It will *not* allow unsecured communication with clients that are not trusted.

- **Server (Request Security)**   Used for all IP traffic. The computer accepts unsecured traffic but always attempts to secure communications by requesting security from the original sender. It will enable unsecured communication with clients that do not respond to the request.

Table 11-1   IPSec Security Services

IPSec Security Property	Description	IPSec Protocol Required
Authentication	A server can verify a message's origin by receiving the credentials of a client. The server determines if the sender is legitimate. The Windows 2000 implementation of IPSec provides multiple methods of authentication for compatibility purposes and remote clients.	AH
Encryption	Encryption ensures that data is only read and processed by the intended recipient. The data is encrypted prior to transmission, which ensures that it cannot be read even if the packet is monitored or intercepted during the transmission. Once the data is received, it is decrypted using the shared key. Payload (data) encryption is not mandatory and can be controlled by IPSec policy settings.	ESP
Non-repudiation	IPSec uses public key technology for digital signing to verify that the sender of the message is the only person who could have sent it. The sender's private key is used to create a digital signature that is sent with message. The receiver uses the sender's public key to verify the digital signature. Because only the sender has possession of the private key, only the sender could have generated the digital signature.	AH
Anti-replay	Anti-replay ensures the uniqueness of each IP packet. Data captured by an attacker cannot be replayed to establish a session or gain information.	AH or ESP
Integrity	IPSec prevents the modification of data in transit, which ensures that the data received is the same as the data sent. Each packet is signed with a cryptographic checksum using a shared key, and only the endpoints have the key used to calculate the checksum. The receiving computer checks the checksum prior to opening the packet; if the packet has changed, the packet fails the checksum test and is discarded.	AH

Predefined policies can be modified using the Security Rule wizard (see Figure 11-4). Once the modified or default policy is ready to be used, make sure the rule in the IP Filter List is checked, and then assign it.

How to Assign a Policy

1. Right-click the policy and select Assign (see Figure 11-5).

2. Make sure the policy is assigned (see Figure 11-6).

Figure 11-4
Security Rule wizard

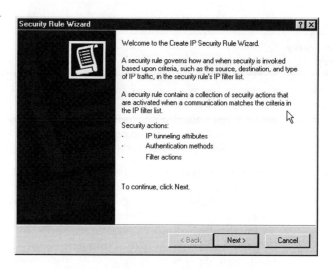

Figure 11-5   Assign the IPSec policy

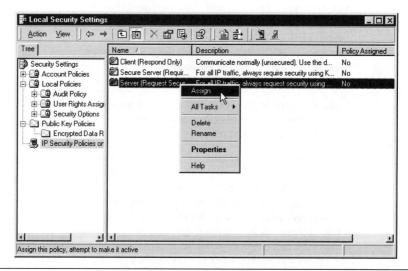

IPSec Implementation Components

Windows 2000 includes a set of security components that make up the Windows security model. These components ensure that applications cannot gain access to resources without authentication and authorization. Components of the security subsystem run in the context of the LSASS.EXE service process and include the following:

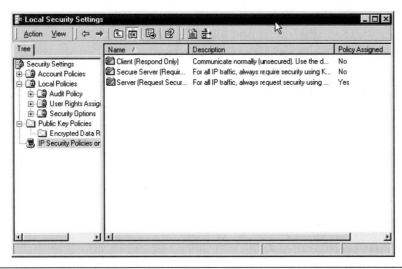

Figure 11-6 IPSec policy assignment

- Netlogon service

- Security Accounts Manager

- The Local Security Authority (LSA) service, which is a Windows 2000 protected subsystem that maintains the data about all aspects of local security on a system

- Secure Sockets Layer (SSL)

- Kerberos v5 authentication protocol

- NT LAN Manager (NTLM) authentication protocol

The security subsystem keeps track of the security policies and the accounts that are in effect on the computer system. In the case of a *domain controller*, which is a computer that has Active Directory installed, these policies and accounts are the ones that are in effect for the domain in which the domain controller is located. They are stored in Active Directory. After the IPSec policy is obtained, it will apply to all IP traffic passing through the system.

IPSec security associations (SAs) define how computers will use IPSec, such as which keys, key lifetimes, encryption, and authentication protocols will be used. Appropriate protection levels should be set to ensure secure data transmissions. As a network designer, you should be mindful of the need to protect the network from outside the network (from outside the firewall) as well as within the network, and IPSec policy settings used with appropriate protection levels can secure internal communications.

Table 11-2 shows the protection provided by authentication and encryption methods supported by IPSec. The encryption algorithms, authentication protocols, and key exchange values are explained in the following sections.

IPSec Encryption Algorithms

The following are the Data Encryption Standard (DES) levels available for IPSec:

- **DES (40-bit)**   Provides the best performance but the least security. Required for transmissions into or out of France.

- **DES (56-bit)**   Provides a performance improvement over 3DES due to shorter key length. Good choice for applications that require low security primarily for exported business traffic.

- **Triple DES (3DES), 3 × 56-bit**   Provides strong security but reduces performance because of key length.

IPSec Authentication Protocols

IPSec supports the Message Digest 5 (MD5) and Secure Hash Algorithm (SHA) authentication protocols. MD5, 128-bit, is less secure than SHA but requires less CPU overhead and has less impact on performance than SHA. SHA, 160-bit, provides stronger security but affects performance. SHA, 160-bit, should be used for U.S. government contracts that require adherence to the Federal Information Processing Standard (FIPS).

IPSec Internet Key Exchange

The Diffie-Hellman Technique (named after its inventors, Whitfield Diffie and Martin Hellman) is a public key algorithm that enables communications based on a shared key. With Diffie-Hellman, the two nodes exchange public information. Then each node

Table 11-2   Relative Protection for the Supported Authentication and Encryption Methods

Protection Level	Authentication (Integrity)	Encryption Level	Diffie-Hellman Group
4 (highest)	SHA-1 (160-bit)	3DES (3 × 56-bit)	1024 bits (medium)
3	MD5 (128-bit)	3DES (3 × 56-bit)	1024 bits (medium)
2	SHA-1 (160-bit)	DES (56-bit)	768 bits (low)
1 (lowest)	MD5 (128-bit)	DES (40-bit)	768 bits (low)

combines the public information along with its own secret information to generate a secret, shared code. Two group levels are available, 768 bits and 1,204 bits. If mismatched groups are specified on peered nodes, key negotiation fails. As in most cases, the larger bit length is harder to crack but requires more CPU cycles to process.

Internet Key Exchange is used between peers to calculate security keys; it uses two protocols, the Internet Security Association and Key Management Protocol (ISAKMP) and the Oakley key generation protocol. These two protocols reduce connection time and generate authenticated keys used to secure information. SAs must be negotiated between peer nodes. You can use Kerberos v5, Public key certificates, or previously agreed upon keys shared as authentication methods when negotiating security associations. Kerberos v5 is the default method for Windows 2000 and can be used for authentication with any clients in a trusted domain running this protocol. Public key certificates can be used when systems are not using Kerberos. An example of this is a trading partner accessing the network through the Internet. Preshared keys should not be used when a large number of systems are involved. Preshared key use is a simple method for systems not running Windows 2000 or using Kerberos v5.

 TIP Select Kerberos v5 if your design includes Active Directory. Use certificates for untrusted domains when Kerberos v5 is not supported.

Designing an IPSec Management Strategy

An IPSec implementation has a dramatic effect on server and network overhead. Due to the nature of the IPSec connections, they can be costly to maintain and implement. If tunneling is used, the tunnel has to be created, which means that someone must provide a list of IP addresses for the server to give out and then, once the connection has been established, it must be maintained. Maintenance not only means making sure the connection stays up, but it means that the system must encrypt and decrypt all these packets, which may degrade performance.

No matter the size of the organization, managing the use of IPSec means striking a balance between information availability for users and protecting information from unauthorized network access.

To properly manage and implement IPSec, you must perform the following steps:

• Assess the risk and determine the appropriate levels of security for the organization.

- Identify and document confidential information and its location and path.

- Define appropriate security policies using the risk management criteria, and implement protection schemes for the identified confidential information.

- Determine how the policies can best be implemented within the existing organization.

- Ensure that management and technology requirements are identified.

- Provide users with secure and efficient access to the appropriate resources based on their needs.

IPSec management is also influenced by the way the networked computer will be used. The required security will be affected by whether the computer is a domain controller, router, remote-access server, file and print server, application server, or intranet or VPN client. Managing and implementing IPSec requires careful planning and assessment, security guidelines, policy enforcement, auditing, and appropriate security policy design and assignment.

There is no exact definition of security standards for communications channels. Nor are there predefined measures that can be taken to provide a secure networking environment. The security measures taken can vary widely, depending on an organization's policies and infrastructure. Review how networking is used in the organization and then tailor the measures to meet the organization's needs.

Defining Security Levels

The following security levels can be considered as a general basis for planning your IPSec deployment:

- **Minimal security** Computers do not exchange sensitive data. IPSec policies are not assigned.

- **Standard security** This is used on servers that store valuable data. Security must not interfere with legitimate users trying to perform their tasks. Use predefined IPSec policies that secure data but do not necessarily require the highest level of security such as Client (Respond Only) and Server (Request Security).

- **High security** Servers providing confidential or secret data are at risk of data communications theft or disruption. Use the predefined Secure Server (Require Security) policy, which requires IPSec protection for all traffic being sent or received. Secure Server (Require Security) includes strong confidentiality and integrity algorithms, perfect forward secrecy (PFS), key lifetimes and limits, and strong Diffie-Hellman groups. Non-IPSec–aware computers or failed security-negotiation communications are blocked.

Designing Negotiation Policies

The negotiation of IPSec connections is managed by Internet Key Exchange (IKE). To ensure successful, secure communication, IKE performs a two-phase operation. The first phase ensures a secure communications channel, and the other negotiates the use of SAs. Encryption and authentication algorithms are used during each phase to ensure confidentiality and authentication during security negotiations. To design policies that stipulate these negotiations, you must understand the basic process presented here.

The design issues consist of making the choices in each area negotiated that will best fulfill the desired level of security for each IPSec connection. These choices will then be translated into IPSec policies and applied to each computer by using group policies. The following are key aspects of an IPSec negotiation:

- Phase I Negotiation
- Diffie-Hellman Group (DH) Exchange
- Phase II Negotiation
- SA Lifetimes
- Perfect Forward Secrecy

The following sections describe various issues and processes associated with each of these key aspects.

Phase I Negotiation

The purpose of the first phase is for the sender to tell the receiver what it would like, and the receiver tells the sender whether it is available. The following items are negotiated as part of the Phase I SA:

- The encryption algorithm (DE or 3DES)
- The hash algorithm (MD5 or SHA)
- The authentication method (certificate, preshared key, or Kerberos v5 authentication)
- The Diffie-Hellman group to be used for the base keying material

The computer's identity is protected if certificates or preshared keys are used for authentication. If Kerberos v5 is used, however, the computer ID is not encrypted until the complete identity payload is encrypted during authentication. The preshared key is considered the least secure option.

Diffie-Hellman Group (DH) Exchange

The DH exchange is part of Phase I and Phase II negotiation. The actual keys are not exchanged, only the base prime number used by the DH exchange. The DH algorithm generates the shared, secret key. At no time are actual keys exchanged. The DH groups, which are groups used to determine the length of the base prime numbers (key material) for the DH exchange, are as follows:

- Group 1, 768-bit

- Group 2, 1024-bit

Once this exchange has taken place, the IKE service on each computer generates the master key used to protect authentication. Without successful authentication, communication cannot proceed. The master key, along with negotiation algorithms and methods, is used to authenticate identities. The identity payload is protected from both modification and interpretation.

When the sender presents an SA offer to the receiver, the responder cannot modify the offer unless there is a rejection. The receiver may either accept the offer or reply with alternatives. Messages during this phase have an automatic retry cycle, which repeats five times. If the IPSec policy allows, fallback to clear is permitted after a short period. Standard SA negotiation begins if a response is received before the cycle times out. There is no limit to the number of exchanges that can take place. System resources only limit the number of SAs formed at a given time.

Phase II Negotiation

Phase II is used to negotiate the SAs that will be used. The second phase actually negotiates the SA connection. The following three steps occur during this second phase:

1. The policy negotiation step is where the IPSec computers exchange requirements for securing the data transfer including the IPSec protocol (AH or ESP), hash algorithm for integrity and authentication (MD5 or SHA), and the encryption algorithm. In this step, a common agreement is reached, and inbound and outbound SAs are established.

2. The session key material refresh rate, or how frequently exchange keys are regenerated by each computer during the lifetime of the SA, takes place according to the scheduled exchange of new information provided by IKE. IKE refreshes the keying material and new, shared, or secret keys are generated for authentication and encryption (if negotiated) of the packets.

3. The SA's security parameters index (SPI), a unique, identifying value, is used to distinguish among multiple security associations, and keys are passed to the IPSec driver.

In this phase, a pair of SAs is created for every SA negotiated. During negotiations, if the time-out limits are exceeded, IPSec will go back to Phase I SA. Of course, Phase I SA can also expire, but because the process is in two phases, the first phase of negotiation and authentication does not need to be repeated. The number of Phase II negotiations can be set using policies.

SA Lifetimes

Phase I SA is cached to enhance performance and to enable multiple Phase II SA negotiations (unless perfect forward security, described next, is enabled for the master key, or the session key policy lifetimes have been reached). If a key lifetime is reached for the master or session key, the SA must be renegotiated.

If the time-out period is reached for Phase I, or the master or session key lifetime is reached, a delete message is sent to the responder. An IKE message tells the responder to expire the Phase I SA. This prevents invalid Phase II SAs from being formed because Phase II SAs are valid until their lifetime is expired by the IPSec driver. The prevention of invalid Phase II SA formation creates Phase I SA lifetime independence. Because only the IPSec driver knows the number of seconds or bytes that have elapsed to reach the key lifetime for Phase II SA, IKE does not expire Phase II SA.

Perfect Forward Secrecy

Perfect forward secrecy (PFS) determines how a new key is generated, rather than when it is generated. Because it is inevitable that keys will be compromised, PFS simply ensures that the compromise of a single key permits access only to the limited data protected by that single key and not to the entire transmission. PFS ensures that a key used to protect a transmission will not enable the attacker to generate additional keys. With knowledge of a key, and the information used to generate new keys, attackers could potentially discover all transmitted information.

The use of master key PFS requires a reauthentication, so use it with caution because its use creates additional overhead for domain controllers. It requires a new Phase I negotiation for every Phase II negotiation that takes place. Session key PFS can, however, be used without reauthentication and requires less overhead.

Because PFS is not a negotiated property, it is not required to be enabled on both the sender and responder in order to work. If the responder requires PFS, and the sender's Phase II SA expires, the responder rejects the sender's message and requires a new negotiation. The sender expires the Phase I SA and creates a new negotiation. However, it is not the use of PFS that is negotiated; it is the SA itself that includes the exchange of base keying information.

> **TIP** The IPSec IKE protocol negotiates security for a Layer Two Tunneling Protocol (L2TP) tunnel using certificate-based authentication. The computer certificates (not user certificates) are used to authenticate and verify that both source and destination computers trust each other. If the IPSec transport security is established successfully, then L2TP negotiates the tunnel and provides access control based on the user's credentials. The IKE helps to make L2TP with IPSec flexible and a secure tunneling option for both client remote-access VPN and gateway-to-gateway VPN tunnels.

Designing Security Policies and Policy Management

IPSec Policy Management is used to create and configure IPSec policies through the Microsoft Management Console. Policies can be managed in four basic ways:

- Active Directory can be used to apply and manage policies centrally in the local domain.

- Active Directory can be used to apply and manage policies centrally in another domain.

- Policies can be managed locally on the computer on which you are running the snap-in.

- Policies can be managed remotely for a computer or domain.

You must add the IPSec Policy Management snap-in to the MMC (see Figure 11-7). A wizard guides you through the snap-in configuration (see Figure 11-8). You can save the IPSec policies' customized console so that you can manage policies at a later date.

Policies Stored in Active Directory

You can assign IPSec policies to the group policy object (GPO) of a computer account, site, domain, or OU. When the IPSec policy is applied to the GPO, the IPSec policy will propagate to any computer account affected by that GPO. IPSec policies that are applied to domain policy will override the locally applied IPSec policy if that computer is a member of the domain. IPSec policies assigned to OUs in Active Directory will override the domain-level policy for any members of that OU and the lowest-level OU in the Active Directory structure. It is best to assign policies at the highest possible level in order to reduce administrative effort and create a consistent application of policies.

PART II

Figure 11-7
IPSec Policy
Management
snap-in

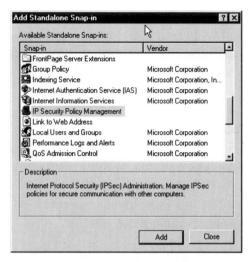

Figure 11-8
IPSec snap-in wizard

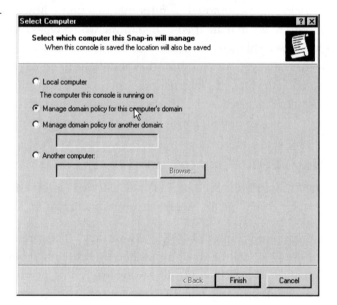

NOTE An IPSec policy remains active on a computer even after the GPO that it has previously been assigned to has been deleted, creating an orphaned IPSec policy. It is best to unassign the IPSec policy before deleting the GPO. If the IPSec policy is not unassigned before the GPO is deleted, the IPSec Policy Agent will use the cached copy.

An IPSec Policy Agent will only check Active Directory for changes or updates to the assigned IPSec policy. If IPSec policies have been changed and assigned to a computer, the Winlogon service will discover the changes during its polling cycle for group policy changes and will notify the IPSec Policy Agent. Then the IPSec Policy Agent will apply the policy to the computer.

Local Computer Policy

Windows 2000 computers have a local computer policy. Group policy settings can be stored on individual computers whether they are part of an Active Directory network or not. Because group policy objects associated with sites, domains, or OUs can overwrite the local computer policy, the local group policy is rarely used in an Active Directory–managed security environment.

Rules Design

The IPSec policies are composed of rules that determine how polices are used. Rules have a list of IP filters that are used to determine which types of packets are allowed to cross through the local computer's interface from the network. These filters control and determine the traffic patterns and how they should be handled. The rules list filters and actions related to the filter. If a match is made between the filter and packet header information, the rule is triggered by the filter actions. Each policy can have multiple rules, and the rules can be active simultaneously. Figure 11-9 shows the default IPSec rules.

Designing IPSec Encryption

When using Encapsulating Security Payload (ESP), you select encryption algorithms in the Rule Properties dialog box. The most common encryption algorithms are

- **Data Encryption Standard (DES), 56-bit key**   This protocol is popular and is part of the IPSec standard. Unfortunately, it is no longer secure due to the small key length. However, because of the relatively low overhead that this protocol requires, it will probably remain in use for some time to come.

- **Triple DES (3DES)**   This protocol simply uses DES three consecutive times in three different ways. This means it takes longer and is more difficult to encrypt and decrypt than DES.

Designing IPSec Filters

As mentioned earlier, *rules* govern how an IPSec policy protects communication. A rule provides the ability to trigger and secure communication based on the source, destina-

Figure 11-9
Default IPSec rules

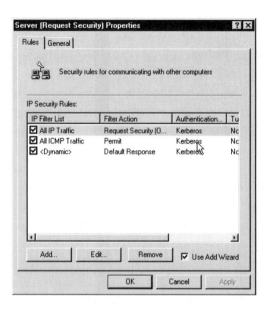

tion, and type of IP traffic, including protocol and port. Rules contain a filter list and the action(s) that take place upon a match with a listed filter.

IPSec filters are the most important part of IPSec policy. They are triggers for negotiating communications and are based on the protocol characteristics; they must be configured properly for communications to be secure. You must decide which specific interfaces the filters should apply to.

After the necessary IPSec filters have been defined, filter actions must be specified. The allowed filter actions are as follows:

- **Pass through** This defines the network traffic that must not be encrypted. IPSec is not applied to this traffic.

- **Block** The traffic that meets the filter definition is discarded. This is used to block hacking attempts using the protocols associated with these hacking attempts.

- **Negotiate** If the IPSec filter is matched, the participants negotiate the type and level of IPSec policy that will be applied to the data transmission.

IPSec filters can be applied to protect network connections, remote access connections, or both. The following is a discussion about the use of IP packet filtering and how it can be used with IPSec.

IP Packet Filtering

Each IP filter list contains a list of filters, and each filter describes a particular subset of network traffic to be secured, both for inbound and outbound traffic. An IP filter can make IPSec sessions mandatory.

In addition to specifying packet encryption and authentication, filters can identify a block of client IP addresses with which the computer can enable communications. Filters can specify individual IP addresses as well.

Inbound Filters

Inbound filters apply to traffic received and enable the receiving computer to match the traffic with the IP filter list. Inbound filters respond to requests for secure communication or match the traffic with an existing SA and process the secured packets.

Outbound Filters

Outbound filters apply to traffic leaving a computer, and they trigger a security negotiation that must take place before traffic is sent. Filters are associated with IPSec rules and help to define the rules. You must have a filter to cover any traffic for which the associated rule applies. For example, if one computer always wants to exchange data securely with another computer, IP filters help the IPSec server recognize whether or not it can talk to a particular computer. The IP filter will either enable or deny access to the IPSec server, depending on the address of the specific computer or the subnet on which it resides.

 EXAM TIP Some port filters require special attention. IPSec uses IP ports 50 and 51 and UDP port 500. These ports should be opened at the firewall if communication is going to occur between a remote user and the VPN server behind a firewall.

IPSec Best Practices

The following are the best practices when using IPSec to protect data transmissions:

- Examine the kinds of information being sent over the network: is it sensitive payroll data, trade-secret information, or e-mail? Some functional areas might require a higher level of security than the rest of the enterprise because of their function. For instance, the Research and Development function will probably have higher security requirements than Inventory Control.

- Determine where sensitive information is stored and how it routes through the network. Also determine which computers require access to this sensitive information. This information provides data about the speed, capacity, and utilization of the network prior to IPSec implementation, which is helpful for performance optimization.

- Identify your likely communication channel scenarios: intranet, remote access, extranets for business partners, or communication between sites (gateway to gateway). The level of security necessary for each scenario should be identified and built into the IPSec design. For example, you may find that only research and development server communications require confidentiality. Design, create, and test the IPSec policies for each scenario in your plan before going live. This enables you to clarify and refine the policies and policy structures that are necessary.

Verifying IPSec Communications

After designing an IPSec communication structure, it is important to verify that IPSec communications are functioning as designed. Several tools are available to help verify that IPSec negotiations are occurring successfully. Table 11-3 identifies the tools and procedures that can be used to verify whether IPSec is active and whether or not IPSec communications are occurring between two nodes.

Table 11-3   IPSec Monitoring and Testing Tools

Utility	Purpose	Analysis and Usage Notes
PING	The Packet Internet Groper utility verifies that a network interface is functioning.	To determine whether successful IPSec negotiations are occurring, PING the IP address of the server computer with which you are trying to communicate. You should receive four replies to the PING. This verifies that you can communicate with your partner. Make sure there is an IPSec filter that encrypts ICMP packets.
IPSec Monitor	This enables you to monitor the operation of IPSec in real time on either a local or remote computer. If an IPSec policy is negotiated for communication, the IPSec policy will be in the Security Associations listing.	Initiate the utility using the RUN command and type **IPSECMON** in the text box. The utility has three panes (see Figure 11-10) and enables you to look at real-time statistics.
Network Monitor	Use Network Monitor to filter all protocols except ISAKMP, AH, and ESP.	If the IPSec protocols do not appear in the capture, the interface is not using IPSec.
Event Viewer	Enable security auditing and check the event log for events related to IPSec.	Check the Security Log for IPSec service messages.
TCP/IP Properties	By displaying the properties for Internet Protocol (TCP/IP), you can see the active IPSec policy.	Type **IPCONFIG /all** at a command prompt. If the computer is running local IPSec policy, the name is displayed in an editable form. If the computer is running a policy assigned through the Active Directory group policy, the name and dialog is grayed out and is not editable.

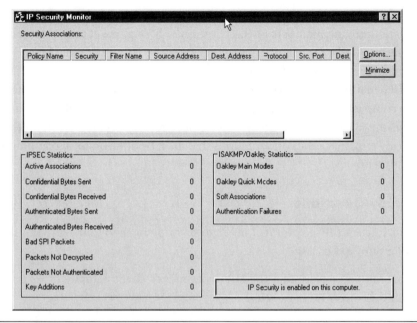

Figure 11-10 IP Security Monitor console

Case Study 11: Protecting the Catywhompus Finance Department Using Internet Protocol Security

In this exercise, determine the IPSec configuration required to appropriately protect the Human Resources department at Catywhompus Construction.

Scenario

The Human Resources (HR) department wants to control which computers are allowed to attempt a connection to the payroll management server. This server has information about salaries and other confidential data. HR wants access to only be granted to members of the HR team.

All client computers in the HR department run Windows 2000 Professional, and the payroll management server is a Windows 2000 server. The HR department and server are located on a separate segment to prevent network-monitoring tools from seeing the

continued

traffic on the HR department's segment. To secure the communications in the HR department, only the members of the HR team will be allowed to communicate with the HR server. All data transmissions to and from the HR server must be encrypted to ensure that they are kept confidential.

The HR department is also connected to the corporate network and wants to prevent portable computers in other departments from connecting to the HR department's segment and the HR server. Additionally, the Information Systems department wants to make it easy to manage the configurations that must be done on local computers in the HR department.

Case Study Questions

1. Which type of IPSec protocol needs to be implemented to meet the needs of the HR group? AH or ESP?

2. How can you ensure that the HR department's client computers are configured with the correct IPSec policies?

3. Which IPSec configuration settings on the HR server are required in order to ensure that all data transmissions are protected based on the HR department needs?

4. Assuming large numbers of transactions and transmissions are occurring on the HR server, what can be done to reduce the processor overhead on the server due to encryption processing?

Suggested Solutions

(Your solutions may vary.)

1. Because Encapsulating Security Payload (ESP) provides for data encryption and Authentication Header (AH) does not, ESP is best for this situation—HR wants all data transmissions encrypted.

2. The HR department's Windows 2000 clients should be placed in the same OU in Active Directory, and a group policy for the OU needs to be configured so that ESP is used for all data transmissions sent to and from the HR server using its static IP address.

continued

3. Using Active Directory, the HR server is placed in an OU where the group policy is defined to require ESP for all transmissions. The transmissions received must come from the local subnet where the HR department server and clients are placed.

4. The server's performance can be improved by installing an IPSec-capable network interface card. This will reduce the load on the server's processes. However, it will possibly increase the cost of the solution.

Chapter Review

Unsecured network communications can provide an opening for attackers. To secure network communications, you can use SMB signing and IPSec. You must have the prerequisite knowledge about communications and the ability to design authentication and encryption integration to implement them.

IPSec is an extension of IP that enables packets to be authenticated and encrypted between two endpoints. The two primary components of IPSec are the Authentication Header (AH) and the Encapsulating Security Payload (ESP). Both can be configured in transport mode or tunnel mode.

Using security policies, you can determine which packets will require IPSec. You have complete control over policies, even though Windows 2000 comes with three default policies to make administration easier. The policies can be applied through GPOs to provide an enterprise IPSec solution. Additionally, tools like IPSECMON, PING, Network Monitor, and Event Viewer can be used to investigate IPSec communications.

Questions

1. If you want to ensure that all Windows 2000 clients will use IPSec if required, where will you deploy the Client (Respond Only) IPSec policy to ensure that all client computers will respond to an IPSec request?
   a. At the OU level
   b. At the site level
   c. On the local computer
   d. At the domain level

2. If you believe the communication failure is IPSec-related, which diagnostic tool should you use first?
   a. IPSECMON
   b. System Monitor
   c. Network Monitor
   d. PING
   e. Event Viewer

3. Where are the IPSec security policies defined?

4. The AH protocol provides for what? (Choose all that apply.)
   a. Confidentiality
   b. Authentication
   c. Integrity
   d. Anti-replay services

5. The ESP protocol provides for what? (Choose all that apply.)
   a. Confidentiality
   b. Authentication
   c. Integrity
   d. Anti-replay services

6. Once an IPSec policy is enabled for a computer, which of the following is true?
   a. All computers are forced to use IPSec when they communicate with the computer.
   b. Communication with that computer will use IPSec if possible, and if negotiations fail, then unsecured communications will take place.
   c. The computer is vulnerable.
   d. Whether IPSec is set to require or suggest will be determined by the IPSec policy.

Answers

1. **D.** Domain-level deployment will ensure that all client computers respond to IPSec requests.

2. **A.** However, PING is a very close second because it is fast and can detect other problems, such as a bad IP stack. Using IPSec Monitor will give you a quick look at the active policy associations and the IPSec statistics.

3. IPSec security policies are defined in Group Policy at the local, site, domain, and OU levels.

4. **B, C,** and **D**. The AH protocol does not encrypt data. ESP provides for encryption.

5. **A, B, C,** and **D**. The ESP protocol provides for all of these, including encryption for confidentiality.

6. **D**. IPSec policies specify whether or not IPSec must be used or is optionally used.

Key Skill Sets

The following skill sets meet the Microsoft Objectives for the 70-220 exam. You learned how to design security for communication channels by using Windows 2000 network capabilities to accomplish the following:

- Design an SMB-signing solution.
- Design an IPSec solution for the following areas:
- An IPSec encryption scheme
- An IPSec management strategy
- IPSec negotiation policies
- Security policies
- IP filters
- Define security levels

Key Terms

Anti-replay
Authentication Header (AH)
Denial-of-service attacks
Diffie-Hellman (DH) group
Encapsulating Security Payload (ESP)
Internet Key Exchange (IKE)
IP Security (IPSec)
IP spoofing
Man-in-the-middle attack
Perfect forward security (PFS)
Security association (SA)
Security Parameters Index (SPI)
Server Message Block (SMB)

PART III

Exam 70-221: Designing a Microsoft Windows 2000 Network Infrastructure

- **Chapter 12** Overview of Designing a Network Infrastructure
- **Chapter 13** Analyzing Business and Technical Requirements
- **Chapter 14** Designing a Network Infrastructure Using TCP/IP
- **Chapter 15** Designing an Automated IP Configuration Solution Using DHCP
- **Chapter 16** Creating a DNS Name-Resolution Design
- **Chapter 17** Designing with WINS Services and DFS
- **Chapter 18** Designing Internet and Extranet Connectivity Solutions
- **Chapter 19** Designing a Wide Area Network Infrastructure
- **Chapter 20** Designing a Management and Implementation Strategy for Windows 2000 Networking

Overview of Designing a Network Infrastructure

This chapter covers the following key mastery goals:

- Identify and briefly describe the core Windows 2000 networking services
- Describe the network service design aspects used to define network design criteria
- Identify the four networking-solutions areas for connectivity and protocol requirements provided by Windows 2000

This chapter provides the baseline knowledge needed to proceed in your preparation for the 70-221 Designing a Microsoft Windows 2000 Network Infrastructure exam. The foundational knowledge contained in this chapter corresponds to the information you will be held responsible for on the certification exam. That is, the information here points you toward what it takes to design a network infrastructure using essential design principles and the technologies provided by Windows 2000. Our goal is for you to gain some key background needed to understand the scope of the creative and technical task before you. That is, the task of designing a network infrastructure and passing the Microsoft certification exam.

Windows 2000 Networking Services Design Overview

So, welcome to the wonderful world of network infrastructure design in the Windows 2000 Server time frame! While the basic principals of sound network infrastructure design, such as the proper use of networking protocols, is valid today (and tomorrow), you may have and will notice things unique to the Windows 2000 Server environment.

Well-Trodden Networking Territory

To be brutally honest, most Windows 2000 MCSEs inherit, rather than create, the networks they work on. That's because, at least in the United States, few firms of any significant size are without a network. There is very little virgin territory out there for the Windows 2000 MCSE.

When you look at a company from a design perspective, you will likely find that significant components of many existing networks have been in place for years. Some of these networks were rolled out rapidly with one goal in mind—to get the network up and running, fast! In other words, they implemented these networks without much thought or credence placed in the design and planning process. This method, while expedient and initially friendly to the accounting statements because of the lower up-front costs, can lead to networks that do not allow for easy access to resources and that often develop into networks that perform poorly. We've often seen this inverse relationship in networking: the faster and cheaper the network was set up, the poorer the network performs over the long run.

Other networks may have designs that simply require enhancements to allow for growth or for the implementation of new services. However, these networks can also impede the implementation of new client/server applications that may be needed for an organization's strategic initiatives. For instance, if a network does not properly implement the Domain Name Service (DNS), then a scalable database will not exist to allow for the centralized management of fully qualified domain name (FQDN) resolution. Without appropriate name resolution on the network, it is very difficult to publish the mission-critical sales data that is needed for a new business initiative. The infrastructure can be a significant impediment if it is not properly designed. While this is better than the first situation we described, the fact is that poorly designed networks can come in many different shapes and sizes.

Because networks often play a fundamental role in an organization's ability to achieve strategic goals and objectives, the ability to design a network-services infrastructure providing functionality, availability, performance, and security to the organization's network is highly valued. A poorly designed computer network is extremely visible in the organization, and even if it isn't the punch line of water-cooler jokes, it can hamper the organization's ability to function at an optimal level.

For example, perhaps during the Windows 2000 MCSE journey through the core exams (which we assume you've taken prior to starting the design series), you learned about Terminal Services. This environment, unique to Windows 2000 Server, demands you think differently than you have in the past about your network design.

This chapter is the first of several in the Exam 70-221 Designing a Microsoft Windows 2000 Network Infrastructure section of the book. The chapters that follow will focus on specific Windows 2000 MCSE exam objectives. Our intent for this first chapter is to provide a networking infrastructure overview that reviews the key processes and strategies for aligning the selection of appropriate infrastructure services with an organization's networking goals and objectives. The key learning objective, other than to introduce networking infrastructure matters, is to emphasize alignment of technical and business considerations in the organization. It's just another way we're weaving the old MCSE and MBA togetherness theme across this book. In case you missed that MCSE and MBA theme previously, early in the book, we spoke about how the designing certification exam series forces the MCSE to think like an MBA in considering the business and technical needs analysis of the organization.

But there's more to this chapter. This overview also identifies the contemporary networking services and components available in the Microsoft Windows 2000 networking model. Most of the discussions will revolve around the following Catywhompus Construction case study.

Case Study 12: Catywhompus Construction Infrastructure Redesign

Catywhompus Construction is a large organization headquartered in Oakland, CA, with five additional locations in New York, Los Angeles, Chicago, London, and Tokyo. Bob Smith is the president and CEO, and he has decided to move boldly into a new era of the business. He and his management team have determined that electronic commerce technologies are key to the future growth and success of Catywhompus. They insist it is critical to ensure that the network infrastructure be in place to meet the following electronic commerce objectives:

- The network protocols used on the wide area network (WAN) must support the flow of communications with customers and trading partners. These protocols must be based on international standards.

continued

- The physical network must provide the bandwidth and addressing schemes required for information exchange.

- Tools and techniques must be implemented to browse through information collections to find relevant information.

- The infrastructure must support electronic transaction systems.

- Information must be collected and organized for easy ad hoc queries.

- Payment authentication systems must be supported.

- Tools and protection must be in place to safeguard the network information flow.

- Employees must have full access to the Internet, and remote users must be able to access the corporate network and its data cache 24/7 from any of its six locations.

- The networking infrastructure must be of sound mind and body. That is, when management decides to move quickly on merger and acquisition opportunities, the network infrastructure must be prepared to handle the merger of different and disparate operating systems.

The management team has indicated that this transformation must take place quickly. Yet, it must not interfere with the existing operations, which have been very profitable for the company. You, a rising star in the Windows 2000 MCSE community, have been hired to design the Catywhompus network to achieve these objectives.

Case Study Questions

1. What design strategies will you use to ensure that all network infrastructure design issues are addressed?

2. What are the critical success factors in designing the Catywhompus network infrastructure?

3. Do you have enough information at this point to know where to start?

4. What network protocols, services, and management techniques will you put into place to achieve these goals?

Remember, the goal of this chapter is to introduce a framework for building a detailed infrastructure design, and to present fundamental services available in a Windows 2000 network that you can use to meet the design objectives for a large network. So go easy on yourself, and don't expect to be able to design the entire infrastructure at this point.

Throughout this chapter, you will have an opportunity to address some of the Catywhompus Construction design issues. You will use the information in the presentations

continued

of the upcoming chapter and, as you move through the subsequent chapters, put the pieces together to create an integrated network infrastructure design. In subsequent chapters, we will also address the design issues for single locations within the Catywhompus network, so we can address small- and medium-sized network design issues, as well.

The Networking Services Deployment Cycle

When we're acting as a network designer, we take our job seriously. We feel we're no less important than the building architect who put care and forethought into designing the building that houses the company's network. The architect certainly took enough time to guarantee that the building wouldn't fall down in a heap of dusty rubble. We want to do the same when it comes to networks we design and sign off on—my goal is to ensure that the implementation of my designs adds value to the organization.

The essential cycle used to deploy a networking-services design has five main phases, as shown in Figure 12-1:

- Design
- Test Design

Figure 12-1
Five key infrastructure design phases

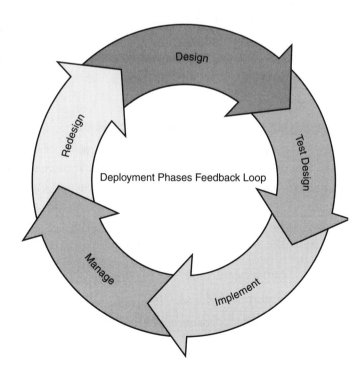

- Implement

- Manage

- Redesign, if needed

Each of these phases breaks down into specific decisions driven by the organization's networking objectives. An organization's distinctive characteristics will make each deployment cycle unique.

For instance, because Catywhompus Construction will be redesigning their network infrastructure, we recommend they thoroughly address each of the five design phases. It is important for a company to process each of the phases to ensure a design's success. By following this process, the designer has a better opportunity to add value to the organization through a quality design. If Catywhompus were to create a high-quality design, but not test before implementation, they might find that the implementation, or the ability to manage the design, is severely hampered. On the other hand, if they work step by step through the key phases, each of the critical design factors can be addressed and managed as needed.

You will have noticed that the design process is displayed as a circle. That's a critical point. The design process is typically ongoing, never truly ending. That is an ambiguous quality that bedevils many old-school MCSEs intent on believing that something has to have a discrete start and finish. Not here, my friend. Even after a network is up and running, the network design is often revisited, at least once per year in a strategic planning mode. A strategic planning mode, we believe, is when you stop focusing on the day-to-day demands of your job and think forward. In plain talk, it's a planning paradigm you embrace.

Designing the Networking Services

When you design a networking services infrastructure, you must follow some general principles that apply to most networking scenarios. You can think of these general principles as being akin to building codes in the construction industry.

When designing, you need to consider the existing infrastructure and then manage the resulting solution to meet the design specifications. Make your fundamental decisions based on the answers to the following questions:

- What is the existing infrastructure of an organization?

- What are the current and near-term goals of the organization?

- What network services are used within the design?

Your comprehensive network designs will vary widely in their overall composition, reinforcing the MCSE adage that network design is more of an art than a science. In fact, many networks designed by MCSEs working independently will look very different. And it's not that these networks are wrong; they're just different! However, they will have common elements if they are based on the answers to those questions.

In the Catywhompus Construction network redesign project, you as the designer will review the existing infrastructure, determine the network objectives, and then choose the network services needed in the network infrastructure design. The key to a successful design is to manage the integration of the new services with the existing infrastructure to achieve the network goals. If, for instance, you note that one of the network objectives is to use dynamic IP configuration on the network, and Catywhompus's current infrastructure includes IP routing, the implementation of DHCP must include some form of IP helper or DHCP relay agent over the routers, and include multiple subnet scopes to provide dynamic client configurations over the routed network.

Start the process of creating a network design by analyzing the current infrastructure of the organization. Then, gain a solid understanding of the goals and priorities of the network functionality. Make sure the network services selected are in alignment with the goals and priorities of the organization while taking into account the current infrastructure of the organization. Review the recommended process in Figure 12-2.

PART III

Figure 12-2
The basis for network design solutions

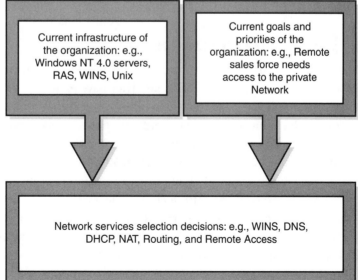

Current infrastructure of the organization: e.g., Windows NT 4.0 servers, RAS, WINS, Unix

Current goals and priorities of the organization: e.g., Remote sales force needs access to the private Network

Network services selection decisions: e.g., WINS, DNS, DHCP, NAT, Routing, and Remote Access

After selecting the network services for design inclusion, you as the almighty MCSE network designer must think about how to integrate these services for use on the network. Because the subsequent management and maintenance of the design will have a dramatic impact on the design's success, you should combine services so that the integration will make managing the network simpler.

Testing the Design

Once the detailed design is complete, validate the design. In the construction industry, many architects will engage in peer review as part of the design process—peer review prevents problems later. Its use in network design serves the same purpose.

Validating the design consists of performing service-unit testing and integrated testing to ensure the proposed system functions as expected. Service-unit testing involves testing the individual services independent of other computers and systems to ensure basic functionality. Integrated testing ensures the functionality, performance, and security of the integrated services within the context of a network and the platforms and servers with which the services will operate.

NOTE Perform testing within a lab environment and test the key applications within the integrated lab environment before implementation. That is, save your skin, and don't perform live testing on a production network.

Implementing the Design

After testing, the design is ready for implementation planning. At this point, Windows 2000 MCSEs are like kids at Christmas! They have planned, designed, tested, and validated. They can't wait to do the real work. We're the same way.

During this critical phase, you configure the network services to meet the design specifications, and part of this involves putting management processes in place to collect information. Let us clarify this important point for you, lest you feel you've been inundated with bureaucratic gibberish. For example, we'll use the Simple Network Management Protocol (SNMP) agent area to make our point. You might choose to install SNMP agents on service devices and a network management console to collect SNMP information. This is commonly done when using a network management tool such as Microsoft Systems Management Server (SMS), Computer Associates UniCenter, IBM's Tivoli, or HP's OpenView. So if you were planning to use one or more of these management tools, you would of course need to implement SNMP.

But we won't leave it at a single example. Rather, much of the Windows 2000 MCSE experience is just beginning for you. Hopefully your experience will be positive, thanks to the planning and design work you've done to get to this stage.

As an example of implementing a design, Catywhompus Construction might require the implementation of Dynamic Host Configuration Protocol (DHCP) to simplify IP configuration management and reduce configuration errors. The implementation would need to meet the functional requirements and management processes would need to be put in place to make sure the service kept working. In the case of DHCP, the DHCP scope would need to be configured to match the client's IP configuration requirements and an SNMP agent would need to be installed to send traps to the network management console. In addition, alerts should be configured to notify administrators if DHCP service errors occurred.

Managing the Network Services

After successfully implementing a network, MCSEs move on to managing the network. It's an honor and duty. It is also the beginning of a different type of work—downstream administrative functions. In this phase of the deployment cycle, you collect data on the continuing operations of the network and analyze this data to determine whether the services are performing according to the design specifications. During this phase, certain actions may be required in order to maintain the network within acceptable tolerances. If the network characteristics differ significantly from the design specifications, the network will need to be redesigned.

At Catywhompus, you can use tools like Network Monitor, Performance Monitor, and others to collect data on the network, and then you can analyze the data in analysis tools like Microsoft Excel. This process helps you manage the design within the specifications and project future capacity problems—this way you can manage proactively instead of fight problems all day. As an MCSE, the choice is yours. We'll take proactivity over problem-solving any day of the week, thank you very much. For instance, if Performance Monitor reflected packet loss on the Windows 2000 DHCP server, adding another DHCP server or increasing system memory could bring DHCP server performance back into design alignment, avoiding larger problems.

Microsoft Windows 2000 Networking Services

Part of the design process is identifying and selecting the networking services to be used, based on the functionality desired by the organization. You translate the company's needs into functional requirements and specifications: Determine what the services will do and how they will do it. This is the basis for all of your design work, so you should make sure this part is clear and well documented!

If Catywhompus Construction required the ability to reach each host on the network using the fully qualified domain name (FQDN), you might recommend they set up a primary and secondary DNS server. This is standard DNS advice and shouldn't surprise you greatly. They might then add to this initial requirement saying that they wanted to do this without adding significant administrative overhead. Remember, networking objectives drive functional requirements, which in this case are now appended to achieve centralized host name resolution as well as lower administrative overhead. In this latter case, satisfying the needs might be for you to specify that the DNS must dynamically register clients in the primary zone to accomplish the FQDN resolution services and minimize overhead.

Microsoft Windows 2000 Server, and other network operating systems (NOSs) offer many networking services. If you've been in the networking profession for more than five years, it might seem shocking how robust modern operating systems, such as Windows 2000, have become. (We remember in the mid-1980s that just being able to share a printer was justification to purchase an NOS. Not only were the business users happy with the network, but the belief was that value had truly been added to the business organization.)

The NOS services in Windows 2000 address significant functional requirements and specifications for networking. Some of the services are fundamental and other services meet specific functional requirements. For instance, TCP/IP is a foundational component for installing Windows 2000 or implementing Windows 2000 Active Directory. Other networking services, such as Remote Authentication Dial-In User Service (RADIUS) and Network Address Translation (NAT), meet specific user-connectivity requirements.

We now take our discussion on a slightly new path, focusing on designing networking services by creating an integrated networking services design (the key point being integrated). So the path to integration in this discussion is: creating the network foundation, IP routing solutions, using remote access and identifying Internet connectivity. We suggest you use these core elements to create your Microsoft Windows 2000 network services design with respect to integration. In Figure 12-3, you will see our view of integrating the network services design: designing the network foundation, designing Internet connectivity, and designing remote access and IP routing solutions.

Lab Exercise 12.1:
Developing a Design Approach

Enough heavy reading for a moment—time for something hands-on. The following lab exercise provides you with a practical opportunity to use the network infrastructure design knowledge you have gained in this chapter.

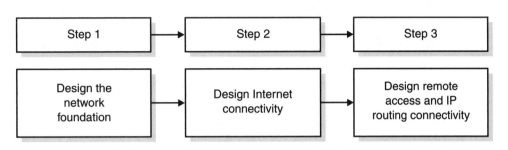

Figure 12-3   Integrating the network services design

The purpose of this exercise is to give you experience determining the network design phases to use. You must identify the phases for the redesign project at Catywhompus Construction and determine the driving forces behind functional requirements. At the end of the exercise are suggested solutions.

1. Determine and define the phased approach that should be used for Catywhompus Construction's network infrastructure redesign. Name each of the five phases and briefly describe the activities associated with each of the five phases.

2. In your design, what are the three core elements you will focus on to achieve an integrated network design?

3. Describe how the Microsoft Windows 2000 networking services are associated with these core elements and how you will determine service requirements for an integrated network design at Catywhompus Construction. Consider elements such as TCP/IP, DHCP, DNS and even topics that will be covered in greater detail in future chapters (Microsoft's enhanced Proxy Server solution called Internet Security and Acceleration (ISA) Server).

Lab 12.1: Suggested Solutions

1. The five key design phases are as follows:
   a. **Design**   Create an integrated design.
   b. **Test Design**   Thoroughly test the design in a lab environment.

       c. Implement the design   Create a functional implementation plan and execute the plan.

       d. Manage the networking design   Monitor and ensure the design meets the design specifications.

       e. Redesign   If the network infrastructure is not meeting the network requirements, it may need to be redesigned.

2. The three core elements that need to be addressed to achieve an integrated design are as follows:

    a. Design the network foundation.

    b. Design Internet connectivity.

    c. Design remote access and IP routing solutions.

3. For each of the core elements (network foundation, Internet connectivity, and remote access and IP routing), you will select services to achieve the objectives within each of these areas and then combine the services to achieve an integrated network infrastructure design. For example, you may combine TCP/IP, DHCP, and DNS services to achieve a network foundation, and then connect Catywhompus Construction to the Internet using the Windows 2000 routing solution combined with a proxy server or ISA Server to achieve an integrated solution.

The Network Foundation

Okay, back to basics for a few minutes. It's healthy to revisit your foundation knowledge, and taking a moment to review here ensures that you will have the necessary technical background before we get to the really good stuff for the Windows 2000 MCSE exams.

At its most elementary level, a network consists of two computers connected to each other (in either a real or virtual way) so they can share data. Basic networking, even at this elementary level, requires services that provide for data transmission. Additionally, you use services to simplify client and server configuration and to provide naming to make it easy to locate resources on the network. The services that provide these three capabilities are the network's foundation: They provide core support for an addressing scheme, automation of client and server configuration, and the resolution of names for network communications.

For example, Catywhompus Construction has a network that relies on NetBIOS name resolution for legacy client support (in the great tradition of Harvard Business School case studies, this information wasn't initially presented, allowing you to discover new facts as you proceed through the case study). This approach, that provided file-sharing support, has been accessible only on one subnet at the corporate head-quarters for many years. Catywhompus uses the NetBIOS Extended User Interface pro-tocol (NetBEUI) to communicate with its file-sharing application, thereby preventing the ability to route the application's traffic over routed WAN connections (NetBEUI traffic cannot be routed). Now management wants all data to be accessible from all international locations over the network.

So a choice confronts you. You must decide what foundational elements and services should be used to meet the objectives. To meet the WAN accessibility requirements, you need to support NetBIOS and you want to ensure that the network protocols used are routable. The Windows 2000 network services that provide these foundational network elements are TCP/IP, DHCP, DNS, and WINS, a NetBIOS name service.

Thinking from both technical and business points of view, consider the matter of running Catywhompus Construction business applications over the WAN. To support the aforementioned legacy core-transaction application requiring NetBIOS, the core elements of TCP/IP and WINS are specifically required to provide WAN support. The core network services will then support these applications, even if the WAN bandwidth needed to support the application has not yet been addressed in the design.

EXAM TIP Microsoft is known to slip references to its Quality of Service (QoS) capability, which allows network managers to manage bandwidth, into Windows 2000 MCSE exams. A QoS-compliant application can be guaranteed a specific amount of bandwidth. The practical reason for implementing QoS is to prevent your business applications from being crowded out by Web surfers. And of course another practical reason to be knowledgeable about QoS is to pass the Windows 2000 MCSE exams!

Base Protocol Support—TCP/IP

TCP/IP is an industry-standard suite of protocols providing communications in an environment that supports these standards. (If you're serious about pursuing the Windows 2000 MCSE designation, it's essential that you commit to memory the role of TCP/IP.) TCP/IP is vendor-independent and provides a routable, enterprise-wide networking protocol that enables access to the Internet as well as to intranet resources. Most of the other core networking services provided in Windows 2000 for workstation naming and configuration, routing, and name resolution rely on TCP/IP to function.

DNS, for host name resolution, and WINS, for NetBIOS name resolution, for instance, rely on TCP/IP to function. Without TCP/IP, most enterprise-wide services will not function.

EXAM TIP Talk about a name game! In the real world, DNS refers to the Domain Name Service. At Microsoft, DNS refers to Domain Name Servers. It may seem like a minor point, but such granular thinking is your path to success on the Windows 2000 MCSE exams.

Automated Client Configuration—DHCP

DHCP is our network buddy—we use it to make our lives easier. We can report with pride that DHCP offers much better performance under Windows 2000 than under prior versions of Windows NT. And we've yet to have any DHCP hiccups, such as phantom DHCP addresses, which we had under Windows NT.

We put DHCP services in our designs to configure core TCP/IP settings automatically. This means users and administrators no longer need to manually configure individual IP addresses for each client computer. Instead, the DHCP server automatically delivers all of the necessary client configuration information to DHCP-enabled clients. If used correctly, DHCP helps to ensure that network clients use correct configuration information, thereby eliminating common IP configuration problems that stem from manual configuring. Additionally, it reduces administrative overload on networks where clients are frequently moved, and it enables client configurations to be updated automatically to reflect changes in network structure or moves between logical subnets.

At Catywhompus Construction, they frequently move users among locations and subnets on a regular basis. At present, they are not using DHCP because the present design does not include dynamic IP client configuration capabilities. Like many technology professionals, the network designers originally wanted to have complete control over the IP addresses that each client used. In this way, the manual IP address configuration approach was used, so when a laptop user travels to another location, the administrator changes the static IP configuration so the user can communicate on the new subnet. But as you might imagine, the manual configuration of IP addresses is burdensome on the technology staff at Catywhompus. Thus the problem was one of administrative overhead for the technology staff. In Windows 2000 Server, DHCP is an excellent solution for this problem. By implementing DHCP as a foundational network improvement, users will be able to move between subnets without manually changing IP configurations.

TIP One thing you are unlikely to see on the Windows 2000 MCSE exams, but which will show up in the real world, is that the basic DHCP scope configuration is not richly configured. Just in case you weren't paying close attention during the core Windows 2000 MCSE exams, a DHCP scope refers to settings. When you install the DHCP service on a Windows 2000 server and then log on from a client configured to receive its IP address dynamically, it will only receive the IP address and subnet mask address. It will not receive default gateway or DNS server values by default. This isn't a big problem if the client machine is newly built, without an existing TCP/IP addressing configuration. This clean client machine will receive its dynamic IP address without incident. However, if the client machine has been previously used on another network and has existing default gateway and DNS settings, the dynamically assigned IP address won't overwrite these specific values. This is a major ouch when trying to fully interact with the Windows 2000 server and Active Directory as efficiently as possible! You've been warned!

Resolving Host Names—DNS

So now let's really get into DNS specifics! DNS is a distributed database system that serves as the foundation for resolving names to IP addresses within and beyond the confines of the enterprise network. Names must be resolved through the client resolver so that network communications can take place.

NOTE Subsequently, the IP address is resolved to the Media Access Control (MAC) address or hardware address using the Address Resolution Protocol (ARP)—even in a routed network.

This DNS system makes it possible to use a fully qualified domain name (FQDN), such as hostname.catywhompus.com on the network. DNS, if enabled properly, uses the FQDN to resolve a host name to an IP address even without the use of a local host file. FQDNs and the hierarchical structure of DNS allow the network designer to create meaningful resource records and implement designs with DNS that will resolve those names. DNS uses a forward lookup query to resolve a name to an IP address and uses a reverse lookup query to resolve an IP address to a host name. DNS client settings can be automatically configured with Microsoft Windows 2000 DHCP options.

Catywhompus Construction has two big problems when it comes to reaching non-NetBIOS named resources. The first problem is that they use host files on the local workstations for host names (aliases) to IP address resolutions. If they change an existing server's IP address or add a new server, they must update each workstation's host file to reflect the change. The second problem is that in many cases the host files are not updated, so users begin to use the IP address of the interface to access the host's resources. This creates a problem when the administrator wants to use a different IP address for the resource.

The DNS service makes it possible to use FQDNs on the network to provide a central host-name resolution service, eliminating the need to modify host files on each machine to keep them synchronized with name or IP address changes. Catywhompus can solve their host-name resolution issues by moving to the use of a DNS server as a core piece of their infrastructure design.

Lab Exercise 12.2: Solving a Name Resolution Design Problem

Let's take a moment to test our understanding of the Catywhompus Construction case study in the context of this chapter. Please review and answer the following questions.

1. Catywhompus, as you know, has a few problems with their current design. One of the issues is that host-name resolution has been managed manually at the client level. This gives rise to name resolution errors as well as an inordinate amount of client configuration management. What can you put into place to reduce the administrative overhead associated with host file updates and to improve the reliability of clients resolving the correct names to IP addresses?

2. How can you ensure that the Catywhompus DNS configuration on its fleet of workstations is updated automatically when a DNS server's IP address changes?

Lab Exercise 12.2: Suggested Solutions

1. Insert DNS services in your network design to eliminate the need for clients to use host files or to know the IP address of server resources. This will mean you can centrally manage the host-to-IP-address resolution table.

2. Use DHCP options to deliver DNS server addresses to the client.

Resolving NetBIOS Names—WINS

As with DNS host names, a NetBIOS name must be resolved to an IP address for Net-BIOS communications to occur effectively, especially in a routed network. NetBIOS names are 16 bytes in length, including a service-type byte, and unlike the hierarchical DNS, the namespace for NetBIOS has only one level, which makes it critical to register unique names and use them only once within a network.

The NetBIOS protocol has been one of the most popular APIs for network applications and services (especially within the peer-to-peer network environments). Therefore, it is necessary to support such NetBIOS API-reliant applications and services, as well as previous Windows clients, including Windows NT 4.0, Windows 95, and Windows for Workgroups, which do not use Active Directory.

In Windows 2000, you can use WINS to support these legacy clients and applications. You can also use DHCP options to automatically configure WINS clients.

So, now we present some more historic tidbits of case study information for you to digest. In the past, Catywhompus Construction designed their networks to resolve NetBIOS names using both a local file called LMHOSTS or simply relying on an additional protocol like NetBEUI to provide for NetBIOS broadcast communications on the local network segment. (Remember that if a name can't be resolved with one method, the other method is automatically used.) The use of LMHOSTS files, like the use of host files can lead to errors in the local file copy of LMHOSTS and significant administrative effort is often required to change host names and IP addresses—this is a big concern at Catywhompus. By using a NetBIOS name server like WINS, you can eliminate the need to use an LMHOSTS file. As the Catywhompus network designer, you should review the requirements for implementing a WINS server. That way you can deliver NetBIOS name-resolution services as needed.

Designing Internet Connectivity

The Internet is a tremendous resource for any organization and can be an integral part of the corporate strategy, especially for e-commerce businesses. Yet, Internet connectivity poses certain security risks that did not exist when the private network was isolated. Additionally, organizations may wish to use a private addressing scheme to avoid wasting costly blocks of public IP addresses. The Network Address Translation (NAT) protocol, which is built into Windows 2000, and Microsoft's Internet Security and Acceleration (ISA) Server are two network services that, if properly used, conceal internal IP addresses for external networks and reduce the costs of registering IP addresses.

We have seen companies connect to the Internet in a variety of ways. One large food company, for instance, connects to the Internet using a Class B address name space along with load-balancing servers over three T-1 lines. (We are of course assuming you recall from the core Windows 2000 MCSE exams what a Class B range is as compared to Class A, C or even D; if not, this topic is covered in Chapter 14.) A small, not-for-profit organization used a NAT server to connect to an ISP using a single public IP address and a 192.168.0.0/24 private network. This allowed for 256 Class C network IDs and 254 hosts per subnet (again, if you don't recall the definitions of private and public networks from the core Windows 2000 MCSE exams, please read Chapter 14). We have also worked with a business that uses a proxy server along with a private address scheme and an external firewall to access the Internet.

As you can see, there are many ways to connect to the Internet, and you will want to integrate the company with the Internet using the most appropriate method. We will discuss each of the essential options here and in the subsequent chapters of this book. We won't be able to discuss every Internet connection option along the way—there are many ways to get from point A to point B when it comes to Internet connectivity. It's likely your firm has a different take on this topic.

Network Address Translation—NAT

This body of matter called Network Address Translation (NAT) is a popular topic on the MCSE exams. NAT is a protocol that is managed through the Routing and Remote Access Service (RRAS) found in Windows 2000 and through the administrative facilities of other operating systems. By translating private internal addresses to public addresses, NAT hides the internally managed IP addresses from the external public network. This reduces registration costs by letting the private organization use unregistered IP addresses for the internal network, with translation to a small number of publicly registered IP addresses. (In other words, you don't need to lease or rent as many "real" IP addresses from your Internet Service Provider to provide complete Internet functionality to all users and workstations on your network.) This can reduce the risk of denial-of-service attacks against internal systems and shield the internal network. That's because any attack is made against the "real" or external IP address that is bound to the router (allowing the internal LAN to largely function unimpeded). NAT also provides Internet connectivity for smaller organizations where simple management and implementation are necessary.

NAT uses a valid IP address registered on a public network to represent a private IP address (possibly one that would be invalid externally) to the Internet. The NAT function changes the IP addresses and port number inside each IP packet, as necessary.

Figure 12-4 shows a specific example of the NAT IP address swapping that is processed on the NAT-enabled router. This is valuable in many different situations. For example, when a host communicates with the WWW server cluster, the NAT translates the IP address in each packet so that the cluster sees the source address as 204.57.0.1, even though the client is at 192.168.0.11. When the cluster responds back to the client, the packet is forwarded to the client back in the private network. NAT translations can be performed by NAT configured on a Windows 2000 RRAS or by other routers with NAT capabilities enabled.

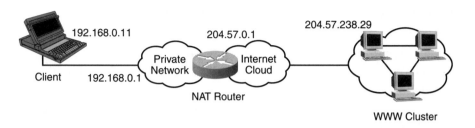

Figure 12-4   NAT IP address translation between public and private IP addresses

PART III

NOTE   As you may suspect, NAT requires more processing power to translate packets than is needed to simply route traffic. Because of the additional overhead, NAT is not recommended for very large networks. Security techniques, such as NAT, are discussed at length in Part II of this book.

Microsoft Internet Security and Acceleration Server

Okay, Microsoft heard you—you need firewall protection. An Internet Security and Acceleration (ISA) server acts as a gateway between your network and the Internet. It manages traffic and determines whether network packets are allowed to pass through to the network. When a client computer makes a request, the ISA server translates the request and passes it on to the Internet or satisfies the request from its cached information. If the ISA server passes the request to the Internet, it will also pass the response back to the client device. ISA server is used like a firewall, or even better, along with a firewall, to protect the private network.

The ISA server's caching capabilities can also improve performance of Internet access through existing connections. Why? Commonly accessed Web pages are stored on the server's hard disks in a cache file and are delivered to the client instead of being retrieved every time over the Internet. To prevent out-of-date information from being used by the client, ISA server can be configured to update these cached Web pages with appropriate frequency.

NOTE   Microsoft ISA Server provides many advanced security features. It is purchased separately from Windows 2000 Server.

Designing Routing and Remote-Access Connectivity

In your network designs, you can and typically will (in this day and age) include the routing and remote-access services provided in Windows 2000. The rich options available in Windows 2000 make it possible to connect private segments at a site level, as well as between sites using leased lines or the Internet. You also have available to you, as the designer, the remote-access capabilities for external users. These capabilities allow external users to connect to the private network using encrypted authentication, encrypted transmission, and tunneling. Windows 2000 allows remote clients to connect to remote-access servers through a variety of hardware, including analog modems, digital subscriber line (xDSL) adapters, and Integrated Services Digital Network (ISDN) adapters, in addition to virtual private network (VPN) connections over a public network such as the Internet.

Remote Access

Remote-access services for Windows 2000 offer integrated direct-dial and VPN access for individuals and branch offices over Point-to-Point Tunneling Protocol (PPTP), IP Security (IPSec), and Layer Two Tunneling Protocol (L2TP). You can create solutions using dial-up or VPN connections to the private network, and you can use a variety of encryption and authentication protocols and methods with Windows 2000 to secure user credentials and confidential data. Windows 2000 also allows for the use of Extensible Authentication Protocols, through which you can load third-party protocols in the form of plug-in modules to support capabilities such as smart cards. Additionally, you may want to include a phone-book publishing service for remote users. You can use the Connection Manager Administration Kit (CMAK) to provide direct access to telephone numbers on mobile devices.

NOTE If you are using the native Windows 2000 RRAS to configure inbound VPN connectivity, be advised that the wizard process closes the other TCP/IP ports from inbound traffic. Basically, if RRAS configures the VPN settings, it believes the Windows 2000 Server machine will be used for this, and only this. This is important to know if you are using your Windows 2000 Server as a Web server. The preferred way to set TCP/IP port settings is to use the ISA server's VPN wizard, which leaves non-VPN TCP/IP ports untouched.

RADIUS and IAS

Organizations that support a variety of dial-up users, that outsource dial-up access, or that engage in joint ventures with other organizations require authentication outside the private network. Remote Authentication Dial-In User Service (RADIUS) is a widely used protocol that provides a solution for these authentication and remote-access accounting requirements. RADIUS is discussed in Chapter 19. The Internet Authentication Service (IAS) should be included to provide a complete RADIUS solution. A perfect example of an organization requiring these services is an Internet service provider (ISP). ISPs require remote-user connection accounting so they can charge subscribers properly.

EXAM TIP Two quick exam points. First, RADIUS, while not wildly popular in the real world, does indeed show up on the Windows 2000 MCSE exams. Second, IAS allows for the use of centralized policy management, which avoids the administrative headaches of working with separate RRAS policies stored locally on each server.

IP Routing

This section is about IP routing, which as you will recall from the Windows 2000 MCSE core exams, is about routing traffic between IP subnets. In your network design, you can use the routing capabilities built into Windows 2000, including creating static or dynamic routing tables. Supported dynamic routing protocols include OSPF (open shortest path first), which uses a link-state routing algorithm, and RIP (Routing Information Protocol), which uses a distance-vector algorithm. Extensive discussion of either of these approaches is beyond the scope of this chapter (and quite frankly, the Windows 2000 MCSE designing exams as a whole) but the information is provided to give you the appropriate context to discuss IP routing. In either case, when connecting to remote locations over connections that are not persistent, you can use demand-dial routing in your design to achieve cost advantages. You can also secure authentication and data encryption using a variety of methods, even over public networks.

NOTE In general, remember that what goes out can come back in with IP routing. Configuring IP routing is a two-way flow, and without an effective firewall, IP routing that is "naked" is truly exposed to the comings and goings of the Internet.

Putting It All Together: Integrating the Network Services Infrastructure

When you are designing the network services infrastructure, you will focus on the functionality needed to accomplish the networking goals. When you create your networking services design, remember that your design will be the basis for the connectivity and protocol requirements of the organization. You are combining multiple networking services in your design to establish a network foundation, to support network-based applications, to provide access to the Internet, and to support remote user access. Once the services are identified, you will produce a network design that is manageable and has clear criteria for security, availability, and performance.

The objective of the management strategy is to ensure the network service accurately reflects your grand vision from a network management perspective. The management tasks you should focus on in the management strategy include:

- Collecting server and network performance data to determine network status.

- Performing data analysis to compare the network status versus the design.

- Optimizing, or making changes based on service variations, to bring the services back into alignment with the design.

Let's assume, just for the sake of argument, that you have completed the design and implementation phases of the Catywhompus network. Despite this accomplishment, much hard work is still ahead. You decide to put network analysis and optimization into place to ensure the network is operating within the parameters of the design. You will use tools like the Performance MMC snap-in on the servers to create performance logs for the servers that provide key network services such as DNS, WINS, DHCP, Remote Access, and so on. You decide to monitor the four key performance areas:

- Memory

- Processor

- Disk subsystem

- Network subsystem

As time passes, you will put the logged performance results into a reference database—the log files will create a measurement baseline that reflects the performance of the network services under normal conditions. If the network subsequently begins to underperform outside the boundaries of the design, the baseline can be used to identify bottlenecks or design issues.

You may find that services are not performing as you expected after a time. You might find, for instance, that under normal loads, the DNS service utilizes approximately 50 percent of the CPU, and that suddenly the usage jumps to 80 percent for an extended period of time. Your performance-management tools can help you identify design problems or optimizations required to get the DNS server back into compliance with the performance requirements.

Creating Performance Monitor Log Files

In this exercise, you will use the Microsoft Windows 2000 performance MMC snap-in to schedule a counter log to monitor key DHCP objects, and then view a log in a graphical Web view on your Windows 2000 system.

In order to show Network Segment Counters, the network driver must be installed first, and in order to do so, you must be logged on as a local administrator or be a member of the Administrators group. If your computer is connected to a network, network policy settings may also prevent you from completing this procedure.

The Network Monitor Driver is available on both Windows 2000 Professional and Windows 2000 Server. If you are running Windows 2000 Server, you can also use Network Monitor to display and analyze the information you collect with the Network Monitor Driver.

How to Install the Network Monitor Driver

1. Click Start | Settings | Control Panel, and double-click Network and Dial-up Connections.

2. Click Local Area Connection and select File | Properties.

3. In the Local Area Connection Properties dialog box (see the following illustration), click Install.

PART III

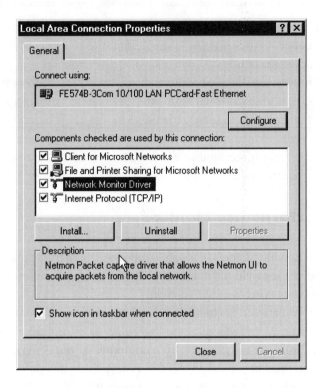

4. In the Select Network Component Type dialog box, click Protocol and then click Add.

5. In the Select Network Protocol dialog box (see the next illustration), click the Network Monitor Driver, and then click OK.

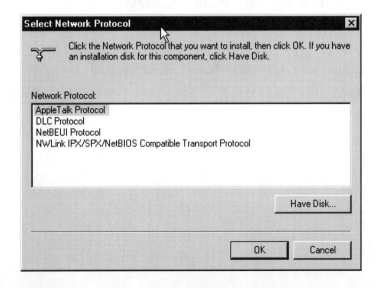

6. If prompted for additional files, insert your Windows 2000 CD-ROM, or type a path to the network location of the files.

7. Click Close. You have now added the Network Monitor Driver.

How to Create a Counter Log Using System Monitor (to monitor important system health matters)

1. Click Start | Programs | Administrative Tools | Performance. (Alternatively, you can click Start | Run, and then type **perfmon** in the Run box, and then click OK.)

2. Expand Performance Logs and Alerts and then click Counter Logs, as shown in Figure 12-5. Any existing logs will be listed in the details pane to the right. A green icon indicates that a log is running; a red icon indicates that a log has been stopped.

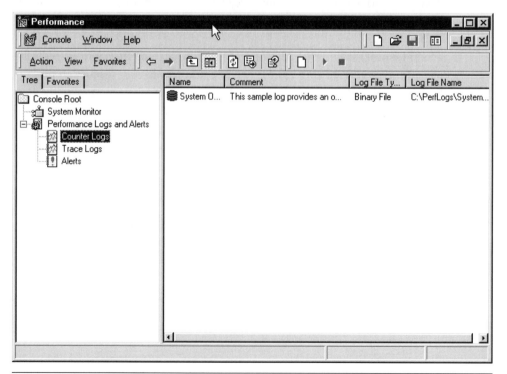

Figure 12-5 System Monitor displaying counter logs

3. Right-click a blank area of the details pane, and select New Log Settings (don't choose the New Log Settings From menu choice!).

4. In the New Log Settings dialog box, type **dhcpbaseline** to name the log file, and then click OK.

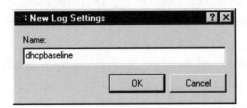

5. The property sheet for dhcpbaseline is displayed. On the General tab, click Add. (Note that you may not have some of these objects if you are not running the same services as the server in the figure.) Select the following objects and counters to log:
   a. Select DHCP and click All Counters; click Add to add the counters to the log
   b. Select IP and click All Counters; click Add to add the counters to the log
   c. Select Memory and click All Counters; click Add to add the counters to the log
   d. Select Network Segment and click All Counters; click Add to add the counters to the log
   e. Select PhysicalDisk and click All Counters; click Add to add the counters to the log
   f. Select Process and click All Counters; click Add to add the counters to the log
   g. Select System and click All Counters; click Add to add the counters to the log
   h. Select TCP and click All Counters; click Add to add the counters to the log
   i. Select UDP and click All Counters; click Add to add the counters to the log

6. Click Close on the Counters dialog box.

7. In the dhcpbaseline property sheet, select an interval of 15 with a units value of seconds in the Sample Data Every section. The dhcpbaseline property sheet should look similar to the one in the following illustration.

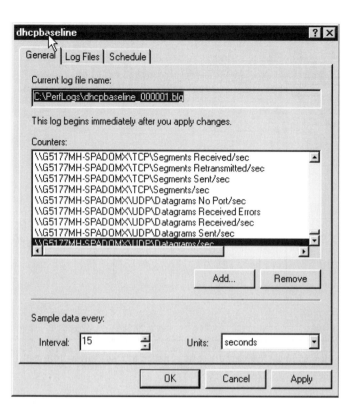

8. If you want to change the default file and schedule information, make the changes on the Log Files tab and the Schedule tab of the dhcpbaseline property sheet. For now, though, leave them at the default values.

9. Note the Current Log File Name and location on the General tab. It should be C:\PerfLogs\dhcpbaseline_000001.blg, or something similar.

10. Click OK. Note that the dhcpbaseline log is entered into the Counter Logs (see Figure 12-6) and the log icon has turned green, indicating that it is started and that you are now logging the performance data you selected.

11. Wait for a few minutes to allow some performance data to be logged. Logging continues even when you close the System Monitor, because System Monitor runs as a service under Windows 2000. Previously, in Windows NT, Performance

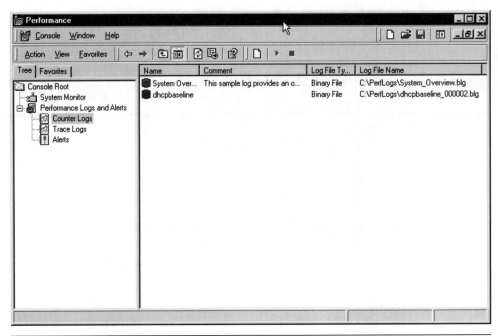

Figure 12-6 The counter log you created appears in the System Monitor.

Monitor (the predecessor to System Monitor), ran as an application (which required it to remain open to work).

12. Right-click the dhcpbaseline icon in the details pane and click Stop.

13. You have now created a baseline log file for the DHCP server. If you start the logging again, it will automatically append data to this log file.

14. To view the captured information in a Web browser (which many of us find more pleasant), right-click the dhcpbaseline icon in the details pane, select Save Settings As, and name the file **DHCPBASELINE1** and click Save. This saves a Web-based view of the log in HTML.

15. You will be able to view the dhcpbaseline file with Internet Explorer or any contemporary Web browser (as shown in Figure 12-7). These can then be posted to a systems status Web page.

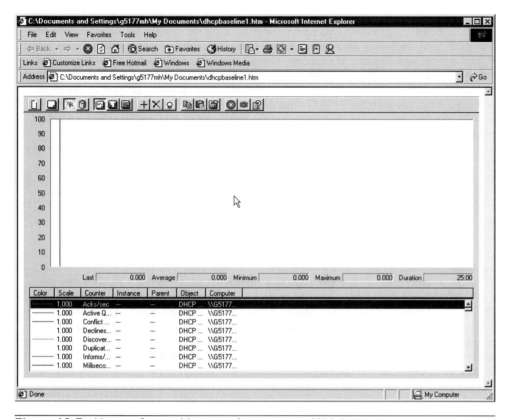

Figure 12-7   Viewing System Monitor information in a Web browser

   TIP   Be careful not to track too many objects at one time. The chart can become cluttered and difficult to read.

Once DHCPBASELINE1.htm is in your Web browser, you can click on a particular counter and type CTRL-H, and that counter will be highlighted in the graphical view above. Also note that other views are available, including the Report view.

NOTE To save the counter settings for a log file or alert file, right-click the file in the details pane and click Save Settings As. You can then specify an .htm file in which to save the settings. To reuse the saved settings for a new log or alert, right-click the details pane, and then click New Log Settings From or New Alert Settings From. This is an easy way to reuse log settings from an alert configuration. To create or modify a log, you must have Full Control permission for the following registry key, which controls the Performance Logs and Alerts service: HKEY_LOCAL_MACHINE\SYSTEM\CurrentControlSet\Services\SysmonLog\Log Queries.

This is just one example of the monitoring tools that can be used to manage the network and help determine whether the network infrastructure is meeting the design specifications. Network Monitor is also an excellent tool for making these determinations.

 NOTE Remember, there are two approaches to optimizing a network. The first focuses on making more bandwidth available to the users by reducing service traffic. The second provides users with better performance by properly implementing network services, which may increase network traffic. Therefore, a properly optimized network is a compromise between allotting bandwidth to the users and improving service response time. Collect data in both of these areas and then evaluate it against the network-services performance standards.

Defining the Network Design Attributes

As a Windows 2000 MCSE, you are implicitly granted some powers. You make design decisions based on the benefits and trade-offs that individual services provide. Four design aspects, which are driven by organization goals (see Figure 12-8), form the structure used to study each of these services:

- **Functionality** This is the essential reason for implementing the networking services. The other aspects of the design are independent of the functionality elements—if the design is not functional, the remaining elements are irrelevant. Therefore, functionality is the foundational element driven by organizational goals.

- **Availability** Your design is available to the extent that users are able to access the functionality provided by the services. You will typically measure this in uptime percentage for the functionality provided. Availability does not necessarily mean that the service is secure or performs well.

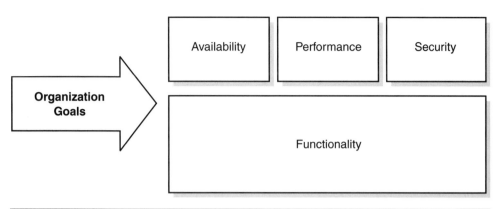

Figure 12-8   The network design attributes

PART III

- **Performance**   Response times specified by the organization's expectations are integral to the design. We have found through experience that certain services must perform within a given amount of time to be useful. You should set performance criteria and evaluate against these expectations. Performance also is dependent on the functionality aspect but need not be secure or exhibit high availability.

- **Security**   The security aspect of your design ensures the data cannot be either viewed or changed by unauthorized people. Your design is secure when you have adequately protected the data through the services. Security is based on the functionality aspect of your design, but is independent of the availability and performance aspects. Security does not ensure availability or meet performance criteria.

To make our point, we will analyze the use of DHCP at Catywhompus within the framework of the four key design goals discussed in this chapter. If one of the design goals is to minimize the administrative burden of client IP configuration and to reduce IP configuration errors, you must decide whether DHCP has the appropriate functionality to achieve these goals. If it does, that functionality becomes the basic reason for using the design. Once functionality is established, you can review the appropriate measures you need to take to improve availability, to ensure adequate performance, and to address security.

The process of creating a design by addressing these four areas for each network service is the essential process used to translate an organization's networking goals into a design. Therefore, we will focus on each of these aspects as we address the key networking services for Catywhompus Construction across this section of the book.

Catywhompus Construction Updates: Infrastructure Redesign

This chapter has painted a broad picture of network infrastructure issues, are important to our sample company, Catywhompus Construction. In the remaining chapters of this section, the Catywhompus case studies will dig deeper into the details of many of the technical issues presented here. For example, the detailed DHCP discussion needed to help Catywhompus make the best possible network infrastructure design decisions will be presented in Chapter 15.

So, it's onward and upward from here for both you and Catywhompus Construction! Chapter 13, up next, will cover the analysis of business and technical needs.

Chapter Review

This chapter is the first chapter of the network infrastructure section, and thus sets the table for the several chapters that follow. Understand that many topics were presented as a high-level in order to paint the picture of what's coming. If you didn't completely understand a technical concept being presented, you can bet the discussion will be revisited in greater detail in forthcoming chapters. The key points to take from this chapter are:

- The organization's goals should drive the network design requirements.
- The network design is the technology "platform" or foundation for the connectivity and protocol requirements of the organization. The following considerations should be included in the design:
  - Establish a network foundation.
  - Provide Internet access.
  - Include remote user access.
  - Support network-based applications.
- The Network Foundation services provided by Microsoft Windows 2000 Advanced Server include:
  - TCP/IP   Industry-standard network protocol suite

- DHCP   Automates and manages TCP/IP configuration

- DNS   Provides server-level host-name resolution services

- WINS   Provides NetBIOS name-resolution services

- When creating a network design, remember to consider functionality, availability, performance, and security when making design decisions.

Questions

1. You are given the task of translating the networking goals of Catywhompus Construction into an effective networking services design. How can you do this?

2. Catywhompus Construction needs a list of the Network Foundation services provided by Windows 2000 Advanced Server. What are the foundation services?

3. Catywhompus Construction wants to provide Internet connectivity to their users. What are three solution options from the information presented in this chapter?

4. Catywhompus Construction has decided to provide remote users with the capability to access private network resources from the Internet. The data will be sensitive, so it must be encrypted, and remote users must be securely authenticated. Which Windows 2000 Advanced Server networking services would assist the organization in achieving these goals?

Answers

1. Obtain the specifications and documentation describing the goals of Catywhompus. Translate these goals into service requirements, and evaluate the functionality, availability, performance, and security requirements of the organization. Use this information to create a design that exceeds or meets the goals of the organization.

2. TCP/IP, DHCP, DNS, WINS.

3. Network Address Translation (NAT), MS Proxy Server 2.0 (or its successor ISA Server), and routed connection.

4. TCP/IP for data transfer; DHCP for address assignment; RRAS for remote access functionality; and VPN connections for data encryption and authentication.

Key Skill Sets

- Know the five design phases within a network infrastructure in order to organize and develop a best-practices design plan.

- Remember that designing a network infrastructure is primarily about addressing the functional requirements of the network through the selection of a network foundation, Internet connectivity, remote access and routing capabilities, and integrating the design.

- You should know the network foundation components and be able to analyze their ability to meet networking goals.

- You should know the Internet and routing and remote access connectivity components to be able to analyze their functionality to meet networking goals.

- Realize that the ultimate goal is to create an integrated networking-services infrastructure design that meets the functional, availability, performance, and security requirements of an organization.

Key Terms

Dynamic Host Configuration Protocol (DHCP)
Domain Name System (DNS)
Logging
Network Infrastructure
Network Operating System (NOS)
Protocol
System Monitor
Transmission Control Protocol/Internet Protocol (TCP/IP)
Windows Internet Naming Service (WINS)

CHAPTER

Analyzing Business and Technical Requirements

This chapter covers these key mastery goals:

- Analyze the business.

- Analyze the existing and planned business models.

- Analyze the company model and the geographical scope. Models include regional, national, international, subsidiary, and branch offices.

- Analyze company processes. Processes include information flow, communications flow, service and product life cycles, and decision making.

- Analyze the existing and planned organizational structures. Considerations include the management model; company organization; vendor, partner, and customer relationships; and acquisitions plans.

- Analyze factors that influence company strategies.

- Identify the total cost of operations.

- Analyze the structure of IT management.

- Evaluate the company's existing and planned technical environment and goals.

- Analyze the impact of infrastructure design on the existing and planned technical environment.

- Analyze technical support structure.

- Analyze existing and planned network and systems management.

- Analyze the network requirements for client computer access.

- Analyze the existing disaster recovery strategy for client computers, servers, and the network.

You will remember that Microsoft has shifted its MCSE certification goals to include business and technical analysis in order to focus the networking professional on what drives the networking and systems needs. This book, at every turn, nook, and cranny, attempts to honor that paradigm shift. With no further ado, welcome to Chapter 13!

 TIP On a career note, understanding the business dynamics of an organization can save your MCSE hide! That is, an awareness and appreciation, if not mastery, of the business side of the organization will keep you happy, healthy, and wealthy as an MCSE professional. We recall a fellow MCSE who was a technical wizard, but who had a nasty habit of walking directly into political minefields at work. He lamented the Windows NT days, when the MCSE certification program emphasized the technical requirements. We suspect that his fears of being unsuccessful in the business realm have only increased under the Windows 2000 MCSE.

Update: Business and Technical Analysis for Catywhompus Construction

You have been hired as part of a consulting group to help Catywhompus Construction implement an improved network infrastructure to support a new strategy to integrate electronic commerce technologies with the existing business to drive future growth. The ability of the management team to integrate technology with the business is key to the success of this strategy. Your team must thoroughly understand the business in order to properly integrate the key technologies and move the business forward. The business model, business processes, and organization structure must be understood to integrate new electronic commerce technologies. You must pore over the corporate organization to help you plan not only for the present network infrastructure, but for the future network as well.

We recommend you avoid designing the network infrastructure in a vacuum. Have you ever proposed a change only to have the modification denied for cost reasons? Although network infrastructure operations are critical, the business decision-makers may conclude that the cost of such technologies as load-sharing or fault-tolerant systems outweigh the potential business impact. For Catywhompus, you must determine these issues prior to design presentation. Here, you will consider how to modify design proposals based on both the business and technical requirements of the business.

continued

Now you will drill down into the nitty-gritty details of the enterprise technical services. One of the biggest problems that arises from an infrastructure design rollout is that legacy services do not work with the new services. You can avoid and address this issue by thoroughly understanding the existing services and current hardware in place. The customer needs of Catywhompus drive the business requirements, and in turn, applications must meet the business requirements. Make sure all of the business applications are identified and that your design recommendations support these key applications.

Once you have developed a solid understanding of the business and technical environment at Catywhompus, your ability to select and integrate the appropriate networking services is enhanced because you now know what you are up against. Without this knowledge, you may disrupt the organization, or more devastatingly, select the wrong services for the situation. While you do not have all of the answers at this point, after you complete this chapter, you should spend some time developing your analysis of the Catywhompus Construction business and technical environment. This exercise will help you practice the skills presented in this chapter.

Analyzing the Business

Your goal as a network infrastructure designer is to deploy a network that adds value to the organization for which you are working. To accomplish this goal, you must understand the existing network infrastructure as well as the existing business model.

Keep in mind that business managers commonly complain that IT people do not understand the business aspects of IT decisions. Similarly, IT people commonly complain that business managers do not understand IT. We suggest that you attempt to find some common ground with the business manager—aim to move the business goals and objectives forward. Relax a little. If you find yourself in the position of constantly protecting your turf, back off and concentrate on getting to know the business. Because of the impact that IT has on business, the business folks will want to know more about IT, and you can help to ensure the success of your design by understanding the business.

Your new design should aim to achieve certain technical goals as well. You need to understand why this infrastructure requires a new design and what goals the new design needs to achieve. We find that once this analysis is complete, the job of determining which Windows 2000 network services to implement is much easier, and the ultimate implementation of the services fires up the business as well as the IT functions.

Analyzing the Geographical Scope and Existing and Planned Business Models

For any company, it is important to analyze a number of areas. You must analyze the geographical scope of the organization and document the number of locations and the user base at each location.

The physical configuration is part of the geographical scope of the company. Some of the physical layout models include regional, national, international, subsidiary, and branch offices. Is there a need for WAN technologies? On the other hand, are LAN technologies sufficient for the physical layout of the organization?

Mobility is also an issue in contemporary organizations. How often does the organization reconfigure its physical structure? Is the organization in a constant state of transition? These are all crucial questions that must be answered because they will influence network design.

Analyzing Business Models

What is a business model? Essentially, it is a set of methods for doing business that allows a company to sustain itself or generate sales. The model defines how the company makes a profit or achieves cash flow by identifying how the company adds value to a specific value chain, which is a group of processes that add value to the end product, and then derives income based on its position in that chain.

It is important to understand the organization's business model and design your network infrastructure to support that model. You must keep your eye on this goal no matter what happens or how deeply you get involved in the technology. As a famous golf teacher once said, "When you swing the club, *take dead aim.*" We cannot overemphasize the importance of following this advice when it comes to understanding and supporting the business model. Doing so will help you in all areas of design. If you build services to support the business model, you lay the foundation for both network design and business success. Remember, *take dead aim.*

Some models are simple. For example, a company buys a widget from one company and then sells it to another. If they keep their costs below their total cash sales, the company realizes a profit.

Other models are much more intricate. Radio broadcasting is an excellent example of an intricate business model. Radio programs are broadcast free to anyone with the ability to receive the signals. The broadcaster is networked intricately with artists, content creators, advertisers, distributors, and listeners. Exactly who makes the money in this model is not always clear. What is clear, however, is that the model works by way of a number of competing factors, and that the broadcaster has a key role in the value chain. Clearly, they must continue broadcasting to make a profit.

If you read the literature on business models, you will find business models categorized in various ways. Because e-commerce and other technologies have given rise to new kinds of business models, it is understandable that the Web is also obliterating, or reinventing, tried-and-true models. One example is the use of auctions. Auctions are a very old business model in use worldwide. Companies like Ebay, Yahoo, and Amazon have rejuvenated the auction model, and many e-commerce businesses now have active auction components, including Amazon. The e-commerce models are implemented in a variety of ways and are supported by an IT network infrastructure.

Business models currently evolve rapidly, and companies also combine various models to create new models. How does this affect a network design? Make sure your design model is flexible and that it supports the rapidly changing business model! Table 13-1 shows several examples of e-business models.

Table 13-1 Typical E-Commerce Business Models

Model	Description
Brokerage	A financial brokerage like ETrade or Schwab, where customers place buy and sell orders for financial instruments, such as stock and bonds. In this model, the broker charges the buyer and/or seller a transaction fee. Travel agents also fit into this category.
Advertising	The Web advertising model is an extension of the traditional broadcasting model. A Web site typically provides free content and services, such as e-mail mixed with banner ads. The ads are often the major source of revenue for the broadcaster. The broadcaster creates content or buys from third parties.
Merchant	Classic retailers of goods and services. Sales may be made based on list prices or through auction. In many cases, such as Egghead, the online store replaces the brick-and-mortar storefronts.
Manufacturer	This model uses the Web to allow manufacturers to reach buyers directly and eliminate intermediaries. The manufacturer model can create cost savings that may or may not be passed on to consumers. Examples of this model include Cisco, Apple, and Microsoft.
Subscription	Consumers pay for access to high-value content, such as the *Wall Street Journal*. Value-added content is essential. Some businesses have combined free content paid for by advertisers with premium content or services for subscribers only.

If you are struggling to define a business's model, asking several questions can jump-start the process. What products does the company sell? What markets do they sell in? What are their distribution channels? Answering these questions will frame the model. If you can relate the new business to one you have seen before, you will be more comfortable with the business, and you may find similarities in how it handles marketing, finance, operations, human resources, management, development, and technology.

You should also review the processes or steps the business takes to complete certain functions. How does it deliver its products? How does it buy products? The business processes will help you to define the business model. Where this approach may run into difficulty is implementing a network solution for a division or department that is part of a global enterprise. Determining such a business model may be way too complex an analysis for the project!

Analyzing Company Geographical Scope

From an IT perspective, it is critical to know the geographical scope (infrastructure) of a business in order to develop its IT infrastructure. If the geographical scope is similar to that of other companies, they may have similar network infrastructure requirements. You should be familiar with regional, national, international, subsidiary, and branch-office geographical scopes.

Regional   A *regional* company tends to operate within a state or several states, dispersed throughout the cities within the region. An example of this is a regional accounting firm or consulting firm that focuses on clients within a region. They may have offices in each of the major cities in one "anchor" state and in targeted cities in adjacent states. For instance, a regional accounting firm located in the state of Washington is headquartered in Seattle with offices in Tacoma, Bellingham, Spokane, Bremerton, and Battleground. They also have offices in Portland and Pendleton, Oregon, and Boise, Idaho. Other examples of regional businesses could be grocery stores, utilities, medical clinics, and law firms operating within a region.

National   An organization with a national scope has a presence throughout the home country. A national company's scope does not go beyond national boundaries, even though they may do business internationally. In Mexico, for example, a food manufacturing and distribution business might not have an equal presence in every state, but it might have some presence in every state with a focus on metropolitan areas. The food business is headquartered in Mexico City with offices in Guadalajara, Puebla, Monterrey, and 10 other cities throughout Mexico. They trade with U.S. companies but do not have locations outside of Mexico. This food business example is a typical national company. Other examples of typical national organizations include engineering firms, government agencies, construction companies, and insurance companies.

International An organization having a presence that crosses international boundaries is said to have an *international* scope. The number of locations tends to be distributed across at least several offices in cities throughout the world. An international organization may have a headquarters in Boston with offices in Tokyo, London, Singapore, and Mexico City. Remember, just because a company has an international presence doesn't mean they have offices throughout the home country—a company may have an international scope without a national scope, and vice versa. The defining element of an international business is the strategic necessity of the international locations.

Subsidiaries *Subsidiary* offices are operations owned by the overall business but not necessarily operated directly by the company. A company will buy strategic companies that can stand alone as subsidiaries.

You might also have seen, or become a victim of, subsidiary fever. In this case, a business will recast its organization so that divisions can operate in the future as subsidiaries. We've personally seen this done to meet regulatory requirements (such as accounting firms spinning off consulting and bookkeeping divisions).

The key decision-making occurs at the subsidiary level, but there is a reporting relationship with corporate headquarters, which requires a connected WAN infrastructure with high-speed site-level connections. The corporation also has other subsidiaries that operate independently. Subsidiaries tend to have unique requirements in that they need to have distributed networking capabilities along with connectivity to the corporate headquarters. Usually, these subsidiaries have unique requirements that fly in the face of the parent's corporate standards. Because of the unique legacy requirements, a subsidiary can get out of compliance with corporate standards and strain network resources, or even ignore corporate standards altogether. This model creates unique challenges for creating centralized network-management practices.

Branch Offices Companies of all geographical scopes and sizes can have branch offices. Typically, these offices are located close to customers, suppliers, or strategic partners. Sometimes these offices are inherited via mergers and acquisitions (with the parent company sometimes not knowing what to do with them). Branch offices can have connections to headquarters, to regional offices, or even to other branch offices, and they have a level of autonomy based on the needs of the operation. The connections can come in many forms, ranging from frame relay to VPN connections over local dial-up.

One example of a branch office is a balloon manufacturer located in Tacoma, Washington. As you can see in Figure 13-1, the balloon manufacturer has branch sales offices in San Francisco, Boston, and Miami. The sales offices are strategically located close to areas where balloon sales are dominant. The sales offices operate somewhat autonomously and vary in size based on the regional market size and the support required. Each of the branch offices is connected to the central office via fractional 256 kilobits per second (Kbps) T1 service.

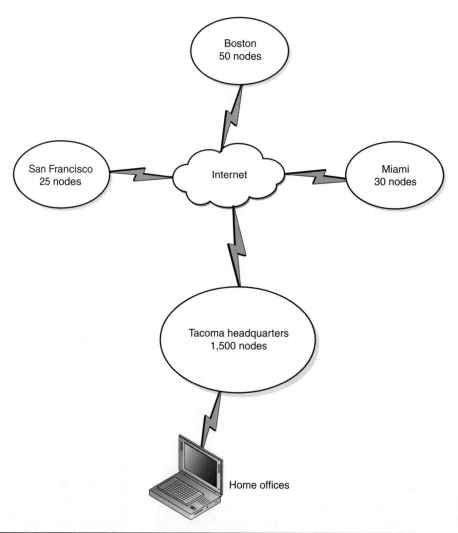

Figure 13-1   Balloon manufacturer branch office map

Analyzing Company Processes

It is important to understand what the company does and how they do it. And while that is a very basic approach to business analysis, it's not uncommon for MCSE consultants to be unsure of what their clients do. We've often felt at a disadvantage when we attempt to help clients work through strategic technology-planning issues and we don't understand the details of their business. It is important to understand an entity's processes in order to understand how technology plays a role in the process.

By *process,* we mean a series of steps that continues without branching, or in which a decision is made between process branches. Process mapping can be one of the most valuable abilities to develop in your personal toolset, and there are some excellent software aids for you to use, such as Microsoft Visio, for creating flowcharts and process maps. Process mapping can help to communicate knowledge about how the business works to decision makers both inside and outside the firm. While doing your analysis, you should either acquire the business flowcharts, if they exist, or develop your own and validate them with the business folks.

There are certain process areas on which you, as a Microsoft Windows 2000 network infrastructure designer, should focus. These areas include information flow, communications flow, service and product life cycles, and decision-making. You need not have detailed knowledge of all business processes, but an overview will help you add value to the business. The IT infrastructure—network service functionality, availability, optimization, and security strategies—should all be designed to support these flows. How can you properly support that which you do not understand and cannot see?

Analyzing Information Flow

How does information flow through the organization? More importantly, how does information flow in relation to certain physical processes? For instance, if a food company receives an order to ship products to a customer, information flow is associated with the physical flow of goods for that order. There will be a purchase order from the customer, an order-entry function, inventory impact, cost accounting, and so on. This may all get processed via Electronic Data Interchange (EDI) or via one of the various e-commerce systems. In any case, this information eventually ends up in a data management system. Therefore, information flow occurs in conjunction with physical processes, and you should identify them.

Also, how does the company get information from one point to another? As basic as that question may sound, it can be rather complex. Trust us, the old Point A to Point B question draws snickers in the conference room, but it's surprisingly difficult to answer. Is there a central database for information storage and processing? Or is e-mail exchange the primary mode of information movement? Maybe an intranet or extranet is used for information transfer. You should also be prepared for the reality that much of a company's information flow might be processed using traditional means, such as paper and word of mouth. You may have an opportunity to help the information flow in these situations by recommending information systems to improve processes.

One piece of advice is to use appropriate tools to develop these information flow maps if they don't already exist. As a network designer, diagramming key information flows is a core part of your work. If you are an MCSE consultant, this activity is valued by the client and is billable. Be prepared to explain and demonstrate how the company moves important information from one point to another and how key information is supplied throughout the organization.

Analyzing Communications Flow

Information moves over communication channels. When it comes to communicating, there are various styles and nuances. Everyone has a unique way of communicating, even when it comes to using technology to communicate. We view communications inside and outside an organization as occurring over various channels, including real-time voice, voice mail, e-mail, real-time chat, streaming video, real-time information sharing (NetMeeting), teleconferencing, and live in person.

In today's organizations, you must develop infrastructure designs to support all of these various channels of communication (including channels we didn't mention). Additionally, some, if not all, of these channels are digitally converging on the network with Voice over IP (VoIP) and teleconferencing over Quality of Service (QoS) allocated bandwidth. For the Microsoft design test, be aware of individual communication styles and make sure you are addressing those needs in the design.

Identifying Service and Product Life Cycles

Now we'll head deep into MBA territory with the product and service life cycle discussion. Product and service life cycles address a product or service's progression from life to death. Figure 13-2 shows a traditional product life cycle. The product is introduced, and then catches on and, if successful, moves into a growth phase. Eventually, there is a sales maturity stage and then decline.

Typically, a marketing strategist will work to phase in new products in order to continue the growth cycle or will restage products to move back down the growth curve and avoid maturation or sustained declines. An example of a product that has been renewed through the continued discovery of new uses is Arm and Hammer Baking Soda. Arm and Hammer continues to find new uses for baking soda, ranging from absorbing

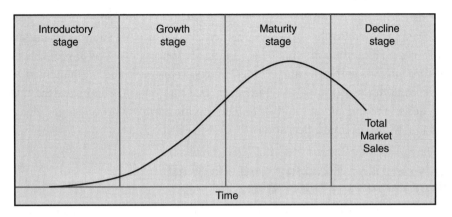

Figure 13-2   Product life cycle

odors to toothpaste. This renewal keeps the product alive and leverages the brand name as well, creatively extending the product life cycle.

Other products and services, such as Microsoft Office, regularly renew through new versions and added capabilities. Be aware of the product life cycles in general, because the time span of the life cycle and staying power of the service determines the infrastructure needed to support it.

Analyzing Decision-Making

Who makes the decisions in an organization? If you know how decisions are made, you can ensure that the network will support quality decisions through the delivery of information and communication. Additionally, it is important to know who makes the decisions in order to gain design-process approvals.

The process and effectiveness of decision-making is affected by the organizational structure, which identifies lines of authority and defines who can make decisions. The traditional hierarchical structures place decision-making at the top. In new networked organizations, decisions are made at all points in the network.

TIP   Don't forget the ways that organizations make decisions informally. Have you ever heard an organization communicate one decision and then seen it act on another? That's the result of the old informal decision-making process at work!

The decision-making process typically begins when a problem is noticed and analyzed. Data pertinent to the problem is gathered, and once the situation is understood as fully as possible, then alternative solutions are developed. After a problem is analyzed through data gathering and synthesis, a choice is made and implemented. This is followed-up with a review of the outcomes. Take the time to chart how the business makes decisions, and get especially familiar with the approval processes and determine who has authority to make decisions.

Analyzing the Existing and Planned Organizational Structures

Before you evaluate the networking infrastructure features, such as those identified in Chapter 12 like DHCP and DNS, you must evaluate the existing and planned organizational structures. How is the company organized? Is it organized by function or by another method? What is the management model? Is it customer-focused or product-focused? Areas to consider include the management model; company organization; vendor, partner, and customer relationships; and acquisition or transition plans. Keep in mind that, from a design perspective, knowing how work flows through the organizational structure will allow you to enhance your design to improve the effectiveness of the organization.

TIP Be sure to act like a seasoned consultant and cast a wary eye at organizational charts and business plans. You can learn just as much observing informal behaviors in the organization, such as who wields power irrespective of their placement in the organizational chart. For example, in a family-run business, the owner's kids may be officially at the bottom of the organizational chart, but don't fall for that old trick.

Identifying the Management Model

Determine how the key areas of the business are managed and what the essential management methods are. How are the affairs of the business, or of a particular segment of the business, organized or controlled?

Managers, as a group, are the decision makers, planners, organizers, leaders, and controllers of the business. Successful managers, especially the directors and executives, effectively and efficiently handle the affairs of the business. Managers must "change hats" frequently and take on various roles as needed. Managers work with and through people while acting as channels of communication inside and outside the organization.

Typically, the management model is defined within the framework of the business model, strategy, and organization. Managers have a variety of styles—some emulate their own managers and some have their own style. These styles range from *autocratic*, which is where the manager directly dictates the way things are done, to *laissez faire*, which means that the manager sets goals and empowers workers to approach projects and solutions in their own way. Management styles are matched with the strategic organizational structure.

Analyzing the Company's Organization

The structure of an organization involves the description of work, or how the work gets done. It also defines the reporting relationships in an organization that can help or hinder an organization's ability to accomplish its goals and objectives. A good structure can provide the organization with certain advantages based on the business strategy and model. The structure's success is judged by how well it facilitates or impedes communication, decision-making, leadership, team relations, and employee motivation.

All organizational structures have two major characteristics: (1) the manner and extent to which labor is allocated among workers, and (2) the mechanisms used for formally coordinating workers. An organizational chart can reflect these essential relationships graphically, and you should review the company's organizational chart to review these formal relationships prior to building network design solutions.

The organizational structure must divide work, must allocate work responsibilities, and the authority accompanying those responsibilities. Some positions have broad task and responsibility definitions; for example, the CEO has a much more generalized set of tasks and responsibilities than the director of training in the sample pizza manufacturer's organizational chart in Figure 13-3. In addition, in a functional organization, one position may perform a few or many tasks and may also oversee another functional area. For instance, the Finance manager's position in an organization often oversees the IS function. Remember, the responsibilities of any position in an organization can have many tentacles, and individual employees can play multiple roles. Also keep in mind that we've presented much of this discussion in the context of formal organizations. Always ask yourself how the informal organization plays into this.

Another thing you should keep in mind is that as a company's positions get more specialized or differentiated, the more coordination is required in order to get the various pieces working together toward common goals and objectives. Without coordination, the organization may or may not be working toward common goals. Therefore, another aspect of the organizational structure to review is the mechanisms used to

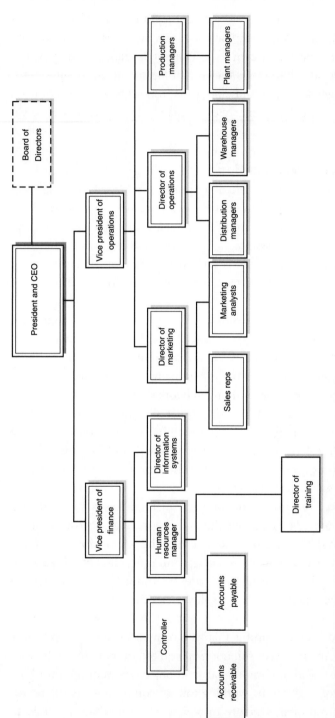

Figure 13-3 Partial organizational chart for a pizza manufacturer

coordinate the various individuals or groups. Some common coordinating mechanisms are as follows:

- **Direct synchronous or asynchronous communication**   Direct communications between positions and groups.

- **Direct supervision**   Chain of command or reporting relationships where the Director reports to the Vice President, the Vice President reports to the CEO, and so on.

- **Standardization of work processes**   Steps are specified for how to do a job. This works well for highly specialized jobs.

- **Output standards**   The required results from work as well as performance standards are specified. Sales quotas being put in place for a sales force is a typical example of this coordination mechanism.

- **Standardization of skill sets**   This identifies the training required to perform the work. (For example, professionals, such as teachers, lawyers, and accountants tend to coordinate their work using standard skill sets in addition to other coordinating mechanisms.)

Review the coordination mechanisms used at different levels in the organization, and remember that these coordination techniques vary at different levels. While levels can use multiple coordination techniques, the lower levels tend to require standardization of work processes, directors use direct supervision, and Vice Presidents rely on direct communications.

To save yourself time as an MCSE seeking to better understand business operations, develop a map showing how the organization's work is divided and coordinated. If you do this, you will again know how to appropriately support the organizational structure with your network communications and infrastructure design. Use your organizational chart and see how the management structure in your organization matches up against both your organizational needs and your network LAN links. Design the infrastructure based on these considerations.

EXAM TIP   When reviewing the case studies for the MCSE certification exams, be sure to study the organizational information provided. Get to know the key managers and their reporting relationships. The more you know about the organization's structure, the better chance you have of correctly answering the questions related to the structure.

Identifying Strategic Relationships

The savvy Windows 2000 MCSE will take this next piece of advice seriously. Take the time to list and understand the current and planned strategic relationships. Today, and in the near future, many of the most dramatic and powerful uses of the IT network involve the ability to go beyond a company's intranet boundaries. These networking capabilities, along with exciting new applications, enable firms to incorporate buyers, suppliers, and partners in the redesign of key business processes.

This redesign can enhance productivity, quality, speed, flexibility, and generate improvements not yet imagined. In addition, new channels of product distribution can be created, and information-based products can be delivered with no physical packaging. These new relationships can shift the competitive position of participating businesses in an industry almost overnight.

How does the business you are working with interact with its partners? Do they use the Internet, extranet applications, EDI, or fax? Help them look for opportunities to leverage networking technology to achieve competitive advantages. Ensure the network design supports their strategic relationships.

Identifying Acquisition Plans

This is one of our favorite business situations to observe. Perhaps it's because we've personally seen many business mergers, both as an employee and as an MCSE consultant. Is the company pursuing acquisitions or are they currently in the middle of an acquisition or new business combination? Maybe they are being acquired or are looking for an acquiring partner. These business activities can significantly affect network infrastructure design requirements. Make sure you know how these changes will potentially, or in reality, affect the connectivity designs you create.

A Windows 2000 deployment under these conditions will undoubtedly require you to understand the existing environment and make plans based on the most likely outcomes. You will also have to look at the potential pitfalls when trying to get approval for the implementation of a new design. Keep in mind, though, that Windows 2000 was built using standards. If you design the infrastructure using best practices, your network will potentially add value even under a new business-combination scenario. Put the work into ensuring your design does not preclude you or the business from integrating another standards-based environment.

Analyzing Factors That Influence Company Strategies

A number of factors influence a company's network strategy, including company priorities, projected growth and growth strategy, relevant laws and regulations, risk tolerance, and total cost of operations. Address each of these at some level in your design, and make sure they are taken into account in the design direction.

Identifying Company Priorities

Each organization has a different set of priorities, and they can be both formal and informal. Organizations approach their IT infrastructure from many different perspectives. For instance, one organization may want to provide an infrastructure making it easier for employees to share information, while another may simply want to make it less expensive to operate the network. Identify the company's unique priorities.

In most cases, in addition to any unique priorities, there are common priorities found at most organizations, such as these:

- The network infrastructure must make it easier for employees to share information resources.

- The network infrastructure must support a global enterprise.

- A new network infrastructure must be faster, more reliable, and easier to manage.

- The network infrastructure must be standards-based and improve existing processes, while supporting emerging business realities, such as heavy reliance on the Internet, a growing mobile workforce, and business collaboration.

- The changes to network infrastructure must minimize impact on end users.

- The network infrastructure must be cost-effective and lower the total cost of ownership and desktop support.

- The network infrastructure must prepare the company for future technologies, with advanced intranet and extranet options.

- The network infrastructure must provide for high security and a low level of granular security administration.

You must identify the company's priorities and develop the appropriate network infrastructure to address those priorities. For example, if an organization needs to make 75 percent of their workforce mobile, you as the designer must focus on mobile solutions like remote access and DHCP settings to support remote users. Here the company's priorities drive the infrastructure design.

Identifying the Organization's Projected Growth and Growth Strategy

An organization's *projected growth* will influence many aspects of your design. The number of users supported by the infrastructure is one area to address. User growth by location will affect the subnet design as well as the placement of services.

You may, for example, have set a performance standard for your DHCP server placement to support 2,500 users per server. If the growth projected for the organization exceeds that limit on individual servers, changes must be made to the DHCP design to accommodate the additional load. This may come in the form of adding additional DHCP servers or increasing the capacity of individual DHCP servers.

The *growth strategy* also influences the network infrastructure design. The issue here is not whether the company will grow, but *how* it will grow. Growth can occur in various areas that can create significant design issues.

Consider a company that provides credit card verification equipment and services. The management team has developed a strategy to grow by increasing the mobility of the sales force and placing them in 20 major metropolitan areas around the country. The projected effect of this new distributed sales-force growth strategy increases credit card processing of sales by 50 percent and is central to creating shareholder value. To enable this growth, the company needs to provide the sales force with portable network devices with secure distributed network connectivity, central data access, collaboration tools, and sales-processing abilities. Currently, the centralized sales organization uses high internal bandwidth but very little direct contact with customers beyond telephone and mail. The sales force wants to maintain the high-bandwidth communications with the headquarters and extend their reach through a decentralized organization to get closer to their customers.

This new growth strategy will have a significant impact on the network infrastructure. The new requirements include remote access with VPN capability, access to corporate data sources 24/7, an Internet Listing Service (ILS) for NetMeeting, and Terminal Services for remote sales transactions. The network infrastructure now becomes strategically important and must operate at high levels of reliability. Therefore, all services must be fault tolerant with no single point of failure on key services. Growth for this company is dependent on a network infrastructure that has the functionality, availability, performance, and security that matches this key growth strategy.

Identifying Relevant Laws and Regulations

So not only are we discretely trying to make you an MBA, but now a lawyer! The basic role of law in network-infrastructure decisions may not be readily apparent on the surface, yet the law constrains an organization in its decisions and limits alternative courses of actions. Certain conduct is illegal, and organizations that commit acts or omissions declared to be illegal are subject to sanctions. There may be fines or imprisonment if the conduct is declared a crime, and sanctions include liability for dollar damages if the conduct involves a wrongful act or breach of contract.

Your network infrastructure decisions must be made within the law on a local, national, and international basis, or sanctions will be imposed and your organization may be severely affected. This is particularly important now that information technology is crossing international boundaries and spanning regions. For example, import and export laws concerning encryption are not standardized from country to country.

The law is part of the foundation for designing the network infrastructure because it influences the infrastructure and the organization's conduct and decisions. Identify any laws constraining your network design, and be prepared to adjust your design as required by the law.

Identifying the Company's Tolerance for Risk

How risk-averse is the organization? Most companies today require a highly reliable network infrastructure. As organizations use networking for strategic reasons, there is little tolerance for infrastructure failure—it can mean lost sales, reduced market position, lost customer goodwill, lost productivity, missed contractual obligations, and loss of competitiveness. This risk of failure can influence shareholder value.

TIP Until you're informed otherwise, consider all companies that you work with or for to be risk-adverse and conservative in nature. Business schools drill into their students the concept of minimizing risk. This is often presented from finance and accounting perspectives, but can include management and political perspectives. While there are exceptions to this rule, firms that embrace risk are truly the exception.

To address this intolerance, network designs must include fault-tolerant and fault-recovery solutions. Fault tolerance allows key network services to continue to function through redundant online systems even with single failures in the system. Examples of fault-tolerant networking solutions include a routing solution that goes over multiple paths, server clustering, and network-service segmentation using multiple servers. Fault recovery allows for recovery after a short period if the service fails. A classic example of this is having a spare router offline, with a backup image available if the router fails. We suggest you propose using a combination of fault-tolerant and fault-recovery solutions in your designs. You should also review the disaster-recovery and contingency plans.

Identifying the Cost of Network Operations

When you design an organization's network infrastructure, the single largest consideration for the business is the return on investment (ROI) the organization expects to achieve from the design. This ROI is reflected in a change to the total cost of computing. Some of the major areas in which companies see cost improvements are management of systems and service/server consolidations.

One of the larger costs in a computing environment is supporting end users and managing desktop configurations. Many support costs originate from a lack of standards across the enterprise and a need to "touch" PCs for configuration and troubleshooting. You should design the network to reduce these costs and lower the cost of computing on a per-user basis. There are many technologies within Windows 2000 to help reduce the number of enterprise servers on the network and manage user-desktop standards.

Analyzing the IT Management Structure

It's now time to take much of the broad discussion so far in this chapter, and apply it to the information technology department. This starts by taking a look at the structural elements of IT management. Traditionally, IT management has been conservative and risk averse—the primary job was to keep systems up and running. Newer models focus on putting cutting-edge technologies in place without fail—IT management must get these systems up, fast and right. The systems must work 24/7.

You will need to consider the type of administration and how it functions in the company with which you are working. You must understand the organization and address network infrastructure requirements at various organizational levels. For instance, the Chief Information Officer's (CIO's) primary objective for the design may be to drive cost out of the systems, whereas the network administrator may want to ensure adequate WAN performance to remote locations.

We make it a practice to get the input from as many key players in the IT organization as possible when developing the network infrastructure design. You will need to interview the key players in the organization and develop an infrastructure design that meets their objectives. Typically, you will interview the IT administration, which is divided into various roles in an organization. Some of the roles include the following:

- **Chief Information Officer (CIO)**   Responsible for the strategic direction of information systems.

- **Director of Information Systems**   Responsible for recommending information-systems solutions and for managing implementations.

- **Network Administrator**   Responsible for the maintenance of networking systems, including WAN and remote access management.

- **End-User Support Manager**   Manages the end-user support group.

We recommend interviewing each of these managers to help determine their goals and priorities for the infrastructure design. You should also obtain their buy-in for the

PART III

ultimate design (though these specific positions or roles may or may not exist, depending on the size of the organization, and there may be other roles in the IT organization that will also impact the design). This consultation particularly helps when developing the goals and objectives of the design. This input can also point out opportunities for existing infrastructure improvements.

Determine whether the organization is centralized or decentralized. How is the IT organization funded? Does the organization outsource any key functions or processes? How are decisions made, and at what levels are they made? Answers to these key questions will help you improve the acceptance of your design.

Identifying the Type of Administration

Many companies over the last 10 years have moved from centralized to decentralized administration and resource management. This is the result of organizations moving from hierarchical structures supported by mainframe technology to networked structures supported by distributed systems.

In the early 1990s, we worked for a food company in Concord, Massachusetts. Initially, the company used an IBM mainframe, and all computers and administration were centrally located. Later, they began acquiring other food businesses and decided to change their IT organization to a decentralized model by placing IT personnel at plant locations and new acquisition locations. Eventually, distributed servers replaced the mainframe. This is typical of how IT organizations restructured in the early 1990s. The move to decentralization gives IT organizations more flexibility and provides improved service to sites outside of headquarters.

Centralized Structure   In a *centralized* IT structure, user management, resources, and administration are found in a central location. Servers, IT staff, and the network infrastructure components are housed and managed centrally. Access may be provided to users outside the central location, but the management of the resources and user accounts is centralized. In this pure model, divisions or departments do not have IT staff or server resources, as shown in Figure 13-4. All of the key IT decisions are made in the central location—every aspect of IT is under central authority.

TIP   While computer experts and many MCSEs think centralized administration is the best way to go, end users often prefer decentralized management models, where they have more control over their technology.

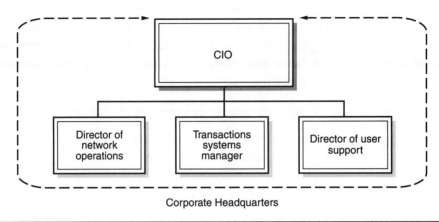

Corporate Headquarters

Figure 13-4   Example of a centralized IT management organization

Decentralized Structure   A *decentralized* IT structure moves resources and user management to smaller sites in an effort to place IT support and access closer to the users. These resource centers have their own equipment, IT staff, networks, and server administrators, along with support technicians. Decentralized organizations tend to have autonomous business units that have significant decision-making authority, as shown in Figure 13-5. This structure tends to provide better site-level support than centralized structures—IT can be more responsive to users. You will often find departmental servers and functional resources for finance, production, human resources, and marketing when IT is decentralized.

NOTE   Decentralized IT management approaches can raise security concerns. This topic is more germane for the discussion of Exam 70-220, "Designing Security for a Microsoft Windows 2000 Network."

Identifying the Funding Model

Let's face it, MCSEs live and breathe by the budget. Without an IT budget, your grandiose Windows 2000 design plans might gather dust.

Spending on IT is receiving increased scrutiny and the demand for accountability is also increasing. This focus is at all levels of the IT organization. The funding for IT comes from many different sources inside and outside an organization, and it varies

Figure 13-5
Example of a
decentralized IT
management
organization

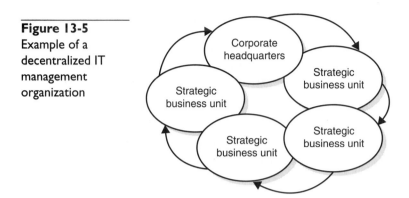

based on the nature of the organization and how it is funded. For instance, a not-for-profit agency must not exceed available funds, while a private sector business budgets for profitability.

Companies build annual budgets for systems projects and projected expenses, usually as part of a larger comprehensive budgeting process. The comprehensive annual budget includes the sales plan, purchasing plan, capital expenditures budget, and cash plan. The budgeted costs in the IT area include hardware, software, upgrades, consulting, and maintenance. If a cost is not included in the annual budget, management must attempt to get an approved variance specifically for the project, so make sure the project has adequate funding, and understand any potential constraints arising from budgetary limitations. For the Microsoft test, remember that these budget constraints can affect the project, especially the implementation timing.

Funding your design begins with a justification of the cost. Remember that upper management approves IT funding and they are looking primarily for a return on investment (ROI) or a strategic advantage that translates into ROI. ROI describes the way an expense will either reduce costs or increase revenue over time to improve profitability or operating cash flow. Project justifications must identify cost savings, problems solved, total cost of ownership reductions, productivity improvements, and so on. The problem that IT folks run into is that with ROI analysis, cost improvements or revenue enhancements must be quantified, and many IT benefits are intangible at first blush. Intangible benefits are very hard to fully quantify. For instance, if you install an EDI system that improves a vendor relationship, you may have difficulty putting a dollar value on the improved relationship. You will have to come up with some creative ways to quantify these improvements. Sometimes the improvements will show up as cost avoidance items, which should be used in the calculation.

TIP There are occasional exceptions where the funding model looks beyond the costs and ROI to the competitive advantage. The IT project may not make the most sense from a strict accounting perspective, but instead is justified for strategic reasons, such as the ability to analyze data (data mining) in ways that competitors cannot.

Once a change is justified, the change must be rolled into a budget including the cash budget. Funding points of contact, which are standard financial planning documents for an organization, include internal expense budgets, capital budgets, or new venture funding. Certain projects will be funded by one of these sources based on the nature and scale of the project. Typically, a company uses capital budgets for new installations or substantial upgrades, and expense budgets for small projects and low-cost project elements.

For instance, 100 Windows 2000 Professional upgrade licenses costing $8,000 would more than likely be expensed in a large company, and be funded from the expense budget. The $8,000 would impact the current fiscal year's operations. On the other hand, 100 new desktop workstations costing $150,000 would be capitalized and depreciated so that only a portion of the cost is expensed during the current fiscal period. Remember, the expensed items will affect current period operations, and capitalized costs are amortized over a longer time period.

Accommodating Outsourcing

Outsourcing is the result of making the classical decision to buy a solution or a combination of services rather than to build it yourself. This buy vs. build decision has accelerated IT advancements within many companies—outsourcers can disseminate and implement more advanced technologies more quickly than in-house IT departments often can. Outsourcing has been commonplace since the late 1990s and can occur at many levels in the IT organization. These levels range from outsourcing the entire IT function to only outsourcing the DNS service for Internet access. Outsourcing of IT, or the fulfillment of IT capabilities by sources outside an organization, is part of the reality of modern systems.

Outsourcers can help businesses complete difficult projects quickly and help fill gaps in professional IT skills. A skilled outsourcer can provide key knowledge to organizations for current and future projects. Outsourcing can be particularly useful for managing remote sites. Local contracted support can be used to avoid travel and costly permanent placements in small locations.

Another commonly outsourced service is product support for desktop applications, as well as PC maintenance and server-hardware maintenance. In addition, since most

ISPs offer Domain Name Services (DNS), many companies have outsourced their DNS to their ISP.

In a Windows 2000 network, DNS plays a critical role—without DNS, the logon services do not function, nor will Active Directory function properly. Your network design decisions should include an analysis of the outsourced services and the infrastructure impact, and especially how you will treat DNS, if outsourced. Your design may include a change to the DNS outsourcing arrangement.

NOTE   Many Windows 2000 MCSEs know outsourcing firsthand, working for firms that provide outsourcing services to traditional companies. Participating in an outsourcing arrangement is often a win-win situation. The company contracting the outsourced MCSEs doesn't have to manage a staff of MCSEs, and the MCSEs get frequently changing and challenging assignments.

Understanding the Decision-Making Process

The decision-making process is usually closely related to the IT organization structure, and understanding this process in the organization will help you move your design changes forward quickly and smoothly.

At what level or position are decisions made? What process do design changes go through to achieve implementation approval? Every organization has a different process, but every quality decision is made through a justification process. The justification process includes technical justification, as well as matching up the technical changes while moving the business forward.

Who are the people involved in the process? Remember that decisions are typically recommended at lower levels and approved at higher levels. A control group also must typically approve decisions if funding is involved in the decision. The decision to go ahead with a project such as an infrastructure design is arrived at with management review.

Watch out for phased projects that have gained management approval without budget review. Sometimes critical phases of a project are delayed or cancelled after significant effort because budgeted funds are not available. You need to have a reduced plan in place to accomplish the fundamental design with reduced enhancements, just in case the money dries up.

Understanding the Change-Management Process

It is time to discuss the change-management process at an organization. If you have done any troubleshooting in your career, you know that one of the first questions to ask when identifying the cause of problems is: "What has changed?" The answer to this question directs you to the cause of the problem and ultimately to the solution. Avoiding changes, or managing them carefully, can prevent problems.

A well-implemented change-management process can improve the reliability of a design implementation and improve the acceptance of the design in a large internetworked organization. If an organization does not have a formal process in place, you should recommend a model for them to use.

Change management is a simple concept that requires tremendous discipline to implement. Change-management programs require you to thoroughly define the recommended system change, and the level of detail of the described change should be appropriate to the change.

A change management process should include the following elements:

- **Detailed change description**   Give a description of changes, including a process flow.

- **Change justification**   Specify why the change is recommended.

- **Change impact statement**   Explain the impact of the changes, including the impact on servers, applications, and users.

- **Network infrastructure changes**   Identify the infrastructure changes that are required.

- **Testing**   Outline the advance and post testing procedures for the change.

- **Time for implementation**   Give an estimate of the time required to implement the changes.

- **Change timing**   Specify when the changes will take place.

- **Implementation team**   Identify who is involved in the project.

- **Stakeholders**   Identify who should approve the changes.

- **Rollback procedures**   Specify procedures for the event of failure.

Documentation and follow-through are the backbone of successful change management. Change-management documents should include an approval process whereby the stakeholders and managers approve the changes. These change documents help to ensure that changes are communicated and coordinated throughout the IT organization.

Change management is especially appropriate for a Windows 2000 network design. Given the interconnected nature of current networks, a Windows 2000 upgrade requires very tight change management and is something you should take very seriously to avoid interoperability issues.

Start by observing the change in a lab environment that attempts to emulate the production environment. Your observations should also include reviewing the effect of planned rollback procedures in the test lab. After the testing is completed in the lab environment, it is time to create a change-management document, as mentioned earlier. If approved, the change should be scheduled and implemented as defined in the document.

This process has many benefits, one of which is that it forces the designer to think through all of the important change elements and create a rollback procedure in case of failure. Additionally, it is always nice to have your "ducks in a row" when integrating a new network operating system as complex as Windows 2000.

Business Requirements Analysis Checklist

Use the following checklist when analyzing business requirements:

- [ ] Analyze the existing and planned business models.
  - [ ] Analyze the company model and the geographical scope. Models include regional, national, international, subsidiary, and branch offices.
  - [ ] Analyze company processes. Processes include information flow, communications flow, service and product life cycles, and decision-making.
- [ ] Analyze the existing and planned organizational structures. Considerations include the management model; company organization; vendor, partner, and customer relationships; and acquisitions plans.
- [ ] Analyze factors that influence company strategies.
  - [ ] Identify company priorities.
  - [ ] Identify the projected growth and growth strategy.
  - [ ] Identify relevant laws and regulations.
  - [ ] Identify the company's tolerance of risk.
  - [ ] Identify the total cost of operations.
- [ ] Analyze the structure of IT management.
  - [ ] Identify the type of administration—centralized or decentralized.
  - [ ] Identify the funding model.
  - [ ] Accommodate any outsourcing in your plan.
  - [ ] Understand the decision-making process.
  - [ ] Understand the change-management process.

Evaluating the Company's Technical Requirements

After a complete analysis of the organization's business model, processes, priorities, and IT management structure, it is fitting to address the planned technical environment and goals. Given the fact that every organization is unique, this phase may be extensive. However, if you are familiar with typical business models, you will likely understand the foundation of a business very quickly. We recommend you work toward a thorough understanding of the existing and planned technical environments, which will lead to a high-quality design solution.

TIP   If you're an MCSE consultant, many billable hours await you here! The technical-requirements analysis is important, and it can take many hours to complete.

For instance, if you know that an organization requires secure Internet access for all users at all locations, you must ensure that the networking services design you create addresses this need appropriately. You may design Internet access through one location using private IP addressing. You may also use a proxy server and a firewall with a Demilitarized Zone (DMZ). Then decide whether to place all external Web and e-mail servers in the DMZ.

The design that you create should address the planned technical environment.

Documenting the Existing Infrastructure Design

You should generate an accurate inventory of the hardware and software the organization uses before you begin designing the network infrastructure. It is impossible to analyze the impact of infrastructure design changes without knowing the existing network's physical and logical topology.

You need to document and assess the following areas of the current network environment:

- Hardware and software

- Network infrastructure

- Network configuration

- File, print, and Web servers

- Line-of-business applications
- Directory service architecture
- Security

Applications such as Network Monitor or Microsoft Systems Management Server are useful for documenting your network. Often, original equipment manufacturers offer troubleshooting or configuration software that is ideal for documenting the configuration of equipment and drivers.

You will be doing a considerable amount of analysis before preparing your network infrastructure design. Focus on analyzing the network infrastructure in preparation for the infrastructure design. Whether you are designing a new network or upgrading an infrastructure, your planning in the area of infrastructure requirements will determine the specific tasks you need to perform in preparation for your infrastructure design implementation.

Documenting Hardware and Software

You must perform hardware and software inventories of all servers and client computers in use on the network. Document all routers, printers, modems, and other hardware, such as RAID arrays and Remote Access Service (RAS) server hardware. Be sure to include such details as BIOS settings and the configuration of any peripheral devices, such as printers, scanners, and input devices. It is also important to record driver versions and other software and firmware information.

Your software inventory should list all applications found on all computers, and include version numbers (or date and time-stamp data) associated with the applications on your system.

TIP Remember to document any service packs applied to the operating system or applications. You can use scripts and a variety of third-party applications to obtain this information from Microsoft Windows networks that use Windows Management Instrumentation (WMI).

Document network configurations for servers and client computers, including all services running on the servers, such as DNS, DHCP, WINS, Remote Access Service, and so on.

TIP Microsoft Systems Management Server can produce detailed reports about the hardware, software, and applications in use in your organization.

Documenting the Network Infrastructure

Any network uses multiple protocols as appropriate. Organizations that maintain an Ethernet network might use a combination of TCP/IP, NetBEUI, SPX/IPX, and others, depending on the networking, authentication, and security needs and capabilities of the operating systems in place. Identify the protocols in use on the network.

As you do so, consider whether any of these protocols can be replaced or eliminated because upgraded clients may no longer need them. For instance, if you replace all clients that use IPX/SPX as part of the migration, you might be able to eliminate the use of the additional IPX/SPX protocol on your network, thereby freeing bandwidth. We strongly recommend simplifying your network by using only the TCP/IP protocol suite, as long as there is no overriding need for additional protocols. Simplify, simplify, simplify to improve performance and reduce management costs.

While you are documenting the current network environment, take special notice of areas where there are currently problems—especially service functionality, availability, performance, or security issues. If you stabilize your network before deploying a new infrastructure, later deployment will be easier, and the new design can be used to solve existing problems or deal with any lack of functionality. You should use a test lab to duplicate problems and configurations, and then apply new solutions to evaluate the impact of deploying your new design, given certain network conditions, including protocols, hardware drivers, and client/server configurations.

When documenting the network infrastructure, you must obtain both hardware data to document the infrastructure's physical structure, and software data to document the existence and configuration of the protocols used on the network. You also need to document the logical organization of the network, the name and address resolution methods, and the existence and configuration of services used. Documenting the location of the network sites and the available bandwidth between them will also assist you in determining performance-improvement opportunities.

Developing physical and logical diagrams of the network will help you organize the information you gather in an understandable and intuitive manner. I have found this useful in creating a gap analysis showing the net changes that will occur in the infrastructure design.

TIP You might recall our earlier discussion in this chapter about using Visio to create diagrams. Please feel free to revisit that discussion now.

Physical Network Diagram The *physical network diagram* should include the following network information:

- Provide details of communication links, including length, grade, and approxima-tion of the physical paths of the communication media.

- Show servers, with NetBIOS/host name, IP address, and server role. Servers can operate in many roles, including primary or backup domain controller, DHCP ser-vice server, DNS server, WINS server, file and print server, router, and application server.

- Show the location of devices such as printers, bridges, switches, miscellaneous com-munications devices, routers, firewalls, and proxy servers that are on the network.

- Identify WAN communication links and the available bandwidth between sites. This could be an approximation or the actual measured capacity, as well as utiliza-tion or saturation level of the WAN links. This is critical for optimizing the network infrastructure design.

- Identify the number of users at each site, including mobile users, and how they move between locations/subnets.

Figure 13-6 shows an example of a physical network diagram for Catywhompus Construction.

Make sure you record the firmware version, throughput, and any special configura-tion requirements for any devices on the network. If you assign static IP addresses to any of these devices, write it down.

Logical Network Diagram   The *logical network diagram* shows the network architec-ture and should include the following information:

- Diagram the addressing scheme and domain architecture, including the existing domain hierarchy and domain names.

- Show the server roles, including primary or backup domain controllers, DHCP ser-vice servers, and WINS servers.

In a Windows NT environment, show trust relationships, including representations of existing trust relationships. Figure 13-7 is an example of a logical network diagram for Catywhompus Construction.

Documenting the Network Configuration

The network configuration includes foundational elements such as IP addressing as well as name resolutions services like DNS. The network configuration creates the net-work's foundation. The following sections show the areas of the network configuration that you need to document.

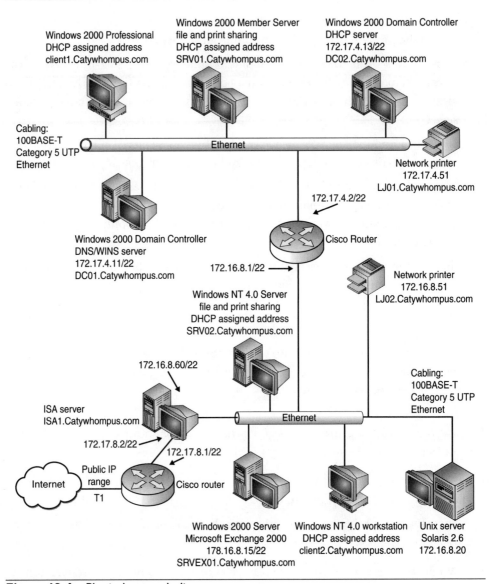

Figure 13-6   Physical network diagram

IP Addressing Methods and Service Configurations   Ensure that you have documented all DHCP service servers on the network, including the following:

• IP addresses that are assigned servers or client computers

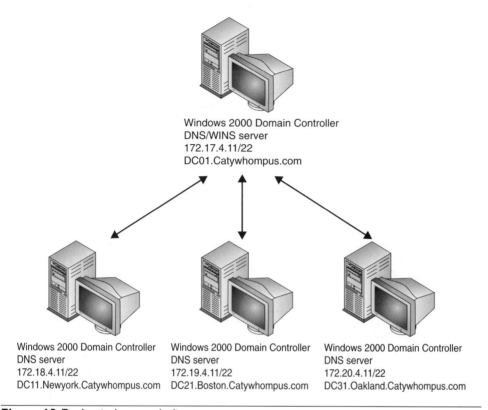

Windows 2000 Domain Controller
DNS/WINS server
172.17.4.11/22
DC01.Catywhompus.com

Windows 2000 Domain Controller
DNS server
172.18.4.11/22
DC11.Newyork.Catywhompus.com

Windows 2000 Domain Controller
DNS server
172.19.4.11/22
DC21.Boston.Catywhompus.com

Windows 2000 Domain Controller
DNS server
172.20.4.11/22
DC31.Oakland.Catywhompus.com

Figure 13-7   Logical network diagram

- DHCP option settings, such as the default gateway

- Scope settings and the location of DHCP servers

- Details of the subnets and hosts on the network

- The number of subnets and hosts on the network

- The IP addresses and subnet masks used on the Internetwork

- The client IP lease duration used on the network

Name Resolution Services   Ensure that you have documented all DNS and WINS servers that are on the network, noting configuration and version information, and hardware details, including the number and type of CPU, memory, disk subsystem, and network subsystem. Note whether any of the DNS servers on the network can support dynamic registration and service (SRV) Resource Records, and whether upgrades for this capability are available from the software manufacturer.

 TIP You may recall from the core Windows 2000 MCSE exams, where the emphasis is placed more on hands-on skills, that not all DNS servers can interact with the dynamic DNS in Windows 2000 Server.

If you have non-Microsoft hosts on the network, pay particular attention to documenting the services they use and provide. Make sure to document services such as the Service Advertising Protocol (SAP) and Routing Information Protocol (RIP) if they are presently in use on the network. Make sure you identify any applications that require NetBIOS on the network.

Routing, Dial-Up Networking, and Internet Connectivity   If there are remote or mobile users (and what company doesn't have either these days!), document the remote access and dial-up configurations. If third-party software is used for mobile users, review and document the configuration of those products. If there are existing VPNs, document the configuration of those connections. Document the configurations and locations of all network routers and Internet connections.

Bandwidth Issues   There's one easy method for MCSEs to document their network bandwidth: just monitor end-user complaints! Or, rather than suffer the angst of your end users, you can use the business- and technical-needs analysis to proactively address bandwidth matters before problems arise.

First, document the network's current bandwidth utilization to establish a gap analysis. You can use Microsoft Network Monitor and a variety of third-party tools to measure bandwidth and utilization metrics, such as frames sent or received, transmit and receive errors, and packets per second. Document the speed of the network links between the organization's site-level segments and between sites.

Look at the logical and geographical dispersion of the organization in terms of bandwidth considerations. Does it have branch offices, or mobile or remote employees? Consider the amount and type of traffic over the organization's communication links. Try to record available bandwidth during the course of low, normal, and high network utilization. This will provide valuable information when developing the new design for performance.

Consider the quality and bandwidth of the existing network wiring and devices, and whether they will support the new design. Are the network devices, such as hubs and cabling, fast enough for the purposes? How fast are the links to geographically dispersed sites?

In your designs, you will match the total bandwidth with bandwidth needs. This is the old "guns and butter" argument of MCSE network bandwidth management. You have to find a balance between the bandwidth that is needed and the bandwidth that can be provided, while living with a reasonable IT budget. The volume of traffic generated on site networks and between sites over WAN links must be analyzed in all situations. WAN links can quickly become bottlenecks if adequate bandwidth is not in place.

An example of this bandwidth analysis is a remote sales office that uses a word processor or spreadsheet as its main desktop application. The application does not generate much network traffic to the branch server, so Category 5 network cabling capable of 100 Megabits per second (Mbps) transmission, matched with 10 Mbps hubs might be acceptable. In the headquarters, applications with shared data, such as client/server databases and accounting systems, are the main desktop applications. These applications generate much more network traffic, and therefore require faster network equipment.

We know you likely recognize that the growing importance of providing Internet access and multimedia on the corporate desktop adds to bandwidth demand. Ethernet networks running shared applications might require Category 5 cable capable of 100 Mbps transmission speed and 100 Mbps switched Ethernet.

Documenting File, Print, and Web Servers

You should also document the configuration details of the file and printer sharing servers, paying particular attention to any unique configurations, such as a RAS server hosting a bank of modems. Document the profile of the server and its primary role in the organization. Is the server an enterprise or a departmental server? You should make note of any special operational requirements of the organization's servers and identify whether any of these servers rely on special protocols or drivers. Again, evaluate the hardware and associated drivers on these computers.

Be sure you locate the printers in the organization and document their configurations. Include ports, drivers, and protocols such as Datalink Control (DLC) running on these servers.

Give special consideration to HTTP and proxy servers. You need to address the security implications in this category of server and the bandwidth each can require. And, as you know by now, Web and firewall activities can place big demands on your infrastructure.

PART III

Documenting Line-of-Business Applications

Here's one of our favorites, as we truly believe that applications largely drive the technology process in organizations. You must identify all mission-critical applications that the organization must have to perform its core mission. Typically, you will find a set of applications, such as a core transaction system, a database application, and an e-mail system, each of which must be operating correctly to achieve the organization's objectives. Compatibility is a key concern for these applications. You will need to ensure that there are no compatibility issues with these applications when testing the new infrastructure design.

Documenting the Directory Services Architecture

Here's an obvious technical planning step, given the emphasis of Active Directory in the Windows 2000 MCSE track: document the existing domain structure. Identify the domain architectures, the users and groups in the organization and their geographical location, and the resource and administrative domains if they are using a Windows NT network. Be sure to document the number of domains and the domain model used for the domain structure. Is it a single domain? A single master? Or a multiple-master domain model? And don't forget to document whether there is a noncontiguous DNS namespace, possibly created by acquisitions, mergers, or other transitions. This information will assist you when you are planning the new directory structure.

Next, identify any other directory services currently running on the network, such as Microsoft Exchange Server directory service extensions, or UNIX BIND. You should also endeavor to identify all of the user accounts that exist for each user. This information will be useful during both the migration to DNS and Active Directory and in maintaining correct functionality between Windows 2000 Active Directory and other directory services. We find that having this account information makes the transition much smoother. And if you take our suggestions to heart, you've got yourself a needs-analysis methodology, putting you in business as an MCSE consultant!

Domain Administration Model   When examining the existing domain structure, document the following information for the network:

- Many networks have multiple-master account domains with many more resource domains, and this should be documented. When migrating or upgrading existing domains, the existing domain structure will influence the new domain structure design.

- Note the existing trust relationships in the network. Identify any domains and trust relationships that will not move into the new directory structure.

- Identify the primary and backup domain controllers on the physical and logical network diagrams. Note their physical locations and configuration details.

- Determine what namespaces exist in the organization to help to create a unique namespace for the organization. Sometimes organizations have multiple namespaces for business reasons or because of mergers and acquisitions. Determining the DNS namespace as the root of the Active Directory hierarchy is an important part of the planning, because it is difficult to change the root namespace after designing the hierarchy.

Document Existing Security

I find that a review of the organization's security standards and how they are implemented is useful, even if the organization is not moving to a new operating system, but it becomes particularly important when an organization does move to a new OS. Review the security standards and procedures for mobile and desktop users, internal and external networks, and dial-up and remote-access accounts.

Find out whether administrative tasks, such as creating users, groups, and file shares, changing passwords, and configuring device and object attributes, are performed by a centralized group or by several groups. What are the specific rights and membership lists of these groups? You will need this information when implementing the new infrastructure design for setting up services, policies, and so on.

Document the types of relationships that currently exist among office locations, business units, and divisions in the organization. Are the administrative tasks in these units shared, or is each unit responsible for administration? Do the user groups extend over company divisions or locations, or does an organizational unit group them? Document what types of information are available to which groups, and whether any significant restrictions are required for certain types of information, such as human resources data.

Document any guidelines regarding appropriate network usage, such as whether staff members can access the Web and for what purposes, and what constitutes prohibited or inappropriate access. The relationships the company has with outside vendors, customers, and business partners affect the security strategy. Answer the following questions about the company's relationships:

- Does the organization have service-level commitments with partners that permit them to access the network?

- What are the policies concerning the external party's access to the network data and resources?

- Can the external parties view data on a read-only basis, or can they modify data on the network?

- How is access restricted to applications?

Document the security and encryption standards currently in place or planned by providing the following information:

- Document security permissions on the network by user and user group.

- Document the organization's password standards—how long a password must be, what the approved combinations of characters are, how long a user is permitted to retain a password, and so on.

- List the security protocols used in the network.

- Document how external users are authenticated over the Internet, dial-up, and WAN links to the private network.

- Document the details of any multiple accounts that exist for a single user.

TIP See the "Exam 70-220: Designing Security for a Microsoft Windows 2000 Network" section in this book for much more on security.

Analyzing Client Computer Access Requirements

This area is critical to the network infrastructure, because after all is said and done, enabling appropriate user access determines network success or failure. If the network is a "not work" as far as the users are concerned, you're outta there! The network exists to supply services and applications to users who can do something with them.

We take a two-pronged approach to analyzing client access. The first prong looks at what clients should be able to do on the network, and the second prong characterizes how they use resources on the network. To put it simply, we will review what they *need* to do on the network and *how* they do it. Knowing a client's needs will help you design the infrastructure to benefit users.

Analyzing End-User Work Needs

It is not necessary to examine all the details needed in the infrastructure to support users. There's simply not enough time in your life as a busy Windows 2000 MCSE to do so. But it is important to examine the right details. Focus on the users and take a user perspective. What resources do they need to reach on the network? What client capabilities do they possess? To do their job, users typically need two things on the network: appropriate access to resources, and the client tools to reach those resources.

In addition to analyzing the services-level support needed by clients, it makes sense to review the point-to-point communications that clients require. These points include local network access and access to the enterprise from a remote location outside the enterprise.

- **Local network access** Users need access to typical file and printer sharing, along with a variety of client-server applications, including e-mail, database, and business-productivity applications. Areas to consider include client configuration, including TCP/IP settings and the operating system, as well as the network architecture with which the client must interoperate. Is the user connected over a WAN or LAN segment? What network protocols are needed to support the client access?

- **Remote location intranet access** Organizations typically have remote locations, and users will need access to resources located at the remote locations. How will they do this? Will they use a leased line between sites? Will users in the local site need to dial up remote sites directly? Identify how users access remote sites.

- **Remote location from outside the enterprise** Many users now access the corporate network remotely. These "road warriors" travel often and may need access to corporate resources including e-mail and files from a laptop or other remote device. They may also need access when traveling internationally. How is their access achieved? Do they use a dial-up connection VPN, a Web browser, or client e-mail software? Users will also access the network from home. How is this access provided? Do they have a company laptop? Access must be supplied in all cases.

Analyzing End-User Usage Patterns

The two key items to monitor are what services are being used on the network, and when they are being used. This analysis will help you determine capacity requirements and let you focus on the network areas that are most relied on by users.

Once the patterns are determined, structure the network to support key activities with the goal of meeting the users' realistic expectations.

Analyzing the Existing Disaster-Recovery Strategy

The disaster-recovery plan is an important "living" document for the enterprise. It should identify who does what as well as the resources needed in case there is a disaster. Most stable companies have these in place to ensure the survival of the enterprise after a disaster. You should review this strategy and then look for ways to improve the disaster recovery plans for the organization. The following discusses some recommended steps for this analysis.

Reviewing the Disaster-Recovery Plan

What provisions exist for the partial or complete loss of data at the organization? Has the organization determined the total cost of rebuilding or replacing the data used?

Check to see that the disaster-recovery plan addresses the following questions:

- What are the costs of reconstructing financial, personnel, and other business data?
- Is there adequate business insurance coverage to replace lost data?
- How long will it take to reconstruct business data?
- How will data losses translate into lost business?
- What does server downtime cost on a per-hour basis?

Address several conceptual areas in a comprehensive disaster-recovery plan. Make sure the company plan for data protection addresses the following questions:

- What data is backed up and how often are backups performed?
- How is critical computer- or other hardware-configuration information protected if it is not saved during normal backups?
- What data needs to be stored on-site, and how is it physically stored?
- What data needs to be stored off-site, and how is it physically stored?
- Are server operators and administrators adequately trained so they can respond quickly and effectively if an emergency occurs?
- Are copies of the disaster-recovery plan kept both on-site and off-site?
- Has the plan for recovering and restoring the organization's critical data been tested?

Testing the Disaster Recovery Plan

Needless to say, testing is an important part of being prepared for disaster recovery. The skill and experience of the administrators and operators is a major factor in getting a failed network back online with minimal disruption to the business. Analyze the following aspects of the disaster-recovery plan:

- Test results with particular emphasis on test failures in the disaster recovery plan.
- The performance of backup restorations.

You can use testing to try to predict failure situations and to practice recovery procedures. Be sure to do stress testing and test all functionality. Some of the failures that you need to test include

- Individual computer components, such as hard disks and controllers, processors, and RAM
- External components, such as routers, bridges, switches, cabling, and connectors

The stress tests that you set up need to include

- Network loads
- Heavy use of file, print, and applications servers
- Heavy use of the network by users who log on simultaneously

Reviewing Recovery Procedures

Check the procedures for getting a computer or network back online after a disaster. Review the operations handbook, which should include the following procedures:

- Performing backups
- Implementing off-site storage policies
- Restoring servers and the network

You should review the documentation when you make design changes to the network—design changes can impact the disaster recovery procedures. Updating the documentation is particularly important when you install new versions of the operating system or change the placement of servers and routers on the network.

 TIP Disaster recovery plans can be an excellent source for identifying existing infrastructure components that are not found in high-level design diagrams.

Reviewing Records of Past Failures

Review the past failure records and their causes. This information can help identify the key failure sources, such as

- Software failure of the operating system or applications on a server or client
- Hardware failure on a network component
- Administrative or user error
- Deliberate damage, such as sabotage or a virus assaults

The following questions can help you analyze failures and the impact the network design will have on handling them:

- How was the problem solved?
- How long would or did the solution take?
- What was the cost of the solution?
- What actions were taken to reduce the recurrence of failure?
- What changes will you make to the network infrastructure that might affect the failure frequency? Changes might include the size of the LAN or WAN or the type or number of the following:

  - Routers
  - Switches
  - Bridges
  - IP configuration services
  - Name resolution services
  - Remote access services

  - Modems
  - Servers
  - Clients
  - Users
  - Administrators
  - External connections

Technical Requirements Analysis Checklist

Use the following as a checklist when analyzing technical requirements:

☐ Evaluate the company's existing and planned technical environment and goals.

☐ Analyze company size and user and resource distribution.

☐ Assess the available connectivity between the geographic location of worksites and remote sites.

☐ Assess net available bandwidth and latency issues.

☐ Analyze performance, availability, and scalability requirements of services.

☐ Analyze data- and system-access patterns.

☐ Analyze network roles and responsibilities.

☐ Analyze security considerations.

☐ Analyze the impact of infrastructure design on the existing and planned technical environment.

☐ Assess current applications.

☐ Analyze network infrastructure, protocols, and hosts.

☐ Evaluate network services.

☐ Analyze TCP/IP infrastructure.

☐ Assess current hardware.

☐ Identify existing and planned upgrades and rollouts.

☐ Analyze technical support structure.

☐ Analyze existing and planned network and systems management.

☐ Analyze the network requirements for client computer access.

☐ Analyze end-user work needs.

☐ Analyze end-user usage patterns.

☐ Analyze the existing disaster-recovery strategy for client computers, servers, and the network.

Case Study 13: Big Time Investments, Inc. Business and Technical Requirements Analysis

You work for an outsourcing IT company and have been assigned to create a design solution for an investment firm called Big Time Investments (BTI), a fictitious company. This is your ticket to the big time, an opportunity to get the IT practical exposure you need to move your network-design career forward. You know you have to understand the business and technology already in place in order to best serve the client. This can be a daunting task! Where do you start?

continued

You must identify the key information that will influence the design. This includes company strategy, organizational structure, IT management capabilities, and technical environment. Current network operations data, such as user traffic patterns and future network requirements, will also affect the design.

Analyze the company processes as well. Processes include information flow, communication flow, service and product life cycles, and decision-making. Review the organization structure and document the following:

- What activities and functions do people perform in the organization?
- Are the activities specialized; are they performed through work units?
- Are work activities standardized?
- Does the organization use a knowledge-management system?
- How are the activities coordinated?
- Is decision-making centralized or decentralized?
- Does the organization's structure match the business strategy, or will the organization go through transformation during the course of network implementation?
- How reliant on network infrastructure is the organization? Is networking the lifeblood of the organization?

The answers to these questions regarding process and organizational structure will have a dramatic impact on infrastructure design. Once you have collected the information, you must transform it into networking objectives that meet business goals and objectives.

In the case of BTI, the company has five international locations and 3,000 employees, and the company's strategy is to improve its sales-support tools and increase its accessibility using Web-based transaction tools. The design requirements are developed from the analysis of this strategy. The requirements must also reflect the physical layout and organizational structure of the firm, which we will discuss in more detail later.

For now, consider the notion that the analysis of business and technical requirements eventually will generate a functional specification for the network. The investment firm's functional specification might require routers, DNS, DHCP, remote access, and so on to accomplish their design requirements. Then, the functional specification will be enhanced for availability, performance, security, and manageability.

continued

Next in the process, you will examine business and IT analysis concepts that will aid in your design development. These ideas will help you understand the key business and technical issues that need to be considered when creating a design solution. Then you will address key design questions that will aid you in creating a network infrastructure for BTI.

Directions

Spend 10 to 15 minutes reviewing the case information about BTI, and pay particular attention to the business and technical requirements. Create your own organizational, process, and network diagrams as needed. Then answer the questions at the end of the case analysis, and compare your findings to the suggested solutions.

Business Background

Originally, the firm was owned by an Englishman who later sold it to a wealthy investor from the United States in 1950. The headquarters was moved from London to New York shortly thereafter. BTI has locations in New York, London, Melbourne, Tokyo, and Mexico City.

The organization of BTI has three strategic business units (SBUs). The first SBU is an investment-banking unit that focuses on investing in start-ups and pre-IPO firms. This unit is responsible for 50 percent of the firm's revenue. The second unit underwrites initial public offerings, and the third is a retail brokerage and financial-services division. The retail division accounts for 20 percent of the $5 billion annual revenues. While the other SBUs are growing at 15 to 20 percent annually, the retail division's sales growth is lagging at 5 to 6 percent growth.

The retail division primarily supports clients with a net worth exceeding $1 million. Each client is assigned a professional investment advisor who manages the client's investment portfolio and provides the client with in-depth investment advice. The key value added here is that the investment advisors work very closely with each client to provide highly personalized investment services. Building trust between clients and advisors is critical to making this part of the business work. The retail division supports approximately 500 clients and each advisor is assigned five or six clients. The CEO, Bob Wells, wants the division to grow at 20 percent per year. His strategy is two-pronged. The first is to increase the volume of existing clients by improving investment recommendations and the second is to gain market share from their nearest competitor.

continued

Ed Davis, the Executive Vice President of retail investments at BTI, made this statement at the all-company meeting in New York: "The retail division must be given dramatically improved technology tools and access, to help our investment advisors make investment recommendations for their clients quickly, based on strong research support. Our outdated paper-based tools must be replaced if we expect to grow this strategically important business. Also, our clients should be able to view their investment accounts 24 hours a day, seven days a week, and move financial instruments as needed."

The executive management agrees with Mr. Davis' assessment and supports a move to automate critical research and client-contact methods. The board of directors, which has approved the enhancements in the current fiscal year's capital and expense budget, supports this new enhancement project.

The firm has one CIO, who oversees the IT organization and manages the strategic IT plans, reporting directly to the CEO. In addition, an IT director for each of the three SBUs reports to the CIO. These IT directors manage the IS functions for their division across all remote locations. Each of the international locations has one network administrator for every 200 users, and they are located at each site. The user population is spread evenly across all five international locations.

Current System

The current systems consist of an IBM AS/400 transaction system built for the business. The AS/400 is only located in New York. All remote sites must access the AS/400 system over the WAN links. A few hundred people use a host-emulation package running over SNA Server to access this important database.

There is also a single domain with 25 Windows NT 4.0 servers running Service Pack 3, five of which are running MS Exchange 5.5 SP3. There are three Netware 4.x file servers in each location, used for a legacy client-analysis application. In each of the five locations, there are BDCs that run WINS and DHCP. The ISP, using an unknown version of BIND through the New York office's Internet connection, provides DNS. All Internet traffic goes through the New York routed connection to the Internet. All international locations connect to New York over 256 Kbps frame relay.

Internal client computers are running Microsoft Windows 95 with the client for Netware and the client for Microsoft Networks. All workstations run IPX/SPX and TCP/IP protocols.

continued

IT Management Sample Interviews

" . . . I am excited about the new strategic direction, and I support the new client applications. There will be significant infrastructure changes required, but I am confident that we can make the necessary changes without disrupting our current business . . . my biggest concern is client confidentiality—how can we improve security?"

CIO

"These new improvements are long overdue. Our network bandwidth has been severely saturated, especially between London and New York. I'm glad to see that our executive management team finally realizes how important these changes are to improving performance."

IT Director, retail sales division

"Three of the five WAN connections are saturated on a regular basis. If we are going to rely on a Web-based application, we will need to do something to improve the performance of the WAN connections."

Network Administrator, New York location

"It took us months to stabilize our SNA server. I support any network improvements as long as it does not undo the work on the SNA server."

AS/400 Administrator

Envisioned System

In order to conduct the day-to-day network operations objectives, the investment firm wants to create a design to accomplish the following:

Application Requirements:

- Provide network support for a mission-critical Web-based application that manages the investment firm's customers and their corresponding stock portfolios.

- Provide network support for a mission-critical Web-based application that allows customers to perform investment trading and other financial transactions over the Internet.

- Authenticate users using a directory-services infrastructure provided by Windows 2000.

- Administrate intranet resources by using a directory-services infrastructure provided by Windows 2000.

continued

- Provide support for mission-critical applications to be available 24/7.

- Provide intranet access to all shared resources without regard to location, including international locations.

Connectivity   The investment firm will require certain connectivity between offices. The design will also provide for the following connectivity:

- Provide for isolation of a firm's intranet from the Internet.

- Provide for Internet access through the headquarters in North America.

- Reserve access to management capabilities for the administrative staff at the firm.

- Provide simultaneous access to Web applications for thousands of customers and brokers through the Internet, using a variety of Web browsers and operating systems.

Please see the two BTI diagrams in Figures 13-8 and 13-9 as samples.

Figure 13-8
Overview of BTI
locations

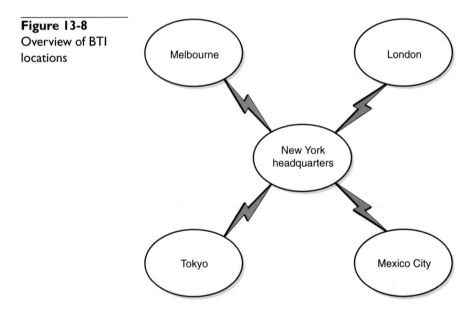

continued

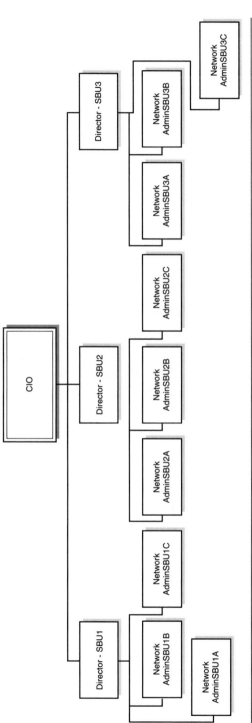

Figure 13-9 IT organizational structure of BTI

continued

Case Study Questions: BTI Analysis

1. What is the geographical scope of BTI?
   a. Regional
   b. National
   c. Branch offices
   d. International

2. Describe the most important business strategy for BTI during this current fiscal year.

3. What products does the BTI retail division sell?

4. Is the IT organization centralized or decentralized? Why?

5. Your fellow consultants recommend replacing the AS/400 system this year. Is this reasonable? Why or why not?

6. Which strategic relationship is BTI trying to improve? Explain the strategy.

7. Which of the following network infrastructure priorities is the most important to the BTI management? Why?
   a. The network servers must all have Microsoft Windows 2000 installed.
   b. The new network infrastructure must minimize the impact on end users.
   c. The network infrastructure must support the global enterprise.
   d. The network infrastructure must make it easier for investment advisors to support clients.

Suggested Solutions

(Note that your solutions may vary from the ones presented here.)

1. D. BTI has an international geographical scope.

2. The most important strategy is to improve the investment tools so the investment advisors can improve investment throughput and gain new customers.

3. Investment advice and portfolio-management services.

4. It is essentially decentralized because there are servers and network administrators in all locations.

5. It is not reasonable. The AS/400 is a legacy system that is not targeted for removal. The network infrastructure must support this system.

continued

6. They are trying to use technology to improve the portfolio managers' effectiveness with client contact. The strategic partnership targeted for improvement is with clients.

7. **D.** Based on the strategic intent of management, the infrastructure must improve client contact as the highest priority.

Chapter Review

To meet the Microsoft certification objectives, we discussed the business and technical requirements of the organization. These objectives require you to look at the big picture. Starting at the top, this means looking at the company's priorities and the business structure. Then you need to look at the structural elements of IT management and the key elements in the decision-making process. An understanding of these areas can help determine whether the design is appropriate for the business.

You need to consider the actual network technologies used on the network because the technical abilities of Windows 2000 will play a major role in implementing the design. Documenting and analyzing the technical environment will help you develop a Windows 2000 network-integration game plan.

You also need to review the users' work habits and requirements to ensure that the design you create supports their needs.

Finally, it is important to review the disaster recovery planning process. This will ensure that your network designs support and enhance the disaster recovery process.

Questions

1. You are a consultant for a firm specializing in the sales of Real Time Operating Systems (RTOS) in the United States and Canada. You have offices throughout the United States, including ones in Los Angeles, San Francisco, Seattle, Denver, Chicago, New York, and Miami. What is your company's geographic scope (choose one only)?

   a. International

   b. Regional

   c. Local

   d. National

2. You work for a bottled juice manufacturer that has a mainframe in a single location called headquarters. Every plant connects to this central location through 56 Kbps leased lines. All IS management is in the central location, along with all resources. What is your IT structure (choose all that apply)?
   a. IS administration is centralized, but resource management is decentralized.
   b. IS administration is centralized, and so is resource management.
   c. User management is centralized, but resource management is decentralized.
   d. User management is centralized and so is resource management.
   e. All users are centrally located.
   f. All users are not centrally located.

3. Which of the following will most reduce the saturation of a WAN connection (choose all that apply)?
   a. Put clients and servers on the same side of a WAN connection.
   b. Reduce the number of different routable protocols in use.
   c. Put clients and servers on the opposite side of WAN connections.
   d. Increase the number of routable protocols because NDIS and ODI support this.
   e. Use data compression between clients and servers over the WAN.
   f. Reduce the services that require traversing WAN circuits.

4. Fred is reviewing network performance logs over time. A particular WAN connection's utilization is hovering around 85 percent, latency has increased by 25 percent, and applications are timing out. What should Fred do?

5. True or False? When designing a network infrastructure, the only area that you should focus on as a designer is the technical requirement. Leave the business analysis to the MBAs and accountants.

Answers

1. **D.** While the company sells in Canada, it does not have locations outside of the United States. They have locations throughout the United States.

2. **B and D.** The IT organization is centralized. All IT administration and resources are centrally located.

3. **A, B, C, E, and F.** Each of these will reduce the saturation of the WAN connection. Increasing the number of protocols, as in answer D, will increase WAN traffic and saturate WAN circuits.

4. Because the technical analysis shows a problem over time and not just a peak situation, it is time for Fred to determine why this is happening. This kind of performance is not acceptable under most conditions.

5. **False.** Business requirements drive the technical requirements of network designs.

Key Skill Sets

- Analyzing the existing and planned business models.

  - Analyzing the existing and planned organizational structures. Considerations include the management model, company organization, vendor, partner, and customer relationships, and acquisitions plans.

  - Analyzing factors that influence company strategies.

  - Analyzing the structure of IT management.

  - Analyzing the company's existing and planned technical environment and goals.

- Analyzing the impact of infrastructure design on the existing and planned technical environment.

- Analyzing the network requirements for client computer access.

- Analyzing the existing disaster-recovery strategy for client computers, servers, and the network.

Key Terms

Business models
Business strategies
Centralized and decentralized organizations
Change-management process
Company processes
Funding models
Organizational structures
Outsourcing

Designing a Network Infrastructure Using TCP/IP

This chapter covers the following key mastery goals:

- Identify and briefly describe the core features and functionality of Windows 2000 TCP/IP networking services

- Understand the potential design issues related to public versus private IP addressing

- Describe the methods and strategies for optimizing the availability of IP routing capabilities

- Develop strategies for securing TCP/IP traffic and for optimizing the performance of IP data transmission

- Apply the comprehensive TCP/IP feature set to a Windows 2000 IP network design

Let's face it, like many companies, Microsoft revises and revises its products until it gets them right. If you've followed the history of Microsoft's network operating systems, you'll recall that it initially emphasized NetBEUI, when Windows NT Advanced Server 3.1 was released, to connect workstations in a workgroup (such as Windows for Workgroups 3.11). Next in line was NWLink IPX/SPX, which repositioned Windows NT 3.5*x* against Novell. It was in the Windows NT Server 4.0 era that the TCP/IP protocol suite arrived front and center. Not surprisingly, Microsoft created Windows 2000 to integrate with and enhance TCP/IP services. You can't even install Windows 2000 Server without the protocol, given its integration with TCP/IP. Services such as DHCP (see Chapter 15) and DNS (see Chapter 16) rely on TCP/IP to function. All of this means you must have a thorough understanding of TCP/IP in order to design Windows 2000 network services.

This chapter will focus on using TCP/IP in your design strategies, starting with an overview of the comprehensive feature set and ending with applied design practice. As in so many things, practice makes perfect, and failure to practice invites failure! So, get ready to put your knowledge to the test when you design the Fromanywhere.com IP network. Don't worry about Catywhompus Construction—we'll update you on this venerable firm at the end of the chapter.

 EXAM TIP The topics discussed in this chapter largely (but not completely) address the topics that were on the TCP/IP certification exam in the Windows NT 4 MCSE era. This is Microsoft's way of slipping TCP/IP into the Windows 2000 MCSE track without creating a dedicated TCP/IP exam.

Introduction to Case Study 14: Fromanywhere.com, Inc. Creating a Network Design for an Internet Startup

In your previous network-services designs, you analyzed an existing network and created a new design based on revised business and technical requirements. Your next assignment is to tackle a new scenario. An Internet start-up company has hired you to design their network-services infrastructure. The business model is a big idea based on providing a small solution. Fromanywhere.com, Inc., wants to take many of the small office activities typically performed by users on a LAN or stand-alone PC, and put them up on a Web site that provides a unified message and storage solution for voice, fax, e-mail, and files. In other words, Fromanywhere.com provides an integrated virtual-office solution for a small office or home office.

Although no one has actually started work on the implementation yet, the funds are available to put users to work in three locations: Denver, San Francisco, and Seattle. In addition, since many of the developers are located in remote locations, provision for VPN access over the Internet must be part of the picture.

All development will need to be tested on intranet servers. Internet operations will be outsourced. The outsourced Internet locations will accommodate the final version of e-commerce applications. Where do you start? Your first assignment, when you

continued

revisit this case at the end of this chapter, is to determine the TCP/IP functionality, availability, performance, and security required by the startup. Then you will endeavor to determine and choose the foundational elements required for the TCP/IP solution. At the end of this chapter, you will consider this case's envisioned solution and develop your own TCP/IP subnet design recommendations for the Fromanywhere.com startup management team.

TCP/IP Background

The Transmission Control Protocol/Internet Protocol (TCP/IP) suite has emerged as the standard for network communications. It is an industry-standard suite of protocols designed for large networks spanning wide area network (WAN) links that was developed in 1969 by the U.S. Department of Defense Advanced Research Projects Agency (DARPA) as the result of a resource-sharing experiment called ARPANET (Advanced Research Projects Agency Network). The original and continuing purpose of TCP/IP was to provide high-speed communication network links. Since 1969, ARPANET has grown into the worldwide WAN known as the Internet.

 NOTE   Many long-time technology and political observers consider TCP/IP, ARPANET, and then the Internet to be the greatest peace-time application of military build-up in the United States from the 1960s through the Reagan administration. That is, the military industrial complex delivered a peace dividend.

Revisiting the history we referred to earlier, we more than remember the early days of Windows NT 3.1 when the default network protocol used for network operating system (NOS) installation was NetBIOS Extended User Interface protocol (NetBEUI). This made it very difficult to scale the network without substituting another protocol, because NetBEUI was not routable. Now TCP/IP is the default for Windows 2000, and it intertwines with the network functionality of the NOS. Because organizations are facing an increased need for Internet connectivity, and connectivity between various platforms is sometimes a crucial functional requirement, TCP/IP is the standard that connects these dissimilar systems. TCP/IP is routable and scalable, it connects dissimilar systems, and it was designed for the Internet. Developers also have the ability to write programs with Windows 2000 using the Windows Sockets for cross-platform client-server application development. Because TCP/IP operates on a wide variety of physical networks, it is often the only protocol meeting the scalability requirements of organizations.

In this chapter, we present the role of TCP/IP in networking infrastructures used in organizations of various sizes including the following three:

- Small office/home office (SOHO)

- Small business

- Medium-sized business

At the end of the chapter, you will have an opportunity to practice designing your own TCP/IP solutions.

TCP/IP Protocol Suite

Microsoft TCP/IP on Windows 2000 enables enterprise networking and connectivity as the foundation of your network infrastructure design. It has the following features:

- TCP/IP is the standard protocol for gaining access to the Internet. The Internet has vast resources built with thousands of networks worldwide, connecting companies, research facilities, universities, libraries, and government agencies.

- It is the most complete and accepted protocol available. Nearly all network NOSs offer TCP/IP support, and most large, routed networks rely on TCP/IP for much of their network traffic.

- It is a technology built for connecting dissimilar systems. Many standard connectivity utilities are available for accessing and transferring data between dissimilar systems, including File Transfer Protocol (FTP) and Telnet.

- It was built as a robust, scalable, cross-platform client/server framework. Microsoft Windows 2000 TCP/IP offers the Windows Sockets interface, an ideal interface for developing client/server applications that can run on Windows Sockets–compliant vendor stacks.

TCP/IP Standards

The standards for TCP/IP are published in a series of documents, each of which is called a Request for Comments (RFC). RFCs describe the internal workings of the Internet. TCP/IP standards are developed by consensus and are always published as RFCs, although not all RFCs specify standards. The RFCs are reviewed by a technical expert, a task force, or the RFC editor, and are then assigned a status that specifies whether a document is being considered as a standard.

Hang in there with us—the discussion of the standards process provides the context for how an initiative such as the TCP/IP protocol becomes a standard.

There are five status assignments for RFCs, as described in Table 14-1.

If a document is under standards consideration, it goes through stages of development, testing, and acceptance known as the Internet Standards Process. These stages have formal labels called maturity levels. Table 14-2 lists the three maturity levels for Internet standards.

Table 14-1 The Five RFC Status Assignments

Status	Description
Required	*Must be implemented* on all TCP/IP-based hosts and gateways.
Recommended	Encourage that all TCP/IP-based hosts and gateways implement the RFC specifications. Recommended RFCs *are usually implemented.*
Elective	Implementation is optional. Its application *has been agreed to* but is not a requirement.
Limited Use	*Not intended for general use.*
Not recommended	*Not recommended for implementation.*

Table 14-2 The Three Internet Standard Maturity Levels

Maturity Level	Description
Internet Standard	The Internet Standard specification (which might simply be referred to as a standard) has a high degree of technical maturity and is characterized by a generally held belief that the specified protocol or service provides significant benefit to the Internet community.
Draft Standard	A Draft Standard must be well understood and known to be quite stable, both in its semantics and as a basis for developing an implementation.
Proposed Standard	A Proposed Standard specification is generally stable, has resolved known design choices, is believed to be well understood, has received significant community review, and appears to enjoy enough community interest to be considered valuable.

When a document is published, it is assigned an RFC number. The original RFC is never updated, so if changes are required, a new RFC is published with a new number. It is important to verify that you have the most recent RFC on a particular topic.

The bottom line is that the Internet Engineering Task Force (IETF) continues to revise and improve the TCP/IP suite of protocols. Microsoft must, in turn, continuously update the TCP/IP implementation to comply with the latest standards. Understand that the standards process is political, much like passing legislation in Congress. Big special interests, such as industry-leading vendors, influence that ultimate appearance of the standard. The good news is that the Windows 2000 MCSE track, in the upper-level designing exams that this book is dedicated to, solidly places politics on your professional radar screen!

TCP/IP Protocol Architecture

TCP/IP protocols map to a four-layer conceptual model known as the *DARPA model*, named after the U.S. government agency that initially developed TCP/IP. The four layers of the DARPA model are Network Interface, Internet, Transport, and Application. Each layer in the DARPA model corresponds to one or more layers of the seven-layer Open Systems Interconnection (OSI) model.

The TCP/IP model and protocol suite are shown in Figure 14-1 for easy reference.

Network Interface Layer

The *Network Interface layer* (also called the *Network Access layer*) is responsible for placing TCP/IP packets on the network medium and receiving TCP/IP packets off the network medium. TCP/IP is generally independent of the network access method, frame format, and medium. As a result, TCP/IP can be used to connect differing network types. We have seen TCP/IP used on many LAN technologies, such as Ethernet and token ring, and WAN technologies, such as X.25 and frame relay.

The Network Interface layer maps to the Data Link and Physical layers of the OSI model. Note that the Internet layer does not take advantage of sequencing and acknowledgment services that might be present in the Data Link layer. Reliable communications through session establishment and the sequencing and acknowledgment of packets is the responsibility of the Transport layer.

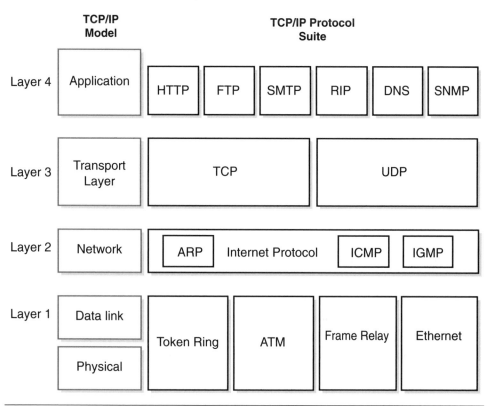

Figure 14-1   TCP/IP protocol architecture

Internet Layer

The *Internet layer* is responsible for addressing, packaging, and routing functions. The core protocols of the Internet layer are IP, ARP, ICMP, and IGMP.

- The Internet Protocol (IP) is a routable protocol responsible for IP addressing, routing, and the fragmentation and reassembly of packets.

- The Address Resolution Protocol (ARP) is responsible for the resolution of the Internet layer addresses to the Network Interface layer addresses, such as hardware addresses.

- The Internet Control Message Protocol (ICMP) is responsible for providing diagnostic functions and reporting errors due to the unsuccessful delivery of IP packets.

- The Internet Group Management Protocol (IGMP) is responsible for the management of IP multicast groups.

The Internet layer is analogous to the Network layer of the OSI model.

Transport Layer

The *Transport layer* (also known as the *Host-to-Host Transport layer*) is responsible for providing the Application layer with session and datagram communication services. The core protocols of the Transport layer are TCP and UDP.

- The Transmission Control Protocol (TCP) provides a connection-oriented, reliable communications service. TCP is responsible for the establishment of a TCP connection, the sequencing and acknowledgment of packets sent, and the recovery of packets lost during transmission.

- The User Datagram Protocol (UDP) provides a one-to-one or one-to-many, connectionless, unreliable communications service. UDP is used when the amount of data to be transferred is small (such as the data that would fit into a single packet), when the overhead of establishing a TCP connection is not desired, or when the applications or upper-layer protocols provide reliable delivery.

The Transport layer encompasses the responsibilities of the OSI Transport layer and some of the responsibilities of the OSI Session layer.

Application Layer

The *Application layer* provides applications with the ability to access the services of the other layers and defines the protocols that applications use to exchange data. The most widely known Application layer protocols are those used for the exchange of user information:

- The Hypertext Transfer Protocol (HTTP) is used to transfer files that make up the Web pages of the World Wide Web.

- The File Transfer Protocol (FTP) is used for interactive file transfer.

- The Simple Mail Transfer Protocol (SMTP) is used for the transfer of mail messages and attachments.

- Telnet, a terminal emulation protocol, is used for logging on remotely to network hosts.

Additionally, the following Application layer protocols help facilitate the use and management of TCP/IP networks:

- The Domain Name System (DNS) is used to resolve a host name to an IP address.

- The Routing Information Protocol (RIP) is a routing protocol that routers use to exchange routing information on an IP routed network.

- The Simple Network Management Protocol (SNMP) is used between a network-management console and network devices (routers, bridges, switches, and hubs) to collect and exchange network-management information.

Another example of an Application layer interface for TCP/IP applications is Net-BIOS. NetBIOS is an industry-standard interface for accessing protocol services, such as sessions, name resolution, and datagrams.

 TIP You should assume that the Physical and Data link layers' infrastructure components are already in place for your design considerations in this chapter.

Key TCP/IP Design Considerations

Windows 2000 TCP/IP has many standard features and services that you should be aware of when developing your infrastructure design.

Windows 2000 TCP/IP Features

Windows 2000 TCP/IP supports the following standard features:

- Ability to bind to multiple network adapters with different media types
- Logical and physical multi-homing
- Internal IP routing capability
- IGMP Version 2 (support for IP multicasting)
- Duplicate IP address detection
- ICMP router discovery
- Multiple configurable default gateways

- Dead gateway detection for TCP traffic

- Automatic Path Maximum Transmission Unit (PMTU) discovery for TCP connections

- IP Security (IPSec) allows enhanced data and authentication encryption

- Quality of Service (QoS) for time-sensitive IP traffic streams, such as streaming media; TCP/IP supports bandwidth reservation using QoS mechanisms

- TCP/IP over ATM services

- Virtual private networks (VPNs)

- Automatic Private IP Addressing (APIPA) automates address configuration for hosts on a single-subnet network allocated from 169.254.0.0/16, which is reserved by the Internet Assigned Numbers Authority (IANA)

In addition, Windows 2000 TCP/IP has the following new performance enhancements:

- Increased default window sizes

- TCP Scalable Window sizes including Large TCP Windows

- Selective Acknowledgments (SACK)

- TCP Fast Retransmit

- Round Trip Time (RTT) and Retransmission Timeout (RTO) calculation improvements

- TCP/IP supports packet-level filtering

- NetBIOS over TCP/IP (NetBT) can be disabled for computers that use only DNS name registration and resolution; these computers can only browse resources on computers that have NetBT disabled and use Client for Microsoft Networks, and Print Sharing for Microsoft Networks components.

 NOTE Typically, NetBT is only disabled on computers such as edge proxy servers or hosts in a firewall environment where NetBT is not desired.

Windows 2000 TCP/IP Services

Windows 2000 provides the following services:

- Dynamic Host Configuration Protocol (DHCP) client and server.

- Windows Internet Name Service (WINS), a network basic input/output system (NetBIOS) name client and server.

- Domain Name System (DNS) client and server.

- Dial-up (Point-to-Point Protocol/Serial Lines) support.

- Point-to-Point Tunneling Protocol (PPTP) and Layer Two Tunneling Protocol (L2TP) used for VPNs.

- TCP/IP network printing (Lpr/Lpd).

- Simple Network Management Protocol (SNMP) agent.

- NetBIOS interface.

- Windows Sockets Version 2 (Winsock2) interface.

- Microsoft networking browsing support across IP routers.

- High-performance Microsoft Internet Information Services (IIS).

- Basic TCP/IP connectivity tools, including Finger, FTP, Rcp, Rexec, Rsh, Telnet, and Tftp.

- Client and server software for simple network protocols, including Character Generator, Daytime, Discard, Echo, and Quote of the Day.

- TCP/IP management and diagnostic tools, including Arp, Hostname, Ipconfig, Lpq, Nbtstat, Netstat, Ping, Route, Nslookup, Tracert, and Pathping; Pathping displays Round Trip Time calculation improvements.

Designing a Functional TCP/IP Solution

When we begin a project that includes designing a TCP/IP solution, we analyze the following:

- How many hosts will require IP connectivity, including multi-homed devices?

- What are the network architectures to consider from OSI layers one and two?

- What is the requirement for public and/or private IP addressing?

- How many WAN connections are required?

- What is the number of physical subnets and routers?

Since Windows 2000 uses TCP/IP for numerous network functions, including authentication and file sharing, getting the answers to these questions is essential to the TCP/IP solution design. Your analysis of the organization's technical requirements should aid in answering most, if not all, of these questions. And as Paul Harvey likes to say on his daily syndicated radio program, "now you know the rest of the story," about why Microsoft emphasizes the business and technical needs analysis for the Windows 2000 MCSE.

When we look at the functional design aspects of a TCP/IP solution, we focus on the basics of IP addressing. You as the designer must know what the Internet accessibility needs are, how many routers are needed, and whether public address access is part of the requirements. Ultimately, you decide on the number of subnets required for each physical location and the number of public and private IP addresses required for the design. You also determine the appropriate IP configuration methodology and must be able to explain the benefits of each method.

IP Addressing Review

To be able to communicate on a network, each host must have a unique IP address, and the size and complexity of a network determines the addressing scheme used for the network. The standard for IP addressing uses a 32-bit address and a 32-bit mask. These two addresses together determine what portion of the address is the host and which is the network. The first part of the address, which is consecutive ones (1's) in the subnet mask, is the network address, and the consecutive zeros (0's) in the subnet mask determine the host portion of the IP address. This is the IP version 4 (IPv4) standard.

Addressing Structures

Depending on the routing protocols used in the infrastructure, you can specify IP addresses using classful IP addressing, variable-length subnet masks (VLSM), and Classless Inter-Domain Routing (CIDR).

Classful IP Addressing   The Internet community originally defined five address classes to accommodate networks of varying sizes. Microsoft TCP/IP supports class A, B, and C addresses assigned to hosts. The class of address defines which bits are used for the network ID and which bits are used for the host ID. It also defines the possible number of networks and the number of hosts per network. This method of determining IP address classes is referred to as the "first octet rule." In addition to defining the classes, it provides an efficient way for layer 3 devices to start interpreting the address. Any address beginning with a zero can be forwarded only to an interface that connects directly or indirectly to a class A network.

- **Class A** addresses are assigned to networks with a very large number of hosts. The high-order bit in a class A address is always set to zero. The next 7 bits complete the network ID. The remaining 24 bits represent the host ID. This allows for 126 networks and 16,777,214 hosts per network.

- **Class B** addresses are assigned from medium-sized to large-sized networks. The 2 high-order bits in a class B address are set to binary 10. The next 14 bits complete the network ID. The remaining 16 bits (last two octets) represent the host ID. This allows for 16,384 networks and 65,534 hosts per network. Table 14-3 illustrates the structure of class B addresses.

- **Class C** addresses are used for small networks and are ideal for subnets. The three high-order bits in a class C address are set to binary 110. The next 21 bits complete the network ID. The remaining 8 bits represent the host ID. This allows for 2,097,152 networks and 254 hosts per network.

- **Class D** addresses are reserved for IP multicast addresses. The four high-order bits in a class D address are always set to binary 1110. The remaining bits are for the address that interested hosts recognize. Microsoft supports class D addresses for applications to multicast data to multicast-capable hosts on a network.

- **Class E** is an experimental address reserved for future use. The five high-order bits in a class E address are set to 11110.

Table 14-3 lists the classes A, B, and C that can be used for class-based network and host IP addresses.

Variable-Length Subnetting   Subnets of different sizes can exist within a class-based network ID. This is suited to real-world environments, where networks of an organization contain different numbers of hosts, and different-sized subnets are needed to minimize the wasting of IP addresses. The creation and deployment of various-sized subnets of a network ID is known as variable-length subnetting and uses variable-length subnet masks (VLSM).

Table 14-3   Primary Class-Based Addresses

Class	Value of the First Octet	Default Mask	Available Networks	Hosts per Network	Host Range
A	1–126	255.0.0.0	126	16,777,214	x.0.0.1-x.255.255.254
B	128–191	255.255.0.0	16,384	65,534	x.x.0.1-x.x.255.254
C	192–223	255.255.255.0	2,097,152	254	x.x.x.1-x.x.x.254

PART III

Variable-length subnetting is a technique of allocating subnetted network IDs that use subnet masks of different sizes. However, all subnetted network IDs are unique and can be distinguished from each other by their corresponding subnet mask.

The mechanics of variable-length subnetting are essentially those of performing subnetting on a default class-based network ID. When subnetting, the network ID bits are fixed and a certain number of host bits are chosen to express subnets.

Classless Inter-Domain Routing (CIDR)   CIDR translates all IP address and subnet masks to binary notation. CIDR divides an IP address into a set of 32 values, in place of the four class-based decimal values. This division allows for more variations in network size and optimizes the allocation of IP addresses. CIDR does not define a default subnet mask based on the IP address. Instead, each host uses a custom subnet mask, and each router is sent the IP address as part of the packet. The router then uses the subnet mask from its routing table to determine the network ID of the destination. This method allows for much greater flexibility in the use of IP addressing.

 TIP   Both VLSM and CIDR require routers that support more advanced routing protocols, such as RIP version 2 and open shortest path first (OSPF). In order to support CIDR and VLSM, routers must be able to exchange routing information in the form of network ID and network mask pairs. RIP for IP version 2 and OSPF are two Windows 2000 routing protocols that support CIDR. RIP for IP version 1 does not support CIDR or VLSM.

Subnet Masks

IP addresses are split into two portions to enable network communications on the local subnet and over routers. Binary subnet masks are composed of contiguous ones (1's) followed by contiguous zeros (0's). The contiguous ones (1's) determine the network ID and the contiguous zeros (0's) determine the host component. In class-based addressing, the subnets are always high-order maximum or low-order minimum values. When using VLSM, you cannot decrease the number of bits for the network ID below the class's subnet mask. For instance, if you are using VLSM with a class B block, the lowest subnet mask value would be 16 bits.

Addressing Guidelines

Not all possible IP addresses can be assigned to host computers. You must consider the following guidelines when you assign an IP address using classes or CIDR:

- The network ID must be unique to the IP network. If you plan on having a direct routed connection to the public Internet, the network ID must be unique to the Internet. If you do not plan to connect to the public Internet, the local network ID must be unique to your private network.

- The decimal value in the first octet of the network ID cannot be 127 (01111111 binary). This is a special address reserved for internal testing, acting as a local loop back to ensure TCP/IP is functioning on the local machine.

- All bits within the network ID cannot be set to 1. All ones (1's) in the network ID are reserved for use as an IP broadcast address (255.255.255.255).

- All bits within the network ID cannot be set to 0. All zeros (0's) in the network ID are used to denote a specific host on the local network and are not routed.

- The binary number for the host ID cannot be all ones (1's), as this is used as the limited broadcast address.

- The host ID cannot be all zeros (0's), as this address denotes the network ID.

- The host ID must be unique to the local network ID.

These guidelines will influence your TCP/IP design whether you choose to use classful IP addressing, CIDR, or classes with variable-length subnet masks (VLSM).

Private Network IP Addressing

When you design your IP network, you will need to determine whether you are going to use public IP addresses for the majority of network hosts or a private IP addressing strategy.

EXAM TIP   Be sure to brand your brain with the fact that both the certification exams and the real world of Windows 2000 demand you have mastery of private and public IP network addressing concepts. It's fundamental in understanding Microsoft products, such as Internet Security and Acceleration (ISA) Server 2000. It's also critical as you look at case studies and the design diagrams on the designing exams in the Windows 2000 MCSE track.

Host interfaces connected directly to the Internet will require public IP addresses, whereas interfaces not connected can use private IP addressing. Remember, if you require access to the Internet, you need at least one public IP address. Table 14-4 shows a comparison of public and private addressing schemes.

Public Addressing Schemes

When hosts connect directly to the Internet, they require a globally unique IP address in order to communicate properly on the network. You can apply for public IP addresses from an Internet service provider or Internet registry. A bound network needs a minimum of one public IP address to access the Internet. The use of a firewall (in the generic sense) is used to improve security when using this scheme. The actual firewall implementation is based on the organization's security requirements and may come in the form of a screened subnet, packet-filtering router, or a packet-inspection firewall.

In most situations, organizations using public addressing schemes either waste IP addresses or find that the original addressing scheme does not anticipate their device growth. I have seen, more than once, thousands of costly IP addresses wasted by organizations acquiring unneeded IP addresses. On the other hand, after you assign all public addresses, new IP device interfaces cannot be added without acquiring additional IP addresses.

Table 14-4 Public vs. Private Addressing Schemes

Scheme	Public	Private
Pros	All hosts can be accessible from the Internet. Addresses can be owned.	Addresses don't need to be purchased. Intrinsically more secure. Scalable.
Cons	Costly to lease. Potentially restricted growth. Security is a greater concern.	Requires filtering, proxy, or network translation device for Internet access.
Use	Large number of hosts require direct access to the Internet. Can be used when there are enough public addresses available.	Few hosts require direct interface to the Internet. Used when enough registered public addresses are not available.

Use public addressing schemes when your organization has either of the following:

- Enough public addresses for host assignment, including room for projected growth
- A large number of host interfaces that require direct Internet access

Private Addressing Schemes

Each IP node on a network connected to the Internet requires an IP address that is globally unique to the Internet. As the Internet grew, organizations connecting to the Internet required a public address for each node on their intranets. This requirement placed a huge demand on the pool of available public addresses.

When analyzing the addressing needs of organizations, the designers of the Internet noted that for many organizations, most of the hosts on the organization's intranet did not require direct connectivity to Internet hosts. The result is that most organizations only required a small number of public addresses for those nodes (such as proxies, routers, firewalls, and translators) that were directly connected to the Internet.

For the hosts within the organization that do not require direct access to the Internet, IP addresses that do not duplicate already assigned public addresses are required. To solve this addressing problem, the Internet designers reserved a portion of the IP address space and named this space the *private address space*. An IP address in the private address space is never assigned as a public address and is not Internet "routable." IP addresses within the private address space are known as *private addresses*. Because the public and private address spaces do not overlap, private addresses never duplicate public addresses.

The private address space specified in RFC 1918 is defined by the following three address blocks:

- **The 10.0.0.0/8 private network** is a class A network ID that allows the following range of valid IP addresses: 10.0.0.1 to 10.255.255.254. The 10.0.0.0/8 private network has 24 host bits that can be used for any subnet scheme within the private organization.

- **The 172.16.0.0/12 private network** can be interpreted either as a block of 16 class B network IDs or as a 20-bit assignable address space (20 host bits) that can be used for any subnetting scheme within the private organization. The 172.16.0.0/12 private network allows the following range of valid IP addresses: 172.16.0.1 to 172.31.255.254.

- **The 192.168.0.0/16 private network** can be interpreted either as a block of 256 class C network IDs or as a 16-bit assignable address space (16 host bits) that can be used for any subnetting scheme within the private organization. The 192.168.0.0/16 private network allows the following range of valid IP addresses: 192.168.0.1 to 192.168.255.254. More trivia. In both BackOffice 2000 and Small Business Server 2000, the default private network addressing is 192.x.x.x.

In addition to the addresses in RFC 1918, the Internet Assigned Numbers Authority (IANA) reserved class B network 169.254.0.0/16 for private addressing.

Because the IP addresses in the private address space will never be assigned by InterNIC as public addresses, routes will never exist in the Internet routers for private addresses. It's also a way for you to be an IP-address conservationist and help save the world's limited supply of IP addresses! Therefore, Internet traffic from a host that has a private address must either send its requests to an Application layer gateway that has a valid public address or have its private address translated into a valid public address by a network address translator before it is sent on the Internet.

Use a private addressing scheme if the organization has

- Insufficient public addresses for all private network hosts
- Few hosts that require direct Internet access

Illegal Addresses

If you have a private intranet with no intention of connecting to the Internet, you can choose any addresses you want. However, if your organization later decides to connect to the Internet, its address scheme might include addresses already assigned by InterNIC to other organizations. These addresses would be ineffective addresses for the public Internet. Connectivity from illegal addresses to Internet locations would then become an issue, because these addresses would not be able to communicate over the routed public network.

For example, suppose your organization chooses an address block already assigned to another entity's use for your intranet address space. The public address routes exist on the Internet routers to route all packets destined to another entity's routers. As long as your organization does not connect to the Internet, there is no problem because the two address spaces are on separate IP networks. If your organization then decided to

continued

connect directly to the Internet and continued to use that public block as its address space, then any Internet response traffic to locations on the public network would be routed to the other entity's routers, not to the routers of your organization. You would then need to redesign your IP-addressing solution to eliminate the illegal addresses.

Subnet Requirements

When we design a network subnet, we have four questions that must be addressed:

- What is the host population on each subnet, and what are the logical host limits of each subnet?
- How many logical subnets can exist for a given subnet mask?
- How many subnets are currently populated with hosts on the network?
- What are the limitations on growth for a given subnet?

Your network design must optimize the number of subnets and hosts per subnet. A quality subnet mask does not hamper expected growth in either subnets or hosts. Adjust your subnet selection to provide for expected network growth. You will balance the number of subnets and hosts per subnet based on setting limits in the design. This is one of the key elements in designing the TCP/IP routed network solution.

Limits on the Number of Hosts per Subnet

Assess the following when setting the host limit per subnet:

- **Future growth** Assess the number of hosts supported by the subnet and determine if it will provide for current performance needs and future growth expectations.
- **Router performance** Evaluate the number of hosts supported by the routers. You do this by dividing the total number of hosts on any network by the number of subnets supported by the routers. If routers limit the number of hosts per subnet, you will have to increase the number of subnets available for the anticipated total network hosts.
- **Network design specifications** Base the design on required performance goals.

You will need to thoroughly analyze router configuration, costs, data flows, bandwidth utilization, and user expectations to meet performance goals. This will require testing production applications for the number of hosts on each subnet to determine if the design will, in reality, meet the performance goals.

Limits on the Number of Subnets

Assess the following when setting the limits on the number of subnets with the subnet mask:

- **Future growth**   Make sure the network growth will be supported by the number of segments provided by the subnet and leave excess room for unexpected subnets.

- **Segment load**   Note the load on each segment and evaluate the number of hosts supported by the router. Ensure that the host load does not exceed the router's capacity.

- **Segment count**   You must include a subnet for WAN connections, and each remote connection requires a subnet.

IP Configuration Approaches

There are effectively four approaches available for configuring a host IP address in Windows 2000. IP addressing and settings can be processed using manual assignment, APIPA automatic assignment, DHCP dynamic assignment, and DHCP manual assignment. The four methods, when applied separately, have a significant impact on TCP/IP functionality and flexibility within the infrastructure. In our experience, all four can have a role to play in your network designs and will influence IP configuration management going forward.

Manual Assignment

All networks have hosts that require manual configuration of IP addresses. For instance, DHCP servers and IP routers require the manual configuration of a network interface of the 32-bit address, subnet mask, default gateway, and so on. Traditionally, servers have fixed IP addresses as well. For instance, name-resolution servers, such as DNS and WINS, use fixed IP addresses.

Automatic Private IP Addressing (APIPA)

The DHCP client has the ability to obtain core TCP/IP configuration settings, along with options like the WINS server IP address, automatically. This ability is expanded in Windows 2000.

A new feature in Windows 2000 is the ability for the DHCP client to obtain an IP address from the IANA reserved network 169.254.0.0/16 if a DHCP service provider is not available on the subnet. The DHCP client will detect a duplicate address to ensure that the address chosen is not already in use. If the address is in use, the client will try another address up to ten times to find one. Once the client finds an available IP address, the client will automatically configure the DHCP interface with this IP address and subnet mask. APIPA does not provide for functionality over a routed network because it will not provide a default gateway for the client. Every five minutes thereafter, the client will attempt to locate a DHCP server on the network and configure the interface with the DHCP settings from the appropriate server, thereby replacing the IANA settings.

DHCP Dynamic Configuration

DHCP is a safe and reliable, centralized and automated configuration method that minimizes configuration errors caused by typographical errors. The network administrator can centrally define global and subnet-level configurations. This method is an excellent choice for DHCP-supported clients and is especially a good choice for remote-access clients and clients that need dynamic configurations due to mobility requirements. Most routers can forward DHCP client requests, which make it possible to scale a network without a DHCP server on every subnet.

DHCP Manual Configuration

Windows 2000 DHCP has the ability to reserve IP address and option settings by Media Access Control (MAC) address. These reservations can provide a solution for tailored option settings for specific nodes. Use this manual method primarily for clients or servers that require fixed IP addresses for applications or services.

NOTE   See Chapter 15 for more details on DHCP.

TCP/IP Design for Improving Availability

You can improve the availability in your network design with redundant or fault-tolerant links between network segments within and between sites. You must use multiple links to increase the potential availability where such improvements are required. Figure 14-2 shows an example of a multipath network—note that Node A can communicate with Node B over two separate paths. Each of the links can also have backup links as well. When selecting multiple links, look to key client-to-server and server-to-server relationships, and create redundant links appropriate to the nature of the communications. Multiple paths will improve the availability of network resources.

In a single-path routing infrastructure, only a single path exists between any two segments in the network. While this may simplify the routing tables and the packet-flow paths, single-path routed networks are not fault-tolerant. It is possible to sense a fault with a dynamic router, but the networks across the failure are unreachable during the fault. A downed link must be restored before packets can be delivered successfully across the downed link or router.

Redundant-path networks are fault-tolerant when dynamic routing is used, and some routing protocols, such as OSPF, can balance the load of network traffic across multiple paths with the same metric value. Redundant-path networks, however, can be more complex to configure and can have a higher probability of resulting in unwanted routing loops. You can also configure cost metrics for different routes to control traffic flow and to avoid high cost routes until they are needed.

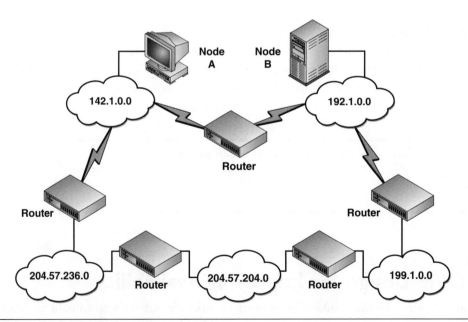

Figure 14-2   Redundant links and paths

TCP/IP Design for Improving Performance

Keeping your performance improvement mindset in place, consider this. When designing TCP/IP solutions, your goal is to reduce the length of time required to transmit an IP packet. You can design for performance by wisely selecting a partition or subnet scheme, analyzing traffic flows, and using appropriate tuning and optimizing techniques, and ensuring priority transmissions using Quality of Service (QoS) mechanisms. The underlying physical network topology selected will set the performance standard of your network design, so select the topology in line with the organization's objectives and growth projections.

Optimizing IP Subnetting

You can use customized subnet masks to implement IP subnetting. In most situations, typical IP class subnets are either too large or too small. Custom subnetting is defined either as subnetting, Classless Interdomain Routing (CIDR), or variable-length subnet masks (VLSM).

With custom IP subnetting, you can go beyond the limitations of default classful subnet masks and use your IP address range to match the organization's performance requirement. One danger is that if the address scheme is too small, many address ranges can exist, and achieving your network design may require complicated routing tables. Therefore, try to minimize the number of routers in the design to improve performance between subnets, but also ensure that there are enough subnets and addresses to support future growth.

Remember, make sure you have included a subnet for each segment of your network bordered by a router, including WAN connections bordered by routers. Figure 14-3 shows a sample network configuration and the segments requiring unique network IDs. Also, keep in mind that VPN connections require public IP addresses in order to create a tunnel into the private network.

By customizing the subnet mask length, you can reduce the number of bits used for the actual host ID. In some cases, you can use default subnet masks for standard-size class A, B, and C networks. Default subnet masks are dotted decimal values that separate the network ID from the host ID of an IP address. For example, if you have a network segment and are using the class A address range starting at 10.0.0.0, the default subnet mask that you would use is 255.0.0.0. Typically, default values for subnet masks are acceptable for networks with no special requirements, where each IP network segment corresponds to a single physical network.

To prevent addressing and routing problems, make sure all TCP/IP computers on any network segment use the same subnet mask. Therefore, in a network with a single subnet mask, all subnetworks will have the same maximum size for host addresses.

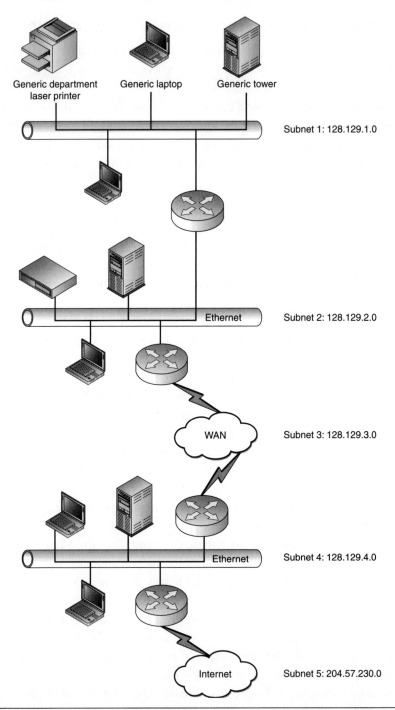

Figure 14-3 Example of a network design requiring two network IDs for WAN connections

Supernetting can also be used in the design as a technique that can allow the combination of multiple IP addresses into a single range of addresses by using the bits belonging to the network address as host bits. This is realized, for example, by altering the default class C subnet mask such that some of the bits that relate to the network address are set to zeros (0's) instead of ones (1's). The CIDR specification, or route aggregation for routers, supports supernetting. To use supernetting in your design, you must use routers that support supernetting. Routers that support RIP 2.0 or OSPF will support supernetting.

Optimizing Traffic on an IP Network

It is important to make sure traffic is optimized on the IP network. You must first analyze the traffic and then identify ways to optimize the traffic in your design.

Traffic Analysis

To understand where configuration and tuning changes will bring performance gains, you must perform traffic analysis. Some network traffic is very simple datagram traffic that requires no response, security, or verification. Other traffic though can be very complex and sensitive to delays in communication. For instance, an example of communication that is sensitive to delays is logon validation, or the setup of a PPTP tunnel that requires acknowledgment before communication can continue. This type of traffic requires somewhat synchronous bandwidth. An example of traffic that is not as sensitive to delays is a Web-based application, where large amounts of data are flowing in one direction and acknowledgments are flowing in the other direction. The bandwidth required in the second case is asynchronous.

TCP/IP Performance

TCP/IP in Windows 2000 can adapt to most network conditions, and Windows 2000 TCP/IP will tune itself dynamically to provide the best throughput and reliability possible. Yet certain design choices can ultimately affect performance, especially in a WAN environment, when links span long distances and bandwidth is precious.

Windows 2000's TCP/IP design provides optimum performance over varying link conditions. Actual throughput for a link depends on a number of variables though, and the most important factors are

- Link speed (bits/second that can be transmitted)
- Propagation delay
- TCP/IP Receive Window Size (amount of unacknowledged data that might be outstanding on a TCP connection)

- Link reliability

- Network and intermediate device congestion

Here are some additional throughput considerations:

- The capacity of a communications channel, also known as a *pipe*, is known as the bandwidth-delay product, and it is the bandwidth (the bit rate) multiplied by round-trip time. If the link has a low number of bit-level errors, the window size for best performance should be greater than or equal to the bandwidth-delay product so that the sender can fill the pipe. Without window scaling, 65,535 is the largest window size that can be specified, due to the 16-bit Window field in the TCP header. Window scaling can be used for window sizes up to 1GB.

- Throughput can never exceed the window size divided by round-trip time.

- If the link has a large number of bit-level errors or is badly congested, using a larger window size might not improve throughput.

- Propagation delay is dependent upon the speed of transmission and latencies in transmission equipment and intermediate systems.

- Transmission delay depends on the speed of the media and the nature of the media-access control scheme, such as CSMA/CD.

- For a particular path, propagation delay is fixed, but transmission delay depends upon the packet size and congestion.

- At low speeds, transmission delay is the limiting factor. At high speeds, propagation delay might become the limiting factor.

If the network you are designing has slow WAN links, the design may require the appropriate placement of authentication and key application servers on both sides of the links to achieve acceptable performance.

Using QoS Mechanisms

This next discussion concerns one of the best, yet least known and used, features in Windows 2000. In certain network communications, the standard network communications, using the first-come, first-served basis for communication does not work. For instance, video conferencing or real-time data applications require immediate response and do not perform well without dedicated bandwidth. QoS within Windows 2000 was created to address this very issue with a number of components and technologies that enable a network administrator to allocate and manage end-to-end network resources.

QoS enables consistent bandwidth results for network traffic, such as video and audio applications and ERP applications that normally use large amounts of network bandwidth. It also helps to control the impact of media traffic that potentially generates large volumes of UDP traffic. Because of this impact, many administrators are backing off the deployment of rich multimedia tools on the network. QoS helps to control the performance impact of this traffic through QoS mechanisms.

QoS is a set of traffic reservation technologies that allow networks to control their traffic efficiently, potentially reducing the costs spent on new hardware resources. Management of the mechanisms works through the Admission Control Service (ACS), an administrative interface of QoS, which allows for the centralized management of QoS policies. These policies determine how you can reserve and allocate priority bandwidth. In the past, QoS has been incorporated into router and switching hardware and must still be supported in the router between a sender and receiver.

You will include QoS in your designs when:

- You have a need to identify criteria for reserving network resources and setting priorities.

- You need to ensure a priority bandwidth reservation that is transparent to the user.

- You have planned applications that will support QoS.

- The routers support Resource Reservation Protocol (RSVP).

The goal of a QoS implementation is to supply guaranteed packet-delivery service to applications or services that require such network traffic management. QoS mechanisms rely on QoS services and QoS protocols. Windows 2000 has the following services and protocols to support QoS: QoS Admission Control Services (QoS ACS), RSVP, and traffic control.

The QoS ACS simplifies subnet administration by implementing:

- Centralized subnet bandwidth policy configuration on a per-user or per-subnet or subnet basis, via the QoS ACS snap-in

- Transparency to users

- The ability to partition subnet resources between low-priority and high-priority traffic

- End-to-end network service with low-delay guarantees

- Interoperability with LAN, WAN, ATM, Ethernet, and Token Ring configurations

- Support for multicast transmission of bandwidth reservation messages

Resource Reservation Protocol (RSVP)

When speaking about RSVP in the context of Windows 2000, we're not speaking about that cute French term for politely letting an inviter know your attendance intentions. Rather, RSVP is a signaling layer-3 protocol, not a routing protocol, making it independent of the underlying network media. It enables the sender and receiver to set up a virtual dedicated connection. Customer networks generally include heterogeneous media, including Ethernet or token ring LAN media, WANs made up of low- and high-speed leased lines, modem links, and ATM technology. RSVP bridges the gap between applications, the operating system, and media-specific QoS mechanisms.

RSVP is a good choice for mission-critical applications, such as Enterprise Resource Planning (ERP) software and video conferencing—these types of applications tend to stream data. Both applications exchange QoS data between fixed end nodes for some degree of persistence. QoS-enabled connections are unidirectional, so to enable a connection with service guarantees for both sending and receiving from a host, two individual QoS-enabled connections are required.

Traffic Control

The good news about the next concept is that it is exactly as it appears. And the road-congestion metaphors you've conjured up in your head from the morning commute are entirely applicable. Traffic control chooses the virtual lane across which the packets travel. A key element of traffic control is establishing the service parameters for a sequence of packets and then treating all member packets as a single flow. Traffic control uses information from the single flow to create a flow with defined QoS parameters, and then creates filters to direct selected packets into this flow.

Traffic control works with the QoS ACS and RSVP to meet the service level and priority required by the bandwidth request.

QoS Example

Here is an example of QoS at work:

1. A client on a network requests QoS. The application used to transmit data supports QoS. The application requests QoS from the RSVP Service Provider (SP).

2. The RSVP SP requests the RSVP service to signal the necessary bandwidth requirements and notifies traffic control that QoS has been requested for this flow. At this point, traffic is currently sent at a best-effort delivery level.

3. An RSVP message is sent to the QoS ACS server, requesting a reservation. The data packets, which are ultimately transmitted from sender to receiver, are not sent at this point, just the RSVP packets.

4. The QoS ACS server verifies that enough network resources are available to meet the QoS level requested, and that the user has the policy rights to request that amount of bandwidth.

5. After verification is complete, the QoS ACS server approves the request and logically allocates bandwidth. The QoS ACS server forwards the request toward the receiver (client).

6. When the RSVP request passes through QoS-supported edge routers, each router keeps track of the resources (bandwidth) that are requested. The bandwidth is not yet physically allocated (RSVP is a receiver-initiated protocol, and bandwidth can only be reserved by the receiver).

7. The request is passed through each network device in the data path before it arrives at the receiver. The receiving client indicates that it wants to receive the data and returns an RSVP message requesting a reservation.

8. When the receiver's request for bandwidth passes through an edge router, it already has cached the information about the requested bandwidth (from the sender's request). The router matches the receiver request with the sender's request and installs the reservation by physically granting the bandwidth. The same process is repeated on each edge router.

9. The reservation is sent back to the sender. The layer-3 network devices (the edge routers) are capable of approving and allocating the physical bandwidth. The reservation simply passes through the layer-2 switch.

10. During this process, the traffic is sent by traffic control on the sender as best-effort. Upon receiving the reservation message, the traffic control on the sending host begins the process of classifying, marking, and scheduling the packets to accommodate the QoS level requested.

11. The QoS Scheduler begins sending the prioritized traffic. The data is handled as priority by all devices along the data path, providing greater speed of throughput and a more successful transmission to the receiving client.

It is key that all routers along the path support the proposed reservation and commit bandwidth resources. If all routers commit the resources, the sender can begin delivering prioritized data.

NOTE Remember that with QoS, you can restrict the bandwidth-draining Flash element that your staff is downloading from the Internet and ensure that the really important traffic, such as the traffic related to your SQL Server and Oracle databases, gets through! Business first, play second is the information-design goal behind QoS.

TCP/IP Security Solutions

The goal of IP network security is to provide access to resources, while preventing unauthenticated users from accessing, intercepting, or modifying transmissions. One of the challenges you will address in any of your TCP/IP designs is to provide for data integrity, confidentiality, and secure authentication. Generic TCP/IP security design solutions come in two essential forms. You, as a network designer, will focus in this chapter on blocking traffic (packet filtering) and encrypting data transmissions as the two primary security solutions used in a TCP/IP design.

 NOTE   Remember that security is discussed at length in the 70-220 section of this book.

Packet Filtering Techniques

Filtering is a useful way to block traffic for an entire network, using a packet-filtering firewall. Global or "edge" packet filtering includes blocking both TCP and UDP ports, as well as certain IP protocols. Firewalls may operate at the network layer (IP packet or datagram) or at the applications level (connection level). Application-level security systems are typically referred to as application gateways. Windows 2000 more specifically allows for the filtering of packets on a host-by-host basis, working at the application layer. Using this filtering method, TCP/IP can block the delivery of IP packets based on the host filter configuration. You will use filtering on specific dedicated servers that provide services on well-known ports, specifically an HTTP service using port 80 and HTTPS using port 443.

A host configured to use a filter may contain some or all of the following configuration settings:

- *Identify the source and destination address of the packet.* These can be configured at a low level, such as a single IP address, or at a global level that encompasses an entire subnet or entire IP subnet classes.

- *Identify the protocol used by the packet.* The default covers all protocols in the TCP/IP protocol suite. However, individual protocols can be configured to meet special protocol requirements.

- *Identify the source and destination port of the protocol for TCP and UDP.* This also defaults to cover all ports, but can be configured to apply to only packets sent or received on a specific protocol port.

Data Encryption Design

IPSec is implemented, as defined by the IETF, as a protocol, not as a service. IPSec uses an authentication header (AH) and an encapsulating security payload (ESP). The AH provides data communication with source authentication and integrity without providing data encryption. The ESP provides confidentiality along with the aforementioned authentication and integrity. With IPSec, only the sender and recipient know the security key. AH is used only when data integrity is needed, and ESP is used when encryption is needed in addition to authentication and integrity.

Since Windows 2000 IP Security operates below the network layer, it is transparent to end users. Both AH and ESP support transport mode where endpoints are not identified because there are multiple computers involved in communication at the same time. They also support tunnel mode where the end points are specified. It is possible to use IPSec alone as a form of tunneling when end systems do not support the use of other VPN tunneling technologies.

IPSec can be implemented either through Active Directory or by using local security settings. Windows 2000 comes with preset policies that define the IPSec role of a particular computer. The preset policies apply to a computer when they are assigned. The following are the default IP Security Policies available on Windows 2000:

- **Client (Respond Only)**   Used to communicate normally (unsecured). This will use the default response rule to negotiate with servers that request security. Only the requested protocol and port traffic with that server is secured.

- **Secure Server (Require Security)**   Used for all IP traffic. It always requires security using Kerberos trust. It will *not* allow unsecured communication with untrusted clients.

- **Server (Request Security)**   Used for all IP traffic. It always requests security using Kerberos trust. It will allow unsecured communication with clients that do not respond to the request.

The *IPSec Policy Agent* is a Windows 2000 service that runs within the Lsass.exe. Windows 2000 includes a set of security components that make up the Windows security model. These components ensure that applications cannot gain access to resources without authentication and authorization. Components of the security subsystem run in the context of the Lsass.exe process, and they include the following:

- Local Security Authority
- Netlogon service
- Security Accounts Manager
- LSA Server service

- Secure Sockets Layer

- Kerberos v5 authentication protocol and NTLM authentication protocol

The security subsystem keeps track of the security policies and the accounts that are in effect on the computer system. In the case of a *domain controller*, which is a computer that has Active Directory installed, these policies and accounts are the ones that are in effect for the domain in which the domain controller is located. They are stored in Active Directory. After the IPSec policy is obtained, it will apply to all IP traffic passing through the system.

IPSec security associations (SAs) define how computers will use IPSec, such as which keys, key lifetimes, encryption, and authentication protocols will be used. Appropriate protection levels should be set to ensure secure data transmissions. As a network designer, you should be mindful of the need to protect the network from outside the network (from outside the firewall) as well as within the network, and IPSec policy settings used with appropriate protection levels can secure internal communications.

Table 14-5 shows the protection provided by authentication and encryption methods supported by IPSec.

IPSec Encryption Algorithms

The following are encryption options:

- **DES, 40-bit**   Provides the best performance, but the least security. Required for transmissions into or out of France.

- **DES, 56-bit**   Provides a performance improvement over 3DES, due to shorter key length. It is a good choice for applications that require low security for exported business traffic.

Table 14-5   Relative Protection for the Supported Authentication and Encryption Methods

Protection Level	Authentication (Integrity)	Encryption Level	Diffie-Hellman Group
4 (Highest)	SHA-1 (160-bit)	3DES (3 × 56-bit)	1024 bits (medium)
3	MD5 (128-bit)	3DES (3 × 56-bit)	1024 bits (medium)
2	SHA-1 (160-bit)	DES (56-bit)	768 bits (low)
1 (Lowest)	MD5 (128-bit)	DES (56-bit)	768 bits (low)

- **Triple DES (3DES), 128-bit**   Provides strong security, but key length reduces performance.

IPSec Authentication Protocols

IPSec supports the Message Digest 5 (MD5) and Secure Hash Algorithm (SHA) authentication protocols. MD5, 128-bit is less secure than SHA, but requires less CPU overhead and has less impact on performance. SHA, 160-bit provides stronger security, but affects performance. SHA, 160-bit should be used for U.S. government contracts that require adherence to the FIPS (Federal Information Processing Standard).

IPSec Internet Key Exchange

The Diffie-Hellman technique (named after its inventors Whitfield Diffie and Martin Hellman) is a public-key algorithm that allows communications based on a shared key. With Diffie-Hellman, the two nodes exchange public information. Then each node combines the public information along with its own secret information to generate a secret, shared code. There are two group levels: 768 bits and 1,204 bits. If mismatched groups are specified on peered nodes, key negotiation fails. As in most cases, the larger bit length is harder to crack, but requires more CPU cycles to process.

Internet Key Exchange is used between peers to calculate security keys; it uses two protocols: the Internet Security Association and Key Management Protocol (ISAKMP) and the Oakley key-generation protocol. These two protocols reduce connection time and generate authenticated keys used to secure information. SAs must be negotiated between peer nodes. You can use Kerberos v5, public-key certificates, or previously agreed-upon keys shared as authentication methods when negotiating security associations. Kerberos v5 is the default method for Windows 2000 and can be used for authentication with any clients in a trusted domain running this protocol. Public-key certificates can be used when systems are not using Kerberos. An example of this is a trading partner accessing the network through the Internet. Preshared keys should not be used when there are a large number of systems involved. Preshared key use is a simple method for systems not running Windows 2000 or using Kerberos v5.

 TIP   Select Kerberos v5 if your design includes Active Directory. Use certificates for untrusted domains when Kerberos v5 is not supported.

Catywhompus Construction Updates

How does the TCP/IP solution discussion apply to Catywhompus Construction? Does it apply to Catywhompus? Of course, the answer is yes. The network at Catywhompus will require a TCP/IP foundation on which the entire network will be built. Although we are not going to build an integrated solution now for Catywhompus, you might want to refer back to some of the issues that Catywhompus may want to address with a TCP/IP solution. For instance, will they use public or private IP addressing? How many hosts will require connectivity? What network architectures will be considered at layers 1 and 2? How many WAN connections are required? This is a good time to go back and analyze Catywhompus. We suggest you consider the key TCP/IP issues during your review.

Case Study 14: Fromanywhere.com, Inc.
Creating a Network Design for an Internet Startup TCP/IP Protocol Architecture

Apply your knowledge to the analysis of a TCP/IP subnet design for a new business venture's network. There are essentially three reasons why people are hired to create a network design: to make money for the company, to save money for the company, or to solve a problem using their unique skills. As a new breed of MCSE, put your newfound MBA hat on and endeavor to address the business as well as the technical reasons for your hire. The management team at Fromanywhere.com needs you to solve a TCP/IP subnetwork design problem and add value to this fledgling business. Spend 10 to 15 minutes reviewing the following additional information, paying particular attention to the subnet design issues, and create your own network diagrams as needed. Then, complete the questions for this case and compare your solutions with the suggested answers.

continued

Envisioned System

Fromanywhere.com, as mentioned earlier, has three locations (see Figure 14-4). The IT management group has generally defined the user counts at each location and developed certain server needs and standards that create design constraints.

Client Traffic Patterns and Information

The current host counts are found in Figure 14-4. The client counts do not include the current year's projected client growth.

Client data flows are projected for intranet access as well as access to the Internet. These include 30 percent client growth expected over the next year. The projected data flows should only utilize 50 percent of the maximum available bandwidth on any link, to provide excess bandwidth for growth or extreme peak WAN usage. Table 14-6 shows the projected data flows between locations.

Design Requirements and Constraints

In order to conduct the day-to-day network operations and achieve the corporate strategic objectives, the firm wants to create a design using Windows 2000 Server.

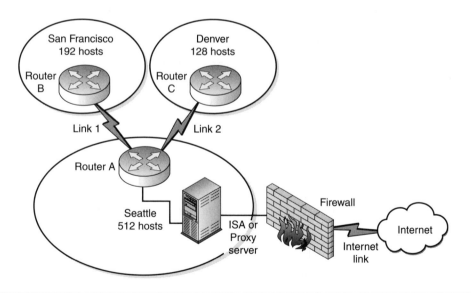

Figure 14-4   High-level Fromanywhere.com network diagram

continued

Table 14-6   Bandwidth Requirements Between Locations

Link	Projected Client Traffic
Seattle local clients only to the Internet	1.544 Mbps
Denver local clients only to the Internet	256 Kbps
San Francisco local clients only to the Internet	512 Kbps
Denver to Seattle (including Internet)	768 Kbps
San Francisco to Seattle (including Internet)	1.024 Mbps

Network Services   DNS will be integrated with Active Directory, and there will be separate DNS namespaces internally and externally. The ISP will maintain the external DNS namespace.

- Microsoft Exchange 2000 will be installed on the network.

- There will be DHCP servers at each location.

- There will be file and print sharing at each location. There will be some file transfer over the WAN connections, but all printing traffic occurs at the site level.

Application Requirements

- Provide network support for a mission-critical, Web-based, application-development environment that allows developers and support personnel to collaborate and develop a new set of virtual office applications.

- Authenticate users using a directory-services infrastructure provided by Windows 2000.

- Administer intranet resources by using a directory-services infrastructure provided by Windows 2000.

- Provide support for mission-critical applications to be available 24/7, 365 days a year.

- Software developers and business managers must be able to access critical applications 24/7, 365 days a year.

- Intranet access must be available to all shared resources without regard to user or resource location.

continued

Connectivity   Fromanywhere.com will require connectivity between offices. The network must also

- Offer high-performance Internet access from all locations.

- Isolate the organization's network from the Internet using Microsoft ISA or Proxy Server, and a firewall.

- The Internet connection must be placed in Seattle.

- Reserve access to management capabilities for the administrative staff at the firm.

- Provide for the support of all hosts shown in Figure 14-4.

- Use 100 Mbps switched Ethernet for LAN connections.

- Use a private address block that uses 172.16.0.0/22. The company prefers to use a private block primarily to handle growth and increase security.

- Use new routers in all locations. Each router can support up to five interfaces. The routers can be stacked or aggregated to create a single logical router.

- The Performance analysis mandates 128 or fewer clients per subnet, so make sure the network is configured appropriately.

- Use one of three T-1 levels for WAN links between locations: fractional 512 Kbps, fractional 1.024 Kbps, or full 1.544 Mbps. You have more flexibility with the ISP connection when selecting the WAN link.

- Establish a link to the ISP for Internet connectivity. The ISP will supply the necessary public addresses for the firewall and ISA/Proxy interface.

Case Study Questions

1. Calculate the projected number of client hosts for each location at the end of year one.

2. Select each link speed (Link 1, Link 2, and the Internet link) by analyzing the client traffic, and also identify the strategy used to ensure clients do not saturate the WAN links through the first year.

3. Given the total number of clients and the number of clients supported by each router interface, determine the number of routers and subnets required for each of the three locations. Explain your rationale for each determination.

continued

4. For each router in your answer for question 3, identify each interface and the associated subnet supported by that port. Using the private IP address block and subnet mask (172.16.0.0/22), show why the port is needed (that is, clients, router links, ISM, and so on) along with the subnetwork address. Determine which IP address scheme is going to be used, and write down which addresses will be used for routers, which for servers, and which for clients.

5. Draw a new network diagram, and show the following items in the diagram: routers, projected client counts, WAN links and speeds, and Internet-connectivity components.

6. Which dynamic routing protocols should be used for the routing connections? (Choose two.)
   a. RIP version 1
   b. RIP version 2
   c. OSPF
   d. Static IP configurations

7. Describe where you would locate the VPN service in your design.

8. How many subnets are supported by the private IP address block and subnet mask (172.16.0.0/22)?

9. What single design change could you make to improve the fault tolerance of the connections between Seattle and the two remote locations?

Suggested Solutions
(Your answers may vary.)

1. Figure 14-4 shows the initial user counts of 512, 192, and 128 for Seattle, San Francisco, and Denver, respectively. Each of these counts needs to be increased by the 30 percent growth rate anticipated in the next year. Count only discrete users (round up). This information will help in creating the subnet design in a later design question.

Location	Projected User Count
Seattle	$512 \times 1.3 = 666$
San Francisco	$192 \times 1.3 = 250$
Denver	$128 \times 1.3 = 167$
Total	1,083

continued

2. Each link speed should be selected to support double the projected bandwidth to meet the 50 percent utilization standard set by the startup's IT group. The selection speeds are also constrained by the T service increment levels:

Link	Link Speed and Type
Link 1 (SEA-SF)	1024 Kbps × 2 = 2.048 Mbps Select full T-1 of 1.544 Mbps (multilinking is not available for this connection). However, this will not meet the 50 percent utilization requirement.
Link 2 (SEA-DEN)	768 Kbps × 2 = 1.544 Mbps Select full T-1 of 1.544 Mbps.
Internet link (SEA-INT)	(1544 Kbps + 512 Kbps + 256 Kbps) × 2 = 4.624 Mbps Select three multilinked full T-1s with a total bandwidth of 4.632 Mbps.

3. Given the total client counts and the number of clients supported by each router interface (a maximum of 128), the following routers and subnets are required for each location to support the new enterprise:

Location	Number of Routers	Number of Segments	Rationale
Seattle	Two stacked routers, Logical A	Nine segments	Six segments for clients, two for links to San Francisco and Denver, and one for the ISA/firewall link
San Francisco	One router, Logical B	Three segments	Two segments for clients, and one for a link to Seattle
Denver	One router, Logical C	Three segments	Two segments for clients, and one for a link to Seattle

4. Table 14-7 reflects a possible IP address-assignment scheme for each segment on the new network.

5. Figure 14-5 shows the revised network diagram.

6. **B and C.** Either will work well. RIP version 1 does not support CIDR.

7. Place the VPN service at the ISM/proxy location.

8. 172.16.0.0/22 supports 64 subnets and 1,022 nodes per subnet. The total possible nodes is 1,022 × 64 = 65,408.

continued

Table 14-7 A Possible IP Address-Assignment Scheme for the New Network

Location	Router	Subnet	Network Address	Purpose	Router Interface	Client Address Range	Server Address Range
Seattle	A	A1	172.16.4.0	Clients	172.16.4.1	x.x.4.100 to x.x.4.228	x.x.4.10 to x.x.4.99
Seattle	A	A2	172.16.8.0	Clients	172.16.8.1	x.x.8.100 to x.x.8.228	x.x.8.10 to x.x.8.99
Seattle	A	A3	172.16.12.0	Clients	172.16.12.1	x.x.12.100 to x.x.12.228	x.x.12.10 to x.x.12.99
Seattle	A	A4	172.16.16.0	Clients	172.16.16.1	x.x.16.100 to x.x.16.228	x.x.16.10 to x.x.16.99
Seattle	A	A5	172.16.20.0	Clients	172.16.20.1	x.x.20.100 to x.x.20.228	x.x.20.10 to x.x.20.99
Seattle	A	A6	172.16.24.0	Clients	172.16.24.1	x.x.24.100 to x.x.24.228	x.x.24.10 to x.x.24.99
Seattle	A	A7	172.16.28.0	Link to San Francisco	172.16.28.1	x.x.28.100 to x.x.28.228	x.x.28.10 to x.x.28.99
Seattle	A	A8	172.16.32.0	Link to Denver	172.16.32.1	x.x.32.100 to x.x.32.228	x.x.32.10 to x.x.32.99
Seattle	A	A9	172.16.36.0	ISM/proxy connection	172.16.36.1	x.x.36.100 to x.x.36.228	x.x.36.10 to x.x.36.99
San Francisco	B	B1	172.16.40.0	Clients	172.16.40.1	x.x.40.100 to x.x.40.228	x.x.40.10 to x.x.40.99
San Francisco	B	B2	172.16.44.0	Clients	172.16.44.1	x.x.44.100 to x.x.44.228	x.x.44.10 to x.x.44.99
San Francisco	B	B3	172.16.48.0	Link to Seattle	172.16.48.1	x.x.48.100 to x.x.48.228	x.x.48.10 to x.x.48.99
Denver	C	C1	172.16.52.0	Clients	172.16.52.1	x.x.52.100 to x.x.52.228	x.x.52.10 to x.x.52.99
Denver	C	C2	172.16.56.0	Clients	172.16.56.1	x.x.56.100 to x.x.56.228	x.x.56.10 to x.x.56.99
Denver	C	C3	172.16.60.0	Link to Seattle	172.16.60.1	x.x.60.100 to x.x.60.228	x.x.60.10 to x.x.60.99

continued

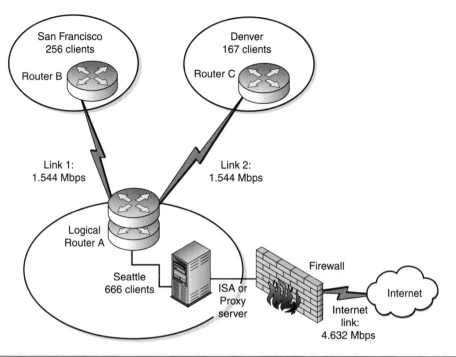

Figure 14-5   Revised Fromanywhere.com network diagram

9. One possibility is to remove the single point of failure at the remote locations by installing a demand-dial or fixed routed link between Denver and San Francisco. This would allow either location to route to Seattle even if the primary link is down.

Chapter Review

This chapter addressed Windows 2000 TCP/IP design issues, starting with a view of the comprehensive feature set, including how to create a suitable subnet design. You then put your TCP/IP network-design knowledge to the test as you designed the Fromany-where.com IP network. You can review this chapter frequently for test preparation, but don't forget to use it as an aid to solving real-world TCP/IP design issues.

Questions

1. Which of the following are valid reasons for using the reserved IP network addresses for private networks? (Choose all that apply.)
   a. Improves the scalability of the subnet and routing design
   b. Proxy servers require the reserved IP network addresses
   c. Improves security because external networks do not have internal address visibility
   d. A large number of host interfaces require direct Internet access
   e. Public address waste can be avoided

2. What two routing protocols are available in Windows 2000 Routing and Remote Access Service?

3. You wish to use a private reserved IP address range in your network design. You have selected the 172.16.0.0 block. What subnet mask would you use to provide 64 networks and 1,022 nodes on each segment?

4. In creating your TCP/IP design, what is your highest priority item to plan for? (Select the best answer.)
   a. A sufficient number of hosts are supported.
   b. An adequate number of networks are supported.
   c. Ample bandwidth for all clients.
   d. Internet access.

5. You are using a class B network address with a subnet mask of 255.255.240.0. Which of the following needs to be supported on all routers in order to allow for proper routing using this subnet mask?
   a. IGRP
   b. VLSM
   c. EAP
   d. OSPF

Answers

1. **A, C, and E.** By using one of the reserved IP address ranges, security and scalability are improved. You also avoid wasting addresses or going through the pains of obtaining more public addresses.

2. RIP 2.0 and OSPF are the default routing protocols.

3. A 22-bit subnet mask would provide 64 subnetworks and 1,022 host addresses per segment.

4. **A.** Remember, every host requires an IP address. You must, therefore, make sure the design provides this as the number one priority. Think of it as a prerequisite to addressing any other design issue.

5. **B.** Routers need to support VLSM (variable-length subnet mask). VLSM support is required on routers when a classless or non-standard subnet mask is used.

Key Skill Sets

In order to achieve the Microsoft objectives for this chapter, you should have learned the following:

- You should be able to identify and briefly describe the core features and functionality of Windows 2000 TCP/IP networking services.

- You should understand the potential design issues related to public versus private IP addressing.

- You should be able to describe the methods and strategies for optimizing the availability of IP routing capabilities.

- You should know how to develop strategies for securing TCP/IP traffic and optimizing the performance of IP data transmission.

- You should be able to apply the comprehensive TCP/IP feature set to a Windows 2000 IP network design.

Key Terms

Automatic Private IP Addressing (APIPA)
Classless Inter-Domain Routing (CIDR)
IP Security (IPSec)
Open shortest path first (OSPF)
Packet filtering
Quality of Service (QoS)
Request for Comments (RFC)
Resource Reservation Protocol (RSVP)
Routing Information Protocol (RIP)
Small office/home office (SOHO)
Variable-length subnet mask (VLSM)

Designing an Automated IP Configuration Solution Using DHCP

This chapter covers the following key mastery goals:

- Integrate DHCP into a routed environment
- Integrate DHCP with Windows 2000
- Design a DHCP service for remote locations
- Measure and optimize a DHCP infrastructure design
- Understand the value and abilities of the Windows 2000 DHCP server as a solution for automating address configuration for network clients of an organization
- Discuss, evaluate, and place DHCP services in small, medium, and large networks including enterprise networks
- Provide support for various client types, including solutions for organizations in transition
- Analyze network design needs and select appropriate strategies to enhance the availability, performance, and security of DHCP designs

Dynamic Host Configuration Protocol (DHCP) is new and improved. It is a service that can now be taken seriously at the enterprise level. Many shortcomings that were frustrating for Windows NT MCSEs have been cured, and other features have been added to take advantage of Windows 2000. For example, DHCP integrates with dynamic DNS in Windows 2000, a key feature for updating the DNS tables.

DHCP reduces the complexity of administering the client IP configurations by providing automated client configuration. With a DHCP Server in a network, the process of configuring IP parameters for DHCP-enabled clients is completely automated and centrally managed. The DHCP server maintains a pool of IP addresses and leases an IP address (along with other settings) to a DHCP client on the network. This address assignment is a dynamic process rather than a static (manually assigned) one. When an address is no longer in use, it is returned to the pool for reallocation. DHCP makes life easier for the network administrator, especially as the network gets larger and more complex. Without dynamic address assignment, clients have to be configured manually, one by one, and carefully to avoid IP addressing errors; manual configuration also requires a static environment where clients do not often move between subnets.

Update: Catywhompus Construction DHCP Design Project

Catywhompus Construction's new network initiatives presented earlier in Chapter 12 have created a demand for a new IP address assignment plan at the company. You have been hired to create this new design and integrate it appropriately on the network. You must first review the existing address assignment design and then create a new design and manage the implementation. Where do you start? We recommend a process that includes identifying the service requirements. In other words, review or create the business and technical requirements, including the diagrams, design limitations, and network requirements. For a Microsoft Windows 2000 DHCP design solution, address the functionality, availability, performance, and security-related issues. Then, create your design scenarios and select your design.

Catywhompus has decided to restructure the existing DHCP-enabled network. The current network configuration provides the following:

- Multiple location support
- Multiple subnet support
- Support for remote access users
- No support on routers for DHCP and BOOTP forwarding

continued

- Mission-critical applications at all locations
- Public network isolation from the Internet with an ISA server used for caching and another used as a firewall

The new design must provide the following:

- All clients must be able to obtain addresses, even if a single link fails.
- All clients must be able to obtain addresses, even if a single server fails.
- DHCP must not be used outside the private network.

You must take into account these new basic requirements. Later in this chapter, you will return to this case to address the following:

- Plan the number of DHCP servers needed.
- Plan the placement of the DHCP servers.
- Plan the number and location of DHCP relay agents.
- Identify the scopes configured on each server and the options required for each scope.
- Determine ways to improve the security, performance, and availability of the DCHP solution.
- Identify ways to manage the DHCP service in the organization.
- Look for ways to combine DHCP and other services on the same server.

Key DHCP Features

It is important for you as a network infrastructure designer to know and understand the key features of DHCP in Windows 2000. DHCP is based on Internet Engineering Task Force (IETF) standards, as defined by Requests For Comments (RFCs) 2131 and 2132. DHCP can automatically configure a client when the client boots on a TCP/IP network and can automatically *push down* configuration settings while the client is running, using the DHCP message-driven protocol.

Management Features

The creation of an address range is defined by what is called a Scope. Scopes in DHCP are key management objects for the management of subnets. You can use the DHCP Manager within the Microsoft Management Console (MMC) to perform local and remote DHCP management tasks. DHCP Manager supports scope properties, super-scopes, and multicast scopes, and TCP/IP client options.

Scope Properties   This is a collection of IP addresses and configuration parameters that are available for lease to DHCP clients. The properties include the following attributes:

- Scope naming
- Ranges of IP addresses used for DHCP lease offers
- Exclusion ranges defining addresses an administrator does not want to offer to clients within the scope
- Subnet mask for the IP address range
- Reservations set to ensure a device can always use the same IP address and optional settings
- Lease length values

Superscopes and Multicast Scopes   The DHCP Manager can be used to define all child scopes and then to create a superscope to provide leases from more than one scope to clients on the same physical subnet. Multicast scopes now allow multicast applications to lease Class D IP addresses from the following ranges:

- 239.255.0.0 to 239.255.255.255
- 239.254.0.0 to 239.254.255.255
- 239.253.0.0 to 239.253.255.255

TCP/IP Client Options   These are client configuration parameters a DHCP server can assign when passing an IP address lease to a client. DHCP Manager can be used to define and add custom option types predefined through RFC 2132.

Enhanced Monitoring and Statistical Reporting

The DHCP Manager provides reporting through graphical representations of server, scope, and client states. System Monitor counters can be used to specifically monitor DHCP server performance. For instance, you can monitor the active queue length to see the number of packets in the processing queue, or you can monitor the number of requests per second to view the rate of DHCP requests received by the DHCP server. These capabilities improve the monitoring that can be done on network DHCP servers.

DNS and WINS Integration

DNS or WINS can be used to register name-to-address mappings dynamically on the network. DHCP and DNS integration will allow pre-Windows 2000 versions and non-Microsoft DHCP clients to have their name-to-address mappings updated dynamically in DNS by the DHCP server when changes occur to their DHCP-assigned address. Your DHCP design strategy should include a plan for implementing DHCP with DNS, WINS, or possibly both.

EXAM TIP   A key advantage to using DHCP in Windows 2000 is its integration with dynamic DNS.

Rogue DHCP Server Detection

It's unlikely that malcontent employees will bring a Windows 2000 server from home and plug it into the corporate network, thus creating a rogue DHCP server that could assign IP addresses. It's also unlikely that foreign security risks are going to engage in IP terrorism, whereby a rogue DHCP server is introduced on your network to assign unusable IP addresses.

Rather, we've seen rogue DHCP servers appear in two ways. First, the training room your company likely has in some building is attached to the corporate network, and a contract trainer sets up the training room with a server that is also a DHCP server. This DHCP server starts to assign rogue IP addresses inadvertently when real users on the corporate network log on. A second case is the overly eager MCSE candidate who brings a server to work or creates a server at his or her desk. Perhaps unintentionally, this server running the DHCP server service is attached to the corporate network, and again you've got a rogue server.

The DHCP service for Windows 2000 prevents rogue Windows 2000 DHCP servers from assigning addresses in conflict with the network design. The Active Directory service allows DHCP service authorization, and if a Windows 2000-based DHCP server is not authorized, the service will not start. The authorization control has no impact on Windows NT 4 or DHCP servers on other operating systems.

User-Specific and Vendor-Specific Option Support

One of the key reasons to plan your DHCP implementation is the wide range of options you can configure. For example, we've worked with a legacy database application (which we won't name, to protect the guilty) at a large client site. This legacy database from the Unix community expected a BOOTP configuration (the Bootstrap Protocol, BOOTP, is a daemon in Unix that dynamically assigns IP addresses). Here, the challenge, which was solved, was to richly configure the DHCP scope.

The solution under Windows 2000 was to use vendor-specific options and user-defined options, called classes, that the DHCP service supports. For instance, this support includes certain options only supported by Windows 2000, such as the option to disable NetBIOS over TCP/IP, which will disable the use of NetBIOS Over TCP/IP (NetBT) on Windows 2000 clients only. Typically, NetBT is only disabled on computers such as edge proxy servers, which are proxy servers between the private network and public network, or hosts in a firewall environment where NetBT is not desired. Windows 2000 allows you to shut off the NetBIOS datagram service, which is connectionless service traffic. These services include the User Datagram Protocol (UDP) port 138, the NetBIOS name service at UDP port 137, and the NetBIOS session service (which is a connection-oriented protocol) at TCP port 139. The use of user- and vendor-specific options makes it possible to use these options without going through IETF approval to add to the standard options.

DHCP Server Clustering

The Windows 2000 Advanced Server clustering service can be used to provide DHCP with a fault-tolerant DHCP solution. Clustering allows two servers to be managed as a single system. As with mirroring, if the primary system fails, the secondary system keeps providing DHCP services to clients.

Multicast IP Address Allocation

The Multicast Address Dynamic Client Allocation Protocol (MADCAP) is included with the Windows 2000 DHCP service. It is used to support the dynamic assignment and configuration of IP multicast addresses on TCP/IP networks. MADCAP is used to enable multicast clients to be a part of multicast groups. The Windows 2000 DHCP service supports both the DHCP protocol and MADCAP. The assignment of MADCAP addresses does not rely on the DHCP dynamic addressing, but does rely on the Windows 2000 DHCP service, so the two protocols operate independently.

DHCP Client Support

Any client device that supports communication with an RFC 2132–compliant DHCP server can be configured dynamically by a Windows 2000 DHCP server. DHCP client support is supplied by the following Microsoft operating systems:

- Microsoft Windows NT Workstation (all release versions)

- Microsoft Windows NT Server (all release versions)

- Microsoft Windows CE (all release versions)

- Microsoft Windows 9x or ME

- Microsoft Windows for Workgroups version 3.11 (with Microsoft 32-bit TCP/IP installed)

- Microsoft Network Client version 3.0 for MS-DOS (with the real-mode TCP/IP driver installed)

- Microsoft LAN Manager version 2.2c

Automatic Client Configuration

The DHCP client in Windows 2000 has the capability to automatically configure an IP address and subnet mask if the DHCP server is unavailable or if the client is started on a non-routed small network where no DHCP server is available to assign addresses. This feature, Automatic Private IP Addressing (APIPA), which uses the reserved IP Address block of 169.254.0.0/16, can be useful for clients on small private networks, such as a small office/home office (SOHO).

 EXAM TIP   Hopefully, we're not talking outside of school here, but the APIPA area is known to appear on the Windows 2000 MCSE exams. Know it!

Local Storage

The Microsoft DHCP client supports local storage. This means that the DHCP clients can keep DHCP information on their own hard disks. If the DHCP server is down, the next time the client restarts, local storage allows the client to use its previously leased address and configuration options.

BOOTP Client Support

Time to pay homage to the Unix community! BOOTP precedes DHCP as a computer configuration protocol. This protocol lets diskless clients obtain their own IP addresses and other boot information needed for networking setup.

The Microsoft DHCP server offers BOOTP support through pointer records in the BOOTP table and supports RFC-951 BOOTP clients. The DHCP Manager can add, delete, and modify records in the BOOTP table. Unlike DHCP, BOOTP does not allow IP address leases, so BOOTP clients assume any IP address granted to them to be permanent. Where BOOTP is used, the range of IP addresses that are reserved for BOOTP services on the network must be excluded from any configured DHCP scopes.

Combining DHCP with Other Services

Windows 2000 DHCP has the capability to integrate with other services to reduce management requirements and extend certain service capabilities on a Windows 2000 network. The key service integrations include Active Directory, DNS, and Routing and Remote Access.

Active Directory Integration

When a Windows 2000 DHCP server attempts to start on the network, part of the startup process includes a query of the Active Directory *DHCPServer* object. The DHCP server's IP address is compared to a list of authorized DHCP servers found in the object's listing. If a match is found, the server computer is authorized as a DHCP server and the service is allowed to complete starting up. If a match is not found, the server has not been authorized on the network and is identified as a rogue, and the service is not allowed to start up. This provides additional assurance that the DHCP server is correctly configured for the network.

When configured correctly, DHCP servers provide an intended service. However, if a rogue DHCP server were to start without proper configuration and authorization, it could lease incorrect IP addresses and configuration information to clients. A client improperly configured by a rogue DHCP server might not be able to reach the Internet or resolve a DNS name because of invalid router addresses, subnet masks, or DNS server.

To authorize a DHCP server in Active Directory, a member of the Enterprise Admins group must authorize the DHCP server. This group has network-wide administrative privileges. Once a DHCP server is authorized, a DHCPServer object exists in Active

Directory, which lists the IP address of the server that has been authorized to provide DHCP services to the network. Once authorized, the DHCP server is allowed to start the DHCP service.

> **EXAM TIP** At least one DHCP server must be installed on an Active Directory domain controller or member server before they can be authorized in the directory server or begin providing DHCP services to clients. It is important that you do not elect to install the first Windows 2000 DHCP server computer as a stand-alone server.

Dynamic Updates in the DNS Namespace

When using DHCP to supply IP addresses dynamically to client computers, it does not make sense to make manual entries into DNS for host-name mappings. Windows 2000 DHCP, however, supports the update of client records in DNS as IP addresses are leased. This integration of DHCP and DNS will allow previous versions of Windows clients and other client operating systems to automatically update DNS through DHCP. This client record integration provides client name resolution through DNS.

Windows 2000 DHCP clients automatically update records in DNS directly, but with other clients, you can use DHCP to enable updates for DNS clients that do not support dynamic updates. See Figure 15-1 for scope-level integration dialog settings in Windows 2000 Advanced Server.

Routing and Remote Access Integration

Routing and Remote Access Service (RRAS) allows a remote-access server to obtain IP address leases from DHCP. The remote-access server can allocate IP addresses from a DHCP server and reserve them for remote-access client use. When a remote-access client connects to the remote-access server, the client is assigned an IP address from the list of reserved addresses. When a client disconnects, the address goes back into the pool of reserved addresses at the remote-access server.

If a DHCP server is not available when RRAS is started, then the DHCP client returns ten addresses in the APIPA range (APIPA was introduced earlier in the "Automatic Client Configuration" section). If the local network is not using APIPA addresses, remote-access clients are only able to obtain point-to-point remote-access connectivity with RRAS.

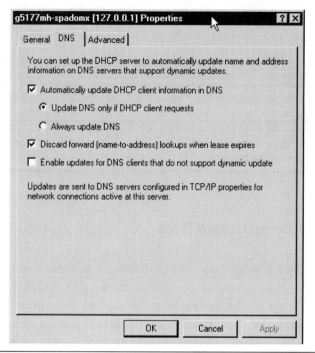

Figure 15-1   DNS integration settings in DHCP Manager

If a DHCP server does become available, the next time IP addresses are needed by RRAS, DHCP-obtained addresses are then allocated to remote-access clients that connect after the DHCP addresses were obtained. Therefore, clients will need to reconnect in order to obtain valid IP configurations from the allocated pool.

The remote-access server can use a specific LAN interface to obtain DHCP-allocated IP addresses for remote-access clients. You can select which LAN interface to use from the IP tab on the properties of a remote-access router (which are accessed with a right-click on the server name) in the Routing and Remote Access snap-in. By default, Allow RAS to Select Adapter is selected so that RRAS randomly selects the LAN interface to use.

If the remote-access server is configured to use the DHCP Relay Agent service, full DHCP configuration settings are available to remote-access clients. If the DHCP Relay Agent service is not set up, the clients will be provided with only the IP address and subnet mask by the DHCP server.

DHCP Design Choices

Your goal in designing a TCP/IP solution is to provide for communication on the IP network. To enable DHCP to deliver IP address and configuration information, you must determine the number of hosts, number of subnets, and network configuration information required on the network. You must determine how the network is subnetted and have the DHCP client option information available to enter into the DHCP service so you can configure the service properly.

Each client must be allocated an IP address and configuration information to enable IP communication. You will use the DHCP Server to maintain the database of IP addresses allocated and available for the defined subnets as well as the TCP/IP options needed for client configuration (including the router address, DNS servers, WINS servers, and so on).

Consider the Catywhompus Construction DHCP design challenge. Once you have determined the host population and number of subnets, you will have some of the essential design information needed to configure a DHCP server to enable IP communication. You will also need other key information, such as the router IP addresses and the location of key services, like DNS and WINS, as well as which computers will be manually configured with static TCP/IP configuration parameters. DHCP is obviously an IP solution that requires information from a number of other services, such as Active Directory, DNS, WINS, and the routing infrastructure in order to be properly designed into the network.

You must make many decisions before developing the DHCP solution because DHCP provides much of the "glue" that puts the IP configuration management pieces together. If these key structural network decisions are not yet determined, final DHCP design decisions should be postponed until the key TCP/IP communications infrastructure decisions are made.

Functional Aspects of Designing a DHCP Solution

DHCP can be used to design an IP configuration service for a small LAN, routed networks, dial-up services, and large enterprise networks. As you design the DHCP solution, you should consider, and provide a determination for, each of the following questions:

- How will DHCP be integrated with other Windows 2000 services, such as DNS, Active Directory, and WINS?

- Which computers will be configured as DHCP clients and which computers will be configured with static TCP/IP configuration parameters?

- Which options, types, and values will be defined for the DHCP clients?

- What are the hardware and storage requirements for each DHCP server, taking into account future dynamic-host population growth? How many DHCP clients will be supported?

- Are there any interoperability issues with existing systems, including the core accounting-transactions systems or human-resource management systems?

- Are there any hardware support issues or software compatibility issues on servers, routers, or switches?

- Will network monitoring tools be used, such as SNMP or Microsoft's Network Monitor?

Using DHCP Servers on the Network

It is important to consider the physical layout (geographical and physical structure) of the network to determine the DHCP server placement in the DHCP design. We do not recommend using the logical groupings as defined by Windows NT or Windows 2000 domains. The placement should be based on the subnetwork configuration and not the account database structure.

A single DHCP server has the capacity to support several thousand DHCP clients. Multiple DHCP servers and/or DHCP relay agent placements are often needed to address fault tolerance, slow links in WAN environments, and multiple broadcast domains created by certain routed and switched environments. When you have multiple DHCP servers, we recommend that you position the servers on different subnets to create a fault-tolerant DHCP solution, rather than placing the DHCP servers in one subnet. The servers should not have the same pool of addresses, because two clients may lease the same IP address on different servers, which would cause an IP address conflict.

Try to use the 80/20 design rule when placing multiple servers on the different subnets: Put 80 percent of the subnet scope on the local DHCP server and 20 percent on the remote subnet. Place the DHCP server with the largest number of IP addresses for a given subnet on the same physical subnet to improve DHCP client performance. If you decide to put two DHCP servers on the same subnet, use distributed or split scopes between the two DHCP servers to provide the best performance. One added benefit of having two DHCP servers on the same subnet is that if one server goes down, the other will continue to supply IP address configurations to clients that require a lease.

CAUTION Make sure these two DHCP servers on the same subnet do not have overlapping IP addresses defined for the same subnet.

Configuring and Selecting TCP/IP Options on the Network

DHCP configuration options can be assigned and managed using different levels for each DHCP server. These levels include default global options, scope options, class options, and reserved client options. The lower-level settings override any settings at a higher level. For instance, scope options override global options; class options override scope and global options; reserved options override global, scope, and class options. Table 15-1 shows the four option levels that can be assigned at each DHCP server.

NOTE If you are designing a large network, take care when assigning global options. These options will apply to all clients leasing an IP address from the DHCP server (unless overridden by lower-level options).

Typically, options are applied from each DHCP server at the global level or the scope level. Customized settings can be applied with one of the class assignments. If you have special client requirements, settings can be applied at a reserved client level.

Table 15-1 DHCP Option Assignment Levels

Options	How Options Are Applied
Default global options	Applied globally for all scopes and classes as defined at each DHCP server. These will be used (if configured) unless scope, class, or reserved settings are applied.
Scope options	Applied to clients that obtain a lease within a given scope. These will be used unless overridden by class or reserved settings.
Class options	Applied to clients that specify a DHCP class ID value when obtaining a lease, unless overridden by a reserved client option.
Reserved client options	Applied to a client that has a reservation in the scope for its IP address. If these options are active and leased, they will override all other DHCP settings.

CAUTION Remember that statically configured values on a client override any DHCP options from any level.

Providing IP Configuration Management to BOOTP and Non-Microsoft Clients

The specifications for your network may include a requirement to support automated IP configurations on clients that are not Microsoft DHCP clients. These clients include nodes that use BOOTP and others that are simply not Microsoft clients. The Windows 2000 DHCP server is backwardly compatible with BOOTP, and it will support clients that are compliant with RFCs 951, 2131, and 2132. This enables support for third-party clients such as RFC 951–compliant BOOTP devices.

The Bootstrap Protocol (BOOTP)

We've mentioned this in passing, but now it's time to learn about BOOTP. The Bootstrap Protocol was originally created for loading IP configuration information on diskless workstations. It was designed to obtain from a BOOTP server all the information required for a computer to become operational on the TCP/IP network. Because a diskless node is not able to store its IP address or the programs that support a sophisticated operating system, IP addresses were not leased by the BOOTP node. Typically, BOOTP servers set up client reservations for the MAC addresses of the BOOTP clients. This allowed for the centralized control over the diskless workstations on the TCP/IP network. BOOTP is similar to DHCP in that BOOTP allows a node to broadcast requests onto a network and obtain required information from a BOOTP server. A BOOTP server listens for incoming BOOTP requests and generates responses from a database of configurations for the BOOTP clients on that network.

EXAM TIP Windows 2000 now supports dynamic BOOTP, which allows you to designate a pool of addresses to be used for BOOTP clients. This allows DHCP to reclaim addresses used in the pool and provides support for more clients from a limited supply of IP addresses. To configure the server to provide IP addresses to BOOTP clients, you must set up a BOOTP address pool within an existing scope on the DHCP server.

The BOOTP headers are sent in UDP datagrams from port 68 on the client and on the server from port 67, just like DHCP. On powering up, the diskless workstation uses a network card with a MAC address to communicate on the local broadcast domain. The mechanism used to find a BOOTP server is broadcast-based, which is fine, provided the BOOTP server is located in that broadcast area. If the BOOTP traffic must cross one or more routers to reach the BOOTP servers, the routers must recognize the broadcast address and support BOOTP relay or BOOTP assist. The traffic that must cross routers includes the configuration of the BOOTP server's IP address that the router should relay to and from the server via unicast traffic.

 EXAM TIP BOOTP is typically presented on MCSE exams as a trick answer. You're not really being tested on BOOTP so much as it is being offered as an answer to throw you off the real answer.

Non-DHCP Clients

The DHCP server allows you to document the non-DHCP clients by entering them as reserved addresses. Since DHCP does not issue these reserved addresses to clients other than the reserved interface, the DHCP server operates as a central documentation repository for the manually assigned IP addresses of DHCP clients.

DHCP Sample Design for a Single Subnet LAN

In a simple LAN environment that does not include routing, a single DHCP server might be all that is required to issue IP address and configuration information for DHCP clients. With a single-server solution, DHCP client requests are delivered from a single scope defining all addresses and options offered to clients on the LAN (see Figure 15-2).

If the management of the company desires a simple LAN without subnets or routing, the small LAN is a prime candidate for a single-server DHCP solution. The primary reason for using this design is the simplicity of DHCP server management. The downside is that there is a lack of fault tolerance for client IP configuration.

You, as the designer, can mitigate this lack of fault tolerance under certain circumstances. For instance, if the LAN is stable and not subject to frequent IP configuration

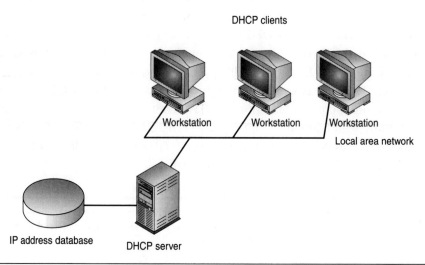

Figure 15-2   Single LAN using DHCP

changes, DHCP leases can be extended so that if the DHCP server goes down, clients would still possess a leased address.

DHCP Example Design for a Large Enterprise Network

Welcome to the big leagues. Large enterprise networks typically use a combination of ISO layer 2 switches and routed networking to achieve network scale. You should plan the physical subnets of the network and relative placement of DHCP servers to reduce broadcast traffic across routers. There may also be WAN links on the network where bandwidth availability must be maximized. DHCP servers should be placed appropriately to maximize response time and minimize the use of WAN links for low-speed traffic.

On large routed networks, DHCP option types and values should be predefined for DHCP clients. It is a best practice to set these options at the scope level because client settings tend to be the same on a subnet.

You can plan to include certain options to meet the needs of a particular group of users. For example, in a medium-to-large network scenario, users may frequently move between locations. If shorter lease durations are used, the IP addresses will be returned to the available pool more frequently. This will help to make more IP addresses available as users move between subnets, and these addresses can then be used for new lease offerings within the subnets.

DHCP Example Design for a Routed Network

Here's a networking law you should tattoo on yourself so it'll be with you forever. One DHCP server must be located on the routed network in order to have a functional DHCP implementation. This rule applies to switched single-subnet networks (using multiple broadcast domains) as well as routed networks.

TCP/IP protocols use two basic techniques for discovering the locations of resources and for communicating between systems to provide a common service. These two techniques rely on broadcast frames and multicast frames.

- *Multicast frames* use bandwidth but are not processed by every node or interface. They only negatively impact network performance when bandwidth is at a premium, especially on slower wide-area links.

- *Broadcast frames* are much more harmful to network station performance. ARP, BOOTP, DHCP, and RIP protocols generate broadcast frames. Every system on a bridged or switched network must process *every* broadcast frame. If the number of broadcast frames increases, performance of every system will degrade noticeably. Routers (and certain switched environments with multiple broadcast domains) provide for the ability to create broadcast domains where broadcasts are limited. This allows a network to scale without the negative broadcast effects being spread throughout the internetwork. Since BOOTP and DHCP are broadcast-based protocols, your DHCP services design must allow clients on separate subnets to reach a DHCP server.

Many contemporary network routers, Windows NT 4, and Windows 2000 provide DHCP relay agents that receive client broadcast frames and relay DHCP messages using unicast frames to a DHCP server. Figure 15-3 shows an example of a routed network using a DHCP relay agent on the router. You must install a relay agent for DHCP for subnets that do not have a local DHCP server, or configure the IP routers to support DHCP/BOOTP forwarding, in order to reach DHCP servers on different subnets.

Relay Agent Deployment

In most cases, routers will support the relay of DHCP/BOOTP traffic when configured with an IP helper address entered for the appropriate DHCP server on the remote network. It is best to configure this capability on the network routers, if possible, but some routers do not support DHCP/BOOTP relay. You may want to consider contacting the manufacturer or installing routers that support this capability.

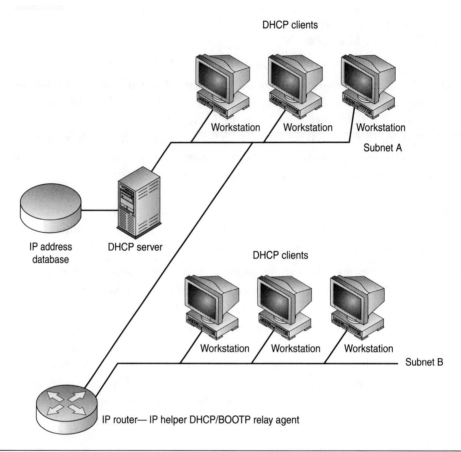

Figure 15-3   Routed network using DHCP with a router implementing a DHCP/BOOTP relay agent

   EXAM TIP   In most cases, it is not a best practice to pass **BOOTP** broadcast traffic over routers.

Alternatively, if a router cannot function as a relay agent, each subnet must have on it either a server that can function as a relay agent or a DHCP server. If you wish to use relay agents, Windows 2000 and Windows NT Server 4 can act as relay agents by installing the DHCP Relay Agent service. You can configure the DHCP relay agent to delay forwarding requests to a DHCP server, so that if there is a local DHCP server on the subnet, it can respond before unicast traffic is generated over the router(s). You can also set the relay agent to forward to multiple DHCP servers. It is not recommended to have more than two DHCP relay agents on a subnet for performance reasons, and it is also not recommended to run a relay agent on a DHCP server because they use the same UDP ports.

DHCP and Routing and Remote Access

Microsoft Windows 2000's RRAS can be used as an IP router supporting DHCP/BOOTP relay using a DHCP Relay Agent protocol. Figure 15-4 shows a Windows 2000 Server RRAS configuration acting as an IP router between subnets A and B. It is also acting as a DHCP relay agent between the DHCP server at 10.0.0.10 on subnet A and the clients on subnet B.

Remember, relay agents use unicast messages, so Windows 2000 must be configured with the IP address of the DHCP server on subnet A in order to relay client messages.

DHCP Server Placement

Where you place DHCP servers on a routed network and the number of DHCP servers required is dependent on the routing configuration, client service requirements, and other network-configuration elements, including connection speed and network architecture. The decision to have more than one DHCP server may also include fault-tolerance requirements for the network. In addition, keep in mind that routed network communications are dependent on proper IP configuration. Place DHCP servers in a way that will provide excellent service availability and DHCP client performance.

When using a single DHCP server, place it on the subnet with the highest population of clients. The other subnets will use DHCP relay agents or routers supporting BOOTP or DHCP forwarding. This is the placement of choice when there are persistent, high-speed connections between subnets.

If you have a routed network that is geographically dispersed with WAN links or demand-dial connections between locations, multiple DHCP servers should be used. You should also use multiple DHCP servers if the client base exceeds the capacity of a single DHCP server solution. A multiple-server solution will accommodate client expansion and improve availability. The routing configuration permits a DHCP server at each location, so that clients are serviced locally. This solution will still require DHCP relay agents or routers supporting BOOTP or DHCP forwarding on the subnets that do not have a DHCP server.

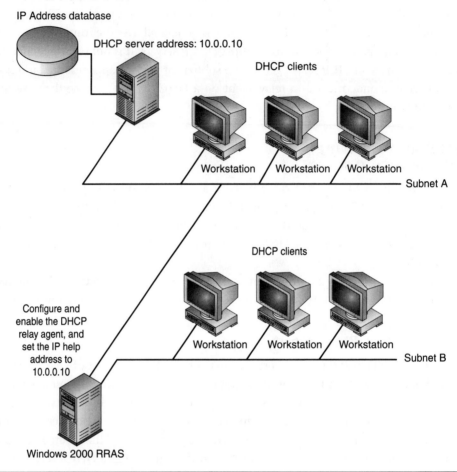

IP Address database

DHCP server address: 10.0.0.10

DHCP clients

Workstation   Workstation   Workstation

Subnet A

DHCP clients

Configure and
enable the DHCP
relay agent, and
set the IP help
address to
10.0.0.10

Workstation   Workstation   Workstation

Subnet B

Windows 2000 RRAS

Figure 15-4   Windows 2000 RRAS relay agents

Creating a DHCP Solution
to Ensure Service Availability

Businesses place a premium on uptime in the networking infrastructure arena. In order
to create a DHCP solution that provides the needed service whenever required, the
design must address fault tolerance. In most cases, a fault-tolerance design will include
redundant DHCP servers.

From a practical standpoint, your best defense against server failure is to make sure
the DHCP servers are internally fault-tolerant. Use standard fault-tolerance technologies

like Disk Mirroring, RAID level 5 (Striping with parity), and redundant power supplies with backup power to ensure the server will tolerate any significant failures. If the server itself has fault-tolerance measures applied, it decreases the need for multiple servers for fault-tolerance reasons only. The following are two primary options available to the designer to improve DHCP service availability:

- Installing multiple DHCP servers that share distributed scopes (superscopes) to prevent the failure of a single DHCP server from hampering the DHCP client lease process.

- Clustering DHCP servers using Windows 2000 Advanced Server to provide higher availability.

Distributed Scope Solution

You can increase the availability of DHCP services by installing more than one DHCP server so that any individual server failure will not prevent DHCP or BOOTP clients from starting. Keep in mind, however, that DHCP itself does not provide a way for DHCP servers to cooperate in ensuring that assigned addresses are unique. You must therefore carefully distribute scopes between multiple servers to avoid duplicate address assignments.

NOTE Take care to ensure that the reservations exist on all DHCP servers when supplying addresses from distributed scopes. If you do not, another DHCP server could lease to clients to reserved addresses from the other DHCP server.

Use the 80/20 model to balance server usage and divide scope addresses between DHCP servers, especially when the two DHCP servers are on separate subnets. Put 80 percent of the address pool on the DHCP server attached to the local subnet and 20 percent on the remote DHCP server that is reached through a DHCP relay agent. This will provide excellent performance for local DHCP clients and fault tolerance in the event that the local DHCP server fails.

NOTE You should set a delay on the DHCP relay agent in the preceding scenario to avoid traffic over the router. This is especially recommended if the remote DHCP server is on the other side of a slow WAN connection.

If there are multiple DHCP servers on the same network segment, or if all subnets use DHCP relay agents, you should allocate the local subnet scope between all servers. Just make sure there is no overlap between the scopes, or you run the risk of assigning the same IP address to two different DHCP clients.

Clustering Solution

A Windows 2000 Advanced Server cluster allows two physical servers to be managed as one logical DHCP server. The clustering service can provide higher availability through immediate recovery in the event of hardware or application failure. Windows clustering can automatically detect server failure and quickly switch over to the surviving server. It requires persistent, high-speed connections between the two servers.

Here's a DHCP design tip you might not have considered. Clustering, in effect, eliminates the need to split scopes. If one server goes down, the entire scope is still available. A common disk holds the DHCP database of address assignments. If the primary active server goes down, the failover server becomes the DHCP server and has complete access to the external database of assigned addresses. In reality, only one node is running as the DHCP server at a time. The clustering services simply provide seamless transition between servers as needed.

 NOTE If a cluster is using an external database, the DatabasePath and Backup-DatabasePath Registry entries in HKEYLOCALMACHINE\SYSTEM\CurrentControlSet\Services\DhcpServer\Parameters must be modified on both nodes in the cluster.

Creating a DHCP Solution to Enhance Performance

When optimizing the performance of your DHCP design solution, you can focus on two primary optimization solutions. The first is to look at individual DHCP servers to maximize their response time to DHCP clients, and the second option is to use multiple servers and enhance the responsiveness of the multiple-server solution.

Increasing Performance of Individual DHCP Servers

When optimizing the performance on a single Windows 2000 DHCP server, keep in mind two important facts:

- The DHCP service on Windows 2000 Server is a multithreaded service and therefore makes use of additional processors and processing power.

- The DHCP database design is optimized to provide fast query-response times. You can improve speed with high-performance disk subsystems, including striped disks.

You should always monitor DHCP server resource usage in the following areas:

- Processor usage

- Memory usage

- Disk subsystem performance

- Network subsystem performance

Additionally, the DHCP server performance counters found in System Monitor are described in more detail in Table 15-2. These counters provide a specific analysis and should be used to monitor and gather information about the DHCP service.

Again, use these counters in System Monitor to determine the proper load for the DHCP server in your environment. This detailed performance analysis will help to provide needed information about your DHCP service in a number of areas during planning and later allow you to manage the design to your specifications.

NOTE You can reduce overall traffic on each subnet by putting each of the network interfaces for a multihomed DHCP server on a different subnet.

You can improve performance on a DHCP server by adding or upgrading CPUs, adding memory, installing high-performance disk subsystems, and installing high-speed network cards or multihoming the DHCP server by adding multiple network-interface cards.

EXAM TIP You can also improve DHCP performance by increasing lease lengths. This will decrease the frequency with which a client contacts the DHCP server for lease renewal. Increasing the lease length will decrease network traffic and decrease the load on the DHCP server.

Table 15-2 DHCP Server Performance Object Counters

Counter	Description
Packets received/sec	Reports the number of message packets received per second by the DHCP server. A large number indicates heavy DHCP-related message traffic to the server.
Duplicates dropped/sec	Reports the number of duplicated packets per second dropped by the DHCP server. This number can be affected by multiple DHCP relay agents or network interfaces forwarding the same packet to the server. A large number here indicates that either clients are timing out too quickly or the server is not responding quickly enough.
Packets expired/sec	Reports the number of packets per second that expire and are dropped by the DHCP server. When a DHCP-related message packet is internally queued for 30 seconds or more, it is determined to be stale and expired by the server. A large number here indicates that the server is either taking too long to process some packets while other packets are queued and becoming stale, or traffic on the network is too high for the server to manage.
Milliseconds per packet (avg.)	Reports the average time in milliseconds used by the DHCP server to process each packet it receives. This number can vary depending on the server hardware and its I/O subsystem. A sudden or unusual increase might indicate a problem, either with the I/O subsystem becoming slower or because of an intrinsic processing overhead on the server computer.
Active queue length	Reports the current length of the internal message queue of the DHCP server. This number equals the number of unprocessed messages received by the server. A large number might indicate heavy server traffic.
Conflict check queue length	Reports the current length of the conflict-check queue for the DHCP server. This queue holds messages without responses while the DHCP server performs address-conflict detection. A large value here might indicate that the Conflict Detection Attempts setting has been set too high or that there is unusually heavy lease traffic at the server.
Discovers/sec	Reports the number of DHCP discover messages (DHCPDISCOVERs) received per second by the server. Clients send these messages when they start on the network and obtain a new address lease. A sudden or unusual increase indicates that a large number of clients are attempting to initialize and obtain an IP address lease from the server, such as when a number of client computers are started at any given time.
Offers/sec	Reports the number of DHCP offer messages (DHCPOFFERs) sent per second by the DHCP server to clients. A sudden or unusual increase in this number indicates heavy traffic on the server.

continued

Table 15-2 DHCP Server Performance Object Counters (*continued*)

Counter	Description
Requests/sec	Reports the number of DHCP request messages (DHCPREQUESTs) received per second by the DHCP server from clients. A sudden or unusual increase in this number indicates a large number of clients trying to renew their leases with the DHCP server. This might indicate that scope lease durations are too short.
Informs/sec	Reports the number of DHCP inform messages (DHCPINFORMs) received per second by the DHCP server. DHCP inform messages are used when the DHCP server queries for the directory service for the enterprise root and when the server is doing dynamic updates on behalf of clients.
Acks/sec	Reports the number of DHCP acknowledgment messages (DHCPACKs) sent per second by the DHCP server to clients. A sudden or unusual increase in this number indicates that the DHCP server is renewing a large number of clients. This might indicate that scope lease durations are too short.
Nacks/sec	Reports the number of DHCP negative acknowledgment messages (DHCPNAKs) sent per second by the DHCP server to clients. A very high value might indicate potential network trouble in the form of improper configuration of either the server or clients. When servers are improperly configured, one possible cause is a deactivated scope. Computers moving between subnets, such as laptop computers or other mobile devices, could cause a very high value.
Declines/sec	Reports the number of DHCP decline messages (DHCPDECLINEs) received per second by the DHCP server from clients. A high value indicates that several clients have found their addresses to be in conflict, possibly indicating network trouble. In this situation, it can help to enable conflict detection on the DHCP server. This should only be used temporarily. Once the situation returns to normal, it should be turned off.
Releases/sec	Reports the number of DHCP release messages (DHCPRELEASEs) received per second by the DHCP server from clients. This number only exists if a DHCP client sends a release to the server. This can occur manually, such as when the IPCONFIG/release command is used at the client computer. Release messages can also be sent by the client if it is configured with the Release DHCP Lease On Shutdown option. Because clients rarely release their addresses, the value of this counter remains low for many DHCP network configurations.

Increasing Performance
by Adding DHCP Servers

If you determine that more than one DHCP server is required for your design, you can use the following strategies to enhance the performance when creating multiple-server solutions:

- Use the 80/20 design rule between subnets, and configure distributed scopes between DHCP servers.

- Put DHCP servers on subnets with the highest number of DHCP clients.

- Locate DHCP servers so that DHCP clients do not have to cross subnets or WAN links.

- Use multihomed servers to reduce network overhead between subnets.

- Optimize individual servers using the performance-tuning suggestions for individual servers described in the previous section.

 TIP The 80/20 rule mentioned previously really comes from the MBA community, more so than the MCSE community. Its original MBA formulation is that you often engage in management by exception (MBE) by virtue of addressing the 20 percent of management issues with 80 percent of your time.

Designing a Secure DHCP Solution

Breaking news! The DHCP service itself is not secure and therefore requires security-management strategies to make it secure. The DHCP service for Windows 2000 is designed to prevent unauthorized servers from starting and potentially creating address-assignment conflicts and errors when combined with Active Directory.

The process of assigning IP addresses on the network must be done carefully and requires significant planning, especially on large routed networks. If a rogue server were to start in this environment, significant effort might be required to correct the problems created by this server. DHCP authorization is one way to control the DHCP protocol through Active Directory.

Preventing Unauthorized Windows 2000 Servers

Although you have read it before, let us repeat that when a Windows 2000 DHCP server attempts to start on the network, part of the startup process includes a query of the Active Directory *DHCPServer* object. The DHCP server's IP address is compared to a list of authorized DHCP servers found in the object's listing. If a match is found, the server computer is authorized as a DHCP server and the service is allowed to complete startup. If a match is not found, the server has not been authorized on the network and is identified as a rogue, and the service is not allowed to start up. This provides additional assurance that the DHCP server is correctly configured for the network.

When configured correctly, DHCP servers provide an intended service. However, if a rogue DHCP server were to start without proper configuration and authorization, it could lease incorrect IP addresses and configuration information to clients. A client improperly configured by a rogue DHCP server might not be able to reach the Internet or resolve a DNS name because of invalid router addresses, subnet masks, or DNS servers.

To authorize a DHCP server in Active Directory, a member of the Enterprise Admins group must authorize the DHCP server. This group has network-wide administrative privileges.

CAUTION   You must carefully manage who you place in the Enterprise Admins group. Remember that just as much damage (if not more) occurs on the inside of the firewall as is caused by intruders on the outside!

Once a DHCP server is authorized, a DHCP server object exists in Active Directory, which lists the IP address of the server that has been authorized to provide DHCP services to the network. Once authorized, the DHCP server is allowed to start the DHCP service.

EXAM TIP   Rogue DHCP server detection does not work if the DHCP servers are running earlier NT versions or DHCP servers from other vendors because authorization will not work. There is no protection from these other rogue server types except to use network monitoring. Authorization requires Active Directory deployment and the installation of the first Windows 2000 DHCP server must be on a Windows 2000 domain controller or member server. In addition, DHCP relay agents should be used to allow DHCPINFORM messages between DHCP servers on separate subnets if the DHCP servers are not installed on domain controllers or member servers.

Security Risks Using DHCP in DMZ Networks

A demilitarized zone (DMZ) or screened subnet is a subnet that separates the public network from the private network. The screened subnet is separated with firewall technologies. Typically, resources that require public access are located within the DMZ to protect the internal network. Using DHCP to make allocated addresses available outside of a firewall creates a security risk if an unauthorized client were to lease one of the addresses to gain access to your network resources. You can minimize the risk by doing the following:

- Limit the address range available to just the number of addresses needed on the subnet.

- Create reservations for the interfaces that require assignments.

- Set extended lease times for IP addresses.

Case Study 15: Officesupplies.com
Upgrading an Existing DHCP Infrastructure

The Chief Technology Officer (CTO) of Officesupplies.com, in Framingham, Massachusetts, manages an environment that provides 24/7 support. Officesupplies.com has a retail bricks-and-mortar business model married to a strong online Internet business. This is a classical "clicks-and-mortar" company that must make sure the legacy transaction system exposed to their online customers is available 24/7.

David Randy, the Chief Information Officer (CIO), has determined that Windows 2000 Advanced Server's improved functionality and performance are required to implement new Web technology promised by Microsoft. He approved the upgrade of all Windows NT 4.0 Enterprise Edition servers to Windows 2000 Advanced Server. You have been hired to review and validate the proposed design changes and manage the DHCP upgrade. Where do you start?

Your first assignment is to determine the functionality and infrastructure impact of this upgrade. After you complete a review of improved DHCP capabilities in Windows 2000 Advanced Server, you will analyze the planned business and technical environment at Officesupplies.com. Then develop your own DHCP design recommendations for the Officesupplies.com IT management team.

continued

Directions

Analyze a DHCP solution within the framework of an existing large routed network. Spend 10 to 15 minutes reviewing the following additional Officesupplies.com information, and pay particular attention to the DHCP design issues. Create your own organizational and network diagrams as needed. Then complete the questions for this case and compare your solutions to the suggested answers.

Scenario

Officesupplies.com developed a new business-to-business (B2B) strategy slated to go online in six months. The company is projecting this new venture will add 15 percent to sales by the second year. The Chief Technology Officer (CTO), Mike Faunas, makes it clear that the B2B applications will operate on top of a solid Windows 2000 infrastructure. The DHCP services must support all users at every site and provide dial-up and VPN support for extranet connections. This new venture has been developed over the last year. The company is large, but management hopes it will be gigantic with the projected growth.

In addition to the Framingham, Massachusetts headquarters, the company has four remote administrative facilities, in Chicago, Miami, Dallas, and Seattle. Headquarters has approximately 2,000 users and each of the remote sites has 1,500 users. T-1 frame relay circuits connect all sites to headquarters. User accounts are held and managed in a Windows NT 4.0 master domain called OSCDOM. All network resources are managed in location-specific resource domains called CHIDOM, MIADOM, DALDOM, and SEADOM. There are three Windows NT 4.0 servers in each remote location and five servers at headquarters. Some servers provide core business applications, along with file and print serving, while others provide Web applications and services. All of the company's e-commerce servers are maintained by an Internet service provider (ISP) on Windows NT 4.0 servers. Currently, there is one DHCP server at headquarters, and the remote locations use DHCP relay agents on Cisco 2600 series routers to obtain IP configuration information.

The company uses the 172.16.0.0/12 private network address. There are two subnets populated with DHCP clients at headquarters and one subnet populated with DHCP users in each of the other four remote locations.

There is a budget to add more servers as needed.

continued

Design Requirements and Constraints

In order to conduct the day-to-day network operations and achieve the corporate strategic objectives, the firm wants to create a design to accomplish the following using Windows 2000 Server.

Envisioned System

Application Requirements

- Provide network support for a mission-critical Web-based application that allows customers to manage their inventories and reorder supplies automatically.

- Provide network support for a mission-critical Web-based application that allows customers and business partners to order and trade office supplies over the Internet.

- Provide authentication of users using a directory services infrastructure provided by Windows 2000.

- Administer intranet resources by using a directory services infrastructure provided by Windows 2000.

- Provide support for mission-critical applications to be available 24/7.

- Ensure that customer service operators can access their critical applications 24/7.

- Provide intranet access to all shared resources without regard to location, including international locations.

Connectivity

The firm will require connectivity between all offices. The design will also provide for the following connectivity:

- Provide for isolation of a firm's intranet from the Internet.

- Provide for Internet access through headquarters in Framingham, Massachusetts.

- Reserve access to management capabilities for the administrative staff at the firm.

- Provide simultaneous access to Web applications for thousands of customers and business partners through the Internet using a variety of Web browsers and operating systems.

continued

Availability

"Users cannot, under any circumstances, experience communications failures from DHCP IP configuration outages. The DHCP solution must be a reliable and fault-tolerant IP address allocation system for workstations 24/7 because of the time zone differences and because the organization has locations across the nation. Servers, printers, routers, and other LAN devices will continue to use static IP configurations," says David Randy, Chief Information Officer.

Performance

DHCP traffic between sites must not strain the costly T-1 circuit's bandwidth. The network group is aware of the fact that these links need upgrading, but the cost is currently prohibitive. The design must minimize the impact of DHCP on these circuits.

Testing shows that the company's standard server hardware supports up to 5,000 DHCP or BOOTP devices on a single server with a 48-hour lease period. Each fully loaded standard server costs $50,000.

Security

The security administrator has this to say about DHCP:

"Because of the competitive nature of the office-supply distribution business, securing our data is critical. Also, there must be a facility to guard against rogue DHCP servers causing IP communication failures. Security administration rights must be easily granted to only DHCP administrators. Also, the DHCP design must not allow clients outside of the organization to obtain internal IP addresses unless they come in over a VPN or RAS connection."

Proposed System

To meet the proposed objectives, place one DHCP server in each remote location and split each scope 80/20. Place 80 percent of the IP addresses on the local subnet's DHCP server and 20 percent on the headquarters' single DHCP server. Nothing else needs to be configured. Future growth is allowed and users will be able to obtain an IP address even if the WAN connections fail between sites.

continued

Chief Technology Officer's Comments

"Let's see if we can find a way to spend less on capital equipment and still provide the required infrastructure. Given our server sizing, it seems like a waste of resources to have a DHCP server in each location. Also, the security issues are still nagging. The proposed design doesn't address the security concerns. What are your thoughts?"

Case Study Questions

1. Based on the comments from the CTO, and your knowledge of the availability, performance, and security requirements, which of the following would you recommend to the CTO? Why?

   a. The proposed design is best. It meets all of the availability requirements. Yes, it will cost $200,000, but it will work. Set the lease period to 24 hours.

   b. The proposed design is a step in the right direction, but the designers didn't go far enough. They must also add a DHCP relay agent in the second subnet at headquarters and integrate DHCP with Active Directory to prevent rogue DHCP servers from starting if they are not authorized.

   c. Add only one DHCP server so there are two DHCP servers at headquarters. Put one DHCP server in each of the two subnets at headquarters and split all scopes 50/50 between the servers for load balancing. Then set up DHCP relay agents on the appropriate router subnet interfaces. Also, add a dial-up backup for all remote locations in case the T-1 connections go down. Integrate DHCP with Active Directory to prevent rogue DHCP servers from starting if not authorized.

   d. Do the same as in answer C, but make the split 80/20 between the DHCP servers at headquarters.

2. You want to use DHCP authorization with Active Directory. In which location or locations should you place a Domain Controller or member server to enable DHCP authorization?

   a. Framingham
   b. Chicago
   c. Miami
   d. Dallas
   e. Seattle

continued

3. Draw a network diagram or describe the network and show your recommended locations for DHCP servers, DHCP relay agents, and the subnets. Describe how the scopes are split between subnets.

4. On your previous diagram, identify the need for redundant WAN links to reduce the possibility of a single point of failure. Also, identify any need for multiple paths between subnets to reduce a single point of failure.

5. Identify at least one strategy to reduce WAN impact.

6. Identify two distinct management strategies to make the DHCP service more secure.

7. Identify two distinct strategies to improve the availability of the DHCP servers.

Suggested Solutions

Note that there is no one right solution for this case study. Your solutions may vary from those suggested.

1. **C.** The most cost-effective setup that will appropriately support the number of users is to place two DHCP servers at headquarters. Remember, the business requirement determined by the CTO must take high priority. Solution C also provides load balancing between the two servers. The communications links will be impacted, but not more than they are now. Later, as the company grows, more DHCP servers could be added to the remote locations for additional fault tolerance and to reduce the impact on the WAN circuits. Answer D is also a viable solution, but answer C is preferred because it provides equal load balancing for the DHCP servers.

2. **A.** There must be at least one Domain Controller or member server to use Active Directory authorization with Windows 2000, and one DHCP server must be participating in Active Directory. In addition, DHCP relay agents should be used to allow DHCPINFORM messages between DHCP servers on separate subnets. This is required if the DHCP servers are not installed on domain controllers or member servers. Since Framingham is the headquarters, it is a likely candidate. Remember, the DHCP servers must be able to communicate with Active Directory using DHCP messages.

continued

3. The locations for the DHCP servers might be as follows:

Framingham	Subnets A, B, and C (subnets A and B have users while C is used for the WAN connection)
Chicago	Subnet D
Miami	Subnet E
Dallas	Subnet F
Seattle	Subnet G

Place two DHCP servers in Framingham on subnet A. Place DHCP relay agents on all other subnets. The relay agents on subnets B, C, D, E, and F will forward DHCP traffic to subnet A DHCP servers. All scopes are split evenly between the two servers.

4. Add a second path between subnets A and B, even though the connection is not a WAN connection. Install backup ISDN or POTS connections between the remote sites and subnet A.

5. To reduce DHCP WAN traffic, you can increase the lease length.

6. To make DHCP more secure:

   • Use Active Directory integration and authorized DHCP servers.

   • Use the DHCP Administrator group to provide administrative capability to DHCP Administrators.

   • Use the DHCP users group to provide read-only access to DHCP trouble-shooters or to people who need access to the DHCP database on a read-only basis.

7. To improve the availability:

   • Use cluster-server support for a highly available solution.

   • Use scope splits to provide fault-tolerant scopes.

Catywhompus Construction Updates: DHCP Design Project

Does the DHCP discussion apply to Catywhompus Construction? The answer is yes, and to find out how, revisit "Case Study 12: Catywhompus Construction Infrastructure Redesign" at the beginning of Chapter 12.

You will recall from Chapter 12 that Catywhompus Construction's current infrastructure includes IP routing, so the implementation of DHCP must include some form of IP helper or DHCP relay agent over the routers and include multiple subnet scopes to provide dynamic client configurations over the routed network. What would your solution be? A big hint would be to revisit the DHCP relay agent discussion in this chapter.

Another issue mentioned in Chapter 12 was that Catywhompus Construction frequently moves users between locations and between subnets. This isn't surprising with several offices around the world and construction projects running in the field. When this issue was last discussed, in Chapter 12, Catywhompus was not using DHCP because of the legacy design. Now that you're firmly grounded in the DHCP design process, we're sure you will join us in agreeing that DHCP is an excellent solution for remote users. By implementing DHCP as a foundational network improvement, users can move between subnets without manual IP configuration changes.

Chapter Review

The Dynamic Host Configuration Protocol reduces the complexity of administering the client IP configurations used on your network by automating client configuration. A DHCP solution provides this automation for hosts on single or multiple subnets. The network designer needs to determine host population, subnet configuration, and network topology, and this information should then be used to develop the DHCP design elements needed for the network scenario. This chapter discussed the appropriate functionality, availability, performance, and security strategies to meet the DHCP solution requirements for the network design.

Questions

1. Your organization has many mobile users that frequently move between subnets. Each of the subnets has a pool of addresses and occasionally users are not able to use the network because the subnet does not have enough available IP addresses. What can be done to ensure that more IP addresses are returned to the pool and that fewer addresses are leased but not used?

2. Your organization is planning to deploy Windows 2000 DHCP servers to reduce the complexity of administering the client IP configurations on your network. The network is a routed network that has many subnets, and you determine that the existing routers do not support BOOTP forwarding. You can upgrade these routers if necessary. Your performance and availability design requirements include the use of only one clustered DHCP server on the network that is not multihomed. The DHCP server only has a network interface on the subnet with the greatest number of users. What must you do to the network to ensure that DHCP config-urations are delivered to all DHCP clients?

3. In the past, your organization has had problems with rogue DHCP servers start-ing on the network and supplying incorrect configurations to clients. You have decided to install your first DHCP server on a stand-alone Windows 2000 server and find that it will not use rogue server detection. What can you do to use DHCP authorization under these circumstances?

4. You are working with a TCP/IP routed network that has four subnets. You have been assigned the job of designing a single DHCP server solution for the organiza-tion. The routers do not support BOOTP forwarding and there is no funding for more than one DHCP server or for router upgrades. How can you design the single-server solution to provide TCP/IP configuration for all clients on the network?

5. You have a very reliable network and have made it so by ensuring fault tolerance for key services. What DHCP fault-tolerant solutions might you implement to ensure that DHCP is as reliable as the rest of the key networking solutions?

6. Since the budget will not support buying another server, what should you do to improve the performance of the server? (Choose all that apply.)
   a. Add another new DHCP server.
   b. Add more RAM on the DHCP server.
   c. Add another processor to the DHCP server.
   d. Add a RAID 5 disk controller.
   e. Decrease the scope lease time on the DHCP server.

7. What fault-tolerance methods can you apply to a Windows 2000 Server DHCP server? (Choose only one answer.)

    a. Put DHCP on a server cluster.

    b. Put DHCP on a multihomed server.

    c. Split the scope between servers on different subnets.

    d. Back up the DHCP database regularly.

8. When Routing and Remote Access Service is configured to obtain DHCP addresses from a Windows 2000 DHCP server, what is the initial IP address block size supplied to the Remote Access server?

    a. 100

    b. 50

    c. 25

    d. 11

    e. 10

9. Your firm's main office is located in Seattle, where your DHCP, DNS, and WINS services are maintained. You support a remote site with 100 users on a separate subnet located in Olympia, Washington, 60 miles away. There are two Cisco 2600 series routers and a pair of AT&T Paradyne CSU/DSUs connecting the T-1 frame relay circuit between these two locations. In the past, there have been very few workstations added or moved in the Olympia site, and the workstations and servers in that location have used manually configured IP address settings. Now, more users want to move between sites easily with their laptops. You correctly configure a Windows 2000 DHCP server in the main office to supply addresses for that subnet and properly configure clients to use DHCP. Yet clients in Olympia still cannot obtain IP configuration information using DHCP. What is the problem? (Choose one answer only.)

    a. The scope is not properly set up on the DHCP server.

    b. The clients are not properly configured using the LMHOST file.

    c. You forgot to add the IP addresses of the DNS and WINS servers to locate the DHCP server.

    d. The DHCP IP address is not configured properly at the client level.

    e. The routers are not configured as DHCP relay agents.

Answers

1. Review the lease length, especially for mobile clients, and reduce the lease length to return moved addresses to the pool. This will ensure that more IP addresses are available for use.

2. Upgrade all routers to support BOOTP forwarding, and configure the routers to forward DHCP requests to the DHCP server. You could also place DHCP relay agents on each subnet.

3. Install DHCP on a Windows 2000 domain controller or member server. Authorization requires integration with Active Directory.

4. Multihome the DHCP server and place an interface on each of the subnets.

5. Use a clustering server or divide the IP address scope between two separate servers using an 80/20 design split. One of the servers would have 80 percent of the IP addresses and the other would have 20 percent.

6. **B.** and **D.** are the only answers that apply because they will both improve server performance—adding more RAM is the best choice. A sudden increase in the rate of packet expiration indicates that the server cannot handle the amount of traffic coming in to the server, or that the server is taking too long to process some packets. You cannot buy another server to improve performance due to budget constrains, and even though Windows 2000 supports Symmetrical Multi-Processing (SMP), you cannot add an additional processor because the server cannot handle multiple processors. If you decrease the scope lease time, you will increase traffic and potentially worsen the performance problem.

7. **C** is the only correct answer because splitting the scope provides online redundancy.

8. **D.** Initially, 11 are supplied—10 for clients and 1 for the service. Once these are used up by clients, additional blocks are supplied in groups of 10.

9. **E.** DHCP traffic is broadcast based. Routers typically do not pass DHCP or BOOTP broadcast traffic unless configured to do so.

Key Skill Sets

- You should understand the value and abilities of the Windows 2000 DHCP server as a solution for automating address configuration for network clients for an organization. This will help you to design functional DHCP solutions.

- You should be able to apply a DHCP solution in various scenarios, including international wide-area internetworks.

- You will now be able to provide support for various client types, including organizations in transition.

- You should be able to select appropriate strategies to enhance the availability, performance, and security of a DHCP design.

Key Terms

Automatic Private IP Addressing (APIPA)

BOOTP

DHCP

Exclusions

Global scope

Local scope

Multicast scope

NetBIOS Over TCP/IP (NetBT)

Relay agent

Reservations

Superscope

User classes

Vendor classes

CHAPTER 16

Creating a DNS Name-Resolution Design

This chapter covers these key mastery goals:

- Understand the value and capabilities of Windows 2000 DNS as a name-resolution solution

- Understand the value and capabilities of the Windows 2000 DNS as it works in combination with WINS, DHCP, and the Windows 2000 Active Directory

- Evaluate DNS technologies and learn to apply a DNS solution to support an organization's namespace requirements

- Analyze network design needs and select appropriate strategies to enhance the availability, performance, and security of a DNS design

This is perhaps the most important chapter in this section of the book, and it covers one of the critical 70-221 exam topics. It's really no surprise—article after article confirms that the Domain Name System (DNS) is near the top of the list of the most needed and respected improvements in Windows 2000. A Windows 2000 DNS Server is Microsoft's new and improved implementation of the industry standard Domain Name System (also known as DNS).

We believe you'll truly enjoy this chapter, as it has practical application to your day-to-day MCSE world. This chapter looks again at much of the content that was previously presented and tested for on the TCP/IP elective exam in the legacy Windows NT MCSE days. The key mastery goals listed earlier track directly to specific goals for Exam 70-221, "Designing a Microsoft Windows 2000 Network Infrastructure."

Update: Catywhompus Construction Requires a DNS Design Strategy

You have been assigned the task of designing a DNS solution for Catywhompus Construction, and it will be a key foundational component of the organization's network. Name resolution is required on a TCP/IP network to locate resources using user-friendly names, rather than IP addresses.

An analysis of the organization's name-resolution needs will be completed at the end of this chapter. You will then review the DNS design requirements needed to support the name-resolution requirements for Catywhompus Construction. Your design will address the functionality, availability, performance, and security aspects of the DNS service. The design will also take into account appropriate opportunities for integrating with other services on the Windows 2000 network that could enhance or extend the functionality of DNS.

Through the course of this chapter, you will learn about tools you need to design the firm's DNS strategy. By the end of the chapter, you will have the information to create a design strategy for this case.

Now you will examine the Windows 2000 DNS design information related to functionality, availability, performance, and security in order to understand the key issues that need to be addressed when creating a DNS solution.

The Domain Name System Solution

It's difficult to fathom an MCSE certification candidate who doesn't know about DNS. But, as time passes, memory lapses, so we are honor-bound to present the DNS story for your enjoyment. The Domain Name System (DNS) is a distributed database system used by most Internet software, such as Web browsers or e-mail applications, to locate servers and other resources. Without name-resolution services, users and applications would have to use IP addresses, rather than user-friendly names, to reach resources in a TCP/IP network.

For example, if an organization did not use a name-resolution method like DNS, employees who wanted to get recent information about their employee-benefits program on the corporate human-resources Web server would have to use a URL that includes the IP address (for example, https://**10.0.0.99**/benefits) instead of a name that is easy to remember (such as, https://info.Catywhompus.com/benefits).

The DNS solves the name-resolution problem by resolving or mapping a user-friendly name to an IP address. DNS can, therefore, serve as the name-resolution foundation in a TCP/IP network.

There are significant reasons for making DNS the key resolution method in your TCP/IP network designs:

- It is the most popular name-resolution method on planet Earth, telephone books aside.

- It provides convenient and easy-to-remember names for users wanting to locate resources. Users do not have to remember IP addresses.

- It offers simplicity—users only need to learn one naming convention to locate resources on the internetwork.

- Consistent server and resource names can be used, even if they have changing IP addresses.

- It is, by design, a highly reliable, hierarchical, distributed, and scalable database that integrates with other Windows 2000 services to extend the name-resolution capabilities.

> **TIP** Take a moment to reflect on how you've used DNS in your organization and as a practicing technology professional. Do you have a war story that is noteworthy? For example, did DNS running on a Unix box allow your Windows clients to interact with Macintosh clients running MacTCP? We're sure a few minutes of walking down DNS-memory lane will allow you to revisit how you've worked with DNS in the past and will provide a historic context as part of your mental framework for tackling this beast of a topic!

New Features in the Windows 2000 Implementation of DNS

The DNS server and client resolver have several new features and many enhancements over previous Microsoft DNS versions. These improvements and changes fall into four categories: resolution, management, performance, and integration. You should become familiar with these improvements, especially if you are upgrading a Windows NT 4.0 DNS network or integrating Windows 2000 DNS into an existing infrastructure.

Resolution Improvements

There are many name resolution enhancements in the Windows 2000 DNS including the following:

- The Windows 2000 resolver (DNS client) attempts to resolve names with DNS prior to attempting to do so using NetBIOS.

- The resolver can query different servers based on the adapters to which they are assigned.

- You can view and flush the DNS resolver cache by using the IPCONFIG command-line tool—use IPCONFIG with the */displaydns* switch to view the DNS cache and the */flushdns* switch to delete the DNS cache contents.

- You can flush the DNS server cache within the DNS console.

If all of the computers on the network are running Windows 2000, WINS (NetBIOS name-resolution service) servers are not needed. Even in a mixed environment, you can configure the DNS server to query WINS for name resolution for DNS clients, and the names can be looked up via DNS.

Management and Performance Improvements

There are many management and performance enhancements in the Windows 2000 version of DNS, including the following:

- The DNS console snap-in provides a graphical interface for managing the DNS services. Many wizards now help with key management tasks.

- The DNS service allows client computers to dynamically update their resource records (RRs) in DNS. Dynamic update reduces the amount of time needed to manually manage zone files by automatically adding host (A) and pointer (PTR) resource records.

- DNS servers can now send and receive incremental zone transfers so that only changes are synchronized between zone files. Bandwidth utilization is improved for server-to-server zone transfers.

- The resolver performs negative caching, which records that a name or type of record does not exist. This eliminates the need to check for a name that the resolver has already determined does not exist.

Integration Opportunities with Other Windows 2000 Services

DNS is required for Active Directory. Also, DNS zones can be integrated into Active Directory, providing reliability and security advantages because the zones are replicated between all Active Directory domain controllers. All of the domain controllers act as primary servers and can receive dynamic client updates. Active Directory also replicates on a per-property basis, so only relevant changes are propagated between servers.

Windows 2000 DNS server is integrated with WINS, and two record types are supported by the Microsoft implementation of DNS: SRV and ATMA.

Service (SRV) resource records enable you to specify the location of the servers for a specific service, protocol, and DNS domain. Thus, if you have two Web servers in your domain, you can create SRV resource records specifying which hosts serve as Web servers, and resolvers can then retrieve all the SRV resource records for the Web servers.

The *ATMA resource record*, defined by the Asynchronous Transfer Mode (ATM) Forum, is used to map DNS domain names to ATM addresses.

Integration into Existing DNS Designs

The Windows 2000 DNS server is RFC-compliant, so it will interoperate with other RFC-compliant products, such as the Berkeley Internet Name Domain (BIND), as well as older versions of DNS. The DNS service in Windows 2000 is a superset of the Internet Engineering Task Force (IETF) standards.

BIND compatibility includes the following:

- Support for SRV resource records supported by BIND 4.9.6 and later.

- DNS zone databases are now dynamically updated, which is supported by BIND 8.1.2.

- Incremental zone-transfer updates, supported by BIND 8.1.2 and later.

Windows 2000 DNS now supports Unicode characters in DNS zones and can still process zone transfers if a zone receives a non-RFC-compliant resource record.

 EXAM TIP We're always up for living on the edge, so here goes. It's our recollection that on Microsoft MCSE exams, including the new Windows 2000 exams, you are not held responsible for standards down to the third digit of the version level. So while we list BIND to the third significant digit, don't waste a great deal of time memorizing version numbers. On a design exam, a better use of your time is to look at the bigger picture.

Now that you understand the importance of DNS and the new features supported by Windows 2000, it is important to review how DNS resolves names. The best way to begin reviewing the resolution process is to understand the key DNS components.

Key Components of DNS

We'll define DNS components as a remedial learning mechanism for MCSE candidates who are weak in this area, but if you are experienced with DNS as a scholar and practitioner, it should be sufficient for you to speed read through this section.

The Domain Namespace

The domain namespace provides the structure of a DNS distributed database. The domain namespace has a hierarchical structure, with each domain having a unique name.

The root domain is at the top, represented by a period.

Below the root domain, the top-level domains can be organizational types, such as *com* or *edu*, or geographical locations, such as *ca* for Canada. Second-level domains are registered to individuals or organizations, such as *Catywhompus* in Catywhompus.com, the Catywhompus Construction domain.

Second-level domains can have many subdomains, and any domain can have hosts. A *host* is a specific node within a domain, such as *webserver01* or *mail01* in the Catywhompus.com domain.

A fully qualified domain name (FQDN) describes the exact relationship between a host and its domain. DNS uses the FQDN to map a host name to an IP address.

Zones

Domains are organized into zones primarily for administrative purposes. A zone is a discrete and contiguous area of the domain namespace. One reason to divide a namespace into zones is to delegate authority for different portions of the space—one very large domain can be difficult to administer. The name-to-IP address data for computers located in a zone is stored in a traditional zone database file on the DNS server.

Name Servers

In traditional or standard DNS, one name server holds the primary zone database file for a zone and is a read-write copy of the database. The primary server is said to have "authority" for making changes to the zone file. In traditional DNS, a copy of the zone file may be stored on other servers for security, availability, and network load-balancing reasons.

These copies are generally referred to as secondary zone database files. The secondary database files are read-only copies of the primary zone files made using a zone transfer process. This allows servers, other than the primary name server, to answer name-resolution queries for that zone.

DNS Resolution Process

Now we'll look at how name servers resolve user-friendly names to numerical IP addresses. It has been our experience that even BackOffice gurus can benefit from revisiting the actual mechanics of DNS, as it's easy to forget how DNS actually works.

The DNS Query

The name-resolution process involves sending a query to one or more name servers to locate the IP address of the requested resource. The query includes the FQDN of the requested resource. Name servers use a computer's FQDN to locate its IP address.

A query that returns an IP address when given a FQDN is a *forward-lookup query*. For example, if a client somewhere on the Internet wants to communicate with the IP address of a server called "webserver01" in the Catywhompus.com domain, the client would query the local DNS server, LOCALDNS01, for the IP address of webserver01.Catywhompus.com (step 1 in Figure 16-1). The local name server for the client checks its zone database to see if it is authoritative for the Catywhompus.com domain. If it is not authoritative, the local DNS server will then begin searching for a name server that has authority for the Catywhompus.com domain. Figure 16-1 shows this name-resolution process.

The local server first sends a query to the root name server, which contains the IP addresses of the top level domain, "com" (step 2 in Figure 16-1). The root name server sends those IP addresses back to the local name server (step 3), which then queries a name server for the com top-level domain (step 4). The com name server receives the query and responds with a referral to the Catywhompus.com name servers (step 5). The local DNS server then sends its request to the Catywhompus.com name servers that contain the zone name-to-IP mapping information for webserver01.Catywhompus.com (step 6). The local DNS server receives the mapping (step 7) and passes the IP address for webserver01.Catywhompus.com to the client (step 8), which allows the client to establish a TCP/IP session with webserver01.

You may discover that DNS servers can send many queries when resolving an IP address for a client. This resolution process will certainly affect your DNS design decisions.

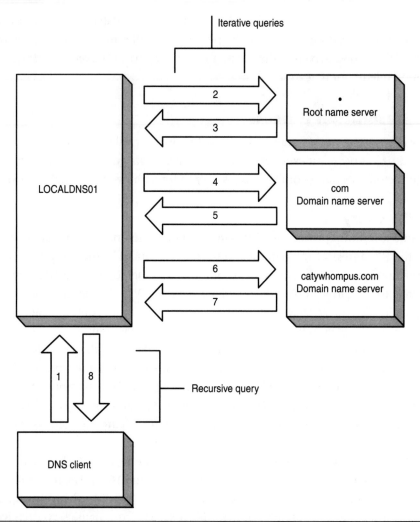

Figure 16-1 Query resolution process initiated by a DNS client

Resource Load-Sharing Control

Versions of BIND 4.9.3, and later DNS servers, including Windows 2000 DNS, use a load-balancing mechanism called round-robin, explained in RFC 1794, to share and distribute loads for network resources (resource servers). Round-robin is a simple form of resource load-balancing that rotates the order of the resource record's (RR) IP address data returned to clients. Round-robin uses multiple RRs for the same queried

DNS domain name. Resouce records come in many forms, but they eventually resolve to IP addresses. The rotation of servers' IP addresses creates this simple form of resource load-balancing. Unfortunately, Round-robin is limited because it does not take into account the state of the servers supplying the data. For instance, if one of the servers is fully loaded, Round-robin will still send a client to that server even if the server cannot provide the resource. This same issue arises when one of the servers is down. Round Robin will still try to send client requests to a server that is down.

> **TIP** If Round-robin is used, it is very important to monitor and fix the resource servers if one is not functioning properly. If one of the resource servers goes down, the DNS server can still send client requests to the downed resource server's IP address.

For example, suppose you have three FTP servers with the same domain name, ftp.catywhompus.com, that all contain the same files and directory structure, and you want to share the load between them. On the DNS server, you would create the following resource records:

ftp.catywhompus.com	A	204.57.236.10
ftp.catywhompus.com	A	204.57.236.20
ftp.catywhompus.com	A	204.57.236.30

Using a DNS server configured to perform round-robin will rotate the order of the "A" resource records when answering client requests. In this example, the DNS server would reply to the first client request by ordering the addresses as 204.57.236.10, 204.57.236.20, and 204.57.236.30. It would reply to the second client response by ordering the addresses as 204.57.236.20, 204.57.236.30, and 204.57.236.10. The rotation process continues until all of the same type of resource records associated with a name have been rotated to the top of the list that is returned in response to client queries.

> **TIP** By default, a Windows 2000 DNS server uses a different method to order the records returned to clients. DNS attempts to find the resource record containing the IP address closest to the client, then returns this IP address first from the list of records. However, you can modify the default so that it performs traditional round-robin.

Windows 2000 DNS servers, by default, use a different method to order the records returned to a client. They attempt to find the resource record containing the IP address closest to the client, returning this resource record first in the list of records. However, you can modify the default so it performs traditional round-robin.

Enabling Round-Robin

You can use round-robin to rotate host resource records ("A" records) that are in a query answer if multiple "A" resource records are found. (For round-robin to work, multiple "A" resource records for the queried name must first be registered in the zone.) If round-robin is not enabled for a DNS server, the order of the response for these queries is static, based on the order of resource records as they are stored in the zone.

Lab Exercise 16.1:
How to Enable Round-Robin

1. Open the DNS Console by selecting Start | Programs | Administrative Tools | DNS.

2. In the console tree, click the applicable DNS server name.

3. Select Action | Properties.

4. Click the Advanced tab.

5. In Server options, you check the Enable Round-Robin check box (it is enabled already by default) and uncheck the Enable Netmask Ordering. Then click OK.

If you leave the Enable Netmask Ordering check box checked, the records will be reordered by their subnet location, and resource records will be rotated using round-robin as the secondary method of sorting the response list. Once round-robin is enabled, DNS will rotate through the multiple "A" resource records rather than using the default method of responding, which is to supply the resource closest to the client. Note that this is done on a per-server basis so you can control round-robin use on different servers, but not at the zone level on the same server.

 CAUTION Round-robin DNS is a solution for enabling a limited form of TCP/IP load balancing for Web servers. Beware, though, that it does not function effectively as a high-availability solution, nor does it affect DNS load balancing. Round-robin DNS uses DNS to map incoming IP requests to a defined set of servers in a circular approach. If a server in the rotation fails, round-robin DNS continues to route requests to the failed server until the server is removed from DNS or the connection times out.

Collecting Information for the DNS Design Decisions

Name-resolution services are key to a client computer's ability to locate network resources on host devices. Windows 2000 DNS allows users to refer to network resources by names complying with the DNS standards. Installing Windows 2000 DNS on the network is also a requirement for using the Windows 2000 Active Directory. DNS can also integrate with other Windows 2000 services to provide additional functionality and name-resolution capabilities.

To design a DNS solution for locating network resources, you have to make some key decisions based on information about the network. Collect the following information for use in creating your DNS design:

- How many DNS clients or users are at each site or location? The number of clients determines how many DNS servers will be needed at each location. Often there is at least one DNS server per location.

- How many locations are there in the organization? Often, but not always, one DNS server is needed at each location.

- Are there any DNS servers, such as Unix or Windows NT 4.0 servers, currently in use on the network? Older DNS servers will not support all of the newer features, like incremental zone transfer.

- Is Active Directory in use or planned for the future? Active Directory integrated zones are available only on Windows 2000 Domain Controllers, and they use the replication capabilities of Active Directory, while maintaining backward compatibility with traditional DNS zones.

Creating a Functional Windows 2000 DNS Strategy

Once you know the functionality your DNS solution needs to provide, you have some decisions to make:

- Select the zone types you will use in the solution.

- Select the appropriate locations for the DNS servers, given the server capacities and zone types selected.

- Select the integration options incuding DHCP, WINS, and Active Directory integration.

- Determine what type of Internet connectivity you need and where the public DNS servers should be placed.

DNS Zones and Zone Types

DNS is critical to the functioning of an Active Directory network and for a contemporary routed network—it makes it possible to locate host services, such as a printer named "myprinter" or a Web site like www.catywhompus.com. Therefore, DNS name-resolution services can stand alone and provide services apart from Active Directory. In any case, a good DNS design can improve the performance of your overall network and reduce the impact of the DNS load on the network.

Zone Basics

A zone, as mentioned earlier, is a contiguous portion of the DNS namespace. The zone file (or the Active Directory) contains a series of records stored on the DNS server. However, zones are not domains. A DNS domain is a branch or a part of the overall namespace, and a zone is a portion of the DNS namespace typically stored in a file or Active Directory. A zone can contain multiple domains. Using the zone, the DNS server uses the zones to answer queries about hosts in the zone when the DNS server is authoritative for that zone.

Zones can be either standard or integrated *primary* zones or standard *secondary* zones. The primary zone is a read/write copy of the zone information, and the secondary zone is simply a copy of the primary zone that is replicated from its configured master. You will note that the standard secondary zone can use a standard primary, an Active Directory–integrated primary zone, or another standard secondary zone as its master server. The Active Directory–integrated zones are always primary, but the standard zones can be either primary or secondary.

You can support Active Directory and traditional DNS name-resolution services by using standard DNS servers as well as Active Directory–integrated zones. You do not have to use integrated zones to support Active Directory. Active Directory will function with Windows 2000 standard zones.

Typically, you will choose integrated zones if Active Directory is in place or will be put in place as part of the long-term directory strategy. In other words, do it if it fits. If you have the luxury of maintaining your DNS information as a text file or as part of a secure and robust relational database (Active Directory), then there really isn't any other choice but integrated. We'll look at the benefits of Active Directory integration shortly.

PART III

EXAM TIP   Remember Microsoft's propensity for testing most heavily on its newest, coolest, and most-promoted features. Active Directory integration is one of the newest, coolest, and more-promoted features. That said, not only will you have exams covering the Active Directory integration issue with DNS, but often the correct answer on the exam incorporates Active Directory integration as the solution to the problem presented (but use your best judgment on that last point).

Standard zones should be selected if integration with existing DNS servers is a high priority and the existing servers will remain primary. The reason you would use standard zones for integration reasons is that they can perform secondary roles, whereas integrated zones cannot. Keep in mind, though, that a domain controller can run all three types of zones at the same time! It could be used as an integrated zone for one domain, a standard primary for another, and a standard secondary zone for yet another domain, all on the same server. Remember, this is only on a Windows 2000 domain controller. The following dialog box shows the zone types available when a new zone is created:

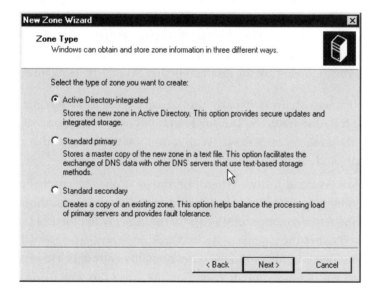

Standard DNS Zones

Standard DNS zones are stored in either primary or secondary zones, which are stored in a text format. Using standard zones facilitates the exchange of DNS data with other

DNS servers that use text-based storage methods. These standard zones follow a single master model, meaning that there is only one primary zone, which has a read/write copy of the zone file, and all other zones are secondary zones with read-only copies.

Unlike the old NT 4.0 days, these zones now support incremental zone transfers so that replication can occur on a net-change basis between master and secondary, or by transferring the entire contents of a zone file. Yes! The Windows 2000 DNS service supports complete and incremental zone transfers.

Standard zones function as clones of BIND-based DNS servers. Standard DNS zones, therefore, have the same benefits and limitations as BIND DNS zones, are highly interoperable with BIND-based DNS servers, and can play a role in designs that require this level of interoperability.

Active Directory–Integrated DNS Storage

As promised, here's the good stuff on Active Directory integration with DNS. When you store a zone in Active Directory, the zone data is stored as Active Directory objects, and these objects get replicated along with other Active Directory–replicated data. Each of the DNS servers becomes a primary DNS server multimaster capable of reading and writing DNS records and receiving dynamic client updates. An Active Directory–integrated zone provides a series of benefits and very few limitations over standard zone functionality. The following are the essential design benefits of using integrated zones:

- **Fault tolerance**   Active Directory multimaster replication provides better fault tolerance for zone transfers. The single master has a single point of failure if the primary zone's server goes down. With a multimaster integrated zone, all servers are primary and each can perform zone replication.

- **Replication compatibility**   When a primary zone is configured as Active Directory–integrated, the zone is stored in Active Directory and the standard DNS zone on the server contains only a copy of the zone. When the DNS server receives a change, it writes the change to Active Directory. Through Active Directory replication, the zone is replicated to the other domain controllers. However, because of the existence of a zone compatibility copy, the server can send its copy of the zone to any secondary server that requests it.

- **Security requirements**   The administrator can set access limits for any zone or record using Access Control Lists (ACLs) to specify users and groups that have authority to modify the zone and zone records.

NOTE Secure dynamic updates require, and are only available for, Active Directory–integrated zones.

- **Ease of management** Once DNS is integrated with Active Directory, you do not have to set up the replication between DNS servers because Active Directory handles the transfer between domain controllers.

- **Faster and more-efficient replication** Active Directory will replicate DNS zone data on a per-property basis, which is the same as for Active Directory data. If the address of a particular host is changed, only the changed information will replicate. This is more efficient than are full zone transfers.

Integrated Zone Storage Location in Active Directory The Active Directory is an object-oriented database stored in the ntds.dit file. The resources in the database are organized in a hierarchical structure, which means every resource, including DNS, is represented by an object. Object classes and attributes are defined in the Active Directory Schema. Figure 16-2 shows the DNS objects in Active Directory.

The following are the DNS objects shown in Active Directory:

Object	Description
dnsZone	The container created when a zone is integrated in Active Directory
dnsNode	A leaf object used to map and associate a name in the zone to resource data
dnsRecord	Attribute of a dnsNode object used to store the resource records associated with the named node object
dnsProperty	Attribute of a dnsZone object used to store zone-configuration information

Lab Exercise 16.2:
How to View Zones Stored in Active Directory

1. On a domain controller, select Start | Programs | Administrative Tools | Active Directory Users and Computers.

2. Select View | Advanced Features.

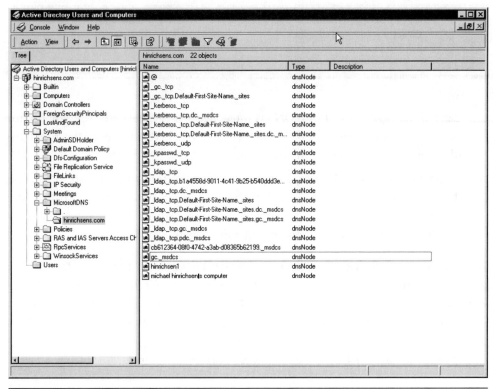

Figure 16-2   DNS objects displayed in the Active Directory

3. Double-click the Domain object, the System object, and then the Microsoft DNS object to display the dnsZone objects (refer to Figure 16-2).

4. Double-click the zone you wish to view.

TIP   If you haven't done this before, take a moment to perform the keystrokes now. If we learned anything at the Online Learning 2000 conference in Denver, Colorado, in the fall of 2000, it's that people learn by doing.

When viewing stored zones, you can see the Active Directory objects in the Users and Computers snap-in. You will notice, though, that this component cannot interpret the values of the dnsRecord attribute. You must view the hierarchy and associated records in the DNS snap-in console component. Table 16-1 shows a comparison of the behaviors of Active Directory–integrated zones and standard zones.

DNS Server Placement and Zone Type Considerations

Two key issues that must be addressed in your DNS design are where to locate servers and what types of zone files should be used on these servers. The following is a discussion related to making decisions in these two key areas.

PART III

Table 16-1   Zone Type Design-Parameter Comparisons

Behavior	Active Directory– Integrated Zone	Standard Primary Zone	Standard Secondary Zone
Master-read/ write abilities	Each AD–integrated zone is capable of both read and write and is considered to be multimaster.	Each primary zone is capable of both read and write and is considered a single master zone.	Each secondary zone is read-only and can be the master for other secondary zones.
Replication	Provided by Active Directory, along with other Active Directory data. It goes in two directions between Domain Controllers.	Occurs in one direction from primary to secondary.	Occurs in one direction from master to the secondary.
Secure updates	Provides ability	Not available	Not available
Interoperability	Treated as a primary zone when interoperating with BIND-based DNS	Functions identically to BIND-based DNS	Functions identically to BIND-based DNS
Zone transfers	Incremental or full	Incremental or full	Incremental or full
Adheres to IETF specifications	Yes	Yes	Yes
Supports dynamic update	Yes	Yes, but there is a single point of transfer failure.	Yes, but there is a single point of transfer failure.

Server Placement

We're not worried about where you physically place your DNS services from a Martha Stewart aesthetic perspective, although we are concerned about security, performance, and availability of DNS functionality. At the physical level, we're only concerned about servers being secure, having plenty of airflow, and being blocked from direct sunlight. What we'll consider here really addresses both logical placement and physical placement.

Placing DNS servers is a key namespace design issue and must be addressed with zone type in mind. Remember, the availability of DNS directly affects the availability of Active Directory and other key services. Clients rely on DNS to be able to find a domain controller, domain controllers rely on DNS to find other domain controllers, and so on. Even if you already have DNS servers deployed on the network, you may need to adjust the placement of servers to meet the needs of your Active Directory clients and domain controllers. You may also need to adjust the number of servers to achieve the appropriate availability and performance.

In general, place your DNS servers at a central location on the network that is accessible to your clients. It is typically most practical to place a DNS server on each subnet. However, there are several factors to consider when deciding where a DNS server is needed:

- Is the DNS server computer also a domain controller or likely to be promoted to one in the future?

- If the DNS server fails, can clients resolve names using an alternate DNS server?

- What other DNS servers or name-resolution options are available if the routed connection stops responding?

For example, if you have a routed LAN and multiple high-speed links that are reliable, you might be able to use one DNS server for a larger, routed network. If you have a high number of clients on a single subnet design, you may want to add more than one DNS server to the subnet to provide backup and failover if the preferred DNS server stops responding.

When determining the number of DNS servers you need to use, assess the effect of zone transfers and DNS query traffic on slower links in your network. Although DNS uses unicast traffic, it does create some traffic between servers and clients. This traffic should be analyzed and characterized, particularly when used in routed LAN or WAN environments.

You have probably experienced a slow WAN link on a corporate network. As part of the DNS server placement planning, you should especially consider the effects of zone transfer over slower links, like those typically used for a WAN connection. Although the DNS service supports incremental zone transfers, and Windows 2000 DNS clients and servers can cache recently used names, traffic considerations are sometimes still an issue, particularly when DHCP leases are shortened and, as a result, dynamic updates in DNS are performed more frequently. One option for dealing with remote locations on WAN links is to set up a DNS server at these locations to provide a caching-only DNS service.

With most installations, you should have at least two server computers hosting each of your DNS zones to provide fault tolerance. Standard DNS was designed to have two servers for each zone: one as a primary server and the other as a backup or secondary server.

This design reportedly goes back to the Cold War in the United States, when the military was still the prime mover and shaker of internetworking activity. In the event of a thermonuclear war, the Internet, based on TCP/IP and DNS, was designed to remain up and running. Part of this redundancy is evidenced in the use of two distinct and separate servers to hold the DNS zone. Consider it another civilian benefit from the military industrial complex. So when making any final determinations about the number of servers to use, first assess the level of fault tolerance you need for your network. And keep that bit of military history in mind.

Generally, it is a best practice to place at least one DNS server in every site, and there's a reason for that. The DNS servers in the site should be authoritative for the locator records of the domains in the site, so that internal network resource queries will stay local and not go out to DNS servers off-site. Domain controllers will also periodically verify that the entries on the primary master server for each service location record (SRV) are correct. Remember, SRV records specify the names of computers running the Windows 2000 Server operating system that offer specific services, such as NETLOGON. The NETLOGON service of Windows 2000 Server–based domain controllers registers its SRV record, thus enabling a query to return the names and addresses of all domain controllers in the enterprise domain. Because of the heavy reliance on DNS servers in a Windows 2000 network, higher speed site-level connections to the DNS server makes a positive impact on overall network performance.

One simple configuration that satisfies all requirements is to use Active Directory–integrated DNS, which will store the locator records for a domain within the domain, and run the Windows 2000 DNS service on one or more domain controllers for each site where those domain controllers appear.

Zone Type and Server Requirements

Select the *standard primary zone* type when you have one of the following DNS server requirements:

- You are using a traditional single-master design and you must set up the first DNS server.

- You need to have a compatible DNS server that is both read/write.

- You need a DNS zone apart from an integrated zone.

Select the *secondary zone* type when you have one of the following DNS server requirements:

- You have a remote site from which users need to resolve names, but you do not want to increase network overhead with a domain controller. The secondary zone can copy the zone file from the Active Directory–integrated zone.

- You need to provide fault tolerance by providing a local copy of the primary zone.

- Use secondary zones in screened subnets for users accessing the zone from the Internet.

Integrating DNS and WINS

You can allow DNS clients to resolve host names found on a Windows Internet Naming Service (WINS) NetBIOS name server. To provide this interoperability, a new record (the WINS record) was defined as part of the zone database file. If a name cannot be resolved on the preferred DNS servers, or using iterative queries to other DNS servers, a WINS-integrated DNS zone will query WINS to look them up. Host names can be resolved through WINS by forwarding unresolved DNS queries to a WINS server for NetBIOS name resolution. (Be careful here because the WINS cannot do DNS resolution.)

This forwarding is established on a by-zone basis. For example, you could have one private zone called internal-catywhompus.com that forwards unresolved queries to WINS, and a public zone called Catywhompus.com that does not forward to WINS, both on the same DNS server.

To accomplish WINS lookup, two specific resource-record types are used and can be enabled for any zones loaded by the DNS service:

- The WINS resource record, which can be enabled to integrate WINS lookup into forward-lookup zones

- The WINS-R resource record, which can be enabled to integrate WINS reverse lookup for reverse-lookup zones

The WINS resource record is specific to Windows 2000 Server and earlier versions of Windows NT Server, and is attached only to the zone. The presence of a WINS resource record instructs the DNS service to use WINS to look up any forward queries for host names or names that are not found in the zone database. This functionality is particularly useful for name resolution required by non-WINS clients, or for the names of computers not registered with DNS.

DNS Lookup Process Using WINS

The DNS lookup process is similar to the DNS query process discussed earlier, but it includes additional steps related to host lookup on the WINS server. The name-resolution process involves sending a query to a WINS lookup-enabled name server to locate the host's IP address. For example, if a client on the local network wants to communicate with the IP address of a server called "WINShost1" in the Catywhompus.com domain, the client would query the local DNS server, LOCALDNS01, for the IP address of WINShost1.Catywhompus.com. The local name server for the client would then check its zone database to see if it is authoritative for the Catywhompus.com domain. If it is not authoritative, the local DNS server will then begin searching for a name server that has authority for the Catywhompus.com domain, beginning with the root name servers.

The local server sends a query to the root name server, which contains the IP addresses of the top level domain, "com." The root name server sends those IP addresses back to the local name server, which then queries a name server for the com top-level domain. The com name server receives the query and responds with a referral to the Catywhompus.com name servers. The local DNS server then sends its request to the Catywhompus.com name servers that contain the zone name-to-IP mapping information for WINShost1.Catywhompus.com. If the authoritative zone does not have a record for the host located in its zone, it will then pass the request to the WINS servers to resolve the request. The local DNS server receives the mapping and passes the IP address for WINShost1.Catywhompus.com to the client, which allows the client to establish a TCP/IP session with WINShost1. This resolution process will certainly affect your DNS design decisions when DNS is integrated with WINS.

NOTE WINS is covered in much greater detail in Chapter 17.

Configuring WINS Lookup Through Zone Configuration

You can enable WINS resolution on a zone to forward names not found by the DNS query. WINS-enabled DNS zone can point to more than one WINS server and the IP addresses of the WINS servers are prioritized so the DNS server can use the closest WINS server first. The prioritization improves performance and the ability to point to multiple WINS servers improves availability of the WINS resolution resources.

You have control over which zones provide integrated WINS resolution on your network. Subdomains can be created to specifically handle the unresolved DNS queries, and you can select whether to use the subdomain for WINS first or the subdomain for WINS last. The ability to use subdomains for WINS lookups will have a significant positive impact on the performance of overall name resolution on the network. Figure 16-3 shows the settings for integrating DNS with WINS.

Integrating with BIND and Windows NT 4.0 DNS Servers

If the organization has existing Windows NT 4.0 or BIND DNS servers, Windows 2000 will integrate with these servers. Windows 2000 DNS is RFC-compliant, so it will interoperate with Windows NT 4.0, BIND 8.2, BIND 8.1.2, and BIND 4.9.7. These servers are treated as standard DNS servers, and they support all zone types except for Active

Figure 16-3

Settings for integrating DNS with WINS

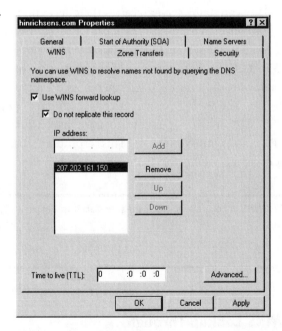

Directory–integrated zones. You can treat these zone types the way you would treat the Windows 2000 standard zone types, except for a few issues that we will address.

Remember, though, that Windows 2000 DNS is a superset of the RFC—Windows 2000 DNS supports features that the other versions do not. Table 16-2, which was taken from the Microsoft Windows 2000 Server help files, compares the feature sets of these five versions of DNS.

The design implications of these features affect the following areas:

- Dynamic updates and secure dynamic updates

- WINS lookup interoperability

- WINS referral

- Zone transfers

- Non-RFC-compliant resource records

- Unicode character-set considerations

- Active Directory support for SRV record types

Table 16-2 DNS Feature Set Comparison

Feature	Windows 2000	Windows NT 4.0	BIND 8.2	BIND 8.1.2	BIND 4.9.7
Support for dynamic update	Yes	No	Yes	Yes	No
Support for UTF-8 character encoding	Yes	No	No	No	No
Support for the IETF Internet Draft "A DNS RR for specifying the location of services (DNS SRV)" (SRV records)	Yes	Yes (with Service Pack 4)	Yes	Yes	Yes
Support for WINS and WINS-R records	Yes	Yes	No	No	No
Support for fast zone transfer	Yes	Yes	Yes	Yes	Yes
Support for incremental zone transfer	Yes	No	Yes	No	No

Dynamic Updates and Secure Dynamic Updates

Dynamic updates allow clients directly, or through DHCP, to enter zone records. Clients and servers running Windows versions earlier than Windows 2000 do not directly support dynamic-zone update. The reason dynamic updating is often included in network design is because it supports Active Directory. It is a best practice to use dynamic updates if you are using Active Directory.

WINS Lookup Interoperability

WINS lookup works best if all authoritative servers are running Windows 2000 or Windows NT 4.0. WINS and WINS-R record types are two special record types that enable forward and reverse lookups to be attempted using WINS servers. This is a Microsoft-specific solution and is not supported on third-party DNS servers that may be used to host a zone.

Take care when replicating these records to BIND DNS servers, because BIND treats these non-RFC-compliant records as invalid. If you use a mixture of Microsoft and BIND DNS servers to host a zone, the mixture may cause database errors or failed zone transfers if the non-RFC-compliant WINS and WINS-R record types are replicated between the zones. You should disable the replication of WINS and WINS-R records.

Lab Exercise 16.3: How to Disable Replication of WINS and WINS-R Records

1. In the DNS console, double-click your server to view its zones.

2. If you want to disable replication in a forward-lookup zone, double-click the Forward Lookup Zone folder. If you want to disable replication in a reverse-lookup zone, double-click the Reverse Lookup Zone folder.

3. Right-click the zone for which you want to disable replication of WINS and WINS-R records, and select Properties.

4. Click the WINS tab.

5. Select the Do Not Replicate this Record check box.

CAUTION   If you do disable replication of WINS and WINS-R records, queries directed to the primary and secondary servers will return different results. When the authoritative primary server is queried for the name of a WINS client, it queries WINS, then returns the result to the client. However, when an authoritative secondary server is queried, it will not have the WINS or WINS-R records in the zone, it will not use WINS servers for lookup, and the record will not be found. The best way to prevent this problem is to configure your DNS servers to use WINS referral, described next.

WINS Referral

If you have a domain that needs to contain WINS lookup resource records, but some of the authoritative name servers for that domain are running third-party DNS implementations, like BIND, you can prevent interoperability problems by disabling WINS replication. The downside to this is that not all servers will be able to resolve using WINS servers, which creates interoperability problems. You can prevent these interoperability problems by creating and delegating a WINS referral zone using a subdomain as mentioned earlier in the section, "Configuring WINS Lookup Through Zone Configuration." This zone does not perform any registrations or updates for DNS; it only handles the referrals of DNS lookups to WINS.

After you have created your WINS referral zone, you must configure your DNS clients to append the WINS referral zone name to unqualified queries. The easiest way is to configure the DHCP server to assign a connection-specific DNS suffix to all DHCP adapters on all computers in your network. That suffix is appended to unqualified queries.

Alternatively, you can specify a domain-suffix search-order list on each client computer. Keep in mind that when you specify a domain-suffix search-order list, your primary DNS suffix and connection-specific DNS suffix are not used unless you specifically add them to the domain-suffix search list. When a Windows 2000–based DNS client looks up a computer by its short name, it appends all the domain suffixes that the DNS client is configured to append, including the domain suffix that must be created for WINS-only lookups.

Having only one WINS-integrated zone provides other advantages as well. When a DNS forward lookup for the host name of a computer uses WINS lookup, the DNS name specified and used in the query explicitly indicates that the source used to resolve the name was a DNS server that uses WINS lookup integration. The limited name space used in the lookup will improve performance by reducing record search times. This integrated solution can also prevent the confusing situation in which DNS queries for different FQDNs resolve to the same WINS client name and IP address. This result can easily occur if you add and configure multiple zones and enable each of them to use WINS lookup integration.

How to Set up a Referral Zone

1. Create a subzone for WINS lookup only, such as wins-only.Catywhompus.com, by using the New Zone wizard, shown next.

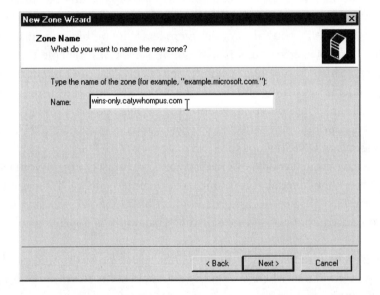

2. Right-click on the wins-only zone as in the preceding dialog box and select Properties. On the WINS tab (shown in Figure 16-4), check the box for Use WINS Forward Lookup.

3. Right-click on the appropriate network interface under Network and Dial-Up Connections, which is found in the Control Panel, and select Properties. Double-click the Internet Protocol (TCP/IP) and click the Advanced button on the General tab; then click the DNS tab. Add an appended DNS suffix in the appropriate box found in Figure 16-5.

4. Alternatively, and preferably, you can configure DHCP to assign a connection-specific DNS suffix to all DHCP clients that is appended as a suffix for all unqualified queries.

Figure 16-4
WINS
forward lookup
Configuration
Tab

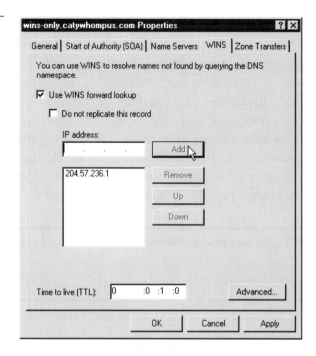

Figure 16-5
Add an appended
DNS suffix.

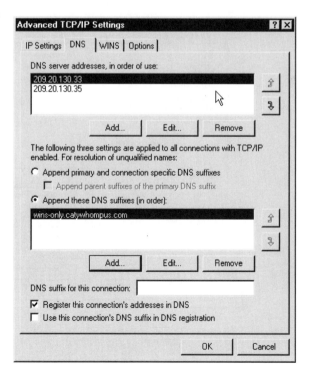

Zone Transfers

Windows 2000 supports *fast zone transfer*, which allows for more than one resource record to be sent per zone transfer. This tends to be more efficient than just sending one record per message. Some third-party DNS servers, including BIND versions earlier than 4.9.5, do not support fast zone transfer.

If you have to interoperate with a secondary server that does not support fast zone transfer, Windows 2000 allows you to disable fast zone transfers on a by-server basis. From the DNS console, select the BIND Secondaries check box (under Server Options) on the Advanced tab of the properties dialog box. This should be done for the server on which BIND secondaries exist that do not support fast zone transfers (see Figure 16-6).

NOTE   The Fast zone transfer setting is disabled for a zone by default.

Figure 16-6
BIND secondaries
check box location

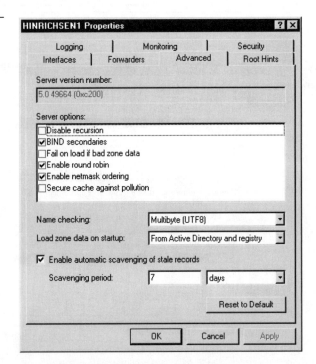

> **TIP** Note that there are DNS servers that do not support incremental zone transfers. With incremental zone transfer, instead of transferring a whole zone, a DNS server can transfer only those portions of the zone that changed since the last time the secondary server was queried. Note the performance impact of using these servers because they will use full zone transfer. This allows for compatibility, but it comes with a performance price.

Non-RFC-Compliant Resource Records

It is possible that a third-party DNS server can support vendor-specific, non-RFC-compliant resource records in a DNS zone. If the primary zone copy is on one of these servers, and the secondary zone is a Windows 2000 DNS server, the Windows 2000 server will drop these non-RFC-compliant resource records, and you will not get support for them on the Windows 2000 secondary.

Unicode Character-Set Considerations

Windows 2000 DNS supports Unicode characters and RFC 2044, which enlarges the character set allowed in DNS names beyond ANSI characters defined in RFC 1123. BIND and Windows NT 4.0 follow RFC 1123, which permits a smaller character set with ANSI characters.

You can enable the enforcement of characters supported by BIND and Windows NT if you have these standard DNS servers in your design. The enforcement of characters means that the replication of records to BIND or Windows 4.0 DNS secondaries compatibility is ensured by the Windows 2000 DNS server.

Active Directory Support for SRV Record Types

Domain controller locators, which are used for the Network Logon service, require a primary DNS server that is authoritative. The DNS server must be authoritative for the names to be registered by the Netlogon server. This ability is actually provided by the service location resource record (SRV RR) housed on the authoritative DNS. The SRV records are special DNS round-robin entries similar to mail exchange (MX) records. If you are using a DNS server with Active Directory and the DNS server does not support a DNS RR for specifying the location of services, you must upgrade your DNS server or add one that supports Active Directory. Also, if you use a DNS server other than Windows 2000, it is a best practice to test for compatibility with Active Directory and DHCP. In addition, it is good to verify your DNS configuration after you install Active Directory.

The DNS database must include locator resource records (SRV, CNAME, and A) to support each domain controller.

The following servers support SRV records:

- Windows 2000

- Windows NT 4.0 Service Pack 4 and later

- BIND 4.9.6 and later

The following servers support dynamic update:

- Windows 2000

- BIND 8.1.2 and 8.2

If you use a third-party server, you cannot use the DNS console, Active Directory integration, secure dynamic updates, aging and scavenging of stale records, or remote administration.

 EXAM TIP Take a moment to commit the preceding lists to memory. You will note that Windows 2000 appears on both lists. BIND appears on both, but note the BIND version numbers.

Internet Access Considerations

Within the framework of a private network, DNS must interact with the Internet in two primary ways.

First, DNS must allow queries from the Internet to reach registered zone authorities for domain name resolution. For instance, if www.Catywhompus.com is going to be resolved for Internet users, a DNS server must be accessible from the Internet. This responsiveness to DNS queries needs to be in place and can be provided by using one of two essential strategies:

- Your Internet service provider (ISP) can place the public DNS entries in a DNS server that the ISP supports. This is a good strategy if the entries are relatively static and the organization does not have a need to directly manage the DNS.

- Place a secondary DNS server in a screened subnet or demilitarized zone (DMZ) that contains entries for the publicly accessed resources.

The second way that DNS interacts with the Internet is when a DNS server forwards iterative queries to root servers or downstream authoritative zones for final resolution. Review Figure 16-1 to see this resolution process. The infrastructure must provide for these forwarded queries and responses.

Existing Namespace Integration Issues

When you are deciding on a namespace-integration strategy for the network, four basic options exist:

- Use the same DNS name for your internal and external networks. Microsoft recommends this strategy; the only drawback is that you must ensure that your DNS implementation supports SRV records. If it doesn't, you will need to upgrade to a version that does, or to a Windows 2000 DNS server.

- Integrate DNS into the existing namespace of your organization by using separate public and private namespaces. The existing namespace will be the public portion, and Windows 2000 DNS will manage the private portion. This improves security because the users outside the organization will not see the private namespace. This also minimizes the impact on the existing namespace.

- Use a subdomain or multiple subdomains of the registered domain to provide a single subdomain for Microsoft DNS servers and clients. This has minimal impact on the existing namespace and allows simple management of coexisting private and public portions of a contiguous namespace.

- Use the same name for both the internal and external DNS, but separate the two by putting one in a screened subnet and manually maintaining the appropriate records in each server. This is the most difficult scenario to manage because it requires manual manipulation of the external DNS database.

Hands-On Section Exercises

An organic milk company (OMC) located in Denver, Colorado, has a series of collection and distribution sites located in Minnesota, Wisconsin, and Michigan. This company allows small, organic dairy farmers to sell through a brand that consolidates these farmers' marketing functions. Each location is connected to the Denver site through a dedicated T-1 WAN connection. On a daily basis, the milk supply information is transferred to corporate headquarters using a Web-based application.

The production facilities constantly monitor production information and consolidate the data in an Oracle database located at headquarters. Distribution centers and buyers from distributors have the ability to access inventories over the Internet using a

Web-based application and can order organic milk on a weekly basis online. Currently, the DNS servers are Windows NT 4.0, and name resolution for FQDNs is provided using the traditional single-master zone model.

Lab Exercise 16.4:
Analyzing DNS Functionality

1. OMC has traditionally used WINS for NetBIOS name-resolution services. If OMC deploys Windows 2000 Active Directory Services along with Windows 2000 DNS in a mixed environment for the near term, how could you allow clients to use Windows 2000 DNS to resolve NetBIOS names?

2. OMC has deployed Windows 2000 and is using Active Directory to provide directory services. In the past, the network administrator has complained that full zone transfers have created performance issues on the WAN connections. A consultant has recommended using Active Directory–integrated zones and placing at least one domain controller with DNS installed at each site to improve the situation. What elements of these suggestions reduce WAN load?

3. The DNS services at one location is based on UNIX BIND DNS servers. The director of information services at that location is unwilling to replace the existing BIND DNS servers. Will this affect the DNS solution?

4. OMC's management has decided not to use the ISP to manage DNS services for DNS queries coming from the Internet because the ISP's DNS has not been reliable. They have decided to place an Active Directory–integrated DNS in their screened subnet. Would you support this decision? Why or why not?

Lab 16.4: Suggested Solutions

1. You can allow DNS clients to resolve host names found on a WINS NetBIOS name server by configuring the DNS server to query WINS for resolution of names not found in the DNS zone.

2. Incremental zone transfers will occur over the WAN links instead of full zone transfers. DNS resolution for the local zone records will occur locally.

3. Yes. Standard DNS zones will need to be used in this location. If there is a delegated zone involved, the Windows 2000–based DNS server needs to support primary or Active Directory–integrated zones as delegated domains. If the zone is a master copy of the zone information on the BIND server, the Windows 2000–based server needs to use secondary zones that replicate from the BIND DNS servers. To support Active Directory, the version of BIND DNS server needs

to be 4.9.6 or later. To support dynamically updated DNS zones, which is recommended for Active Directory support, BIND 8.1.2 or later is required. Finally, to support incremental zone transfers, the version of BIND needs to be 8.1.2 or later.

4. It is fine to place a DNS server in a screened subnet, but you should recommend that for security reasons, they use a standard secondary zone that is read-only, rather than jeopardizing the read/write DNS on the domain controller by subjecting it to security risks in the screened subnet.

Availability Considerations in Windows 2000 DNS Designs

Always keep in mind that your network is only as strong as its weakest link. In a Windows 2000 network, DNS availability is a key concern because many services rely on DNS name resolution. For instance, Active Directory requires DNS for a user to log on, to find resources, and so on. Without DNS, clients will not be able to log on to the network. The DNS specifications address fault tolerance, which means that the tools are in place within the DNS system to allow you to address fault tolerance very directly in your design.

Two primary areas are addressed by these DNS availability solutions:

- A WAN link or other network connection going down
- One or more DNS servers going down

The first obvious fault-tolerance solution for both of these issues is to use multiple DNS servers with zone replication, and assign multiple DNS server addresses to clients for DNS lookup. This requires additional hardware, but you can place additional DNS servers at remote locations to ensure DNS availability in the event of a WAN link or router failure. Put simply, having a DNS server on both sides of most WAN connections is the safest design. This solution also addresses the effect of a single DNS server going down, given correct zone replications.

The second fault-tolerance solution is to use cluster servers to provide name-resolution services in the event that a single DNS server fails. This method increases the availability of a single DNS server. Clustered servers should be configured to share a cluster drive so that both nodes have access to the most recent zone database file. Failed servers can be restored more quickly from a cluster drive because there is no need to resynchronize. The availability is at site-level only, because clusters require persistent high-speed links. Clustering enhances the availability of the DNS design solution.

Optimization Strategies in Windows 2000 DNS Designs

The DNS design you create will be measured directly by two primary factors: How long does it take a client to resolve via a DNS query? What is the impact of query traffic and replication traffic on network bandwidth?

When we create an optimized DNS design, we endeavor to improve the performance of the service and reduce the impact of the service on network bandwidth by addressing these three issues in the process:

- **Server capacity** Create a strategy to improve the performance of individual DNS servers.

- **Client resolution** Reduce DNS client query-resolution time.

- **Zone replication** Reduce DNS server query and zone-replication impact on the network.

The following sections address ways of improving the performance of your DNS design.

Server Capacity Optimization

The first step that you should take when optimizing a DNS server is to size the DNS server to match the client load placed on the server. Because each DNS server loads the configured zones into memory at initialization to provide fast access to zone information, increasing RAM on the server will usually provide the biggest performance improvement, rather than providing a faster processor or improving hard-drive capabilities. The amount of RAM needed in the server is based on a number of load variables:

- The services the server provides on the network

- Whether the server is a domain controller

- Whether the server is used for file and print services

- How many clients the server supports

- How many server relationships the server has, and the nature of the traffic

- How many DNS queries the DNS server needs to handle simultaneously

Make note of the RAM required to support DNS alone, and add that to the RAM requirements of the other services supported on the server. In a typical environment, DNS uses RAM as follows:

- Approximately 100 bytes for each resource record within each zone on the server

- Approximately 4MB for the DNS server itself, before zones are created

For example, if a DNS server is supporting 2,000 resource records, the RAM needed for the service would be calculated as follows:

$$4MB + (100 \text{ bytes} \times 1,500 \text{ records}) = 4.2MB \text{ of RAM}$$

You should also review the other hardware, including the processor, disk subsystem, and network subsystem, to increase processing and network transfer rates. Be aware, though, that when you improve the performance of any one component of a system, it may impact another. Continue to monitor performance directly after you have enhanced one area to ensure that an unresolved bottleneck has not developed in another component.

For instance, if the network card was previously a bottleneck for client traffic, and you replace the NIC, you may find that the processor or memory is now bottlenecked because of the increased network service load. Continue to monitor and test even in the lab environment prior to implementation.

Monitoring Server Performance

DNS servers are of critical importance, especially for Active Directory and Internet access. Monitoring their performance can help in the following ways:

- Providing a useful benchmark for predicting, estimating, and optimizing DNS server performance

- Troubleshooting DNS servers where server performance has degraded either over time or during periods of peak activity

Windows 2000 Server provides a set of DNS server performance counters that can be used with System Monitor to measure and monitor various aspects of server activity, such as the following:

- DNS server performance statistics, such as the number of overall queries and responses processed by a DNS server

- User Datagram Protocol (UDP) or Transmission Control Protocol (TCP) counters, for measuring DNS queries and responses using either of these transport protocols

- Dynamic-update and secure dynamic-update counters for measuring registration and update activity generated by dynamic clients

PART III

- Memory usage counters for measuring system memory usage and memory-allocation patterns created by operating the server computer as a Windows 2000 DNS server

- Recursive lookup counters for measuring queries and responses when the DNS Server service uses recursion to look up and fully resolve DNS names on behalf of requesting clients

- WINS lookup counters for measuring queries and responses made to WINS servers when the WINS lookup integration features of the DNS Server service are used

- Zone-transfer counters, including specific counters for measuring all zone transfer (AXFR), incremental zone transfer (IXFR), and DNS zone update notification activity

Each of these DNS Server performance counters is described in more detail in the following sections. These counters provide a specific analysis and should be used to monitor and gather information about the DNS service. This detailed performance analysis will help to provide needed information about your DNS in a number of areas during planning and later allow you to manage the design to your specifications.

All Zone Transfer (AXFR) Counters

Field	Description
AXFR Request Received	The total number of full zone-transfer requests received by the DNS Server service when operating as a master server for a zone
AXFR Request Sent	The total number of full zone-transfer requests sent by the DNS Server service when operating as a secondary server for a zone
AXFR Response Received	The total number of full zone-transfer requests received by the DNS Server service when operating as a secondary server for a zone
AXFR Success Received	The total number of full zone transfers received by the DNS Server service when operating as a secondary server for a zone
AXFR Success Sent	The total number of full zone transfers successfully sent by the DNS Server service when operating as a master server for a zone

DNS Server Memory Counters

Field	Description
Caching Memory	The total amount of system memory in use by the DNS Server service for caching

continued

DNS Server Memory Counters (*continued*)

Field	Description
Database Node Memory	The total amount of system memory in use by the DNS Server service for database nodes
Nbtstat Memory	The total amount of system memory in use by the DNS Server service for Nbtstat
Record Flow Memory	The total amount of system memory in use by the DNS Server service for record flow

Dynamic-Update Counters

Field	Description
Dynamic Update NoOperation	The total number of no-operation/empty dynamic-update requests received by the DNS server
Dynamic Update NoOperation/sec	The average number of no-operation/empty dynamic-update requests received by the DNS server in each second
Dynamic Update Queued	The total number of dynamic updates queued by the DNS server
Dynamic Update Received	The total number of dynamic-update requests received by the DNS server
Dynamic Update Received/sec	The average number of dynamic-update requests received by the DNS server in each second
Dynamic Update Rejected	The total number of dynamic updates rejected by the DNS server
Dynamic Update TimeOuts	The total number of dynamic-update time-outs of the DNS server
Dynamic Update Written to Database	The total number of dynamic updates written to the database by the DNS server
Dynamic Update Written to Database/sec	The average number of dynamic updates written to the database by the DNS server in each second

Incremental Zone-Transfer (IXFR) Counters

Field	Description
IXFR Request Received	The total number of incremental zone-transfer requests received by the master DNS server
IXFR Request Sent	The total number of incremental zone-transfer requests sent by the secondary DNS server

continued

Incremental Zone-Transfer (IXFR) Counters (*continued*)

Field	Description
IXFR Response Received	The total number of incremental zone-transfer responses received by the secondary DNS server
IXFR Success Received	The total number of successful incremental zone transfers received by the secondary DNS server
IXFR Success Sent	The total number of successful incremental zone transfers of the master DNS server
IXFR TCP Success Received	The total number of successful TCP incremental zone transfers received by the secondary DNS server
IXFR UDP Success Received	The total number of successful UDP incremental zone transfers received by the secondary DNS server

Notification Counters

Field	Description
Notify Received	The total number of notifies received by the secondary DNS server
Notify Sent	The total number of notifies sent by the master DNS server

Recursion Counters

Field	Description
Recursive Queries	The total number of recursive queries received by the DNS server
Recursive Queries/sec	The average number of recursive queries received by the DNS server in each second
Recursive Query Failure	The total number of recursive query failures
Recursive Query Failure/sec	The average number of recursive query failures in each second
Recursive TimeOuts	The total number of recursive query sending time-outs
Recursive TimeOuts/sec	The average number of recursive query sending time-outs in each second

Secure Dynamic-Update Counters

Field	Description
Secure Update Failure	The total number of secure updates failed on the DNS server

continued

Secure Dynamic-Update Counters (*continued*)

Field	Description
Secure Update Received	The total number of secure-update requests received by the DNS server
Secure Update Received/sec	The average number of secure-update requests received by the DNS server in each second

TCP Counters

Field	Description
TCP Message Memory	The total TCP message memory used by the DNS server
TCP Query Received	The total number of TCP queries received by the DNS server
TCP Query Received/sec	The average number of TCP queries received by the DNS server in each second
TCP Response Sent	The total number of TCP responses sent by the DNS server
TCP Response Sent/sec	The average number of TCP responses sent by the DNS server in each second

Total (Overall Performance) Counters

Field	Description
Total Query Received	The total number of queries received by the DNS server
Total Query Received/sec	The average number of queries received by the DNS server in each second
Total Response Sent	The total number of responses sent by the DNS server
Total Response Sent/sec	The average number of responses sent by the DNS server in each second

UDP Counters

Field	Description
UDP Message Memory	The total UDP message memory used by the DNS server
UDP Query Received	The total number of UDP queries received by the DNS server
UDP Query Received/sec	The average number of UDP queries received by the DNS server in each second

continued

UDP Counters (*continued*)

Field	Description
UDP Response Sent	The total number of UDP responses sent by the DNS server
UDP Response Sent/sec	The average number of UDP responses sent by the DNS server in each second

WINS Lookup Counters

Field	Description
WINS Lookup Received	The total number of WINS lookup requests received by the server
WINS Lookup Received/sec	The average number of WINS lookup requests received by the server in each second
WINS Response Sent	The total number of WINS lookup responses sent by the server
WINS Response Sent/sec	The average number of WINS lookup responses sent by the server in each second
WINS Reverse Lookup Received	The total number of WINS reverse-lookup requests received by the server
WINS Reverse Lookup Received/sec	The average number of WINS reverse-lookup requests received by the server in each second
WINS Reverse Response Sent	The total number of WINS reverse-lookup responses sent by the server
WINS Reverse Response Sent/sec	The average number of WINS reverse-lookup responses sent by the server in each second

Zone-Transfer Counters

Field	Description
Zone Transfer Failure	The total number of failed zone transfers of the master DNS server
Zone Transfer Request Received	The total number of zone-transfer requests received by the master DNS server
Zone Transfer Start of Authority (SOA) Request Sent	The total number of zone-transfer SOA requests sent by the secondary DNS server
Zone Transfer Success	The total number of successful zone transfers of the master DNS server

Query Resolution Optimization

End users and management will view your DNS design as highly successful if you reduce query-resolution time because query resolution is the primary business purpose for providing DNS. You can use caching-only DNS servers, delegated zones, forwarders, and load balancing to improve query-resolution performance in various situations.

Using Caching-Only Servers

All DNS name servers cache queries that they have resolved. Caching-only servers are simply DNS name servers that only perform queries, cache the answers, and return the results to clients. They do not contain zones, and the information that they contain is limited to what has been cached while resolving queries. By locally caching DNS requests, the DNS server can respond to clients quickly from cached information, and the impact on WAN traffic is reduced.

The cache information is obtained over time as client requests are serviced. However, if you are dealing with a slow WAN link between sites, this option might be ideal because, once the cache is built, traffic decreases over the WAN connection. This should only be used if DNS records are relatively static so that frequent changes do not result in resolution failures.

Frankly, using caching-only servers only improves performance over other types of DNS servers because caching servers reduce the impact of zone replication over slow WAN connections. Consider using caching-only servers if DNS zone replication will overuse WAN links.

Delegating Zones

DNS provides the option of dividing up the namespace into more than one zone if a particular zone gets saturated by organizational growth. These delegated zones can then be stored, distributed, and replicated to other DNS servers. When deciding when to divide your DNS namespace to make additional zones for performance reasons, consider the option of dividing one large zone into smaller zones for distributing traffic loads among multiple servers, which will improve DNS name-resolution performance.

If, for any of these reasons, you could benefit from delegating zones, it might make sense to restructure your namespace by adding zones. When choosing how to structure zones, you should use a plan that reflects the structure of your organization.

When delegating zones within a namespace, be aware that for each new zone you create, you will need delegation records in other zones that point to the authoritative DNS servers for the new zone. This is necessary both to transfer authority and to provide correct referral to other DNS servers and clients.

Using Forwarders

DNS servers can be configured to send all recursive queries to a selected list of *forwarder* DNS servers. Windows 2000 DNS can be configured to use forwarders on the Forwarders property page of the server properties. Servers in the list of forwarders provide recursive lookups rather than iterative lookups for any queries that a DNS server receives and cannot resolve based on its local zones. A DNS server configured to use forwarders essentially behaves as a DNS client using recursive lookups, which are sent to its forwarders.

Using forwarders is an excellent way to reduce iterative traffic when access to remote DNS root servers requires the use of a slow link, such as a relatively slow link to the Internet. In this situation, using forwarders can cut down on expensive traffic over the low-speed link in two ways:

- Using forwarders reduces the number of overall queries that get sent across the slow link.

- When the DNS server used as a forwarder for your internal network receives a query for a remote name on the Internet, it can directly contact remote servers on the Internet using recursion.

Forwarders provide a way to share information about remote names with a group of DNS servers located in the same area. Rather than having each server send queries through a firewall and out to the Internet, all DNS servers can be configured to forward queries to one DNS server (placed in a screened subnet) that makes the necessary queries to the remote servers. In the process, the forwarder builds up a cache of Internet DNS names from the responses it receives. As local DNS servers continue to forward queries to the forwarder, it answers more queries from its cache like a caching-only server.

The DNS server can also be configured to use forwarders so that forwarding is used before any other means of resolution is tried. If the list of forwarders fails to provide an answer, a DNS server will attempt to resolve the query itself, using iterative queries and standard recursion.

Load Balancing

Adding more DNS servers can allow client queries to be distributed across servers to improve DNS query performance. Having more DNS servers provides zone redundancy, thereby enabling DNS names in the zone to be resolved for clients if a primary DNS server stops responding. New DNS servers can also be placed so as to reduce DNS network traffic. For example, adding a DNS server to the other end of a low-speed WAN link can be useful in managing and reducing network traffic.

Reducing the Impact of Server-to-Server Traffic on the Network

The single biggest way to improve DNS replication traffic across WAN links is to upgrade the DNS servers to the latest versions of BIND, for Unix servers, and Windows 2000 DNS, for Windows servers. This will allow for incremental zone transfers, which are more efficient than full zone transfers, and will also allow for fast zone transfers, which compress the zone-replication data. Also, if your zone data is fairly static, you can use a replication schedule for secondary servers that allows for zone transfers during non-peak hours. These two strategies reduce the amount of traffic and frequency, especially over slow WAN connections.

Security Strategies in DNS Designs

Time for an MCSE candidate no-brainer. Your network will rely heavily on the name-resolution capabilities of DNS, not only for Active Directory, but for Internet and host-name resolutions across the internetwork. You must safeguard DNS and the network from malicious attacks, while providing appropriate access to the DNS services.

With Windows 2000 and other operating systems, you can secure DNS on both public and private networks. Over public networks, DNS zone-replication traffic can be transmitted using encryption and secure communications, such as IPSec, VPNs, and Active Directory. You can also provide access to DNS services by restricting DNS access and using subnets screened by firewalls.

Secured Dynamic Update

The DNS zone information needs to be protected from unauthorized updates, especially on servers that allow dynamic updates. Without server dynamic updates, host records could be modified and key communications would be interrupted. Secure dynamic updates are only supported on Active Directory–integrated zones. When you create an Active Directory–integrated zone, it is configured to allow only secure dynamic updates by default. If you create the zone as a standard zone and then convert it to an Active Directory–integrated zone, it retains the original configuration for non-secure dynamic updates or for no dynamic updates.

Lab Exercise 16.5:
How to Configure Secure Dynamic Update

1. In the DNS console, right-click the zone you want to configure for dynamic update, and click Properties.

2. In the Allow Dynamic Updates drop-down list, select the Only Secure Updates option.

Controlling Update Access to Zones

With secure dynamic update, only the computers and users you specify in an Access Control List (ACL) can create or modify dnsNode objects within the zone. By default, the ACL gives create permission to all members of the Authenticated User group, the group of all authenticated computers and users in an Active Directory forest. This means that any authenticated user or computer can create a new object in the zone. Also by default, the creator owns the new object and is given full control of it.

You can view and change the permissions for all DNS objects on the Security tab for the object, from within the Active Directory Users and Computers console, or through the properties of zone and resource record in the DNS console.

Lab Exercise 16.6:
How to View the ACL for a dnsZone
or dnsNode Object

1. In the DNS console, right-click the zone or record you want to view, and click Properties.

2. Click the Security tab.

DNS Dynamic Updates from DHCP
and Windows 2000

If you have specified that DHCP servers within the network dynamically update DNS from DHCP for clients, you can set up the permissions so that only DHCP is authorized to update DNS zones. This works well for networks that have operating systems other than Windows 2000, and if setting permissions at another level is too unwieldy.

You may wish to allow individual Windows 2000 workstations to update DNS directly if the computer has a manually assigned IP address and you want the node to register in DNS. You can also allow direct updates if there is a limited security risk to having individual nodes register directly.

DNS Zone Replication

Past concerns about good, old-fashioned terrorism have been replaced by concerns about cyber-terrorism. Fortunately, DNS server-to-server traffic can be secured using IPSec, VPN tunnels, or encrypted transmissions for Active Directory–integrated zones.

Windows 2000 can provide for the use of IPSec using IP security policies. VPN connections can be set up using Remote Access features. If you use Active Directory–integrated zones exclusively, you automatically inherit the security features of Active Directory, which includes the encryption of all replication data between servers.

DNS in Screened Subnets

DNS servers are often integrated into screened subnets to provide Internet accessibility and protect internal resources. The following are recommended best practices when placing DNS servers in screened subnets:

- Place only servers with secondary zones in screened subnets because they are, by nature, read-only zone copies.

- Do not place Active Directory–integrated zones in the screened subnet.

- Use IPSec or a VPN tunnel to encrypt all DNS traffic between the primary zone and the secondary zone if either zone is located on the private side of the subnet.

- Ensure that DNS servers on the private side of the subnet communicate only over a secure connection with the DNS server in the screened subnet. Only allow internal clients to access the private DNS servers; the DNS server in the screen subnet should not be able to access the private DNS servers because it is difficult to secure this traffic.

- Only allow queries from the Internet or secure internal queries from DNS servers to reach the DNS servers on the screened subnet.

Hands-On Section Exercises

Two years after you created the original DNS design for the organic milk company (OMC), the company was very happy with your work and decided to retain you to help again, because they have a new problem—growth.

As you'll recall, the company is located in Denver, Colorado, and has a series of and distribution sites located in Minnesota, Wisconsin, and Michigan. Each location is connected to the Denver site through a dedicated T-1 WAN connection. Many users and managers complain that these connections are too slow, and occasionally mission-critical name-resolution services fail. They are also concerned that there are certain instances where DNS records mysteriously disappear from the Active Directory–integrated DNS database located in the screened subnet.

You are asked by the Director of Information Systems to analyze the business and technical requirements and provide design suggestions to improve their DNS design.

Lab Exercise 16.7: Enhancing DNS Availability, Performance, and Security

1. The Director of Information Systems has stated that the system must be available 24/7 because of production and order requirements and time-zone differences. What precautions can be taken to ensure DNS will function on this basis?

2. The increased load on the Internet connection requires that the DNS traffic between the DNS server in the screened subnet and DNS servers on the Internet be minimized. What configuration changes can be made to the DNS on the screened subnet to reduce traffic to the Internet?

3. OMC's network team places an Active Directory–integrated DNS in their screened subnet. What changes, if any, would you make to this configuration?

Lab 16.7: Suggested Solutions

(It's OK if your answers vary.)

1. Use multiple DNS servers with zone replication using either standard DNS zones or Active Directory–integrated zones. You can place additional DNS servers at remote locations to ensure DNS availability in the event of a WAN link or router failure. Set up client computers to point to the DNS on the local subnet as primary and on a remote subnet for secondary to provide fault tolerance.

2. Configure forwarders on the DNS server to reduce iterative query traffic over the relatively slow link to the Internet. Using forwarders in this situation can cut down on expensive traffic over the low-speed link by reducing the number of overall queries that are sent across the slow link.

3. Make the following changes to the configuration:
   - Use a DNS server with standard secondary zones rather than jeopardize the read/write DNS on the Active Directory–integrated zones.
   - Configure firewalls to permit DNS queries only from the Internet.
   - Encrypt all replications using IPSec or VPN for zone replication between the private network DNS servers.

Catywhompus Updates: DNS Analysis Steps

Catywhompus Construction requires a DNS solution for locating network resources. When creating a design solution for the new e-commerce initiatives at Catywhompus, you have to make some key decisions based on information about the network. Collect the following information for use in creating your DNS design:

- How many DNS clients or users are at each site or location? The number of clients determines how many DNS servers will be needed at each location. Often, there is at least one DNS server per location.

- How many locations are there in the organization? Often, but not always, one DNS server is needed at each location.

- Are there any DNS servers, such as Unix or Windows NT 4.0 servers, currently in use on the network? Older DNS servers will not support all of the newer features, like incremental zone transfer.

- Is Active Directory in use or planned for the future? Active Directory–integrated zones are available only on Windows 2000 DNS servers, and they use the replication capabilities of Active Directory, while maintaining backward compatibility with traditional DNS zones.

Once you know the functionality your DNS solution needs to provide, you have some decisions to make:

- Select the zone types you will use in the solution.

- Select the appropriate locations for the DNS servers, given the capacities and zone types selected.

- Select the integration options including DHCP, WINS, and Active Directory integration.

- Determine what type of Internet connectivity you need and where the servers should be placed.

Once you have designed the base functionality, look for ways to improve availability, performance, and security. Make sure to consider the following best practices:

continued

- Make sure you have at least two servers supporting each zone. These can be either primary and secondary copies, or two Active Directory–integrated copies of zones.

- If possible, use Active Directory–integrated zones. This provides for improved records replication and dynamic updates.

- Improve traffic and performance by using load-balancing with secondary servers and/or caching-only servers to reduce the load on key DNS servers.

Now, develop your own design based on your analysis.

Case Study 16: The Environmental Consulting Group Needs a DNS Design Strategy

Now you will apply your new knowledge of DNS design. Review the following case information for the Environmental Consulting Group (ECG), and pay particular attention to the business-application support and technical requirements. The design and integration of DNS is driven by the business needs, so be sure you first understand the business requirements. Next, you will review the high-level physical network diagram for ECG and the key offices. Then you will complete an analysis worksheet and complete the hands-on strategy analysis and design worksheet for the ECG scenario.

Scenario

The Environmental Consulting Group (ECG) is preparing to upgrade much of its network to Windows 2000 from Windows NT 4.0. All of the client operating systems will be upgraded to Windows 2000 from Windows 98 over the course of a two-year period, so any network solution, including DNS, must support both client operating systems for a period of time. You are a consultant for the firm and are assigned the task of evaluating the deployment of the mission-critical name-resolution services. The organization has requested that you evaluate the current name-resolution services, and redesign the services as needed to leverage the advantages of upgrading to the Windows 2000 operating system.

continued

The internal consultants often refer to ECG as a "virtual" organization and use other choice words when their managers are within earshot. Locations include a corporate headquarters, seven regional offices, and many small offices/home offices (SOHOs). The central office is where the executive management team is located, along with support staff and the financial management group. Most of the staff at headquarters, except for the financial group, travels to regional offices on a regular basis.

The seven regional offices are managed by a director of operations and they support the individual consultants and small offices dispersed within each region. The individual consultants operate as independent agents or are hired by the company and move between regional offices regularly, depending on project assignments—the agents are often members of multiple cross-functional teams. The SOHOs connect to the Internet through dial-up connections if there is a single consultant or network address translators if there are multiple agents in a small office.

ECG Design Requirements and Constraints

The Director of Information Systems has provided investigative data regarding the current network operations. This analysis includes traffic patterns, network application usage analysis, user requirements, and projected growth or structural changes. You must consider these in developing your design. ECG uses a number of applications to provide information on a day-to-day basis. ECG also has specific connectivity requirements between locations, as well as DNS-specific requirements. All of the business and technical requirements must be provided for in the DNS design.

The analysis of current operations and growth projections reveal the following requirements:

- Terminal server support for remote users accessing a file-sharing database over slow dial-up connections.

- Support for a Web-based knowledge-management system of environmental issues, governmental policies, and solutions. This data is replicated between the central office and regional offices.

- Support for a Web-based financial management system.

- All mission-critical applications must be available 24/7 to support consultants in the field and emergency support services.

These are the technical requirements:

- Seamless network access to all shared files, resources, and Web-based applications on regional office servers and the main office servers.

continued

- Internet access must be provided for the central and regional offices.

- There must be support for connectivity between the seven regional offices and the central office over the Internet.

- The consultants must be able to connect to the regional offices over dial-up Internet connections.

- All private offices must be secure from external tampering and therefore, isolated from the public network.

ECG has the following integration requirements:

- ECG is installing Active Directory and would like to take advantage of Active Directory's ability to provide increased fault tolerance, security, easier management, and efficient zone replication.

- Host names for shared resources on Windows 2000 professional and Windows 98 must be available, and the host names for these resources must be resolved through DNS.

- The internal and external namespace must be the same so that there is no need to manage two separate namespaces.

These are the DNS-specific requirements:

- DNS forward-query response times must allow application response time to improve. Based on testing, the DNS servers on the approved server hardware will support up to 1,500 clients per server with reasonable response times.

- The DNS solution must provide for increased fault tolerance, security, easier management, and efficient replication of zone data.

- DNS reverse lookup is not required for client computers.

ECG Diagrams

Figures 16-7, 16-8, and 16-9 show the layout of the existing ECG network. Use these diagrams when developing your DNS solution.

continued

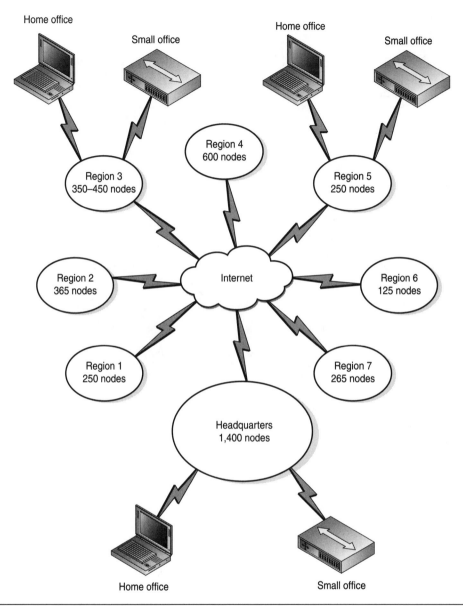

Figure 16-7   ECG's high-level physical and network diagram

continued

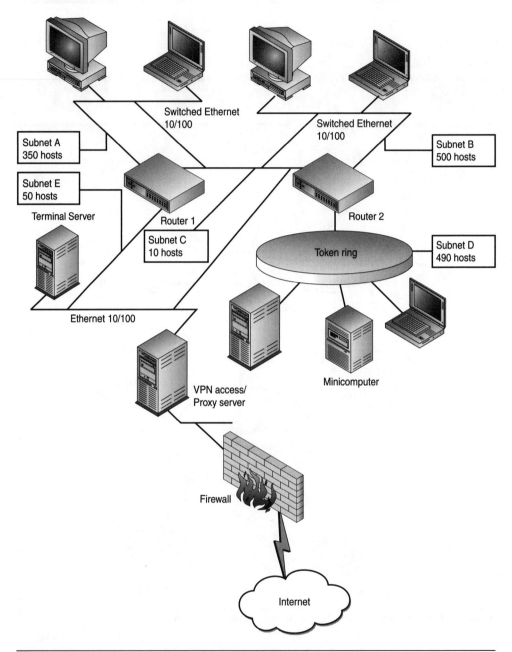

Figure 16-8 ECG's central office network diagram

continued

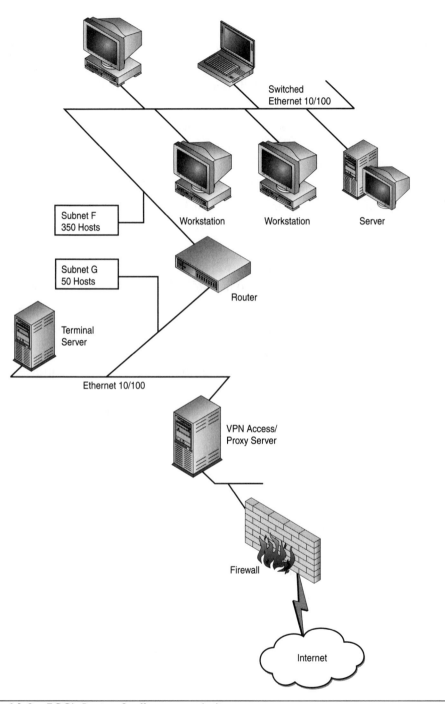

Figure 16-9   ECG's Region 3 office network diagram

continued

Case Study Questions

1. You have taken the Active Directory–integrated zones integration requirement to heart and believe it is the best solution for a variety of reasons. Name at least four reasons why ECG should use integrated zones. Should they use them exclusively in all situations?

2. ECG needs to create a location plan for DNS servers. Based on the current network structure and the reliability business requirements, identify the quantity, type, and location of each DNS server for the headquarters and Region 3 office. Also, address how clients in the various subnets will contact DNS servers.

3. ECG wants to be sure that all nodes, including clients and servers, have resource records in DNS and are available from any DNS server on the network. How would you create the design to accomplish this objective?

4. What design enhancements can you add to ensure DNS server availability in the case of a single DNS failure, and how does this change your DNS location design?

5. If the small offices have limited bandwidth over the WAN connection to the Internet, how can you configure the DNS servers at those offices to minimize traffic related to zone transfers?

6. What type of zones would you put in the screened subnets to provide Internet accessibility? Why?

7. Recommend a zone-replication strategy for the network.

Suggested Solutions

Be aware that your solutions may vary.

1. Active Directory–integrated zones are the best solution for the following reasons:

   - **Fault tolerance** Multimaster replication provides better fault tolerance for zone transfers.

   - **Security** The administrators can set access limits for zones and zone records.

   - **Ease of management** Replication is automated by the domain controllers.

   - **Fast and efficient replication** DNS will use incremental zone replication.

NOTE Active Directory–integrated zones should not be used in the screened subnets.

continued

2. Server placement

Office	DNS Server Number	Server Location	Justification for Placement
Headquarters	DNS1, DNS2	Subnet C	Place servers centrally and use two servers to provide the required load balancing and fault tolerance.
Region 3	DNS3, DNS4	DNS3 and DNS4 in subnet F	Place on the largest client subnet and use two servers to provide load balancing and fault tolerance.

3. Enable dynamic DNS updates from the DHCP server. This will support both Windows 2000 clients and Windows 98 clients.

4. Make one DNS server in each of the eight main locations be a cluster-aware DNS server. This will increase the hardware requirements in each location and improve server recovery.

5. You could ensure that they are caching-only DNS servers to eliminate zone transfers.

6. Use Windows 2000 DNS servers as the corporate standard DNS server to ease management, and then set up a secondary zone with incremental zone transfers so there is read-only zone information in the screened subnet.

7. Use the efficient and secure zone transfers available in the Active Directory–integrated zones.

Chapter Review

DNS provides the core name-resolution services on a network and has particular significance on a Windows 2000 network; and the DNS area receives some of the greatest attention on the 70-221 exam. The functionality and key features reviewed in this chapter include interoperability features, as well as enhanced functionality related to design issues. Windows 2000 DNS availability, performance, and security enhancements were also discussed.

Questions

1. When assessing the number and location of DNS servers for a WAN, which of the following is the most important information to use, from a network-design standpoint? (Choose one only.)
   a. For business reasons, the DNS services need to function 24/7 because they provide mission-critical name-resolution services to support company sales.
   b. The Director of Information Systems wants to replace the BIND DNS servers with Windows 2000 DNS servers.
   c. DNS reverse lookup is required for client computers.
   d. The existing DNS servers are over three years old and must be replaced.

2. Which of the following are reasons to use Active Directory–integrated zones? (Choose all that apply.)
   a. Active Directory–integrated zones are more secure and should be used in the screened subnet.
   b. Active Directory–integrated zones provide improved fault tolerance for zone transfers because all servers are primary and can perform zone replication.
   c. Active Directory–integrated zones are compatible with standard secondary zones on Windows NT 4.0 or BIND 4.9.7.
   d. Active Directory–integrated zones provide faster and more efficient replication than Windows NT 4.0.

3. Which of the following will most improve DNS server performance by minimizing zone transfer traffic over a WAN connection? (Choose one answer only.)
   a. Use delegated zones.
   b. Configure forwarders.
   c. Configure a secondary zone Windows 4.0 DNS server.
   d. Configure a standard primary zone Windows 2000 DNS server.
   e. Configure an Active Directory–integrated zone.
   f. Use a caching-only DNS server.

4. What is the security advantage of making the DNS zone files Active Directory-integrated?

5. True or False? When designing a DNS naming solution for a business, technical requirements take priority over the business requirements.

Answers

1. **A.** Network infrastructure designs must be based on business requirements first, and this states a key business requirement.

2. **B, C,** and **D.** A is not correct because Active Directory–integrated zones are read/write and pose security risks in screened subnets.

3. **F.** A caching-only DNS server will not perform zone transfers.

4. The administrator can set access limits for any zone or record using Discretionary Access Control List entries (DACLs) to specify users or groups that have access to modify the zone or zone records. Secure dynamic updates are only supported by Active Directory–integrated zones.

5. **False.** In network design, business needs drive the technical requirements.

Key Skill Sets

- You should be able to evaluate DNS as a solution for name resolution in order to appropriately integrate DNS into an infrastructure design.

- You should be able to evaluate and create a DNS solution to support an organization's namespace requirements.

- You should be able to select appropriate strategies to secure DNS services.

- You should be able to select appropriate strategies to enhance the availability of DNS.

- You should be able to select appropriate strategies to improve the performance of DNS.

- You should be able to design a DNS deployment strategy based on the business and technical requirements of the organization.

Key Terms

Berkeley Internet Name Domain (BIND)
Domain Name System (DNS)
Dynamic DNS
Record
Resource record (RR)
Service Location Record (SRV)
Subnet
Windows Internet Naming Service (WINS)
Zone

Designing with WINS Services and DFS

This chapter covers the following key mastery goals:

- Design NetBIOS name resolution services
- Evaluate WINS as a solution for NetBIOS name resolution
- Evaluate and create a functional design for baseline name resolution
- Design and select appropriate strategies to secure a WINS solution
- Develop and implement appropriate strategies to improve WINS availability
- Improve WINS performance
- Design a Distributed File System (DFS) strategy
- Design the placement of a DFS root
- Design a DFS root replica strategy

The Microsoft WINS Solution

The Windows Internet Naming Service (WINS) is a service that maps NetBIOS names to IP addresses. This capability is crucial for any network containing computers based on older Windows architectures, including Windows NT or Windows 9x. Microsoft created WINS following the RFC 1001 and RFC 1002 guidelines (which Microsoft essentially created). The goal of WINS is to aid clients in resolving NetBIOS names, as opposed to fully qualified domain names (FQDNs), to IP addresses. If you ping hostname.domain.com, host name resolution will return the IP address of the FQDN. On the other hand, if you ping netbiosname, NetBIOS name resolution will return the IP address of the NetBIOS name. A NetBIOS name needs to be resolved to an IP address so that communication can take place using the IP address.

EXAM TIP   This is a more important chapter than you may think. More than one Windows 2000 MCSE candidate has made the mistake of assuming that WINS went away with the Windows NT Server 4.0 era. Such is not the case. WINS is on the current Windows 2000 MCSE exams, if for no other reason than to serve as both a technical and cultural tie to the past.

You may remember that NetBIOS defines a software interface, along with a naming convention. NetBIOS is, however, not a network protocol. The NetBEUI (NetBIOS Extended User Interface) protocol, introduced by IBM in 1985, was created to provide a protocol for programs designed around the NetBIOS interface. However, NetBEUI is a small protocol that is broadcast-based and efficient for a small LAN but has no networking layer and is therefore not routable. Bottom line? NetBEUI will not scale.

In order to scale networks, routable protocols like TCP/IP or IPX/SPX must be used. Along comes the capability to provide the NetBIOS interface on routed networks by creating NetBIOS over TCP/IP (NetBT). The capability to provide NetBT extends the reach of NetBIOS client/server programs to the WAN and also provides improved interoperability with various other operating systems and applications that rely on the NetBIOS interface.

WINS Background

As discussed in Chapter 16, name resolution is an essential part of network administration, whether the network uses DNS or WINS. Name resolution enables you to search or browse your network and connect to resources using names such as "laserprtr001" or "fileserver01" rather than memorizing an IP address. Remember, IP address memorization would be even less practical when using DHCP for address assignment because of dynamic IP address assignments.

One of the early developments of DHCP was WINS support. Whenever the NetBIOS name and supported computer are dynamically assigned a new IP address, the change is transparently logged in WINS. When you connect to fileserver01 from another node, you can use the name fileserver01 rather than the new IP address because WINS keeps track of the changing IP addresses associated with that name in a server database.

WINS was created to solve the problems of NetBIOS broadcast-based name resolution and the burden of maintaining LMHOSTS files because most contemporary networks span broadcast domains. Using LMHOSTS files for name resolution will maintain and store the mapping of a NetBIOS name to an IP address in a static format, making it a management chore to maintain changes (especially in a DHCP environment with a short lease duration).

With a broadcast-based name-resolution system such as NetBIOS, larger networks become more congested as hosts come online and broadcast messages to all other nodes to resolve IP addresses. Remember, if we are not able to segment the network by creating broadcast domains, networks will not scale. Broadcasts should not be allowed to cross routers because of all of the congestion created by broadcasts, meaning that names can only be resolved locally. Therefore, the beauty of WINS is that it enables NetBIOS traffic to traverse broadcast domains without using broadcasts or LMHOSTS files.

WINS is built on a standard protocol defined by an IETF RFC that performs name registration, resolution, and tombstoning (WINS records marked for deletion) using unicast messages to NetBIOS name servers across routers. This enables the system to work across routers and eliminates the need for an LMHOSTS file, restoring the dynamic nature of NetBIOS name resolution and allowing the system to work effectively with DHCP. DHCP can supply WINS server addresses to clients so that when dynamic addressing through DHCP creates new IP addresses for computers that move between subnets, the reconciled WINS database will automatically track the changes.

The network-wide Windows 2000 WINS system includes a WINS server, WINS clients, WINS proxy agents to support non-WINS clients, a WINS database, and a WINS management console. These components are critical to designing a WINS solution, and each is described in this chapter.

As mentioned earlier, WINS is compatible with the protocols defined for NetBIOS name servers (NBNS) in RFCs 1001 and 1002, so it is interoperable with other RFC-compliant NBNS implementations. Another RFC-compliant implementation of the client can talk to the WINS server and, similarly, a Microsoft TCP/IP client can talk to other implementations of the NBNS.

 EXAM TIP Because the Microsoft Windows 2000 WINS server-to-server replication protocol is not specified in the RFCs, the WINS server does not interoperate with other server implementations of NBNS for replication. Data cannot be replicated between the WINS server and the non-WINS NBNS. Because replication interoperability is not supported, complete enterprise-wide name resolution cannot be guaranteed.

NetBIOS Name Resolution

Before we get to actually designing a WINS solution, hang in there while we review the nitty-gritty of NetBIOS name resolution. This may not seem fun, but you truly need to understand the foundation before building that house.

NetBT is the process of effectively mapping a unique NetBIOS name to an IP address. The NetBIOS namespace is flat, not hierarchical, which means that all names must be unique in the namespace. Resources are identified by NetBIOS names that are registered dynamically when computers start, services start, or a user logs on.

As a user or administrator, you can specify the first 15 bytes or characters of a Net-BIOS name through the configuration of the operating system, but the 16th byte is reserved for the NetBIOS resource type (00–FF hex). Therefore, a *full NetBIOS name* is a 16-byte address used to identify a NetBIOS resource on the network.

A NetBIOS name is either a unique or group name. When a NetBIOS process communicates with a specific process on a specific computer, a *unique name* such as a server service name is used. When a NetBIOS process communicates with multiple processes on multiple computers, a *group name* such as a workgroup or domain name is used.

NetBIOS Names Reference

Tables 17-1 and 17-2 contain additional details of the 16-character NetBIOS names used by Microsoft networking components when registering unique and group names.

The NetBIOS name acts as an OSI model session-layer application identifier. This enables two applications on different nodes to open, use, and close a session or structured dialog between two nodes. For example, the NetBIOS service sessions operate over TCP port 139. All NetBT session requests are addressed to TCP destination port 139. When identifying a NetBIOS application with which to establish a NetBIOS session, the NetBIOS name is used. Also, NetBT datagrams use UDP port 138, and name lookups use UDP port 137. Additional ports are used by the WINS system, and they will be addressed later, based on the associated service.

An example of a process using a NetBIOS name is the file and print-sharing server service on a Windows 2000–based node. When the server starts, the server service registers a unique NetBIOS name based on the computer's name. The exact name used by the server service is the 15-character computer name plus a 16th character of 0x20. If the computer name is not 15 characters long, it is padded with spaces up to the 15 characters required. Other network services also use the computer name to build their Net-BIOS names, so the 16th character is used to uniquely identify each service, such as the redirector, server, or messenger services.

When a user initiates a file-sharing connection by a NetBIOS name to a Windows 2000–based server, the server service on the file server specified corresponds to a specific NetBIOS name specific to that service. For example, when you attempt to connect to the computer called FILESERVER, the NetBIOS name corresponding to the server

Table 17-1   NetBIOS Unique Names

Format	Description
computer_name[00h]	Registered by the Workstation service on the WINS client. In general, this name is called the NetBIOS computer name.
computer_name[03h]	Registered by the Messenger service on the WINS client. The client uses this service when sending and receiving messages. This name is usually appended to the NetBIOS computer name for the WINS client computer and to the name of the user logged on to that computer when sending messages on the network.
computer_name[06h]	Registered by Routing and Remote Access on the WINS client (when the Routing and Remote Access Service is started).
domain_name[1Bh]	Registered by each Windows 2000 Server domain controller running as the domain master browser. This name record is used to enable the remote browsing of domains. When a WINS server is queried for this name, a WINS server returns the IP address of the computer that registered this name.
computer_name[1Fh]	Registered by the Network Dynamic Data Exchange (NetDDE) services, it appears only if the NetDDE services are started on the computer.
computer_name[20h]	Registered by the Server service on the WINS client. This service is used to provide points of service for the WINS client to share its files on the network.
computer_name[21h]	Registered by the Routing and Remote Access Client service on the WINS client (when the Routing and Remote Access Client is started).
computer_name[BEh]	Registered by the Network Monitoring Agent Service and appears only if the service is started on the WINS client computer. If the computer name has fewer than 15 characters, plus symbols (+) are added to expand the name to 15 characters.
computer_name[BFh]	Registered by the Network Monitoring Utility (included with Microsoft Systems Management Server). If the computer name has fewer than 15 characters, plus symbols (+) are added to expand the name to 15 characters.
user_name[03h]	Usernames for the currently logged-on users are registered in the WINS database. Each username is registered by the Server service component so that the user can receive any net send commands sent to that username. If more than one user logs on with the same username, only the first computer logged on with that username registers the name.

Table 17-2   NetBIOS Group Names

Format	Description
domain_name[00h]	Registered by the Workstation service so that it can receive browser broadcasts from LAN Manager–based computers.
domain_name[1Ch]	Registered for use by the domain controllers within the domain and can contain up to 25 IP addresses.
domain_name[1Dh]	Registered for use by a master browser; there is only one master browser per subnet. Backup browsers use this name to communicate with the master browser to retrieve the list of available servers from the master browser. WINS servers always return a positive registration response for *domain_name*[1D], even though the WINS server does not register this name in its database. Therefore, when a WINS server is queried for *domain_name*[1D], the server always responds with a broadcast address, which forces the client to broadcast to resolve the name.
group_name[1Eh]	A normal group name. Any computers configured to be network browsers can broadcast to this name and listen for broadcasts to this name to elect a master browser. A statically mapped group name uses this name to register itself on the network. When a WINS server receives a name query for a name ending with [1E], the WINS server always returns the network broadcast address for the local network of the requesting client. The client can then use this address to broadcast to the group members. These broadcasts are for the local subnet and should not cross routers.
group_name[20h]	A special group name called the Internet Group is registered with WINS servers to identify groups of computers for administrative purposes. For example, "printersg" could be a registered group name used to identify an administrative group of print servers.
__MSBROWSE__ [01h][01h]	Registered by the master browser for each subnet. When a WINS server receives a name query for this name, the WINS server always returns the network broadcast address for the local network of the requesting client.

service is "FILESERVER <20>" (the padding uses the space character). Before a file-and print-sharing connection can be established, a TCP connection must be created, and in order for that to happen, the NetBIOS name "FILESERVER <20>" must be resolved to an IP address.

To view the NetBIOS names registered by NetBIOS processes running on a Windows 2000 computer, type **nbtstat -n** at the command prompt.

NetBIOS Node Types

Windows clients can use several methods for locating the NetBIOS resources on the network. These methods include the following:

- NetBIOS name cache (cache on the local network node)
- NetBIOS name server (a WINS server or other NBNS server)
- IP subnet broadcasts
- Static LMHOSTS files
- Static HOSTS files
- DNS servers

The method by which NetBIOS names are resolved to IP addresses depends on the node's configured *NetBIOS node type*. RFC 1001 defines the NetBIOS node types, and they are listed in Table 17-3. These node types determine how nodes will resolve Net-BIOS names to IP addresses and whether WINS will be used for the resolution.

Table 17-3   NetBIOS Node Types

Node Type	Description
B-node (broadcast)	B-node uses broadcasted NetBIOS name queries for name registration, discovery, and release. B-node has two major problems, even though it requires virtually no configuration: it creates a great deal of traffic and routers are typically not configured to forward broadcasts, so only a Net-BIOS name on the local subnetwork can be resolved using broadcasts. Enhanced B-nodes can also query the LMHOSTS file, should broadcast resolution fail.
P-node (point-to-point)	P-node uses a NetBIOS name server (NBNS), such as WINS, to resolve the NetBIOS name. P-node does not use broadcasts; instead, it queries the name server directly. One requirement for P-node is that all nodes must be configured with the IP address of the NBNS, and if the NBNS is offline, computers are not able to communicate even on the local network except by using resolutions found in the node's NetBIOS name cache.
M-node (mixed)	M-node is simply a combination of B-node and P-node. Initially, an M-node functions as a B-node. If it is unable to resolve a name by broadcast, it uses WINS or another NBNS to resolve the name.
H-node (hybrid)	H-node is just a combination of P-node and B-node. Initially, an H-node functions as a P-node. If it is unable to resolve a name through the Net-BIOS name server, it uses a broadcast to resolve the name. Windows machines that are configured to use WINS are by default H-node types.

PART III

Windows 2000–based computers are B-node by default and become H-node when configured for a WINS server. Windows 2000 initially uses the NetBIOS name cache but also uses a local database file called LMHOSTS to resolve remote NetBIOS names. Both LMHOSTS files, as well as WINS, have benefits over the broadcast method. Since resolutions are sent directly to the WINS server, there is no need for the additional traffic generated by broadcasts on the subnet. The node type can be viewed from a command prompt by typing the command **ipconfig /all**.

WINS at Work

The client-to-server WINS process is simple and easy to understand because there are four parts: NetBIOS name registration, NetBIOS name renewal, NetBIOS name discovery, and NetBIOS name release. The four client-to-server communication steps are illustrated in Figure 17-1.

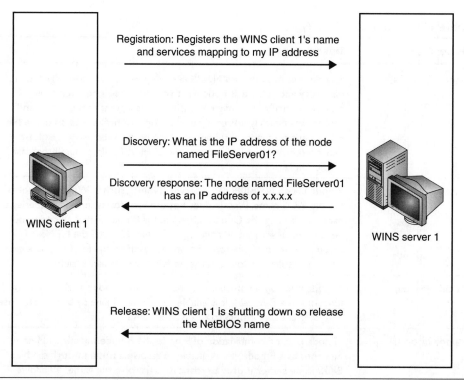

Figure 17-1   The client-to-server WINS communication process

- **NetBIOS name registration**   When a WINS client starts up, it directs a message to the WINS server requesting the WINS server to register its NetBIOS name to IP address mapping. If accepted, the mapping is given a time to live (TTL), and the name is registered.

- **NetBIOS name renewal**   Once 50 percent of the TTL expires, the client will attempt to renew the TTL for its NetBIOS name.

- **NetBIOS name discovery**   When a WINS client attempts to establish a session with a destination host, a directed message is sent to the WINS server requesting an IP address for the host from the WINS name-resolution services. If the record exists or has been registered and is in good standing, the WINS server will reply with the IP address of the destination host.

- **NetBIOS name release**   When the WINS client shuts down properly, the client sends a directed message to the WINS server releasing its NetBIOS name. The WINS server sets the TTL of the corresponding record to zero and marks the record. Once the record is released, the name is available for use by another node.

Creating a WINS Design

In Windows 2000, your network no longer needs to use WINS and NetBT if you have only Windows 2000 servers, Windows 2000 clients, or most versions of Unix. Instead, Windows 2000 DNS server should be used to resolve names to IP addresses. However, if routed networks must support or use legacy systems, such as Windows NT 4.0, Windows NT 3.*x*, Windows 3.*x*, Windows 9*x*, or Microsoft TCP/IP clients, WINS is still required, because these systems use NetBIOS name resolution and NetBIOS session setups for key services, including file and print sharing. Also, if the network must support applications that rely on the NetBIOS interface to function properly, WINS can be used to provide an NBNS for efficient NetBT, needed for WAN communications.

 EXAM TIP   Let us highlight a critical point. The Windows 2000 MCSE certification exams will test you in the context of WINS in legacy settings. It would be unlike Microsoft to test you over WINS in the context of Windows 2000, where dynamic DNS is the preferred name-resolution mechanism.

The bottom line here is that these networks will need to support WINS until such time as all clients and servers are migrated to Windows 2000 or an operating system that does not require NetBIOS name support. In addition to legacy NetBIOS operating system support, keep in mind that certain third-party applications may also require NetBIOS interface support—in these cases, use testing and vendor verification before assuming that you can remove NetBIOS support. Given this situation, you must still provide support for NetBIOS on the network even if the operating systems themselves do not require NetBIOS name resolution.

If NetBIOS name resolution is required, you should keep certain design considerations in mind. You will need to determine the number of servers you need for WINS and the location of these servers, given router locations and client placement on the subnets. A single WINS server can support a small network of 10,000 NetBIOS clients or less. WINS has some very explicit guidelines, but your design must address the functionality, availability, performance, and security aspects of the WINS service in order to develop a rounded WINS service design. Each of these areas will be discussed in this chapter.

Initial WINS Design Steps

To design your WINS strategy for server-based NetBIOS name location, some initial steps should be taken. First, from the network, collect the configuration data that you will need to ultimately make the design decisions for your WINS solution. Then pinpoint the features that will provide the functionality required in the design. Remember, as a consultant interested in adding value to a client's network services, always look for creative ways to optimize the design with new features. Finally, identify opportunities to integrate WINS with other Windows 2000 services in a way that will benefit the design.

Initial Assessment

Remember, WINS is not required in a single-segment LAN (a single *broadcast domain*), but it is beneficial, in any environment, to reduce the reliance on broadcast traffic to resolve NetBIOS names.

WINS implements a distributed database for NetBIOS names and their corresponding addresses. WINS servers are updated with client names and WINS servers will replicate the entries (NetBIOS names/IP address mappings) to other WINS servers. This specific set of mechanisms ensures unique NetBIOS names and makes it possible for servers to provide more localized resolutions and registrations for clients while distributing the mappings across the enterprise.

Your initial WINS assessment must include the number of hosts, the resource requirements, and the routing configuration. Your design will eventually address the following issues once the overall network infrastructure requirements and configuration have been determined:

- The quantity and location of WINS servers with the non-routed or routed network

- WINS database replication methods and schedules

- Configuration options for the WINS servers and clients

- The need and placement of WINS proxy agents for non-WINS clients to ensure unique NetBIOS names

Initial Feature Analysis

To develop a complete WINS solution for your network, you must understand the core Windows 2000 WINS features. WINS core features provide name-resolution capabilities, RFC compliance, burst-mode name registration, multiple WINS server support, DNS integration, and centralized administration. Keep in mind that these essential features provide the WINS design foundation, and additional features will be discussed in depth throughout this chapter.

Integration Opportunities Analysis

A WINS infrastructure integrates with DHCP and DNS. This integration provides name resolution for hosts with an allocated dynamic IP address. The integration enables DNS servers to forward unresolved DNS queries to WINS servers for the resolution of names using potentially dynamic IP addresses. (For more information on DNS integration, see Chapter 16.) It also enables DNS resolution of legacy versions of Windows. Additionally, you can configure WINS clients to send a NetBIOS name query to a DNS server for unresolved queries. The integration of WINS and DNS makes it possible for DNS to forward host-name resolution requests to WINS. Therefore, if a host is not registered in DNS, it can be resolved in the WINS namespace. The DNS server can then return the IP-to-host mapping for a DNS client's query.

DHCP integration enables client computer name registrations to be updated in WINS for clients with dynamically assigned IP addresses. Automated registration eliminates the need to manually configure WINS, which all but eliminates client configuration errors. You can register NetBIOS names in WINS through DHCP clients and servers.

Designing a Functional WINS Solution

A functional WINS solution can be put into place to support a LAN or a routed network that supports WINS clients, as well as to support non-WINS clients that require NetBIOS name resolution. You can also incorporate multiple WINS servers, called *replication partners*, to provide load-balancing and fault-tolerant NetBIOS name-server solutions on the network.

PART III

Before diving into the function of WINS service designs, you should consider the new features found in Windows 2000. After reviewing the new features, the functional requirements for each of the following will be addressed: WINS on LANs that do not use routing, WINS on routed networks, WINS client features and considerations, supporting non-WINS clients, and using multiple WINS servers.

New WINS Features

The new implementation of WINS provides a number of features that combine to make the Windows 2000 WINS an improvement over Windows NT 4.0 for managing dynamic NetBIOS name resolution across a routed TCP/IP network. The new features include the following:

Persistent Connections This configurable feature enables each WINS server to maintain a persistent connection with one or more replication partners to eliminate the overhead of opening and terminating connections and to increase the speed of replication.

Manual Tombstoning Use of the manual tombstoning feature marks a record for deletion so that the tombstone state for the record is replicated across all WINS servers, preventing an undeleted copy of the record on a different server database from being repropagated.

Improved Management Tools The WINS Manager is fully integrated with the Microsoft Management Console (MMC), providing a more user-friendly and powerful environment for viewing and managing WINS information.

Enhanced Filtering and Record Searching These functions help locate records of interest by showing only those that fit specific criteria. This is particularly useful for analyzing very large WINS databases.

Dynamic Record Deletion and Multiselect Managing the WINS database is made easier with dynamic record deletion along with its capability to select multiple records when managing the database. Dynamic and static records can be deleted, and the point-and-click interface makes it possible to delete files with nonalphanumeric characters that could not be handled from the command line.

Record Verification and Version-Number Validation Two tools are available for quickly checking the consistency between various WINS servers. The tests are done by comparing the IP addresses of a NetBIOS name query returned from different WINS servers, or by examining the mapping tables for owner address to version-number consistency.

Export Function   The Export command can be used to place WINS data into a comma-delimited text file that can be imported into Microsoft Excel, reporting tools, scripting applications, and so on for analysis and reporting.

Increased Fault-Tolerance   Windows 2000 and Windows 98 enable a client to specify more than two WINS servers (up to a maximum of 12 addresses) per interface. The extra WINS server addresses are used only if the primary and secondary WINS servers fail to respond.

Dynamic Reregistration   WINS clients can now reregister their NetBIOS name-to-IP address mapping without rebooting the server.

WINS on LANs That Do Not Use Routing

Remember, non-routed networks do not require a WINS server because NetBIOS name resolution can be accomplished using broadcasts. In fact, this is the method used by default in small peer-to-peer networks that don't have a server providing a more sophisticated name-resolution mechanism. However, in order to improve the performance of these smaller LANs, we recommend using a WINS server because it enables the use of a unicast protocol for NetBIOS name resolution, which can help to eliminate much of the NetBIOS-related broadcast traffic.

To accomplish this on a non-routed LAN, consider implementing the following two steps:

1. Enable as many WINS clients as possible.

2. Install at least one WINS server to provide WINS services on the network.

Remember that a single WINS server can support up to 10,000 users for NetBIOS name-resolution requests, so a server that provides other services on a small LAN, like a domain controller, can often handle the WINS workload. However, in larger installations, a dedicated WINS server is often recommended, along with at least one replication partner. Larger networks may require more, depending on the server loads. In either case, you must consider configuring at least an additional (or second) computer running Windows 2000 Server as a secondary, or backup, WINS server for clients.

If you use only two WINS servers, you can very simply set them up as replication partners of each other. For a simple solution, set them up as push/pull partners and make replication automatic. On a small network you can enable automatic partner configuration by selecting the check box on the Advanced tab of the Replication Partner Properties dialog box. This will automatically find the other WINS servers on the network through multicasting and configure them as replication partners. If a server is discovered and added as a partner through multicasting using this automatic method, it is removed as a replication partner when WINS is shut down properly. For this reason, WINS restarts can impact network and WINS performance. Also, multicasting needs to be supported across all routers. Therefore, for performance reasons, this should only be used on networks with a small client base.

The Windows 2000 client, and other legacy Windows clients, is by default a hybrid node client if it is configured to use a WINS server. This makes it possible for the client to use a WINS server using unicast traffic first, and then to eventually fall back to broadcasts or even DNS if the WINS server or LMHOSTS file does not contain the needed IP mapping.

WINS on Routed Networks

On routed networks, broadcast domains are limited, and the primary reason WINS exists is to provide network-wide NetBIOS name registrations and resolutions. To put it simply, WINS makes it possible to reach NetBIOS resources over routers—the unicast protocol that WINS uses provides this capability.

One of the key design considerations for WINS is to ensure broadcast traffic is not generated unless a failure occurs or non-WINS clients are used. Before you install the WINS server(s) on the routed network, consider the number of WINS servers required for fault-tolerance and replication, the client performance issues over slower links, and how you might minimize the impact of client-to-server and server-to-server traffic over routers.

Consider the position of servers on the routed LAN to reduce name queries across subnets as well as registration and response traffic between subnets. Name requests and responses that occur at the daily startup of computers must pass through the traffic queues on the routers, which can cause significant delays at peak times.

Roving users between subnets also present challenges on the routed network. When a user shuts down a computer and moves to another subnet or location, starting the computer on the new subnet with a different primary WINS server can generate name-challenge traffic for WINS. Often, the name registration request is answered with a "Wait for Acknowledgment" message. There is a challenge to the IP address currently existing in the database, assuming the TTL has not expired on the earlier record. When there is no challenge reply after three attempts (as expected), the challenge is successful and the new primary WINS server updates the name registration along with a version ID update. This new version ID indicates that the entry must be replicated from the new WINS server to the other WINS partners. As you might suspect, this causes a tremendous amount of traffic on the network and potentially over WAN connections.

You can estimate the WINS client traffic based on how WINS clients behave. Consider this traffic and the corresponding network topology and router configuration when determining where to place WINS servers. In WAN environments where bandwidth cost is at a premium, place WINS servers to optimize client response times and minimize database convergence times. WINS convergence time is the time it takes for a new entry in one WINS server to replicate to other WINS servers. If database convergence times are too far apart, users may not gain access to resources during server configuration changes.

EXAM TIP Although Windows 2000 clients will support up to 12 WINS servers, most networks really only need one or two. The second server is often used as a backup in case the first server fails. So, minimize the number of WINS servers on the network by using only as many as are needed to support the client count.

WINS Client Features and Considerations

Thanks to Microsoft's built-in client support for WINS, all versions of Windows support a WINS client, which will reduce broadcasts due to NetBIOS name resolution. The Windows 2000 WINS client provides the capability to support up to 12 WINS servers using unicast packets. The Windows 2000 client will also support multiple node types defined in RFC 1001.

To reduce renewal traffic, increase the NetBIOS name-registration renewal period above the default, which is six days. Also specify more than one WINS server in the client's configuration to provide WINS redundancy in case of WINS server failure or WAN connection failures.

Supporting Non-WINS Clients

Although you will probably never need to support non-WINS clients, you will probably run into the need of supporting one of these guys on a Microsoft exam. Some (non-Microsoft) clients are not able to work with WINS servers, yet they require the ability to perform NetBIOS name resolution. For resources not on the local subnet, these non-WINS clients need to have names resolved and requests resolved even if they cannot register their names dynamically.

You can use a number of methods to support non-WINS clients, including the following:

- Place a WINS proxy agent on the subnet containing non-WINS clients. The WINS proxy agent receives the broadcast-based interactions with non-WINS clients and forwards the broadcast-based requests to a WINS server configured on the proxy-agent computer.

- Include static WINS or LMHOSTS entries to enable name resolution on remote subnets.

- Enable NetBIOS broadcast traffic over the routers on a routed network. (This is not recommended because it degrades segmentation benefits.)

 NOTE The WINS proxy agent receives the broadcast-based NetBIOS name-service interaction from non-WINS clients and forwards the request in unicast form to a remote WINS server. The WINS proxy agent can be set up on any WINS-enabled Windows computer, but you should not have more than two WINS proxy agents on a single subnet for performance reasons. The WINS proxy agent should be included on subnets that have non-WINS clients and no WINS server.

When supporting NetBIOS on non-WINS clients, it is best to manually register the NetBIOS names in the WINS server to ensure the uniqueness of NetBIOS names on the network—the WINS proxy agent will not perform this registration. Once these are manually registered, WINS clients will be able to resolve these resources. If you use LMHOSTS files, you can use a centrally managed LMHOSTS file for these static entries, using a #include in the client's file. From a design standpoint, any subnets that contain non-WINS clients and do not have any WINS servers require at least one WINS proxy agent.

Using Multiple WINS Servers

Using multiple WINS servers can help to localize WINS client queries and registration. Although the client-to-server traffic and load is localized, it is best to ensure consistent name resolution across the internetwork by setting up the servers to replicate their locally acquired mappings to the other WINS servers participating in the WAN environment.

Configuring Replication   Configuring WINS replication correctly is essential to an efficient WINS-capable network. The most important features of a proper WINS configuration are described in the following sections.

Automatic Replication Partner Configuration   A WINS server can be configured to automatically accept other WINS servers as its replication partners. When a server uses automatic partner configuration, it finds other WINS servers as they join the network and adds them to its list of replication partners. This is possible because each WINS server announces its presence on the network through regular multicast announcements. These announcements are sent as Internet Group Management

Protocol (IGMP—a protocol that manages host membership in IP multicast groups) messages for the multicast group address of 224.0.1.24 (the multicast IP address reserved for use by WINS servers).

When WINS uses automatic replication configuration, it monitors the traffic for these multicast announcements. When it detects a new server, it automatically does three things:

1. Adds IP addresses for discovered servers to its list of replication partners.

2. Configures any discovered servers to be both push and pull partners.

3. Configures pull replication with discovered servers to occur every two hours.

If a remote server is discovered and added as a partner through multicasting, it is removed as a replication partner when WINS is shut down properly. Manual partner configuration is often used instead so that partnerships are maintained through restarts. To manually configure replication with other WINS servers, configure each partner server using the WINS management console or add the WINS snap-in through a user-defined MMC.

So when should you use automatic partner configuration? It is most useful in single-subnet environments. It can also be useful for situations in which the available network for WINS multicast traffic is expanded by configuring routers to forward WINS multicast traffic between routed subnets. For IP multicasting to span routers across a routed network, multicast routing protocols are used to communicate host group information so that each router supporting multicast forwarding is aware of which networks contain members of which host groups.

Because periodic multicast announcements between WINS servers add traffic to your network, automatic partner configuration is only recommended if you have three or fewer WINS servers installed on the reachable network.

Replication Between Untrusted Domains   WINS replication can be set up between WINS servers in untrusting domains without requiring a valid user account in the untrusting domain. To configure replication, administrators for each WINS server must use the WINS management console to configure their controlled WINS server to enable replication with the WINS server in the remote domain. This method ensures localized control over WINS replication partners.

Replication Across WANs   Selecting the right replication interval requires careful consideration. The WINS server database should be replicated frequently enough that the downtime of a single WINS server does not affect the integrity of the replicated mapping information. However, you want to minimize the impact of database replication on network performance. If the replication interval is too short, the impact can become significant.

You also need to consider the topology of your network along with the database-convergence requirements of the network. If your network has multiple hubs connected by relatively slow WAN links, configure replication between WINS servers on the slow links to occur less frequently than replication between WINS servers on fast links. This reduces traffic across the slow links and reduces competition between replication traffic and client name queries.

Replication Convergence Time   When deploying WINS servers, you must choose an acceptable convergence time for your network. If a WINS client registers its name with the WINS server WINS-A, other WINS clients can query WINS-A for this name and get the name-to-IP address mapping. WINS clients that query any of the other WINS servers do not get a positive response until the entry is replicated from WINS-A to WINS servers WINS-HUB, WINS-B, and WINS-C. WINS-C is configured to start replication when the update count exceeds the push threshold or when the pull replication interval expires on its WINS pull partner, WINS-A. The update count is the number of changes to database entries required to trigger push replication.

Sometimes name-query requests succeed before the convergence time has passed. For example, this happens when the entries are replicated over a shorter path than the worst-case path and the client has multiple WINS server entries. It also happens when an update-count threshold is passed before the replication interval expires; this results in earlier replication of the new entry.

Replication Partners and Network Configuration   Choosing whether to configure another WINS server as a push partner or pull partner depends on several considerations, including the specific configuration of servers at your site, whether the partner is across a wide area network (WAN), and how important it is to distribute changes throughout the network immediately.

You can use a hub-and-spoke configuration, and we're not talking bicycle wheels here. This is done by configuring one WINS server as the "central" server and all other WINS servers as both push partners and pull partners of this hub server. Such a configuration ensures that the WINS database on each server contains up-to-date data through the hub server.

You can select other replication partner configurations to meet the particular needs of your site. However, you should consider using the recommended best practices that follow in the next section for WINS replication.

Best Practices for WINS Replication

Configuring replication correctly can avert many problems, and doing so enables a group of WINS servers to function more effectively.

Configuring Push/Pull Replication Partners   In general, push/pull replication is the simplest and most effective way to ensure full WINS replication between partners. This also ensures that the primary and secondary WINS servers for any particular WINS client are push and pull partners of each other, a requirement for proper WINS functioning in the event of a failure of the primary server of the client.

For most WINS installations, avoid the use of limited-replication partnerships (push-only or pull-only) between WINS servers. In some large enterprise WINS networks, limited-replication partnering can effectively support replication over slow network links. However, when you plan limited WINS replication, pay attention to the design and configuration. Each server must still have at least one replication partner, and each slow link that employs a unidirectional link should be balanced by a unidirectional link elsewhere in the network that carries updated entries in the opposite direction.

Using a Hub-and-Spoke Design for Replication and Convergence   Convergence is a critical part of WINS planning. The central question of convergence time for a WINS network design is "How long does it take for a change in WINS data at one WINS server to replicate and appear at other WINS servers on the network?" The answer is the sum of the replication periods from one server to the next over the path containing the longest replication periods.

In most cases, the hub-and-spoke model provides a simple and effective planning method for organizations that require full and speedy convergence with minimal administrative intervention. For example, this model works well for organizations with centralized headquarters or a corporate data center (the hub) and several branch offices (the spokes). Also, a second or redundant hub (that is, a second WINS server in the central location) can increase the fault tolerance for WINS.

The convergence time for the system is the sum of the two longest convergence times to the hub when using a hub-and-spoke model. For instance, if WINS-Spoke_A and WINS-Spoke_B replicate with WINS-HUB every 45 minutes, and WINS-Spoke_C and WINS-Spoke_D are configured to replicate every two hours, the convergence time is four hours.

Replication Across a Firewall   At times, and especially in some large networks, WINS replication is wanted across a firewall. WINS replication occurs over TCP port 42.

This port must not be blocked on any intermediate network device between two WINS replication partners when using replication across packet-filtering devices.

Performance Enhancements for Multiple Servers To improve replication performance in high-bandwidth networks, you must configure persistent connections between partners. In Windows 2000, you can configure each WINS server to maintain a persistent connection with one or more replication partners. This will increase the speed of replication by eliminating the overhead of opening and terminating connections to replication partners.

Enhancing WINS Availability

The WINS server database, much like Active Directory–integrated DNS, inherently provides fault-tolerant service because it is replicated among multiple WINS servers in a LAN or WAN. This replicated database design also prevents users from registering duplicate NetBIOS computer names on the network, which improves availability. In practice, even small networks should have more than one WINS server to enable the load-balancing of NetBIOS name queries and registration, and to provide WINS database redundancy, backup, and failure recovery.

WINS server failures basically come in two types:

- **Server failure**   A WINS server might malfunction, or it might be downed for maintenance.
- **Network failure**   Routers or network links can fail.

The failure of an individual WINS server within a network affects multiple WINS servers. To plan for these outages, determine expected or worst-case lengths of time any given WINS server could be out of service on the network, and factor in the length of both planned and unexpected WINS server outages. Also, consider what happens to WINS clients if their primary WINS server fails to respond. By maintaining and assigning certain levels of secondary WINS servers (up to 12 total), you can significantly reduce the effects of a single WINS server failure. In addition, clustering can provide further fault-tolerance.

Using Segmented Configurations

Here is a tip that you will find very useful if you have a failed WINS server. When a link or router between two subnets fails, replication between two WINS servers may well be interrupted or prevented by the link failure. However, a segmented WINS configuration can provide many of the services of a fully functional system, because clients using the hybrid node type can resolve addresses from names. Local WINS servers and/or broadcasts resolve most name queries.

TIP Most quality WAN configurations have key server resources located close to clients on the same subnet.

The only names that cannot be resolved when there is a link failure are new entries that were registered remotely or those that have been updated since the network was separated due to link failure. Entries are not dropped at scavenging time when the owning WINS server cannot be reached. To restore the segmented network to full functionality when the hardware of the regular WINS server fails, install the WINS service on another computer using the same WINS and TCP/IP configuration, and restore the database by forcing replication from a replication partner.

Improving Fault Tolerance

As indicated earlier, Windows 2000 and Windows 98 provide an extra measure of fault tolerance by enabling a client to specify more than two WINS servers (up to a maximum of 12) per interface through either the DHCP or the WINS option under Administrative Tools. The additional WINS servers resolve names only if the primary and secondary WINS servers fail to respond. If one of the additional WINS servers answers a query, the client caches the address of the WINS server that responded and uses it the next time the primary and secondary WINS servers fail to resolve the name. This feature is enabled by default in NetBT. However, if this feature is activated for too many computers, the result is excessive duplication of name queries, resulting in performance degradation.

Using WINS Clustering

Using Windows 2000 clustering on a WINS server can improve the availability of a single WINS server. Availability is the upside. The downside is that the availability comes at a higher cost because clustering requires more computing resources than using multiple WINS servers for load-balancing and fault-tolerance. Assess your high-availability needs. If you find that a single WINS server will require a highly available configuration, consider using clustering to dramatically enhance a single server's availability. Remember, as with all clustering, the servers in the cluster require persistent, high-speed connections between all servers in the cluster. Also, although a cluster guards against hardware or system failure, it will not guard against database corruption.

PART III

Optimizing WINS Performance

To optimize the WINS design for performance, begin by estimating the amount of network traffic between WINS clients and WINS servers under normal circumstances, including high-utilization times (like Monday morning start-ups). Do the work to predict and monitor the following:

- WINS registration and renewal due to daily client start-ups
- Roving users and the effects of their moves between subnets on a routed network
- NetBIOS names often registered by WINS clients
- WAN links and the effect they have on replication and convergence

The WINS design you create will be measured directly by two primary factors: How long does it take a client to resolve via a WINS query? And what is the impact of query traffic and replication traffic on network bandwidth?

When we create an optimized WINS design, we endeavor to improve the performance of the service on and between servers and to reduce the impact of the service on network bandwidth by addressing these three issues in the process:

- **WINS server capacity**   Create a strategy to improve the performance of individual WINS servers.
- **Client resolution**   Reduce WINS client query-resolution time.
- **WINS database replication**   Reduce the impact of WINS server query- and zone-replication on the network.

Optimizing WINS Server Capacity

The first step you will want to take is to size the WINS server to match the client load. Because each WINS server loads the WINS database into memory at initialization to provide fast access to zone information, increasing RAM on the server will usually provide the biggest performance improvement, rather than providing faster processor or hard-drive capabilities. The amount of RAM needed in the server is based on a number of load variables:

- What additional services does the server provide on the network?
- Is the server a domain controller as well?
- Is the server used for file and print services?

- How many clients does the server support?

- How many server-replication relationships does this server have, and what is the nature of the traffic? Is it the hub or the spoke in a hub-and-spoke configuration?

- How many WINS queries and registrations will the WINS server need to handle simultaneously?

Make note of the RAM required to support WINS alone, and add it to the RAM requirements of the other services supported on the server.

You should also review the other hardware, including processor, disk subsystem, and network subsystem, to increase processing and network transfer rates. Be aware, though, that when you improve the performance of any one component of a system, it may impact another. Continue to monitor performance after you have enhanced one area to ensure that an unresolved bottleneck has not developed in another component. For instance, if the network card was previously a bottleneck for client traffic, and you replace the NIC, you may find that the processor or memory is now bottlenecked because of the increased network service load. Continue to monitor and test even in the lab environment prior to implementation.

> **TIP**   Using the new burst-mode name registration in Windows 2000 can improve performance if periods of high activity saturate the server.

For the Windows 2000 Server, the WINS Server service includes a set of performance counters that can be used to monitor various types of server activity using System Monitor. After WINS is installed on a Windows 2000 Server, the WINS performance counters in Table 17-4 are available for use in monitoring server activity.

> **TIP**   To provide granular security for WINS performance counters, a member of the local Administrators group can use values for the following Registry key to deny or modify permissions, determining who can view the System Monitor counters used for WINS on the server computer: HKEY_LOCAL_MACHINE\System\CurrentControlSet\Services\WINS\Performance.

PART III

Table 17-4 WINS Performance Counters

Performance Counter	Description
Queries/sec	The rate per second at which NetBIOS name queries are received by the WINS server. A large number indicates heavy WINS-related message traffic to the server.
Releases/sec	The rate per second at which NetBIOS release messages are received by the WINS server.
Successful Queries/sec	The rate per second at which NetBIOS name queries are successfully processed when received by the WINS server.
Successful Releases/sec	The rate per second at which NetBIOS release messages are successfully processed when received by the WINS server.
Total Number of Conflicts/sec	The rate per second at which all name conflicts are detected by WINS. This total is determined by averaging the sum of all unique- and group-name conflicts.
Total Number of Registrations/sec	The rate per second at which all name registrations are detected by WINS. This total is determined by averaging the sum of all unique- and group-name registrations.
Total Number of Renewals/sec	The rate per second at which all name renewals are detected by WINS. This total is determined by averaging the sum of all unique- and group-name renewals.
Unique Conflicts/sec	The rate per second at which unique-name conflicts are detected by the WINS server. This total is determined by averaging conflicts for unique names only.
Unique Registrations/sec	The rate per second at which unique-name registrations are detected by the WINS server. This total is determined by averaging registrations for unique names only.
Unique Renewals/sec	The rate per second at which unique-name renewals are detected by the WINS server. This total is determined by averaging renewals for unique names only.

WINS Client Resolution

The following list of simplifications will help eliminate many performance issues:

- *Turn off services on network clients that are not needed* (to reduce WINS registrations). These include server, messaging, network monitoring agent, and NetDDE. Note that there are some dependency relationships, so you may only need to disable the server service in many cases.

- *Use WINS-enabled clients whenever possible to reduce NetBIOS broadcasts.*

- *Only one computer on a subnet should be configured as a WINS proxy agent.* Because each WINS proxy on a network relays every NetBIOS broadcast that it receives, configuring more than one proxy per subnet can affect routers and WINS server performance.

- *Increase the TTL and caching duration on relatively static networks.*

Improving WINS Database Replication Performance

The following suggestions can improve the performance of the WINS service on a variety of network topologies:

- Add multiple WINS servers and distribute the client load across multiple servers.

- Place servers on either side of WAN connections, and configure them as push/pull partners.

- Assign primary WINS servers to clients on their local subnet.

- Pay special attention to the bandwidth required for server-to-server replication, and plan link capacity to meet the traffic requirements of WINS servers.

- Use persistent connections to maintain server-to-server connections that will enable less session set-up traffic during replications.

- Set replications to occur during non-peak hours over saturated WAN links.

- Reduce the server services running on the network, especially on client computers where possible, because fewer registrations will reduce the amount of replication traffic.

Securing a WINS Solution

Your network may rely heavily on the name-resolution capabilities of WINS over a public network like the Internet. You must safeguard WINS and the network from malicious attacks while providing appropriate access to the WINS services. With Windows 2000, you can secure WINS on both public and private networks. Over public networks, WINS replication traffic can be transmitted using encryption and secure communications, such as IPSec and VPNs. You also can provide access to WINS services by restricting WINS access and by screening subnets with firewalls.

PART III

WINS in Screened Subnets

WINS servers can be integrated into screened subnets to provide Internet accessibility and to protect internal resources, especially for the Common Internet File System (CIFS), which uses the NetBIOS interface to make data shareable across the Internet. Because CIFS relies on the NetBIOS interface, you can use WINS to provide resolution services for these resources. The following are the recommended best practices when placing WINS servers in screened subnets:

- Consider making the WINS server in the DMZ a pull partner with the corporate WINS server on the other side of the firewall.

- Use IPSec or a VPN tunnel with high encryption settings to encrypt all WINS traffic between the external and internal WINS servers.

- Only enable WINS servers on the private side of the subnet to communicate over a secure connection with the WINS server in the screened subnet. Also only enable internal clients to access the private WINS servers, not the WINS server in the screened subnet, because it is more difficult to secure this traffic.

- Only enable queries from the Internet or secure internal queries from WINS servers to reach the WINS servers on the screened subnet.

EXAM TIP   Open ports 137 (UDP and TCP), 138 (UDP), and 139 (TCP) for name service and connections across the firewall. RFC 1002 can provide additional information regarding the needed ports.

Designing a Distributed File System (DFS) Strategy

The Microsoft distributed file system (DFS) enables system administrators to make it easier for users to access and manage files that are physically distributed across a network; DFS also makes administration easier. DFS provides a single logical view of distributed physical storage on the network. With DFS, you can make files that are distributed across multiple servers appear to users as if they reside on one server or can reside in the Active Directory. DFS, at its most elementary level, creates pointers to shared files on many different servers. This makes it possible for users to reach resources through one location without knowing the actual physical location of files.

This will work as long as the client has the capability of connecting to the resource in its native format. In other words, DFS isn't a gateway, and it doesn't perform protocol translation—it is primarily a pointer repository or a system for maintaining links and redirecting clients to the requested files.

For example, if you have art files shared across multiple servers in a domain, you can use DFS to make it appear as though all of the files reside on the shares of a single server. This eliminates the need for users to remember the multiple locations on the network where they will find the information they need. There is a server component that is called a *DFS root* and a separate client component.

DFS is very powerful, and you should consider creating a design solution for DFS if any of the following apply:

- You want to make it easy to deliver shared file resources on the network.
- Users who access shared folders are distributed across a site or multiple sites.
- Most users require access to multiple shared folders.
- Server load-balancing could be improved by redistributing shared folders.
- Users require uninterrupted access to shared folders.

Using the DFS console, you can implement a distributed file system on servers in one of two ways:

- Create a stand-alone distributed file system.
- Create a domain-based distributed file system.

DFS Architecture

In addition to the server-based DFS component of Windows 2000, the client component is required to use DFS. The administrator can configure the DFS client to cache a DFS root referral or a DFS link for an explicit duration. A computer running the DFS client must be a member of the domain for the DFS root, and this affects root placement.

The DFS client component runs on a number of different Windows platforms. Platform compatibility for DFS client versions and their associated platforms are discussed next.

DFS Platform Compatibility

Table 17-5 shows what Microsoft Windows 2000 Help has to say about DFS shared folders or replicas' (which are replicated shared folders) platform compatibility.

Table 17-5 DFS Platform Support

Platform	Will the Operating System Support a DFS Client?	Will the Operating System Support a Host DFS Root?
Unix or NetWare file servers	No	No
DOS, Windows 3.x, Windows for Workgroups, and NetWare servers	No	No
Windows 95	Yes, download client for DFS 4.x and 5.0	No
Windows 98	Yes, DFS 4.x and 5.0 (stand-alone) client included; download client for DFS 5.0 (domain-based)	No
Windows ME	Yes, DFS 4.x and 5.0 (stand-alone) client included; download client for DFS 5.0 (domain-based)	No
Windows NT 4.0 and Service Pack 3	Yes, DFS 4.x and 5.0 (stand-alone) client included	Yes, stand-alone server only
Windows 2000 Professional	DFS 5.0 client included	No
Windows 2000 Server	DFS 5.0 client included	Yes, stand-alone and domain-based server or domain controller

DFS Features

DFS provides several important features:

- Ease of file access
- Availability
- Server load-balancing
- Security

Ease of File Access

Users can have easy access to files with the distributed file system. They can go to one location on a server or query the Active Directory on the network to access files, even though the files may be physically spread across multiple servers. The administrator can change the physical location of a shared folder and users will not be affected by the change, because the link name remains the same. The user accesses the folder in the same way as before, because the location of the file looks the same.

Availability

If a domain-based DFS root is configured, users maintain access to files through automatic publishing of the DFS topology to Active Directory. This aids in providing DFS visibility to users of all servers in the domain. As an administrator, you can replicate DFS roots and DFS shared folders. DFS roots are placed on a server, and links to shared folders are reflected in the root. The replication enables you to duplicate DFS roots and DFS shared folders on servers in the domain. Using this replication, users can still access their files through DFS, even if one of the physical servers on which the DFS root resides becomes unavailable.

Server Load-Balancing

Within a domain, the DFS topology is automatically published to Active Directory, thus providing synchronization of DFS topologies across host servers by default. This provides load-balancing for the DFS root and supports the optional replication of DFS shared folders.

Adding a DFS link to the DFS root can expand the DFS topology. The only limitation on the number of hierarchical levels in a DFS topology is imposed by the limit of 260 characters for any file path on Windows 2000. A new DFS link can refer to a shared folder with subfolders, or to an entire Windows 2000 volume, using hidden shares or explicit drive shares. With sufficient permissions, a user can access any local subfolders that exist in or are added to a DFS shared folder. A DFS root can support multiple DFS shared folders that are physically distributed across a network.

DFS Topology   A DFS topology consists of a DFS root, one or more DFS links, and one or more DFS shared folders to which each DFS link points. The host server is a domain server on which a DFS root lives. DFS roots can be replicated by creating root shares on other servers in the domain. This provides file availability when the root host server is unavailable.

To users, a DFS topology provides cohesive and transparent access to the network resources they need. To the system administrator, a DFS topology is a single DNS namespace; with domain-based DFS, the DNS names for the DFS root shares resolve to the host servers for the DFS root.

Security

Aside from creating the necessary administrator permissions, the DFS service does not implement any additional security measures, beyond what the Windows 2000 system provides. The permissions assigned to a DFS root or DFS link determine who can add a new DFS link.

Permissions to a shared folder are not related to the DFS topology. If there is a DFS link named SharedDocuments, and you have permission to access a particular DFS shared folder to which SharedDocuments points, you can access all other DFS shared folders in the group of DFS shared folders whether or not you have the actual permission to access those other shared folders. However, having permission to access these shared folders does resolve whether or not you have access to any of the information within the shared folders. This access is determined by standard Windows 2000 security.

To put it simply, security is enforced by the underlying file system when a user tries to access a DFS shared folder and its contents. A FAT volume provides share-level security, while an NTFS volume provides full Windows 2000 security.

NOTE To support synchronization of DFS shared folders, the referenced resource for a DFS shared folder must be located on a Windows 2000 NTFS partition.

Key DFS Terms

The following terms are important in understanding DFS:

- **DFS topology** This is the DFS hierarchy as reflected in the DFS administrative console. It includes roots, shared folders, and replica sets. It is not, however, the view seen by users, which is the DFS namespace.

- **DFS root** This is the share at the root of the DFS topology that starts a DFS tree-like namespace. These roots can be configured using domain-based roots or stand-alone roots. From an enterprise standpoint, you will typically use the domain-based roots. Stand-alone roots are best for earlier implementations of DFS. A domain-based DFS can have multiple roots, but each server can have only one root. Root placement and replication are key elements that need to be addressed in the DFS root design.

- **Root replica** A server can duplicate the DFS root to provide improved availability. The host DFS server controls the referrals to clients for shared folders. Remember, replicas can be used for DFS links as well.

- **DFS link**   These are the pointers that create connections to shared folders or other DFS roots. Mapping a DNS or NetBIOS name to the UNC of the target share will create this link.

- **DFS shared folder**   These are shared files that can exist at the root level on a domain-based DFS or that can be referred to by a DFS link.

- **Replication policy**   These are the rules that facilitate the regular replication of files between computers where replication has been enabled. Replication through Active Directory is supported at the root and child-folder levels of a domain-based DFS. Remember that a stand-alone DFS cannot take advantage of replication.

Placing a DFS Root

You can create a DFS root on a Windows 2000 File Allocation Table (FAT) or NTFS partitions. A FAT file system does not offer the security advantages of NTFS. It also does not enable automatic replication, which is a design consideration when choosing where to place the DFS root. When creating a DFS root, you have the option of creating either a domain or stand-alone DFS root.

Here are the essential attributes of a *domain-based DFS root*:

- It must be hosted on a Windows 2000 domain controller.
- DFS topology (overall logical hierarchy) is automatically published to Active Directory.
- It can have root-level DFS shared folders.
- It supports root and file replication through the File Replication Service (FRS).

Here are the essential attributes of a *stand-alone DFS root*:

- It does not use Active Directory or FRS.
- It cannot have root-level replicas.
- It has a limited hierarchy. A standard DFS root can have only a single level of DFS links.

Using the DFS console, you specify a shared folder to assign as the DFS root. This creates the DFS root. Users can access any subfolders of this shared folder, in addition to accessing the shared folder. Replicating a DFS root to another server in the domain ensures that if the root hosting server becomes unavailable for any reason, the distributed file system associated with that DFS root will still be available to users.

To replicate a DFS root, you start the DFS console and select New Root Share from the DFS Root menu. This starts the Root Share wizard. You can add a DFS link at the root of the DFS topology. Note, though, that if the target folder of the DFS link is not a Windows 2000 folder, the target folder cannot have subfolders. You can assign a maximum of 1,000 DFS links to a DFS root.

Each shared folder that is added to the DFS has an associated client-caching length assigned. The caching duration determines the caching TTL of the shared folder information on the client. When the caching TTL elapses, the DFS client must access the DFS host server to update the referral information. You can adjust the caching length to balance the factors of client use and network traffic associated with a shared folder.

For each DFS link, you can create a set of DFS shared folders to which the DFS link points. Within a set of DFS shared folders, you add the first folder to the set when you create the DFS link, using the Distributed File System console. Subsequent DFS folders are added using the console's New Shared Folder dialog box.

The maximum number of DFS shared folders allowed in a set of shared folders is 32. Within a set of DFS shared folders, you can choose which folders will participate in replication. If you add DFS shared folders for domain-based DFS roots, you also need to do the following:

- Set the replication policy among the shared folders.

- Check the replication status.

DFS Root Replica Strategy for High Availability

Now that the DFS root is established, you have the option of ensuring that the content of folders is always available to users by replicating that content to other root shares or DFS shared folders in the domain. You can replicate both DFS roots and DFS shared folders using FRS. Replication copies the content of one DFS root to another root share, or from one DFS shared folder to another DFS shared folder.

Replicating a DFS root to another server in the domain ensures that if the host server becomes unavailable for any reason, the distributed file system associated with that DFS root is still available to domain users. To replicate a DFS root, you start the Distributed File System console and select New Root Share from the DFS Root menu. This will start the Root Share wizard.

When replicating a DFS shared folder, DFS stores a duplicate copy of the contents of the original shared folder in another shared folder. Replicating a DFS shared folder involves two steps:

1. Add the DFS shared folder to a DFS link, and specify that the folder will participate in replication.

PART III

2. Set the replication policy for the set of DFS shared folders associated with the link just created.

The replication of DFS shared folders can be performed either manually or automatically. For domain-based DFS, you can enable DFS to automatically replicate the contents of a DFS shared folder to other folders in the set of DFS shared folders. The content of the DFS shared folders is synchronized as changes to the DFS shared folders occur.

You enable automatic replication by using the Replication Policy window of the DFS console. Although it is invisible to users, DFS uses the *File Replication Service* (FRS) to perform the replication function. FRS, by default, synchronizes the contents of the DFS shared folders at 15-minute intervals. Within a set of DFS folders, FRS manages updates across the folders that are specified to be replicated.

When creating a replication policy, select one of your DFS shared folders as the initial master. This will then replicate the shared folder's contents to the other DFS shared folders in the set. For domain-based DFS, if FRS management of DFS shared folders is not enabled, the same content in all of the DFS shared folders must be maintained manually.

For stand-alone DFS, you can only use manual replication. Automatic replication is only available for files stored on NTFS volumes on Windows 2000 servers. Other types of files, such as FAT files, must be replicated manually. Within a set of DFS shared folders, mixing automatic and manual replication is not recommended. Use either automatic replication or manual replication exclusively within a set of DFS shared folders to ensure the integrity of the contents through synchronization.

Case Study 17: Catywhompus Construction, Inc. Restructuring WINS

Spend 10 to 15 minutes reviewing this case study. Create diagrams as needed and then complete the hands-on strategy analysis and case-study questions at the end of this case.

Scenario

You have been hired as a consultant to assist Catywhompus Construction (CC) in redesigning their Oakland location's network infrastructure. (See Figure 17-2 to view

continued

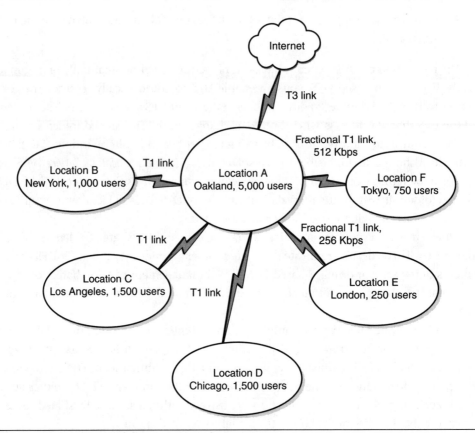

Figure 17-2 Overall CC network configuration

the overall Catywhompus network configuration. Then review Figures 17-3 through 17-8, which show the network configurations for each of the Catywhompus locations.)

Catywhompus has decided to restructure the existing network and wants to provide backward compatibility with legacy systems. WINS will provide name-to-address resolution for NetBIOS client requests and will enable legacy Windows-based clients to find key Windows-based services on their routed network. Catywhompus wants to use this service to preserve its investment in existing Windows clients and to provide scalable administration of the NetBIOS namespace.

On the network, Windows 2000–based servers must point to WINS servers to ensure that proper NetBIOS name registration occurs for client queries or lookups. As time passes, it is likely that the role of WINS will diminish in importance as the legacy Windows clients are replaced by Windows 2000 clients.

continued

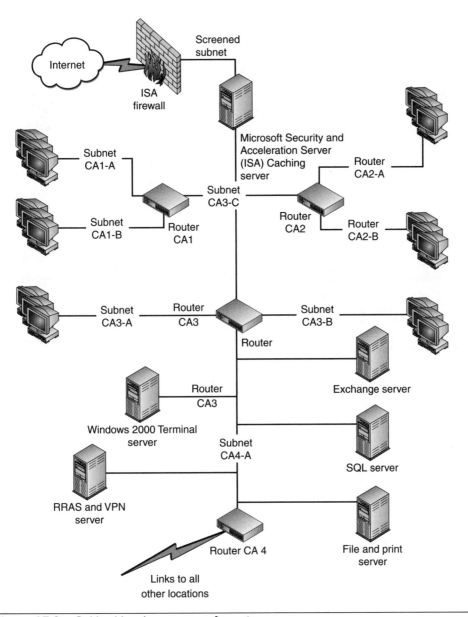

Figure 17-3   Oakland headquarters configuration

continued

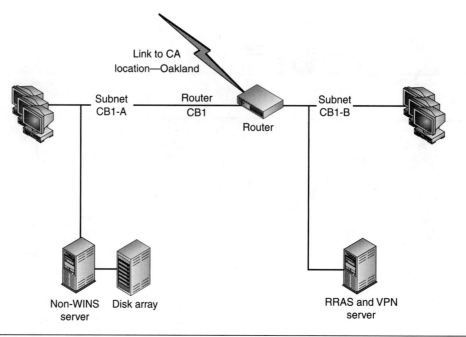

Figure 17-4   New York location B

Legacy Environment

As a best practice, Catywhompus Construction has kept accurate and up-to-date network and server configuration records for its legacy environment. This will greatly reduce the time that would otherwise be required to collect the information.

Catywhompus has included details in its documentation that are specific to how the legacy WINS infrastructure and network components have been deployed. The documentation includes the following:

- WINS servers and those servers' replication schedules
- Switches
- Hub routers
- Leased lines
- Satellite networks

continued

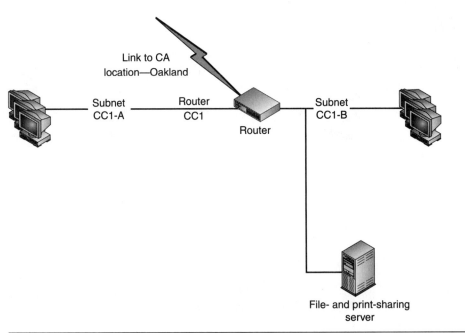

Figure 17-5 Los Angeles location C

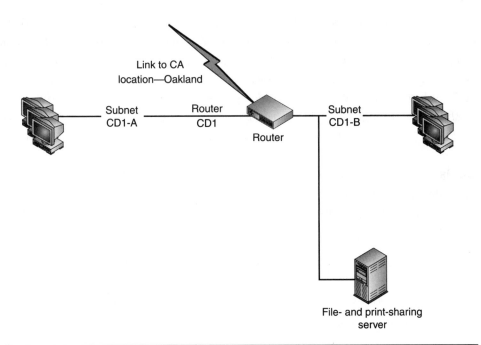

Figure 17-6 Chicago location D

continued

Figure 17-7
London location E

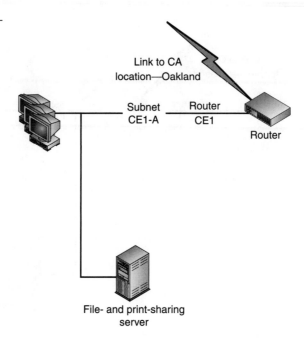

Prior to upgrading the internal computing infrastructure, Catywhompus documented its legacy environment. The documentation consisted of complete and accurate inventory records, server placement, hardware and software standards, and logical and physical architecture diagrams. The documentation and diagrams helped Catywhompus develop goals for deploying Windows 2000 Server and execute the deployment carefully and thoughtfully. The documentation included detailed information on server placement, WINS replication, client configuration, and server configuration.

Goals for the Deployment

After documenting and reviewing the legacy WINS environment, Catywhompus created the following goals for deploying Windows 2000–based WINS within the company:

- Use WINS as an interim solution for name resolution until dynamic DNS is fully deployed.

- Standardize WINS server configurations throughout the company. Each WINS server should support no more than 3,000 users.

continued

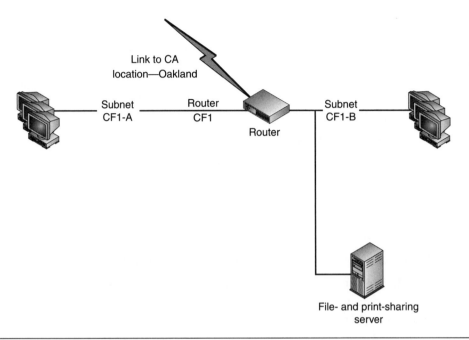

Figure 17-8   Tokyo location F

- Retain all existing WINS server placements.

- Improve the availability, fault-tolerance, and performance of the WINS environment.

- WINS redundancy must be set up such that there is no single point of failure, except the routers. To put it simply, there must be at least one WINS server in each location.

- WINS servers must be placed to minimize traffic across subnets from both client registrations and queries as well as synchronization traffic.

- WINS servers will be set up as single-function servers to improve performance and ease the disruption to the network when they are eventually decommissioned.

- Add NetBIOS name-resolution support for non-WINS clients as appropriate.

- Legacy non-WINS clients are on each subnet, along with a non-WINS legacy server with a proprietary drive array at the New York location B.

continued

Case Study Questions

List the actions and choices necessary to create a WINS solution for the given design goals:

1. Select the quantity and placement of the WINS servers based on the current and future requirements.

2. Describe the WINS replication strategy that should be used on the network.

3. Locate the WINS proxy agents needed to support the solution.

4. Describe the WINS client requirements.

5. Identify the options to improve WINS availability.

6. Identify options to improve WINS performance.

7. Select the appropriate security options for WINS replication traffic.

8. In this design scenario, where would you place the DFS root? Why?

Suggested Solutions

(You may find that your answers vary somewhat from these.)

1. A minimum of seven WINS servers is required; one at each spoke location in the hub-and-spoke model, and two at the Oakland location A. In location A, place one WINS server in Subnet CA3-C and the second in Subnet CA4-A, which places them centrally and offers some measure of fault-tolerance. Place one WINS server in each of the following subnets: CB1-A, CC1-A, CD1-A, CE1-A, and CF1-A. This will provide for consistent placement between locations, because all locations have a C*x*1-A subnet. It is always best to standardize when possible.

2. Create partnerships manually. Automatic partner discovery is not appropriate because of the extensive WAN connections. Design the WINS server in CA4-A as the hub of the WINS replication partnerships and set up push/pull replication between all of the spoke WINS servers and the hub WINS server. You will have to test the replication schedule to determine if any database-convergence delays will impact client communications, and select an appropriate schedule to diminish the impact.

3. Since non-WINS clients are on every subnet, place a WINS proxy agent on every subnet that doesn't have a WINS server, excluding WINS connections and screened subnets to ensure proper communications for these clients, which exist

continued

on all subnets. The total required is 10 WINS proxy agents. You may consider putting a WINS proxy agent on the subnets that do have WINS servers on them as well to provide a measure of fault tolerance.

4. Use the default registration-renewal period. Six days should work fine. Set up each client with three or four WINS servers for redundancy, make the closest WINS server the primary, and load-balance the rest of the WINS servers.

5. You could use clustering, but the current design provides both online fault-tolerance as well as load-balancing. The only candidate for clustering might be the hub WINS server on subnet CA3-C because of the replication delays if it fails.

6. You could increase the TTL on clients or schedule replication traffic for off hours.

7. No WINS servers are placed in screened subnets, so it is not necessary to use IPSec or a VPN solution.

8. Based on the information available, place the root on a domain controller and create a domain root. Target the initial root placement in subnet CA3-C where most servers are centrally located.

Chapter Review

Even though WINS is not the future of Microsoft server-based networking, it is part of the exams along the Windows 2000 MCSE path. WINS enables NetBIOS name resolution to occur over TCP/IP using a NetBIOS name server. This helps to reduce broadcast-based resolution and reduces the administrative burden of maintaining LMHOSTS files because of the dynamic registration that takes place for WINS-enabled clients. Keep in mind that if all clients are Windows 2000, you may be able to use Windows 2000 DNS exclusively in most circumstances. However, if the network must support legacy clients, such as Windows NT or Windows 9.x, WINS (or LMHOSTS files) may be necessary in a routed network.

WINS design should include a functional analysis as well as decisions with regard to availability, performance, and security. You should assess how many users require support on the network and use WINS servers to meet those user needs. Use multiple WINS servers for fault-tolerance, and install WINS proxy agents to support non-WINS clients.

DFS will provide needed management and user visibility by providing a single share point where users can map to shares without regard for the share's location.

Two essential root types are available: domain level and server level. Domain-level roots are recommended for the Windows 2000 enterprise; server-level roots are really for backward compatibility. Shares and roots can be replicated across the domain to provide a highly available DFS solution.

Questions

1. Which of the following are the benefits of using WINS? (Choose all that apply.)
   a. Dynamic IP configuration
   b. Dynamic NetBIOS name registration
   c. Server-based NetBIOS name resolution
   d. Broadcast traffic is reduced.
   e. The NetBIOS interface over TCP/IP functions more effectively over the routed network.

2. You are responsible for configuring WINS name resolution for all the computers on the network. Two WINS servers on the network are on the same subnet. The routers are not configured to forward NetBIOS broadcasts. Six total subnets are on the entire IP network, and each has a mixture of WINS and non-WINS clients. How many WINS proxy servers must be configured to meet your objective, and where should they be placed?
   a. Six, one WINS proxy agent on each subnet
   b. Five, one on each subnet that does not have a WINS server
   c. One WINS proxy agent on the same subnet as the WINS servers
   d. None are needed for Windows 2000.

3. You have two Windows 2000 WINS servers on different subnets, and you want to replicate their databases to ensure NetBIOS name resolution across subnets. What is the best way to configure these servers to synchronize their databases? (Choose the best answer.)
   a. Set the primary WINS server of each server to point to the other server.
   b. Install DNS on each server.
   c. Install and configure DHCP on one of the servers.
   d. Configure one server as a pull partner of the other, and configure the other server as a push partner.
   e. Turn on FRS on both WINS servers.
   f. Configure each WINS server as both a push and pull partner with the other WINS server.

4. You have 1,000 NT 4.0 workstations and 200 Windows 98 workstations on a routed network. You need to provide NetBIOS name resolution for these legacy systems. What two options do you have?
   a. LMHOSTS file
   b. DNS
   c. DHCP
   d. WINS

5. You have Unix hosts that are non-WINS–compliant on one subnet. The Unix hosts run NetBIOS services that all clients need to reach using NetBIOS names including Windows 98 and Windows NT 4.0. What two steps should be taken to ensure these clients can reach the Unix host?
   a. Place a WINS proxy agent on the same subnet as the Unix host.
   b. Install the Microsoft Unix Client.
   c. Create a static unique entry for the Unix host in WINS.
   d. Upgrade the Unix host to Windows 2000.

6. Two types of DFS roots can be created. Which is more useful for a highly available DFS solution?
   a. Stand-alone
   b. Domain-based
   c. Internet-based
   d. Active Directory–integrated

7. You are trying to set up a link replica on a server in the domain that contains the same data as the original DFS link, but the link-replica operation is not working. Which of the following are problem candidates? (Choose all that apply.)
   a. The FRS service is not started on the second computer.
   b. The second server is in a different domain but still in the same forest.
   c. The second server is a Windows NT 3.51 server.
   d. The second server has FAT partitions only.

Answers

1. **B, C, D,** and **E.**

2. **B.**

3. **F.**

4. **A** and **D.** DNS will also be used in the NetBIOS name-resolution sequence (last).

5. A and C.

6. B.

7. C and D.

Key Skill Sets

You should be able to perform the following tasks to meet the Microsoft Objectives for the 70-221 exam:

- Evaluate WINS as a solution to NetBIOS name resolution.
- Evaluate and create a functional design for baseline name resolution.
- Select the appropriate strategies to secure a WINS solution.
- Select the appropriate strategies to improve WINS availability.
- Select the appropriate strategies to improve WINS performance.
- Design a DFS strategy:
  - Design the placement of a DFS root.
  - Design a DFS root replica strategy.

Key Terms

Burst-mode name registration
Convergence time
DFS root
DFS root replica
Distributed file system (DFS)
Domain-based root
File Replication Service (FRS)
Initial master
Link
Link replica
LMHOSTS file
NetBIOS
Node type
Push/pull partner
Stand-alone root
Windows Internet Naming Service (WINS)
WINS proxy agent

CHAPTER 18

Designing Internet and Extranet Connectivity Solutions

This chapter covers the following key mastery goals:

- Evaluate NAT as a solution for Internet connectivity
- Evaluate and create a functional design for baseline Internet connectivity
- Select appropriate strategies to secure a NAT solution
- Select appropriate strategies to enhance Internet connection availability
- Select appropriate strategies to improve Internet connectivity performance
- Evaluate the use of ICS as a NAT method for appropriate situations
- Understand the purpose and need for a network firewall when connecting an enterprise to the Internet
- Select appropriate hardware-based or software-based firewalls
- Evaluate Proxy Server or ISA as a solution for Internet connectivity
- Evaluate and create a functional design for baseline Internet connectivity
- Select appropriate strategies to secure a Proxy Server or ISA solution
- Select appropriate strategies to enhance Proxy Server or ISA availability
- Select appropriate strategies to improve Proxy Server or ISA performance
- Understand how Routing and Remote Access Service (RRAS) can be integrated into an Internet connection solution to provide remote-user connectivity

Update: Internet Connection for Catywhompus Construction

Catywhompus Construction will require a new Internet connectivity solution that allows for 24/7 access that is both fast and secure. The key functionality needed includes control over users' access to Internet resources from all locations. Since Catywhompus Construction is a large enterprise, you will need to take this into account when you determine the appropriate Internet connectivity solution. Use the information presented in this chapter and then later determine the appropriate solution for this scenario. Once this is determined, you will then create a design that functions as needed and provides the required security and availability.

The value of Internet connectivity is clear to many organizations and to business leaders around the world. To business leaders, the Internet presents a huge opportunity and market to tap. The Internet potentially gives companies an effective means for communicating with internal and external customers, along with business partners. Whatever the motivation, businesses now treat the connection to the Internet as a mission-critical set of network service capabilities. One of Microsoft's primary design strategies for Windows 2000 was to create an operating system that supports comprehensive Internet connectivity. In this chapter, the focus is on analyzing the various features and components of Windows 2000's Internet, extranet, and intranet connectivity solutions. Your Internet connectivity design must be developed with care, in order to provide the correct strategic fit with the organization's networking objectives.

To enable an appropriate Internet design solution, the components of the solution must be determined and then integrated as part of the network infrastructure. The Internet-connectivity components reviewed in this chapter include Network Address Translation, Connection Sharing, Proxy Server (2.0 and ISA), firewalls, and Routing and Remote Access. Once the basic Internet-access infrastructure is established, IIS 5.0 and Internet Mail access through Exchange 2000 is addressed along with network load balancing. The standard Internet services used by an organization can be implemented on the network.

Firewalls and Web and mail access are addressed at a fairly high level in this chapter. Remember that the focus for the Microsoft test is on "designing." Do not get caught up in the details of the implementation and installation of the Internet-connectivity components. Instead, focus on understanding the essential capabilities and limitations of the technologies presented, and evaluate their ability to meet business's technical needs. As in the other Windows 2000 network-infrastructure design chapters, review the functionality of each solution and make sure it fits with the company's overall network strategy. Once the functionality fit is determined, identify ways to enhance the availability, performance, and security of the solution. Keep in mind the simple fact that sometimes the key functionality includes the service's ability to provide availability, security, and performance.

Firewalls

When an organization is connected to a public network like the Internet, there is a real risk of public users gaining access to the local network and its internal, confidential, or secret data. To create a secure Internet connectivity design, network resources need to be protected from viruses, hackers, and unauthorized access. Additionally, there is a risk that denial-of-service (DoS) attacks can flood the network with more information than the network can process, thereby preventing essential services from functioning properly. These risks can result in embarrassment as well as lost revenue. Security is a very real concern when a company connects to the Internet, and firewall services are key design elements in Internet connectivity solutions.

A *firewall* is a generic term for a device or for software services that use a variety of methods to control incoming and outgoing network traffic to create secure private networks. A firewall is typically a combination of hardware and software that, when designed and implemented properly, can reduce the risk of unauthorized network access. While firewalls can be used in scenarios that require the separation or filtering of traffic between networks, they are most often used to control the flow of traffic between an intranet and the Internet (see Figure 18-1).

The flow of traffic through a firewall is both inbound and outbound. *Inbound traffic* is traffic that passes from the Internet to the private network. This traffic can be controlled by a firewall to protect internal resources. *Outbound traffic* is traffic that passes from the private network to the Internet. This traffic can also be controlled to restrict internal users or systems from accessing certain public network resources. Firewalls can and do control the flow of traffic in both directions, and most companies need to control this flow in both directions.

The theory is that firewalls are placed at the connection point between internal (trusted) networks and networks from "the outside world" (untrusted). In practice, a

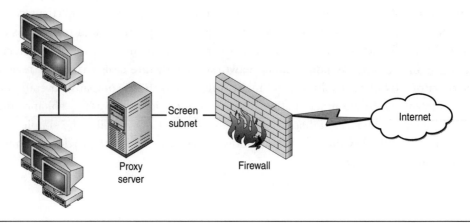

Figure 18-1 A network firewall between the Internet and the internal network

firewall must provide the perfect balance between safety and convenience. A firewall could be configured to block all traffic in and out of the organization. This would be relatively safe but would defeat the purpose of having the Internet connection. On the other hand, if a firewall were configured to allow all traffic from any source to pass through the connection, the firewall's purpose of controlling access would be defeated. This setup would be very convenient for users, while providing no additional security.

The ideal firewall solution will begin by blocking all traffic as the starting point, and then it can be configured to allow traffic when there is a clear need and set of rules for access. For example, if your users must have unlimited access to HTTP and HTTP-Secure Sockets Layer (SSL) or the HTTPS protocol, you would allow port 80 for HTTP and port 443 for any requests from the internal network on the firewall. Because these are the only ports open, the user would not be able to use FTP over the common FTP port 21.

NOTE In reality, this simplistic example is not foolproof because many hacker programs designed to infiltrate a network can be configured to use a common port like port 80 (which is used for HTTP) or port 443 (which is used for HTTPS). Also, it does not allow for other services, such as DNS, so it is quite useless!

Before selecting a firewall solution, you must thoroughly understand the existing network environment. During the planning process, collect the following information:

- What incoming traffic is authorized?

- What outgoing traffic is authorized?

- What protocols are supported?

- Where are users located?

- What services are being used on the network?

Again, this is where clearly defined goals and objectives must be identified if the appropriate firewall solution is to be selected for implementation. As with most network technologies, firewall solutions vary in complexity and cost.

Please remember this: firewalls are not foolproof. They are one component of a security plan that must be evaluated and certified for the enterprise. In addition, it is best to use a combination of firewall technologies at different OSI layers to create multiple lines of defense against public-user incursion.

Common Firewall Technologies

There are a number of common firewall technologies for controlling incoming and outgoing network traffic. As a network designer, your designs will be much more secure if you implement an appropriate combination of these technologies. Table 18-1 describes the general firewalls you can set up and discusses the advantages and disadvantages of each.

Table 18-1 Common Firewall Technologies

Technology	Description
Packet-filtering firewalls	These routers can restrict incoming and outgoing traffic to the local network by filtering unauthorized source IP addresses and port numbers.
Dynamic packet-inspection firewalls	Software at the device validates TCP/UDP session information before opening a connection. The stateful packet-inspection firewall keeps track of the packet's state. A stateful-inspection firewall can let you block all incoming traffic while allowing all outgoing traffic. This type of firewall provides advanced capabilities over the packet-filtering firewall because it tracks traffic based on the session layer of the OSI model.
Application-proxy firewalls or gateways	Application-level gateways are considered to be the most secure type of firewall. They operate at the application and presentation layers of the OSI model.

Packet-Filtering Firewalls

A packet-filtering firewall or router works at the network layer of the OSI model. It is one of the first generation of firewalls, and it checks each packet passing through an interface and either discards the packet or allows it to pass, depending on the packet-filtering policies configured. Most packet-filtering routers are multihomed and typically have two network interfaces. When used as an Internet firewall, the router will have one network interface connected to the public Internet and the other connected to the internal network or to a screened subnet.

The firewall essentially acts as a traffic director by delivering packets to the appropriate destination and discarding or blocking those that are filtered. Rules or policies are defined using the network header of the protocol stack being filtered based on the following criteria:

- Source address
- Destination address
- Packet type
- Source port
- Destination port
- Router interface

For instance, you could set up complex rules that allow users to access an FTP server from the Internet, but only from one particular group of users from a given subnet. If you set up these rules, the packet will only be forwarded if it matches an allowance rule.

- **Advantages**   Packet-filtering provides low-level control over each packet traversing the Internet connection. Each component of the IP packet is checked against a set of rules and is filtered based on that information. The firewall can discard packets with spoofed IP addresses and is often difficult to bypass because it is placed at the connection point. Many routers, including Windows 2000 RRAS, include the capability to filter packets.

- **Disadvantages**   It can be difficult to configure packet filtering, which can lead to holes in the firewall. Also, certain applications can get through the firewall by using a common port that is not blocked. There may also be other ways to bypass the firewall, including dial-up or remote-access connections.

 TIP   Because common ports are often left open on a packet filtering firewall, additional security measures should be added to counteract the use of common ports to bypass the firewall. It is important not to depend exclusively on the firewall for security.

- **Design Fit**   Packet-filtering firewalls are best for smaller networks that don't have critical security needs. While these kinds of firewalls are being replaced by more advanced stateful-inspection firewalls, you can use common routers from Cisco, Lucent, and even Microsoft's Routing and Remote Access server for packet filtering as long as all other unnecessary network services are disabled (such as the NetBIOS interface).

Dynamic Packet-Inspection Firewalls

A dynamic (stateful) packet-inspection firewall can keep track of network connections that pass through it, so the firewall can apply a set of criteria for allowing or denying traffic. The packet's state is inspected by the firewall and uses this information to identify the packets. As an example, this firewall will let you block all incoming traffic while allowing all outgoing traffic. Because the firewall keeps track of the internal requests as they go out, all requested incoming data is allowed through until the connection is closed. (This is where the session layer of the OSI model comes into play.) Only the solicited incoming data is allowed to pass through the firewall.

The manner in which the connection state is tracked will depend on whether the packets are TCP or UDP. The firewall is not always concerned about the "connection" as much as the state of the packets.

 NOTE   Do not confuse this firewall with Network Address Translation, which is addressed later.

The configuration of this firewall is more complicated than for packet-filtering firewalls, but stateful packet inspection is both powerful and flexible. For instance, if you have an FTP service, you can direct incoming traffic to port 21 to only the server specified.

- **Advantages**   Stateful inspection offers the ability to check IP packet fields, such as source address and port number. It has the ability to verify the packet based on previous communications, which allows return packets. It can verify the state of a packet based on the application information and will allow for detailed logging information.

- **Disadvantages**   The only disadvantage is the speed limitation, resulting from the inspection overhead. Over time, though, as hardware speeds improve, this cost will become less noticeable.

- **Design Fit**   Dynamic packet-filtering firewalls are best for networks with critical enterprise-level security needs. These types of firewalls are replacing less-advanced packet-filtering firewalls. Often they include additional firewall technologies, such as packet filtering and application proxy services. Cisco's PIX firewall is an example of this technology, along with Microsoft's new Internet Security and Acceleration Server, which provides multilayered traffic screening, including packet, circuit, and application-level filtering. There are many companies selling firewalls, including Check Point, CyberGuard, and Network Associates.

Application-Proxy Firewalls or Gateways

Application proxies don't actually allow traffic to flow between the networks to which they are connected. Instead, they accept traffic from a client application, such as a Web browser, on port 80 and then set up a separate connection to the destination server while operating on the client's behalf. This hides the internal network from the Internet and provides a level of shielding for the local network. The connection and redirection is transparent to the user once the client is configured to use the proxy server.

Some of the common applications that use proxy firewalls include:

- HTTP
- HTTPS/SSL
- SMTP
- POP3
- IMAP
- NNTP
- Telnet
- FTP
- IRC

 TIP   Most proxy firewalls have the added benefit of providing a local cache copy of frequently requested information. This caching often offsets the additional overhead related to the gateway translations and can speed up the retrieval of static data dramatically. Additionally, the caching can improve the performance of the Internet connection because the proxy server doesn't require as much remote data fetching.

Application proxies can also add a measure of security by requiring connections only by authenticated users. This restricts connections so that only known users can have outgoing connections.

- **Advantages**   Proxies can log the source and destination address of connections and provide useful information if an attack occurs. They can restrict the use of outgoing traffic to certain protocols. They can restrict access to specific groups of users or IP addresses.

- **Disadvantages**   Client components must be installed and configured because the traffic must pass through a gateway operating at the higher levels of the OSI model. The traffic requires software configuration beyond the network layers. Remember, there may be situations where not all applications and protocols operate over a proxy connection.

- **Design Fit**   As with the other common firewalls, application proxy services are often combined with other firewall technologies, or they can be stand-alone solutions that are often found adjacent to the local network on the inside of a screened subnet or demilitarized zone (DMZ). Again, there are a number of vendors that provide application firewalls, including Cisco, Network Associates, and Nortel Networks. Later in this chapter, the Microsoft Proxy Server will be addressed in detail.

Firewall Placement

For the greatest strength and benefit to the organization, the firewall should be placed directly between the internal network and the Internet or external network. If possible, the firewall should be placed on the single line of connection between the two. In addition, all of the internal hosts should connect through this point to the public network.

The firewall should then be configured to allow only certain communications to pass through its interfaces. This may seem like a no-brainer, but actually there are justifications for placing hosts outside the firewall, for example, when you want to offer services to the Internet on a host, but you don't want to expose the internal network.

Demilitarized Zones or Screened Subnets

Firewall configuration often involves setting up an additional subnet that is both accessible to the internal network as well as the external network (as illustrated earlier in Figure 18-1). This "buffer" is referred to as a demilitarized zone (DMZ) or screened subnet. The DMZ is only used if you need to make certain resources available to the public network, such as a Web server or an FTP server, and you are not using shared or co-location services (that is, you are not outsourcing network and server management).

The advantage of the DMZ is that you can limit external access to the DMZ and only allow outgoing traffic or only responses to outgoing queries. This offers internal security and still provides public resources in the DMZ. In essence, the results are very similar to having two firewalls: one between your internal network and the DMZ, and one between the DMZ and the Internet. You can also use a proxy server for the internal interface, and a stateful firewall on the outside interface of the DMZ. From a design standpoint, this is the recommended configuration for the Microsoft exams.

Routing and Remote Access

The Routing and Remote Access Service (RRAS) is a key component in Microsoft's Internet-connectivity strategy. Windows 2000 with RRAS becomes a multiprotocol router supporting a variety of routing protocols and services. Through RRAS, the designer can configure LAN-to-LAN, LAN-to-WAN, VPN, Network Address Translation, dynamic routing services, DHCP Relay Agent, and dial-up/VPN services, along with Internet Connection Sharing (ICS). Many capabilities are now centralized in the RRAS group of services. Two new features in the Windows 2000 version of RRAS provide Internet connectivity for small and medium networks using Network Address Translation.

Network Address Translation (NAT) provides a small to medium-sized network with a single interface that has at least one public IP address that connects to the Internet and provides IP address-translation services between public and private IP addresses. NAT also provides IP address assignment and proxy-name resolution services to internal network clients so that full-blown DHCP, DNS, and WINS services may not be needed for smaller environments.

Internet Connection Sharing (ICS)—you can think of ICS as "NAT light"—provides a small network with an easy-to-configure but limited interface that connects small office/home office (SOHO) clients to the Internet. ICS provides DNS name resolution, automatic address allocation, and a single IP address range for IP distribution. ICS is not a flexible solution.

Additionally, the remote-access component of RRAS provides remote users with access to intranet, as well as outbound Internet, resources through a variety of connection types, including dial-up and virtual private network (VPN) connections. Many of the details of remote-access and routing capabilities are covered in detail in other chapters of this book, including Chapter 19. The Connection Sharing design components of RRAS are explored in the "Internet Connection Sharing" section of this chapter.

Windows 2000 Network Address Translation

A router that provides Network Address Translation is not technically a firewall but has some attributes of a firewall. The NAT router translates a group or range of private IP addresses on an internal network to one public address that is shared and sent out to the Internet. It, in essence, hides the private internal IP addresses from external visibility.

Once installed and configured, Windows 2000 Network Address Translation allows computers on a small network, such as a SOHO, to share a single Internet connection. The Windows 2000 server on which NAT is installed acts as a network address translator, a simplified DHCP server, a DNS proxy, and a WINS proxy. NAT allows host computers to share one or more publicly registered IP addresses, which helps to conserve public address space and has the added benefit of requiring very few public address acquisitions, thereby lowering costs.

As background information, there are essentially two types of connections that can be made to the Internet using Windows 2000's RRAS capabilities: routed connections and translated connections. When planning for a *routed connection*, you will need one or more public IP addresses from your ISP to use on the external router interface of your network. This is necessary because the internal (private) addresses are translated to the (public) IP addresses provided by the ISP. The ISP may also provide the IP address of the DNS server you need to use (or you can set up your own DNS server—see Chapter 16 for information on DNS design). You can either statically configure the IP address configuration of each host computer, or use a DHCP server, which automates the host IP configuration process.

The Windows 2000 NAT router needs to be configured with a minimum of two interfaces. One network adapter is configured for the internal network (100BaseT Ethernet, for example) and one interface needs to be configured with an Internet connection such as a modem, xDSL device, cable modem, or T-1 line.

NAT gives you a more secure network because the addresses of your private network are hidden from the Internet. The shared computer, which uses NAT, does all of the translation of Internet addresses in and out of your private network. However, be aware that the NAT computer does not have the ability to translate all packets. This is because some applications use IP address fields outside the standard TCP/IP header fields. Therefore, the following protocols do not work with NAT:

- Kerberos V5—Active Directory uses Kerberos V5, so domain controllers cannot replicate through a Network Address Translator

- Internet Protocol Security (IPSec) packets that use IP header compression

- IPX/SPX or NWLink

- Simple Network Management Protocol (SNMP)

- Lightweight Directory Access Protocol (LDAP), which Active Directory requires

- Microsoft's Remote Procedure Call (RPC)—many Microsoft Management Control (MMC) snap-ins use RPC

- Component Object Model (COM) or Distributed Component Object Model (DCOM)

 TIP For applications that use these protocols not supported by the NAT routing protocol, use a routed Internet connection or proxy server.

Designing a Functional NAT Solution

When creating a functional NAT solution, answers to the following questions will provide the foundation for your Internet connectivity and provide the basis for NAT implementation:

- Where will the NAT server be placed, and what NAT server interface options, including IP address, persistence type, and data rate, will be used?

- What are the appropriate automatic IP address-assignment and DNS name-resolution feature options to implement?

To keep resource costs to a minimum for a SOHO network, only one Windows 2000 server is needed. Depending on whether you are running a translated or routed connection, this single server is all that is needed for NAT, APIPA, Routing and Remote Access, or DHCP.

NAT Server Placement

The NAT server is placed between network segments (see Figure 18-2), which localizes network traffic and helps to create a secure environment. NAT is appropriate for non-

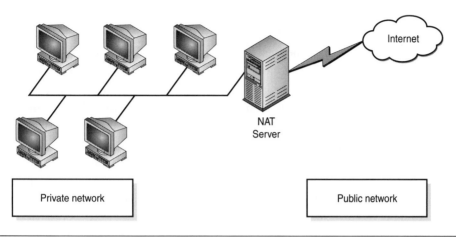

Figure 18-2   A NAT network

routed network environments where all users have the same access privileges but where private IP addressing is required for all computers. Place the NAT server within the private network to do the following:

- Create a screened subnet within a private network to aid in the protection of confidential data.

- Allow the exchange of network packets between dissimilar network architectures or segments, such as an Ethernet segment, Token Ring segment, or xDSL segment. You'll choose NAT when you want to exchange traffic between two dissimilar network segments, but the expense and complexity of Microsoft ISA Server or Microsoft Proxy Server is not desired.

- Isolate the network traffic to source, destination, and intermediate network segments.

NAT Interface IP Address and Subnet Mask
The following issues must be addressed for each interface:

- Each interface must have an IP address and subnet mask.

- The IP address selected and the subnet mask must both be within the range of valid IP addresses for the network, and they must match the subnet mask assigned to the network segment that is directly connected to the interface.

NAT Data Rate and Persistence

Each of the NAT server network interfaces connects to a network segment. The segment may be either a private or public network. The data rates for these network segments can vary widely, and you will need to identify and specify the data rate and persistence for each interface so that the NAT server can connect to network segments as required. The NAT server will easily handle the translation, even though dissimilar network architectures and data rates are used on the different network interfaces.

Typically, the data rate for a private network segment is determined by the LAN technology or network architecture. These private network segments are most often persistent connections that are "always on." For instance, you may have connection speeds of 16 megabits per second (Mbps) for Token Ring or 100 Mbps for Fast Ethernet.

Public segment connections tend to vary more widely—they can be persistent or non-persistent. These network segments are based on LAN and various demand-dial or WAN technologies. A dial-up modem connection is an example of a demand-dial interface, and the data rate is determined by the speed of the modem or underlying technology. Network segments are at times based on LAN technologies, such as xDSL, and demand-dial interfaces, such as VPN connections, can be used over a LAN technology infrastructure. The following are situations where you should include demand-dial interfaces in your design:

- When connection costs are based on connection time
- When authentication is required for a connection

NAT Server Options

The DHCP allocation functionality in NAT enables all DHCP clients in the private network to automatically obtain an IP address, subnet mask, default gateway, and DNS server address from the NAT computer. If you have any non-DHCP computers on the network, then statically configure their IP address configuration. To provide the best IP-address manageability on the private network, you must configure NAT client computers such that they obtain their TCP/IP configurations automatically. When computers are started, the NAT server can then configure the TCP/IP options of the DHCP-enabled computers.

The following TCP/IP options and settings are configured on the DHCP client computers:

- The IP address is set to an address from the range of 192.168.0/24.
- The subnet mask is set to 255.255.255.0.
- The DNS server option is set to the IP address of the NAT private interface.
- The default gateway is set to the IP address of the NAT private interface.

Automatic Private IP Addressing (APIPA) can also be used in Windows 2000 and Windows 98 to automatically configure computers on the private network. When you use APIPA, the IP address for the NAT server's private network interface must be selected from the range of APIPA addresses.

CAUTION Ensure that DHCP servers do not provide IP configuration for the private network when enabling the automatic IP addressing feature. If the DHCP servers and NAT server attempt to configure DHCP-enabled computers, IP configuration conflicts will occur.

The name-resolution feature of NAT forwards DNS name-resolution requests to DNS servers belonging to the organization or to its ISP. This DNS-proxy capability can be used in your design when other private-network servers do not provide DNS name resolution or when the private network consists of a single, non-routed network. The DNS servers serve the NAT server, which serves the clients. The NAT server resolves requests for the private system name.

Designing for NAT Availability and Performance

Performance of the NAT server depends on several factors, so you should monitor the hardware, software, and network-connection utilization to make optimization choices. Use Windows 2000 System Monitor to monitor the processor, memory, disk subsystem, and network subsystem, which can all reveal bottlenecks that can typically be remedied with hardware upgrades or configuration changes. (See Chapter 13 for more information about System Monitor.)

It is important to dedicate a system to running NAT. This prevents other applications running on the server from consuming resources or causing system instability, which will potentially lead to an unscheduled shutdown. A dedicated NAT server is your primary defense against system instability.

Since the NAT system often connects to a public network, the connection to the Internet can be improved by making it persistent and by using multiple connections for redundancy. For example, the primary connection can be a T-1 frame-relay connection with an ISDN connection used for backup. This provides a consistent connection that is always on and also provides for a lower-speed backup with the ISDN connection in case the frame-relay connection fails. Also, the traffic can be distributed across multiple connections to the public network.

NAT Security Considerations

The default security that NAT provides will adequately protect private network resources and ensure that they are not available to public Internet users by hiding the private address space from Internet users. NAT interface security can be enhanced beyond the default security, by the use of packet filtering, port mapping, and VPN connections.

Access restrictions can be specified with Routing and Remote Access Service filters, which can be used to grant or block access by IP address and/or protocol. Filters can be applied to the private or public interface on the NAT server to allow or disallow packets to pass through the interface specified. Multiple filters can be used in combination to address almost any security requirements, which allows the NAT server to act as a packet-filtering firewall. The filter design can be based on any combination of the following:

- Source IP address or range of addresses
- Destination IP address or range of addresses
- IP port number

You can design the filters to either accept or reject packets. You can also manage any of the filters assigned to the NAT interface.

 CAUTION Verify that the public and private interface filters do not conflict with each other. An inadvertent conflict may prevent IP traffic from passing through the NAT server.

Outbound Internet Traffic

If the traffic from the private network is outbound on the Internet interface, the NAT server first determines whether or not an address/port mapping, static or dynamic, is in place for the packet. If it doesn't exist, a dynamic mapping is created. The NAT server creates a mapping depending on whether there are single or multiple public IP addresses available.

If a single public IP address is available, the NAT server requests a new unique TCP or UDP port for the public IP address and uses that mapped port. If there are multiple public IP addresses available, the NAT performs private-to-public IP address mapping. For multiple public IP addresses, the ports are not translated. When the last public IP address is needed, NAT will switch to performing address and port mapping as if there were a single public IP address.

Inbound Internet Traffic

For traffic to the private network that is inbound on the Internet interface, the NAT first assesses whether an address/port mapping, static or dynamic, exists for the packet. If a mapping does not exist for the packet, it is discarded by the NAT.

This behavior protects the private network from malicious users on the Internet. The only way that Internet traffic is forwarded to the private network is either in response to traffic initiated by a private network user that created a dynamic mapping or because a static mapping exists so that Internet users can access specific resources on the private network, such as a Web server on port 80 or 443.

After mapping, the NAT will check for an editor and call upon one if necessary. After editing, the NAT modifies the TCP, UDP, and IP headers and forwards the frame using the private network interface.

VPNs and Network Address Translators

Using VPN connections to authenticate and encrypt data transferred across public networks can improve restricted access to resources. Secure connections can be installed in order to secure traffic between remote users and private network resources. PPTP is the only VPN tunneling protocol supported over the NAT server. Since L2TP uses IPSec to encrypt the IP header, NAT cannot perform address translation for this protocol.

Internet Connection Sharing

As mentioned earlier, you can think of Internet Connection Sharing (ICS) as the Microsoft Windows 2000 implementation of "NAT-light" (RFC 1631). The ICS service enables a company to set up a single computer to act as a shared access point to the Internet. Private-side clients route requests through the ICS server as the default gateway. The ICS server handles the translating of the private request into a request that can be passed to the Internet.

ICS works well for small organizations or home offices—the fully configurable version of NAT is intended for larger organizations and organizations that require more configuration flexibility. ICS offers the following benefits to an organization:

- Small network Internet access—public IP addresses are not needed for every client computer accessing the Internet.

- IP address and name resolution is provided by ICS so that separate DHCP and DNS services are not needed.

- Private IP addresses are hidden from the Internet.

- Installation is simple.

Web Caching with a Proxy Server

Connecting the private network to the Internet can be a risky proposition. With Windows 2000, this risk in some ways is heightened (if appropriate security measures are not implemented on the network) primarily because Windows 2000 has enhanced interoperability features with various types of systems. Windows 2000's design focuses heavily on Internet-based standard protocols, such as LDAP and DNS, to accomplish this high level of interoperability. Microsoft proxy and ISA servers provide Internet access services that can be used to improve the management of the Internet connection.

What Does a Proxy Server Do?

Like NAT, a *proxy server* acts as a control point that isolates certain types of traffic and controls the level of access to the private network from the public network. By using a proxy server as a control mechanism at the edge of the internal network, you can ensure your private network environment is secure and control access by users or groups.

A "proxy" is something that acts as a go-between or acts on your behalf. The proxy server acts as a gateway for computers on the network that need to make an Internet connection. A proxy server serves as the single connection to the Internet while protecting the internal network and controlling access to the Internet. This dual function solves the two primary problems associated with Internet access: Internet connection vulnerability and controlling internal users' access to the Internet.

A proxy server is the only computer directly connected to the Internet. Internal network computers make their requests to the proxy server. The proxy server then makes requests to Internet resources directly and fulfills the client requests. Again, like NAT, only the public IP address and proxy server information is exposed on the public Internet, thus protecting the internal network.

Protecting the Network

The proxy server design decisions are based on the security requirements of the network. The primary role of the proxy server is to protect the internal network from the Internet.

A proxy server placed at the edge of the network needs at least two network interfaces: one connected to the internal network and one connected to the Internet. It is important that the proxy server does not forward packets—to put it simply, the proxy server should not have routing turned on. The proxy server should act as a gateway that, instead of forwarding packets from the client to the Internet, converts packets so that the origin of the request is not included in the packets that may be sent to the Internet or processed from the proxy cache. The proxy server creates a newly formulated packet that then goes out to the Internet, and the Internet resource server then returns the requested information to the proxy server, which in turn sends the requested information to the original requesting client.

The functionality of a proxy server occurs primarily at the application layer of the Open Systems Interconnect (OSI) model and works primarily as a gateway.

Microsoft Proxy Server

Microsoft Proxy Server's current version, at the time of writing, is 2.0 and was upgraded to Microsoft Internet Acceleration (ISA) Server in 2001. The Proxy Server name was dropped by Microsoft because ISA provides firewall services in addition to caching services. So, Proxy Server does not really exist in a version beyond 2.0. For Proxy Server to run, it must be loaded on Windows NT or Windows 2000. ISA server will only run on Windows 2000. Also, Proxy Server requires Microsoft's Internet Information Server (IIS) and is managed using the Microsoft Management Console (MMC) snap-in. Proxy Server is compatible with IIS versions 3.0 and greater.

Proxy Server allows you to restrict Internet and private-network traffic so you can limit the access of private-network users to Internet resources, and at the same time limit Internet user's access to private network-based resources. You can grant Internet access to authorized users.

You can also establish filters that discard packets based on cascading rules. The proxy server also allows for the interception of certain inbound requests and determines whether the requests must be forwarded to a resource on the local network. A proxy

PART III

server can be used at the edge of the private network to isolate the private network from the public network, and it can be used in a screened subnet to provide the required level of network security.

The proxy server intercepts FTP and HTTP requests from internal users for Web objects, such as graphics or Web pages, and saves the retrieved Web objects in a local cache on the proxy server if configured to do so. When a private-network user requests an Internet-based resource using HTTP or FTP, the proxy server checks the local cache to see if the request is already stored. If the request is found in the local cache and is up to date, the object is provided to the client without a call to the Internet resource. In this case, an Internet request is not necessary. From a performance standpoint, the additional overhead of the proxy server can be offset by the improved performance achieved by caching.

The proxy server integrates with a new or existing Windows 2000 network by supporting both WinSock and non-WinSock clients. It also supports the IPX/SPX protocols on private networks and integrates with the Active Directory service accounts in Windows 2000 to provide single-logon access for users on Windows computers. Also, RRAS can provide support for persistent as well as non-persistent connections using a demand-dial interface. This provides the ability to reduce connect charges.

 NOTE A special Install wizard was released by Microsoft to fix a Proxy Server 2.0 installation so that it is compatible with Windows 2000.

On the client side, Internet Explorer 5.0 is all that is required for HTTP and FTP traffic. Install the Proxy Server Client (WSP) for any Windows-based Internet application that uses wsock32.dll or NWLink. For Unix and Macintosh clients, SOCKS4-compatible applications are supported.

The Local Address Table

The Local Address Table (LAT) is an important component of the proxy server, especially from a performance perspective. The LAT determines whether an IP address is on the internal or external network.

The LAT needs to contain all of the IP address ranges from the internal network. When a client needs to connect to a resource, the LAT is consulted to see if the address is internal or external. If the LAT contains the destination address, it is on the internal network, and the client can use a direct connection. If the address is not in the LAT, the address is considered to be part of the external network, and the proxy server will process the packets.

There is a LAT on both the proxy server as well as the client, and the client's LAT is generated at the server. If the internal or external network addresses change, the LAT must be updated.

Preparing for Proxy Server

Before incorporating Proxy Server into a network, certain changes may be needed to prepare the network, once planning is completed. IP addressing is one issue that usually needs to be resolved. The proxy server with a direct Internet connection must use at least one valid public IP address, which can often be obtained from an ISP.

The proxy server sits on the edge of the network and allows clients to use a range of private IP addresses. A proxy server can also be used between WAN connections within a private network.

Designing a Functional Proxy Server Solution

There are three areas on which to focus when creating the functional proxy server solution: proxy server placement, proxy server interface configuration, and client access solutions. Each of these areas will require decisions that will create the specifications for the proxy server design. Later, you will optimize the design to create a highly available and secure proxy server.

Proxy Server Placement

The Web-object caching provided by Proxy Server is used to reduce the use of high-cost bandwidth within a private network, and between the private network and the Internet. When a proxy server is used within a private network, screened subnets are created to protect confidential data and to localize more traffic. When used at the edge of the private network, the private network is screened from the public network, which protects confidential private data. In all cases, the proxy server allows traffic to be exchanged between dissimilar network segments, such as ISDN on the public segment and Ethernet or Token Ring on the private segment.

Proxy Server Interface Configuration

Each proxy server in the network design must have at least one interface. Most proxy servers have more than one, which allows them to connect to dissimilar network segments.

NOTE If the proxy server only requires caching, or if the proxy server provides IPX-to-TCP/IP translation, only one interface is needed.

The following issues must be addressed for each interface:

- Each interface must have an IP address and subnet mask.
- The IP address selected and the subnet mask must both be within the range of valid IP addresses for the network, and they must match the subnet mask assigned to the network segment that is directly connected to the interface.

Proxy Server Data Rate and Persistence

Each of the proxy server interfaces connects to a network segment. The segment may be either a private or public network. The data rates for these network segments can vary widely, and you will need to identify and specify the data rate and persistence for each interface so that the proxy server can connect to network segments as required. The proxy server will easily handle the translation, even though dissimilar network architectures and data rates are used on the different network interfaces.

Typically, the data rate for a private network segment is determined by the LAN technology or network architecture. These private network segments are most often persistent connections that are "always on." For instance, you may have connection speeds of 16 Mbps for Token Ring or 100 Mbps for Fast Ethernet.

Public segment connections tend to vary more widely—they can be persistent or non-persistent. These network segments are based on LAN and various demand-dial or WAN technologies. A dial-up modem connection is an example of a demand-dial interface, and the data rate is determined by the speed of the modem or underlying technology. Network segments are at times based on LAN technologies, such as xDSL, and demand-dial interfaces, such as VPN connections, that can be used over a LAN technology infrastructure. The following are situations where you should include demand-dial interfaces in your design:

- When connection costs are based on connection time
- When authentication is required for a connection

Proxy Server Client

Proxy server client requirements must be determined so that you can select the appropriate client setup and software. As mentioned earlier, there is a Local Address Table

(LAT) on the server. When computers on the private network have Proxy Server client software installed, they have a local copy of the LAT. The proxy clients query the local LAT to determine how to direct private or public requests. Private network requests are sent directly to the resource destination without using the proxy server. Public requests are sent to the proxy server.

The default gateway for client computers on the private network can be set to point to the proxy server or proxy-server array (a logical grouping of proxy servers that are revealed as one logical address to clients). You should make client configuration changes based on the kinds of applications used on the client. Use Table 18-2 to make client configuration decisions.

Designing for Proxy Server Availability and Performance

When configuring demand-dial connections, specify the data rate and the persistence of the connection. With DSL, you can set up a demand-dial VPN tunnel.

Active content caching makes the most commonly requested objects available to clients without needing to retrieve the content from the Internet when the client makes a request. This improves the performance of the WAN or Internet connections. The server will retrieve objects automatically during low-traffic periods if configured properly. Active caching conserves disk space but adds an additional load to the proxy server's CPU.

If you configure the server to use *passive caching*, objects are retrieved when the client makes a request, and the content is stored in the cache until the content's TTL expires. The proxy server's passive caching uses fewer CPU cycles but requires more disk space than active caching.

Table 18-2   Client Configuration Requirements

Client Setup	Client Application Requirements
Microsoft Internet Explorer 5.0 and later	HTTP and FTP traffic only. Packet and domain filters. Operating systems that support Internet Explorer 5.0.
WSP Proxy Server Client	All IP traffic or an operating system that supports WinSocks. IPX/SPX-based networks. Packet and domain filters.
SOCKS	All SOCKS-supported IP protocols. Operating systems that support SOCKS.
No client software	All IP protocols. Set the default gateway to point to the proxy server.

Multiple servers can be configured as a proxy-server array for fault tolerance. If a member of the array fails, the remaining servers will still provide proxy services. Because the Web objects cache is spread across the array, the cache is lost only on the failed server. It is important to set all of the proxy servers in the array to use the same array name, and they should belong to the same Active Directory domain and site.

Multiple proxy servers can be set up for network load balancing, which provides all servers with a single IP address used by clients making requests. When one of the proxy servers fails, the others will continue processing client requests. Proxy servers can also be chained together hierarchically so that requests are forwarded from one proxy server or array to another.

NOTE Round-robin DNS can be used to provide fault tolerance for proxy servers. However, using round-robin doesn't provide the same performance enhancements, such as the Windows 2000 network load-balancing solution. A hardware load balancer would also work well to provide performance enhancements. These two load-balancing solutions take into consideration the state of the proxy server's capabilities.

Proxy Server Security Considerations

While Proxy Server improves Internet performance with caching, it also plays an extensive and powerful security role. The majority of the Proxy Server services provide for internal network security. The proxy server is a gateway for Internet connections, and therefore granular controls can be placed on the Internet connections, which can be as fine as specifying which services are available, which users can use these services, and which sites users can access.

Proxy Server allows administrators to control outbound users' access to the Internet. The administrator can control access levels to Internet resources by users or groups of users. The administrator can also set which domains, sites, and IP address ranges can and cannot be accessed.

Active Directory Integration

Proxy Server integrates with Active Directory services provided in Windows 2000 by allowing an administrator to set Internet service access levels. Not everyone on the internal network may need all services provided on the Internet. As an example, your organization may have a group of common users that only need access to a corporate Web site on the Internet but do not need to connect to other Internet resources or use FTP. The ability to control service-level access, such as FTP, is found in Proxy Server.

In addition to service control, Proxy Server can be set to control Internet site access. Your company may decide that only certain sites can be accessed and block all others. Proxy Server can control what sites are accessed using either domain names or IP addresses.

Inbound Internet Traffic

Inbound traffic can be controlled with Proxy Server by not allowing packets originating from the Internet to pass through the external interface. Packet filtering closes all inbound ports to prevent external computers from passing the external interface to reach internal computers. Because Proxy Server is a gateway for all Internet traffic, it can watch for attempts to access internal systems.

Packet filters are often only implemented on the external interface to the Internet. Because all ports are closed by default, an administrator needs to create exceptions that will allow ports to be open to provide services to the network. Packet filters can be dynamic or static. A *dynamic filter* opens ports as needed and then closes the port. *Static filters* open ports and then leave them open. Proxy Server uses dynamic filters by default because they are more secure.

Comparing Internet-Connection Sharing Solutions

It is important to select the appropriate Internet-connection-sharing solution for your organization. The solution should be selected based on size, functionality, and budgetary constraints. Table 18-3 can help you choose the most appropriate solution for your organization.

Table 18-3   Selecting an Internet Access Solution

Customer Requirements	NAT Supported	ICS Supported	Proxy Server Supported
Share one IP address among several computers	Yes	Yes	Yes
No additional software purchase needed	Yes: built-in	Yes: built-in	No: purchased separately

continued

Table 18-3 Selecting an Internet Access Solution (*continued*)

Customer Requirements	NAT Supported	ICS Supported	Proxy Server Supported
Web objects caching is used	No	No	Yes
An IP address range other than 192.168.0.0 must be used on the internal network	Yes	No	Yes
DHCP or DNS servers can be used on the network	Yes	No	Yes
Advanced filtering and firewall capabilities are required	No	No	Yes
Special client software components may be required	No	No	Yes
You must use IPSec	No	No	Proxy Server's Web caching and filtering can be used, but not its NAT feature. IPSec can be used with a routed connection.

Case Study 18:
Designing Internet-Access Methods

Spend 10 to 15 minutes reviewing this case study. You will make Internet connectivity recommendations for two companies.

Scenario

You are a consultant for a small consulting company that helps connect businesses to the Internet. Currently, Kim's Modeling Agency and the courthouse in Mount Vernon are your responsibility.

Kim's Modeling Agency focuses on managing minority models for Internet-based advertising. They need to connect 25 computers currently configured as a LAN to the Internet. All computers are running Windows 9x. They wish to connect to the Internet without making significant changes to client software. Security is not a primary

continued

concern, but you must address security and protect your client's private network. The controller for the company is very concerned that confidential information, such as payroll records and the telephone numbers of the models, remain inaccessible to other employees and external Internet users. One of the users on the network acts as a part-time administrator for the network.

The courthouse in Mount Vernon, Washington, has an established network with 90 computers running Windows 9*x*, Windows NT Workstation 4.0, and Windows 2000 Professional. There are three servers running in a Windows NT 4.0-based network. The courthouse requires high levels of security on its servers because of the court documents and legal records. The courthouse employees access the Internet via modems attached to their local computers using Earthlink.net accounts. You must create a more cost-effective and secure solution for Internet access. The courthouse has a full-time network administrator.

Case Study Question

What are your recommendations for these two scenarios?

Suggested Solution

(Your answer may vary.)

In the first scenario, the best solution is to install a Windows 2000 server and set up either NAT or ICS. ICS would probably be the simpler solution for this environment because the DHCP allocator could easily be used to configure DHCP clients on the network. The server would require two interfaces. The internal interface should match the network architecture on the LAN (probably 10 or 100 Mbps Ethernet) and the second interface should use xDSL or ISDN. On the server, you would configure ICS.

The second scenario is more complex and has much higher security requirements. First, the individual modem access is a serious security breach and must be terminated immediately. Since there is a full-time administrator on staff, a more complex Internet connectivity scheme can be used in the environment. With the number of users on staff, it would make sense to use a proxy server's caching capabilities to improve the performance and security of the network. We recommend either upgrading one of the NT 4.0 servers to Windows 2000 or installing a new Windows 2000 server on which to run Proxy Server or ISA. Using Active Directory, you can configure access-control levels and apply filters for improved security.

You could either use xDSL or frame relay on the Internet external connection. It is important that the proxy server be configured to block all unwanted traffic from passing through the external interface.

Catywhompus Construction Updates: Internet Connection

Catywhompus has extensive documentation about their existing network. This documentation, in addition to interviews with personnel at the company will help to determine the best solution for Catywhompus. Your research reveals the following:

- Active Directory is used as the directory services for Catywhompus.

- New servers can be purchased to provide controlled Internet connectivity.

- Internet connectivity is required 24/7 at all locations.

- Management is concerned that employees' access to the Internet is controlled at a user level.

- Internet connections can use dedicated connections.

- All locations must be isolated or screened from the Internet.

This situation requires either a routed solution with additional firewall technology or proxy servers. Your job now is to build a design for Catywhompus. You and your team will need to address the following design decisions:

- Determine the naming convention and placement of each proxy server on the network. Make sure you justify your placement decisions.

- Determine the server and client options required for your solution. Make sure that the appropriate levels of functionality, availability, performance, and security are addressed in your configurations.

Chapter Review

This chapter explored the key technologies available in Windows 2000 for connecting to the Internet, with a specific focus on firewalls, Proxy Server, NAT, and ICS.

The firewall discussion provided a look at the various technologies and terminology used by firewall designers. The primary goal is to understand the various types of firewalls and how the Windows 2000 solutions map to the existing firewall technologies.

Network Address Translation (NAT) and Internet Connection Sharing (ICS) provide appropriate Internet connection capabilities for small companies. We reviewed the design issues associated with using NAT on the network.

Finally, Proxy Server was analyzed as an enhancement over NAT that provides increased security and performance when connecting to the Internet.

Questions

1. What is the first thing you should do when starting to plan your Internet access solution?
   a. Review the wiring of the network.
   b. Upgrade the workstations to Windows 2000 Professional.
   c. Use Microsoft Visio Enterprise to auto-discover all of the devices on the network and do a complete audit of the network.
   d. Diagram the existing network.
   e. Rewire the existing network to Category 5 UTP.

2. Why would you consider using firewall technologies in the final solution when creating your design?
   a. You must use firewalls when connecting to the Internet.
   b. It gives you the ability to share a connection to the Internet.
   c. It helps to secure your network from potential intruders.
   d. It means you don't need DNS or DHCP servers.

3. Due to the company's growth and increased Internet usage, Internet performance is too slow at the main office and each branch office of a company. What proxy server solutions can help this situation? (Choose the two best answers.)
   a. Set up DNS for round-robin entries.
   b. Create a proxy array at the main office.
   c. Enable packet filtering on the LAN proxy server.
   d. Connect the proxy servers at the branch offices to the Internet.

4. A proxy server array is used at the corporate headquarters. What performance and availability enhancements does an array provide?
   a. Caching
   b. Fault tolerance
   c. Filtering
   d. Chaining

5. Which of the following is true of a typical firewall configuration? (Choose all that apply.)
   a. Packets can be blocked based on IP address.
   b. Packets can be blocked based on port number.
   c. Packets can be blocked based on protocol.
   d. Packets can be blocked based on the source and destination.

6. You want to use the automatic method of configuring a shared Internet connection. What should be chosen?
   a. Microsoft Proxy Server
   b. Network Address Translation
   c. Internet Connection Sharing
   d. Routing Information Protocol
   e. Open shortest path first

7. Which of the following is true of Network Address Translation (NAT) but not of Internet Connection Sharing (ICS) in Windows 2000? (Choose all that apply.)
   a. It can be used in conjunction with DHCP and DNS server on the network.
   b. It is configured via the Routing and Remote Access console.
   c. It must use addresses from the following IP network: 192.168.0.0.
   d. It is included in both Windows 2000 Professional and Windows 2000 Server.

Answers

1. **C.** It is best to audit the network to determine the best course of action for the Internet connection.

2. **C.**

3. **B and D.**

4. **A and B.**

5. **A, B, C, and D.**

6. **C.**

7. **A and B.**

Key Skill Sets

You should be able to perform the following tasks to meet the Microsoft Objectives for the 70-221 exam:

- Evaluate NAT as a solution for Internet connectivity.
- Evaluate and create a functional design for baseline Internet connectivity.
- Select appropriate strategies to secure a NAT solution.
- Select appropriate strategies to enhance Internet connection availability.
- Select appropriate strategies to improve Internet connectivity performance.
- Evaluate the use of ICS as a NAT method for appropriate situations.
- Create a Web-caching solution using Microsoft Proxy Server 2.0 or Internet Security and Acceleration (ISA) Server 2000.
- Evaluate Proxy Server as a solution for Internet connectivity.
- Evaluate and create a functional design for baseline Internet connectivity.
- Select appropriate strategies to secure a Proxy Server solution.
- Select appropriate strategies to enhance Proxy Server availability.
- Select appropriate strategies to improve Proxy Server performance.
- Understand the purpose and need for a network firewall when connecting an enterprise to the Internet.
- Select appropriate hardware-based or software-based firewalls.
- Understand how Routing and Remote Access Service (RRAS) can be integrated into an Internet connection solution to provide remote-user connectivity.

Key Terms

Application-layer gateways
Circuit-level gateways
Firewalls
Network Address Translation (NAT)
Packet-filtering routers
Proxy array
Proxy Server
Routing

PART III

CHAPTER 19

Designing a Wide Area Network Infrastructure

This chapter covers the following key mastery goals:

- Create a wide area network infrastructure design
- Design a functional routing solution with Routing and Remote Access Service (RRAS) to connect locations and provide for private network connectivity
- Select appropriate strategies to enhance availability, improve performance, and secure an RRAS routing design
- Design a virtual private network (VPN) strategy
- Design a functional VPN solution
- Select appropriate strategies to enhance availability, improve performance, and secure a VPN design
- Integrate authentication with Remote Authentication Dial-In User Service (RADIUS)
- Design a functional RADIUS solution
- Select appropriate strategies to enhance availability, improve performance, and secure the RADIUS design
- Design a demand-dial routing strategy

The future of wide-area networking involves technologies that are now being refined and, frankly, still being defined. Broadband networking in the near term, and distant future, involves an increasing need for high-bandwidth communications. The Public Switched Telephone Network (PSTN) set the stage early, and still remains in place to handle voice beautifully, along with limited data applications. However, it offers limited bandwidth and is relatively slow in establishing connections. Additionally, it is expensive for data-intensive applications.

The conventional public data networks (PDNs) introduced significant improvements over PSTN. Yet PDNs still rely heavily on the PSTN model for connectivity (for example, using local loops, data nodes co-located with voice switches, and common transport facilities). The next entry is the broadband network model, which is still emerging. Although some broadband network technologies are quite immature, they are being rapidly deployed as the backbone for many developing countries. Broadband networks again rely on the voice model to some extent. Some broadband technologies are intended specifically for data transmission, while others are designed to support the full range of voice, data, video, and image traffic. These technologies include xDSL, ADSL, CATV, and SONET. The broadband network services include Frame Relay, SMDS, ATM, B-ISND, and AINs.

In today's business environment, it is quite common to have branch offices, distribution centers, and various dispersed locations that need to be connected to the corporate network. The speed and bandwidth required to connect to these locations has enabled businesses to operate in many new and more competitive ways. Surely, the continued growth trends of services for dispersed network services like video conferencing and telecommuting will increase the requirements for WAN infrastructure and network services.

In this chapter, we'll look at the key services for remote access and WAN connectivity, and at how Windows 2000 and the Active Directory play a key role in making these services work reliably and securely. Here, we will discuss key design points related to dial-up remote access, Remote Authentication Dial-In User Service (RADIUS), virtual private networks (VPNs), and Routing and Remote Access Service (RRAS). The importance of these capabilities is obvious as they change how almost any business operates. In many cases, a business cannot survive without these capabilities. The ability to reliably link remote users to network resources is surely one of the most required tasks of network-infrastructure designers, and the Microsoft designing exams focus on that need.

Update: Wide Area Network Design for Catywhompus Construction

Catywhompus Construction will require a routing and VPN end-user connectivity solution that allows for 24/7 access. The key functionality needed includes VPN and

continued

dial-up connectivity for remote users. The IT team also wants to outsource its dial-up, yet centrally manage user authentication and accounting. Since Catywhompus Construction is a large enterprise, you will need to take this into account when you determine the appropriate WAN connectivity solution. Use the information presented in this chapter and then later determine the appropriate solution. Once this is determined, you will then create a design that functions as needed and provides the required security and availability.

Connecting Private Networks Using RRAS

The WAN extends the network beyond a single geographic location and traditionally consists of a number of LANs connected via WAN technologies. There are three primary areas to look at when reviewing WAN technologies: physical links, VPNs, and WAN protocols.

Full-time and direct physical links between sites can come in many forms. Sites can be linked using early technologies, such as Basic Rate Interface Integrated Services Digital Network (BRI-ISDN) or the Public Switched Telephone Network (PSTN, such as a dial-up that never hangs up). Companies needing higher speeds with low latency and full-time solutions typically purchase T-carrier lines (T-1, T-2, and T-3), but newer technologies, such as DSL and cable modems, can be used to achieve similar results with much better costs per bit of transferred data. This makes high-speed WAN connectivity affordable for small offices/home offices (SOHOs).

Virtual private networks are another form of WAN connectivity. A VPN creates a connection using encryption that securely "tunnels" the data transmissions through an existing public or private network. VPN connections can create "private" network connectivity, which can generate significant cost savings over traditional direct physical links, especially over long distances. A low-cost local point of presence (POP), or access point, can eliminate the need for high-cost intermediary T-carrier providers. So, why hasn't the VPN become the standard for WAN connectivity? Primarily because the Internet doesn't allow for Quality of Service (QoS) guarantees. Many businesses require guaranteed bandwidth between locations and have a low tolerance for latency. Also, there is a certain amount of fear regarding the ability of hackers to intercept and decode important data transmitted over the VPN. Therefore, to make VPNs a viable WAN option, it is important to provide the proper bandwidth through the local access points and be sure the encryption level for authentication and data transmission is adequate for the business requirements.

When designing connectivity between LANs, there are WAN connectivity components or technologies that are needed to complete the network infrastructure beyond just the physical connection. The WAN links must have a remote access or line protocol, such as Point-to-Point Protocol (PPP), in place to encapsulate the Network Control Protocol (NCP). NCPs establish and configure the transmission protocol, such as TCP/IP, IPX, NetBEUI, and AppleTalk. TCP/IP, for instance, is encapsulated using the line protocol PPP between end points.

There are various remote-access protocols, but the Windows 2000 RRAS service supports PPP as the primary standard for most remote-access computing. RRAS can be both a PPP server and client. The PPP standards permit advanced features that are not available with older standards, such as SLIP. PPP supports multiple NCPs, multiple authentication protocols, dynamic IP addressing, encryption, and compression. PPP provides clear advantages over SLIP, which does not provide these capabilities. For instance, a Windows 2000 RRAS PPP connection can support TCP/IP, NetBEUI, and AppleTalk, along with dynamic IP configuration with DHCP and encrypted authentication with MS-CHAPv2.

The Point-to-Point Tunneling Protocol (PPTP) is an extension of PPP. PPTP adds enhanced security and multiprotocol communications over the Internet by using the new Extensible Authentication Protocol (EAP). PPTP and the Layer Two Tunneling Protocol (L2TP) are used to create secure VPN connections. Any Windows 2000–based network connection that will communicate with another network over a VPN must have a server running either PPTP or L2TP and Routing and Remote Access.

 EXAM TIP   You must understand the difference between virtual links and VPNs. A VPN requires encryption, but establishing a virtual link with L2TP does not ensure encryption like PPTP. L2TP sets up the virtual link, but you need a standard encryption method such as IP Security (IPSec) to ensure that data transfers are encrypted as they move through the L2TP virtual link.

If you want a Windows 2000 server that is either a member server or domain controller to function as a remote-access server, the server must have Routing and Remote Access Service (RRAS) installed and enabled. RRAS is installed by default with Windows 2000, but is by default disabled. RRAS is really a collection of networking services that provides administrative control over the protocols, interfaces, and mechanisms related to routing and remote-access functionality. These services provide for remote dial-up, virtual private networking, routing between two or more network cards, and many other capabilities that are not addressed specifically in this chapter.

Knowing how to enable and configure RRAS is an important part of understanding how to manage the routing and remote-access capabilities in Windows 2000.

Installing and Configuring RRAS

There are two steps to take when implementing RRAS: install and then enable. The installation of RRAS essentially requires you to enable it using the Microsoft Management Console (MMC). Prior to implementing this set of powerful capabilities found in RRAS, you, as the network designer, must make design decisions about the various roles the RRAS server is going to play. For instance, is the server going to become a multi-homed router or a dial-up server? These key decisions will be addressed in detail throughout this chapter.

The following lab exercise takes you through the procedure for installing and configuring basic RRAS on Windows 2000. You will gain familiarity with adding the RRAS plug-in though MMC, identifying connection types, configuring connection types, and running the configuration wizard.

Lab Exercise 19.1:
Install RRAS and Configure

1. To add the Routing and Remote Access snap-in, select Start | Run, type **MMC**, and click OK. This will open the Microsoft Management Console.

2. From the Console menu, select Add/Remove Snap-In (see the following illustration).

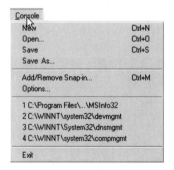

3. Click the Add button and scroll though the list of available snap-ins. Double-click the Routing and Remote Access snap-in (see Figure 19-1) to place it in the list of snap-ins.

Figure 19-1
Routing and Remote
Access in the list of
snap-ins

4. Click the Close button, and then click OK. The Routing and Remote Access snap-in is now installed in MMC (see Figure 19-2).

5. Right-click the Routing and Remote Access snap-in to bring up the context menu. Select Add Server. This gives you the opportunity to add one or more servers in a variety of ways.

6. Select the This Computer radio button and click OK.

7. Expand the Routing and Remote Access snap-in, and you will see the name of the server or servers listed.

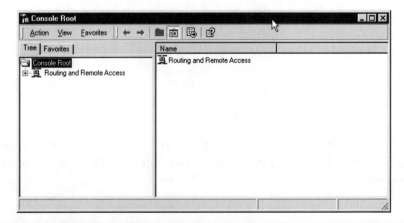

Figure 19-2 Routing and Remote Access installed in MMC

8. Now right-click the server you just added to display the context menu for this server. Assuming this Routing and Remote Access server has not been configured, you will select Configure and Enable Routing and Remote Access. This will launch the Routing and Remote Access Server Setup wizard (see Figure 19-3). Click Next once the RRAS Setup wizard is displayed.

9. At this point, you can select from one of several common configurations, which gives you the option of setting up a remote-access server, a VPN server, or a network router. You can also manually configure the server. Select the Remote Access Server radio button and click Next (see Figure 19-4).

Figure 19-3
The Routing and Remote Access Server Setup wizard

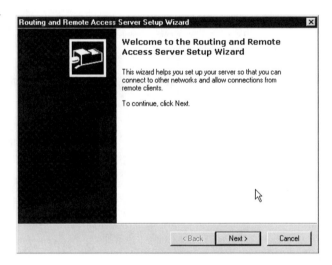

Figure 19-4
The Common Configurations page of the RRAS Setup wizard

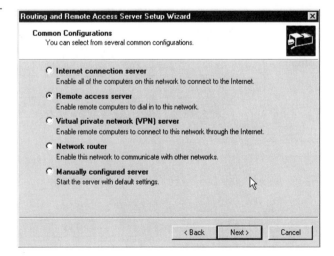

10. The Remote Client Protocols page is displayed (see Figure 19-5). TCP/IP is displayed by default, and you have the option of adding other protocols if the other protocols, such as NWLink, are installed on the target server. Leave TCP/IP selected and click Next.

11. If you have more than one network interface installed, the Network Selection page will be displayed next (see Figure 19-6). Select the network segment you want to access by way of the remote-access service, and click Next.

12. The IP Address Assignment page is displayed next (see Figure 19-7), and you can select the IP address assignment method for remote clients. You can use either

Figure 19-5
The Remote Client Protocols page of the RRAS Setup wizard

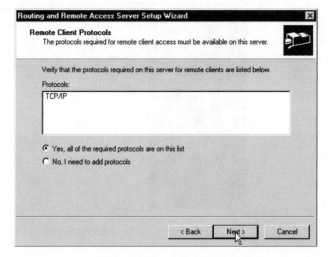

Figure 19-6
The Network Selection page of the RRAS Setup wizard

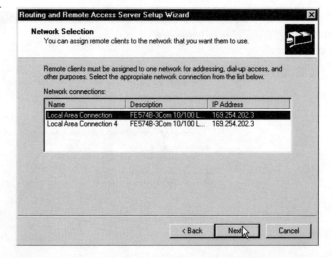

Figure 19-7
The IP Address
Assignment page of
the RRAS Setup
wizard

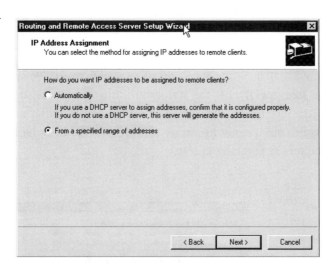

DHCP or select from a specified range of addresses. Click From a Specified Range of Addresses and click Next.

13. Click the New button on the IP Address Assignment page and in the New Address Range dialog box shown in the following illustration to add a range and address count that is compatible with the RAS server IP settings for that server. You can also just put in the beginning of the address range and then enter the number of addresses, and the value for the End IP Address field will be calculated automatically, as shown in the following illustration. Click OK, and the range of addresses you selected will appear in the next dialog box. Click Next.

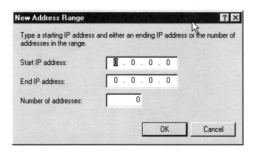

14. The Managing Multiple Remote Access Servers page is now displayed. You can now choose to configure this remote access server to use RADIUS. Click the Yes, I Want to Use a RADIUS Server radio button, and then click Next (see Figure 19-8).

15. On the RADIUS Server Selection page (see Figure 19-9), add the RADIUS server name (use a FQDN if the name resolution occurs with DNS) in the Primary RADIUS Server field. On a production server, you will also set up a shared secret password, but it is not necessary for this exercise. Click Next. The wizard will verify the servers you have entered.

Figure 19-8
Setting up a
RADIUS server

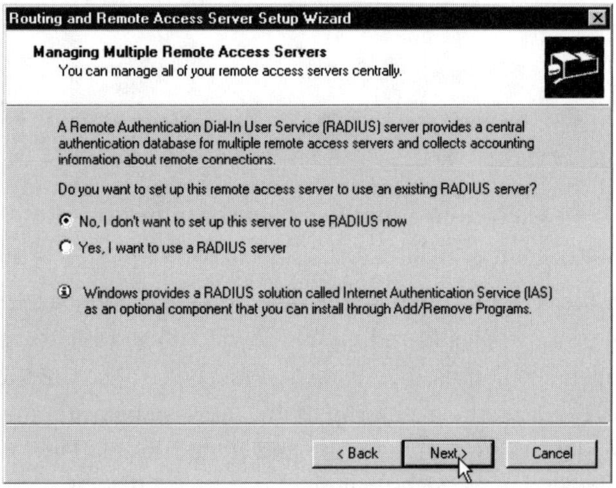

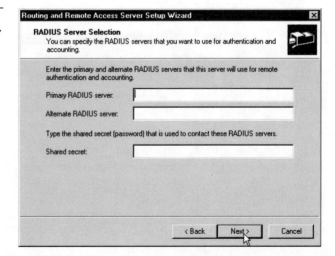

Figure 19-9
The RADIUS Server
Selection page of
the RRAS Setup
wizard

16. The Routing and Remote Access Server Setup wizard now completes its work. Select Finish (see Figure 19-10). You will receive a DHCP message requesting a verification of the address pool. Click OK, and then RRAS will start and the server's icon will turn green if configured properly.

Figure 19-10
RRAS setup
completion

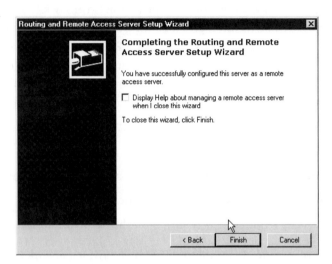

As you can see in this lab, many of the design elements are managed through the RRAS snap-in, along with the configuration wizard. Throughout the rest of this chapter, the design elements related to WAN connectivity will be explored. Keep in mind that most of the functionality is managed through the tools you have just been using to configure RRAS.

Routing for Connectivity Between Private Networks

Routing is defined as the procedure or process of finding a path from a source to a destination across broadcast domains. Routing uses addressing information present in a network packet to determine the path that packet should take to reach its destination. If the source and destination hosts are on different logical networks, routing is required for the data to reach the destination.

Larger networks use a network-segmentation method called *subnetting*, because it is impractical to use one set of addresses for the entire network. Because of broadcast traffic, collisions, and other limitations, it is impractical to put all systems in a large network on the same logical subnet. As networks increase in size, so does the addressing complexity.

You can segment a TCP/IP network by dividing the IP address range into subnets. Routers forward data from one subnet to another. Additionally, you can use routing or bridging to connect dissimilar network architectures, such as Ethernet, ATM, and Token Ring. Routing on the private network requires a network protocol that is routable.

Routing is provided by the RRAS features in Windows 2000. The routing solution provided by Windows 2000 connects private networks. RRAS capabilities protect network resources using technologies including encryption and authentication.

When designing a routing solution using RRAS, you must make certain key design decisions. This decision process includes identifying the key features of RRAS that will meet the design requirements to take advantage of opportunities to integrate RRAS with other network services. When creating a design for a routed private network, consider the following:

- The number of locations and their geographic dispersion
- The number of nodes or hosts at each location, including router interfaces
- The routing protocols needed in each location
- The security requirements required for the network connections

Routing is an appropriate solution for most private networks that are geographically dispersed, that have a wide range of user base sizes, and that support industry-standard routing protocols, such as open shortest path first (OSPF), Routing Information Protocol (RIP), or Internet Group Management Protocol (IGMP). Routing is also appropriate if there are router-authentication and data-encryption requirements, such as router-to-router authentication and transmission encryption.

Windows 2000 RRAS Features

A router that is dedicated to routing and has hardware in place specifically designed and optimized for routing is called a *hardware router*. A router in the form of a computer with software like Windows 2000 Server that is not dedicated to performing routing, but potentially performs routing as one of its various processes is a *software router*.

 NOTE The Windows 2000 router service is a software router.

The key features of RRAS fall into three main categories:

- Multiple protocol support
- Security
- Existing network integration

Multiple Protocol Support   Table 19-1 identifies the transport protocols that RRAS supports and the benefit of supporting that protocol.

Table 19-2 identifies the routing protocols that RRAS supports and how these protocols might affect the routing design.

Table 19-1   Transport Protocols Supported by Routing and Remote Access

Transmission Protocol	Why It Is Important
TCP/IP	Cross-platform support; it is the industry-standard routable protocol
IPX/SPX	Supports NetWare clients and servers
AppleTalk	Supports Macintosh clients and servers

Table 19-2   Routing Protocols Supported by Routing and Remote Access

Routing Protocol	Purpose
IGMP	Internet Group Management Protocol. This allows network hosts to participate in multicasting.
OSPF	Open shortest path first. A dynamic link-state algorithm–based routing protocol that is more efficient than RIP. It transmits net changes to routing tables rather than the entire table.
RIP for IP	Routing Information Protocol for IP. A dynamic distance-vector algorithm–based routing protocol that uses considerable overhead due to routing-table broadcasts every 60 seconds.
RIP for IPX	Routing Information Protocol for IPX. Similar to RIP for IP, but it supports IPX/SPX.
SAP	Service Advertising Protocol. Proprietary broadcast-based protocol developed by Novell and used by IPX/SPX clients or servers to broadcast their resources.

Security Enhancements   RRAS has several functions to enhance network security. The following list provides an overview of these enhancements.

- Mutual router authentication to prevent unauthorized routers from receiving data
- Private network isolation using packet filtering
- Traffic between routers can be encrypted over public and private networks

Network Design Integration   RRAS supports various network interfaces, such as modems, ISDN, ADSL, T-1, T-3, or SONET. While integrating with the existing network, RRAS supports IP and IPX/SPX. Multi-protocol support allows clients to communicate using IP and IPX/SPX, and routing protocols can exchange routing-table information with existing OSPF or RIP routers.

Integration Benefits of a Windows 2000 Router

Active Directory–integration provides Kerberos version 5 protocol certificates and user accounts for router authentication. It also permits browsing and managing remote-access servers by using Active Directory–based tools, such as the RRAS administrative tool. Remote-access policies give administrators the ability to control connections based on time of day, group membership, type of connection, and other criteria. The Layer Two Tunneling Protocol (L2TP) provides gateway-to-gateway encrypted connections, secured by IPSec.

The router integrates with RRAS to provide connections using demand-dial. RRAS can also secure and control traffic by using IP filters. The router itself can also provide authentication and the encryption of data transmitted between routers.

Designing a Functional Routing Solution

Essential decisions need to be made about the routing design. The key decisions include where to place the routers, what the IP address configuration for the router should be, whether to use static or dynamic routing tables, and, if dynamic is appropriate, which dynamic routing protocol to use. Additionally, the blocking and passing of certain types of broadcast traffic must be addressed. This specifically includes DHCP traffic. The use of DHCP relay-agent options will affect the routing design and whether DHCP broadcast traffic is passed. For example, if the relay agent (an IP helper) is used, DHCP broadcast traffic does not need to be passed.

Private-Network Router Placement

One of the goals of routing is to place routers between network segments such that network traffic is localized. In other words, traffic stays within the extended private network. When placing routers within the private network, you want to ensure that network traffic only travels between the source, destination, and intermediary network segments, which are network devices with the ability to forward packets between portions of the network, such as bridges, switches, and routers.

You also want to place routers so that packets can be exchanged between dissimilar network architectures (such as Ethernet, Token Ring, and asynchronous transfer mode) found at times on different network segments. It is also important to use routers to create screened subnets to protect confidential or secret data. Another design consideration is whether the network connections are persistent (highly available) or demand-dial connections. The type of network connection impacts router performance.

There are times when routers are placed at the edge of a network (often between the private network and the Internet) so that an organization can exchange data over the public network using VPN technologies or in order to isolate the private network with packet filtering. Routers are also placed on the edge of a private network to exchange data with the private network and the Internet. See Figure 19-11 for examples of typical router placements.

Network-Router Integration

A network router will always have multiple interfaces so that it can route between subnets. Typically, they have two interfaces that connect two subnets. Each of the interfaces can be connected persistently to a network segment or connected using demand-dial interfaces.

The router interface connects to a public or private network segment. The data rate and persistence of the interfaces needs to be specified so that the router can connect to the corresponding network segment. The configuration of each interface will also require an IP address and subnet mask:

- The IP address must be a valid address (within the range) assigned to the network segment connected to the interface.

- The subnet mask must match the network segment to which the interface is attached.

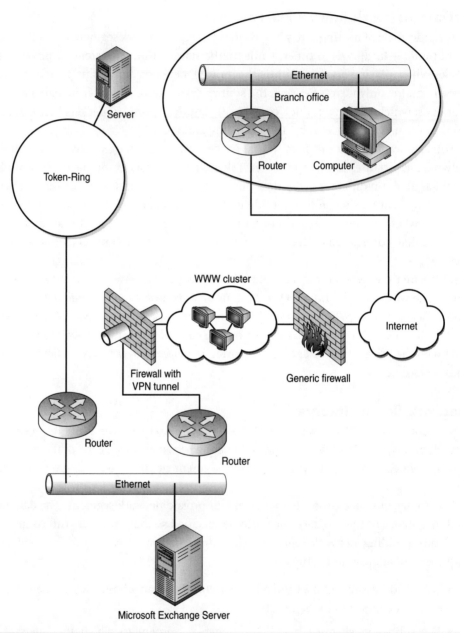

Figure 19-11 Examples of router placements

Most private network segments are persistent connections based on LAN (site-level) technologies with relatively high data rates, such as Gigabit Ethernet (1 Gbps) or 100-Mbps Ethernet (100 Mbps). Public network segments are often based on LAN and demand-dial connections that can be either persistent or demand-dial. Typically for a small business, the private side uses LAN technologies that are persistent, and the public segment uses demand-dial interfaces that are non-persistent. An example of this would be a LAN interface using 100-Mbps Ethernet for the private interface and a demand-dial 56-Kbps modem set to dial on demand.

There are also technologies that enable VPN demand-dial interfaces in a routing solution that can be created over a public segment, such as a demand-dial VPN connection over a frame-relay T-1 connection. Demand-dial interfaces are often included when an exchange of authentication information is needed; such as with a VPN tunnel or when toll charges accumulate if the public segment is active. Take, for example, two locations that must be connected to each other across the Internet. A common solution is to configure a VPN tunnel over the segment connected to the Internet with a persistent technology like DSL (see Figure 19-12). In this case, the LAN interface would be a 10-Mbps Ethernet connection supporting the DSL network segment with a demand-dial VPN tunnel to perform authentication and encrypt data routed to and from the remote network.

Static and Dynamic Routing

Router communication is one of the most important considerations when planning the routed network. For example, router-to-router communication enables the routers to

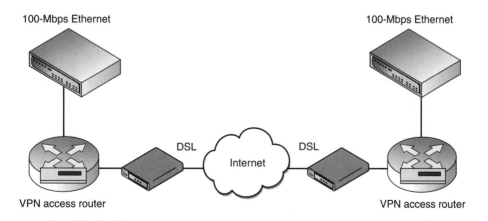

Figure 19-12 Two networks connected using DSL and a demand-dial VPN

update routing-table information so that routers can forward packets to their proper destinations. Routers that share routing-table information use dynamic routing protocols to accomplish information sharing. Examples of dynamic routing protocols include the Routing Information Protocol (RIP), which is designed for a small to medium-sized internetwork, and open shortest path first (OSPF), which can be used for very large-scale network designs.

 EXAM TIP Routes for demand-dial interfaces must be manually added because neither RIP nor OSPF support them. Note also that the automatic entering of static routes for demand-dial interfaces is known as auto-static updates and is supported by the Windows 2000 router. Auto-static updates are supported when you use RIP for IP, RIP for IPX, and SAP for IPX, but not OSPF.

If the network design does not include one of the routing protocols, static routing entries need to be added manually to the routing table so that routers can forward packets to their destinations. Static routing is an option when it is desirable to reduce network overhead generated by dynamic routing protocols, such as RIP and OSPF, or to increase security. Static routing should be avoided when it generates levels of management overhead that are unacceptable because of the amount of resources required or the frequency of changes.

 NOTE You can include static and dynamic routing in the same design so that the amount of routing information transmitted between routers is controlled.

The following are situations in which you could include static routing in the routing design:

- When there are very few ongoing changes to the routing-table information
- When you want to improve security by preventing the transmission of routing table information
- When you need to reduce traffic created by dynamic routing protocols
- When you want to add a default route or route of last resort to the demand-dial interface

If you decide to use static routing, a default route entry (also known as the route of last resort by some router vendors) needs to be created so that all IP packets with desti-

nations outside the private network will be forwarded through the demand-dial connection. The advantage of using a default route is that the entry needs to be added only
once. The downside is that any traffic, including unreachable local traffic, is forwarded
through the interface.

Auto-static routing is a combination of static routes and RIP for IP. An administrator
or designer can use a schedule when a demand-dial connection is established so that
static routing entries are automatically updated. Auto-static routing controls the
amount of traffic generated for these entries and also reduces the amount of management required to update static routes. One advantage of auto-static routes is that
unreachable destinations do not cause an unneeded demand-dial connection. The disadvantage is that availability problems can occur if auto-static updates are not performed frequently enough.

Designing Using RIP

RIP for IP has universal availability and is extremely simple to configure and deploy.
Going by the requirements of larger corporate networks, however, RIP is very limited.
Its only measure of performance of a route (metric) or of the selection of a route is hop
count, which is the number of routers between a given point and the destination network.

RIP's biggest shortcoming, when using Windows 2000 routing, is its inability to scale
beyond 14 hops. The maximum hop count used by RIP routers is 15. Networks that are
16 hops or more away are considered unreachable. Because RRAS in Windows 2000 considers all non-RIP learned routes, such as static route entries, to be a fixed hop count of
2 instead of 1, the maximum number of hops is reduced from 15 to 14. Also, as the network grows in size, the periodic updates create traffic, and broadcast (found in RIP version 1) announcements made by each RIP router can cause excessive traffic. RIP does not
traditionally respond well to network failures and has a relatively high recovery time.
However, the Windows 2000 router implementation of RIP version 2 has some improvements over the previous versions. RIP v2 supports multicast announcements, simple
password authentication, and more flexibility in subnetted and Classless Inter-Domain
Routing (CIDR) environments. The Windows 2000 router supports RIP v1 and v2.

The following is a list of features and design suggestions for the Windows 2000
router implementation of RIP:

- You can select which RIP version to run on each interface for incoming and outgoing packets.

- Algorithms are used to avoid routing loops and to speed recovery of the routed
  network when topology changes occur.

- Route filters can be implemented for choosing which networks to announce or accept.

- Router-to-router filters can be implemented for choosing which router's announcements are accepted.

- Route aging timers can be set to force periodic updates.

- Password authentication is supported.

RIP uses the hop count to determine the best route, but using the number of routers to be crossed as the basis for selecting the best route may lead to undesired routing behavior. To prevent slow links from being chosen simply because they have a low hop count, you can assign an additional cost to the slow interface. For example, if you assign a cost of 2 to the slow interface (rather than the default of 1), then the best route can be chosen for link speed. If the faster link goes down, the slow link is chosen as the next best route.

When using RIP, you should use version 2 because of the improvements over version 1, such as multicasting and password authentication. If there are routers in your inter-network that do not support RIP v2, you can mix RIP v1 and v2. However, remember that RIP v1 does not support CIDR or VLSM implementations. If the network is using a mixture of RIP version routers, the Windows 2000 router interfaces can advertise by using either RIP v1 or v2 broadcasts and accept either RIP v1 or v2 announcements.

If RIP v2 simple password authentication is used, then you must configure all of the RIP v2 interfaces on the same network with the same password (which is case-sensitive). You can use the same password for all the networks in the enterprise, or the password can be different for each network as long as neighbors know the password.

If you use RIP to perform auto-static updates across demand-dial links, each demand-dial interface must be configured to use RIP v2 multicast announcements and to accept announcements. If not, the router on the other side of the demand-dial link does not respond to the RIP request for routes sent by the requesting router. Since RIP is primarily a broadcast (v1) or multicast-based (v2) protocol, non-broadcast technologies, such as frame relay, require special configurations. To ensure that RIP traffic is received by all of the appropriate endpoints on the cloud, you must configure the frame-relay interface to unicast its RIP announcements to all of the appropriate endpoints in a single adapter configuration. With multiple adapters, each frame-relay virtual circuit appears as a point-to-point link with its own network ID, and the endpoints are assigned IP addresses from a designated IP network ID. Because each virtual circuit is its own point-to-point connection, you can either broadcast (assuming both endpoints are on the same IP network ID) or multicast RIP announcements.

In summary, RIP should be used over static routing when it is appropriate to reduce the management overhead caused by static route maintenance. It should be used if routing-table information changes frequently, if demand dial interfaces are used, if existing routers use RIP, or if there will be no more than 14 hops between routers. Choose RIP v2 if the network includes VLSM, CIDR, multicast routing-table updates, or simple password authentication between routers.

Designing Using OSPF

Open shortest path first (OSPF) is a routing protocol for use within an autonomous system (see Figure 19-13) or a network under one overall management control. It is designed for dynamically exchanging routing information within a large or very large network. Unlike RIP-for-IP routers, OSPF routers maintain the routing map of the network using a *link-state database*. Network updates are shown in the link-state database, and only changes are advertised and synchronized between routers. The biggest advantage of OSPF is that it is efficient. OSPF requires very little network overhead, even in very large networks. The biggest disadvantage of OSPF is its complexity; OSPF requires proper planning and is more difficult to configure and administer than the alternatives.

OSPF uses a shortest path first (SPF) algorithm to compute routes in the routing table. The SPF algorithm computes the shortest (least cost) path between the router and all the networks of the network. SPF-calculated routes are always loop-free.

> **NOTE** In OSPF, "open" means "openly published and not controlled by a single manufacturer." The core protocol is really shortest path first.

Instead of exchanging routing table entries like RIP routers, OSPF routers maintain a map of the network that is updated after any change to the network topology. This map, called the link-state database, is synchronized between all the OSPF routers and is used to compute the routes in the routing table. Neighboring OSPF routers form an adjacency, which is a logical relationship between routers to synchronize the link-state database.

Changes to network topology are efficiently flooded across the entire network to ensure that the link-state database on each router is synchronized and accurate at all times. Upon receiving changes to the link-state database, the routing table is recalculated. As the size of the link-state database increases, memory requirements and route computation times increase.

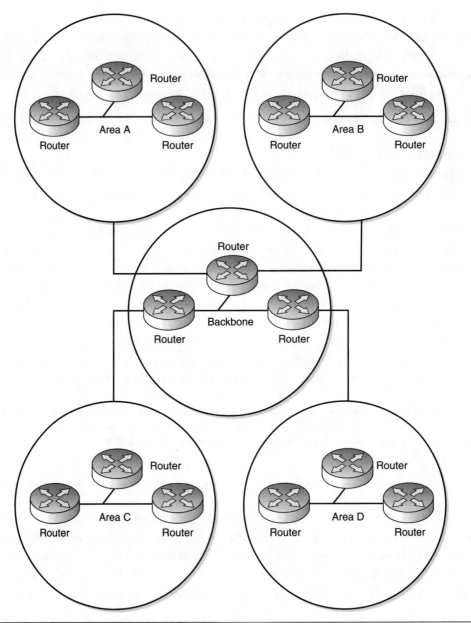

Figure 19-13   Autonomous system network

To address this scaling problem, OSPF divides the network into *areas* (collections of contiguous networks) that are connected to each other through a backbone area. Each router only keeps a link-state database for those areas that are connected to the router. Area-border routers (ABRs) connect the backbone area to other areas.

OSPF has the following advantages over RIP:

- OSPF-calculated routes are always loop-free.
- OSPF can scale to large or very large networks.
- Reconfiguration for network topology changes is faster.

The Windows 2000 router implementation of OSPF has the following features:

- Route filters for controlling interaction with other routing protocols
- Dynamic reconfiguration of all OSPF settings
- Coexistence with RIP
- Dynamic addition and deletion of interfaces

The Windows 2000 router does not support the use of OSPF in a demand-dial configuration that uses nonpermanent, dial-up links. If you are using multiple IP routing protocols, configure only a single routing protocol per interface.

In summary, choose OSPF when dynamic routing is necessary, existing routers are OSPF-compliant, there are over 50 subnets, or there are redundant paths between subnets.

You can use the three hierarchical levels described next to subdivide and simplify the design.

OSPF Design Considerations

Three hierarchical levels of OSPF design are available, and these areas should be considered before you implement OSPF:

- Autonomous-system design
- Area design
- Network design

Autonomous-System Design   All of the OSPF routers in the organization define the OSPF autonomous system. The OSPF autonomous system is a collection of networks that share a common administrative authority. By default, only OSPF routes that are related to directly connected network segments are considered part of the autonomous system. Autonomous systems are subdivided into OSPF areas.

The following guidelines are recommended when designing an OSPF autonomous system:

- Make the backbone area a single high-bandwidth network.
- Subdivide the OSPF autonomous system into areas that can be summarized.
- If possible, subdivide your IP address space into a network/area/subnet/host hierarchy.
- Create *stub areas* whenever possible. Stub areas do not maintain routes to external autonomous systems, but use a default route.
- Avoid *virtual links* whenever possible. Virtual links are created if two routers belong to the same area, but are not connected to the same backbone.

Area Design   The following guidelines are recommended when designing each OSPF area:

- Keep areas under 100 networks for performance reasons.
- Ensure that all areas are assigned network IDs that can be expressed as a small number of summary routes within an area.
- If an area can be summarized with a single route, make the area ID the single route being advertised.
- Ensure that multiple area-border routers (ABRs) for the same area are summarizing the same routes.
- Ensure that there are no back doors between areas and that all inter-area traffic crosses the backbone area.

Network Design   The following guidelines are recommended when designing each network:

- Assign router priorities so that the least-busy routers are the designated router and backup designated router.
- Designate link costs to reflect bit rate, delay, or reliability characteristics.
- Assign a password.

Comparing RIP and OSPF Using Windows 2000 Routing

Each routing protocol has advantages and drawbacks. Depending on the configuration and size of a network, one protocol may be required over another. Table 19-3 compares OSPF and RIP.

Designing Using IGMP

IP provides a mechanism for sending and receiving IP multicast traffic. IP multicast traffic is sent to a single destination IP address, but is received and processed by multiple IP hosts. A host listens for a specific IP multicast address and receives all packets sent to that IP address. IP multicast is more efficient than IP unicast or broadcast for one-to-many delivery of data because only one copy of the data is sent. Unlike broadcast, the traffic is only received and processed by computers that are listening for multicast transmissions.

The set of hosts listening on a specific IP multicast address is called a *host group*. Hosts can join and leave the group at any time. There are no limitations to the size of a host group, and a host group can span IP routers across multiple network segments. This configuration does require IP multicast support on IP routers and the ability for hosts to register themselves with the router using the Internet Group Management Protocol (IGMP). A host can send traffic to an IP multicast address without belonging to the corresponding host group.

Multicast routing—the transmission of multicast listening information—is provided by multicast routing protocols. Windows 2000 does not provide any true multicast routing protocols, although it does support multicast-capable routers on the network.

Table 19-3   RIP vs. OSPF

Protocol Attribute	RIP	OSPF
Hop-count limits	Has a router hop limit of 14 in Windows 2000	Unlimited
Convergence of routing information	Slower than OSPF	Faster than RIP
Router table updates	High overhead and affects performance	Efficient and optimized updates
Path determination	Use hop-count metrics	Uses link state or bandwidth to determine routes

You can use the Windows 2000 IGMP routing protocol, IGMP router mode, and IGMP proxy mode to provide multicast forwarding in a single-router intranet or when connecting a single-router intranet to the Internet. However, the Windows 2000 IGMP routing protocol that uses IGMP router mode and IGMP proxy mode is not the same as a multicast routing protocol. A true multicast routing protocol is required for multicast forwarding and routing support in a multiple-router intranet. Routing and Remote Access IGMP is enabled by configuring the IGMP router mode and IGMP proxy mode interfaces to provide multicast-forwarding support in multiple-router intranets.

EXAM TIP For an intranet that connects multiple networks using a single router, enable IGMP router mode on all router interfaces to provide multicast-forwarding support between multicast sources and multicast listening hosts on any network. If the Windows 2000 router is attached to the multicast backbone or Mbone (the multicast-capable portion of the Internet) through an ISP, you can use IGMP proxy mode to send and receive multicast traffic to and from the Internet.

In summary, IGMP is used when existing routers are multicast-capable, the IGMP clients are connected directly to the same subnet, and multicast traffic needs to pass to and from the Internet for applications like NetMeeting and Windows MediaPlayer. Windows 2000's RRAS has two modes of support for multicast backbone or Mbone (the multicast-capable portion of the Internet), which listens for all multicast traffic on all attached networks. However, router mode cannot propagate group listening to other multicast-capable routers.

 NOTE The IGMP routing protocol provided with RRAS will not propagate multicast group listening information to other multicast-capable routers and is not a true multicast-protocol router.

Securing Private Network Connections

RRAS can improve IP routing security in a number of different ways:

- You can encrypt data.
- You can require the mutual authentication of remote routers.

- You can restrict the traffic between private networks or public networks by using IP filters.

- You can prevent the interception or viewing of confidential or secret data transmitted across public networks by using IPSec tunnels.

- You can use VPN tunnels for authentication and encryption, using PPTP tunnels with MPPE encryption or L2TP tunnels using IPSec encryption.

- You can authenticate routers to prevent unauthorized routers from intercepting or receiving data. Router authentication can be accomplished using RIP-for-IP or OSPF passwords, demand-dial authentication, or IPSec Machine Certificates. In your design, RIP-for-IP or OSPF passwords can be implemented to authenticate routers only if clear-text password exchange is acceptable and all routers use the same protocols.

 NOTE IPSec Machine Certificates provide a high degree of security, but it should only be used when all routers support IPSec, and a Certificate Authority is available to issue machine-based certificates. IPSec provides authentication and protection against spoofing when using the Authentication Header (AH) protocol, but it does not encrypt the data. IPSec Encapsulating Security Payload (ESP) or tunnels can be used to protect confidential data. Tunnel mode is used for point-to-point communication, while transport mode can communicate with multiple computers simultaneously. When L2TP is used, machine-based authentication is possible using certificates.

Optimizing a Router Design for Availability and Performance

The following are ways to design your routing solution to provide for high availability and enhanced performance:

- Dedicating a computer to be used as a router can enhance the availability and performance of routing. When a computer is sharing tasks among several applications, performance is degraded and its stability may be at risk.

- Use persistent connections to eliminate reconnection times associated with demand-dial interfaces.

- Your design should also include multiple connections and routers to reduce the chance of network downtime in the event a connection fails.

RRAS Solutions Using Demand-Dial Routing

When creating a demand-dial routing solution, the following actions should be taken:

- Demand-dial routing designs should specify what accounts will be used when performing authentication.

- You must set remote access security restrictions and make note of the routing capabilities of the remote access servers.

- The demand-dial interface used in each location should be identified.

- Design and document how many adapters, phones lines, modems, and ports are required to support remote locations.

Designing Remote-User Connectivity

Remote access allows users to dial into a Routing and Remote Access server from a remote location as if they were connected directly to the local network. To design a remote-access solution, you must determine the client requirements and how Routing and Remote Access should be configured to meet those requirements. How many dial-up clients must be supported? What types of resources are clients required to access? Are the resources both on the corporate network and on the Internet? What are the client authentication, encryption, and connection protocols needed on the network? What are the connection technologies and speed requirements?

Using a modem, users can access the corporate network. This is called *dial-up remote access*. Dial-up remote access is usually accomplished with a line protocol such as PPP. Remote access can also come in the form of a dial-up connection to the office that is over a public network, often implemented using a VPN. A VPN provides a secure communications channel across a network and can secure data from end to end or from a network-access server to the private network. VPNs enhance connection data security by authenticating remote users prior to data exchange, encrypting authentication credentials, and encrypting the data transmitted.

The Remote Access server in Windows 2000 provides client access to an organization's resources using dial-up connections. It provides support for various transport protocols, such as TCP/IP, NWLink, NetBEUI, and AppleTalk. It also supports the proprietary Microsoft RAS line protocol that supports dial-up clients by using the NetBEUI protocol. When using the Microsoft RAS line protocol, the RAS server acts as a NetBIOS gateway for these clients, but lacks the support for TCP/IP.

The Remote Access server also supports various WAN technologies, including PSTN, ISDN, and X.25. The security protocols support secured authentication and data encryption. The RAS server negotiates authentication and encryption levels with PPP-based remote-access clients. For authentication, Routing and Remote Access supports the Microsoft Challenge Handshake Authentication Protocol (MS-CHAP), MS-CHAPv2, CHAP, Extensible Authentication Protocol–Transport Level Security (EAP-TLS), the Shiva Password Authentication Protocol (SPAP), and the Password Authentication Protocol (PAP).

Companies can improve their users' productivity through remote connectivity by using Windows 2000 RRAS. When clients are located off-site, this service can provide them with remote access to resources on the internal network and can help maximize speed and security. The Windows 2000 client makes it significantly easier than previous client versions of Windows for users to remotely connect to networks. It is now easier to establish VPN and dial-up connections.

With the Network Connection wizard, users can create new types of connections. The connection setup is also automated (see Figure 19-14).

Clients who do not want to use remote-access VPNs can dial directly into your corporation's remote access server to gain access to resources. The advantage of this method is that you can use a simple dial-up connection without having to use an ISP. The disadvantage is the potential long-distance charges.

Figure 19-14
The Windows
2000 Network
Connection wizard

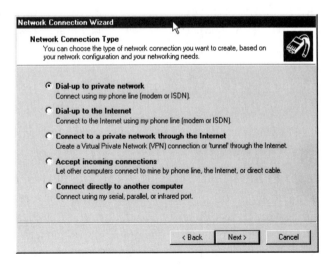

Designing a VPN Strategy

Remote clients in today's advanced networks can access resources using VPN protocols. Although Windows 2000 supports the widely used Point-to-Point Tunneling Protocol (PPTP), it also enables a secure connection using the Layer Two Tunneling Protocol (L2TP), which provides the necessary link, in conjunction with IPSec, which provides encryption. Using L2TP and IPSec, secure tunnels can be constructed through the remote client's Internet connection from a remote point of presence (POP), enabling the client to send and receive data that is secure over the public network segments.

IPSec is designed to encrypt data as it travels between two computers, protecting it from interception and interpretation while on the network. Once it is determined how the two computers will trust each other, the computers can specify how they will secure their traffic. This configuration is managed as an IPSec policy that an administrator creates and applies on the local computer or by using Group Policy in Active Directory. Windows 2000 has IPSec support built into L2TP so that all that has to be created is a VPN connection using L2TP from the remote computer to the VPN server.

To use IPSec on Internet or network clients, the IPSec policies need to be applied on both hosts that are exchanging the data. If a remote user is dialing in through the client's local ISP, then that client and the VPN server called must both be running the IPSec protocol.

There are two essential VPN connection designs: compulsory and voluntary tunnels. *Compulsory tunnels* are initiated by the RAS server and are preconfigured and device-initiated. Compulsory tunnels do not require tunneling support at the client level, and client authentication is user-based, with the optional use of Remote Authentication Dial-In User Service (RADIUS). The *voluntary tunnel* design is an ad hoc tunnel that is initiated by the dial-up user and requires client support for the tunneling protocols used. The connections for voluntary tunnels do not need intermediate RAS servers to support tunneling. The two main encryption protocols used with a VPN include Microsoft Point-to-Point Encryption (MPPE) with PPTP and IPSec with L2TP.

MPPE is used with PPTP. MPPE is used to encrypt PPP frames, and PPTP is a tunneling protocol that was developed by Microsoft and others. It has not been widely adopted by the Internet community, but it is a de facto industry-standard tunneling protocol that was first supported in Windows NT 4.0. PPTP is, in fact, an extension of PPP, with authentication, compression, and encryption improvements. A PPTP frame is a PPP frame carrying the MPPE-encrypted data with a Generic Routing Encapsulation (GRE) header. The data can be an IP datagram, an IPX datagram, or a NetBEUI frame. PPTP ports can be created on the Routing and Remote Access server. You must determine how many simultaneous PPTP connections are required in the VPN server design based on the peak load of the server.

The IP Security Protocol (IPSec) is an open suite of cryptography-based protection services and security protocols that relies on L2TP for encrypted authentication and compression. IPSec is used to encrypt data, and L2TP is a draft tunneling protocol that is currently not an approved industry standard. L2TP encapsulates the original payload inside a PPP frame and provides compression. The compressed frame is then encrypted using IPSec and is transported inside a UDP packet. L2TP ports can be created on the Routing and Remote Access server. You must determine how many simultaneous L2TP connections are required in the VPN server design.

 NOTE IPSec does not require L2TP to operate in tunnel mode. Tunnel mode is used for interoperability with other routers or end systems. IPSec tunnel mode is not actually supported for clients in a remote-access situation.

If the clients cannot support PPTP or L2TP directly, compulsory VPN tunnels can be selected. If clients do support VPN tunnels, then use voluntary VPN tunnels to provide data encryption.

Designing Remote-Access Dial-Up Solutions

The client/server dial-up designs should specify which users will be granted remote-access capability. The design should also address remote-access policy restrictions by user or group. Make sure to specify how many adapters, phones lines, modems, and ports are needed for client-connection support, based on the peak load of the server. When designing a dial-up solution, consider the following:

- What is the total throughput required by the remote-access clients? Be sure to review the peak throughput required, and make sure the LAN interface on the remote access server has sufficient capacity to handle this traffic.

- When possible, try to use the Windows 2000 native mode domain policies, which provide greater flexibility over mixed-mode policies.

- How many concurrent dial-up sessions must be supported? If PPP multi-link and Bandwidth Allocation Protocol (BAP) are being used, a client can request additional lines, so it may be necessary to have more than one connection device per client.

- How will the TCP/IP client configuration be handled? Will it use DHCP, RAS allocated, or fixed IP addresses?

Designing a Dial-Up or VPN Solution in a Routed Network

It is important to choose a dial-up or VPN solution based on the needs of the business. Use the information from the following discussion when choosing either a dial-up or VPN solution.

A dial-up solution should be considered when all of the following situations exist:

- Access over a VPN connection outweighs the costs associated with dial-up. This will often occur when most dial-up is not long distance.

- Access over a VPN connection is an unacceptable security risk for the organization.

- Security policies require the use of caller ID or callback.

- The Internet connections available do not provide adequate throughput during peak periods.

- The client requires additional bandwidth using multi-link or BAP.

The VPN solution should be considered in the following situations:

- The variability and latency of Internet speeds are not a concern.

- Access to the private network by way of the Internet is an acceptable security risk.

- The organization's Internet connections will support the total bandwidth required for the concurrent VPN client connections.

- Money needs to be saved on RAS infrastructure and long-distance dial-in costs.

Performance and Availability Design Considerations

You can improve the performance of your remote access server design as the number of remote-access clients grows. You can improve the performance of the individual RRAS servers, or you can segment the solution across additional servers in the network design as the client base grows. The use of multiple remote access servers to distribute the client load across servers can be accomplished by placing both additional remote access dial-up servers and VPN servers in a load-balanced configuration using round-robin DNS or other load-balancing configurations.

When using a multiple-server remote-access solution, the goal is to distribute clients across multiple servers. This can be accomplished by associating different telephone numbers with different servers. The Microsoft Connection Manager allows the distribution of a dial-up phone book for multiple client-access numbers. This phone book can be automatically updated whenever a client connects using a Web-based Connection

Point Services server. The Connection Manager client component can be created using the Connection Manager Administration Kit wizard (see Figure 19-15).

Improving the Performance of a Remote Access Server

When trying to improve the performance of a RAS server, position it on the subnet with the most client-accessible resources in a switched, non-routed LAN to minimize the amount of unicast traffic flowing across all segments and to minimize cross-subnet traffic in routed networks with multiple routers. Also, position the RAS server in a single segment, non-switched LAN when clients are only allowed access to resources on the RAS server.

EXAM TIP Do not try to combine a VPN server using L2TP tunnels with IPSec running on a Network Address Translation (NAT) server. The NAT server will be unable to read the encrypted IP headers.

Security Considerations

An effective security design for remote access includes a configuration that authenticates users and manages remote-user settings when a client attempts to use the network. The security plan should include the protection of specific resources from

Figure 19-15
The Connection
Manager
Administration Kit
wizard

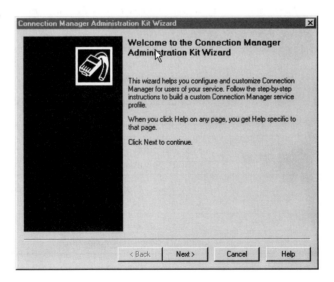

inappropriate user access, yet provide management resources to maintain rights and permissions. The security features described in this section address the remote access security design goals for an organization.

Authentication Protocols

Routing and Remote Access support the authentication protocols described in Table 19-4 to help reduce unauthorized access and provide authentication flexibility.

Restricting Access on a Private Network

Network resources can be secured by limiting access to a remote access or VPN server only. Using static routes that are defined only to specific subnets where access is granted can also restrict resources. This can be set by user or server policy. Access can also be permitted to all resources on the routed network to which the remote access server is attached. This restriction or access capability can only be applied at the server level and will apply to all clients connected to that server.

Placing a RAS Server in a Screened Subnet

Place a RAS server in a screened subnet in any of the following situations:

- Security policies in the organization specify that all client access must take place through a screened subnet or firewall.

Table 19-4   Authentication Protocols Supported by Routing and Remote Access

Authentication Protocol	Design Use
MS-CHAP	Provides encrypted authentication for Microsoft Windows 95, Windows 98, Windows NT 4.0, or Windows 2000
MS-CHAPv2	Provides encrypted authentication for Windows 2000
EAP-TLS	Provides encrypted authentication support for a smart card
CHAP	Provides encrypted authentication for remote-access clients using various operating systems
SPAP	Provides encrypted authentication support for Shiva LAN Rover software
PAP	Provides unencrypted authentication for clients that will not support other protocols

- The majority, if not all, of the resources accessed by the remote clients exists in the screened subnet.

- The RAS server itself contains data published to the public over the Internet, or clients make VPN connections to the private network.

Placing a VPN Server Outside the Firewall

Place a VPN server outside the firewall in any of the following situations:

- Confidential or secret data is protected behind the firewall, and only access by way of VPN server transmissions is allowed through the firewall.

- The integrity of the network security will not be compromised if you expose the VPN server directly to the Internet.

- Allowing access to the complete range of VPN IP addresses through the firewall creates an unacceptable risk.

VPN Best Practices

The following are the best practices for VPN design. They are based on recommendations from Microsoft Product Support Services:

- Use a DHCP server to obtain IP addresses; the VPN server should be configured to use DHCP to obtain IP addresses for client use. If a DHCP server does not exist, and you have a single subnet, configure the VPN server with a static IP address pool from the subnet to which the VPN server is attached. If you have multiple subnets and a routed infrastructure, configure the VPN server with a static IP address pool from a separate subnet or an IP range other than the one to which the VPN server is attached. Then ensure that the appropriate static-routing entries or enterprise-routing protocols, such as OSPF or RIP, are configured on the VPN server.

- Enforce the use of strong authentication through policies by using strong passwords that are more than eight characters long and that contain a mixture of uppercase and lowercase letters, numbers, and permitted punctuation. The use of strong passwords is more resistant to dictionary attacks, which try a series of common words used for passwords. Only use EAP-TLS with smart cards for remote-access VPN connections, although EAP-TLS works with registry-based certificates. If using MS-CHAP, use MS-CHAPv2.

NOTE Make sure you obtain the latest MS-CHAP client updates from Microsoft.

- Use the strongest level of encryption that your situation allows you to put in place. Use strong or the strongest encryption for VPNs in North America. Outside of North America, use basic encryption.

 NOTE The strongest encryption is only available with North American versions of Windows 2000.

Dial-Up Best Practices

The following best practices for implementing and configuring the remote access server are based on recommendations from Microsoft Product Support Services:

- Use a DHCP server to obtain IP addresses; the remote access server should be configured to use DHCP to obtain IP addresses for remote-access client use. If a DHCP server does not exist, and you have a single subnet, configure the remote access server with a static IP address pool from the subnet to which the VPN server is attached.

- Enforce the use of strong authentication through policies by using strong passwords that are more than eight characters long and that contain a mixture of uppercase and lowercase letters, numbers, and permitted punctuation. The use of strong passwords is more resistant to dictionary attacks that use a series of common words. Only use EAP-TLS with smart cards for remote-access VPN connections, although EAP-TLS works with registry-based certificates. If using MS-CHAP, use MS-CHAPv2. Make sure you obtain the latest MS-CHAP client updates from Microsoft.

- Use one remote-access policy for a user. If a user requires a multi-link connection, all connections will be given the same policy as the first connection.

Designing a Remote-Access Solution Using RADIUS

Remote Authentication Dial-In User Service (RADIUS) is a client/server protocol that enables remote access servers acting as RADIUS clients to submit authentication and accounting requests to a RADIUS server. RADIUS provides centralized control over remote dial-in connections through three key services: *authentication, authorization,* and *accounting.* Dial-up clients connect to network-access servers (also known as RADIUS clients), which in turn use a RADIUS server to access user-account information and check remote-access *authentication* credentials. If the user's credentials are valid and the connection attempt is authorized, the RADIUS server *authorizes* the user's access based on specified conditions or policies, passes the authentication information back to the NAS, and logs the remote-access connections as *accounting* events.

The use of RADIUS allows the remote-access user-authentication, authorization, and accounting data to be maintained in a central location, rather than on each network access server (NAS). This helps to secure access and centralize administrative control over remote connections. The Internet Authentication Service (IAS) on Windows 2000 allows companies to outsource the remote-access infrastructure to ISPs while retaining control over user authentication and authorization, as well as accounting. In a homogeneous Windows 2000 environment, users connect to RADIUS-compliant NASs, such as a Windows 2000–based computer running the Routing and Remote Access Service, which in turn, forwards authentication requests to a centralized Windows 2000 server running IAS. The IAS server can use either Active Directory or Windows NT 4.0 for the authentication of user accounts (see Figure 19-16).

 NOTE RADIUS protocol specifications are found in RFCs 2138 and 2139.

RADIUS features the use of different types of IAS configurations that can be created using Internet technologies, such as

- Remote dial-up access to your network through a remote access server (NAS)
- Extranet access for business partners
- Internet access
- Outsourced corporate access through ISPs

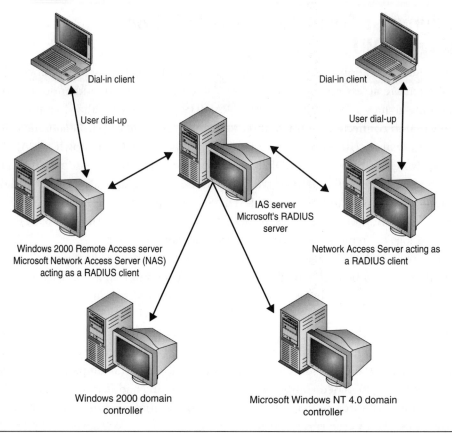

Dial-in client

Dial-in client

User dial-up

User dial-up

IAS server
Microsoft's RADIUS
server

Windows 2000 Remote Access server
Microsoft Network Access Server (NAS)
acting as a RADIUS client

Network Access Server acting as
a RADIUS client

Windows 2000 domain
controller

Microsoft Windows NT 4.0 domain
controller

Figure 19-16   A remote-access network using the Microsoft implementation of RADIUS

Integrating Authentication
with RADIUS

First, let's take a detailed look at the RADIUS authentication process and then review the IAS implementation. When a remote-access user presents authentication information to the RADIUS client or NAS, the RADIUS authentication process begins. The RADIUS client authenticates by using RADIUS.

If the remote-access user were to send credentials using CHAP, the RADIUS client would create a RADIUS Request packet containing the user's name, password, the ID of the client, and the port ID the user is accessing. CHAP encrypts the password.

The RADIUS Access-Request packet is sent to the RADIUS server. If no response is returned within a certain length of time, the request can be re-sent a number of times.

This traffic uses UDP at the transport layer. The RADIUS client can also forward requests to an alternative server or servers in the event that the primary server is down or unreachable. An alternative server can be used either after a number of tries to the primary server fail or in a round-robin fashion.

In the case of RRAS, multiple RADIUS servers can be added and prioritized as authentication providers. If a primary RADIUS server does not respond within a three-second time period, RRAS automatically switches to the RADIUS server with the next highest score.

The RADIUS (IAS) server receives the request and then validates the sending RADIUS client (RAS server). The RADIUS client validation involves verifying that the RADIUS Access-Request packet was, in fact, sent from a preconfigured RADIUS client. If digital signatures are enabled for the RADIUS client, and it is a valid RADIUS client, the digital signature in the packet is checked using the shared secret.

If the RADIUS client is valid, the RADIUS server consults a database of users either in the local security database or from a directory server database (Active Directory, if it is a Windows 2000 server) to find the user whose name matches the request. The user account contains policy settings to allow user access—this may include password verification but can also specify basic user-access permissions. If any authentication or authorization condition is not met, the RADIUS server sends an Access-Reject packet in response, which indicates that this user request is invalid. However, if the conditions are met, the configuration values for that user are entered into a RADIUS Access-Accept packet that is delivered to the RADIUS client. These values contain RADIUS attributes and the necessary values to provide the dial-up services.

NOTE If a request from a RADIUS client (RRAS server) is received by a RADIUS server (IAS server) without a shared secret, the request is discarded.

IAS Authentication

Different RADIUS servers handle different aspects of the task when authenticating and allowing access to a secure network. A NAS operates as a client of an IAS server (refer back to Figure 19-16—the NAS passes user information to "partner" IAS servers. IAS receives user connection requests, authenticates the user, authorizes the connection attempt, and then returns all configuration information for the NAS to deliver dial-up service to the user. When a user attempts to connect to a network, the NAS tries to negotiate a connection with the remote-access client by using the most secure protocol first, then working down to the least secure protocol. For example, the NAS tries to negotiate a connection by using EAP, then MS-CHAP, then CHAP, and finally PAP.

The IAS server verifies the RADIUS Access-Request packet by checking the source IP address. The digital signature in the packet is checked using the shared secret if a valid RADIUS client sent the Access-Request packet, and if digital signatures are enabled for the RADIUS client.

Shared Secret

A shared secret is a special password between the RADIUS server and the RADIUS clients with which the RADIUS server is partnered. Each IAS server must have a shared secret for each NAS. The following rules must be followed to set up a shared secret:

- Shared secrets are case-sensitive.
- A shared secret must be exactly the same at both servers.
- Secrets can use any standard characters or any special characters.

When the NAS does not get a response from the IAS server within its time-out period, it retries and then disconnects the user if the retry fails. If the IAS server cannot connect to the user database source or cannot find the domain controller the user belongs to, the packet is discarded. The RADIUS proxy is then able to retransmit the request to the backup IAS server, which then attempts to authenticate the user against the domain's database.

 NOTE Backup IAS servers provide fault-tolerance for the primary IAS server(s).

If verification of the digital signature is successful, assuming digital signatures are available, the IAS server queries the domain controller for user-credential validation. Given that the user credentials are authentic, the IAS server checks the connection attempt against the remote-access policies and the dial-in properties of the user's account to make a determination as to whether the request will be authorized. If the connection attempt matches the conditions of at least one policy and the user-account dial-in properties, IAS sends a RADIUS Access-Accept message to the NAS that sent the Access-Request message. The Access-Accept message authorizes the connection. However, the message also contains connection parameters derived from the remote-access policy profile settings and account dial-in properties. The NAS uses this authorization data to set up the connection based on the IAS authorized parameters.

Clearly, if the user is not authorized or the connection attempt does not match conditions in at least one policy, or matches policy conditions that deny access, NAS will receive an Access-Reject message from IAS. The NAS will then disconnect the user.

Why Use IAS?

IAS offers various features and benefits for dial-up users:

- **Authentication** IAS uses the PPP authentication protocols supported by Windows 2000. IAS has an authentication protocol for nearly every client. AppleTalk Remote Access protocol authentication is supported for Apple Macintosh clients. IAS can authenticate using Windows NT 4.0 and Windows 2000 domains, as well as local security databases on individual servers.

- **Authorization** Using remote-access policies, you can centrally control access based on variables like the time of day or the phone number the user calls from.

- **Accounting** This implementation of the RADIUS service provides for the logging of successes, rejection attempts, account lockouts, and network usage.

- **Outsource the NAS** Rather than buy and maintain banks of modems and hardware, a company can leverage the availability of dial-up access through an ISP. It is possible to forward to the corporate IAS server the authentication and accounting requests from users connecting to the ISP's NAS.

Designing a Functional RADIUS Solution

Place RADIUS clients or NAS servers as near as possible to the remote users, thereby creating a local point of presence. This will help to reduce or eliminate incremental dial-up costs, reduce administrative costs by delegating administration to network administrators in the local region, and help to reduce confidential or secret data exposure.

RADIUS servers should be placed as close as possible to the Active Directory server or user-database server that provides the user-account authentication. The network connection to this database should be localized to the same site and within the same private network. This will help to prevent unauthorized access to the user-account database. You can also encrypt all data transmissions between the RADIUS servers and the IAS, as well as the IAS servers with the directory servers, using IPSec or VPN tunnels to increase account-transmission security.

It is possible to use an ISP's NAS to outsource dial-up support for remote-access users. Local users access the organization's RADIUS server, which performs user authentication, through the RADIUS client installed on the ISP's network.

Dial-up remote-access connections within the organization's network are used when the organization's security policies require additional security, such as callback or caller ID, or when VPN access through the Internet is prohibited or deemed to be an unacceptable security risk. Using a remote access server within the corporate network requires maintaining a pool of telephone lines, modems, and other communications equipment.

VPN connections can be included in the network design when the Internet connection's bandwidth is sufficient to support VPN traffic.

RADIUS Fault-Tolerance and Performance Solutions

It is possible to enhance the availability of a RADIUS design so that remote dial-in users can nearly always connect to network resources. To design for RADIUS client availability, install multiple RADIUS clients and servers, and give dial-up users primary and secondary phone numbers. Make sure there are adequate telephone lines and modems to handle the user load. Register the redundant RADIUS clients with the RADIUS server to help guarantee proper authentication and accounting. Finally, make sure the redundant RADIUS servers all use the same Active Directory database rather than using the local security database to ensure the user accounts are available for authentication.

To design for improved RADIUS clients using VPN connections, use multiple RADIUS clients (NAS servers) with network load-balancing or round-robin DNS entries to distribute the load across multiple RADIUS clients. If one of the servers is down, another may be available to serve the VPN client.

RADIUS authentication and accounting performance can be improved by adding RADIUS servers as needed, upgrading the hardware on existing servers, and reducing the level of logging and accounting detail. It is important for the RADIUS server to have a high-speed, persistent (preferably site-level) connection to the global catalog server. If appropriate, you can install IAS on the global catalog server to reduce network bandwidth requirements and potentially improve authentication performance. However, the individual RADIUS server's performance needs to be monitored using a performance monitor to make sure it is not a local bottleneck.

Security Considerations for RADIUS

Your goal as a RADIUS solution designer is to provide remote-access users with access to private network resources with a secure RADIUS solution. You will need to protect confidential and secret data by securing the channels between remote-access clients, the RADIUS client, and the RADIUS server. As with any computer on the network that is potentially open to attack, the RADIUS clients and servers should be protected. Certain configuration options, including firewalls, passwords that are difficult to guess, and physical security, should be part of the security plan.

Authentication is a critical part of RADIUS security, and it can take place from any domain accessible to the Windows 2000 server, including Windows NT 4.0 domains, Windows 2000 domains, and domains accessible through explicit or implicit trust relationships. RADIUS only supports a single default domain, but users can specify other authentication realms if necessary.

Use long, difficult-to-crack phrases for the shared secret between the RADIUS client (NAS) and server (IAS). (Shared secrets of 16 characters with a mixture of uppercase and lowercase letters and punctuation are recommended.) It is also recommended that connections between the RADIUS client and the server encrypt all data and authenticate using a VPN tunnel or IPSec. Use the most secure authentication protocol that is appropriate for the situation. Using EAP or MS-CHAP is more secure than other protocols that send passwords in an easy-to-read or decrypted format, such as clear text or PAP. Also, disable all protocols not required, because if authentication protocols are negotiated in order of strength, a rogue RADIUS client could slip in with a less secure protocol that could pass secret data in clear-text format.

It is best to specify the remote-access policies on the RADIUS server. This helps to centralize the applied remote-access policies. Both the RADIUS client and server use remote-access policies along with a user account's dial-up properties to grant authorization. The RADIUS server policies will apply to the dial-up client—while a user is connected, RRAS matches the connection to the settings of the user account and remote-access profile. As long as they match, the connection will stay alive. Also, use the account-lockout feature to limit the number of attempts a user can make at authentication. This can help prevent dictionary attacks.

An IAS server can be used with a firewall or within a screened subnet. This is important when using an IAS server to authenticate VPN connections. Be sure to allow UDP packets to pass through the firewall for ports 1812 and 1645 for authentication, and ports 1813 and 1646 for accounting. The appropriate ports also need to be open for the IPSec or VPN tunnel.

Case Study 19: Wide Area Network Design for Catywhompus Construction

Catywhompus has extensive documentation about their existing network. This documentation, in addition to interviews with personnel at the company, will help to determine the best wide area network solution for Catywhompus. Your research reveals the following:

- Active Directory is used as the directory services for Catywhompus.

- New servers can be purchased to provide controlled wide area network and dial-up connectivity.

- Internet connectivity is required 24/7 at all locations.

- Management is concerned that remote employee's access to the network is controlled at a user level and that authentication and data are both encrypted.

- Network connections must use dedicated connections except for dial-up connections.

- All locations must be isolated or screened from the Internet.

This situation requires a routed solution for the internal network. It will also require dial-up as well as VPN connections for remote users. Your job now is to build a design for Catywhompus. You and your team will need to address the following design questions:

Case Study Questions

1. Routing and Remote Access is installed and configured on a Windows 2000 server in your design. You must add another network interface card to the server, and you want to connect its segment to the rest of the segments on the existing network. How would you accomplish this?

2. There is a demand-dial routing strategy in place. Until a month ago, the routes were performing well and were manageable. This month, 10 routes have been added. Can you simplify this process? How?

3. Remote users want to connect to the organization's network, but are outside the state. The toll-free number costs the company a significant amount of money

continued

annually, and the user has a local point of presence for Internet access. Is it possible to bypass the toll charges on the toll-free line? How can you provide access for this user?

4. What is the possible solution for remote users who need to gain access to resources on the network segment other than the segment where the Routing and Remote Access server resides?

5. What are the steps that must be completed on a Windows 2000 network if RADIUS needs to be implemented?

Suggested Solutions
(Your answers may vary.)

1. Add a static route from the Routing and Remote Access Snap-in in the Microsoft Management Console.

2. Enable auto-static updates using RIP for IP.

3. Set up a VPN connection for the user and have the user establish a VPN connection after they make a connection to their local POP.

4. Enable a dial-in interface to use Routing and Remote Access by establishing a static route to the other network segments.

5. IAS must be installed, and the RADIUS client must be configured to use IAS for authentication.

Chapter Review

Wide area networking and remote access services are mission-critical for many businesses today. The services provided by the networking infrastructure must support secure and reliable resource access from any location. The Microsoft exam objectives for these areas were addressed in this chapter. We looked at the key design issues related to routing, remote-user connectivity, and centralized remote-user management capabilities.

We worked step-by-step through an analysis of the key design issues related to the capabilities found in Windows 2000 because these areas are so important in the real world and for the exam. Initially, network-to-network connections were analyzed, and routing in Windows 2000 was analyzed from a network-design standpoint. We looked at software router configuration and the importance of designing a functional WAN infrastructure. Then dial-up and VPN connectivity was discussed. Then RADIUS was reviewed, which allows an administrator to use logon validation via remote, dial-up connections as an integral part of centralized management and remote security.

Questions

1. How do you add Windows 2000 Routing and Remote Access to a server?
   a. Using the RRAS snap-in in the Microsoft Management Console
   b. Control Pane | Add-Remove Programs
   c. As part of the RRAS option pack
   d. During installation of the operating system

2. Two network interface cards have been added to a server, and you want the server to route RAS users to these new segments as well as the existing segments. How is this accomplished?
   a. Nothing needs to be done. Windows 2000 handles this dynamically and configures it for you.
   b. From the Routing and Remote Access snap-in in the MMC, select the server and select New Static Route. Configure the route.
   c. From the RRAS snap-in in the MMC, expand the server, expand IP routing, right-click the static routes, and select New Static Route. Configure the route.
   d. From a command prompt, type the appropriate routing information.

3. Sites Y and Z need to replicate data across an expensive WAN link, but do not need to replicate synchronously or at all during the day. A dedicated WAN link is costly. Which of the following is the best choice to allow sites Y and Z to replicate while minimizing cost?
   a. A NAS needs to be installed.
   b. A VPN connection for a remote dial-in user can be used.
   c. Demand-dial routing can be used.
   d. Install a RADIUS client and server.

4. The corporation requires the use of encryption on your VPN connections. Which of the following should you use?
   a. PPP
   b. PPTP
   c. L2TP
   d. SPAP

5. To which server does the remote-access policy group apply?
   a. Only Routing and Remote Access servers
   b. Domain controllers
   c. Member servers
   d. All domain computers

6. When designing a Windows 2000 routing solution, you must decide which rout-ing protocol to use. Since your internal network already consists of Windows NT 4.0 routers without RRAS, which dynamic routing protocol can you use to com-municate without reconfiguring the older routers?
   a. OSPF
   b. RIP v1
   c. RIP v2
   d. PPTP
   e. L2TP
   f. IPSec

7. The VPN servers must take on multiple roles for the Accounting department at your organization. You don't want to have a VPN server provide too many services in addition to dial-up VPN services. What other services can be installed on the server to provide for the services leverage?
   a. An OSPF IP router
   b. A Microsoft Exchange 2000 server
   c. A Microsoft SQL 2000 server
   d. A dial-up server

8. An ISP needs help deploying the RADIUS service. It has servers that use Windows NT 4.0, Windows 2000, and Unix. Which servers can be used as a RADIUS client or NAS?
   a. Windows NT 4.0
   b. Windows 2000
   c. Novell Netware 5.*x*
   d. Unix
   e. All of the above

9. An ISP chose to use Windows 2000 as its RADIUS client (NAS). What needs to be installed and configured in order to set up the Windows 2000 servers as RADIUS clients?
   a. IAS
   b. NAS
   c. Routing and Remote Access
   d. PPTP

10. You are the design consultant for a large ISP that has approximately 90,000 dial-up users. The ISP wants to conserve resources and provide speedy authentication. What is acceptable to run on the IAS server?
    a. Microsoft System Management Server
    b. An e-mail server
    c. Active Directory
    d. Microsoft SQL Server

Answers

1. **D.** Routing and Remote Access is installed by default in an inactive state. It must be configured using the snap-in to be activated.

2. **C.** Static routes are added by selecting Static Route from the context menu of the IP routing object under the server name. This could also be done with ROUTE ADD from the command prompt.

3. **C.** A demand-dial route will only incur charges while in use during off hours.

4. **B.** PPTP provides Microsoft Point-to-Point Encryption. L2TP requires IPSec for encryption.

5. **A.**

6. **B.** Windows NT 4.0 routers without RRAS installed with the option pack will only support RIP v1.

7. **A and D.** It is not uncommon to make this server a router as well as a dial-up server. It is not recommended to provide key database and e-mail services on this server for performance, availability, and security reasons.

8. **E.** RADIUS is an open standard. All of these systems support this standard.

9. **C.** A Windows 2000 server RADIUS client needs to have Routing and Remote Access configured.

10. **C.** It may be possible to gain some performance improvements by running Active Directory on the IAS to improve user-authentication performance. However, while this is the best answer, take care that the IAS has adequate memory and processing capabilities to handle the load of IAS as well as Active Directory global catalogue. Also, disk contention could be an issue for 90,000 or more users.

Key Skill Sets

The following skills sets meet the Microsoft Objectives for the 70-221 exam:

- Design a wide area network (WAN) infrastructure.
  - Design a Routing and Remote Access routing solution to connect locations.
  - Evaluate Routing and Remote Access as a solution for private network connectivity.
  - Evaluate and create a functional IP router design.
  - Select appropriate strategies to secure a routing solution.
  - Select appropriate strategies to enhance the availability of routing solutions.
  - Select appropriate strategies to improve routing performance.

- Design a virtual private network (VPN) strategy.
  - Design an implementation strategy for dial-up remote access.
  - Select solutions for remote access using Routing and Remote Access.
  - Evaluate and create a functional design for remote access.
  - Select appropriate strategies to secure remote access connections.
  - Select appropriate strategies to enhance remote access availability.
  - Select appropriate strategies to improve remote access performance.

- Integrate authentication with Remote Authentication Dial-In User Service (RADIUS).
  - Select solutions for remote access using RADIUS.
  - Evaluate and create a functional design for remote access using RADIUS.
  - Select appropriate strategies to secure a RADIUS solution.
  - Select appropriate strategies to enhance the availability of RADIUS solutions.
  - Select appropriate strategies to improve RADIUS performance.

- Design a demand-dial routing strategy.

Key Terms

Bandwidth Allocation Protocol (BAP)

Challenge Handshake Authentication Protocol (CHAP)

Extensible Authentication Protocol (EAP)

Internet Authentication Service (IAS)

Layer Two Tunneling Protocol (L2TP)

Microsoft Challenge Handshake Authentication Protocol (MS-CHAP)

Network Access Server (NAS)

Open shortest path first (OSPF)

Password Authentication Protocol (PAP)

Point-to-Point Tunneling Protocol (PPTP)

Remote Authentication Dial-In User Service (RADIUS)

Routing Information Protocol (RIP)

Shiva Password Authentication Protocol (SPAP)

Virtual private network (VPN)

Designing a Management and Implementation Strategy for Windows 2000 Networking

This chapter covers the following key mastery goals:

- Design a strategy for monitoring and managing Windows 2000 network services, including global catalog, LDAP services, certificate services, DNS, DHCP, WINS, Routing and Remote Access, Proxy Server, and Dfs
- Design network services that support application architecture
- Design a plan for the interaction of Windows 2000 network services, such as WINS, DHCP, and DNS
- Design a resource strategy
- Plan for the placement and management of resources
- Plan for growth
- Plan for decentralized resources or centralized resources

This chapter represents the final preparatory chapter for Exam 70-221, "Designing a Microsoft Windows 2000 Network Infrastructure." You should take a moment to savor the journey. Not only does this chapter address the last bit for the 70-221 exam, but if you have taken all exams in order, this chapter should represent the end of your beloved Windows 2000 MCSE process. That is, one more exam and your MCSE "Welcome Kit" should be in the mail from Microsoft! But first things first. You have to complete this chapter and then go take the exam itself.

Managing any network requires developing a management plan that will allow for the detection of changes in network services. A quality network-management plan will use strategies and processes to detect certain changes in a network and will identify an action plan for when changes are detected. The plan will define the processes and procedures that will make it possible for the network administrator to identify and respond appropriately to service variations. Verifying network services to ensure they are in compliance with the design specification requires monitoring and testing.

Network Services Management Strategies

Although it is important to monitor design compliance to anticipate design changes, the highest priority in network management is to respond to network or service failures proactively. Therefore, the main goal of the management plan must be to identify warnings before they become problems, and to detect and correct critical events, such as network or service failures, when they occur. A warning sign might be CPU usage on the DNS server consistently being above 75 percent, while a critical event might be the failure of a network interface card in the RRAS server. The reaction plans for these two situations are significantly different and will probably require different response times.

Typically, immediate detection and response is required when one of the following occurs:

- A server or service becomes unavailable.
- Client capabilities fail due to network service failures.
- Key threshold values are exceeded.
- Performance is outside the design specifications.

NOTE The plan itself should contain actions, processes, and procedures that detect network variations and should contain the policies associated with deploying personnel to resolve issues as the need arises.

The plan should do the following:

- Define strategies to respond to service interruptions and variations.
- Identify the monitoring and testing required to ensure that network and services coincide with the network design specifications.
- Allow for the expansion and growth of the network.

The key to a quality management plan is defining management processes that detect network service issues while they are warnings and before a failure occurs.

Identifying Management Processes

Management processes must be put in place to readily monitor the current status of the network services against the baseline status, to analyze the data collected, and to identify trends to help verify that the network services fall within the parameters of the infrastructure design. A system for responding to changes, using a product such as Microsoft's Systems Management Server (SMS) for monitoring and data collection, should also be implemented to bring network services back in line with design specifications.

It is important to schedule regular monitoring audits of network services' performance and security. The plan should, for instance, include the manual testing of network load-balancing failover response of clustered servers by taking one of the cluster servers down to test results.

The five main process steps (see Figure 20-1) required to manage the network services are essentially as follows:

1. *Identify what to manage.* Decide what to manage and what not to manage. Target the network services in your design.

2. *Monitor the network services.* It is important to establish the baseline performance. Use tools like a network monitor or performance monitor, along with other tools, to gather information and check the status of the servers and network services.

3. *Analyze the information.* Use real-time collection tools and analyze the data provided by these tools.

4. *Develop a response strategy.* Once problems are detected, you must have a plan to respond to the problems.

5. *Redesign network services as needed.* Times will occur when network monitoring and analysis results in the need to make changes to the network infrastructure design.

Monitoring the Network Services Status

Throughout your testing of the regular operation of the network services, analyze how service uptime, performance, and service interactions are affected. The Performance Console, Performance Logs, and Alerts can be used for this purpose. Scripting can also be used to automate the analysis.

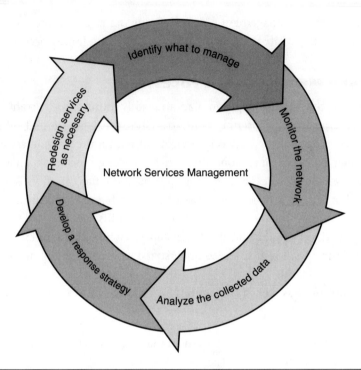

Identify what to manage

Monitor the network

Analyze the collected data

Develop a response strategy

Redesign services as necessary

Network Services Management

Figure 20-1 Network services management process

Data Collection

Data should be collected from multiple points within your network infrastructure. This information is usually delivered to a central management point by one of two methods:

- **In-band data collection** Status data travels the same network that provides services. It is possible that the traffic from collecting this data can impact the network if large amounts of data are collected, and the data can be lost in the event of a network services failure. This method should be used when the network has redundant paths.

- **Out-of-band data collection** Status data is gathered via separate physical network connections. The failure of network services or components being monitored does not affect data collection. Use this method when the network topology is not fault-tolerant.

Centralized Data Collection With *centralized data collection*, data is collected and analyzed at a central location (usually a host running specialized management tools). This method generates increased traffic and can affect network performance. In the event of a network failure, status data may be lost. Centralized data collection (that is, a collection on a local computer from remote computers that you are monitoring) is simple to implement because only one logging service is running. You can collect data from multiple systems into a single log file, but this causes additional network traffic and may be restricted by available memory and disk storage on the local computer.

Distributed Data Collection A *distributed data collection* strategy entails accumulating data on multiple nodes within the network infrastructure where it is processed before being forwarded to a management node. This reduces the burden of the management node and allows localized responses to failures. Use this strategy when design planning calls for the independent operation of locations. Distributed data collection (that is, data collection that occurs on the remote computers you are monitoring) does not have the memory and network-traffic problems of a centralized collection. However, it does result in data availability delays because of the data transfer required to the local collection server.

Tools and Utilities

Event notification is provided by specialized software (Performance Alerts and SNMP) that monitors a service and generates an event when a predefined threshold has been exceeded. These software monitors not only generate events in the form of event-log entries, they can also notify administrators of problems via e-mail or pager, and even restart failed services and servers if necessary.

The tools and utilities listed in Table 20-1 are useful for analyzing the network status.

The event types listed in Table 20-2 can also help when monitoring a given system.

Performance Console System Monitor, found in the Performance Console, can be used to collect real-time data and logs. It is best to run System Monitor remotely because running System Monitor on the system being monitored can affect the integrity of the status data.

Performance Logs are used to log events over a period of time (creating reports and establishing performance baselines), and for event notification. Choose the appropriate counters for the service you are monitoring (DNS, DHCP, Active Directory, WINS, and so on) and establish a management process for analyzing the results. This will help you determine whether your network services are within design specifications.

Table 20-1   Useful Network Tools

Utility	Function
NBTSTAT	Displays protocol stats and current TCP/IP connections using NetBIOS over TCP/IP.
NETDIAG	Performs a series of tests that help to isolate network connectivity problems. It can also diagnose the state of a network client. This is found in the \support\tools folder on the Windows 2000 CD.
NETSTAT	Displays TCP/IP protocol statistics and current connections.
Network Monitor	This packet sniffer monitors all network traffic sent to and from the computer it is running on. The Microsoft Systems Management Server version can capture all data.
NSLOOKUP	This is used for troubleshooting DNS problems (host name resolution failure).
PATHPING	This combination of PING and TRACERT helps to pinpoint where packet loss is occurring.
PING	This is used to troubleshoot IP connectivity.
TRACERT	This is used to trace the path taken from the host to the destination router.

Table 20-2   Event Types and Functions

Event Type	Function
Error	Indicates problems (failure of services) that may lead to a loss of functionality.
Information	Is an entry made upon the successful operation of an application, driver, or service.
Warning	Identifies an event that may indicate future problems.
Success Audit	Indicates that successful access to an audited resource has taken place.
Failure Audit	Indicates that an unsuccessful attempt to access an audited resource has taken place.

Setting up a Performance Monitor configuration is an important first step in evaluating a service's performance. You can choose to view data in a graph or collect the data in log files for use in other applications, such as Microsoft Excel or Microsoft SQL Server.

Graph views are excellent for real-time monitoring of a local or remote computer, or for viewing log-file results. Use logs for record keeping and monitoring over extended periods. On remote computers, logged data can be exported for generating reports and can be presented as graphs or histograms using System Monitor. Logging is a useful way to monitor multiple computers.

Start by monitoring the activity of the following components:

- Memory

- Processors

- Disks

- Network

Table 20-3 shows the recommended counters to use when monitoring a server. When examining specific resources, you should also include counters for the associated performance object.

If some of the counters listed in the table are not available on your computer, verify that you have installed the necessary services or applications to activate the counters.

Table 20-3   System Monitoring Objects and Recommended Counters

Object	System Aspect Monitored	Counters to Monitor
Disk	Usage	Physical Disk\ Disk Reads/sec, Physical Disk\ Disk Writes/sec, LogicalDisk\ % Free Space
Disk	Bottlenecks	Physical Disk\ Avg. Disk Queue Length (all instances)
Memory	Usage	Memory\ Available Bytes
Memory	Bottlenecks or leaks	Memory\ Pages/sec, Memory\ Page Reads/sec, Memory\ Transition Faults/sec, Memory\ Pool Paged Bytes, Memory\ Pool Non-paged Bytes
Network	Usage	Network Segment\ % Net Utilization
Network	Throughput	Protocol Transmission Received/sec
Processor	Usage	Processor\ % Processor Time
Processor	Bottlenecks	System\ Processor Queue Length, Processor\ Interrupts/sec

NOTE Logical-disk counter data is not collected by the operating system by default. To obtain performance counter data for logical drives or storage volumes, type diskperf -yv at the command prompt. By default, the operating system uses the diskperf -yd command to obtain physical drive data.

When monitoring remote computers, note that the remote computer will only allow access to user accounts that have permission to access it. In order to monitor remote systems from your computer, you must start the Performance Logs and Alerts service from the Local System account to a Domain account using an account that has permission to access the remote computers you want to monitor. Figure 20-2 shows how to access the Performance Logs and Alerts service, and Figure 20-3 shows how to modify the Log On tab of a Domain account for the service.

When you save the logged data in a database, the information can be queried and included in reports. Using analysis tools, you can run parameter queries to analyze the data. You can also use logs for trend analysis and capacity planning.

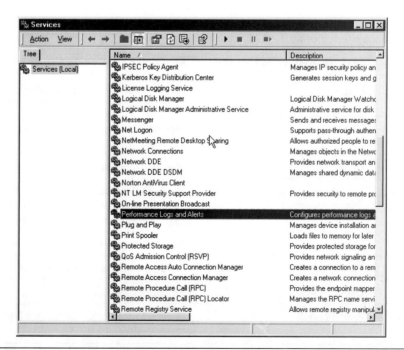

Figure 20-2 Performance Logs and Alerts service access

Figure 20-3
Performance Logs
and Alerts service
logon account
modification

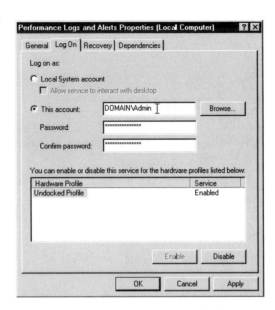

Simple Network Management Protocol (SNMP)

Support for Simple Network Management Protocol (SNMP) services may play a large part in your network design. Hubs, routers, and switches in your existing network infrastructure are often managed by SNMP. Many Windows 2000 services have Management Information Bases (MIBs) that enable SNMP monitoring of Windows 2000 network services. It can be used to remotely configure devices and services, monitor network performance, and detect faults.

SNMP agents are the software and hardware that support SNMP. They all have a defined MIB, which is a configuration database they read data from and write data to. Status information can be collected interactively from an SNMP Manager console or as an SNMP trap (an event generated by the SNMP Manager).

Acquiring Data with Scripting and Programming Solutions

You can acquire data on the status of services on local and remote systems through Windows Management Instrumentation (WMI). It provides a central-integration point for accessing status data from multiple sources within a computer. Use it when scripted or programmed access is needed for performance counters and events, but direct intervention with the services is not desired. It is started by default on Windows 2000 systems but must be manually started on Windows 9x and Windows ME systems.

Using Scripts and Programs for Data Collection and Analysis

Many administrators run scripts or batch files to read accumulated performance data (application logs, event logs, and performance logs) and generate event notifications when certain preprogrammed thresholds are exceeded. We recommend using Windows Scripting Host in combination with popular languages such as VBScript and JScript to monitor and manage network services.

Data collected in the form of log files, event logs, and so on can be imported into Microsoft Excel to provide visual representations in the form of spreadsheets, it can be imported into Microsoft Access or SQL Server databases for analysis, or it can be analyzed using a custom program or third-party solution.

Custom-programmed applications can be created to manage network services as well. They can take the form of stand-alone executables, ActiveX DLLs, MMC snap-ins, and COM components. These programs can automate data collection and analysis, maintenance, and event notification as needed.

Analyzing the Information

The network status can be determined by analyzing real-time statistics and logged statistics. Two essential data-analysis modes can be used: analysis of an isolated point in time or trend analysis to predict future needs. These two types are called manual and automated.

Manual Analysis

Manual analysis can be used as the basis for the investigation of a service on the network and can also be used for capacity planning. As an example, the monitoring staff can review the amount of memory used by DHCP and DNS on a weekly basis and predict when the service will require more memory capacity.

Automated Analysis

Automated analysis can be used when an automated response will correct the network variance. Often, this kind of analysis is done when the response to failure must be immediate and accomplished without manual intervention. This kind of analysis will frequently provide an alternative service source, such as an alternate route for network traffic.

Reactive and Proactive Response Strategies

Responses that occur after an event notification are called *reactive responses*, and they are used in a design if there is fault-tolerance built into the network service using clustering or load-balancing or if limited downtime can be tolerated by the business. Reactive responses are usually triggered by events such as a help-desk call, e-mail notifications, performance-counter-related events, and warnings from management and monitoring systems.

Proactive responses anticipate an issue before it really becomes a problem. These responses are based on implementing management processes that predict future resource usage limits and failures. Proactive responses rely on the collection and analysis of status information on performance, services, network-traffic load, and security. Include proactive responses in your design strategy when downtime must be minimized and prior warning of resource issues or limitations and performance-related failures is essential.

Combining Networking Services

After gaining an understanding of each network service individually, it is useful and practical to find ways to combine the services. To run each service on a separate server would make Microsoft (and your server vendor!) happy, but will probably upset the finance folks in the organization because of the cost and high number of servers on the network. This, in turn, also increases the complexity of the network design. If possible, it is important to try to combine services on a single server.

This solution has the benefit of reducing network traffic related to services communicating locally. However, this combination of services does not fit large organizations that need to eliminate single points of failure. Also, certain services do not function well, or even work, when combined on a single server.

Benefits of Combining Networking Services

Combining services (for example, DHCP and WINS services) on the same server cluster can reduce the number of computers needed, which results in cost savings and reduced management overhead. When services are combined properly, performance, availability, and security can also be improved.

Services should be combined when any of the following is true:

• The organization's goal is to reduce the number of computers.

• Existing computer hardware resources will support the combined services.

• Combining services enhances performance, availability, and security.

Constraints on Combining Networking Services

The most common concern when combining services on a single computer is hardware resources. It is important to recognize which services use which resources and combine them properly so that the use of resources on the server is balanced. For instance, you might try combining a CPU-intensive service with RAM-intensive services. Table 20-4 shows the general resource usage of network services.

Also, the presence of certain applications running on a system may make it impractical to combine with other services because of conflicts. For instance, NAT and DHCP cannot be combined on the same server.

Table 20-4   Resource Usage for Networking Services

Service	RAM	CPU	Network	Disk
DHCP	Low	High	Low	High
DHCP Relay Agent	Low	Med	Med	None
DNS	High	Med	Low	High
IAS	High	Med	Low	None
IPSec	Low	High	Low	None
ISA or Microsoft Proxy 2.0	High	High	High	High
NAT	High	High	High	None
Remote Access Server	High	High	High	None
RRAS Router	High	Med	High	None
VPN	Low	High	Low	None
WINS	Low	Low	Med	High
WINS Proxy	Low	Low	Low	None

With dynamic DNS, the DHCP service performs frequent DNS updates. If the services are on separate machines, network traffic is generated whenever updates are performed. If there is a large volume of updates, consider combining the services on the same machine to reduce network traffic.

The layout of physical networks may also prevent the combination of services. Services may be combined when the clients that access them are in the same geographic location as the system providing the services. If the routers and network segments between the clients and the systems running combined services can support the extra traffic, then it may be acceptable to have some geographic separation.

 EXAM TIP   Avoid combining application services like Microsoft Exchange and SQL Server with networking services like DHCP, DNS, WINS, and RRAS. Practically speaking, it is considered a best practice to keep network services and application services on separate servers.

Security Issues Related to Combining Services

Services that define screened subnets (ISA and RRAS) should be isolated. When these computers connect to the public Internet, only those services required to create the screened subnet should be combined. Services running inside screened subnets should only be combined when all users accessing the system require the same network resources at the same security level.

Combining services running inside a private network often works best. These systems are at low risk as security systems and are in place on other systems dedicated to the task.

Combining Networking Services That Are Cluster-Aware

DHCP and WINS are cluster-aware services and automatically store critical data on cluster-based drives. These services will automatically failover when the primary system in the cluster goes down. Always make sure that cluster-aware services are set up for automatic failover, which is the default when defining cluster resources.

Services that do not support the Cluster API are referred to as *cluster-unaware*. If cluster-unaware applications meet the TCP/IP and remote-storage requirements, you can still use them in a cluster and can often configure them to fail over.

PART III

Whether cluster-aware or not, services that keep significant information in memory may not work well for clustering because memory is lost at failover. The outcome is similar to you restarting a server or the server suffering a power failure.

When working with services that are cluster or not cluster-aware, make sure that both servers have been configured for automatic failover and that critical data is stored on a *shared* cluster drive.

Optimizing Performance by Combining Services

The exchange of information between services can be reduced by combining services on a single computer. However, when services are combined on a single server, the resource usage on the server increases. It is important not to constrain the performance of the networking services on the individual server. We'll look at how to combine services to reduce network traffic and optimize service load on individual servers.

Combine services when any of the following are true:

- The combination of services does not cause functionality or availability to fall below design specifications. For instance, it is acceptable to combine DHCP, DNS, and WINS as long as the services function.

- When there are more instances of the service on different servers than are needed. Instead of running many individual instances of DNS or DHCP, they can be consolidated on fewer servers to reduce network traffic.

- The networking services separately exchange a large amount of data between servers. For instance, if a DHCP server performs dynamic DNS server updates on a separate server, they could be combined to reduce the traffic between servers.

The performance of combined networking services on a given server is based on the resources that are available to allow service functionality. As a best practice, you should load services on a server that has the appropriate resources for each service running on the server, including CPUs, memory, disk subsystem, and network subsystem. For example, certain services require a lot of memory but very little hard disk space. Then make sure, through monitoring, that the services continue to perform to the design specifications.

Catywhompus Construction, Inc. Updates

Catywhompus, our beloved sample company, is celebrating the completion of your Windows 2000 MSCE right along with you. Catywhompus has made the entire journey with you. While you've earned your Windows 2000 MCSE, Catywhompus, as a representative client site, has benefited from the Microsoft design methodology, including this chapter on designing a management and implementation strategy addressing infrastructure matters.

To complete your consulting engagement with Catywhompus Construction, define a management strategy for network services and look for opportunities to combine services and optimize the use of server resources.

Chapter Review

In this chapter, you learned about network management methods and how to combine network services. The management procedures should be built into the design plan with a high priority on responding to service failures. To optimize network performance, you must predetermine the performance levels required for all services deployed. Once the services are deployed, they must be monitored, either in real time or using logs and manual or automated analysis.

You also learned how to create a response plan when network-service performance falls outside the limitations of acceptable performance. Additionally, you learned that trend analysis can help identify issues before they become emergencies. The proactive response is an element that should be included in the design.

The differences, advantages, and disadvantages of centralized and decentralized data-collection strategies were identified, and they will help you develop a practical monitoring plan. You also learned about valuable tools you can use to collect and analyze network data. SNMP is a standard management solution for data collection across the network.

Finally, combining networking services is a potential strategy for simplifying the network, reducing network traffic, and improving the efficient use of server resources.

This reduces the number of servers that must be managed and potentially allows for more user data bandwidth by reducing service traffic on the network. This must be balanced with the need to provide sufficient performance, functionality, security, and the availability of key networking services.

Questions

1. You are a consultant hired by a company to create a network management plan. You want to include, in the plan, specifications related to gathering data about CPU usage for DNS processes. Which tool should be specified?
   a. SNMP Console
   b. Event Viewer
   c. Performance Logs and Alerts
   d. Network Monitor

2. You want to determine whether the 100-megabit Ethernet network requires an upgrade to gigabit Ethernet. To do this, you must centrally monitor and review packet information traversing the network. Which two tools are the best to use to perform this data collection?
   a. SNMP
   b. System Monitor
   c. Network Monitor
   d. PING

3. You are working on a problem with communications between two offices in different cities. You find that communication is fast at certain times during the day, and at others it is slow, based on user comments. The offices are connected to each other using VPNs over the Internet. You want to gather detailed information about the routes that packets take during the slow time of day. Which utility can you use to check the routes that packets are traveling on at a given time?
   a. NSLOOKUP
   b. NETSTAT
   c. TRACERT
   d. PING

4. You are a consultant for a company that has six locations. You are asked to provide a monitoring system for critical network services at the organization's locations. The monitoring support staff is centralized at the headquarters, and the monitoring must not impact the WAN links. Which two of the following are appropriate for collecting the data?

     a. Use centralized data collection.

     b. Use out-of-band data collection without demand-dial routing modem connections.

     c. Use out-of-band data collection with the polling of remote sites by using demand-dial routing modem connections.

     d. Use distributed data collection automated with a script.

5. You are performing a security audit of the network. The results of the audit show that an ISA server is running additional network services. What is the best course of action to take?

6. An organization has experienced phenomenal growth over the past 12 months. Users are beginning to complain that performance is slow when they try to resolve a host name. The organization has DNS, WINS, and DHCP running on a single Windows 2000 server. Which of the following can improve the performance of a single server running these services? (Choose all that apply.)

     a. Upgrade the CPUs.

     b. Upgrade memory.

     c. Upgrade the disk subsystem.

     d. Upgrade or reconfigure the network card or other key network subsystem components that the server is attached to, such as the switch's port speed.

     e. Put WINS on a separate server.

Answers

1. C.

2. B and C.

3. C.

4. C and D.

5. Identify the services running on the ISA server, and if there is confidential information provided by the service, move the services onto the private network and take it out of the screened subnet. Make sure there is no confidential or secret information at risk on the ISA server.

6. **A, B, C,** and **D.** Moving WINS to another server is a multiple-server solution, not a single-server solution.

Key Skill Sets

The following skills sets meet the Microsoft Objectives for the 70-221 exam:

- Design a strategy for monitoring and managing Windows 2000 network services. Services include global catalog, LDAP services, certificate services, DNS, DHCP, WINS, Routing and Remote Access, Proxy Server, and Dfs.

- Design network services that support an application architecture.

- Create a design a plan for the interaction of Windows 2000 network services, such as WINS, DHCP, and DNS.

- Design a resource strategy addressing the following issues:
  - Plan for the placement and management of resources.
  - Plan for growth.
  - Plan for decentralized resources or centralized resources.

Key Terms

Clustering
Event Viewer
Failover
In-band data collection
Network Monitor
Out-of-band data collection
Performance Monitor objects
Proactive
Reactive
Simple Network Management Protocol (SNMP)

PART IV

Bringing It All Together

■ **Chapter 21**   The Holistic Windows 2000 Design Process

The Holistic Windows 2000 Design Process

Welcome to the end (or nearly the end) of your Windows 2000 MCSE journey. It's been a long road fraught with the occasional fright (perhaps taking the difficult certification exams) and lots of hard work. The purpose of this chapter is to quickly summarize many of the key points raised during the course of this book. We think you'll enjoy taking a few minutes before your pending Windows 2000 MCSE celebration to reflect on the entire certification journey and the contents of this book. It's likely that you may have one or two exams left before you complete the Windows 2000 MCSE title, so please keep the champagne on ice just a little longer. And as if you needed more good news, we've decided to eliminate the "Questions" section from the end of this chapter, believing you've likely reached your limit with testing mechanisms.

Building Blocks

It's interesting to revisit the method behind the Microsoft madness in developing and deploying the Windows 2000 MCSE program. You'll recall that Microsoft has really divided the Windows 2000 MCSE journey into two legs. This first leg of the journey focuses on core information with tests on implementing the Windows 2000 Professional and Server operating systems. You are also introduced to the implementation of Active Directory and networking infrastructures. The partner Osborne/McGraw-Hill book in the *All-in-One* series, entitled *MCSE Windows 2000 All-in-One Core Exams Guide* (Marcus Barton, ISBN: 0072127473) is your road map to successfully navigating the first leg of your Windows 2000 MCSE journey. The second leg of the journey is the design exams that are, of course, the focus of this book.

TIP It's important to appreciate that not all technology professionals in the MCSE community agree with Microsoft's Windows 2000 MCSE program structure. For example, the notion that you would study for and pass an exam on Active Directory at the implementation level before addressing design considerations strikes some as odd. But whether you agree with Microsoft's testing plans or not, you really have little say in the existing program. Those with the gold make the rules, and in this case, Microsoft is the keeper of the gold.

After you study for and pass the Windows 2000 MCSE core exams, assuming you take your exams "in order" as suggested by Microsoft, you'll be in a position to benefit most from this book with its focus on the three upper-level planning exams on Active Directory, security, and network infrastructure. At least, that has been our master plan, and we're sticking to it!

Active Directory

The Active Directory part of this book (Part I) closely maps to the testing objectives of Exam 70-219, "Designing a Microsoft Windows 2000 Directory Services Infrastructure." As such, you've been exposed to business and technical needs analysis, along with technical Active Directory design considerations from an MCSE candidate point-of-view. This was, of course, by design (no pun intended). However, at this risk of raining on your Windows 2000 MCSE graduation party, we want to both acknowledge your accomplishment in passing this exam and offer a little Active Directory tough love in a fatherly way. The content you are held responsible for on the 70-219 Active Directory exam is from the MCSE and Microsoft perspective. There is much awaiting you, especially learning experiences, in working with Active Directory. No one book or exam could hope to fully prepare you for the ins and outs you'll discover in implementing Active Directory at the enterprise level.

We like to think that the first section of this book and the 70-219 exam prepare and qualify you to learn more about Active Directory. It is important that our comments aren't taken out of context here. We're not implying that this book or the 70-219 exam are somehow inadequate. Rather, our comments are akin to the Socratic advice offered to young attorneys by law professors: "Now that you've completed law school, you don't know anything about the law, but you're prepared to go out and learn about the law." That is, law school gives you the tools to become a lawyer. Likewise, the first part of this book, combined with successfully passing the 70-219 exam, has given you the tools to go forth and learn about Active Directory.

Security

Talk about an area that will never be static—security remains one of the great challenges in all network planning and deployment scenarios. The bad guys often have a half-step head start on the good guys (like you, the Windows 2000 MCSE). We believe that at a pragmatic level, no exam or book can truly remain current in the security area, as the field changes daily with each new threat and attack. However, the goal of both Microsoft's Windows 2000 MCSE program, with an examination on security, and Part II of this book, was to provide the tools you can use to synthesize, understand, and then capitalize on significant developments in the security area. In other words, perhaps the bad guys have a smaller head start on you, as a result of your becoming a Windows 2000 MCSE.

NOTE It is interesting to note that the security design exam, officially called 70-220, "Designing Security for a Microsoft Windows 2000 Network," is a first for Microsoft in its MCSE program. With prior renditions of the MCSE program, you had exams focused on the operating system and server applications (not unlike today). There was also an exam on TCP/IP, but not one dedicated strictly to security.

Network Infrastructure

Last, and certainly not least, in the Windows 2000 MCSE track is Exam 70-221, "Designing a Microsoft Windows 2000 Network Infrastructure." This was covered in Part III of this book, which focused on core network technology planning issues, as well as the exploitation of Microsoft technologies in Windows 2000 Server. However, it is also interesting to note that it is this examination area where Microsoft has essentially rolled in its legacy examination on TCP/IP (although the core exams are also sprinkled with legacy TCP/IP tidbits as well).

Common Elements

The three exams have similar business and technical requirements sections, and this offers some benefits. Although it's an oversimplification to say that if you learn business and technical requirements on one exam, you'll know the area for all of the exams, you will better understand business and technical requirements the second and third times you encounter the topics. Perhaps the greatest benefit with respect to the common business and technical requirement elements is that directory services (Active Directory), security, and network infrastructure are all intertwined. Pragmatically speaking, you, the MCSE candidate, benefit from such common elements in managing your time while studying and taking exams. This is one opportunity to leverage up and better understand business and technical requirements the second and third times you encounter these topics. We don't know about you, but as active learners, we greatly benefit from the repetition of these areas in the design area of the Windows 2000 MCSE track.

However, you'll be relieved to know that careful consideration was given to the question of how best to present the common elements of the three design exams covered in this book. The notion that a base business and technical requirements section would be copied and pasted three times to fill pages wasn't even considered. Rather, the business and technical requirements sections in each of the three exam sections of this book are handled differently each time. This gives you different perspectives on what business and technical requirements really are. More importantly, the different treatment of this common topical area reflects how work is accomplished in the real world. If you ask three experienced Windows 2000 MCSEs what business and technical requirements mean to them, you'll get three distinct answers.

 TIP   One design exam oddity that is being actively debated amongst Windows 2000 MCSEs is why Microsoft placed the 70-220 security exam in the middle of the designing exam series. Those who live and breathe security as a niche truly believe that you can't design a security solution until all of the other pieces, such as infrastructure and directory services, are in place. In fact, it was actively debated among the authors and editors of this book whether the security section should be the last section of this book. However, compliance to the suggested exam completion order was considered important (even though there is consensus that security is one of the last design areas).

Next Steps—Life as an MCSE

So, sheepskin in hand (that is, your completed MCSE transcript), you're ready to light the world on fire! Go get 'em. But first, a couple of thoughts to consider . . . Remember that you've been provided with a rich set of tools. These tools are both a blessing and a curse. Used with care and a commitment to continued learning, the MCSE tool kit you've created is sure to lead you to profitable endeavors. However, the reckless application of your MCSE tools with disregard for reason and study will certainly lead to system failures and a trail of wreckage behind you.

Regarding the role of the Windows 2000 MCSE, we've never felt that holding the MCSE designation makes you a true expert in the Microsoft networking field. Rather, the MCSE designation communicates to the marketplace that you've paid your dues and you know where to go to get the answer. You also have an above-average understanding of Microsoft networking solutions. However, reverting back to our lawyer example from earlier in the chapter, it remains our contention that a Windows 2000 MCSE should regularly perform research, much like a lawyer visits the law library to look up a fact or judgment. And just as a lawyer isn't expected to know everything about the law, an MCSE shouldn't be held to the standard of knowing everything about Windows 2000 Server. Let us tell you, if that's the standard our clients and employers hold us to, all of us Windows 2000 MCSEs are in trouble!

It behooves you to not only be a life learner in the MCSE community, taking a course here and passing another exam there, but also to participate at a higher level. This includes engaging in activities, such as attending monthly user-group meetings. One such group is the BackOffice Professional Association (www.bopa.org), a group that is dedicated to Microsoft solutions and requires that you be a Microsoft certification holder to join.

Finally, as a professional, you should attend professional conferences once or twice per year. One of the best conferences is the Techmentor conference hosted by *Microsoft Certified Professional Magazine* (www.mcpmag.com). There are several other conferences to select from, including those hosted by IDG (www.idg.com) and *Windows 2000 Magazine* (www.winntmag.com).

Catywhompus Construction, Inc. Updates: A Final Look

And at long last, we take one final look at Catywhompus Construction, the sample company used during the course of this book. The idea behind Catywhompus was to offer a reliable and consistent milepost as you started your journey through the Windows 2000 MCSE Designing exams. Catywhompus has been the ideal framework for showing you how to apply the design discussion presented herein. More importantly, Catywhompus (along with other case study companies in this text) has prepared you for the lengthy case studies presented on the Windows 2000 MCSE exams (where the challenge is often reading comprehension as much as technical know-how).

Chapter Review

Congratulations are in order. You've worked hard to be able to earn the Windows 2000 MCSE. It is the hope of the authors of this book that we've contributed in ways large and small to the success of your journey. Now go forth and provide solutions!

PART V

Appendixes

■ **Appendix A** More Case Study Analyses and Questions
■ **Appendix B** MCSE Certification Specifics
■ **Appendix C** Case Study Analysis Approach

More Case Study Analyses and Questions

This appendix presents several case studies and questions with answers for your Windows 2000 MCSE study effort. The case studies are presented first. Following that, exam-like questions (and answers) are presented. Enjoy!

Four Case Studies for Analysis

In this section of Appendix A, you are presented four lengthy case studies to read and complete. These case studies draw on a wide spectrum of the information presented in this book. Good luck!

Case Study A-1: Infrastructure

This is a case study about XYZ.com and draws on the infrastructure discussion in this book.

Organizational Structure

XYZ.com is a startup applications service provider (ASP) based in New York. It aims to host and maintain applications and offer online access to popular software. XYZ.com's target market is small businesses, home offices, and individuals looking for key enterprise applications that are cost-effective and have minimal infrastructure requirements.

continued

781

Its target market also includes mobile workers using notebook computers with limited resources. Industry analysts have predicted the application-hosting business to grow to a multi-billion dollar industry within a decade. ASPs, such as XYZ.com, offer companies administrative and cost benefits by using the Internet to access enterprise software.

Technical Analysis

XYZ.com offers two various software applications over the Internet, accessible with only a Web browser and a 56 Kbps or faster connection.

The company is using Windows 2000 to deliver continuous availability and fast performance to the applications and data. When evaluating possible platforms, the company selected Windows 2000 as their solution because of the business benefits it offers, including the wide availability of Windows-based applications and the familiar Windows interface, which means a short learning curve for customers and for the staff members at XYZ.com who will be administering the site.

The company needs to resolve issues related to memory management, integrating service packs into the operating system, and efficiently deploying terminal emulation. Terminal emulation is particularly important for the company because a terminal/host architecture is necessary for the customers to use XYZ.com's server-based resources from remote PCs. The functionality of the operating system should provide effective and powerful solutions to address these issues.

XYZ.com turned to Windows 2000 for the features and benefits of high-end corporate systems. High-level scalability and system uptime are important considerations for drawing and retaining customers. The operating system must also offer easy-to-use features, such as easy integration between software components, clustering with a single Internet logical name and IP address, and offline maintenance capabilities that will not disturb cluster operations. These features would allow XYZ.com to manage the Web site and handle any surges in customer usage efficiently and cost-effectively.

Interviews with Employees

Jeremy Jones, an XYZ executive said "In order to seize the enormous opportunity in the consumer and small business market, we need a rich, robust technological foundation that will scale as the business grows."

The manager of the IT department, Randy Reeves, says, "The technology solution should offer great reliability for the vital information of customers. It should also be easy for the small IT department at XYZ.com to manage."

An important belief in the company is "If we're down, we lose business. We need to design and build a solution to provide the kind of reliability and availability we need to attract and retain customers."

continued

The network administrator of XYZ.com is of this opinion: "With the system we design using Windows 2000, we must be able to offer a service that is very flexible for customers. There must be no limitation on the number of applications a customer uses, and the requirements for the client systems must be minimal—all they need is a browser that can run on a PC, a Mac, or even a net appliance."

"The load on the system is going to vary from user to user," Jeremy says. "But our service must respond adequately at all times for our customers. We need a solution that will deliver 24/7 performance."

Goals

The company's goal is to give customers easy access to applications—access to their applications and data when they need it. XYZ.com aims to design and provide a system with no single point of failure. In addition, their objective is to prevent customers from dealing with problems related to downloading software, installing it, and handling compatibility issues.

Solution

The company has 66 Intel-based servers, some of which are equipped with quad and eight-way processors. Windows 2000 Advanced Server is deployed on all of them.

Active Directory enables fast access to applications, allowing large numbers of customers to be served in real time and to begin using applications almost immediately. XYZ.com operates multiple data centers for managing surges in customer sign-ups, but is able to use Active Directory to consolidate all new-customer information into a single hierarchical structure that is easily managed and backed up. Active Directory offers many different options for defining and carefully managing specific privileges and policies for both groups and individual users. It enables XYZ.com to efficiently manage the tens of thousands of users anticipated by its business plan through a single, consistent interface due to its distributed networked design. It also offers a central site for managing network security by allowing the operating system to readily verify a user's identity when he or she attempts to access the company's site.

Case Study Questions

1. You are a member of the IT department at XYZ.com. You decided to install Windows 2000 DHCP server to reduce the complexity of administering the client IP configurations used on your network. Which one of the following options would you consider implementing at XYZ.com, keeping in mind the CEO's absolute requirement with regard to attracting customers?

continued

    a. Put DHCP on a multihomed server.

    b. Back up the DHCP server regularly.

    c. Split the scope between servers on different subnets.

    d. Put DHCP Server on a server cluster.

Answer: C. The most important aspect of XYZ.com is its reliability and availability to its customers. The CEO is, therefore, interested in a robust fault-tolerant network design. Splitting the scope provides online redundancy and thus, fault tolerance. The server version of Windows 2000 does not support clustering. It is available only in Windows 2000 Advanced Server. Multihoming provides limited fault-tolerance and back-ups are a fault-recovery solution.

2. The business model of XYZ.com demands that its clients access the company's resources remotely. Which of the following configurations could be beneficial for XYZ.com to implement?

    a. Automatic Private IP Addressing

    b. DHCP manual configuration

    c. DHCP dynamic configuration

Answer: C. Automatic Private IP Addressing (APIPA) does not provide for functionality over a routed network because it will not provide a default gateway for the client. Windows 2000 DHCP has the ability to reserve IP address and option settings by Media Access Control (MAC) address. These reservations can provide a solution for tailored option settings for specific nodes, and this manual method is primarily used for clients or servers that require fixed IP addresses for applications or services.

DHCP is a safe and reliable configuration method that minimizes configuration errors caused by typographical errors because TCP/IP configuration is centralized and automated. This method is an excellent choice for DHCP-supported clients and is an especially good choice for remote-access clients, and clients that need dynamic configurations due to mobility requirements.

3. The computers running Windows 2000 Server have been configured as routers to manage communications between locations. The computers have been configured to use Routing Information Protocol (RIP) version 2. The company currently operates multiple data centers for managing surges in customer sign-ups and plans to increase their number next year. You, as the network architect, decide to switch to the routing protocol open shortest path first (OSPF) in preparation for the integration of the new facilities into the network. You decide that RIP and OSPF should coexist until OSPF is installed on all routers. If a route to a remote network is learned through both RIP and OSPF, which route will be chosen when a user attempts to access a computer on the remote network?

continued

a. The route that was learned from OSPF

b. The route learned from the protocol that is configured as the preferred protocol

c. The route with the lowest metric

d. The route that was learned from RIP

Answer: B. The route that is learned by the preferred routing protocol is used. You define a preferred routing protocol by configuring a preference level. This is configured with the Routing and Remote Access snap-in. The path from the source with the lowest value in the Rank field on the Preference Levels tab is chosen.

If there are multiple routes learned by each routing protocol, the route with the lowest metric for that protocol will be the route that is included in the IP routing table. Since the definition of a metric varies with each routing protocol, the metric is not the determining factor when comparing routes learned from different protocols. The route that was learned from RIP is chosen only if RIP is configured as the preferred routing protocol. The route that was learned from OSPF is chosen only if OSPF is configured as the preferred routing protocol.

4. XYZ.com uses load balancing on Web servers and clusters its SQL Server database to ensure uninterrupted operation 24/7, 365 days a year. It uses advanced clustering and load-balancing features that enable loads to be distributed to multiple servers, as well as failover capabilities that complete a transaction in process if another server fails. Which related service must be manually reconfigured on another server in the cluster if the primary server for the service fails?

a. Dynamic Host Configuration Protocol (DHCP)

b. Proxy Server

c. Domain Name System (DNS)

d. Windows Internet Naming Service (WINS)

Answer: C. DHCP, WINS, and Proxy Server are all cluster-aware applications. If the primary server for any of these services fails, another server in the cluster provides automatic failover support. DNS is not a cluster-aware application, so you need to manually enable the DNS server service on another computer in the cluster if the server on which DNS is running fails. You can minimize the time needed to bring the other server online if you store the DNS zone files on the cluster drive.

5. Active Directory in Windows 2000 enables XYZ.com to manage network security. What are the other options that you, as a network administrator, can use to protect your network from attacks from within the company and enable secure links between the various subnets that you have created? Which of the following techniques can you employ to satisfy the administrator's requirement? (Choose all that apply.)

continued

PART V

a. Use packet filtering.

b. Use IPSec.

c. Use Kerberos.

d. Use certificates.

Answer: B, C, and D. The goal of IP network security is to provide access to resources, while preventing unauthenticated users from accessing, intercepting, or modifying transmissions. Filtering is a useful way to block traffic for an entire network using a packet-filtering firewall. Using this filtering method, TCP/IP can block the delivery of IP packets based on the host filter configuration. The packet-filtering mechanism is generally used to prevent malicious users outside the company's intranet from entering the network. You can use IPSec, Kerberos (a default method for authentication in Windows 2000), or public key certificates (generally used when the systems are not using Kerberos).

6. Considering the mantra of the company, and its importance to be available 24/7 to attract and retain customers, which of the following would you suggest when setting up a DHCP solution for XYZ.com? (Choose all that apply.)

a. Position DHCP servers on the same subnet.

b. Position DHCP servers on different subnets.

c. Use the 80/20 design rule of placing multiple servers on the same subnet.

d. Design a single-server solution.

e. Install multiple DHCP servers sharing distributed scopes.

f. Cluster DHCP servers using Windows 2000 Advanced Server.

Answer: B, E, and F. Multiple DHCP servers and DHCP Relay Agent placements are often needed to address fault tolerance, slow links in WAN environments, and multiple broadcast domains created by certain routed and switched environments. When you have multiple DHCP servers, you must position the servers on different subnets to create a fault-tolerant DHCP solution, rather than placing the DHCP servers in one subnet. The servers should not have the same pool of addresses, because two clients might lease the same IP address on each server, which would cause an IP address conflict situation.

You must use the 80/20 design rule when placing multiple servers on the different subnets and not on the same subnet. The 80/20 design rule puts 80 percent of the subnet scope on the local DHCP server and 20 percent on the remote subnet. Good performance can be accomplished if you put two DHCP servers on the same subnet and use distributed scopes between the two DHCP servers. Another benefit of having two DHCP servers on the same subnet is that if one server goes down, the other will continue to supply IP address configurations to clients.

continued

The primary reason for using a single-server design for a simple LAN is the simplicity of DHCP server management. The downside of not using a single-server solution is there is a lack of fault tolerance for client IP configuration.

Clustering of DHCP servers using Windows 2000 Advanced Server can also provide higher availability.

7. The CEO stated that the site must be available 24/7 to keep their clients and to attract new clients. What are the precautions that can be taken to ensure DNS will function on this basis? (Choose all that apply.)

    a. Use multiple DNS servers with zone replication that are Active Directory–integrated zones.

    b. Set up client computers to point to the DNS on the local subnet as primary.

    c. Configure clustered servers to share a cluster drive.

    d. Use multiple DNS servers with zone replication that are standard secondary zones.

Answer: A, B, C, and **D.** Multiple DNS servers with zone replication using either standard DNS zones or Active Directory–integrated zones can ensure DNS availability. You can also place additional DNS servers at remote locations to ensure DNS availability in the event of a WAN link or router failure. Client computers can be set up to point to the DNS on the local subnet as primary and on a remote subnet for secondary for fault tolerance. Clustered servers can be configured to share a cluster drive so that both nodes have access to the most recent zone database file. Failed servers can be restored more quickly from a cluster drive because there is no need to resynchronize.

8. XYZ.com has some BIND servers on their network. To provide customers with easy access to applications when they need it, a high level of interoperability between BIND-based DNS servers and Windows 2000 DNS servers is required. Which of the following zones would you create to achieve this interoperability?

    a. Standard DNS zones

    b. Integrated DNS zones

    c. BIND DNS zones

Answer: A. Standard zones function as clones of BIND-based DNS servers and therefore, have the same benefits and limitations as BIND DNS zones. Standard DNS servers are, therefore, highly interoperable with BIND-based DNS servers and can play a role in designs that require this level of interoperability.

continued

9. The network administrator at XYZ.com wants to configure a round-robin DNS as the primary method of sorting the resource list. He follows these steps:

I   Open the DNS Console (Select Start | Programs | Administrative Tools | DNS).

II   Click on the applicable DNS server name in the console tree.

III   Select Action | Properties.

IV   Click the Advanced Tab.

V   In the server options, check the Enable Round-Robin check box and the Enable Netmask Ordering check box.

VI   Click OK.

What do you think about this solution?

a. The solution is right and will work.

b. The solution is wrong and will not work.

c. The solution is partly right and requires additional steps.

Answer: B. To enable round robin on a Windows 2000 DNS server, the Enable Netmask Ordering check box in step V must be unchecked. If the Enable Netmask Ordering is left checked, the records will be reordered by their subnet location, and resource records will be rotated using round robin as the secondary method of sorting the response list.

10. Multiple links are required to increase potential availability of the various applications at XYZ.com by its clients. The manager of the IT department is considering setting up a routing infrastructure. In comparison to multipath networks, what are the benefits of a single-path routing infrastructure that the manager should consider? (Choose all that apply.)

a. Simplification of the routing tables

b. Balancing of the network traffic load

c. Simplification of packet-flow paths

d. Complex configuration

e. Low probability of routing loops

f. Provides fault-tolerance

Answer: A and E. In a single-path routing infrastructure, only a single path exists between any two segments in the network. This will simplify the routing tables and the packet-flow paths. However, these single-path routed networks are not fault-tolerant. It is possible to sense a fault with a dynamic router, but the networks across the failure are unreachable during the fault. Redundant path networks, however, can be more complex to configure and can have a higher probability of routing loops.

Case Study A-2: Infrastructure

This is an infrastructure case study based on the imaginary company called Any Vehicle. A hint for you to be the most successful that you can with this case study: You will draw most of the information you need from the last part of the book focusing on Exam 70-221.

Organizational Structure

AnyVehicle is a car manufacturer headquartered in New York and operating only in the northern United States. It has 250 stores in its dealer network, and it wants to provide and support information exchange between the various dealers and the company. By doing this, AnyVehicle expects to improve customer service and significantly reduce internal labor costs. Proper connectivity and efficient information exchange must enable a 30 percent decrease in information delivery time.

AnyVehicle has made plans to develop an expansive dealer information program explaining the benefits acquired from streamlining communications and information distribution between the corporate headquarters and the 250 dealers. The solution must link AnyVehicle's national headquarters in New York with its entire North American dealership network to provide fast, accurate sales, financing, and service information to improve customer service, while saving dealerships time and money.

The AnyVehicle's project team consists of the marketing manager, the sales manager, the networking manager, two network engineers, and key representatives from the various dealers.

Until now, the dealers sent vehicle and parts orders, warranty information, and other details to headquarters through the post, which was very time consuming. The headquarters, too, sent information, such as application updates, service diagnostics, and bulletins to the dealers on magnetic tape, CD-ROM, floppy disks, and paper by post. This was a very inefficient manner of exchanging information. The information was usually outdated by the time the dealers received it, due to the time required to create and distribute the materials. Another problem was ensuring that the information reached the appropriate person or department at the dealership.

Technical Analysis

The various dealerships operate on a wide range of hardware and software platforms, and if they had any IT support staff, it was minimal. As a result, the company had to make sure that the solution they came up with was extremely easy to use and easy to manage, due to the sheer number of dealers involved.

continued

PART V

The project team identified two key tasks that the solution must accomplish:

- The existing network must support TCP/IP applications.
- Each dealership must be able to link devices from the service, parts, sales, and business offices. This could be achieved by establishing a TCP/IP LAN.

The company chose Windows 2000 as its network operating system, due to Windows' built-in Internet, intranet, and communications services that will support AnyVehicle's long-term information technology (IT) strategy. The Windows 2000 operating system's user interface makes it very easy to deploy and manage and thus helps reduce training costs. In addition, its high performance can help speed up information distribution.

The company has a Web site and is planning to offer each dealer a free Web page that will link back to the company's Web pages. This setup will enable customers not only to locate a dealer from the main manufacturer's Web sites, but also to jump from the dealer's Web page back to the brand site for more information on specific products. Customers can also establish a relationship with a dealer through e-mail.

Currently, there are approximately 300 Windows NT 4.0 workstations and 250 Windows 98 workstations on the routed network.

Interviews with Employees

The need to get information to the dealers in a timely, consistent manner as the volume of information increased became the top priority, according to Tim Frasier, the Project Manager for AnyVehicle's new project. Frasier further explains, "We want dealers to present consistent and fresh information to the consumer, regardless of the cost, features, and benefits of the vehicles, or the latest service diagnostics."

According to Robert Ervin, the network manager, "All the project team members evaluated two other network operating systems before we decided on Windows 2000. We chose Windows 2000 because it meets virtually all of our requirements. We could set up and manage our intranet very quickly and efficiently. The new Windows 2000 user interface makes administration easier and can help reduce training time."

"One of the big reasons we went with Windows 2000 is that we want to be absolutely Internet-compatible. We want our retail stores to be easily accessible to customers electronically," notes Frasier.

The sales manager, Derrick Mathias, notes, "There is a lot of room for improvement in productivity throughout the dealership. We know that today about 50 percent of the time spent with a customer is spent trying to figure out the price of a product. In this new environment, we can present that information immediately."

continued

Ervin also points out that the company is currently looking at creating intranet applications to be used within the dealerships. They also intend to survey dealers to find out if they will be interested in offering additional features, such as service scheduling and inventory availability, through their home pages.

Goals

The system must improve overall productivity, and in particular, the company's service to its customers. Enabling dissemination of service bulletins and diagnostic software from the headquarters as soon as a service problem is discovered and resolved can shorten the resolution of those problems for subsequent customers. This can improve customer service as well as profitability for the dealer. The Windows 2000 interface is a very open system, such that it can potentially work with other business-critical applications within the dealership, thus providing a tightly integrated solution that supports quicker service for customers and reduces costs for the dealer. In addition, Windows 2000's support for centralized management enables the IT department at the New York headquarters to monitor and manage performance of all servers remotely from their offices in Detroit, Chicago, Portland, and so on, and make any midstream adjustments necessary to optimize the system. This can keep support costs down as well.

Solution

The solution is to implement a Windows 2000 architecture that will facilitate communication and the exchange of real-time information. The company plans to have Windows 2000 run on an application server located at each dealership. Each server ties into a TCP/IP LAN at the dealership and connects to AnyVehicle's corporate headquarters.

This system includes built-in Internet and intranet capabilities. It will also work with a variety of dealer information software systems running on the variety of platforms already in place at the dealerships. It is extremely fault-tolerant, and since dealerships do not typically have IT support staff, they need a robust operating system that can take a number of faults without bringing the whole network down and that can recover without intervention. Since the solution provides remote-control capabilities, it can be managed from a central site, so the dealerships do not have to worry about managing the system.

Case Study Questions

1. Keeping in mind the goals of the organization, if the dealers have limited bandwidth over the WAN connection to the Internet, how can you configure the DNS servers at those offices to minimize traffic related to zone transfers?

continued

PART V

a. Use delegated zones.

b. Configure an Active Directory–integrated zone.

c. Configure forwarders.

d. Use caching-only DNS servers.

e. Configure a standard primary zone Windows 2000 DNS server.

Answer: D. By locally caching DNS requests, the DNS server can respond to clients quickly from the cache, and the impact on the WAN is reduced, thereby minimizing traffic over the WAN connection. Only a caching-only DNS server will not perform zone transfers.

2. Why would the network manager at AnyVehicle want to implement Active Directory–integrated zones? What are all the reasons why he should believe integrated zones to be an excellent choice? (Choose all that apply.)

a. Fault tolerance

b. Integration with existing primary DNS servers

c. Security

d. Ease of management

e. Fast and efficient replication

Answer: A, C, D, and **E.** Active Directory–integrated zones provide many benefits, including multimaster replication, which provides better fault tolerance for zone transfers. It offers better security, because administrators can set access limits for zones and zone records using Access Control Lists (ACLs) to specify users and groups that have authority to modify the zone and zone records. It enables ease of management, because the domain controllers automate replication. It also provides fast and efficient replication due to the incremental zone replication. If integration with existing primary DNS servers is a high priority, standard zones must be selected, because integrated zones cannot perform secondary roles.

3. The project team has charted out a solution to help achieve its business goals. On analyzing AnyVehicle's organization and network requirements, what is the highest priority item to plan for, in creating the TCP/IP design as planned by the project team?

a. Adequate number of networks are supported.

b. Ample bandwidth for all clients.

c. Internet access.

d. Sufficient number of hosts are supported.

Answer: D. Every host requires an IP address and, therefore, this must be the number-one priority when designing the network.

continued

4. The DHCP, DNS, and WINS servers are maintained at the headquarters in New York. Fifty of the 250 dealers are located in a region 100 miles away from New York. These dealers are on a separate subnet, and there are two Cisco 2600 series routers and a pair of AT&T Paradyne CSU/DSUs connecting the T-1 frame relay circuit between these two locations. In the past, there have been very few work-stations that were added or required to move between various dealers. The work-stations and servers have used manually configured IP address settings. Now, more users want to move between dealers and sites easily with their laptops. In spite of correctly configuring a Windows 2000 DHCP server in the main office to supply addresses for that subnet and to properly configure clients to use DHCP, clients in the site still cannot obtain IP configuration information using DHCP. What is the problem? (Choose one.)

   a. The DHCP IP address is not configured properly at the client level.
   b. The IP addresses of the DNS and WINS servers that locate the DHCP server have not been added.
   c. The routers are not configured as DHCP relay agents.
   d. The scope is not properly set up on the DHCP server.
   e. The clients are not properly configured using the LMHOSTS file.

Answer: C. DHCP traffic is broadcast-based. Routers typically do not pass DHCP or BOOTP broadcast traffic unless configured to do so.

5. The organization has two WINS servers on different subnets, and one of the net-work engineers who is part of the project team wants to replicate their databases to ensure NetBIOS name resolution across subnets. What is the best way to con-figure these servers to synchronize their databases?

   a. Install and configure DHCP on one of the servers.
   b. Install DNS on each server.
   c. Configure each WINS server as both a push and pull partner with the other WINS server.
   d. Set the primary WINS server of each server to point to the other server.
   e. Turn on the File Replication Service on both WINS servers.
   f. Configure one server as a pull partner with the other, and configure the other as a push partner.

Answer: C. The primary reason WINS exists to is to provide network-wide NetBIOS name registrations and resolutions. Push/pull replication is the simplest and most effective way to ensure full WINS replication between partners. This also ensures that the primary and secondary WINS servers for any particular WINS client are push and pull partners of each other, a requirement for proper WINS functioning in the event of a failure of the primary server of the client.

continued

PART V

6. A NetBIOS name resolution needs to be provided for the computer systems as stated in the technical analysis. What are the two options that can enable this name resolution?

   a. LMHOSTS file

   b. DNS

   c. DHCP

   d. WINS

Answer: A and **D.** Windows 2000 initially uses the NetBIOS name cache, but also uses a local database file called LMHOSTS to resolve remote NetBIOS names. Both LMHOSTS files as well as WINS have benefits over the broadcast method.

WINS was created to solve the problems of NetBIOS broadcast-based name resolution and reduce the burden of maintaining LMHOSTS files, because most contemporary networks span broadcast domains. Using LMHOSTS files for name resolution will maintain and store the NetBIOS name to IP address mapping in a stored static format. WINS allows NetBIOS traffic to traverse broadcast domains without using broadcasts or LMHOSTS files.

7. AnyVehicle's project team is considering designing a DFS solution at its headquarters because they want to make it easy to deliver shared file resources across the network and enable other dealers to access the shared folders that are distributed. Which of the following is/are more useful in determining a highly available solution so that users can have uninterrupted access to shared folders?

   a. Active Directory–integrated solution

   b. Stand-alone solution

   c. Internet-based solution

   d. Domain-based solution

Answer: D. By configuring a domain-based DFS root, users can maintain access to files through automatic publishing of the DFS topology to Active Directory. Replication of the DFS roots and DFS shared folders is possible. DFS roots are placed on the server, and links to shared folders are reflected in the root. The replication allows duplication of DFS roots and DFS shared folders on servers in the domain. Using this replication, users can still access their files through DFS, even if one of the physical servers on which the DFS root resides becomes unavailable.

8. The network engineers are in the process of optimizing a WINS design. They are particularly concerned with improving the performance of the service on and between the servers, and reducing the impact of the service on the network bandwidth. Which of the following are issues that will address these concerns? (Choose all that apply.)

continued

    a. Reduce WINS database replication.

    b. Provide a faster processor.

    c. Reduce client resolution time.

    d. Increase the RAM on the server.

Answer: A, C, and **D.** Improvement in performance can be achieved by improving the performance of individual WINS servers. Since each WINS server loads the WINS database into memory at initialization to provide fast access to zone information, increasing RAM on the server will usually provide the biggest performance improvement, rather than providing faster processor or hard drive capabilities. Reducing DNS client query-resolution time and DNS server query and zone replication can improve performance.

9. You have been hired as a network consultant at AnyVehicle for the new project that it is undertaking. On analyzing the existing network, you learn that the current backup procedure for domain controllers running Windows NT Server 4.0 is to do a normal backup each Friday and Tuesday and an incremental backup each of the other days, including weekends. The domain controllers will be upgraded to Windows 2000 Server to create a Windows 2000 domain. You want to ensure that the domain controllers can be recovered if any key system data becomes corrupt. You develop procedures to use a batch file to run the NT backup utility with the system state switch. Which two types of backup should you use in the batch file when saving system state data?

    a. Normal

    b. Daily

    c. Copy

    d. Differential

    e. Incremental

Answer: A and **C.** When you select the system state option, you must use normal or copy as the backup type. An incremental backup only saves data that has been modified since the last normal or incremental backup. A differential backup only saves data that has been modified since the last normal or incremental backup. A daily backup only saves data that has been modified on the day the backup is being done. When backing up system state data, you must back up all of the system state data to ensure consistency, so incremental, differential, and daily backup types are not supported.

continued

10. On hearing about the new project, the network manager learns that management has approved the acquisition of a cluster of four servers running Windows 2000 Advanced Server. Management asks you to determine which service should be installed on the cluster to benefit from the load-balancing feature of Windows 2000. To take advantage of load balancing, what service do you think the network manager should install on the clustered servers?

a. Dynamic Host Configuration Protocol (DHCP)

b. Proxy Server

c. Windows Internet Name Service (WINS)

d. Domain Name System (DNS)

Answer: B. Proxy Server would benefit the most from load balancing. DNS can be configured with a single IP address for the cluster, and once an external client attempts to connect to this IP address, one of the servers in the cluster responds to the request, alternating the load among the servers. DHCP and WINS are cluster-aware services that benefit primarily from the failover services of a cluster rather than from the load-balancing services. DNS is not a cluster-aware application, so you must manually enable the DNS server service on another computer in the cluster if the server on which DNS is running fails. You can minimize the time needed to bring the other server online if you store the DNS zone files on the cluster drive.

Case Study A-3: Network Address Translation and Proxy

The following is a case study focusing on Network Address Translation and the use of a Proxy server. It is based on the fictional company Fly Away Airlines.

Organizational Structure

Fly Away Airlines is one of the large airlines operating in the United States. The company offers more than 1,500 departures daily to 106 domestic and 57 international destinations. It operates hubs in Chicago, Houston, and Cleveland, and provides extensive service throughout the United States, Europe, and Asia. With more than 26,500 employees around the world, Fly Away Airlines operates a large and sophisticated corporate network. It operates in an operation-critical environment where the timely

continued

transfer of data is crucial to efficient service and to provide customers with the very best flight experience.

The company needs to communicate time-sensitive information about flight operations and fares more efficiently than is possible by fax and rudimentary file transfers. Currently, the network infrastructure of the company is a group of Novell LANs developed for a specific business need, such as revenue management, scheduling, and flight operations. All of them are connected to the host system, but not to each other. This setup caused increased demands for hardware and support, creating unnecessary costs and hindering the integration of applications and information-sharing among divisions.

Technical Analysis

Fly Away operates on a client/server model with 24 Compaq ProLiant 1500 and Compaq ProLiant 4500 server computers at three corporate sites, connected over a WAN running Windows NT Server 4.0 and Microsoft Exchange Server, supporting approximately 2,600 desktop PCs running Microsoft Windows 95.

Fly Away is adding ProLiant 1500 and 4500 servers as needed. Fly Away also plans to redeploy an inventory of 486/66 computers back to the desktop that it had warehoused two years ago, upgrading them with Pentium processors. At the desktop, users typically have 486DX processors with 16MB of RAM and a 500MB hard disk, set up with Windows 95 and Microsoft Office for Windows 95. Fly Away's corporate headquarters has the bulk of the LANs, 41 servers. The two other locations have only a few LANs between them.

Like many large, geographically dispersed companies, Fly Away uses a variety of methods to connect its remote users and sites to the corporate network. The company uses frame relay to connect large sites; direct dial is available for local users; and the 800 number dial-up connections is the method of choice for Fly Away's remote users who did not have access to the corporate LAN.

Interviews with Employees

Veronica Cooper, Fly Away's Vice President and Chief Information Officer remarked, "We realized that we could gain a big business advantage from better employee communications and from sending decision support data around the network, allowing different groups to share the same data."

According to Thomas Miller, Fly Away's Chief Technology Officer, "From a technical standpoint, Fly Away would like to have a server that has multipurpose capabilities so that I only have to learn one server operating system to run all my applications.

continued

PART V

In addition, duplication of servers, like multiple file servers, application servers, and so on, is costly for administrative sites and reservation centers, and is currently a major obstacle to rolling out a network solution to airport locations."

"With offices at 100 locations throughout the United States, we could not possibly afford to put an administrator at each site," Steve Edwards, Director of Human Resources notes. "Centralized management tools will help reduce our cost of administration."

Miller adds, "We want something that provides great interoperability with other hardware and software solutions."

Goals

"We have a very simple goal," Miller explains. "To cut our current remote access costs in half." Fly Away is also zealous about data security. Jones is emphatic, "It's paramount that we protect and encrypt this data. Right now, data is crossing third-party networks that Fly Away does not directly control. Security is Fly Away's responsibility."

Fly Away's remote sales representatives rely on a strategic sales application to perform sales analysis and give them the information they need to retain more corporate accounts and get more business. These knowledge workers need quick, reliable, and secure access to the corporate network so they can use the sales application, e-mail, and other applications. They also need to book their own flights to travel to meet their customers.

"Pilots and flight attendants need to remotely access the scheduling system to do trip 'bids' and trade trips with other flight personnel," says Cooper. "All this creates a huge volume of network traffic. And since the data is very sensitive, it needs to be encrypted."

Fly Away wants to reduce the number of servers and streamline its system support. It also wants to provide its employees with the tools to more efficiently serve a larger volume of customers. "Our focus is to make Fly Away flights the best flight experience in the entire industry. Every decision we make, including technology, is focused on that goal," Edwards concludes.

Solution

The solution is to develop and deploy a Windows 2000 Server–based solution to its three corporate sites. Fly Away will then extend this solution to up to 75 airport sites and four reservation centers in the United States over the next three years.

To achieve these goals, the company is moving from disconnected LANs to one cohesive Microsoft Windows 2000-based network. Fly Away is planning to implement a corporate-wide solution based on the Microsoft Windows 2000 network operating

continued

system to reduce the number of server computers by 50 percent and reduce related support and administration costs. In a major effort to stem rapidly rising remote-access costs, Fly Away Airlines plans to use Microsoft Windows 2000 virtual private networking (VPN) to connect its sales force and other remote users to the corporate network.

"With Windows 2000, we can go into small airports with 5 to 20 users and set up a single server to run the applications and deliver file and print services and logon facilities," Miller observes. Providing all services with a single operating system is also expected to reduce training and administration costs because LAN administrators will only have to learn one system.

Fly Away regards the architecture in Microsoft BackOffice products as a flexible toolset for a wide range of future applications. Miller explains, "With the BackOffice family and the Windows 2000 operating system, Microsoft offered the most efficient and most cohesive solution for our business needs."

The company also plans to use Microsoft Internet Information Server, included with Windows NT Server, to set up an intranet, which will improve collaboration and enable the sharing of information, such as corporate policies, job opportunities, and job-related data, throughout the organization. This system can also be used to keep airport personnel up to date on changes in operations or security procedures resulting from special FAA regulations. Fly Away plans to use Microsoft Exchange Server for other inter-airport communications, such as sending alerts about passengers with special needs from the departure gate of one airport to the arrival gate of another.

"By keeping our agents and our managers fully informed, we can make the customer experience at the airport much better," Cooper says. "With regard to the Internet, in addition to our existing home page, we hope to eventually add an active home page to enable customers to make direct flight reservations."

According to Miller, "Windows 2000 provides us with extra capabilities to keep our systems integrated and our data secure, so we're going to take advantage of it."

Case Study Questions

1. Fly Away wants all of its employees at Chicago, Houston, and Cleveland to be able to access the company's resources via the Internet. Since the data is very confidential and since some of the data is also exposed to outsiders, it is very concerned about security. Taking these conditions into consideration, along with Fly Away's organizational and technical set-up, which of the following features in Windows 2000 would you use to enable this setup with as little trouble as possible, and in order to allow better management?

continued

    a. Proxy Server

    b. NAT

    c. ICS

    d. DMZ

Answer: A. NAT and ICS are useful for smaller networks. For enabling network management for the entire Fly Away network, Proxy Server would be the way to go, since it provides all the benefits that the company is looking for. The DMZ is not a feature, but a manner in which the Web servers are set up in the network to create a secure network.

2. Taking into consideration Fly Away's organizational setup, the solution it wishes to implement, and Cooper's remarks, Miller decides to secure the network by following these steps:

    I   Have a host of Web servers, and create a DMZ with them.

    II   Put a proxy server between the DMZ and the Internet.

    III   Place a firewall between the proxy and the DMZ.

What do you think of the solution?

    a. It is a good solution.

    b. The solution will work, but there's a better way to do it.

    c. It is a bad solution and will not protect the network.

Answer: C. The solution stated would not protect the internal network, since Proxy Server does not provide the level of control that is required to prevent unauthorized users from entering the private network. A firewall must be placed as the first entry point for Internet users. A proxy server is used to act as a very good filter, and therefore, it must be placed ahead of your private network, but behind your firewall to secure your network.

3. Miller decides to use NAT in Cleveland to enable the employees from that site to connect to the network from home. What do you think are the reasons that Miller chose NAT to design such a solution? (Choose all that apply.)

    a. Enable replication in Active Directory.

    b. Connect users to the Internet.

    c. Enable better integration with DNS servers.

    d. Connect disparate types of network segments.

    e. Enable better integration with DHCP servers.

    f. Create a screened subnet for Web servers.

    g. Enable multiple routing.

continued

h. Convert private addresses into public ones.

i. Enable increased security with IPSec.

Answer: B, D, F, and H. NAT (Network Address Translation) is a multifunction service for smaller networks. It enables users on a private network to connect to a public network by converting private addresses to public ones. It also connects disparate types of network segments, such as Ethernet to ISDN. NAT has the following restrictions:

- No other DHCP or DNS servers can be run on the network other than NAT.

- IPSec protocol cannot be used over NAT.

- The network must be a single, non-routed network.

- NAT cannot be used to replicate Active Directory, because Kerberos v5 is not supported by NAT and Kerberos v5 is used by Active Directory.

4. NAT would talk to only a particular set of reserved IP addresses. Fly Away wants to set this up at Chicago, and these are the addresses that are available:

I	192.168.0.0-192.168.255.255
II	192.168.0.0-192.168.24.255
III	255.255.255.255
IV	255.255.255.0

Which combination of IP addresses can Fly Away use?

a. I and III

b. I and IV

c. II and III

d. II and IV

Answer: D. NAT needs to talk to the reserved IP address 192.168.0.0-192.168.24.255, subnet mask 255.255.255.0.

5. There are many issues, like determining redundancy characteristics, planning for disaster recovery, and so on, when dealing with Internet connectivity. However, the most important issue is simply to get connected in the first place. Therefore, how can the network administrator at Fly Away's office in Cleveland design telephony solutions like RRAS to connect the network's users to the Internet? Why would he consider setting up a demand-dial connection on the public side of the NAT setup? (Choose all that apply.)

continued

a. The company is connected 24/7 to the Internet, and users connect to the company via an ISP.
b. He wants to set up a VPN connection to enable secure access.
c. The company has an ISDN line and wants to reduce costs.
d. He wants to set up an inexpensive, high-speed link.
e. The company has an existing inexpensive, high-speed link.

Answer: A, B, C, and **D.** Demand-dial RRAS is used when you have users who dial into their respective ISPs using their telephone line, and you want to provide them with Internet connectivity by setting up an inexpensive high-speed link to an ISP. If a demand-dial connection through RRAS is set up, the users get connected when they access the NAT. NAT can use multiple interfaces on the public side, and therefore, it is perfect for setting up an inexpensive high-speed link to an ISP. If the company is charged every minute for the ISDN line, it would cost a lot, and NAT can help reduce these costs by setting up a demand-dial connection. Demand-dial is also useful when you need to pass connection information over the wire, such as when you have a VPN connection that requires authentication.

6. When setting up NAT, the network administrator wants to increase the level of security. Of the following, what do you think the administrator can do to increase the security? (Choose all that apply.)
a. Set up RRAS IP filters.
b. Provide an IP address pool containing the private network IP addresses of servers that NAT is allowed to connect to.
c. Use L2TP for a VPN connection.

Answer: A and **B.** NAT's security can be augmented by setting up RRAS IP filters to restrict incoming and outgoing IP address ranges by protocol (FTP, for example). This is done by setting up IP address pools to allow Internet or VPN users to be able to access resources on the private network. VPNs can be used to restrict private network access, but since IPSec is not allowed through NAT, you cannot use L2TP for your VPN connection, but must instead rely on PPTP and a PPP connection.

7. Miller has set up ICS at Houston, but on testing, he realizes that company employees cannot access a resource from home, as intended. What can the possible reasons for this be? (Choose all that apply.)
a. There is a DHCP server on the same network.
b. There is a DNS server on the same network.
c. He had configured other computers in the network with static IP addresses.
d. The server with ICS enabled is not a member of a domain.

continued

    e. The server with ICS enabled is a member of a domain.

    f. One cannot "dial in" to ICS.

Answer: A, B, C, and **E.** Once ICS is enabled, it uses the same DHCP pool that is used by NAT, which is why you would not want any other DHCP or DNS servers on the network. You also cannot have computers on the internal network that are configured with a static IP address. It can only be used for incoming connections on a stand-alone server, and if the server is a member of a domain, you will be prompted to use RRAS for this. You can "dial in" to the ICS.

8. Cooper wants to allow users to access the internal network, as is mentioned in the solution adopted by the company. What are the things that she should be concerned about when setting up a DMZ to do what she needs? (Choose all that apply.)

    a. How to set up NAT and ICS

    b. Allowing SMTP traffic, but no HTTP traffic through the firewalls

    c. Having a one-way pull scenario for servers in the DMZ

    d. Managing fault tolerance and load balancing

Answer: B, C, and **D.** Designing a corporate Web presence with a DMZ indicates that less robust services like NAT and ICS would not be advisable for use in a demanding situation. E-mail servers would not be placed on a DMZ, but would be placed inside the corporate network. Therefore, to enable internal users to receive e-mail, SMTP traffic must be allowed into the network. You would also want to configure a one-way pull scenario in the DMZ, so that users cannot modify WINS or DNS entries in the DMZ. Considerations like fault tolerance and network load balancing on the Web servers in the DMZ are very important.

9. Miller is trying to get a Proxy Server installation finalized, but users don't seem to be obtaining an IP address from the server. What do you think is causing the problem?

    a. The DHCP scope is not configured correctly.

    b. The proxy server's private NIC is not in the correct subnet.

    c. Proxy Server does not do any DHCP server work.

    d. The DHCP service has been stopped.

Answer: C. Proxy Server does not do DHCP work, like NAT and ICS do, and you will have to separate the DHCP server for this kind of work.

10. Based on the company's goals and Miller's and Cooper's comments, which of the following should be done to manage the corporate network? (Choose all that apply.)

continued

PART V

a. Use NAT.

b. Get users to dial in to ISPs and use PPTP.

c. Connect the smaller sites, like Cleveland and Chicago, with DSL technology to supply high-speed WAN bandwidth.

d. Use L2TP and IPSec for access by remote users and sites.

e. Enable ICS.

Answer: B, C, and **D.** The company's goal is to reduce its remote-access costs and increase the level of security. Both goals can be satisfied by encouraging users to dial in to ISPs and use PPTP to create a secure tunnel, and by increasing the level of security using L2TP and IPSec across WAN circuits. Another cost-effective solution is to connect the small sites with high-speed bandwidth. NAT and ICS should not be used for large corporate networks, but for smaller networks.

Case Study A-4: Security

This final case study in the Appendix concerns a publishing entity. The focus is security, which is the middle section of this book and, of course, the focus of the 70-220 exam.

Organizational Structure

Medicine Publishers, founded in 1950, is a leading publisher of trade science, medical, and allied health books, journals, and electronic media. Its operations are segregated into distinctive product lines and said operations grow increasingly complicated as the company absorbs employees from the smaller specialty publishers it acquires. It has about 700 employees, all based in the medical-science publishing house in Detroit. The publications are sold primarily to wholesalers rather than to readers.

This year, the company will publish about 100 new editions, not including software, in addition to about 28 professional journals and updates to 430 existing volumes in the fields of science, medicine, surgery, pharmacy, chiropractic, dentistry, veterinary medicine, nursing, allied health (such as nutrition and physical therapy), test preparation, and reference. Its publications in English remain its core product line, in spite of its continuous expansion by acquiring other companies, one recent acquisition being a small French publisher.

continued

In the early 1990s, the company began producing software, CD-ROMs, and videos, as well as putting products online. It has a public Web site over which it sells about 3,000 books, journals, and electronic products. The company had listed its products online for nearly three years, and customers could even order through the site, but the transactions weren't secure, and the online listings were constantly out of date.

Executive Vice President Jerry Andreesen states, "The company, like its competitors, is currently facing a shrinking market. Managed care has prompted its ultimate customers, health-care professionals, to pare down their own spending. Therefore, once individuals are out of medical school, they, as health-care professionals, choose books in only two, or at most three, categories instead of buying books in their specialty and five other areas. For this reason, the company expects some fallout in its own industry over the next two years. The focus on containment of health-care costs in North America, Europe, and Japan will also continue to serve as a drag on our market's growth and cause further industry consolidation in medical publishing."

Technical Analysis

To counter competition in the early '90s, Medicine Publishers looked to the Internet. Like everyone else, the company initially focused on its public Web site. Erected in November 1995, the site put the company's entire catalog online, but the information got "stale" and thus, lost value even before the hard-copy catalog saw print. Why is this? Because the information was updated only once a month. This behavior, which appeared to be tardy, hardly set the scene for the company to provide the high-speed, high-accuracy customer service that executives deemed critical to the company's survival. The executives realized they needed a single cradle-to-grave repository of information about every product, accessible around the clock from anywhere in the world.

In order to keep up with the competition, it is important that the company provide quick information and speed up its printing process. The company is, therefore, planning to deploy Windows 2000 Professional and Windows 2000 Server in its organization to create an intranet and enable strong online sales. The company is in the process of finalizing its designs to start rolling out the Windows 2000 platform on both desktops and the back end during the second fiscal quarter. Currently, only a handful of employees have desktop Internet access.

Interviews with Employees

Anna Francis, an associate Marketing Manager states, "We want to do more productive work rather than spend time answering the questions asked by the salespeople. It is time consuming. We would like to spend more time talking with customers and expedite our processes."

continued

PART V

"Currently, the information is scattered all over the company, and not everybody has access to it," says Mark Thias, Director of Network Services. "The most important documents, the initial publishing proposal, and a product-information newsletter that is published twice a year for the sales department, are handled on paper. Nobody keeps a master copy, which means that a book editor and a marketing manager might each update their own copies of the initial publishing proposal with revised publication dates, without bothering to inform each other about the changes. To find out when the book will actually appear in print requires plugging into 'the informal network'—that is, making phone call after phone call to find the right person with the right date."

Francis also adds, "Things are tougher for salespeople who pitch products to the company's customers, primarily wholesalers and college professors. Since their heavy paper-stuffed binders were updated only twice a year, they, too, typically hit the phones, calling marketers at the Detroit headquarters to get accurate information."

Ted Taylor, a manager in the company's Publishing Resources Group, says "I have at least 50 items on my wish list for upgrades and enhancements to the existing system. For example, tying the intranet into the company's fulfillment systems, and expanding its offerings for international users."

He also adds, "We want an information repository, not a workflow product. We want to streamline and speed up existing processes, not create new electronic ones. We're not trying to become a technology company. We still want to be a publishing company. We want to do something that will promote greater efficiency and productivity, as well as spawn lucrative new opportunities."

Thias underscored the need for good security, "The company needs to set controls, such as passwords, so that only certain employees can gain access to particular areas of the system; only a high-level editor should be able to increase the number of complimentary book copies, for instance, while only a top communications specialist can rewrite catalog text. We also want any behavior that's taking place across the network to be secure."

Goals

Medicine Publishers recognized a few years back that it needed to move quickly to sharpen its competitive edge. The company wants to improve its in-house processes, collaboration, and communication between its employees and with customers. It wants to do business faster, better, and cheaper.

The company's goal is to have a single integrated source of information where the company's employees can access a lot of information about every Medicine Publisher book, journal, CD-ROM, video, and software product—from initial proposal to final inventory.

continued

Solution

The company is in the process of completing the development of a customized database containing all product information, from author contact information to product costs to catalog text. It plans to roll this out using Windows 2000.

Each department would be responsible for entering its own information. People in marketing, editorial, production, administration, finance, sales, creative communications, and customer service can have access to the same "master copy" of the information. If somebody updates a file—for example, to move up a publication date, increase a page count, adjust a price—everybody else can quickly find out.

The developers are distributing a wallet-sized brochure to everyone in the company, listing early champions and trumpeting the intranet's benefits: "Instead of stacks of paper, hard-to-read handwriting, and conflicting facts, you can have a clear view of each journal, book, or electronic product. You can search for one product, or a group of products, by title, author, specialty, and more."

This intranet will not only centralize all the data required by marketers, but it also will let them quickly disseminate new competitive intelligence to salespeople, who in turn can use it to close deals. For example, the latest information on similar books produced by rivals, comments from readers, and suggested sales strategies based on the product's features and benefits can be shared among marketers and salespeople quickly and efficiently. It will also allow marketers to incorporate new information about products. Excerpts can be keyed into the product record, giving salespeople yet another selling point. And if, even with all the available information, salespeople need additional help, they will be able to find out whom to contact, because each record lists all employees associated with that particular product.

This will also streamline the print-catalog production process. Since all product information in the catalog will be updated automatically through the company network, the production process for the hard-copy catalog can be cut from four months to a matter of weeks.

Francis finally states, "Sales reps will not need to call me for information, book prices, page counts, details about the author and so forth, because they can get the most current information themselves from the Web anytime. It will give me the opportunity to do more meaningful, and ultimately, more profitable things with my time. It also means traveling more often to meet customers in locations as distant as Germany or Jamaica."

continued

Case Study Questions

1. The company will face some "hiccups" or mild challenges when setting up Windows 2000 in setting up an intranet. Which of the following do you think are the "hiccups" that will be encountered? (Choose all that apply.)
   a. Employee resistance to new technology.
   b. Limited employee knowledge on using new technology.
   c. No support from management.
   d. No intrinsic business value.
   e. An intranet cannot be set up using Windows 2000.

Answer: A and B. Employee resistance to new technology is evident from the fact that the developers are distributing a wallet-sized brochure to everyone in the company, listing early champions and trumpeting the intranet's benefits. This is to gain employee acceptance and to educate them on the benefits of an intranet. The business value from the intranet is clearly stated and is considered a positive influence on the company. There is no information regarding support from management. An intranet can be set up using Windows 2000.

2. What do you think the company's growth strategy is based on? (Choose all that apply.)
   a. Acquiring publishers catering to non-medical areas, such as fiction, business, and so on
   b. Acquiring publishers in medicine-related fields
   c. Expanding internationally
   d. Expanding nationally

Answer: B and C. Although the company is based in Detroit, it has publishers all over the world. The company's growth strategy is to acquire small publishers and expand internationally. The company acquires specialty publishers in the medicine field, and it recently acquired a French publisher. The Executive Vice President's concern about the containment of health-care costs in North America, Europe and Japan, which will affect the company's growth, reveals the global operations of the company.

3. Referring to the solution the company plans to adopt, what do you think is the kind of administration decision-making the company is following?
   a. Centralized
   b. Decentralized
   c. Centralized with little bit of decentralization

Answer: B. The intranet allows centralization of data, but the company believes in decentralized administration. It plans to allow each department to be responsible for entering and updating its own information.

continued

4. After analyzing the case study, which of the following do you think is true of Medicine Publishers? (Choose all that apply.)
   a. Medicine Publishers' information flows across the organization.
   b. Medicine Publishers' information flows across the organization, down from the management to the employees.
   c. Medicine Publishers' product and catalog information can be accessed only by management.
   d. Medicine Publishers' product and catalog information can be accessed by the editors, salespeople, finance people, customer service, and management.

Answer: A and D. Information does flow across the organization, since everyone can access the product catalog information and a few select personnel can update it, too. People in marketing, editorial, production, administration, finance, sales, creative communications, and customer service can have access to the same "master copy" of the information.

5. The company will be increasingly using the intranet and the Internet for its daily business activities, which may cause various kinds of problems that directly affect business. What are the problems or threats the company may have to encounter? (Choose all that apply.)
   a. Password cracking
   b. Pornography
   c. Loss of data integrity
   d. Data theft
   e. Duplicate versions of the same data
   f. Wire-born viruses
   g. Trojan horses
   h. Credit card fraud
   i. Misuse of company time

Answer: A, C, D, F, G, and H. Pornography, duplicate data, and misuse of company time do not affect the business directly. The intranet does allow for centralization and prevents duplication of data. Password cracking, loss of data integrity, data theft, wire-born viruses, Trojan horses, and credit card fraud are concerns that will directly affect the publisher's business and, therefore, need to be taken care of.

6. The company is very concerned about securing its network. It is also concerned about preventing unauthorized access to its network. Which of the following features in Windows 2000 can enable the company to authorize and authenticate its users? (Choose one.)

continued

PART V

   a. ACLs, Kerberos, PKI, NTLM, RADIUS

   b. RADIUS, LM, PKI, NTLM, L2TP, NTLM v2

   c. Kerberos, NTLM, RADIUS

   d. Kerberos, NTLM, PKI

Answer: A. L2TP is a tunneling protocol, not an authorizing or authenticating mechanism. Only A includes all the features that will allow authorization and authentication of users.

7. Mark Thias, when interviewed, mentioned the use of passwords. The users of the system, the employees, are not technologically savvy and they could compromise their passwords. Which of the following are issues that Thias needs to be concerned about? Which of the following issues should the users be educated about? (Choose all that apply.)

   a. A copy of the SAM might be found on a backup tape and fed into a password-cracking program.

   b. Users might write down their passwords and leave them in the most obvious places (tape the note to their desk).

   c. NTLM does not have a strong security algorithm.

   d. A copy of the NT SAM might be found in the repair directory, and then be copied and fed into a password-cracking program.

   e. Users might pick very easy passwords.

Answer: A, B, D, and **E.** Users, especially ones who aren't technologically savvy, tend to use easy passwords or write them down someplace so that they can remember them. The Windows NT SAM may be found on a carelessly stored emergency repair disk (ERD) or backup tape and then be used to obtain passwords.

8. The company recently acquired BooksForU, a medical publisher in Britain. BooksForU will operate in Britain and serve the European markets. It will, however, need to communicate with Medical Publishers' headquarters in Detroit to access the company information and update the company about its dealings in Europe. Currently, it has a Windows 98 and Unix client environment. The migration to Windows 2000 will take place at BooksForU only after the change is effected at the headquarters. Medical Publishers wants to smoothen the migration as much as possible. In addition to the goals stated previously, it wants to do the following:

continued

I   Install and support a single client operating system for ease of maintenance and rapid deployment.

II   Reduce deployment and management costs by using a single server image.

III   Create a centralized IT administration model, allowing for distributed control to lower levels.

IV   Provide interoperability with existing Unix servers and use a common security protocol.

Windows 2000 Professional provides the client operating system needed, and creating a single Windows 2000 Server image for rapid deployment will address that issue. What Windows 2000 features should be incorporated into the design to address the remaining goals?

a. Active Directory, NTLM, DNS

b. Active Directory, Kerberos, DNS Dynamic Update

c. Systems Management Server, Remote Install services, Intellimirror

d. Active Directory, Kerberos, IPSec

Answer: B. Active Directory allows administrators to delegate control for specific elements within Active Directory to individuals or groups. This eliminates the need for multiple administrators to have authority over an entire domain. Domain Name System (DNS) dynamic update protocol provides interoperability with existing Unix servers. Dynamic update enables DNS client computers to register and dynamically update their resource records with a DNS server whenever changes occur. This reduces the need for manual administration of zone records, especially for clients that frequently move or change locations and that use DHCP to obtain an IP address.

Kerberos security, the default Windows 2000 authentication mechanism, works on both platforms. Kerberos is a multi-vendor standard, so it allows secure interoperability and the potential for a single sign-on between Microsoft implementations and other vendor environments.

The Windows NTLM protocol was the default for authentication in Windows NT 4.0. It is retained in Windows 2000 for compatibility with clients and servers that are running Windows NT 4.0 and earlier. It is also used to authenticate logons to stand-alone computers that are running Windows 2000. Both Windows 98 and Windows NT 4.0 must use the NTLM protocol for network authentication in Windows 2000 domains. Computers with Windows 2000 use NTLM when they are authenticating to servers that are running Windows NT 4.0 and when they are requesting access to resources in Windows NT 4.0 domains. NTLM is not UNIX-compatible.

continued

DNS, by itself, does not provide interoperability with existing Unix servers. The dynamic update protocol is required. IntelliMirror, Remote Install Services, and Systems Management Server are client-management features and automated client install and upgrade technologies. They do not address the requirements of the scenario. IP Security (IPSec) is a Windows 2000 implementation allowing secure network communications. There is no Unix interoperability with IPSec.

9. Roderick Adams, an engineer in the Network Services group plans to use cable modems on five PCs in the company. Any employees in the company can use these PCs to access the Internet. What are the security issues that he needs to consider before installing the modems?
   a. The PCs and modems create a backdoor into the company network.
   b. Users might be able to access each other's e-mail.
   c. A user may be able to access the last user's file.
   d. Users may leave sensitive information in the PC area.

Answer: A. Cable modems and wireless modems are doors into the internal network, and if they are not locked down properly with the use of firewalls or other security products, the security of the network is compromised. Cable modems do not cause users to access another user's e-mail or to access the last user's file.

10. Of the following, which may be the reasons for Medicine Publishers to consider decentralizing its IT operations and administration? (Choose all that apply.)
   a. To reduce company overhead
   b. To enable expansion of the network
   c. To reduce expenditures
   d. To clearly align IT with its specialty publishers located at various locations

Answer: B and D. Decentralization involves increased expenditure, and since administrators are required at various locations, it may also increase administrative overhead. Local administrators will be able to better understand and respond to the needs of the specialty publishers. Decentralized administration can also enable network expansion, especially if the company's growth strategy is through acquisitions, as is the case with Medicine Publishers.

Exam Questions on the Topics Presented in this Book

This section contains over 50 questions on the topics in this book. The questions are presented in a traditional question and answer format. The questions are broken down into the following areas:

Encrypting File System:	6 questions
Auditing:	3 questions
Public Key Infrastructure:	11 questions
Internet Protocol Security:	6 questions
Active Directory Services:	27 questions

Encrypting File System (Six Questions)

XYZ Company is a small sales company with 200 employees. Most of the company employees are field sales reps who are given laptops to enable them to have roaming access to their company's network that runs on Windows 2000. The company is very concerned about the security and confidentiality of its data.

Steve is a field sales rep who is always on the go and is very security conscious. He has most of his folders encrypted using EFS on his office machine. He has to go to a conference where many of his competitors will be present and where he will have to study and edit the company data based on the presentations given at the conference. He's worried that if his laptop, containing the data, is stolen, important company data could be misused against them. To protect the important contents, he copies the encrypted folder (containing the important files) to his laptop, which has encryption enabled. On copying, he notices that the contents of the file are in clear text.

1. What are the possible reasons that this could have happened? (Choose all that apply.)
    a. The operating system on the laptop is Windows 98.
    b. The file was copied to an NTFS partition on the laptop.
    c. Windows NT 4.0 is running on the laptop.
    d. The file was copied to an unencrypted folder.
    Answer: A and C. EFS can be enabled only on NTFS volumes, and if a user moves a file to another folder, the file retains its encryption state, regardless of whether the destination folder is encrypted or unencrypted. EFS does not support encryption and decryption on a FAT or FAT32 volume.

Tim is in the sales department of ABC Company, which has 500 employees based in Seattle. The company is on a Windows 2000 network and has file encryption enabled. The computers in the various departments are running either on Windows 95/98 or on Windows NT. Tim wants to encrypt some files on his computer, but he knows that there are some files that cannot be encrypted. He contacts you in the IT department.

2. What will your response be? Which of the following files can you not encrypt? (Choose all that apply.)
   a. Files on NTFS volumes
   b. System files
   c. Compressed files
   d. Read-only files
   e. Files on FAT volumes

   Answer: B, C, D, and **E.** You cannot encrypt a system file because the user's encryption key isn't available during the boot process, so if you encrypt system files (for example, system DLLs or the Registry), you could not boot into Windows 2000. (However, it is interesting to note that future versions of Windows, such as Windows 2002, will let you encrypt system files.) You cannot encrypt files or folders that are compressed—to do so, you must uncompress the file or folder, and then you can encrypt it. In addition, you cannot encrypt read-only files. EFS does not support encryption and decryption of files or folders on a FAT volume.

You are part of the IT department at company X, which has 500 employees located in St. Louis. All the computers in the organization are connected on a Windows 2000 network. The company is divided into five organizational units—Accounting, Production, IT, Sales, and HR. The company policy states that the employees in the Sales department must not be allowed to keep any files secret from the company. You, as a domain administrator, need to follow this policy, and therefore, you decide to disable EFS on all computers in the Sales organizational unit.

3. What do you do?
   a. Create a No Recovery Policy.
   b. Create a Recovery Agent Policy.
   c. Create an Empty Recovery Policy.

   Answer: C. Recovery agents are users that administrators designate to recover encrypted files. The recovery agents use their certificates and public keys to decrypt the files. Administrators can define three types of recovery policies:

- The Recovery Agent Policy takes effect when an administrator adds one or more recovery agents.

- The Empty Recovery Policy causes no one to be designated as a recovery agent; in this case, EFS is turned off.

- The No Recovery Policy means that you have deleted the group recovery policy so that the local machine administrators can control data recovery by using default local policy.

Note that creating an empty policy is different from having no policy. If you have no recovery policy, local machine administrators can still define their own policies.

4. Bob is a part of the Accounting department of company X, and he has an encrypted folder on the corporate server. Who can access the folder? (Choose all that apply.)
   a. Bob
   b. The domain administrator
   c. Any user who has access to the server
   d. A registered recovery agent
   Answer: A and **D**. When you use EFS to encrypt the files on your computer, an EFS public key encrypts the files, and an EFS private key decrypts the files. Therefore, only the user who encrypts the file or folder can access an encrypted NTFS folder. If your computer is a member of a Windows 2000 domain, the domain administrator can designate certain users as EFS recovery agents who can also access the encrypted NTFS folder. Users cannot share encrypted files.

5. Alice wants to encrypt a file on the remote server with remote encryption enabled. To ensure that the file will be saved as encrypted on the remote server, she encrypts the file using EFS and then sends it across the network.
   a. The solution is optimal—it will work as intended.
   b. The solution will not give the desired result.
   c. The requirement is unrealistic.
   Answer: B. EFS can be used to encrypt files on remote servers. However, it does not encrypt data that is transmitted over the network. IPSec or SSL offer the ability to encrypt all data that must be transferred over the network. EFS can only encrypt files on the hard disk. To obtain the required result, Alice will need to send the file over to the remote server using SSL or IPSec and then encrypt the file with EFS.

6. Clara has lost her private key and cannot open the encrypted file on her machine, so she contacts the IT department. John is the administrator of the domain under which Clara's machine falls. He takes the following steps to enable Clara to access the file whose encryption keys are lost:

I   He asks Clara to send the encrypted file to the recovery agent, who takes a backup and moves the backup file to a secure system.

II   The recovery agent then imports Clara's recovery certificate and private key.

III The backup file is then restored and decrypted with Windows Explorer or cipher command-line utility. The plain-text file is then sent to Clara.

What do you think about the action taken by John?
a. It is an outstanding solution.
b. It is a satisfactory solution, but there is a better way to do it.
c. It is no solution at all.

Answer: A. The recovery agent has a special certificate and associated private key that allow data recovery for the scope of influence of the recovery policy. If domain user Clara loses her private key, she cannot open the files she encrypted with that key. The recovery agent will be able to back up the encrypted file that Clara sent via e-mail, move the backup copy to a secure system, and import Clara's recovery certificate and private key. The recovery agent will then be able to restore the backup file, decrypt the file with the private key, and send the plain-text file back to Clara.

Auditing (Three Questions)

Corey is the administrator of a Windows 2000 domain of an e-commerce company that provides office supplies to other businesses. He has secured the network by installing firewalls and proxy servers. Recently, there was a time when the internal network had to be shut down for a while because someone had tried to break into the intranet. This cost the company a lot of money, and Corey suspected this to be the work of two disgruntled employees who had been fired two days before the incident took place. Corey wants to find out if the disgruntled employees are to blame and prevent any random attacks that may be made to gain entry into the internal network.

1. To satisfy Corey's requirement, what do you think are the issues that must be audited?
a. Audit logon and logoff failures
b. Audit object access
c. Audit account management
d. Audit logon and logoff successes

Answer: A. Establishing an audit trail is an important facet of security. Auditing logon and logoff failures provides a way to track unauthorized users trying to gain entry into the system. Monitoring logon and logoff successes will help in determining if the credentials of a particular user are stolen. Auditing object access will only determine whether correct permissions have been assigned, whereas auditing account management will enable the administrator to identify tasks, such as the renaming, enabling, or disabling of user passwords.

You are the administrator of the corporate server of a start-up company that has developed a new product based on a new technology. The company is in the process of patenting the technology, and the company is, therefore, keeping quiet about the issue to prevent any of its competitors or employees (other than a select few) from knowing about the product. You have secured all the information to prevent any unauthorized access to files. Since you believe in being proactive, you want to enable auditing and study the resulting information.

Required Result You want to obtain details on attempts to open, close, or delete sensitive files.

Optional Result You want to obtain details on the incorrect permissions set on the files.

Proposed Solution You enable the audit policy setting Audit Privilege Use in your group policy object (select the appropriate GPO, Computer Configuration | Windows Settings | Security Settings | Local Policy | Audit Policy). Then, set the size and behavior of the security log and use the file's Properties dialog box to configure the specific levels of access for each user or group you want to track (open the Properties dialog box for the files in question, select the Security tab, click the Advanced button, select the Auditing tab, and click Add to add an audit entry for a specific user or group).

2. What do you think of the proposed solution? (Choose one option.)
   a. The solution will satisfy both the required and the optional result.
   b. The solution will satisfy only the required but not the optional result.
   c. The solution will satisfy only the optional result.
   d. The solution will not satisfy either result.
   Answer: D. Enabling the Audit Privilege Use audit policy setting will not give the desired results because this setting tracks whether a particular user has exercised a privileged right, such as changing the system time. The correct policy setting is Audit Object Access, which gives the ability to audit access to a particular file, folder, or printer.

Catywhompus Construction, Inc., is a contractor company specializing in commercial construction. It is based in Oakland, California, and has 10,000 employees worldwide at six locations: New York, Los Angeles, Chicago, London, Tokyo, and its Oakland headquarters. The major departments in each of these locations are Human Resources, Finance and Accounting, Project Management, Marketing, Construction, and Operations. The company has a Windows 2000–based network, and all the sites are linked via a WAN. Remote construction sites are linked via a VPN connection over the Internet. Professional staff members often connect to the company via the VPN from home and while traveling. You are the administrator in charge of Catywhompus for operations in the United States.

3. What are the events that must absolutely be audited to meet the need for a high-security environment by detecting threats to the system? (Choose all that apply.)
   a. Audit system events, such as system restarts, shutdowns, and so on.
   b. Audit the success and failure of users logging on.
   c. Audit privilege use, such as changing the system time.
   d. Audit failures and successes to access various objects (file, folder, printer).
   e. Audit policy changes, such as changes made to users' security options or audit policies.

   Answer: B and **D.** The absolute minimum requirement of a medium- to high-security environment must be to track the success and failure of users to log on, and the use of resources. This is an absolute minimum in detecting any threat to the network.

Public Key Infrastructure (11 Questions)

You are the domain administrator (in Oakland, California) for Catywhompus Construction, which was profiled in the last question (of the previous section). The corporate headquarters in Oakland needs (1) to allow full control on the operations at the other locations, (2) to allow for transparent user validation and authentication between the various locations, and (3) to enable employees to connect to the company via the VPN.

Proposed Solution   Install a root CA for each office, and create subordinate CAs to issue certificates to users within their domain.

1. What do you think of this solution? (Choose one option.)
   a. The proposed solution is outstanding and will satisfy all the desired requirements.
   b. The proposed solution will satisfy none of the desired requirements.

   Answer: A. A root CA is meant to be the most trusted type of CA in an organization's Public Key Infrastructure (PKI). Typically, both the physical security and the certificate issuance policy of a root CA are more rigorous than those for subordinate CAs. If the root CA is compromised or issues a certificate to an unauthorized entity, then any certificate-based security in your organization is suddenly vulnerable. Therefore, to ensure maximum security, there should be one root CA installed at the headquarters, and subordinate CAs at the various locations to issue certificates to the employees. This will enable transparent validation and authentication to employees between different locations. If root CAs are installed at each location, there is a tremendous decrease in security, and each location will have to install the other root CAs as a trusted root.

As the domain administrator of Catywhompus Construction at its headquarters in Oakland, you have decided to install a CA hierarchy for the intranet. You decided on (1) installing a root CA and CAs to implement the certificate policy, and (2) issuing CAs to clients.

2. To ensure the utmost security, which combination of CAs should be kept offline?
   a. Root CA and certificate policy CAs
   b. Certificate policy CA and issuing CAs
   c. Root CA and issuing CAs
   d. Root CA only

   Answer: A. The first business-policy decision to be made is to select the CAs, both internal and external. The next decision is to design the CA hierarchy, which is usually a three-level architecture, as described. For utmost security, it is recommended that the root CA and the certificate policy CAs (the first and the second levels in the architecture) be kept offline, and thus, protected. The third-level CAs, which are the issuing CAs, can be internal or external and must be the only ones exposed.

You are the administrator at Catywhompus in Oakland, and you want to publish certificates for the users on your internal network to enable them to send secure e-mail to each other and to have Web-based authentication. You install an enterprise CA to issue certificates to users and computers within the same domain. However, you realize that the enterprise CA will not work because of an error.

3. What could the error be? (Choose all that apply.)
   a. The users and computers are not part of a Windows 2000 domain.
   b. No Active Directory service is installed.
   c. Windows 2000 DNS service is not installed.
   Answer: A, B, and **C.** The enterprise CA requires the following:

   • Windows 2000 DNS service installed (required by Active Directory)

   • Windows 2000 Active Directory installed, since enterprise policy places information in the Active Directory

4. Your business requires extreme security—both internally (within the organization) and externally (from your customers and business partners). You decide to install a PKI to enable security and smooth integration, and you decide to set up a root CA, a CA for implementing the certificate policy, and a third level of CAs to issue the certificates. For issuing certificates to the employees, you decide to install an internal CA managed by the IT department; for the external users (customers and partners), you decide to have an external CA. The reasons are as follows:

   I   Internet transactions and software signing might require third-party certificates to establish public credibility.
   II   Third-party CAs (compared to the CA managed by the company) can offer more security, since they specialize in issuing certificates.
   III You do not have Windows 2000 installed, so you cannot manage the PKI.

   What do you think are the right reasons for the external CA to manage certificates to be issued to the external end-users? (Choose any one.)
   a. Reason I only
   b. Reasons I and II
   c. Reasons I and III
   Answer: A. The only reason why you might want to have third-party CAs is to ensure public credibility for Internet transactions and software signing. Third-party CAs do not provide better security than could the company. You can still have a PKI with stand-alone CAs. You only need Windows 2000 to install an enterprise CA.

You are the manager of the IT department at the New York office of Catywhompus. You have to install an enterprise subordinate CA with the Root CA installed at the headquarters in Oakland. You notice that the CA cannot be installed and in addition, you as an administrator, cannot access the CA server to find out the cause of the problem.

5. What are the plausible reasons for such a situation to happen? (Choose all that apply.)
    a. The enterprise subordinate CA does not have a parent CA.
    b. Windows 2000 DNS Services is not installed on the enterprise subordinate CA.
    c. Windows 2000 Active Directory Services is not installed on the CA.
    d. You have no enterprise administrator privileges on the DNS, Active Directory, and CA server.

Answer: B, C, and **D.** To install an enterprise subordinate CA, the prerequisites are

- A parent CA, which could be an external commercial CA or a stand-alone CA

- Windows 2000 DNS Service installed (required by Active Directory)

- Windows 2000 Active Directory installed since enterprise policy places information in the Active Directory

- Enterprise administrator privileges on the DNS, Active Directory, and CA servers

XYZ hospital has a total of 10,000 employees located at Seattle, New York and Houston. The hospital is on a Windows 2000–based network. There is a VPN that connects the three locations. The hospital officials are keen on accepting new technology that will enable tight security. The doctors and the nurses and other select employees from the three locations need to log in to the hospital network from outside the hospital premises, for example from home. The hospital requires transparent user validation and authentication and is very concerned about security. As the CTO of the company, Bob decides to install an Enterprise Root CA as against a stand-alone Root CA.

6. What do you think are the reasons for Bob to take such a decision? (Choose all that apply.)
    a. Seamless integration with Active Directory that enables better management of certificates issued.
    b. Smart card logon is possible, providing more security.
    c. Enterprise CA can enable issuance of certificates to members outside the organization (hospital supplier, etc.).

Answer: A and **B.** The certificates are to be issued to only members within the organization. An enterprise CA will enable seamless integration with Active Directory, thus allowing transparent user validation and authentication. A stand-alone CA, which could be internal or external, is typically used to issue certificates outside of a corporation's enterprise network. To enable extreme security, only the enterprise CA can support the use of smart cards. The hospital has no plans of enabling outside parties to beconnected to the network and Enterprise Root CAs can issue certificates to only subordinate Enterprise CAs that operate only within the organization.

XYZ organization is very concerned about the security within and outside the company network—the intranet and the extranet. Therefore, the domain administrator, Mark, sets up a Windows 2000 PKI—a two-level architecture for issuance and management of certificates for the employees. He is aware of the potential risk in exposing the trust within the CA hierarchy and therefore, he decides to use special-purpose cryptographic hardware for the issuing CA, maintain it in a locked vault, and operate it on an offline mode.

7. What is your view of the decision to protect the trust in the CA hierarchy?
    a. An excellent decision, which will protect the CA hierarchy form being compromised.
    b. A very bad decision and will not protect the CA hierarchy within the organization from being exposed.
    c. The solution/decision is unrealistic and cannot be achieved.
    Answer: B. The Root CA must be protected and kept offline, and its signing key should be secured by special-purpose cryptographic hardware and kept in a vault to minimize the potential of key compromise. Issuer CAs must not be kept offline since they insulate the root CA from attempts to compromise its private key by malicious individuals.

Meanwhile, back at Catywhompus, you are the administrator in charge of network operations in the United States. There is an enterprise root CA at the main office, and there are issuing CAs at each of the other offices.

8. What are the benefits provided by the multiple issuing CAs at the six locations? (Choose all that apply.)
    a. Separate certificate policies for different categories of users and computers, or for organizational and geographic divisions.
    b. To meet site, network, and server requirements, you can distribute certificates for provision of redundant services.
    c. Multiple issuing CAs provide the distribution of certificate load.
    d. Ability to turn off a particular section of the CA hierarchy.
    Answer: A, B, C, and D. Multiple issuing CAs enable you to establish various certificate policies depending upon an entity's role in the organization. It also

enables network connectivity between multiple physical sites that might dictate a requirement for multiple subordinate CAs to meet usability requirements. You can set up an issuing CA to provide certificates to each distinct category, department, or site. A particular section of the CA hierarchy can be turned off without affecting established root trust relationships or the rest of the hierarchy. It also enables distribution of certificate load and provision of redundant services.

Slow and non-continuous network links between sites can require each issuing CA at each site to meet certificate-services performance and usability requirements. You can deploy issuing CAs to distribute certificate load as necessary to meet all site- and network-connectivity load requirements.

Deployment of multiple CAs enables uninterrupted issuance of certificates in the event of failure of any CA.

Your company, Z, has a partnership with ABC Company (who provides temporary workers) that needs to access some internal Web pages. ABC Company has its one CA that issues certificates to its employees. After installing the company's CA as a trusted root in your enterprise, you can set a rule to map the users from ABC Company and give them access rights so that the user accounts can access the Web pages.

9. To enable this mapping, what must you, as an administrator at company Z, undertake:
   a. One-to-one mapping
   b. Many-to-one mapping
   c. User principal name mapping

   Answer: B. Many-to-one mapping maps many certificates to a single user account. Therefore, after installing ABC Company's root certificate as a trusted root in your enterprise, you can set a rule that maps all certificates issued by that CA to a single Windows 2000 account, and then set access rights for the account so that all the users from this account can access the particular Web pages. User principal name mapping is a special case of one-to-one mapping. One-to-one mapping maps only a single user certificate to a single Windows 2000 user account. In this particular case, the one-to-one mapping would be difficult to manage, since permissions for each user account from the ABC Company would have to be set, which is tedious.

You are the administrator of XYZ Company, which has 420 employees, and all of them are on a Windows 2000–based network. The company has installed Windows 2000 Certificate Services to enable transparent user authentication and validation by issuing certificates to all its users. You want to revoke Alice's certificate because she has been fired from the company. You want to prevent her from accessing any of the resources. The steps to be taken to achieve this are as follows:

Step 1 Log on to the system as an Administrator, open Certification Authority (choose Start | Programs | Administrative Tools | Certification Authority). Next, in the console tree, choose Issued Certificates (Certification Authority (*computer*) | *CA name* | Issued Certificates). Then, in the details pane, click Alice's certificate. Choose Action | All Tasks | Revoke Certificate. The Certificate Revocation dialog box is displayed. In the drop-down list, click the reason for the revocation. Click Yes after you select the correct reason code.

Step 2 Right-click the Revoked Certificates folder. Select All Tasks and then choose Publish | Select Publish and click OK.

10. To prevent Alice from accessing any resources, which one of the following options should you employ?
    a. Step 1 and step 2
    b. Only step 1
    c. Only step 2
    d. Neither step 1 nor step 2
    Answer: A. In Certificate Services, revoking a certificate means you are marking an issued certificate in the database as being revoked. Revocation of certificates is a mechanism for invalidating a certificate prior to its natural expiration. Applications that check the revocation status of a certificate prior to use can then make a more informed decision about certificate validity and can determine what process to perform. It is important to note that revoking a certificate is not sufficient to make this information available to applications. That requires creating and publishing a Certificate Revocation List (CRL).

Alan is a new employee in the Human Resources group of XYZ Company. All the members of the HR department communicate via secure e-mail. He wants to obtain a certificate from the stand-alone CA to enable secure e-mail between him and other members in the HR department. For this purpose, he performs the following steps:

I   Open an MMC console that contains Certificates.
II   In the Certificates console, right-click the Personal node.
III In the shortcut menu, select All Tasks | Request New Certificate. The Certificate Request wizard launches. Click Next.
IV   Select the certificate template. Select User. Click Next.

V   Enter a friendly name or a description, if desired. Click Next.

VI   Click Finish to send the certificate request to the CA.

VII   Click Install Certificate to install the certificate to the certificate store.

11. What do you think of this procedure? (Choose one option.)

    a. The procedure will enable Alan to successfully send secure e-mails.

    b. The procedure will not enable Alan to successfully send secure e-mails because an important step is missing.

    c. The procedure will not work because it is incorrect in this situation.

    Answer: C. To obtain a certificate, the certification authority must be installed as either a root or subordinate enterprise Certificate Authority (CA). You can use the procedure listed here to request certificates from an enterprise CA only. To request certificates from a stand-alone CA, you need to request certificates via Web pages. A Windows 2000 CA has its Web pages located at http:*servername*\certsrv, where *servername* is the name of the Windows 2000 server hosting the CA.

Internet Protocol Security (Six Questions)

You want to create a new security method to enable encryption, but not at the cost of performance. Keeping this in mind, you take the following steps:

I   In the IP Security Policy Management snap-in, right-click the policy you want to modify, and select Properties.

II   Select the rule you want to modify, and then click Edit.

III   On the Filter Action tab, click the filter you want to modify, and then click Edit.

IV   Click the Security Methods tab, and click Add to add a new security method.

V   Click Custom, and then click Settings.

VI   Click Data Integrity and Encryption (ESP).

VII   Click SHA-1 for the algorithm you want to use for data integrity.

VIII   Click on DES as the algorithm for confidentiality.

1. Will these steps enable encryption without affecting performance? (Choose one option.)

    a. Encryption is not enabled at all.

    b. Encryption is enabled, compromising performance.

    c. Encryption enables data privacy without much compromise in performance.

Answer: C. ESP (Encapsulating Security Payload) provides both integrity and encryption (ensuring the confidentiality of data), whereas AH (Authentication Header) only provides integrity of data. For integrity, the algorithm SHA-1, which uses a 160-bit key value, provides stronger protection than MD5, which uses a 128-bit key value. The 3DES algorithm, for confidentiality, provides the highest security, but carries a huge performance overhead.

You are the domain administrator for Catywhompus. You want to manage the IPSec policies for this computer's domain members, and so you undertake this process:

I   Click Start | Run and type **MMC**. Then click OK.

II   In the MMC snap-in that appears, select Add/Remove Snap-In from the Console menu. Click Add.

III   Select the IP Security Policy Management snap-in and then click Add.

IV   To manage the policies, select Local Computer.

V   Click Finish, then Close, and OK.

2. Will this process enable management of the IPSec policies in your domain?
    a. Yes, all the steps are right.
    b. No, all the steps are wrong.
    c. Most of the steps are right.
    Answer: C. These steps will not satisfy the requirement, since step IV must specify "click Manage Domain Policy For This Computer's Domain," which will enable management of all IPSec policies for any domain members. Clicking on Local Computer will only enable management of the computer on which the present console is running.

The IPSec driver receives the active IP filter list from the IPSec Policy Agent, and then matches every inbound and outbound packet against the filters in the list. When a packet matches a filter, it applies the filter action. Outbound and inbound processing uses the negotiated security association (SA) and keys. If multiple SAs are present, the driver uses the Security Parameters Index (SPI) to match the correct SA with the correct packet.

When an outbound IP packet matches the IP filter list with an action to negotiate security, you expect the following to happen:

I   The IPSec driver queues the packet, then notifies Internet Key Exchange (IKE), which begins security negotiations with the destination IP address of that packet.

II   Once the negotiations have successfully completed, IKE provides the IPSec driver with the parameters for the SA, including the session keys.

III   The IPSec driver secures the queued outbound IP packet and sends it to the network card for transmission.

IV   If the negotiation failed, the IPSec driver tries to renegotiate.

3. You as the domain administrator managing the IPSec policies at XYZ Company, must determine which of the preceding steps is incorrect. (Choose any one.)

   a. Statement I
   b. Statement II
   c. Statement III
   d. Statement IV

   Answer: D. Statement IV is incorrect because if the negotiation for the outbound packet fails, the IPSec driver does not try to renegotiate—it discards the packet.

ABC Company has 2,000 employees located in New York. The company is on a Windows 2000 network, and it values security among its employees, especially among the employees in the finance department. Alice is the system administrator and is configuring the security for all the departments. There is an IPSec policy in place for the Finance department, but she wants to change the current configuration to always enable high-security communication between the employees in the Finance department. Incoming, unsecured communications from other departments must not be blocked, but all outgoing communications and subsequent two-way communications must be secured.

Alice prefers to have total control over the entire configuration, and to satisfy her requirements, she undertakes the following steps:

I   In IP Security Policy Management, right-click the policy that has to be modified, and click Properties.

II   Click the rule that contains the IP filter list to be modified, click Edit, and then click the Filter Action tab.

III   Uncheck the Use Add Wizard check box, and then click Edit to reconfigure a filter action.

IV   Click Permit.

V   Check the Accept Unsecured Communication, But Always Respond Using IPSec check box.

VI   On the Addressing tab, select Destination Address, then highlight a specific IP address.

VII   Select the Session key Perfect Forward Secrecy check box.

VIII On the General tab, type a unique name.

IX   Type in a Description, type a description for this filter.

4. Will Alice achieve highly secure communication within the Finance department with these steps? (Choose one option.)

   a. Highly secure communication is achieved and optimized with these steps.

   b. Highly secure communication will be achieved only if an additional step is included.

   c. Highly secure communication will be a problem until some steps in the solution are configured in the right manner.

   Answer: C. Step IV should not be to click Permit, since high-security will not be requested for and applied to packets which will cause receiving and sending of packets in clear text. To configure high-security (that is, to provide security for packets that match the filter used), the filter action must be to negotiate security from the list of security methods in the Security Method preference. All the other steps are correct and will enable secure communication within and between the Finance department and the others.

ABC insurance company has 12,000 employees and is located at three locations around the country. The various offices are networked with Windows 2000, and the company values security among its employees, especially among members of its legal departments in all locations. Bob is the system administrator at the headquarters and is configuring the security for the legal departments. There is an IPSec policy in place, but he wants to manually edit it to enable authenticated and encrypted communication between the legal departments, a new requirement that was not included earlier. Bob takes the following steps:

I   In IP Security Policy Management, right-click the policy that has to be modified, and then click Properties.

II   Click the rule that contains the IP filter list to be modified, and then click Edit.

III   Click the IP filter and click Edit.

IV   Clear the Use Add Wizard check box, and then click Add.

V   On the Addressing tab, select Source Address followed by Any IP Address.

VI   On the Addressing tab, select Destination Address, and then select a specific IP address.

VII   Select the Mirrored check box.

VIII In the Description field, type a description for this filter.

5. What do you think the result of these steps will be? (Choose one option.)

   a. The proposed solution will enable secure communication between members of the legal departments.

   b. There are some steps in the proposed solution that are configured in the wrong manner, so these steps will not enable secure communication between members of the legal departments.

   c. There are some steps in the proposed solution that are missing, so secure communication between members of the legal departments will not be possible.

   Answer: B. Step III is wrong—there is no IP filter that had been selected earlier in the IP filter list.

You need to edit the existing IPSec policy that enables secure communication between your branch offices interconnected on a Windows 2000 network. You decide to increase the level of security, and the following are the goals you undertake to provide:

- Confidentiality
- Authentication
- Integrity

These are the steps you perform:

I   In IP Security Policy Management, right-click the policy you want to modify, and then click Properties.

II   Click the rule you want to modify, and then click Edit.

III   On the Filter Action tab, click the filter you want to modify, and then click Edit.

IV   Click the Security Method button, and then click Edit.

V   Click High.

6. What do you think the result of these steps will be? (Choose one option.)

   a. The proposed solution will provide confidentiality, authentication, and integrity.

   b. The proposed solution will not provide confidentiality, authentication, and integrity.

   c. The proposed solution will only provide authentication and integrity.

   Answer: A. High (ESP) will use the ESP (Encapsulating Security Payload) protocol to encrypt the data, which provides confidentiality using the 56-bit DES algorithm, 128-bit MD5 for the integrity algorithm, and default key lifetimes. AH (Authentication Header) will only provide authentication and integrity, whereas ESP provides confidentiality, too.

Active Directory Services
(27 Questions)

You are the domain administrator for Catywhompus. Catywhompus is in the process of acquiring an established company that needs to retain its original name.

1. To ensure smooth integration of the two companies, what would you suggest?
   a. Create organizational units.
   b. Create domain trees in the same forest.
   c. Create domain trees in separate forests.

   Answer: B. Creation of domain trees in the same forest will enable both the companies to maintain their original domain names without changing their internal structure. In addition, you can ensure a trusted relationship between the companies to enable smooth interaction between them.

You, as a domain administrator for an international company, are aware of the benefits of Active Directory forests. Forests are typically used if your company has subsidiaries that require separate namespaces, if your company merges with another company, and so on. A forest is a collection of domain trees that also provide benefits to the organization. You have implemented four domain trees in your forest, based on the three locations that your company has offices in—Paris, Milan, and New York.

2. What do you think are the characteristics that are typical of those domain trees in the forest? (Choose all that apply.)
   a. All the domain trees share common schema.
   b. All the domain trees share the global catalog.
   c. All the domain trees in the forest have transitive hierarchical Kerberos trust relationships.
   d. All the domain trees in the forest have one-way hierarchical Kerberos trust relationships.

   Answer: A, B, and C. A set of one or more domain trees that forms a non-contiguous namespace forms a forest. All the domain trees in a forest share a common schema, configuration information, and global catalog, and they trust each other through transitive, hierarchical Kerberos trust relationships.

ABC Company is a retailer of office supplies and has 2,000 employees located in Seattle. The company is on a Windows 2000 network. The company believes in just-in-time inventory and requires tight integration with its suppliers and customers. Bob is the administrator, and he wants to provide the third parties with access to the company's namespace by setting up one-way trusts between the domains.

3. What structure would you prefer with respect to the design of the domain tree structure for this particular purpose?
   a. Create an additional forest.
   b. Add an organizational unit to the existing domain tree.
   c. Create a separate domain.

   Answer: A. To give outsiders access to the company's namespace, it is better to operate with several forests in your namespace. This enables you to carefully assign the access rights, and you can also set up explicit one-way trusts between the domains involved from each forest. This way, you can monitor the interaction.

You are responsible for planning and designing the Active Directory structure for your organization, which is a multinational company. Your company is in the process of partnering with another company that operates an entirely different business, but will have to access your company's network resources (files, folders, printers, applications, etc.). You want to allow the partner company to have access, but you also want to isolate the existing schema, configuration information, and global catalogs from the other company. In addition, you also want to connect the domains via one-way explicit trusts.

4. What do you do? You create an additional:
   a. Domain tree
   b. Forest
   c. Site
   d. Organizational unit

   Answer: B. Creating additional forests will result in isolation of the existing schema, configuration information, and global catalogs, and can enable connection between the domains via one-way explicit trusts.

ABC Company has 20,000 employees located worldwide in New York, London, and Japan. The company is operating on a Windows 2000 network, and the links between the various locations are very slow, and each office has different security requirements. In addition, the organization is decentralized, with each location operating as a separate entity, managing users and resources with completely different sets of administrative personnel. Alice is in charge of designing the Active Directory implementations.

5. For such a situation, which of the following would be ideal?
   a. Multiple domains
   b. Single domain
   c. Single domain with multiple OUs

Answer: A. More than one domain is necessary if an organization is decentralized, because each domain will need to adhere to different policies, and the individual domain administrators will need control of their domains. Multiple domains are also required because each domain has differing security policies and each domain forms a security boundary. A single domain would also entail the need for a lot of bandwidth for replication purposes, and we know the link between the various locations is slow, which would present a problem.

XYZ insurance company is operating on a Windows 2000 network. The company has created an additional forest to interact with its partners who require access to its resources. You are the administrator, and you want to provide the partners with access to the company's namespace. You are aware that they operate on a Windows NT 3.5 network.

6. What kind of a trust would you implement?
   a. Transitive Kerberos trust
   b. Explicit one-way trust
   c. Explicit transitive trust

   Answer: B. Explicit one-way trusts enable domains that are members of Windows NT 3.5 or 4.0 domains to have access to a particular Active Directory domain. The explicit one-way trust relationship limits the scope of authenticated access to the member domain.

You are designing the naming scheme for the domains in a forest that has many domain trees. These domain trees help in separating the various branches of the parent company. While deciding on a naming scheme, you know that you must decide on a name that is easily recognizable and meaningful to your organization.

7. In addition, which of the following are important namespace design factors that would apply to this situation of selecting the names for the branches? (Choose all that apply.)
   a. Name domains on countries
   b. Name domains on departments
   c. Name domains on buildings
   d. Name domains on divisions
   e. Name domains on groups
   f. Name domains on cities

   Answer: A and F. The life of a domain is at least 3–6 years, whereas that is not the case with divisions, departments, and groups, which could be renamed and reorganized many times. A good namespace design should be capable of withstanding company reorganization without the need to restructure the domain hierarchy. A naming strategy based on the other options can result in regular changes to the hierarchy, which will cause difficulty in managing the various domains.

ABC Company is a software company that has sales offices worldwide, and these offices are connected to the main office via a WAN on a Windows 2000 network. The sales offices are franchised to different individuals and organizations. The software development is done in a single location at Houston, Texas. The company operates in a centralized manner and, therefore, does not believe in allowing the various sales offices to have individual control. The sales offices will be child domains of the parent company and will be assigned permissions and rights by the IT department at Houston.

8. What should the basis be for creating the child domains? (Choose all that apply.)
    a. Organization name
    b. Franchise name
    c. Continent name
    d. Country name

    Answer: C and D. The first layer of domains should be relatively stable by design, so you would be better off using continent and country names as domain names. Organization and franchise names may change and, therefore, are not suited as names for an upper layer in the Active Directory domain structure.

Mike is the administrator of company X, which is headquartered in London, but has branch offices in California, Sydney, and Tokyo. He is planning the design and naming of the Active Directory structure. He has designed the first layer of domains on the basis of the countries, and he is now designing the second layer of domains in the domain tree because of the many branch offices that operate independently of the main office. Each office handles multiple projects that need to be incorporated into the design.

9. On what basis should Mike create the namespace or the second layer of domains?
    a. The business units
    b. The location of the branches
    c. The names of the various projects

    Answer: B. The second layer of the domains must be based on the location of the branches because the business units and projects are different at each branch, and they may change often, which will cause restructuring of the entire Active Directory structure.

You are the administrator of a multinational company that operates in five major locations (London, Tokyo, New York, Sydney, and Paris). Each location has four busi-

PART V

ness units (Human Resources, Sales and Marketing, Development and Research, and Accounting). You, as an administrator, are designing the Active Directory structure that will best depict a decentralized management system for this company, keeping in mind that the company ultimately must have centralized control over the operations.

10. Of the following three options, which one would you select?
   a. Use a single domain tree solution.
   b. Use a multiple forest solution.
   c. Use a single forest solution.

   Answer: C. A decentralized management system involves business units of the parent organization that maintain individual control. Therefore, the best solution would be to create domain trees based on the locations in one forest, which will have one schema and configuration structure, and one global catalog, and so on. This will enable centralized control, but also permit decentralized management by delegating authority to the individual locations.

Bob is designing the Active Directory for his company. He is not sure about the restrictions on the naming strategy, especially with regard to the characters that are allowed when naming the domains.

11. What characters are not allowed as a part of the domain name? (Choose all that apply.)
   a. Backslash
   b. A–Z, a–z
   c. Period
   d. 0–9
   e. Hyphen
   f. Underscore

   Answer: A, C, and F. Only alphabet letters A–Z, a–z, numbers 0–9, and the hyphen are allowed as characters in a domain name.

You are the administrator in charge of Catywhompus for network operations in the United States. You decide to design and create various zones based on location.

12. What are the possible reasons for you to make such a decision? (Choose all that apply.)
   a. Keep local DNS information near the region (geographically) to the DNS name that requires this information most often.
   b. For load balancing.
   c. To provide a redundant source for name resolution.
   d. To provide better replication.

Answers: A, B, and C. In Windows 2000, Active Directory domain trees have a contiguous namespace, which can be in one zone, such as individual zones on a per-domain basis. Establishing zones based on the physical structure of the company generally keeps the local DNS information close to the region that requires the DNS name most often. Partitioning of a namespace into multiple zones can also help in load balancing and can eliminate a single point of failure by providing a redundant source for name resolution. However, many zones means increased replication traffic, which may be a disadvantage.

You are a company with three locations in the country, housing a total of 1,000 employees. Each location has four departments: Human Resources, Marketing, Sales, and Engineering.

Required Result You wish to delegate administrative responsibility to the IT departments at the various locations, but retain complete control over the operations at the locations.

Optional Result The engineering department requires full control of its operations.

Solution You create a single domain tree with different OUs for the various locations. You create another level of OUs consisting of the various departments.

13. What do you think of the solution? (Choose one option.)
    a. The solution will satisfy both the required and the optional result.
    b. The solution will satisfy only the required, but not the optional result.
    c. The solution will satisfy only the optional result.
    d. The solution will not satisfy either result.
    Answer: A. By creating a hierarchy of OUs, delegation of administration is easier, yet the central IT department can retain a tight grip on the environment. By assigning control at the OU level, tracking permission assignments is easy.

Alice is the domain administrator of company M. The company is on a Windows 2000 network operating in a mixed mode. The company conducts its operations in the United States only, and is located at various locations in the country. Employees from each location have to access resources at the other locations. The various locations are part of different domains within the same forest. Alice is in the process of creating groups.

Requirement   To assign permissions to various users in the organization to allow access to resources in any domain.

Solutions at Hand

I   Create universal groups.

II   Create global groups.

III   Create domain local groups.

14. Which solution should Alice carry out? (Choose one option.)
    a. Solution I
    b. Solution II
    c. Solution III

    Answer: B. Global groups will need to be created, since the organization is operating in a mixed mode. Universal groups are applicable only to native mode domains, and domain local groups will allow users to access resources only in one domain.

15. In the previous question, if the entire network operated in a native mode, why might it not be feasible to exclusively create universal groups without dealing with the other security groups in the organization? (Choose all that apply.)
    a. Increased bandwidth usage.
    b. The group and its members appear in the GC.
    c. Universal groups cannot be exclusively created—other groups also have to be created.

    Answer: A and **B.** Using universal groups alone may not be feasible because the universal group and all of its members appear in the GC, which causes one change to be replicated to all GCs in the forest and can result in heavy bandwidth usage. Small organizations can use universal groups exclusively and avoid dealing with global and local groups.

Corey is an administrator at Catywhompus, a construction company with 10,000 employees worldwide, specializing in commercial construction. She has designed and created a forest with domain trees based on the office locations (New York, Los Angeles, Chicago, London, Tokyo, and Oakland) and business units (Human Resources, Finance and Accounting, Project Management, Marketing, Construction, Operations). The company has a WAN linking all sites on a Windows 2000 network operating in a mixed mode. She wants to collect users, computers, and other groups into manageable units.

Requirement   Corey wants to assign permissions to enable access to resources (file shares, printers, and so on).

Solution
I   Create security groups.

II   Create distribution groups.

16. Which of the following is correct? (Choose one option.)
   a. Solution I is correct, but II is incorrect.
   b. Solution II is correct, but I is incorrect.
   c. Solution I and II are correct.
   d. Solution I and II are incorrect.

   Answer: A. The permissions are assigned once to the security groups, instead of several times to each individual user. Each account added to a security group receives the rights and permissions defined for that security group (this, of course, is no surprise). Working with security groups instead of with individual users helps simplify network maintenance and administration. Contrast this with how distribution groups work. Distribution groups can only be used as e-mail distribution lists and have no security function. They cannot be used to filter group policy settings.

For security groups operating in a mixed mode:

I   Global groups can contain only user accounts from the same domain.

II   Domain local groups can contain global groups from the same domain and user accounts from any domain.

17. Which of the following is correct? (Choose one option.)
   a. Statement I is right, but II is wrong.
   b. Statement II is right, but I is wrong.
   c. Statements I and II are right.
   d. Statements I and II are wrong.

   Answer: A. For security groups in mixed mode, global groups can contain only user accounts from the same domain. Domain local groups can contain global groups from any domain and user accounts from the same domain.

You have a Business Operations group that consists of Sales, Marketing, and Customer Relations responsibilities. You create these groups, assign appropriate rights to each group, and make each of them group members of the Business Operations group.

PART V

18. Which of the following are correct? (Choose all that apply.)
    a. The groups inherit the rights assigned to the Business Operations group.
    b. The groups inherit the rights assigned to each of the other groups.
    c. The rights assigned to the Business Operations group override the permissions assigned to individual groups.
    d. The rights assigned to the individual groups have precedence over the rights assigned to the Business Operations group.
    Answer: A and **D.** Child groups inherit the rights assigned to the parent group, and the individual rights assigned to the child groups take precedence over the rights assigned to the parent group.

As a domain administrator, you are aware of the limitations of the group policy object (GPO).

19. Which of the following statements are true? (Choose all that apply.)
    a. Multiple sites and OUs may use a single GPO.
    b. GPOs are inherited across domains.
    c. Multiple GPOs may be associated with a single OU.
    d. GPOs are not inherited.
    Answer: A, C, and **D.** GPOs are per domain and cannot be inherited across domains. Multiple GPOs can be associated with a single site, domain, and organizational unit, and vice-versa.

Clara is the domain administrator of Company Y, and while planning the Active Directory for the company's Windows 2000 network, she decides on implementing the Group Policy structure.

20. What are the possible reasons for doing so? (Choose all that apply.)
    a. Automate software installation.
    b. Manage security settings.
    c. Redirect folders to the server.
    d. Implement scripts.
    Answer: A, B, C, and **D.** Group policies can be used to richly configure a user's environment, including selectively assigning and publishing applications to desktop systems, managing security settings to define a security configuration, folder redirection (to redirect to an alternate location any of the special folders that represent the user's desktop), and assigning scripts to run when the computer starts or shuts down, or when users log on or off.

ABC Company has one domain that spans a multisite WAN. This WAN is comprised of one site in Germany and one in New York, each with one domain controller. Directory information must be widely distributed, but this must be balanced with the need to optimize network performance. If directory updates are constantly distributed to all other domain controllers in the domain, they will consume the company's network resources.

21. How does Windows 2000 use sites and replication change control to optimize replication? (Choose all that apply.)
   a. Occasionally re-evaluating which connections are used
   b. Using multiple routes to replicate changes
   c. Replicating all the information on each DC

   Answer: A and **B.** Active Directory uses the most efficient network connections by occasionally re-evaluating which connections are used, and by using multiple routes to replicate changes, it provides fault tolerance. Replication costs are minimized by only replicating changed information and not replicating all the information on each DC.

When a new child domain or the root domain of a new domain tree in an existing forest is created, some roles are automatically assigned to the first domain controller in the new domain.

22. Which of the following are automatically assigned roles? (Choose all that apply.)
   a. Relative Identifier Master
   b. Schema Master
   c. Primary Domain Controller (PDC) Emulator
   d. Domain Naming Master
   e. Infrastructure Master

   Answer: A, C, and **E.** When you create the first domain in a new forest, all of the single operations master roles are automatically assigned to the first domain controller in that domain. However, when you create a new child domain or the root domain of a new domain tree in an existing forest, the first domain controller in the new domain is automatically assigned only the Relative Identifier Master, Primary Domain Controller (PDC) Emulator, and the Infrastructure Master. Since there can be only one Schema Master and one Domain Naming Master in the forest, these roles remain in the first domain created in the forest and are not assigned when a child domain or a new domain tree is created in the forest.

Your organization has multiple sites, and you have designed and created one domain with multiple domain controllers for purposes of fault tolerance. You select two domain controllers that are direct replication partners and are well connected to each other, and you make one of the domain controllers the operations master domain controller and the other the standby operations master domain controller so that the standby operations master domain controller can be used in case of failure of the operations master domain controller. In typical domains, both the Relative Identifier Master and Primary Domain Controller (PDC) Emulator roles are assigned to the operations master domain controller.

In a very large domain, like the one that exists in your organization, you notice that the load on the operations master domain controller requires separating the roles. The following are some of the things that can be done to reduce the peak load on the PDC emulator:

I   Place the RID Master and the PDC emulator roles on separate domain controllers.

II   Assign the Schema Master and the Domain Naming Master roles to different domain controllers.

23. What should you do to reduce the peak load on the PDC emulator?
    a. I and II
    b. Only I
    c. Only II

    Answer: B. In a very large domain, the load on the PDC Emulator can be reduced by placing the RID Master and the PDC Emulator roles on separate domain controllers.

You want to separate the Infrastructure Master role from the operations master, and you decide to separate the Infrastructure Master role to another domain controller in the domain.

24. What are the issues that you must take care of when you assign the Infrastructure Master role?
    a. Assign the Infrastructure Master role to any domain controller in the domain that is not a global catalog.
    b. Assign the Infrastructure Master role to any domain controller in the domain that is a global catalog.
    c. Assign the Infrastructure Master role to any domain controller that is not a global catalog, but that is well connected to a global catalog in the same site.

Answer: C. Unless there is only one domain controller in the domain, the Infrastructure Master role should not be assigned to the domain controller that is hosting the global catalog. If the Infrastructure Master and global catalog are on the same domain controller, the Infrastructure Master will not function. The Infrastructure Master will never find data that is out of date, so it will never replicate any changes to the other domain controllers in the domain. If both the domain controllers in a domain are also hosting the global catalog, all of the domain controllers will have the current data and it does not matter which domain controller holds the Infrastructure Master role.

When designing and implementing the Active Directory structure, you observe that you cannot create objects in Active Directory.

25. What do you think is the cause for this?
    a. The Primary Domain Controller Emulator is not available.
    b. The Infrastructure Master is not available.
    c. A Relative Identifier Master is not available.
    Answer: C. When objects cannot be created in Active Directory, the RID Master is not available, which may be caused by a network connectivity problem. It may also be due to a failure of the computer holding the RID Master role. This problem can be solved by resolving the network connectivity problem or by repairing or replacing the RID Master computer. It may also be necessary to seize the RID Master role.

When designing and implementing the Active Directory structure, you observe that clients that do not have Active Directory client software installed cannot log on to the network.

26. What do you think is the cause for this?
    a. The Primary Domain Controller Emulator is not available.
    b. The Infrastructure Master is not available.
    c. A Relative Identifier Master is not available.
    Answer: A. When clients that do not have Active Directory client software installed cannot log on to the network, the Primary Domain Controller Emulator is not available. This may be caused by a network connectivity problem or it may also be due to a failure of the computer holding the Primary Domain Controller Emulator role. This problem can be solved by resolving the network connectivity problem or by repairing or replacing the Relative Identifier Master computer. Alternatively, it may also be necessary to seize the Relative Identifier Master role.

When designing and implementing the Active Directory structure, you observe that changes to group memberships are not taking effect.

27. What do you think is the cause for this?
    a. The Primary Domain Controller Emulator is not available.
    b. The Infrastructure Master is not available.
    c. A Relative Identifier Master is not available.

    Answer: B. When changes to group memberships are not taking effect, the Infrastructure Master is not available. This may be caused by a network connectivity problem, or it may also be due to a failure of the computer holding the Infrastructure Master role. This problem can be solved by resolving the network connectivity problem or by repairing or replacing the Relative Identifier Master computer. Alternatively, it may also be necessary to seize the Relative Identifier Master role.

MCSE Certification Specifics

This appendix is focused on the MCSE designation itself. Not only are exam-specific objectives listed, but we share several insights about Microsoft's new Windows 2000 MCSE track and what it means to be an MCSE. Let's get started.

Microsoft's New Certification Track

Microsoft has revamped its MCSE program under Windows 2000 to focus on the enterprise. This is a significant change from the MCSE program several years ago, when workgroup servers and Microsoft Mail 3.x were legitimate areas of focus. The new certification track focuses on the enterprise architect as the role model for MCSEs. The enterprise architect will have sufficient technical depth to accomplish assigned tasks, but will also have the vision to plan and design solutions. The enterprise architect may not be the person who implements their own solutions, leaving that to lower-level IT department employees. Contrast this with MCSEs of a product release cycle ago, where a premium was placed on completing tasks.

The MCSE program under Windows 2000 has grown by one more exam, meaning you must now pass seven exams to become certified on the full track. Past MCSE programs required you to pass six exams.

> **NOTE** If you are an existing MCSE under the Windows NT 4.0 track, and you have all of the Windows NT 4.0 core exams (Windows NT Workstation 4.0, Windows NT Server 4.0, Windows NT Server 4.0 in the Enterprise), you can take the 70-240 Microsoft Windows 2000 Exam for MCPs Certified in Microsoft Windows NT 4.0. This comprehensive and accelerated exam replaces the four core Windows 2000 exams and leaves only one elective exam for updating your NT MCSE to the Windows 2000 MCSE.

The Windows 2000 MCSE exams are broken into core exams and elective exams. As you can see in Table B-1, the first four exams are core exams, then there is an unusual core/elective combo level (which the Microsoft Web site for certification and training identifies as "Plus 1"), where you select from one of three exams. Interestingly, the two exams that you don't select at the core/elective combo level are then made available as two of the limited number of true elective exams.

Whew! And you thought life was complicated under the old Windows NT 4.0 MCSE track. The Windows 2000–based MCSE track requires careful study and planning.

Your Commitment to Getting Certified

It has been our experience as MCT instructors, MCSE title holders, and technology consultants that the certification path is a one- to two-year journey with emotional, physical, and mental peaks and valleys. Earning the Windows 2000 MCSE requires a significant commitment of time and energy on behalf of the MCSE candidate. Loved ones suffer from the time taken away from family. Employers suffer from having the MCSE unavailable for work while attending classes. The most comparable experience we can offer is that obtaining the Windows 2000 MCSE is akin to earning a Masters degree. And regrettably, just as you have some college dropouts, you will also see the trail of certification success littered with MCSE candidates who fell short on the climb.

Role of Real-World Experience

After earning the Windows 2000 MCSE, you could, of course, argue that the journey has only started. It is now time to back that paper certificate with bona fide real-world work experience and know-how. The Windows 2000 MCSE track, more than any other MCSE program promoted by Microsoft, emphasizes real-world experience over strict academics. It is in the real world, not the testing booth, where you will truly make your mark as a superior Windows 2000 MCSE. Don't forget that for a single moment.

Table B-1   Windows 2000 MCSE Track

Exam	Exam Type
Exam 70-210: Installing, Configuring, and Administering Microsoft Windows 2000 Professional	Core—Required
Exam 70-215: Installing, Configuring, and Administering Microsoft Windows 2000 Server	Core—Required
Exam 70-216: Implementing and Administering a Microsoft Windows 2000 Network Infrastructure	Core—Required
Exam 70-217: Implementing and Administering a Microsoft Windows 2000 Directory Services Infrastructure	Core—Required
Exam 70-219: Designing a Microsoft Windows 2000 Directory Services Infrastructure	Plus-1 Core/Elective level (pick one from this classification level)
Exam 70-220: Designing Security for a Microsoft Windows 2000 Network	Plus-1 Core/Elective level (pick one from this classification level)
Exam 70-221: Designing a Microsoft Windows 2000 Network Infrastructure	Plus-1 Core/Elective level (pick one from this classification level)
Exam 70-219: Designing a Microsoft Windows 2000 Directory Services Infrastructure	Elective exams (pick two elective exams)
Exam 70-220: Designing Security for a Microsoft Windows 2000 Network	Elective exams (pick two elective exams)
Exam 70-221: Designing a Microsoft Windows 2000 Network Infrastructure	Elective exams (pick two elective exams)
Exam 70-222: Migrating from Microsoft Windows NT 4.0 to Microsoft Windows 2000	Elective exams (pick two elective exams)
Exam 70-223: Installing, Configuring, and Administering Microsoft Clustering Services by Using Microsoft Windows 2000 Advanced Server	Elective exams (pick two elective exams)
Exam 70-225: Designing and Deploying a Messaging Infrastructure with Microsoft Exchange 2000 Server	Elective exams (pick two elective exams)

continued

PART V

Table B-1 Windows 2000 MCSE Track (*continued*)

Exam	Exam Type
Other Windows NT Server 4.0-era electives (Microsoft Exchange, SNA Server, Proxy Server, IIS, SQL Server, etc.)	As of late 2000, these elective exams are accepted and count toward elective credit on the Windows 2000 MCSE track. This is expected to change as these exams are retired. Given the dynamic nature of this matter, you are advised to consult two Web sites for the latest information: www.microsoft.com/trainingandservices and www.mcpmag.com.

Opportunities for MCSEs

Tremendous opportunities exist today for MCSEs, despite the large numbers of MCSE title holders (over 330,000 as of this writing). These are good days in MCSE-land, and as the old saying goes, "you got to shoot while the ducks are flying." Let us be the first and not last to reiterate that the ducks are truly flying in the MCSE community. It has been our experience that the following general opportunities exist for MCSEs, although everyone is different and may not fit into these three categories:

- **In-house positions** You may be a salaried network administrator, engineer, or enterprise architect. Needless to say, the hours are long, but the pay is good. In-house positions are typically more secure than being self-employed and typically offer the opportunity to master one system well. In-house positions vary from working full-time for medium-sized companies, up to the largest enterprises. In a medium-sized organization, the in-house role for the MCSE tends to be that of butcher, baker, and candlestick maker, where the duties are varied. That is because, in smaller organizations, the MCSE may well be the lone technology resource. At the enterprise level, you are likely a member of a technology team and, while your days are filled and busy, your role is focused on one or two specific areas.

- **Consultant** Earning the Windows 2000 MCSE and some bona fide work experience allows you to pursue a lucrative career as an MCSE consultant. Perhaps you will serve a portfolio of clients including small, medium, and large businesses. Or perhaps you'll act in a contractor capacity, serving one large enterprise client for several months straight. A couple of key observations about consulting are that you typically enjoy more variety than in-house employees, given the different clients you serve. This variety tends to increase your skill set more rapidly than other MCSE career tracks because you are seeing more systems at a given time, and thus, more technology problems. Those of us who have made MCSE consulting a career track often lament that we're only brought in to solve problems, and that's not too far from the truth. And while MCSE consulting is certainly fun, exciting, and financially rewarding, it has downsides that drive technically proficient MCSE titleholders into in-house staff positions.

The negatives of MCSE consulting include communicating, marketing, and management. In the delivery of professional services, clients are asking for a relationship, not just a break-fix service call. This relationship should be communicative and consultative. A great MCSE consultant may not be the bright bulb technically (although more than sufficient technical skills are required), but this individual will be, shall we say, well spoken. Exceptional oral and written communication skills are mandatory. Second is the matter of marketing. MCSE consultants are truly surprised at how much time must be spent marketing to develop new business. Just as political candidates, who run for office to debate the issues of the day, end up in a basement dialing-for-dollars for hours, MCSE consultants spend a lot of time dialing for dollars! Lastly, once you get the work and do the work as an MCSE consultant, you've got to manage the work. Management functions include project management, site reports, billings, and the dreaded collections process. But all in all, MCSE consulting represents a great career opportunity for MCSE consultants.

- **Trainer** Microsoft Certified Trainers (MCTs) are instructors who deliver Microsoft-approved courses to help MCSE candidates earn their certification title. It's likely you've taken a certification course delivered by an MCT in your MCSE candidacy (most MCSE candidates take one or more classroom-based MCSE courses). One requirement for becoming an MCT is that you hold the MCSE title, so this is an employment avenue for you to consider once you've earned your Windows 2000 MCSE. And the pay isn't bad either! The nice thing about teaching is that, when the class ends Friday at 5:00 P.M., that is typically the end of the trainer's commitment. This is a nice way of saying "no pager calls over the weekend" (the bane of existence for many MCSE professionals).

Compensation

Ah, the money issue. Many MCSEs are attracted to the certification path by the *Microsoft Certified Professional Magazine* annual salary survey, which has pegged annual MCSE salaries in the mid- to high-$60,000 range for the past several years (late 1990s/early

21st century). Excerpts of the most recent salary survey (August 2000) are presented here courtesy and permission of *Microsoft Certified Professional Magazine*. In fact, to read the entire salary survey (with all of its colorful charts), which we highly recommend, visit www.mcpmag.com.

Smart Money! 5th Annual Salary Survey

In *MCP Magazine*'s U.S. Salary Survey, everyone's a winner this year—except perhaps the hiring managers who must deal with a rising tide of IT salaries. Despite a doubling in the number of MCSEs in the past year and a huge increase in the numbers of MCPs overall, our fifth annual salary survey shows compensation holding strong for all Microsoft Certified Professionals. In line with general increases in the IT industry driven by strong demand, salaries for MCSEs, for example, are up four percent, from a base salary last year of $65,100, to this year's $67,800.

Almost half of respondents reported no change in income because of certification, but a fifth reported significant jumps. For example, nearly a third of MCTs reported increases of over 25 percent as a result of certification. The MCSE+Internet title also paid off—25 percent of recipients of that certification reported a pay jump of over 25 percent.

Certification appears to boost salary approximately 4 percent from a non-certified IT worker to one holding the entry-level Microsoft title of MCP. (For comparison purposes, we included in the survey a group of non-certified technical professionals working toward their first Microsoft certification.)

The compensation picture is considerably different, though, for someone just entering the IT field. Those with a year or less of experience, as 23 percent of our respondents reported, and who have passed a single Microsoft exam, and thus hold the entry-level Microsoft Certified Professional title, reported an average base salary of $45,800. Experience, as always, is the key differentiator in salary, followed by area of the country and job function. Other factors, including age and gender, also play into the salary equation.

The Windows 2000 Price Tag

Our hot spot for salaries this year is Microsoft Certified Systems Engineers working with Windows 2000. When we collected our survey results in April, Win2K had only recently shipped. We asked MCSEs to indicate whether they had started working with

continued

the new OS or not, and whether they planned to get certified on it this year. (All MCSEs must re-certify on Windows 2000 by the end of 2001. We wanted to measure the early adopters.) Those already focusing on Win2K and planning to certify early are earning somewhat more than MCSEs working with NT 4.0. But it's too soon to conclude that Win2K work pays more than expertise with NT 4.0. In another year, given the same pattern, we might be able to conclude that; but for now, the reason is probably this: More experienced (and thus higher paid) MCSEs are assigned the choicest and most difficult projects. High on the list is working with any new OS or software, hence the salary difference.

The Value of Experience

As always, our survey emphasizes the tight relationship between pay and time on the job. It also highlights how quickly the certification program has grown. Respondents, who represent a statistical sampling of all MCPs in the U.S., have an average of 5.5 years of experience—down from 6.6 years in 1999. In particular, average experience among those holding the MCSE title has dropped almost a full year, from 6.8 to 5.9. Last year, notably, we saw a surprising rise in average experience among MCSEs and speculated that the program might be attracting more experienced IT workers expanding on Novell and Unix-centered skill sets. This year, it appears that the huge influx of newcomers into the certification program is pulling down the average. For example, MCSEs have grown from around 140,000 worldwide when we conducted our survey last spring, to over 260,000 today. Microsoft's program overall includes at least 800,000 certified individuals worldwide, up from about 500,000 a year ago.

Internal vs. External

We consistently found a big difference in salary between those who work in corporate IT/IS supplying internal services to other employees and those who primarily supply external services (working for solution providers, value-added retailers, and systems integration companies). IT professionals supplying external services averaged $73,000 in base salary, 20 percent above the $60,600 of those who supply services primarily to corporate IT departments. Part of the reason may be that companies tend to use more experienced people for outside assignments. Also, working with outside clients may demand more skills and expertise than working with internal employees.

Also, our survey showed that companies supplying external services tend to have a higher percentage of IT workers with expensive talents, including security, Unix, and programming skills.

continued

Bonuses were also higher for those at external service firms, averaging $5,700 a year vs. $4,500 for those supplying internal services.

Finally, our survey shows that those working with Windows 2000 now, and planning to certify this year, are making more than those who aren't. For now, we conclude that it's because the most experienced people are getting assigned to Win2K rollouts. But some analysts have predicted that Win2K skills will be in huge demand if companies deploy the new OS at the predicted rates. Add to that Microsoft's attempts to raise the MCSE bar for Win2K and you can be assured that Windows 2000 skills will be a valuable rarity, at least for a while.

Linda L. Briggs, Editor-in-Chief
Microsoft Certified Professional Magazine

TIP   To read the entire *MCP Magazine* Salary Survey and view the charts that accompany this story, visit www.mcpmag.com.

Ongoing Certification Requirements

Don't underestimate the role of maintaining the MCSE certification. Our certification dates back to Windows NT Server 3.5*x*, and we can attest that Microsoft's certification cycle demands you re-certify every 24 months or so. In many cases, such a re-certification may only require taking and passing one exam. This is most often the case when an elective exam has been retired and no longer counts toward your overall MCSE certification title. We've been the victim of the individual certification upgrade exams for BackOffice applications, such as SQL Server.

The other type of ongoing re-certification requirement, one that occurs less frequently, is when the underlying operating system is significantly upgraded. We have both witnessed and participated in this certification upgrade cycle when Windows NT 3.*x* became Windows NT 4.*x* and again when Windows NT 4.*x* became Windows 2000. This type of certification requirement occurs every three to five years, in our estimation.

It has been our experience that wholesale changes to the MCSE program will also determine how often you have to take more certification exams. For example, between the Windows NT 4 era and Windows 2000 era, the baseline MCSE increased from six exams to seven exams (assuming you enjoyed no test exemptions). And periodically, Microsoft will announce more certification categories, such as the "plus Internet" (+Internet) designation. These are premium designations above and beyond the baseline MCSE title that will require you to take more exams initially and perhaps upgrade more often.

 NOTE An interesting fact of life that we have observed as MCSEs who hold other vendor certifications is the "harder they come, the harder they fall" theory. That is, if you want to be an overachiever in the certification realm, not only do you have to take more exams on the way up the certification ladder, but you're also subject to far more re-certification requirements. A case in point is that the Novell CNE program had a major re-certification requirement in mid-2000. That was immediately followed by the MCSE re-certification requirements that really started in mid-2000 and will be enforced by the end of 2001.

Life as an MCSE Professional

You're working hard to complete your Windows 2000 MCSE, in part by reading and studying with this book. So what type of life awaits you afterwards? We have four sage observations from the field to share with you.

Work

It has been our experience that most MCSE candidates who are successful in completing the Windows 2000 track are already employed in the technology industry. For these people, life will change only slightly. They will still get up in the morning and go to work. These individuals might enjoy a pay raise, new job title, or even land a new job as a result of their Windows 2000 MCSE title.

Others use the MCSE track to get a job in the technology field. These are the career changers who will see their lives dramatically impacted by their MCSE title. Perhaps they will earn more pay than before. Perhaps they'll work harder in a new technology job than they have previously in other jobs. Work awaits you, no matter who you are.

Continuing Education

Many MCSEs, after earning the certification title, are "turned on" to go learn more. This might include another vendor's certification, such as those offered by Cisco. It may well be that the MCSE will go to the local college to take classes in project management, general management, marketing, or accounting. As a professional, which MCSE title holders clearly are, it's paramount and in your best interest to continue your studies and be a life learner. Not only will you perform better in your chosen field, but having more information and knowledge is the fast track to the top as a knowledge worker.

Conferences

It is likely you already know that many professions have trade groups and hold conferences that benefit their members. In the United States, doctors belong to the American Medical Association, a trade group that hosts many conferences. Lawyers belong to the American Bar Association and attend conferences periodically. While there is no governing body for MCSEs like that for lawyers and doctors, there are conferences to attend. First and foremost would be the TechMentor conference sponsored by *Microsoft Certified Professional Magazine* (www.mcpmag.com). This is *the* convention for MCSEs and is held semi-annually. It rotates between major U.S. cities, and there are rumors that this conference might be held at international sites in the future.

User Groups

Don't overlook your local user group as an outlet for your professional activities. All successful professionals know that you have to circulate in your peer group to make good things happen in your career. You can find computer user groups by asking at local computer resellers in your area. We belong to two user groups: BackOffice Professionals Association (www.bopa.org) and the West Sound Technology Professionals Association (www.wstpa.org). You should join a couple yourself.

Certification Exam Objectives

Finally, to arm you for MCSE certification success, we present the following Windows 2000 MCSE exam objectives. Here, you will find the exam objectives for the four core exams and the three designing exams discussed in this book (70-219, 70-220, 70-221). Carefully review these objectives so you can both manage your time efficiently and manage your expectations. By efficient time management, we mean that you should minimize the time you spend studying non-certification topics during your push to earn the Windows 2000 MCSE title. The exam objectives help keep you focused. By expectation management, we mean that you can look over these exam objectives and be neither surprised nor disappointed on an exam by a topic that was or was not covered.

Exam 70-210: Installing, Configuring, and Administering Microsoft Windows 2000 Professional

Candidates for this exam operate in medium to very large computing environments that use Windows 2000 Professional as a desktop operating system. They have a minimum of one year's experience implementing and administering any desktop operating system in a network environment.

Installing Windows 2000 Professional

- Perform an attended installation of Windows 2000 Professional.
- Perform an unattended installation of Windows 2000 Professional.
  - Install Windows 2000 Professional by using Windows 2000 Server Remote Installation Services (RIS).
  - Install Windows 2000 Professional by using the System Preparation Tool.
  - Create unattended answer files by using Setup Manager to automate the installation of Windows 2000 Professional.
- Upgrade from a previous version of Windows to Windows 2000 Professional.
  - Apply update packs to installed software applications.
  - Prepare a computer to meet upgrade requirements.
- Deploy service packs.
- Troubleshoot failed installations.

Implementing and Conducting Administration of Resources

- Monitor, manage, and troubleshoot access to files and folders.
  - Configure, manage, and troubleshoot file compression.
  - Control access to files and folders by using permissions.
  - Optimize access to files and folders.
- Manage and troubleshoot access to shared folders.
  - Create and remove shared folders.
  - Control access to shared folders by using permissions.
  - Manage and troubleshoot Web server resources.

- Connect to local and network print devices.

  - Manage printers and print jobs.

  - Control access to printers by using permissions.

  - Connect to an Internet printer.

  - Connect to a local print device.

- Configure and manage file systems.

  - Convert from one file system to another file system.

  - Configure file systems by using NTFS, FAT32, or FAT.

Implementing, Managing, and Troubleshooting Hardware Devices and Drivers

- Implement, manage, and troubleshoot disk devices.

  - Install, configure, and manage DVD and CD-ROM devices.

  - Monitor and configure disks.

  - Monitor, configure, and troubleshoot volumes.

  - Monitor and configure removable media, such as tape devices.

- Implement, manage, and troubleshoot display devices.

  - Configure multiple-display support.

  - Install, configure, and troubleshoot a video adapter.

- Implement, manage, and troubleshoot mobile computer hardware.

  - Configure Advanced Power Management (APM).

  - Configure and manage card services.

- Implement, manage, and troubleshoot input and output (I/O) devices.

  - Monitor, configure, and troubleshoot I/O devices, such as printers, scanners, multimedia devices, mice, keyboards, and smart-card readers.

  - Monitor, configure, and troubleshoot multimedia hardware, such as cameras.

  - Install, configure, and manage modems.

  - Install, configure, and manage Infrared Data Association (IrDA) devices.

  - Install, configure, and manage wireless devices.

  - Install, configure, and manage USB devices.

- Update drivers.

- Monitor and configure multiple processing units.

- Install, configure, and troubleshoot network adapters.

Monitoring and Optimizing System Performance and Reliability

- Manage and troubleshoot driver signing.

- Configure, manage, and troubleshoot the Task Scheduler.

- Manage and troubleshoot the use and synchronization of offline files.

- Optimize and troubleshoot performance of the Windows 2000 Professional desktop.

  - Optimize and troubleshoot memory performance.

  - Optimize and troubleshoot processor utilization.

  - Optimize and troubleshoot disk performance.

  - Optimize and troubleshoot network performance.

  - Optimize and troubleshoot application performance.

- Manage hardware profiles.

- Recover systems and user data.

  - Recover systems and user data by using Windows Backup.

  - Troubleshoot system restoration by using Safe Mode.

  - Recover systems and user data by using the Recovery Console.

Configuring and Troubleshooting the Desktop Environment

- Configure and manage user profiles.

- Configure support for multiple languages or multiple locations.

  - Enable multiple-language support.

  - Configure multiple-language support for users.

  - Configure local settings.

  - Configure Windows 2000 Professional for multiple locations.

- Install applications by using Windows Installer packages.

- Configure and troubleshoot desktop settings.

- Configure and troubleshoot fax support.

- Configure and troubleshoot accessibility services.

Implementing, Managing, and Troubleshooting Network Protocols and Services

- Configure and troubleshoot the TCP/IP protocol.

- Connect to computers by using dial-up networking.

  - Connect to computers by using a virtual private network (VPN) connection.

  - Create a dial-up connection to connect to a remote-access server.

  - Connect to the Internet by using dial-up networking.

  - Configure and troubleshoot Internet Connection Sharing.

- Connect to shared resources on a Microsoft network.

Implementing, Monitoring, and Troubleshooting Security

- Encrypt data on a hard disk by using Encrypting File System (EFS).

- Implement, configure, manage, and troubleshoot local Group Policy.

- Implement, configure, manage, and troubleshoot local user accounts.

  - Implement, configure, manage, and troubleshoot auditing.

  - Implement, configure, manage, and troubleshoot account settings.

  - Implement, configure, manage, and troubleshoot account policy.

  - Create and manage local users and groups.

  - Implement, configure, manage, and troubleshoot user rights.

- Implement, configure, manage, and troubleshoot local user authentication.

  - Configure and troubleshoot local user accounts.

  - Configure and troubleshoot domain user accounts.

- Implement, configure, manage, and troubleshoot a security configuration.

Exam 70-215: Installing, Configuring, and Administering Microsoft Windows 2000 Server

Candidates for this exam operate in medium to very large computing environments that use the Windows 2000 Server operating system. They have a minimum of one year's experience implementing and administering network operating systems in environments that have the following characteristics:

- Supported users range from 200–26,000+.

- Physical locations range from 5–150+.

- Typical network services and applications include file and print, database, messaging, proxy server or firewall, dial-in server, desktop management, and Web hosting.

- Connectivity needs include connecting individual offices and users at remote locations to the corporate network and connecting corporate networks to the Internet.

Installing Windows 2000 Server

- Perform an attended installation of Windows 2000 Server.

- Perform an unattended installation of Windows 2000 Server.

  - Create unattended answer files by using Setup Manager to automate the installation of Windows 2000 Server.

  - Create and configure automated methods for installation of Windows 2000.

- Upgrade a server from Microsoft Windows NT 4.0.

- Deploy service packs.

- Troubleshoot failed installations.

Installing, Configuring, and Troubleshooting Access to Resources

- Install and configure network services for interoperability.

- Monitor, configure, troubleshoot, and control access to printers.

- Monitor, configure, troubleshoot, and control access to files, folders, and shared folders.

  - Configure, manage, and troubleshoot a stand-alone distributed file system (DFS).

- Configure, manage, and troubleshoot a domain-based distributed file system (DFS).

- Monitor, configure, troubleshoot, and control local security on files and folders.

- Monitor, configure, troubleshoot, and control access to files and folders in a shared folder.

- Monitor, configure, troubleshoot, and control access to files and folders via Web services.

- Monitor, configure, troubleshoot, and control access to Web sites.

Configuring and Troubleshooting Hardware Devices and Drivers

- Configure hardware devices.

- Configure driver signing options.

- Update device drivers.

- Troubleshoot problems with hardware.

Managing, Monitoring, and Optimizing System Performance, Reliability, and Availability

- Monitor and optimize usage of system resources.

- Manage processes.

  - Set priorities and start and stop processes.

- Optimize disk performance.

- Manage and optimize availability of system state data and user data.

- Recover systems and user data.

  - Recover systems and user data by using Windows Backup.

  - Troubleshoot system restoration by using Safe Mode.

  - Recover systems and user data by using the Recovery Console.

Managing, Configuring, and Troubleshooting Storage Use

- Configure and manage user profiles.

- Monitor, configure, and troubleshoot disks and volumes.

- Configure data compression.

- Monitor and configure disk quotas.

- Recover from disk failures.

Configuring and Troubleshooting Windows 2000 Network Connections

- Install, configure, and troubleshoot shared access.

- Install, configure, and troubleshoot a virtual private network (VPN).

- Install, configure, and troubleshoot network protocols.

- Install and configure network services.

- Configure, monitor, and troubleshoot remote access.
  - Configure inbound connections.
  - Create a remote access policy.
  - Configure a remote access profile.

- Install, configure, monitor, and troubleshoot Terminal Services.
  - Remotely administer servers by using Terminal Services.
  - Configure Terminal Services for application sharing.
  - Configure applications for use with Terminal Services.

- Configure the properties of a connection.

- Install, configure, and troubleshoot network adapters and drivers.

Implementing, Monitoring, and Troubleshooting Security

- Encrypt data on a hard disk by using Encrypting File System (EFS).

- Implement, configure, manage, and troubleshoot policies in a Windows 2000 environment.

PART V

- Implement, configure, manage, and troubleshoot Local Policy in a Windows 2000 environment.

- Implement, configure, manage, and troubleshoot System Policy in a Windows 2000 environment.

- Implement, configure, manage, and troubleshoot auditing.

- Implement, configure, manage, and troubleshoot local accounts.

- Implement, configure, manage, and troubleshoot Account Policy.

- Implement, configure, manage, and troubleshoot security by using the Security Configuration Tool Set.

Exam 70-216: Implementing and Administering a Microsoft Windows 2000 Network Infrastructure

This certification exam measures your ability to install, manage, monitor, configure, and troubleshoot DNS, DHCP, Remote Access, Network Protocols, IP Routing, and WINS in a Windows 2000 network infrastructure. In addition, this test measures the skills required to manage, monitor, and troubleshoot Network Address Translation and Certificate Services.

Installing, Configuring, Managing, Monitoring, and Troubleshooting DNS in a Windows 2000 Network Infrastructure

- Install, configure, and troubleshoot DNS.
  - Install the DNS Server service.
  - Configure a root name server.
  - Configure zones.
  - Configure a caching-only server.
  - Configure a DNS client.
  - Configure zones for dynamic updates.
  - Test the DNS Server service.
  - Implement a delegated zone for DNS.
  - Manually create DNS resource records.
- Manage and monitor DNS.

Installing, Configuring, Managing, Monitoring, and Troubleshooting DHCP in a Windows 2000 Network Infrastructure

- Install, configure, and troubleshoot DHCP.
  - Install the DHCP Server service.
  - Create and manage DHCP scopes, superscopes, and multicast scopes.
  - Configure DHCP for DNS integration.
  - Authorize a DHCP server in Active Directory.
- Manage and monitor DHCP.

Configuring, Managing, Monitoring, and Troubleshooting Remote Access in a Windows 2000 Network Infrastructure

- Configure and troubleshoot remote access.
  - Configure inbound connections.
  - Create a remote-access policy.
  - Configure a remote-access profile.
  - Configure a virtual private network (VPN).
  - Configure multilink connections.
  - Configure Routing and Remote Access for DHCP Integration.
- Manage and monitor remote access.
- Configure remote-access security.
  - Configure authentication protocols.
  - Configure encryption protocols.
  - Create a remote-access policy.

Installing, Configuring, Managing, Monitoring, and Troubleshooting Network Protocols in a Windows 2000 Network Infrastructure

- Install, configure, and troubleshoot network protocols.
  - Install and configure TCP/IP.

PART V

- Install the NWLink protocol.
- Configure network bindings.
- Configure TCP/IP packet filters.
- Configure and troubleshoot network protocol security.
- Manage and monitor network traffic.
- Configure and troubleshoot IPSec.
  - Enable IPSec.
  - Configure IPSec for transport mode.
  - Configure IPSec for tunnel mode.
  - Customize IPSec policies and rules.
  - Manage and monitor IPSec.

Installing, Configuring, Managing, Monitoring, and Troubleshooting WINS in a Windows 2000 Network Infrastructure

- Install, configure, and troubleshoot WINS.
- Configure WINS replication.
- Configure NetBIOS name resolution.
- Manage and monitor WINS.

Installing, Configuring, Managing, Monitoring, and Troubleshooting IP Routing in a Windows 2000 Network Infrastructure

- Install, configure, and troubleshoot IP routing protocols.
  - Update a Windows 2000–based routing table by means of static routes.
  - Implement Demand-Dial Routing.
- Manage and monitor IP routing.
  - Manage and monitor border routing.
  - Manage and monitor internal routing.
  - Manage and monitor IP routing protocols.

Installing, Configuring, and Troubleshooting Network Address Translation (NAT)

- Install Internet Connection Sharing.

- Install NAT.

- Configure NAT properties.

- Configure NAT interfaces.

Installing, Configuring, Managing, Monitoring, and Troubleshooting Certificate Services

- Install and configure Certificate Authority (CA).

- Create certificates.

- Issue certificates.

- Revoke certificates.

- Remove the Encrypting File System (EFS) recovery keys.

Exam 70-217: Implementing and Administering a Microsoft Windows 2000 Directory Services Infrastructure

This certification exam measures your ability to install, configure, and troubleshoot the Windows 2000 Active Directory components, DNS for Active Directory, and Active Directory security solutions. In addition, this test measures the skills required to manage, monitor, and optimize the desktop environment by using Group Policy.

Installing, Configuring, and Troubleshooting Active Directory

- Install, configure, and troubleshoot the components of Active Directory.

  - Install Active Directory.

  - Create sites.

  - Create subnets.

  - Create site links.

  - Create site-link bridges.

- Create connection objects.
- Create global catalog servers.
- Move server objects between sites.
- Transfer operations master roles.
- Verify Active Directory installation.
  - Implement an organizational unit (OU) structure.
- Back up and restore Active Directory.
- Perform an authoritative restore of Active Directory.
- Recover from a system failure.

Installing, Configuring, Managing, Monitoring, and Troubleshooting DNS for Active Directory

- Install, configure, and troubleshoot DNS for Active Directory.
  - Integrate an Active Directory DNS with a non-Active Directory DNS.
  - Configure zones for dynamic updates.
- Manage, monitor, and troubleshoot DNS.
- Manage replication of DNS data.

Installing, Configuring, Managing, Monitoring, Optimizing, and Troubleshooting Change and Configuration Management

- Implement and troubleshoot Group Policy.
  - Create a group policy object (GPO).
  - Link an existing GPO.
  - Delegate administrative control of Group Policy.
  - Modify Group Policy inheritance.
  - Filter Group Policy settings by associating security groups to GPOs.
  - Modify Group Policy.
- Manage and troubleshoot user environments by using Group Policy.
  - Control user environments by using Administrative Templates.
  - Assign script policies to users and computers.

- Manage and troubleshoot software by using Group Policy.
  - Deploy software by using Group Policy.
  - Maintain software by using Group Policy.
  - Configure deployment options.
  - Troubleshoot common problems that occur during software deployment.
- Manage network configuration by using Group Policy.
- Deploy Windows 2000 by using Remote Installation Services (RIS).
  - Install an image on a RIS client computer.
  - Create a RIS boot disk.
  - Configure remote installation options.
  - Troubleshoot RIS problems.
  - Manage images for performing remote installations.
- Configure RIS security.
  - Authorize a RIS server.
  - Grant computer-account creation rights.
  - Pre-stage RIS client computers for added security and load balancing.

Managing, Monitoring, and Optimizing the Components of Active Directory

- Manage Active Directory objects.
  - Move Active Directory objects.
  - Publish resources in Active Directory.
  - Locate objects in Active Directory.
  - Create and manage accounts manually or by scripting.
  - Control access to Active Directory objects.
  - Delegate administrative control of objects in Active Directory.
- Manage Active Directory performance.
  - Monitor, maintain, and troubleshoot domain controller performance.
  - Monitor, maintain, and troubleshoot Active Directory components.
- Manage and troubleshoot Active Directory replication.

- Manage intersite replication.

- Manage intrasite replication.

Configuring, Managing, Monitoring, and Troubleshooting Active Directory Security Solutions

- Configure and troubleshoot security in a directory services infrastructure.

  - Apply security policies by using Group Policy.

  - Create, analyze, and modify security configurations by using Security Configuration and Analysis and Security Templates.

  - Implement an audit policy.

- Monitor and analyze security events.

Exam 70-219: Designing a Microsoft Windows 2000 Directory Services Infrastructure

This certification exam measures your ability to analyze the business requirements and design a directory services architecture, including:

- Unified directory services, such as Active Directory and Windows NT domains.

- Connectivity between and within systems, system components, and applications.

- Data replication, such as directory replication and database replication.

In addition, the test measures the skills required to analyze the business requirements for desktop management and to design a solution for desktop management that meets business requirements.

Analyzing Business Requirements

- Analyze the existing and planned business models.

  - Analyze the company model and the geographical scope. Models include regional, national, international, subsidiary, and branch offices.

  - Analyze company processes. Processes include information flow, communication flow, service and product life cycles, and decision-making.

- Analyze the existing and planned organizational structures. Considerations include management model, company organization, vendor, partner, and customer relationships, and acquisition plans.
- Analyze factors that influence company strategies.
  - Identify company priorities.
  - Identify the projected growth and growth strategy.
  - Identify relevant laws and regulations.
  - Identify the company's tolerance for risk.
  - Identify the total cost of operations.
- Analyze the structure of IT management. Considerations include type of administration, such as centralized or decentralized, funding model, outsourcing, decision-making process, and change-management process.

Analyzing Technical Requirements

- Evaluate the company's existing and planned technical environment.
  - Analyze company size and user and resource distribution.
  - Assess the available connectivity between the geographic location of work sites and remote sites.
  - Assess the net available bandwidth.
  - Analyze performance requirements.
  - Analyze data- and system-access patterns.
  - Analyze network roles and responsibilities.
  - Analyze security considerations.
- Analyze the impact of Active Directory on the existing and planned technical environment.
  - Assess existing systems and applications.
  - Identify existing and planned upgrades and rollouts.
  - Analyze technical support structure.
  - Analyze existing and planned network and systems management.
- Analyze the business requirements for client computer desktop management.
  - Analyze end-user work needs.

PART V

- Identify technical support needs for end users.
- Establish the required client computer environment.

Designing a Directory Services Architecture

- Design an Active Directory forest and domain structure.
  - Design a forest and schema structure.
  - Design a domain structure.
  - Analyze and optimize trust relationships.
- Design an Active Directory naming strategy.
  - Establish the scope of the Active Directory.
  - Design the namespace.
  - Plan DNS strategy.
- Design and plan the structure of organizational units (OUs). Considerations include administration control, existing resource domains, administrative policy, and geographic and company structure.
  - Develop an OU delegation plan.
  - Plan Group Policy object management.
  - Plan policy management for client computers.
- Plan for the coexistence of Active Directory and other directory services.
- Design an Active Directory site topology.
- Design a replication strategy.
- Define site boundaries.
- Design a schema-modification policy.
- Design an Active Directory implementation plan.

Designing Service Locations

- Design the placement of operations masters.
  - Considerations include performance, fault tolerance, functionality, and manageability.
- Design the placement of global catalog servers.

- Considerations include performance, fault tolerance, functionality, and manageability.

- Design the placement of domain controllers.

  - Considerations include performance, fault tolerance, functionality, and manageability.

- Design the placement of DNS servers.

  - Considerations include performance, fault tolerance, functionality, and manageability.

  - Plan for interoperability with the existing DNS.

Exam 70-220: Designing Security for a Microsoft Windows 2000 Network

This certification exam tests the skills required to analyze the business requirements for security and to design a security solution that meets business requirements. Security includes:

- Controlling access to resources
- Auditing access to resources
- Authentication
- Encryption

Analyzing Business Requirements

- Analyze the existing and planned business models.

  - Analyze the company model and the geographical scope. Models include regional, national, international, subsidiary, and branch offices.

  - Analyze company processes. Processes include information flow, communication flow, service and product life cycles, and decision-making.

- Analyze the existing and planned organizational structures. Considerations include management model, company organization, vendor, partner, and customer relationships, and acquisition plans.

- Analyze factors that influence company strategies.

  - Identify company priorities.

  - Identify the projected growth and growth strategy.

- Identify relevant laws and regulations.

- Identify the company's tolerance for risk.

- Identify the total cost of operations.

- Analyze business and security requirements for the end user.

- Analyze the structure of IT management. Considerations include type of administration, such as centralized or decentralized; funding model; outsourcing; decision-making process; and change-management process.

- Analyze the current physical model and information security model.

  - Analyze internal and external security risks.

Analyzing Technical Requirements

- Evaluate the company's existing and planned technical environment.

  - Analyze company size and user and resource distribution.

  - Assess the available connectivity between the geographic location of work sites and remote sites.

  - Assess the net available bandwidth.

  - Analyze performance requirements.

  - Analyze the method of accessing data and systems.

  - Analyze network roles and responsibilities. Roles include administrative, user, service, resource ownership, and application.

- Analyze the impact of the security design on the existing and planned technical environment.

  - Assess existing systems and applications.

  - Identify existing and planned upgrades and rollouts.

  - Analyze technical support structure.

  - Analyze existing and planned network and systems management.

Analyzing Security Requirements

- Design a security baseline for a Windows 2000 network that includes domain controllers, operations masters, application servers, file and print servers, RAS servers, desktop computers, portable computers, and kiosks.

• Identify the required level of security for each resource. Resources include printers, files, shares, Internet access, and dial-in access.

Designing a Windows 2000 Security Solution

• Design an audit policy.

• Design a delegation of authority strategy.

• Design the placement and inheritance of security policies for sites, domains, and organizational units.

• Design an Encrypting File System (EFS) strategy.

• Design an authentication strategy.

  • Select authentication methods. Methods include certificate-based authentication, Kerberos authentication, clear-text passwords, digest authentication, smart cards, NTLM, RADIUS, and SSL.

  • Design an authentication strategy for integration with other systems.

• Design a security group strategy.

• Design a Public Key Infrastructure (PKI).

  • Design Certificate Authority (CA) hierarchies.

  • Identify certificate server roles.

  • Manage certificates.

  • Integrate with third-party CAs.

  • Map certificates.

• Design Windows 2000 network services security.

  • Design Windows 2000 DNS security.

  • Design Windows 2000 Remote Installation Services (RIS) security.

  • Design Windows 2000 SNMP security.

  • Design Windows 2000 Terminal Services security.

Designing a Security Solution for Access Between Networks

• Provide secure access to public networks from a private network.

• Provide external users with secure access to private network resources.

- Provide secure access between private networks.
  - Provide secure access within a LAN.
  - Provide secure access within a WAN.
  - Provide secure access across a public network.
- Design Windows 2000 security for remote-access users.

Designing Security
for Communication Channels

- Design an SMB-signing solution.
- Design an IPSec solution.
  - Design an IPSec encryption scheme.
  - Design an IPSec management strategy.
  - Design negotiation policies.
  - Design security policies.
  - Design IP filters.
  - Define security levels.

Exam 70-221: Designing a Microsoft Windows 2000
Network Infrastructure

This certification exam tests the skills required to analyze the business requirements for a network infrastructure and to design a network infrastructure that meets business requirements. Network infrastructure elements include:

- Network topology
- Routing
- IP addressing
- Name resolution, such as WINS and DNS
- Virtual private networks
- Remote access
- Telephony solutions

Analyzing Business Requirements

- Analyze the existing and planned business models.

  - Analyze the company model and the geographical scope. Models include regional, national, international, subsidiary, and branch offices.

  - Analyze company processes. Processes include information flow, communication flow, service and product life cycles, and decision-making.

- Analyze the existing and planned organizational structures. Considerations include management model, company organization, vendor, partner, and customer relationships, and acquisition plans.

- Analyze factors that influence company strategies.

  - Identify company priorities.

  - Identify the projected growth and growth strategy.

  - Identify relevant laws and regulations.

  - Identify the company's tolerance for risk.

  - Identify the total cost of operations.

- Analyze the structure of IT management. Considerations include type of administration, such as centralized or decentralized, funding model, outsourcing; decision-making process, and change-management process.

Analyzing Technical Requirements

- Evaluate the company's existing and planned technical environment and goals.

  - Analyze company size and user and resource distribution.

  - Assess the available connectivity between the geographic location of work sites and remote sites.

  - Assess net available bandwidth and latency issues.

  - Analyze performance, availability, and scalability requirements of services.

  - Analyze data- and system-access patterns.

  - Analyze network roles and responsibilities.

  - Analyze security considerations.

- Analyze the impact of infrastructure design on the existing and planned technical environment.

  - Assess current applications.

- Analyze network infrastructure, protocols, and hosts.
- Evaluate network services.
- Analyze TCP/IP infrastructure.
- Assess current hardware.
- Identify existing and planned upgrades and rollouts.
- Analyze technical support structure.
- Analyze existing and planned network and systems management.
- Analyze the network requirements for client computer access.
  - Analyze end-user work needs.
  - Analyze end-user usage patterns.
- Analyze the existing disaster-recovery strategy for client computers, servers, and the network.

Designing a Windows 2000 Network Infrastructure

- Modify and design a network topology.
- Design a TCP/IP networking strategy.
  - Analyze IP subnet requirements.
  - Design a TCP/IP addressing and implementation plan.
  - Measure and optimize a TCP/IP infrastructure design.
  - Integrate software routing into existing networks.
  - Integrate TCP/IP with existing WAN requirements.
- Design a DHCP strategy.
  - Integrate DHCP into a routed environment.
  - Integrate DHCP with Windows 2000.
  - Design a DHCP service for remote locations.
  - Measure and optimize a DHCP infrastructure design.
- Design name-resolution services.
  - Create an integrated DNS design.

- Create a secure DNS design.
- Create a highly available DNS design.
- Measure and optimize a DNS infrastructure design.
- Design a DNS deployment strategy.
- Create a WINS design.
- Create a secure WINS design.
- Measure and optimize a WINS infrastructure design.
- Design a WINS deployment strategy.
- Design a multi-protocol strategy. Protocols include IPX/SPX and SNA.
- Design a distributed file system (DFS) strategy.
  - Design the placement of a DFS root.
  - Design a DFS root replica strategy.

Designing for Internet Connectivity

- Design an Internet and extranet access solution. Components of the solution could include Proxy Server, firewalls, Routing and Remote Access, Network Address Translation (NAT), connection sharing, Web server, or mail server.
- Design a load-balancing strategy.

Designing a Wide Area Network (WAN) Infrastructure

- Design an implementation strategy for dial-up remote access.
  - Design a remote access solution that uses Routing and Remote Access.
  - Integrate authentication with Remote Authentication Dial-In User Service (RADIUS).
- Design a virtual private network (VPN) strategy.
- Design a Routing and Remote Access routing solution to connect locations.
  - Design a demand-dial routing strategy.

Designing a Management and Implementation Strategy for Windows 2000 Networking

Design a strategy for monitoring and managing Windows 2000 network services. Services include global catalog, Lightweight Directory Access Protocol (LDAP) services, Certificate Services, DNS, DHCP, WINS, Routing and Remote Access, Proxy Server, and DFS.

- Design network services that support application architecture.

- Design a plan for the interaction of Windows 2000 network services, such as WINS, DHCP, and DNS.

- Design a resource strategy.

  - Plan for the placement and management of resources.

  - Plan for growth.

  - Plan for decentralized resources or centralized resources.

Case Study Analysis Approach

The new designing exams from Microsoft, 70-219, 70-220, and 70-221, are not revolutionary in that they are not a significant departure from the past. Yet they are *evolutionary* to the extent that they expand the use of the scenario-based questions of the past. The scenario questions have evolved into *Caselets*. Caselets often begin by describing a detailed scenario and supplying a proposed solution for the situation. This introductory material is followed by a series of exam questions that you are required to answer regarding the Caselet. Although the skills and knowledge necessary to answer these questions are similar to the past scenario-based questions, this new Caselet method offers new challenges for the test taker. The objective of this appendix is to describe these challenges and propose strategies to help you achieve your best score on the exams. Therefore, we present you with study and testing tips for the designing exam series.

Clearly, you have your own learning style and should continue to use methods that have worked for you in the past, especially if they have been successful. However, over the years, our team has helped many students get certified, and the methods or techniques presented here have met with consistent long-term success. On the other hand, we are not magicians; you will have to work hard to pass these new tests, and you will have to prepare carefully using a variety of methods, including a significant amount of hands-on experience. So create a plan that works for you, and consider the various approaches presented in the following sections when developing your individual study plan.

Case Study Method

The case study method was developed at the Harvard Business School and is now the educational standard for applied business and technical training. The case study method seeks to accomplish three essential objectives:

- Case studies are an opportunity to test your knowledge of Windows 2000 functionality and key design issues.

- Case studies are an opportunity to test your ability to apply your design knowledge.

- Case studies are an opportunity to test your ability to comprehend potentially complex real-world situations that, by their very nature, include conflicting network infrastructure, directory, and security-design priorities.

Knowing these objectives helps you to create a preparation plan to help you achieve Windows 2000 Active Directory, security, and network-infrastructure design certification.

Caselets usually have seven or eight sections that include a description of the organization and the goals and objectives of management, including IT management. Detailed descriptions and graphic representations of the existing technical environment are almost always available. This is followed by a description of the goals of the network, along with a proposed design solution. Once the case is presented, you must answer a series of questions based on your comprehension of the case and your knowledge of the subject matter.

Management Value

Historically, network design and operations management has been the domain of the network engineer—technical knowledge was required in order to make operating decisions. This belief has been widely held in the industry and was reflected in the topics included in most IT training programs: operating system installation and configuration, enterprise technologies, desktop and server management, and so on. Now real-life situations described in the pages of this book show that once the technical analysis has been performed, there virtually always remains a set of management decisions that must be made, and that will require more than just technical knowledge. This new case study method is geared to teach you how to improve your situation-analysis and decision-making skills. The case study method can help you become a better IT manager and network designer. In the final analysis, our goal is to help you become a more effective IT systems manager.

We hope to do this by making you aware of the major design elements of Windows 2000 networking. We will do this by helping you understand the range of choices open to the designer, by exposing the interconnections between different aspects of the Windows 2000 operating system, and by constantly giving you practice in decision-making in the face of complexity, ambiguity, and often annoying real-world detail. These cases do propose problems such as "What is the best way to configure DNS replication?" or "How should WINS queries be optimized?" and my recommendation is that you develop answers for these questions. Yet for each of the cases, the same critical question should be asked: "What can be done, if anything, to make the network operation run more effectively or efficiently?" Often, questions of efficiency come down to issues of cost and cost control. Questions of this nature typically are addressed by technical specialists.

However, low cost is not the only desired output from a network operation. It must also be effective. In the final analysis, effectiveness means getting the right job done and getting the complete job done while meeting or exceeding all of the performance criteria. Effectiveness also includes addressing interoperability issues—you may be designing at the department level within a larger enterprise or may need to allow B2B over the Internet, which carries larger interoperability issues and priorities. There can be many non-cost design goals for a Windows 2000 enterprise installation, but five are of particular interest because of their wide applicability:

- Functional quality

- Response time

- Fault-tolerance

- Security

- Manageability

There are always different ways to design and manage an operating system. One design may be the lowest-cost option, for example, but it may not produce consistently available functionality. On the flip side, the design that results in the highest security may suffer from high cost and reduced performance. Also, a system with excellent response times may not have the flexibility needed by the organization. Faced with these alternatives, how should you decide which is the "best" system? Which is the most effective design?

The answers to these questions will always depend on the context of the business and will be decided by the network designer wearing both business and technical specialist hats. The answers require a thorough understanding of the competitive needs of the firm. This means the first question that must be asked when dealing with any design issue is "What does the organization have to do to succeed?" Only when this agenda has been set (traditionally a task for managers, not technical specialists) can the effectiveness of the network design and resulting operation be assessed. As you work through the networking design cases in this book, our hope is that these considerations will be foremost in your mind.

How to Approach a Case

The cases in this book are designed to encourage you to deal with the operating system as a whole. Given adequate time, the successful IT manager will examine all aspects of a problem before deciding on a course of action or a solution, and will review each situation from a variety of different perspectives.

Focus on the information system:

- What information must the workforce have to do their jobs?

- What information must managers and other workers have in order to make decisions?

- How is information collected, assembled, and communicated?

A good understanding of information flows and decision systems is essential for a full understanding of a network operation.

Read the case for understanding. You can start with the highlights and then drill down and try to develop an understanding of the case's key issues, which include both business and technical requirements, along with identified technical constraints. Make physical notes of key issues on the scratch paper provided, and make sure you understand the context of the issues at hand.

Consider a given solution, and address as many alternative solutions as seems reasonable. Once you understand the situation and address possible scenarios, you are ready to answer questions and develop your preferred solution.

Move quickly through the questions and scan the content of the questions. Make mental notes to yourself so you'll develop a focus for the case. Remember, there may be a fair amount of information in the case that is unrelated to the situation at hand, so you will need to filter out irrelevant information from the raw case material when developing your answers. Try to avoid spending a lot of time on information that will not help you effectively answer the questions.

GLOSSARY

This glossary serves the MCSE candidate by drawing on terms from a number of disciplines, including business, the world of consulting, and Microsoft BackOffice technologies. To be honest, an MCSE certification candidate must know the language of the trade. This glossary is your guide to MCSE-speak.

A

Access Control Entry (ACE)   An Access Control Entry is a specific entry in the Access Control List (ACL). Access Control Entries identify what resources a user may access and with what permissions (read/write, read-only, and so on). This is an Active Directory and security term.

Access Control List (ACL)   An Access Control List shows which users can access and use a network resource. This is an Active Directory and security term.

Account Domain   A domain in Windows NT 4.0 that maintains the domain user accounts database. It typically trusts a resource domain. This is a Windows NT term.

Active Directory   The directory services solution in Microsoft Windows 2000 Server. It is the primary topic of this book. And, of course, this is a directory services term.

Active Directory Services Interface (ADSI)   This is an application programming interface (API) that exposes Active Directory to developers seeking to extend Active Directory's functionality. For example, applications access Active Directory via ADSI. This is an Active Directory term.

Add-In   A mini program that runs in conjunction with a Web browser or other application that enhances the functionality of that program. In order for the add-in to run, the main application must be running as well. This is a general computing term.

Address Book   Displays recipient names (mailboxes, distribution lists, custom recipients, and public folders) in the directory. The Address Book can contain one or more address lists. See also *Global Address List*. This is a Microsoft Exchange term.

Agent   Agent has two meanings. First, it can be an application that runs a process. Second, it is an entity that learns a user's preferences and then independently executes tasks based upon those parameters. Agents include Web spiders and other forms of technology that retrieve and filter information for the user. This is a general computer term.

American National Standards Institute (ANSI)   A standards board responsible for proposing and approving many technical standards within the United States. This is a general computer term.

Application Programming Interface (API)   It is a set of protocols, routines, and tools for building software applications. It is used to send commands to the underlying operating system. This is a programming term.

Attribute   This is a descriptive parameter that defines an object. Objects have both required and optional attributes. This is both an Active Directory and a database term.

Auditing   The process an operating system uses to detect and record security-related events, such as an attempt to create, access, or delete objects (files, directories, and so on). This is an operating system term.

Authentication   Validation of a user on a network so that access to resources can be granted. A user ID and password are generally needed for authentication. This is a security term.

B

Backbone   A high-powered network segment that connects individual LANs together. It can be deployed in a single building or across multiple buildings in a campus environment. This is an infrastructure term.

Bandwidth   The amount of data that a communications system can carry in a discrete amount of time. The more casual definition refers to how many projects a person can think about or work on at once, as in "she's got a lot of bandwidth." In general, this is a networking term.

Batch, Batch Files, Batch System   *Batching* is the practice of storing transactions for a period of time before they are posted for processing, typically overnight. Many batch-processing systems are giving way to online transaction systems so that business users see results quickly and can respond to fast-changing business situations. This is a data processing term.

Beta Test   Volunteer customers perform testing of software shortly before the formal release of a product. Beta testing is designed to uncover problems that may appear in actual business use but cannot be found through internal tests. If beta testers find serious problems, the developer fixes those and conducts more beta tests before releasing the software commercially. This is a general technology term.

Bindery   NetWare 3.*x* had a flat-file database as its directory (containing user and security information). The bindery approach was replaced with Novell Directory Services (NDS) starting with NetWare 4.*x*. This is a networking term.

Bookmark   A pointer to a particular Web site. Within browsers, you can bookmark interesting pages so you can return to them easily. This is an Internet usage term.

Boundarylessness   The idea that solutions to business problems should encompass everyone involved, whether inside or outside the formal borders of a corporation. This is a high-level technology planning term.

Bridgehead Server One server within an Active Directory site that handles all intersite (between site) directory replication. Delta Active Directory information is compressed and replicated to other sites. Likewise, all updates from other sites are received by the bridgehead server. A key point is that after a bridgehead server receives an update, it replicates this update to the domain controllers (DCs) inside its site (intrasite replication). This is an Active Directory term.

Broadband A term indicating wider bandwidth than the standard. It originated in the telecommunications world where it referred to the opposite of baseband, but is commonly used to describe a variety of systems with considerable bandwidth. This is a network infrastructure and telecommunications term.

C

Cable Modem A modem that sends and receives data at high speed through a coaxial television cable instead of telephone lines, as with a slower conventional modem. This is a network infrastructure and telecommunications term.

Cache A region of memory where frequently accessed data can be stored for rapid access. This is a general computing term that is typically used when discussing hardware.

Canonical Name This is a DNS resource record identifying an alias (nickname) given to a network host. This is a networking term specific to DNS.

Child Domain These are lower-level or subordinate domains that branch down from the parent (root) domain. This is an Active Directory term.

Circular Log System event and transaction log files that are configured to overwrite the oldest entries when the log reaches a specified size. This is a database term that is also used in Active Directory.

Client A computer on a network that accesses resources provided by another computer called a server. A *dumb client*, or *dumb terminal*, is limited in capability. A *smart client*, or *PC*, also provides computing power for work that logically should be done on the client instead of the server. This is a general computing term.

Console Tree A tree of categories and objects relevant to a particular server. This tree is found on the left pane of MMC. This is a Windows 2000 term.

Container This is an Active Directory object that contains other objects and containers. The most common Active Directory container is the organizational unit (OU), but sites and domains are also containers. This is an Active Directory term.

Cookies These are files stored on your hard drive by your Web browser, containing information about your browsing habits, like what sites you have visited or which newsgroups you have read, and so on. This is an Internet term.

Cost When configuring an Active Directory site link, you can assign costs to particular paths that allow Active Directory to select the optimal path, given costs, connection speed, and availability. This is an Active Directory term (although the word "cost" also has a different meaning in the business community).

Cross-Link Trust This represents the transitive trust relationship you create between domains residing in the same forest. This is an Active Directory term.

D

Data Mining   This is the process of identifying commercially useful patterns or relationships in databases or other computer repositories through the use of advanced statistical tools. This is a database term.

Datastore   Simply stated, this is a database file. This is of course a database term.

Data Table   This is a table storing specific Active Directory data, such as users, groups, computers, and so on. This is a database term.

Data Warehouse   This is a database that can access all of a company's information. While the warehouse can be distributed over several computers and may contain several databases and information from numerous sources in a variety of formats, it should be accessible to users through simple commands. This is a database term.

Defragmentation   All hard disks are subject to fragmentation in which files are spilt up and partially stored in multiple locations. With defragmentations, files are optimized by being placed in one storage location and often compacted. This is a general computer term.

Desktop   The graphical representation of a user's work environment. In the Microsoft Windows environment, it is the background of the screen upon which items such as icons, folders, and dialog boxes appear. This is a general computing term.

Details Pane   The right pane of MMC, detailing a selected item on the console tree. This is a Windows 2000 term.

Digital Certificate   An electronic ID card that verifies a user's credentials, allowing the user to communicate with network resources. This is a security term.

Digital Nervous System   The digital processes that enable a company to perceive and react to its environment, to sense competitive challenges and customer needs, and to organize timely responses. A digital nervous system is distinguished from a mere network of computers by the accuracy, immediacy, and richness of the information it brings to knowledge workers and the insight and collaboration made possible by the information. No company has a perfect digital nervous system today; rather, it's an ideal use of technology in support of business. This is a technology planning and marketing term.

Digital Subscriber Line (DSL)   A regular twisted-pair telephone line that carries digital rather than analog signals, increasing the bandwidth of the line. Also known as xDSL (for DSL, ADSL, IDSL and other basic DSL variations). This is a networking and telecommunications infrastructure term.

Directory-Enabled Network (DEN)   A directory services-aware network. For example, this might be Cisco routers that could be configured and managed by Active Directory. This is a directory services term.

Distinguished Name (DN)   Specified by the X.500 standard, this is a naming convention that employs a pattern of abbreviations to define the full path to an object in Active Directory. Such a path might appear as DC=com/DC=gpcm/CN=PL5/CN=JohnS. This is a directory services term.

Distributed Applications   Applications that harness the processing power of multiple computers in order to run. This is a general computing term.

Distributed Query   Any SELECT, INSERT, UPDATE, or DELETE statement that references tables and rowsets from one or more external OLE DB data sources. This is a SQL Server term.

Domain   An Active Directory object that defines a boundary for administrative or security purposes. This is a Windows 2000 term.

Domain Controller (DC)   A Windows 2000 Server that performs domain user authentication tasks. This is an Active Directory and Windows 2000 Server term.

Domain Name System (DNS)   The default name resolution service in Windows 2000 Server. It is a required service for Active Directory. DNS maps a host name to an IP address and vice versa. This is a networking term.

Dumb Terminal   A terminal that does not run programs locally and typically is capable of displaying only characters and numbers and responding to simple control codes. This is a general computing term.

Dynamic DNS   DNS tables are automatically (not manually) updated when dynamic DNS is implemented (it is implemented on a zone-by-zone basis). This is a Windows 2000 term.

E

E-Commerce (Electronic Commerce)   Commercial activity that takes place by digital processes over a network. Most new business-to-business and business-to-consumer transactions are being delivered over the Internet. This is a business and Internet term.

Electronic Data Interchange (EDI)   A set of standards controlling the transfer of business documents, such as purchase orders and invoices, between computers. EDI has eliminated paperwork for many large businesses but is generally too complex for small and medium-sized businesses. New Internet-based transactions are likely to be built on XML instead of EDI. This is a general computing and business term.

Encryption   A term that applies to the use of mathematical algorithms to scramble and unscramble digital messages. Through various encryption schemes, such as private key, public key, and key escrow, digital messages are protected in transit so that only the sender and receiver can read them. This is a security term.

Enterprise Resource Planning (ERP)   Software used in a number of industries to coordinate sales and order information with the manufacturing system in order to accurately schedule production, fully utilize capacity, and reduce inventory. This is a technology planning term.

Executive Information System (EIS)   A set of tools designed to organize information into categories and reports for senior executives. Many EIS systems were difficult to integrate with other corporate information systems. Today, EIS usually stands for *Enterprise Information System* and is designed to provide information to a wider range of people in an organization. This is a technology planning term.

Explicit Trust   This is a one-way trust between domains wherein Tree One can access resources in Tree Two but not vice-versa. This is an Active Directory term.

Extensible   Active Directory is an *extensible* database, which means it can be modified and expanded. This is an Active Directory term.

Extensible Storage Engine (ESE)   The database engine for Active Directory. Active Directory is based on ESE. This is an Active Directory term.

External Trust   One-way, nontransitive trusts that administrators can create for users to access resources in another domain (both Windows 2000 and Windows NT). This is a networking term most closely associated with Active Directory in this book.

Extranet   An extension of a corporate intranet using Web technology to facilitate communication with the corporation's suppliers and customers in order to enhance the speed and efficiency of the business relationship. See also *intranet*. This is an Internet technology term.

F

Fault Tolerance   Technology with redundancy to minimize the chance for downtime. This is a networking infrastructure term.

Feedback Loop   A system to gather reactions from customers about a product or service in order to create a continuous cycle of improvements, more feedback, and more improvements. This is a general planning term often used in both business and technology.

File Transfer Protocol (FTP)   A set of rules for exchanging files between computers over the Internet. This is an Internet and TCP/IP term.

Firewall   A term used for the wall of software that keeps unauthorized users outside of a network. It can also restrict company users on an internal network from partaking in activities such as Web browsing. This is a security term.

First-Wins Conflict Resolution   A merge-replication conflict-resolution method in which the winner is the one who first submitted the change. This is a SQL Server term.

Flexible Single Master Operation (FSMO)   The master copy of data for service changes that can take place on only one DC at a time. The first DC to be online is the operations master, an approach known as Flexible Single Master Operation (FSMO). This is an Active Directory term.

Forest   A grouping of domain trees (with separate namespaces) that you join together with transitive-trust relationships. This is an Active Directory term.

Frequently Asked Questions (FAQs)   Pronounced "facts." A common feature of Web sites, including answers to common questions related to that site. This is a general computing term.

Front End   A term that pertains to everything that a user sees on the screen. It is contrasted with *back-end* software, which runs on a network server or mainframe. This is a general computing term.

Fully Qualified Domain Name (FQDN)   The full path pointing to network objects (for example, machine01.main.gpcm.com). This is a DNS and Active Directory term.

Functional Active Directory Model   This is an Active Directory design that accommodates a variety of organizational structures. Domains may be grouped by department, division, or project. This is an Active Directory term.

G

Gantt Chart   A bar chart that shows individual parts of a project as bars against a horizontal time scale. Gantt charts are used as project-planning tools for developing schedules. This is a project scheduling term.

Garbage Collection   The periodic (default is 12 hours) automatic cleanup of the Active Directory database. Activity includes deleting unused log files, and tombstoning and defragmenting the database file. This is an Active Directory term.

General Directories   Web directories that offer information in a logical, category-based manner. Unlike spider indexes, they rely on submissions from site creators and present that information in a subject-based, hierarchical manner. This is an Internet term.

Geographic Model   A popular Active Directory design based on geographic boundaries (such as domestic and international locations). This is a planning term.

Global Address List   This is an organization-wide address book in Microsoft Exchange Server. This is an e-mail term.

Global Catalog (GC)   This is an Active Directory searchable index that enables users to search for objects on the network without knowing the exact location of the object (for example, what domain they are in). The GC is a partial or subset replica of Active Directory. This is an Active Directory term.

Group Policy   Extensive user and computer settings that apply to a site, domain, or OU on a Windows 2000 network. This is an Active Directory term.

Group Policy Object (GPO)   This is a set of user and computer configurations that is stored as an object in Active Directory. This is an Active Directory term.

Groupware   Software that enables a group of users on a network to collaborate on a particular project. Groupware software supports common office functions, such as e-mail, collaborative document development, scheduling, and tracking. This is an e-mail term.

H

Heterogeneous Data   Data stored in a data store other than SQL Server. This is a SQL Server term.

Hit   A client computer request for an image or file from a Web server. Hits are a common measure of Web site popularity. This is an Internet term.

Horizontal Integration   A business model for the computer industry in which each layer of technology—chips, systems, software, solutions, and service—is provided by a different set of companies. Fierce competition in each area drives technology ahead rapidly and creates a high-volume, low-price model. Compare vertical integration. This is a business and technology term.

Host   First, this is a client machine when used in the context of TCP/IP, DNS, and Active Directory. Previously this term was used to identify the main computer in a system of computers or terminals, usually a mainframe. This is a general computing term.

Hypertext Markup Language (HTML)   The language used to format documents for viewing with a browser on the user's machine or on a network, including the Web. HTML tells browsers how to display type and images to the user and describes responses to user actions, such as activation of a link by a mouse click. This is an Internet term.

I

Inflection Point   In mathematics, the term that describes the point at which the shape of a curve shifts from concave to convex; in business, the term that describes a sudden and massive change in a business market or technology use. Popularized by Intel Chairman Andrew Grove. This is a business technology term.

Information System, Information Services, Information Technology, IT The formal name for a company's data processing department. This book uses the acronym IT to refer to all aspects of a company's central computing department and systems. This is a general computing term.

Information Work A phrase coined by MIT's Michael Dertouzos to describe the transformation of passive data into active information by human brains or software. This is a general technology term.

Inheritance The passing along of characteristics (properties such as group policy settings) from parent domains and OUs to child objects in the Active Directory tree hierarchy. This is an Active Directory term.

Instant Messaging A communications service that enables a user to create a private chat room with another user. It typically alerts the primary user whenever other selected users are online for the initiation of immediate chat sessions. This is an e-mail and communications term.

Institutional Intelligence, Institutional IQ, Corporate IQ A measure of how easily a company can share information broadly and how well people within an organization can build on each others' ideas and learn from past experiences. This is a business term.

Integrated Services Digital Network (ISDN) A set of digital communications standards that transmit voice, data, and video over standard phone lines at up to 128 Kbps. This is a networking infrastructure term.

Internet Engineering Task Force (IETF) The primary Internet standard governing board. This is a general computing term.

Internet Protocol (IP) The technical specification that governs the sending of data across the Internet. Standardization of most networks on IP in the last several years has made possible for the first time an efficient worldwide network for exchanging data. As phone systems become digital, IP connections will be used for both voice and data. This is a networking term.

Intersite Replication This refers to Active Directory directory updates between DCs across different sites. This is an Active Directory term.

Intranet A network designed to organize and share information and carry out digital business transactions within a company. An intranet employs applications associated with the Internet, such as Web pages, browsers, e-mail, newsgroups, and mailing lists, but are accessible only to those within the organization. This is an Internet term.

Intrasite Replication This refers to Active Directory directory updates between DCs across the same site. This is an Active Directory term.

J

Java A multi-platform, object-oriented language developed by Sun Microsystems. This is a programming term.

Java Application A Java application is a program written in the Java programming language. This is a programming term.

Just-In-Time A system of inventory control based on the Japanese kanban system, in which materials are delivered just in time for manufacturing. The better the information system between a company and suppliers, the less inventory the company has to stock and the lower its costs. This is a business term.

K

Kerberos   Windows 2000's default security-authentication protocol. This is a security term.

Key Distribution Center (KDC)   This is a Kerberos security service running on DCs that distributes tickets and keys to control network resource access. This is a security term.

Kiosk   A freestanding PC that provides information to the public, usually through a multimedia display. Kiosks will become a common way for government agencies to provide services to citizens who do not have PCs or Internet access. This is a business technology term.

Knowledge Management   A concept that pertains to the use of information management technology to cultivate the accumulated expertise within an organization. This technology often provides features that bolster communication, coordination, and collaboration. This is a business technology term.

Knowledge Worker   Employees whose fundamental task is analyzing and manipulating information. PC systems can turn more employees into knowledge workers by giving them better information about the processes they are carrying out. This is a business technology term.

L

LAN Internetwork   The connection of disparate and geographically dispersed LANs so that they function as a single enterprise system. This is a networking infrastructure term.

Latent Guaranteed Consistency   Transactional consistency level in which all participating sites are guaranteed to have the same data values that were achieved at the publishing site at some point in time. This is a SQL Server term.

Leaf   An Active Directory object that terminates. That is, it can't contain other objects (for example, printers). This is an Active Directory term.

Leaf Node   Lowest level of the index tree of a clustered index; storage location of the index entry of a nonclustered index. This is a SQL Server term.

Legacy Application or System   A computer system that remains in use after an organization installs more modern technology. Compatibility with legacy systems is important when new software is installed. Legacy systems based on mainframe computers are being replaced in many organizations by PC-based architectures. This is a business technology term.

Lightweight Directory Access Protocol (LDAP)   A highly regarded Internet standard that enables applications such as Web browsers to find and retrieve information from a directory-services database. LDAP is a more popular, efficient, and less cumbersome form of the X.500 Directory Access Protocol (DAP). This is a directory services term.

Link Table   Maintains links between Active Directory attributes and objects. This is an Active Directory term.

Local Area Network (LAN)   A group of PCs, servers, printers, and similar devices connected over a network in a relatively limited geography. This is a networking term.

Logical Structure   This is the nonphysical view of Active Directory that maps Windows 2000 and Active Directory technical features to organizational processes and structures. This is an Active Directory and a database term.

M

Messaging Application Programming Interface (MAPI)   A standard interface that Exchange and Microsoft Outlook components use to communicate with one another. This is a Microsoft Exchange term.

Meta Data, Metadata   Data about data. For example, the title, subject, author, and size of a document constitute metadata about the document. This is a database term.

Middleware   Software that sits between two or more types of software and translates information between them. This is a technology term.

Migration   A transition from an older hardware platform, operating system, or software version to a newer one. This is a technology planning term.

Mirror Site   An Internet site set up as an alternate to a busy site; contains copies of all the files stored at the primary location. This is an Internet term.

Mixed Mode   A Windows 2000 network that contains Windows NT Server 3.51 and 4.0 servers in the same domain that operates in mixed mode (not native mode). This is an Active Directory term.

Moore's Law   Intel co-founder Gordon Moore's rule of thumb, which has turned out to be true so far, that microprocessors would double in processing power every 18 to 24 months. This is a technology term.

Multipurpose Internet Mail Extensions (MIME)   A standard that enables binary data to be published and read on the Internet. The header of a file with binary data contains the MIME type of the data; this informs client programs (such as Web browsers and mail packages) that they connect and process the data as straight text. This is a Microsoft Exchange term.

N

Namespace   A logically structured naming convention in which all objects are contiguous. Note that all names in a namespace share the same root domain. This is an Active Directory term.

Native Mode   A Windows 2000 network where all servers run Windows 2000. This is an Active Directory term.

Nested Containers   A container inside a container. Typically, you will see OUs nested inside of OUs. This is an Active Directory term.

Netiquette   The dos and don'ts of online communication. In the online world, which is devoid of subtle hints like inflection and body language, netiquette makes communication clearer and more precise. Netiquette examples include short titles, brief descriptions, and proper spelling. This is a business and Internet term.

Novell Directory Services (NDS)   Novell's highly regarded directory services offering. Used in the NetWare operating system from version 4.0 forward. This is a directory services term.

O

Object   In Active Directory, a component such as a computer, group, printer, or user that contains attributes. This is an Active Directory term.

Object Class   Simply stated, a computer is one type of object class, and a user is another. Also known as metadata or schema objects. This is an Active Directory term.

Object Identifiers   ANSI-assigned numbers (dotted decimal, just like the Dewey decimal system in libraries) for each object class and attribute. This is a programming term.

Online Analytical Processing (OLAP)   A database capable of handling queries more complex than those handled by standard relational databases, through the ability to view data by different criteria, intensive calculation capability, and specialized indexing techniques. This is a database term.

Open Database Connectivity (ODBC)   This Microsoft-based solution provides a communications mechanism for data management between databases, specifically relational and nonrelational databases. This is a SQL Server term.

Open-File Backup   While a database remains online and accessible, it can be backed up. This is a SQL Server term.

Organizational Unit (OU)   A fundamental component in Active Directory, an OU is a logical container inside a Windows 2000 domain used for organizational and administrative purposes. For example, the marketing department in a firm may be identified in Active Directory by the Marketing OU. This is an Active Directory term.

OSI   An acronym for Open Systems Interconnect Reference Model. A communications model developed by the International Organization for Standardization (ISO) to define the services provided by a LAN. It includes seven layers of LAN services that can be implemented in a modular fashion. This is a networking term.

P

Paperless Office   The idealized office in which information is entirely stored, manipulated, and transferred digitally rather than on paper. This is a business consulting term.

Parent-Child Trust   This is simply a transitive trust relationship between the parent and the child container. This is an Active Directory term.

Parent Domain   This is a domain that has child domains beneath it. Note the root of a tree is always a parent domain. This is an Active Directory term.

Pessimistic Concurrency Control   Form of concurrency control that places shared locks on tables. This is a SQL Server term.

Physical Structure   In the physical realm of Active Directory. This speaks to the actual network configuration, sites, devices, and connectivity (bandwidth). This is a networking term used in Active Directory planning.

Plug-In   A small application that extends the built-in capabilities of your Web browser. Examples include Macromedia's Shockwave, providing animation, and RealAudio, offering streamed sound files over the Internet. This is a computing term.

Point-of-Sale (POS)   The place in a store where goods are paid for. Computerized scanners for reading tags and bar codes, electronic cash registers, and other special devices record purchases. POS systems connected with digital analysis tools enable real-time analysis of sales and faster response to changing customer demand. This is a business term.

Point-to-Point Tunneling Protocol (PPTP)   A tunneling protocol that encapsulates IP, IPX, or NetBEUI protocols inside IP packets. This is a networking term.

Portal   A Web site that becomes a user's primary starting point for access to the Internet. AOL, MSN, and Yahoo! are examples of portal sites. This is an Internet term.

Post Office Protocol Version 3 (POP3)   Enables users with POP3 clients to retrieve mail from their Exchange Inbox. This is a Microsoft Exchange term.

Propagating Updates   The forced exchange (replication) of Active Directory delta database information between DCs inside of a domain. This is an Active Directory term.

Pull Subscription   Subscription in which the subscriber asks for periodic updates of all changes at the publisher. This is a SQL Server term.

Push Subscription   Subscription in which the publisher propagates the changes to the subscriber without a specific request from the subscriber. This is a SQL Server term.

R

Re-engineering   The design of new business processes, usually in conjunction with digital systems, to improve corporate responsiveness to changing business conditions. This is a business consulting term.

Relative Distinguished Name (RDN)   This is X.500-based and is the portion of an object's name that is distinct from the object path. This could be thought of as a subset or a part of the distinguished name (DN). This is an Active Directory term.

Replication   The exchange of Active Directory delta database information on a periodic basis between DCs. Replication results in data consistency between DCs. This is an Active Directory term.

Replication Latency   The time period from start to finish of the replication process to all DCs. The latency period is often referred to in the context of the very brief period of time that DCs can be out of synch while the replication process is occurring. This is an Active Directory term.

Resource Domain   In Windows NT, a resource domain contained resources such as printers and computers. Resource domains had trust relationships with accounts domains in Windows NT. In Windows 2000, resource domains are typically converted to OUs. This is a networking term.

Resource Record   These are DNS record entries that clients use to access resources via name resolution. This is a networking term.

Root Domain   In Active Directory, the first domain you create is the root domain and is typically displayed graphically as being at the top of the Active Directory domain hierarchy. This is an Active Directory term.

Router   An internetworking device that uses Network Layer Protocol information to route data from one LAN to another. This is a networking term.

S

Safe Mode   Only minimal drivers are loaded when safe mode is selected when starting Windows 2000. This is typically used for troubleshooting. This is a Windows 2000 term.

Schema   Generally a collection of rules for naming directory objects and defining object properties and attributes. Active Directory uses the term to refer to the definitions of all object classes, categories, and corresponding attributes that are maintained in Active Directory. This is an Active Directory and general database term.

Schema Cache   The memory cache area of a Windows 2000 Server that contains a copy of Active Directory. This results in faster performance. This is an Active Directory term.

Search Engines   Software applications that help users find information through the use of keywords or concepts. These applications are free to users with Web access. Examples include AltaVista and Yahoo! This is an Internet term.

Security Accounts Manager   In Windows NT, this was the database that contained user accounts and security information. This is a security term in the legacy Windows NT operating system.

Security Identifier (SID)   A unique identification number (like a serial number) for Active Directory objects on a Windows 2000 network. This is a security and Windows 2000 term.

Semantic Entity   English query entity used to establish semantic relationships between tables, table elements, and so on, allowing the user to type database queries in English language phrases, which are then translated into SQL statements. This is a SQL Server term.

Sequential Log   Service transactions and events are recorded to this log in the order that they occur. This is both an Active Directory and SQL Server term.

Server   A computer system that controls access to a network and network resources, such as printing and file sharing. Some servers provide access to information in databases or on Web sites, while others coordinate the flow of data and computer processes among other servers and back-end systems. See also *Three-Tier Computing*. This is a network consulting term.

Session Ticket   This is the encrypted information that the server examines to validate the client as an authenticated domain member. If a domain client requests access to a server resource, the Key Distribution Center (KDC) returns a sessions ticket to the client computer. The server then decides whether to validate the client for access to that resource. This is a security term.

Simple Mail Transfer Protocol (SMTP)   A protocol used by the Internet Mail Service to transfer messages between an Exchange site and an SMTP messaging system, such as the Internet. This is a Microsoft Exchange term.

Site   When IP subnets are grouped and connected (typically a high-speed connection) in Windows 2000. Sites are a physical network component. This is an Active Directory term.

Site Link   The connection between sites. Replication occurs over a site link. This is an Active Directory term.

Site Link Bridge   This is a connector between two site links. A site link bridge basically creates a replication path between available site links. This is an Active Directory term.

Skunkworks   Any small team that goes off by itself to develop a new product outside of a company's normal development processes. Named for the secret group at Lockheed that developed a number of high-technology aircraft. This is a business consulting term.

Smart Card   A credit card containing an integrated circuit that gives it a limited amount of "intelligence" and memory. Smart cards are being used for identification and to encode information such as a person's medical history. This is a security term.

Soft-Boiled Egg Rule   The principle that software should be simple enough that a user can do most transactions in less than three minutes, or about the time that it takes to soft-boil an egg. This is an analogy used in business consulting.

Spam   The electronic form of junk mail. The gerund, *spamming*, is the process of arbitrarily sending a message to a large number of people. This is an Internet e-mail term.

Subdomain   Also known as *child domain*, this is a domain that has a parent domain. This is an Active Directory term.

Subnet   A segment of an IP network. This is a network consulting term.

Supply Chain   A phrase describing all the companies involved in delivering a product to consumers. Paper-based systems or old digital systems make communication difficult and create slow, complicated business processes. Compare to the term *value network*. This is a popular business consulting term.

Switch   A multiple-port device that links several LANs and provides packet filtering between them. This is a network infrastructure term.

Synchronization   The process of making different directory services (for example, NDS and Active Directory) contain the same database information. This term is also used in SQL Server.

T

T1   A network link that transmits data at a rapid 1.5 Mbps. It refers exclusively to the signaling speed, rather than the medium of the network. The European equivalent is E1, which transmits at 2 Mbps. This is an infrastructure term.

Task Worker   Employees assigned to a single, repetitive task with little autonomy. Modern business principles encourage the use of technology to automate many tasks and redesign others to take advantage of a worker's skills. MCSE consultants would use this term in a business context.

Three-Tier Computing   A computing architecture in which software systems are structured into three networked tiers or layers: the client or presentation layer, the business logic layer, and the data layer. PCs usually provide the presentation layer. PC servers in the middle tier, or business logic layer, coordinate interactions between the user (client) and the back-end data tier. The data tier often includes a variety of PC and non-PC systems. This is a common technology consulting term.

Throughput   A measure of the data transfer rate through a communications system, of the data processing rate in a computer system, or the production rate of other systems. This term is common in network consulting.

Ticket Granting Ticket   This is a Kerberos object that contains authentication information and key information for accessing resources. Whenever a user authenticates, the Key Distribution Center (KDC) sends a ticket-granting ticket (TGT) that contains authentication information. The client host then caches the TGT information until access is needed to the domain resources. The TGT is presented, and an access request is generated. This is an Active Directory and security-related term.

Time to Market   The amount of time it takes a company to go from concept to initial shipment of a product. This is a business consulting term.

Tombstone   This is typically an object in a database that has been identified or marked for removal (for example, a user object). In Active Directory, tombstoned objects remain for 60 days after being marked. This is a database term.

Topology   Represents the physical shape of a network, including star, bus, or ring. This is a networking term.

Total Cost of Ownership (TCO)   The cost of owning, operating, and maintaining a computer system. TCO includes the up-front costs of hardware and software, plus the costs of installation, training, support, upgrades, and repairs. Industry initiatives designed to lower TCO include centralized network management of PCs, automated upgrades, and "self-healing" PCs. This term is widely used in MCSE consulting.

Transactional Consistency   State of affairs in which all sites are guaranteed to have the same data values at the same time. This is a SQL Server term.

Transactional Replication   Replication method in which transactions (INSERT, UPDATE, or DELETE statements) executed on one computer are replicated to another computer. This is a SQL Server term.

Transitive Trust   This is a bidirectional trust relationship between two domains. This is an Active Directory term.

Tree   In Active Directory, this is the hierarchical grouping of domains inside a contiguous namespace. This is an Active Directory term.

Tree-Root Trust   This is the transitive trust relationship between trees in a forest. This is an Active Directory term.

Trigger   An action that causes a procedure to be carried out automatically when a user attempts to modify data. This is a SQL Server term.

Trust or Trust Relationship   This is the way in which domains are joined or related. This is an Active Directory term.

U

Uniform Resource Locator (URL)   A virtual signpost on the Web that marks the location of a home page or Web site. This is an Internet technology term.

User Principal Name (UPN)   Commonly thought of as the e-mail address for a user. It is the user's logon name and the user's logon domain name. This is an Active Directory term.

V

Value Network, Value Chain Initiative   A web of partnerships enabled by digital information flow so that a company and all its suppliers can easily communicate and act together. In a value network, everyone who touches the product—from the retailer, to distribution, to transportation, to manufacturing—must add value, and communications go both forward as well as back among all companies involved. Compare *supply chain*. This is a business technology term.

Verb Phrasing   English query phrasing that expresses a verbal relationship, for example, "authors write books." This is a SQL Server term.

Vertical Integration   An older business model for the computer industry in which most layers of technology—chips, systems, software, solutions, and service—were provided by a single vendor. Sales volumes were low, and switching costs for customers were high, because every piece of the solution would have to change. Compare *horizontal integration*. This is a common term in business consulting.

Video Conferencing   Teleconferencing in which video images are transmitted along with sound. This is a computing term.

Video-on-Demand   The ability to play movies or other recorded events whenever the user wants, rather than at the times set by broadcasters. This is a computing term.

W

Webcasting   The use of the Web to distribute news and information. One of the most popular webcasters is The Pointcast Network, which delivers customized news feeds and animated advertising to users throughout the day. This is an Internet term.

Web Lifestyle, Web Workstyle   The new way of living and working that will become common as consumers and workers take advantage of digital devices and digital connections to transform the way they work, and their approach to living. Once the infrastructure is in place, unforeseen applications will emerge, just as the telephone, radio, television, and computer emerged only after electrical use became commonplace. This is a business and Internet term.

Windows 32   The application programming interface (API) used by developers to create software that operates on the Microsoft Windows family of operating systems. This is an operating system term.

Windows CE   A scaled-down version of Microsoft Windows designed for use with handheld PCs, other digital companions, and embedded devices. This is an operating system term.

Windows NT, Windows 2000   Microsoft's operating system designed primarily for business use. Originally named Windows NT, the product has been renamed Windows 2000. This is an operating system term.

Wizard   An outstanding, creative programmer, a power user, or software help system that guides users through each step of a particular task, such as opening a word-processing document in the correct format for a business letter. This is a general Microsoft technology term.

INDEX

Symbols

.net initiative, 29
3DES algorithm, 384
80/20 rule, DHCP networks, 540

A

ABRs (Area Border Routers),
    OSPF, 725
access
  restrictions
    dial-up networks, 736
    security groups, 211
  security planning, 168
Access-Accept packets, RADIUS, 741
Access-Reject packets, RADIUS, 741
Access-Request packets, RADIUS, 740
accountability, security planning, 169
accounting
  policies, 214
  RADIUS, 739
accounts, network security, 144–145
ACLs (Access Control Lists), 582, 612
acquisition plans
  business model analysis, 52
  network design, 446
ACS (Admission Control Services),
    TCP/IP QoS, 511

actions, audit policies, 235–236
active content caching, 693
Active Directory, 3, 15–17, 78
  ADSI (Active Directory Services
      Interface), 9, 28, 100
  attributes, 15
  authentication, system resource
      access, 206
  business advantages, 29
  child domains, 12
  complete trust domain systems, 108
  contiguous namespace, 90
  delegating authority, 243
  desktop appearance policies, 99
  DHCP integration, 536
  different domain names, 92
  directory services, 4–5
  disjointed namespace, 90
  DNS, 79, 90–92, 587
    forwarders, 93
    incremental zone transfers, 582
    integrated zone servers, 130–131
    network design, 579
    zones, 580–581
  domain controller server
      placement, 127
  domains, 11, 83–84
  dynamic updates, 592
  forests, 11, 79–81

897

global catalog, 79
group policies, 97
holistic design process, 774
implementing, scope of services,
    25–26
integrated zones, 580–583
IPSec, 377–378
  assigning policies, 373
  authentication protocols, 376
  DH exchange, 380
  encryption algorithms, 376
  IKE, 379
  ISAKMP, 376–377
  local computer policies, 384
  negotiation policies, 379–380
  PFS, 381
  policy storage, 382
  predefined policies, 372
  rules, 384
  SAs, 375, 381
  security levels, 378
Kerberos authentication, 207
LDAP, 27, 79, 100
learning curve analysis, 7
logon/logoff scripts, 97
meta-information, 6
multi-master replication, 79
multiple master domain systems,
    107–108
namespace, 89
naming domains, 87
NTFS, 79
open environment, 28
operations masters, 114–119
OUs, 13–15, 93–96
parent domains, 12
password policies, 207
permissions, 88
planning delegation structure,
    243–244
proxy server integration, 694
registering names, 92

replication, 5–6
  data, 100
  strategies, 101
root servers, 93
scalability, 78
schemas, 80, 83, 103–105
scope, 88
single domain systems, 106
single master domain systems,
    106–107
sites, 16
  boundaries, 102–103
  topology, 100
SRV RRS, 597–598
technical needs analysis, 70
trees, 11, 79
trusts, 79, 82, 85
universal groups, 84, 89
viewing stored zones, 583
Windows 2000, 20
workstation policies, 99
X.400, 8
X.500, 7–8, 27
AD objects, permissions, 248
addresses, DHCP servers, 341
administration, security planning,
    169, 222–223
Administrator accounts, network
    security, 145
ADSI (Active Directory Service
    Interface), 100
  Active Directory relationship, 28
  directory services, 9
agents, SNMP, 294–295, 761
AHs (Authentication Headers),
    IPSec, 371
algorithms
  DES versions, 384
  encryption, 317, 376, 384
analyzing business
    requirements, 33–34
  acquisition plans, 52

branch offices, 41
communications flow, 45
customer relationships, 51
decision making processes, 46
existing company structures, 34, 47
geographical scope, 35, 42
growth strategies, 53
information flow, 44
international scope, 39
national scope, 37
partner relationships, 51
planned company structures, 34, 47
regional scope, 35–36
risk tolerance, 54
service life cycles, 46
subsidiaries, 39–41
TCO (Total Cost of Operations), 54
vendor relationships, 51
analyzing network management
    data, 755
analyzing security requirements, 197
attacks, 198–201
current environment, 198
IP spoofing, 201
performance baselines, 202
potential vulnerabilities, 198
security templates, 202
viruses, 199
analyzing TCP/IP network traffic, 509
analyzing technical needs, 57–58
Active Directory issues, 70
bandwidth utilization, 64
client desktop issues, 72
connectivity, 62
data access patterns, 66–67
domain controllers, 62
global catalog servers, 63
home computer resources, 61
link speed, 64
net available bandwidth, 64
performance, 65
replication, 64
security issues, 69

site placement/structure, 62
systems management, 72
technical support structure, 71
upgrades, 70
users, 60
anti-hacking measures, security
    planning, 187
APIPA (Automatic Private IP
    Addressing), 504
Application layer
attacks, communications
    security, 365
TCP/IP, 492–493
application-proxy firewalls, 678–679
applications
inventory, security planning, 175
security, 221–222
TCP/IP networks, 520
architecture
network, security planning, 171
TCP/IP, 490
areas, OSPF, 725–726
ARPANET (Advanced Research Projects
    Agency Network), 487
AS (Authentication Service), Kerberos
    authentication, 262
ASs (Autonomous Systems), OSPF
    routing design, 726
assigning IP addresses, 499
ATMA resource records, DNS, 573
attributes
directory services, 15
network design, 400, 426–427
audit account logon events, 235
audit account management
    events, 235
audit action events, 240
audit directory service access
    events, 235–236
audit logon events, 236
audit object events, 236–237,
    242–243
audit policies, 169, 223

actions, 235–236
audit events, 240–243
change events, 236
checking Security log, 234
domain controllers, 240
domain-wide, 240
local hard disk access, 237
objects, 236
planning, 233
servers, 241
Windows 2000, 233
workstations, 242
audit process tracking events, 236
authentication
certificates, 260
clear text passwords, 269
DA (Digest Authentication), 269
dial-up networks, 736
dial-up remote access routing, 731
IPSec, 330, 376
Kerberos, 207, 261–263
NTLM, 264–265
RADIUS, 266–267, 739–740
security planning, 168
smart cards, 265–266
SSL, 269
VPNs, 335–336
authoritative DNS servers, SRV RR
support, 597–598
authority, delegating, 243–244
authorization
RADIUS, 739
remote access, 353
security planning, 169
authorized servers, DHCP
networks, 555
auto-static routing, 721
automated analysis, network
management, 762
automated client configuration,
DHCP, 410

automatic replication partner
configuration, WINS, 642
AXFR counters, DNS, 604–605

B

bandwidth
domain controller servers, 127
technical analysis, 464–465
utilization, 64
Banyan StreetTalk, 8
baselines, security needs analysis, 202
best practices, IPSec, 387
Big Time Investments, Inc.,
business/technical requirements
analysis, 473–477
binary subnet masks, IP addresses, 498
BIND (Berkeley Internet Name
Domain)
DNS compatibility, 573
Windows 2000 integration, 590
block filter, IPSec, 385
blocking group policy inheritance,
251–252
BOOTP clients, DHCP network design,
536, 542–543
boundaries, domains, 84
branch offices
business model analysis, 41
network design, 437
bridgehead servers, 124
brokering, meta-directories, 10
business analysis, 432–433
acquisition plans, 446
branch offices, 437
business models, 434
centralized IT structure, 451
change management, 456
communications flow analysis, 440

company
  organization analysis, 443–445
  priorities, 447
  processes analysis, 439
  strategies, 446
decentralized IT structure, 452
decision making analysis, 441, 455
existing organization structure
      analysis, 442
fault tolerance/recovery, 449
geographical scope, 434
growth issues, 447–448
information flow analysis, 439–440
international scope, 437
IT issues, 450–454
laws and regulations, 448
management models, 442
national scope, 436
network operating costs, 449–450
outsourcing, 454
planned organization structure
      analysis, 442
product life cycles, 440
regional scope, 436
requirements checklist, 457
risk analysis, 449
ROI, 449
service life cycles, 440
strategic relationships, 446
subsidiaries, 437
business applications, Windows 2000
      implementation, 18–19
business cases, network security, 143
business factors, security
      planning, 160
business managers, IT
      business/technical analysis, 433
business models, 434–435
business requirements analysis, 33–34
  acquisition plans, 52
  branch offices, 41
  communications flow, 45

company
  models, 35
  organization, 48
  priorities, 53
  processes analysis, 44
customer relationships, 51
decision making processes, 46
existing organizational
      structures, 34, 47
geographical scope, 35, 42
growth strategies, 53
information flow, 44
international scope, 39
legal issues, 54
management models, 47
national scope, 37
partner relationships, 51
planned models, 34
planned organizational
      structures, 47
product life cycles, 46
regional scope, 35–36
risk tolerance, 54
service life cycles, 46
subsidiaries, 39–41
TCO (Total Cost of Operations), 54
vendor relationships, 51

C

caching site content, proxy servers, 311
caching-only servers, DNS, 130, 609
capacity optimization, DNS
      servers, 602
CAs (Certificate Authorities), PKI
  disaster recovery, 276
  hierarchies, 271
  installing, 273
  Active Directory design, 114, 133
  business analysis, 432–433
  concepts behind case study, 777

DHCP network design,
    530–531, 563
DNS, 570
    analysis setup, 615
    zone planning, 129
global catalog servers, 123
infrastructure redesign, 428
Internet connections, 672, 698
IPSec implementation,
    384, 389–390
name resolution problems, 412
NetBIOS name resolution via
    WINS, 413
network management planning, 767
secure remote access, 359
security
    attacks, 228
    planning, 192
    remote connections, 310
TCP/IP implementation, 518
technical needs analysis,
    74, 432–433
WAN design, 704, 746
Windows 2000 security,
    232, 304–305
WINS restructuring, 659–664
centralized data collection, network
    management, 757
certificates
    authentication, 260
    file recovery, 257
    PKI
        Enterprise CAs, 282
        expiration, 281
        issuing, 278
        life cycles, 277
        management, 277
        renewing, 281
        revoking, 279
        third party root CAs, 281–284
change management, IT funding, 456
CHAP (Challenge Handshake
    Authentication Protocol), 336

checklist for group policy
    planning, 270
child domains, Active Directory, 12
CIDR (Classless Inter-Domain
    Routing), IP addresses, 498
CIFS (Common Internet File System),
    file sharing security, 315, 366
classful IP addresses, 496–498
clear-text passwords, 269
CLI (Command Line Interface),
    transferring operations masters to
    other domain controllers, 120
Client (Respond Only) policy,
    IPSec, 372
clients
    access analysis, 468
    desktop, technical needs analysis, 72
    DFS, 653, 658
    DHCP, 535
    proxy servers, 692
    RADIUS, 267, 743
    TCP/IP, 519
    VPNs, 334, 343–345
    WINS design, 634, 650–651
clustering
    DHCP, 534, 550
    WINS, 647
com name servers, DNS, 575
communications flow, 45, 440
communications security,
    networks, 146, 363
    attacks, 365
    data modifications, 364
    eavesdropping, 364
    IP spoofing, 364
    IPSec, 369–371
    transport mode, 370
    tunnel mode, 370
    password cracking, 365
    SMB signing, 366–368
complete trust domain systems,
    Active Directory, 108

complexity requirements for
     passwords, 208
compromised access key attacks, 365
compulsory tunnels, VPN design, 732
Computer objects, Active Directory, 14
computer resources, technical needs
     analysis, 61
configuration data, replication, 100
configuring
    DHCP, 341, 541–543
    DNS, 578
    host IP addresses, 504–505
    Internet Connection Server, 312–314
    IPSec, 333
    proxy server interfaces, 691
    RAS, 347, 350
    RIS, 292
    RRAS, 707–711
    security, 203, 224
    SNMP agents, 295
    Terminal Services, 300
    VPNs, 334–336, 342
    WAN routing, 713–714
    WINS, 590, 594
connections
    Internet, 672–673
        application-proxy firewalls,
            678–679
        Catywhompus Construction, 672
        designing, 682
        DMZs, 679
        dynamic packet-inspection
            firewalls, 677
        firewall placement, 679
        firewalls, 673–676
        gateways, 678
        ICS, 680
        incompatible protocols, 681
        NAT, 680–687
        network design, 413
        proxy servers, 688–690
        routed, 681
        RRAS, 680

        screened subnets, 680
        translated, 681
    IPSec, 332
    NetBIOS file sharing, 630
    remote, security, 310
    security planning, 171
    TCP/IP networks, 521
    technical needs analysis, 62
    Terminal Services, 302
    VPNs, 732
Contact records, Active Directory, 14
content filtering, proxy servers, 311
contingency plans, security
     planning, 159
contract employees, technical
     needs analysis, 60
corporate business plans,
     security planning, 160
corporate financial reports,
     security planning, 161
counter logs, Network Monitor,
     421–423, 426
CRLs (Certificate Revocation
     Lists), 280
CTLs (Certificate Trust Lists), 283
current environment, analyzing
     security needs, 198
Custom objects, Active Directory, 15
custom subnet masks, TCP/IP
     networks, 507
customer relationships, business
     model analysis, 51

D

DA (Digest Authentication), 269
data
    access methods, security
        planning, 175
    access patterns, technical needs
        analysis, 66–67

collection, network
management, 756
directory services, 15
loss, security planning, 159
modifications, communications
security, 364
data rates
NAT segments, 684
proxy servers, 692
DDNS (Dynamic DNS), 132
decision making
business model analysis, 46
IT funding, 455
network design, 441
default policies, IPSec, 318–319
default route entries, 720
Delegation of Control wizard,
95, 245, 248
delegation, 243–244
authority, 243
DNS zones, 609
OUs, 94
deleting group policies, 251
demand dial routing, 730
denial of service attacks, 199, 365
deployment schedule, security
design, 152
DES algorithm (Digital Encryption
Standard), IPSec levels, 376, 384
design analysis, TCP/IP networks, 495
design phase
infrastructure, 401–403
security design, 151
designing DHCP networks, 539
80/20 rule, 540
adding servers to improve
performance, 554
authorized servers, 555
broadcast frames, 545
clustering service, 550
distributed scope, 549
DMZs, 556

large enterprise networks, 544
multicast frames, 545
relay agents, 545
routed networks, 545
RRAS, 547
security, 554
servers, 540, 547, 550–551
service availability, 548
single subnet LANs, 543
unauthorized servers, 555
designing DFS networks, 652
client caching, 658
clients, 653
file access, 654
FRS, 659
links, 657
replication policies, 657
roots, 653, 656–658
security, 656
server load balancing, 655
shared folders, 657
topologies, 655–656
designing dial-up networks, 733–738
designing directory services, 77
Active Directory, 78
ADSI, 100
complete trust domain
systems, 108
contiguous namespace, 90
different domain names, 92
disjointed namespace, 90
DNS, 79, 90–93
domains, 83–84
forests, 79–81
global catalog, 79
LDAP, 79, 100
multi-master replication, 79
multiple master domain
systems, 107–108
namespace, 89
naming domains, 87
NTFS, 79

OUs, 93–94
permissions, 88
registering names, 92
replication, 100–101
root servers, 93
scalability, 78
schemas, 80, 83, 103–105
scope, 88
single domain systems, 106–107
sites, 100–103
trees, 79
trusts, 79, 82, 85
universal groups, 84, 89
desktop appearances, 99
group policies, 97
logon/logoff scripts, 97
OUs, 94–96
workstation policies, 99
designing DNS networks, 579
incremental zone transfers, 582
optimizing, 602
servers, 602–604
zones, 580–581
designing Internet connections, 682
application-proxy firewalls,
678–679
DMZs, 679
dynamic packet-inspection
firewalls, 677
firewalls, 672–676, 679
gateways, 678
ICS, 680
incompatible protocols, 681
NAT, 680–687
proxy servers, 688–690
routed, 681
RRAS, 680
screened subnets, 680
translated, 681
designing networks
acquisition plans, 446
attributes, 400, 426–427

bandwidth, 464–465
branch offices, 437
business models, 434
centralized IT structure, 451
change management, 456
client access analysis, 468
communications flow analysis, 440
company analyses, 439, 443–447
decentralized IT structure, 452
decision making, 441, 455
developing approach, 406–408
DHCP, 410
directory services
documentation, 466
disaster recovery analysis, 470
DNS, 411
domain administration models, 466
end user needs analysis, 469
existing organization structure
analysis, 442
fault tolerance/recovery, 449
foundations, 408–409
geographical scope of
organization, 434
growth issues, 447–448
hardware design, 459
IAS, 417
information flow analysis, 439–440
infrastructure, 397–404, 418, 458
integration, 406
international scope, 437
Internet connectivity, 413
IP addresses/service
configurations, 462
IP routing, 417
ISA Server, 415
IT issues, 450–454
legal issues, 448
logical network diagrams, 461
management issues, 418, 442
name resolution issues, 412, 463
NAT, 414

national scope, 436
NetBIOS name resolution, 412–413
network infrastructure
    documentation, 460
network operating costs, 449–450
outsourcing, 454
past failure records analysis, 472
performance logs, 418–419
physical network diagrams, 460
planned organization structure
    analysis, 442
product life cycles, 440
protocol support, 409
RADIUS, 417
regional scope, 436
remote access, 416, 464
requirements checklist, 457
risk analysis, 449
ROI, 449
routing, 416
security documentation, 467
server documentation, 465
service life cycles, 440
software design, 459
strategic relationships, 446
subsidiaries, 437
designing PKI, 271
designing proxy servers, 691
designing RADIUS networks, 739–744
designing routing, 716
    auto-static, 721
    demand dial routing, 730
    dial-up remote access, 730–731
    dynamic routing, 720
    IGMP, 727–728
    OSPF, 723–726
    private network placement, 717
    RIP, 721–722
    router interfaces, 717
    subnet masks, 717
    static routing, 719–720

designing security, 151–153
    analyzing plan, 179
    disaster recovery plans, 188
    discovery process, 151
    end user needs, 180
    hotspots, 189–191
    proactive anti-hacking, 187
    security policy problems, 184
    specific vulnerabilities, 182
    staff training, 183
    technical support structure, 179
    user issues, 179, 185–186
designing VPNs, 732–733, 737
designing WANs, 703–714
designing WINS networks, 635
    automatic replication partners, 642
    clients, 641, 650–651
    clusters, 647
    DMZs, 652
    fault tolerance, 647
    hub and spoke design, 645
    link failures, 646
    multi-server performance, 646
    non-routed LANs, 639
    non-WINS clients, 641–642
    performance optimization, 648–650
    replication, 637, 642–645, 651
    routed LANs, 640
    screened subnets, 652
    segments, 646
    servers, 646–649
    untrusted domain replication, 643
Desktop appearance policies, 99
detection and response, network
    management, 754
developing network design
    approaches, 406–408
DFS (Distributed File System), 652
    availability, 655
    clients, 653, 658
    domain-based roots, 657

file access, 654
FRS, 659
links, 657
replication policies, 657
roots, 653, 656–658
security, 656
server load balancing, 655
shared folders, 657
topologies, 655–656
DH exchange, IPSec, 380
DHCP (Dynamic Host Configuration
    Protocol), 529
    DNS dynamic updates, 612
    NAT options, 684
    networks, 410, 530–531
        Active Directory, 536
        BOOTP support, 536
        clients, 535
        clusters, 534
        configuring, 541–543
        designing, 539–540
        DNS, 533, 537
        MADCAP, 534
        monitoring, 532
        multicast scopes, 532
        Relay Agents, server addresses, 341
        rogue server prevention, 533
        RRAS, 537
        scope properties, 532
        statistical reporting, 532
        superscopes, 532
        TCP/IP client options, 532
        Server Performance Object
            counters, 552–553
        WINS, 628
diagramming network structure,
    security planning, 171
dial-up network design, 733–738
dial-up remote access, 730–731
Digital Nervous System, Windows
    2000 Server, 29

digital signatures, SMB.
    See SMB signing.
directory services, 3, 77
    Active Directory, 78
        ADSI, 100
        complete trust domain
            systems, 108
        contiguous namespace, 90
        different domain names, 92
        disjointed namespace, 90
        DNS, 79, 90–93
        domains, 83–84
        forests, 79–81
        global catalog, 79
        LDAP, 79, 100
        multi-master replication, 79
        multiple master domain
            systems, 107–108
        namespace, 89
        naming domains, 87
        NTFS, 79
        OUs, 93–94
        permissions, 88
        registering names, 92
        replication, 100–101
        root servers, 93
        scalability, 78
        schemas, 80, 83, 103–105
        scope, 88
        single domian systems, 106
        single master domain systems,
            106–107
        site boundaries, 102–103
        site topology, 100
        trees, 79
        trusts, 79, 82, 85
        universal groups, 84, 89
    ADSI (Active Directory Services
        Interface), 9
        attributes, 15
        child domains, 12

components, 4–5
data, 15
desktop appearance policies, 99
domains, 11
forests, 11
group policies, 97
LDAP protocol, 9
logon/logoff scripts, 97
meta-information, 6
OUs, 13–17, 94–96
parent domains, 12
sites, 16
trees, 11
workstation policies, 99
X.400, 8
X.500, 7–8
disabling WINS records
    replication, 592
disaster recovery, 188, 470
    CAs, 276
    EFS, 255
    operations masters, 121
discovery process, security design, 151
distinguished names, X.500, 8
distributed data collection, network
    management, 757
distributed scope, DHCP network
    design, 549
DMZs (Demilitarized Zones), 679
    DHCP networks, 556
    security planning, 172
    WINS design, 652
DNS (Domain Name Service),
    128, 569–570
    Active Directory, 79
        integrated zones, 580–582
        planning, 90–92
    ATMA resource records, 573
    availability issues, 601
    AXFR counters, 604–605
    BIND compatibility, 573
    caching-only servers, 130, 609

Catywhompus Construction
    analysis setup, 615
com name servers, 575
DHCP dynamic updates, 612
domain namespace, 574
dynamic update counters, 605
enhancements for growth, 613–614
external zones, 131
fast zone transfers, 596
fault tolerance, 601
forward-lookup queries, 575
forwarders, 610
FQDNs, 406
functionality analysis, 599–600
incremental zone transfers, 582
integrated zone servers, 130–131
internal zones, 131
Internet interaction, 598
IXFR counters, 605–606
load balancing, 610
local DNS servers, 575
local name servers, 575
lookup zones, 130
name resolution, 412, 569–571, 575
name servers, 574
namespace integration, 599
network design, 411, 579
non-RFC compliant RRs, 597
notification counters, 606
optimizing network design, 602
overall performance counters, 607
primary zones, 580
query resolution optimization, 609
recursion counters, 606
resolver, 572
root domains, 574
root name servers, 575
round-robin load balancing,
    576–578
RRs, 576
screened subnets, 613
second-level domains, 574

secondary zones, 580, 588
secured dynamic updates,
    606, 611–612
security options, 285, 611
servers, 131–132, 586–587,
    603–604
    capacity optimization, 602
    server to server traffic, 611
service integration, 573
SRV records, 573
Standard Primary zone servers, 130
Standard Secondary zone
    servers, 130
standard zones, 581, 587
TCP counters, 607
top-level domains, 574
total counters, 607
UDP counters, 607
unauthorized access protection, 286
Unicode character set support, 597
WINS, 588
    lookups, 589, 608
    referral zones, 593–594
zones, 574, 580, 608–609
DNS forwarders, Active Directory, 93
domain controllers
    audit policies, 240
    networks, 134
    operations masters, 119–121
    servers, 125–127
    SMB signing, 368
    technical needs analysis, 62
domain local groups, 209
Domain Naming Masters, 117–121
domain-based roots, DFS, 657
domain-wide audit policies, 240
domains
    Active Directory, 11–12, 83
    administration models, technical
        analysis, 466
    boundaries, 84
    data replication, 100

namespace, 89–90, 574
naming, 87
trust relationships, 212
DoS attacks (Denial of Service), 673
down services, security planning, 159
drivers, Network Monitor, 419
dynamic IP addresses, VPNs, 336
dynamic packet filters, proxy
    servers, 695
dynamic packet-inspection
    firewalls, 677
dynamic record deletion, WINS, 638
dynamic reregistration, WINS, 639
dynamic routing, 720
dynamic updates
    Active Directory, 592
    DNS
        counters, 605
        DHCP, 537
        secured, 611–612

E

e-commerce, business models, 435
EAP (Extensible Authentication
    Protocol), 335, 706
eavesdropping, communications
    security, 364
EFS (Encrypting File System), 150,
    213, 253
    disaster recovery, 255
    network security, 150
    protecting files during transfers, 254
    recovery agents, 257
    recovery policies, 256–257
    system planning, 254–255
encapsulation, VPNs, 334
encryption, 213, 317
    algorithms, IPSec, 376, 384, 516
    files, 258
    security, 165, 325–326

TCP/IP networks, 515
Terminal Services, 299
VPNs, 335, 732–733
end to end security model, IPSec, 369
end user needs, security planning, 180, 469
endpoints, IPSec tunnels, 371
enterprise CAs, 273, 282
enterprise trusts, third party CAs, 283
ESP (Encapsulating Security Payload), IPSec, 371, 384
evaluation phase, security design, 152
Event Logs, 218
event monitors, 757
Everyone groups, 210
expiration, PKI certificates, 281
explicit trusts, Active Directory, 85
export function, WINS, 639
exportation of encryption programs, security planning, 165
external DNS zones, 131
external trusts, Active Directory, 85

F

failed events, audit policies, 238
fast zone transfers, DNS, 596
fault tolerance
  Active Directory integrated zones, 582
  network design, 449
  RADIUS, 744
  TCP/IP, 506
  WINS, 639, 647
feedback phase, security design, 152
file recovery certificates, securing, 257
file sharing
  connections, NetBIOS, 630
  security, CIFS, 366
File System groups, 218

files
  encrypting, 258
  protecting during transfers, 254
filter actions, IP filter lists, 328
filter lists, security rules, 323, 326
filtering
  content, proxy servers, 311
  Filtering records, WINS, 638
  IPSec, 385–386
  TCP/IP packets, 514
firewalls, 172, 311, 673–676
folders, encryption, 258
forcing group policy inheritance, 253
forests
  Active Directory, 11, 79–81
  Domain Naming Masters, 117
  global catalog servers, 122–124
  Infrastructure Masters, 118
  PDC Emulators, 118
  RID Masters, 119
  Schema Masters, 115–117
forward lookups, DNS, 130, 575
forwarders, DNS, 610
FQDNs (Fully Qualified Domain Names), DNS, 406, 411, 627
Fromanywhere.com exercise, TCP/IP network design, 486, 514–523
FRS (File Replication Service), DFS, 659
FSMO servers (Flexible Single Master Operations). See operations. masters, 113
full NetBIOS names, 630
functionality analysis, DNS, 599–600

G

gateways, 311, 678
geographic models, security planning, 162

geographical scope
    business model analysis, 35, 42
    network design, 434
global catalog
    Active Directory, 79
    servers
        bridgehead servers, 124
        Catywhompus Const, 123, 134
        placement, 122–123, 128
        technical needs analysis, 63
global groups, 210
Graph views, network
        management, 758
group accounts, network security, 144
group policies, 97
    accounts, 214
    auditing, 234
    Event Logs, 218
    File System groups, 218
    inheritance, 249–250
    IP Security Policies groups, 221
    local policies, 214
    planning checklist, 270
    processing order, 250
    Public Key Policies groups, 221
    Registry groups, 218
    removing, 251
    restricted groups, 218
    SMB signing, 368
    system services, 218
groups
    Active Directory, 14
    names, NetBIOS, 630–632
    permissions, 88
    remote access, 354–356
    universal, 89
    zone-admin, 285
GUI (Graphical User Interface),
        transferring operations masters to
        other domain controllers, 120

H

hackers, security planning, 178
hardware
    documentation, technical
        analysis, 459
    inventory, security planning, 175
    routers, 714
hierarchies, PKI CAs, 271
holistic network design
        process, 773–775
home computer resources, technical
        needs analysis, 61
host groups, IGMP routing design, 727
Host Integration Server, 148
host IP addresses, 504–505
host name resolution, DNS, 128
hotspots, security planning, 189–191
hub and spoke WINS design, 645

I

IAS (Internet Authentication Service)
    network design, 417
    RADIUS, 741–743
ICS (Internet Connection Sharing),
        680, 687
IGMP (Internet Group Management
        Protocol), routing design,
        727–728
IIS server (Internet Information
        Services), 269
IKE (Internet Key Exchange),
        lPSec, 379
illegal IP addresses, 502
Implementation phase,
        infrastructure, 404
in-band data collection, network
        management, 756
inbound filters, IPSec, 386

inbound Internet traffic
 NAT, 687
 proxy servers, 695
inbound replication servers, 124
inbound traffic, firewalls, 673
information flow, business model
 analysis, 44, 439–440
information security models, security
 planning, 171
Infrastructure Masters, 118
inheritance, group policies, 249–253
inside attacks, security needs
 analysis, 201
installing
 CAs, 273
 drivers, 419
 RIS, 287–288
 RRAS, WANs, 707
 SNMP agents, 295
 VPNs, 336–338, 343–345
integrated zones, Active Directory,
 580–583
inter-site connectivity, security
 planning, 173
inter-site replication, 101
interception attacks, 199
interfaces
 NAT, 683–684
 proxy servers, 691
 routers, 717
 RRAS support, 716
intermediate CAs, PKI, 272
internal DNS zones, 131
Internet
 DNS interaction, 598
 standards, 489
Internet Connection Server, 312–314
Internet connections, 413, 672–673
 Catywhompus Construction
  example, 672
 DHCP options, 681–687
 DMZs, 679

firewalls, 673–679
gateways, 678
ICS, 680
NAT, 680–684
proxy servers, 688–689
RRAS, 680
screened subnets, 680
Internet layer, TCP/IP, 491
Intersite Topology Generator, inbound
 replication servers, 124
intra-site replication, 101
inventory areas, performance
 baselines, 202
IP addresses, 496–498
 assignment guidelines, 499
 binary subnet masks, 498
 CIDR, 498
 host configuration, 504–505
 illegal addresses, 502
 private, 501
 public, 499–500
 router interfaces, 717
 subnet masks, 498
 technical analysis, 462
 VLSMs, 497
 VPNs, 336
IP filter lists, 323, 326
IP routing
 network design, 417
 RRAS, 728–729
IP Security Policies groups, 221
IP spoofing
 communications security, 364
 security needs analysis, 201
IPSec (Internet Protocol Security),
 214, 254, 317, 364
 AHs, 371
 assigning policies, 373
 authentication, 330, 376, 517
 Client policies, 319
 communications security, 369–371
 components, 374

configuration testing, 333
connection types, 332
default policies, 318–319
DH exchange, 380
encryption algorithms, 376, 516
ESP, 371, 384
filters, 385
IKE, 379
implementation, 377–378
inbound filters, 386
Internet Key Exchange, 517
IP filter lists, 327–328
ISAKMP, 376–377
local computer policies, 384
negotiation policies, 379–380
operation modes, 331
outbound filters, 386
packet filtering, 386
PFS, 381
policies, 321–326, 372, 382
protecting files during transfers, 254
rules, 384
SAs, 318, 375, 381
security levels, 378
Server policies, 319
transport mode, 318
tunnel mode, 318
tunnels, endpoints, 371
VPNs, 335, 733
IPSec Policy Agent, TCP/IP
    networks, 515
IPSec Policy Management snap-in, 382
ISA (Internet Acceleration Server),
    689–690
ISA Server (Internet Security and
    Acceleration), 311, 415
ISAKMP (Internet Security Association
    and Key Management Protocol),
    318, 377
IT staff issues, 179, 433
IXFR counters, DNS, 605–606

K

Kerberos authentication, 207, 261–262
    AS (Authentication Service), 262
    KDC (Key Distribution Center),
        261–262
    NTLM compatibility, 264
    policies, 263
    smart cards, 265–266
    TGS (Ticket Granting Service), 262
Kim's Modeling Agency, Internet
    connection case study, 696–697

L

L2TP (Layer Two Tunneling
    Protocol), 335, 706
large enterprise networks, DHCP
    network design, 544
LAT (Local Address Table), proxy
    servers, 690
LDAP (Lightweight Directory Access
    Protocol), 100
    Active Directory, 27, 79
    directory services, 9
    meta-directories, 10
lifetimes, IPSec SAs, 381
link failures, WINS design, 646
Link State database, OSPF, 723
links
    DFS, 657
    WANs, 705
LMHOSTS file, NetBIOS, 634
load balancing, DNS, 576–578, 610
loading system images remotely, 287
local DNS servers, 575
Local groups, 209
local hard disk access audit
    policies, 237
local name servers, DNS, 575
local policies, 214

Local Security Settings tool,
    audit policies, 234
local storage, DHCP clients, 535
logging
  network management, 758
  network performance, 418–419
  Security log properties, 238
logical layout of network services,
    security planning, 174
logical network diagrams, technical
    analysis, 461
logon/off scripts, 97
lookups
  DNS zones, 130
  WINS, 590, 594

M

MADCAP (Multicast Address Dynamic
    Client Allocation Protocol), 534
man in the middle attacks
  communications security, 365
  security needs analysis, 201
managing networks, 405
  automated analysis, 762
  centralized data collection, 757
  data collection, 756
  detection and response, 754
  distributed data collection, 757
  event monitors, 757
  graph views, 758
  in-band data collection, 756
  logging, 758
  management processes, 755
  manual analysis, 762
  MIBs, 761
  monitoring network services
      status, 755
  out of bound data collection, 756
  performance counters, 759

performance logs, 757
Performance Monitor, 758
proactive responses, 763
response strategies, 755
scripts, 762
SNMP agents, 761
System Monitor, 757
WMI, 761
manual analysis, network
    management, 762
manual tombstoning, WINS, 638
mapping third party PKI
    certificates, 284
masquerade attacks, security needs
    analysis, 201
MD5, IPSec, 376
meta-directories, 9–10
meta-information, directory services, 6
MIBs (Management Information
    Bases), network management, 761
Microsoft
  Host Integration Server, 148
  Proxy Server, 311, 689–690
monitoring
  DHCP, 532
  DNS, 603–604
  network services, 755–766
Mount Vernon courthouse, Internet
    connection case study, 696–697
MPPE (Microsoft Point-to-Point
    Encryption), 335, 732
MS-CHAP, 336
multi-domain networks, 133
multi-master replication, 79
multicast forwarding, IGMP routing
    design, 728
multicast frames, DHCP network
    design, 545
multicast scopes, DHCP, 532
multicasts, RIP routing design, 722

multiple master domain systems,
    Active Directory, 107–108
multiple protocol support, RRAS, 715
multiple WINS servers, WINS
    design, 642

N

name cache, NetBIOS, 634
name resolution
    DNS, 128, 569–571, 575
    NetBIOS, 630
    WINS, 628
name servers, DNS, 574
names, NetBIOS, 630
namespace, Active Directory, 89–90
naming domains, 87–89
NASs (Network Access Servers),
    RADIUS, 739
NAT (Network Address Translation),
    311, 680–681
    design issues, 682
    DHCP options, 684
    inbound Internet traffic, 687
    incompatible protocols, 681
    interface IP addresses, 683
    network design, 414
    outbound Internet traffic, 686
    persistence, 684
    proxy servers, 688–689
    routed connections, 681
    security issues, 686
    segment data rates, 684
    server performance, 685
    translated connections, 681
    VPNs, 687
NBNS (NetBIOS Name Servers), WINS
    compatibility, 629
NDS (Novell Directory Services), 8, 77
needs analysis checklist, 60–72
negotiate filter, IPSec, 385

negotiation policies, lPSec, 379–380
nesting security groups, 211
net available bandwidth, technical
    needs analysis, 64
.net initiative, 29
NetBEUI (NetBIOS Extended User
    Interface), 487
NetBIOS
    file sharing connections, 630
    LMHOSTS file, 634
    name cache, 634
    name resolution, 412–413, 630–632
    nodes, 633
    WINS, 635
NetBT (NetBIOS over TCP/IP), 628
Netlogon service, 123
Network Access layer. See Network
    Interface layer.
network design
    acquistion plans, 446
    attributes, 400, 426–427
    bandwidth, 464–465
    branch offices, 437
    business models, 434
    centralized IT structure, 451
    change management, 456
    client access analysis, 468
    communications flow analysis, 440
    company analyses, 439, 443–447
    connections, security planning, 171
    decentralized IT structure, 452
    decision making, 441, 455
    developing approach, 406–408
    DHCP, 410
    directory services
        documentation, 466
    disaster recovery analysis, 470
    DNS, 411–412
    domain administration
        models, 466
    end user needs analysis, 469

existing organization structure
    analysis, 442
fault tolerance/recovery, 449
foundations, 408–409
geographical scope of
    organization, 434
growth issues, 447–448
hardware documentation, 459
IAS, 417
information flow analysis, 439–440
infrastructure, 397–404, 418, 458
integration, 406
international scope, 437
Internet connectivity, 413
IP addresses/service
    configurations, 462
IP routing, 417
ISA Server, 415
IT funding, 452–454
IT management structure, 450
legal issues, 448
logical network diagrams, 461
management models, 442
name resolution services, 463
NAT, 414
national scope, 436
NetBIOS name resolution, 412–413
network infrastrucuture
    documentation, 460
network operating costs, 449–450
outsourcing, 454
past failure records analysis, 472
performance logs, 418–419
physical network diagrams, 460
planned organization structure
    analysis, 442
product life cycles, 440
protocol support, 409
RADIUS, 417
regional scope, 436
remote access, 416

remote/mobile users, 464
requirements checklist, 457
risk analysis, 449
ROI, 449
routing, 416
security documentation, 467
server documentation, 465
service life cycles, 440
software documentation, 459
strategic relationships, 446
subsidiaries, 437
Network Interface layer, TCP/IP, 490
network management, 405
automated analysis, 762
centralized data collection, 757
combining services, 763–766
data collection, 756
detection and response, 754
distributed data collection, 757
event monitors, 757
graph views, 758
in-band data collection, 756
logs, 758
management processes, 755
manual analysis, 762
MIBs, 761
monitoring network services
    status, 755
out of band data collection, 756
performance counters, 759
performance logs, 757
Performance Monitor, 758
proactive responses, 763
response strategies, 755
scripts, 762
security planning, 176
SNMP agents, 761
System Monitor, 757
WMI, 761
Network Monitor, driver installs, 419
network roles, 67–68, 180–181

network security, 309
   administrator accounts, 145
   business cases, 143
   CIFS, 315
   communications, 146
   EFS, 150
   firewalls, 311
   gateways, 311
   group accounts, 144
   Internet access, 310
   Internet Connection Server, 312
   IPSec, 317
   life cycle, 151
   operating systems, 146
   physical aspects, 145
   PKI, 149–150
   proxy servers, 310
   RADIUS, 149
   Recovery Agent, 150
   remote connections, 310
   technical issues, 144
   third party integration, 147
   tremote users, 148
   user accounts, 144
   user-level security, 315
   VPNs, 149
network services
   combining, 763–766
   monitoring, 755–762
   TCP/IP clients, 520
   Windows 2000, 405–406
networks
   delegating authority, 243
   DFS, 652–659
   DHCP, 530–537
   DNS, 579
      caching-only servers, 609
      fault tolerance, 601
      forwarders, 610
      FQDNs, 406
      incremental zone transfers, 582
      load balancing, 610
      namespace integration, 599
      screened subnets, 613
      security, 611
      WINS integration, 588–589, 593
      zones, 580, 586–587
   proxy servers, 691
   RAS, 346–347
   TCP/IP, 485–487
   VPNs, 333–336
   WANs, 703–714
   Windows 2000, 353
nodes, NetBIOS, 633
non-DHCP clients, DHCP network
      design, 543
non-RFC-compliant RRs, DNS, 597
non-routed LANs, WINS design, 639
non-WINS clients, WINS design,
      641–642
nontransitive trusts, 212
Notification counters, DNS, 606
Novell NDS (Network Directory
      Services), 8
ntdsutil.exe, transferring operations
      masters to other domain con-
      trollers, 120
NTFS (New Technology File
      System), 254
NTLM (NT LAN Manager), 264–265
number assignments, RFCs, 490

O

Oakley protocol, 318
object types, Active Directory, 13
objects, audit policies, 236
Officesupplies.com, DHCP
      upgrades, 556–561
one-way trusts, 212
operating systems, network
      security, 146

operation modes, IPSec, 331
operations masters, 113–115
  disaster recovery, 121
  Domain Naming Master, 117
  Infrastructure Master, 118
  PDC Emulator, 118
  permissions, 120
  RID Master, 119
  roles, 114, 119–121
  Schema Master, 115–117
  transferring roles, 120
OSPF (Open Shortest Path First),
      routing design, 723–726
oubound filters, IPSec, 386
OUs (Organizational Units)
  Active Directory, 13–15, 93–96
  delegation plans, 94
  permissions, 96
outbound traffic
  firewalls, 673
  NAT, 686
overall performance counters,
      DNS, 607

P

packet filtering
  IPSec, 386
  TCP/IP networks, 514, 518
parent domains, Active Directory, 12
pass through filter, IPSec, 385
passive caching, proxy servers, 693
passwords
  clear text, 269
  complexity requirements, 208
  cracking, 365
  security policies, 207
past failure records analysis, 472
PDAs, replication, 5–6
PDC Emulators, 118
PDNs (public data networks), 704

PDS Emulators, 120
performance
  DHCP servers, 550–551
  dial-up networks, 734–735
  NAT servers, 685
  proxy servers, 693
  RADIUS, 744
  routers, 729
  TCP/IP networks, 507
performance baselines, 202
performance counters, 650, 759
performance logs, 418–419, 757
Performance Monitor, network
      management, 758
performance monitoring,
      DNS servers, 603–604
performance optimization, WINS
      design, 648
permissions
  AD objects, 248
  groups, 88
  operations masters, 120
  OUs, 96
  Terminal Services connections, 302
persistence
  NAT segments, 684
  proxy servers, 692
  WINS connections, 638
PFS (Perfect Forward Secrecy),
      lPSec, 381
phases of network design, 402
physical links, WANs, 705
physical machine security, network
      security, 145
physical network diagrams, technical
      analysis, 460
physical security models, security
      planning, 171
pipes, TCP/IP networks, 510
PKI (Public Key Infrastructure),
      149, 271

CAs (Certificate Authorities), 271–273, 276
  certificates, 279–281
  Enterprise CAs, 273, 282
  intermediate CAs, 272
  issuing CAs, 272
  network security, 149–150
  root CAs, 272
  stand-alone CAs, 273
  third-party CAs, 281–284
policies
  auditing, 233–243
  desktop appearances, 99
  disaster recovery, 256–257
  group, 249–252
  groups, 97
  IPSec, 319–326, 373, 382–384
  Kerberos authentication, 263
  passwords, 207
  security. *See* policies for security.
  workstations, 99
policies for security, 206
  account policies, 214
  Active Directory, 207
  authentication, 206
  Event Logs, 218
  File System groups, 218
  group policies, 214
  IP Security Policies groups, 221
  local policies, 214
  password policies, 207
  Public Key Policies groups, 221
  Registry groups, 218
  remote access, 208
  resource access control, 209
  restricted groups, 218
  security groups, 209–211
  smart cards, 208
  user system resource access, 206
  Windows 2000, 231–233
PPP (Point-to-Point Protocol), WANs, 706

PPTP (Point-to-Point Tunneling Protocol), 706
  protecting files during transfers, 254
  VPNs, 334, 732
  WANs, 706
predefined policies, IPSec, 372
preventing unauthorized DNS access, 286
primary zones, DNS, 580
printer objects, Active Directory, 14
private address space, IP addresses, 501
private IP addresses, 499–501
private names, DNS zones, 124, 131
private networks
  router placement, 717
  VPN connections, 334
proactive responses, network management, 763
problems with security policies, 184
processing order, group policies, 250
properties, Security log, 238
protecting files during transfers, EFS, 254
protocols. *See* specific protocol.
Proxy Server 2.0 (Microsoft), 311
proxy servers
  active content caching, 693
  Active Directory integration, 694
  clients, 692
  data rates, 692
  designing, 691
  dynamic packet filters, 695
  inbound Internet traffic, 695
  LAT, 690
  NAT, 688–689
  passive caching, 693
  persistence, 692
  security, 310, 694
  static packet filters, 695

PSTNs (Public Switched Telephone
    Networks), 703
public IP addresses, 500
Public Key Policies groups, 221
public names, DNS zones, 124, 131
push/pull replication, WINS
    design, 645

Q

QoS (Quality of Service), TCP/IP
    networks, 510–513
queries, DNS, 575, 609

R

RADIUS (Remote Authentication
    Dial-In User Service),
    149, 266–267, 417, 704
    client/server trust, 267
    network design, 417, 739–745
    network security, 149
RAS (Remote Access Service),
    346–347, 350, 736
reboots, Windows 2000, 19
records
    DNS, 612
    WINS verification, 638
recovering from disaster
    operations masters, 121
    policies, 256–257
Recovery Agent, 150
    EFS disaster recovery, 255
    security, 257
recursion counters, DNS, 606
redesigning infrastructure, 399–400
redundant links, TCP/IP, 506
referral zones, WINS, 593–594
registering names, Active Directory, 92
Registry groups, 218

relative distinguished names, X.500, 8
Relay Agents, DHCP, 545
remote access, 353
    dial-up networks, 733–738
    group policies, 354–356
    network design, 416
    security
        connections, 310
        policies, 208
    VPNs, 334
remote authorization, 353
remote system image loading, 287
remote users
    network security, 148
    technical analysis, 464
removing group policies, 251
renewing PKI certificates, 281
replication, 5–6
    across firewalls, 645
    across WANs, 643
    convergence time, 644
    DFS, 657–659
    DNS zones, 613
    inter-site, 101
    intra-site, 101
    multi-master, 79
    partners, 637, 644
    policies, DFS, 657
    push/pull, 645
    strategies, 101
    technical needs analysis, 64
    WINS design, 642
Request packets, RADIUS, 740
resolving DNS names, 128, 572, 575
resource access control, security
    groups, 209–210
response strategies, network
    management, 755
restricted groups, 218
restricting access, dial-up
    networks, 736
reverse lookup zones, DNS, 130

revoking PKI certificates, 279–280
RFCs (Requests for Comments),
    489–490
RID Masters (Relative Identifier),
    119–121
RIP (Routing Information Protocol),
    721–722
RIS (Remote Installation
    Services), 286
  configuring, 292
  installing, 287–288
  remote system image loading, 287
  security options, 293
risk tolerance, 449
  business model analysis, 54
  security planning, 166
roles
  operations masters, 114–120
  PKI certificates, 273
roots
  CAs, PKI, 272
  DFS, 653, 656
  DNS, 574–575
  domain-based, 657–658
  servers, Active Directory, 93
round-robin load balancing, DNS,
    576–578
routed networks, designing
  DHCP, 545
  WINS LANs, 640
router interfaces, 717
routers, 714
routing design, 416, 716
  auto-static routing, 721
  demand dial routing, 730
  dial-up remote access, 730
  dynamic routing, 720
  IGMP, 727
  improving availability, 729
  improving performance, 729
  IP. See IP routing.
  OSPF, 723–726

private network placement, 717
RIP, 721–722
router interfaces, 717
static routing, 719–720
WANs, 713–714
RRAS (Routing and Remote Access
    Service), 537, 704
  demand dial routing, 730
  DHCP, 537, 547
  interface support, 716
  IP routing, 728–729
  multiple protocol support, 715
  security, 716
  WANs, 706–711
RRs (Resource Records)
  DNS, 576
  non-RFC-compliant, 597
RSVP (Resource Reservation
    Protocol), 512
rules, IPSec filters, 384–385

S

SAKMP, IPSec, 376–377
SAs (Security Associations),
    IPSec, 318, 375, 381
SBUs (strategic business units), 475
Schema Masters, 115–121
schemas
  Active Directory, 80, 83
  data replication, 100
  modification policies, Active
    Directory, 103–105
scope of services
  Active Directory, 25–26, 88
  DHCP, 532
screened subnets, 680
  DNS, 613
  WINS design, 652
scripts
  network management, 762
  second-level domains, DNS, 574

Secondary zones, DNS, 580, 588
secure dynamic update counters,
    DNS, 606
Secure Server (Require Security)
    policy, IPSec, 372
security
    administration, 222–223
        accounts, 145
    applications, 221–222
    auditing, 223
    communications, 146, 363–370
    DFS, 656
    DHCP, 554
    dial-up networks, 735
    DNS, 285, 611–612
    documentation, technical
        analysis, 467
    EFS, 150, 213
    encryption, 213
    files
        recovery certificates, 257
        sharing, 366
        encryption, 258
    groups, 209–211
        accounts, 144
        policies, 270
    IP routing, 728–729
    IPSec, 214
        levels, 378
    ISAKMP, 318
    life cycle, 151
    NAT, 686
    needs analysis, 197–202
    Oakley, 318
    operating systems, 146
    physical machine security, 145
    PKI, 149–150, 271
    proxy servers, 694
    RADIUS, 149, 745
    Recovery Agent, 150, 257
    remote users, 148
    RIS, 293
    RRAS, 716

Security log, 234, 238
    share-level, 315
    SNMP, 294, 297–298
    TCP/IP networks, 514
    technical issues, 144
    third party integration, 147
    user accounts, 144
    VPNs, 149, 732
Security Configuration and Analysis
    tool, 202–203
security of networks, 309
    CIFS, 315
    firewalls, 311
    gateways, 311
    Internet access, 310
    Internet Connection Server, 312
    IPSec, 317–319
    proxy servers, 310
    remote connections, 310
    user-level security, 315
security planning, 158
    administration, 169
    application inventories, 175
    auditing, 169
    authentication, 168
    authorization, 169
    data
        access methods, 175
        loss, 159
    disaster recovery plans, 188
    DMZs, 172
    down services, 159
    end user needs, 180
    firewalls, 172
    hackers, 178
    hardware inventories, 175
    hotspots, 189–191
    information security models, 171
    inter-site connectivity, 173
    network connections, 171
    network management, 176
    upgrades, 176

security policies
  account policies, 214
  Active Directory, 207
  authentication, 206
  domains, 212
  Event Logs, 218
  File System groups, 218
  group policies, 214
  IP Security Policies groups, 221
  local policies, 214
  password policies, 207
  Public Key Policies groups, 221
  Registry groups, 218
  remote access, 208
  resource access control, 209
  restricted groups, 218
  smart cards, 208
  system services, 218
  TCP/IP networks, 515
  user system resource access, 206
  Windows 2000, 231–233
security rules, Windows 2000,
    321–323
security templates, 202, 224
Server (Request Security) policy,
    IPSec, 372
Server Performance Object counters,
    DHCP, 552–553
servers
  Active Directory integrated zone,
      DNS, 130–131
  audit policies, 241
  com name, 575
  DHCP, 540, 550–551, 554
    addresses, Relay Agents, 341
  dial-up networks, 735
  DNS, 130–132, 285, 586–587,
      602–604, 609–610
  domain controllers, 125–127
  failures, WINS design, 646
  global catalog, 128
  inbound replication, 124

  local name, 575
  NAT, 685
  RADIUS, 267, 743
  remote access, 347, 350
  RIS, 288
  root name, 575
  VPNs, 334–338, 342
  zones, 130
services
  DHCP, 536, 548
  network, 763–766
  TCP/IP networks, 520
session limits, Terminal Services, 300
SHA (Secure Hash Algorithm),
    IPSec, 376
share-level security, 315
shared folder objects, Active
    Directory, 15
shared secrets, RADIUS, 742
shortcut trusts, Active Directory, 85
signing, SMB, 316
single domain networks, 133
single master domain systems,
    106–107
single subnet LANs, 543
site boundaries, Active Directory,
    102–103
smart cards
  authentication, 265–266
  security policies, 208
SMB signing (Server Message Block),
    315–316, 364
  communications security, 366
  implementing, 368
sniffer attacks, communications
    security, 365
SNMP (Simple Network Management
    Protocol)
  agents, 294–295
  managers, 294
  security, 294
  security options, 297–298

SNMP agents, 761
social engineering attacks, 198
software documentation, technical
    analysis, 459
software routers, 714
SRV records (Service Resource
    Records)
  Active Directory, 597–598
  DNS, 573
SSL (Secure Sockets Layer), 269
staff training, security planning, 183
stand-alone CAs, PKI, 273
standard zones, DNS, 581
  incremental zone transfers, 582
  Primary zones, 587
  Secondary zones, 130
  servers, 130
standards
  Internet, 489
  TCP/IP, 488
static packet filters, proxy servers, 695
static routing, 719–720
statistical reporting, DHCP, 532
status assignments, RFCs, 489
storage locations, Active Directory
    integrated zones, 583
stored zones, Active Directory, 583
strategic relationships, network
    design, 446
stub areas, OSPF routing design, 726
subnet masks
  IP addresses, 498
  router interfaces, 717
  TCP/IP networks, 507
subnets
  screened, DNS, 613
  TCP/IP networks, 503
subsidiaries
  business model analysis, 39–41
  network design, 437
subzones, WINS lookups, 594
successful events, audit policies, 238

superscopes, DHCP, 532
synchronization, meta-directories, 10
system images, loading remotely, 287
System Monitor
  counter logs, 421–423, 426
  DNS server performance
      monitoring, 603
  network management, 757
system resources, Active Directory, 206
system services groups, 218
systems management
  security planning, 177
  technical needs analysis, 72

T

TCO (Total Cost of Operations)
  business model analysis, 54
  security planning, 167
TCP counters, DNS, 607
TCP/IP
  Application layer, 492–493
  architecture, 490
  DHCP
    clients, 532
    network design, 541
  Internet layer, 491
  network design, 409
  Network Interface layer, 490
  protocol suite, 488
  standards, 488
  Transport layer, 492
  Windows 2000 features, 493–495
TCP/IP networks, 485–487
  applications, 520
  CIDR, 498
  classful IP addresses, 496
  clients, traffic patterns, 519
  connections, 521
  custom subnet masks, 507
  design analysis, 495

encryption, 515
fault tolerance, 506
host IP addresses, 504–505
IP addresses, 496–503
IPSec, 516–517
IPSec Policy Agent, 515
packet filtering, 514, 518
performance, 507–509
pipes, 510
QoS, 510–513
redundant links, 506
security, 514–515
services, 520
subnet masks, 498
traffic, 509
VLSMs, 498
templates, security, 224
Terminal Services, 296–298
connection permissions, 302
encryption, 299
session limits, 300
Windows 2000, 22
test phase
infrastructure, 404
security design, 151–153
third party integration, network
security, 147
third party root CAs, 281–284
threats to security, 178
tolerance for risk, security
planning, 166
top-level domains, DNS, 574
topologies, DFS networks, 655–656
Total counters, DNS, 607
traffic
Internet, 673
IP filter lists, 327
TCP/IP clients, 519
Windows 2000, 512
transferring files, protecting, 254
transferring operations masters,
120–121

transit networks, VPNs, 334
transitive trusts, 82, 85, 212
Transport layer, TCP/IP, 492
Transport mode, IPSec, 318, 370
trees, Active Directory, 11, 79
Triple DES algorithm, 384
Trojan horses, 199
trust relationships
domains, 212
RADIUS client/servers, 267
Tunnel mode, IPSec, 318, 331, 370
tunneling protocols, VPNs, 334
tunnels
IPSec endpoints, 371
VPNs, 334, 732
two-way trusts, 79, 82, 213

U

UDP counters, DNS, 607
unauthorized DNS access, 286
unauthorized servers, DHCP, 555
unicasts
RIP routing design, 722
WINS messages, 629
Unicode character set, DNS, 597
unique names, NetBIOS, 630–631
Universal groups, Active Directory,
84, 89, 210
untrusted domain replication, 643
updates, dynamic, DHCP DNS, 537
upgrades
security planning, 176
technical needs analysis, 70
User objects, Active Directory, 14
user-level security, 315
users
accounts, network security, 144
administrative access, 223
remote access, 353
security planning, 179

special access issues, 222
system resource access, 206
technical needs analysis, 60

V

vendor relationships
business model analysis, 51
DHCP options, 534
verifying WINS records, 638
viewing
Active Directory stored zones, 583
DNS zones/records, 612
viruses, security needs analysis, 199
VLSMs (Variable Length Subnet
Masks), IP addresses, 497
voluntary tunnels, VPN design, 732
VPNs (Virtual Private Networks),
333, 704
clients, 334, 343–345
configuring, 334–336
design, 732–733, 737
NAT, 687
private connections, 334
remote access, 334
security, 149
servers, 334
configuration, 342
dial-up networks, 737
installing, 336–338
transit networks, 334
tunnels, 334
WANs, 705
Windows 2000 support, 23

W

WAN design (Wide Area Networks),
703–706
physical links, 705
PPP, 706

PPTP, 706
routing, 713–714
RRAS, 706–711
VPNs, 705
Web caching, 688
Windows 2000
Active Directory, 3, 17
dynamic updates, 592
SRV RRs, 597–598
APIPA (Automatic Private IP
Addressing), 504
audit policies, 233
authentication, 260, 265–266, 269
BIND integration, 590
CIFS (Common Internet File
System), 315
DDNS (Dynamic DNS), 132
delegating authority, 243
DMZs (Demilitarized Zones), 679
DNS (Domain Name Service),
571–582
fast zone transfers, 596
fault tolerance, 601
monitoring server performance,
603–604
unauthorized access
protection, 286
Unicode character set
support, 597
zone-admin groups, 285
zones, 574, 580
domain controller server
placement, 125
EFS (Encrypting File System),
150, 253–255
firewalls, 679
global catalog servers, 123–124
IAS (Internet Authentication
Service), 417
ICS (Internet Connection
Sharing), 680, 687
implementation, 18–20
Internet Connection Server, 312–314

Internet connections, 672
  application-proxy firewalls,
    678–679
  dynamic packet-inspection
    firewalls, 677
  firewalls, 673–674
  gateways, 678
  packet filtering firewalls, 676
IP filter lists, 327–328
IP routing, 417
IPSec, 317
  authentication methods, 330
  configuration testing, 333
  connection types, 332
  operation modes, 331
  policies, 318–319
ISA Server, 415
Kerberos authentication, 261–264
NAT (Network Address
  Translation), 680–687
network design, 398–414
  attributes, 426–427
  infrastructure integration, 418
  management strategies, 418
  performance logs, 418–419
Network Monitor, driver install, 419
network security, 309
  firewalls, 311
  gateways, 311
  Internet access, 310
  proxy servers, 310
  remote connections, 310
  SAs, 318
networking services, 405–406
operations masters, 115–120
PKI (Public Key Infrastructure)
  CAs (Certificate Authorities),
    271–273, 276, 282
  certificates, 277–281
  CRLs (Certificate Revocation
    Lists), 280
  third-party CAs, 281–284

planning delegation structure,
  243–244
proxy servers, 688–690
RADIUS, 266–267, 417
RAS (Remote Access Service),
  346–347
Recovery Agent, 150
remote access, 353, 416
RIS (Remote Installation Services),
  286–288, 292–293
routing, 416
RRAS (Routing and Remote
  Access), 680
RSVP (Resource Reservation
  Protocol), 512
screened subnets, 680
security, 285, 294
  encryption, 325–326
  policies, 231–233
  rules, 321–323
SSL (Secure Sockets Layer), 269
System Monitor, counter logs,
  421–423, 426
TCP/IP
  applications, 520
  authentication protocols, 517
  client traffic patterns, 519
  connections, 521
  encryption, 515
  features, 493
  IPSec, 515–517
  network services, 520
  packet filtering, 514, 518
  performance, 509
  QoS, 510–513
  security, 514–515
  services, 495
Terminal Services, 296–299
traffic control, 512
user-level network security, 315
Windows 2000 Server
  Digital Nervous System, 29
  networking services, 406

RRAS (Routing and Remote Access
  Service), 312
software routers, 714
Windows Pocket PC operating
  system, 6
WINS (Windows Internet Naming
  Service), 588, 627
  client to server process, 634
  designing system, 635
    automatic replication partner
      configuration, 642
    clients, 641, 650–651
    clusters, 647
    DMZs, 652
    fault tolerance, 647
    hub and spoke, 645
    link failures, 646
    multiple servers, 642, 646
    non-routed LANs, 639
    non-WINS clients, 641–642
    performance counters, 650
    replication, 637, 642–645, 651
    routed LANs, 640
    screened subnets, 652
    segments, 646
    server capacity optimization,
      648–649
    server failures, 646
    untrusted domain
      replication, 643
  DHCP support, 628
  disabling records replication, 592
  DNS, 533, 588–589
  dynamic record deletion, 638
  dynamic reregistration, 639
  export function, 639
  fault tolerance, 639
  filtering records, 638
  lookups via zone config, 590
  manual tombstoning, 638
  multiselection of records, 638

  name resolution, 628
  NBNS compatibility, 629
  NetBIOS, 635, 412–413
  persistent connections, 638
  records verification, 638
  referral zones, 593–594
  unicast messages, 629
WINS Manager, 638
WinSock clients, 690
wizards
  Delegation of Control, 95
  Windows 2000 support, 24
WMI (Windows Management
  Instrumentation), 761
workstation policies, 99, 242
worms, security needs analysis, 199

X

X.400 directory services, 8
X.500
  Active Directory relationship, 27
  directory services, 7–8
  meta-directories, 10

Z

Zone servers, Active Directory
  integrated, 130–131
Zones
  Active Directory
    integrated, 580
  configuring for WINS lookups, 590
  DNS, 574
    external, 131
    incremental transfers, 582
    internal, 131
    lookup, 130
    network design, 580

placement, 586–587
planning, 129
primary, 580
replication, 613
same public/private names,
124, 131
secondary, 580, 588
standard, 581

standard primary, 587
update access, 612
viewing access, 612
transfers
DNS counters, 608
fast, 596
WINS referral, 593

INTERNATIONAL CONTACT INFORMATION

AUSTRALIA
McGraw-Hill Book Company Australia Pty. Ltd.
TEL +61-2-9417-9899
FAX +61-2-9417-5687
http://www.mcgraw-hill.com.au
books-it_sydney@mcgraw-hill.com

CANADA
McGraw-Hill Ryerson Ltd.
TEL +905-430-5000
FAX +905-430-5020
http://www.mcgrawhill.ca

**GREECE, MIDDLE EAST,
NORTHERN AFRICA**
McGraw-Hill Hellas
TEL +30-1-656-0990-3-4
FAX +30-1-654-5525

MEXICO (Also serving Latin America)
McGraw-Hill Interamericana Editores S.A. de C.V.
TEL +525-117-1583
FAX +525-117-1589
http://www.mcgraw-hill.com.mx
fernando_castellanos@mcgraw-hill.com

SINGAPORE (Serving Asia)
McGraw-Hill Book Company
TEL +65-863-1580
FAX +65-862-3354
http://www.mcgraw-hill.com.sg
mghasia@mcgraw-hill.com

SOUTH AFRICA
McGraw-Hill South Africa
TEL +27-11-622-7512
FAX +27-11-622-9045
robyn_swanepoel@mcgraw-hill.com

**UNITED KINGDOM & EUROPE
(Excluding Southern Europe)**
McGraw-Hill Publishing Company
TEL +44-1-628-502500
FAX +44-1-628-770224
http://www.mcgraw-hill.co.uk
computing_neurope@mcgraw-hill.com

ALL OTHER INQUIRIES Contact:
Osborne/McGraw-Hill
TEL +1-510-549-6600
FAX +1-510-883-7600
http://www.osborne.com
omg_international@mcgraw-hill.com